'This truly is a remarkable book. Give [...] is beyond "an essential read", but, in r [...] READ" for everyone connected with th [...] reading of the entirety of this book en [...] and understand an array of diverse e [...] the cognitive enactment of promotin[...] the fostering of good relations between the Protected Characteristics from within. This is because the content of *Diverse Educators* makes visible those experiences which are often overlooked and made systemically invisible within education and society. When linked with the Equality Act 2010, the power of this book is realised because it demonstrates how, by thinking and working collectively, education is absolutely integral to the building of a fair and socially just society which includes everyone and leaves no one behind.'

Claire Birkenshaw, Lecturer in Childhood and Education at the Carnegie School of Education, Leeds Beckett University

'This book is a powerful tool containing the richness of lived experiences and the insight to move education practice on. An essential read for anyone involved in education.'

Rachel Boyle, Head of Interdisciplinary Studies at Leeds Beckett University

'I thought this was an impressive collection of voices, viewpoints and ideas which not only covers each Protected Characteristic individually, but also addresses the importance of intersectionality. An important read for everyone working in education, from trainee teachers and ECTs to experienced headteachers.'

Sarah Brownsword, Lecturer in Primary Education, Primary PGCE Course Co-Director, UEA

'This book makes an important contribution to an important topic. With its diverse range of passionate and expert contributors, each of whom brings a powerful personal narrative and perspective, this book is a must-read for anyone working in or with schools.'

Andy Buck, Founder of Leadership Matters

'A comprehensive and insightful book that lays out a path to move from 'intention to action' in relation to inclusion within our schools. Such a wide range of lived experiences and knowledge make this a must read for anyone who is serious about creating sustainable cultural change and legacy.'

James Coleman, Head of Operations and Training, NASBTT

'A powerful collection of narratives offering valuable perspectives from across the protected characteristics and beyond. There should be a copy of this in every school.'

Serdar Ferit, CEO of Lyfta Education

'An upstanding and brave manifesto, diverse in its capture of global consciousness which weaves a golden thread of collective agency and supports by providing the tools for sustained systemic challenge and change. This will be the handbook for proactive DEI leaders who have identified the "burning need" in their establishments and those of us who are impatient to mainstream that change.'

Karen Giles, B.Ed. (Hons), NPQH, FCCT, Interim Executive Headteacher

'Ambitious in scope and, appropriately, diverse in perspective. I learned something valuable on every page.'
Russell Hobby, CEO Teach First

'Wow. This book is full of deep analyses of so many diversity issues yet also remains practical and down-to-earth. I have worked in education all my life but this book helped me to look afresh at so many key aspects and I learned a lot. You can choose to read the whole thing but also use it as a reference guide when particular issues come to the forefront. Teachers and educators will find it invaluable. Very impressive.'
Steve Munby, Visiting Professor, Centre for Educational Leadership, University College London

'This is a powerful resource for educators everywhere. A wide range of concise contributions with 'key takeaways' are included with areas for deep reflection and strategies for practical implementation. We are treated to positive inclusive examples and personal stories that illustrate the power of language and action in smashing stereotypes. Highly recommended for school leaders and for teachers who seek to offer a learning environment where marginalised ideas and voices are truly heard.'
Dame Alison Peacock, Chief Executive Chartered College of Teaching

'This is a powerful collection of voices, views and stories, bringing together a thought-provoking range of genuinely diverse perspectives. These rich experiences, shared generously and openly, are anchored in a firm belief that we are able to change things for the better: a true manifesto.'
Hilary Spencer, CEO at Ambition Institute

'In a sector that lacks diversity of thought, representation and lived life experiences this book has the potential to make a great contribution. Its content is as diverse as its subject – giving the reader a huge range of perspectives and food for thought. What they all have in common though is a very practical, constructive approach giving actionable advice that has the potential to make a real difference.'
Samantha Twiselton, Director of Sheffield Institute of Education

'A genuinely extraordinary book. This is a careful exploration of all of the important complexity of diversity in schools. Hannah and Bennie have assembled a diverse array of knowledgeable and experienced writers who carefully pick apart each characteristic and educate us with warmth, wisdom and passion. In each chapter we're asked to reflect, we connect with stories that are sometimes inspiring, sometimes heartrending, and we're given plenty of evidence to contemplate. I can't wait to recommend it to colleagues and friends.'
David Weston, Chief Executive of the Teacher Development Trust

DIVERSE EDUCATORS:

A Manifesto

Edited by

HANNAH WILSON & BENNIE KARA

UNIVERSITY OF
BUCKINGHAM
PRESS

Published by University of Buckingham Press,
an imprint of Legend Times Group
51 Gower Street
London WC1E 6HJ
info@unibuckinghampress.com
www.unibuckinghampress.com

The right of the above editors to be identified as the editors of this work has been asserted in accordance with the Copyright, Designs and Patents Act 1988. British Library Cataloguing in Publication Data available.

Cover design: Blue Hall

ISBN (paperback): 9781915054982
ISBN (ebook): 9781915054999

Diversity is being invited to the party. Inclusion is being asked to dance.

Verna Myers

We all should know that diversity makes for a rich tapestry, and we must understand that all the threads of the tapestry are equal in value no matter what their color.

Maya Angelou

Intersectionality draws attention to invisibilities that exist in feminism, in anti-racism, in class politics, so, obviously, it takes a lot of work to consistently challenge ourselves to be attentive to aspects of power that we don't ourselves experience.

Kimberlé Williams Crenshaw

ACKNOWLEDGEMENTS

We would like to say a massive thank you to our eleven Chapter Editors who have worked closely with their team of contributors to shape each chapter of the book. We appreciate the time, energy, experience and expertise you have each invested in this project.

Equally, we would like to express our heartfelt gratitude to all of the one hundred and five contributors who have shared their lived experience with us. Each contribution enables our readers to develop understanding of the issues they, and colleagues in the school system, have navigated.

We started Diverse Educators in 2017, but in the 2020-21 academic year (and in the middle of a global pandemic) we moved from being a hashtag, a twitter handle and an annual grassroots event into a fully-fledged organisation. We would like to acknowledge the support of our partners to enable this to happen: Alliance for Learning Teaching School Hub, The Carnegie School of Education at Leeds Beckett University, The Global Equality Collective, Lyfta and Teacheroo for helping our growth.

Finally, we would like to share our appreciation to the #DiverseEd network. To everyone who has attended or spoken at an event, to each person who has written or read a blog, to each follower and amplifier on social media: we thank you for sharing our vision for a more diverse, equitable and inclusive education system for all.

Hannah Wilson and Bennie Kara
Co-Founders, Diverse Educators
www.diverseeducators.co.uk

CONTENTS

THE STORY OF DIVERSE EDUCATORS

HANNAH WILSON

THE BEGINNING

Co-founding #WomenEd nearly seven years ago, as a Deputy Headteacher in London, catapulted me into the education grassroots world. Our successful arrival quickly led to the birth of the network's siblings in #BAMEed, #LGBTed and #DisabilityEd – four networks serving as affinity groups for each identity group in education and their allies. Around this time a lot of my network was involved in leading or contributing to the DfE's Equality and Diversity Grants, which was system funding that Teaching Schools could bid for to support existing and aspiring leaders from under-represented groups. A group of us came together and initiated the Diversity Roundtables around this time to forge connections and collaborations across different individuals and organisations working in the DEI space.

THE JOURNEY

As I started my first headship, I pulled back from being one of the national strategic leads of WomenEd as it was becoming nearly a second full-time and unpaid job that was taking up a lot of time and energy – a point I will raise again in my commitment about remuneration for DEI work. I was also keen to pass the baton on to women from the burgeoning network to lean in as I leaned out. I was also in the process of relocating to Oxfordshire from London. Being involved in the grassroots scene, I could not have imagined the opportunities and introductions that I would gain from this voluntary role. My network had grown exponentially and I had a number of diverse role models, mentors and coaches who had taken me under their wing as critical friends – inspiring, empowering and challenging me on my journey as a woman leader in education. I had not anticipated that I would be offered roles and be able to recruit from a talented diverse network of connections as a result of joining Twitter, blogging and attending grassroots events. Becoming the founding Headteacher of a start-up school in a new trust, in a new locality, in a new region brought with it a few challenges which I will explore later, but it also brought about an opportunity for us to bring to life a vision for an education with diversity, equity and inclusion at the core of the school's vision. 'Us' at this point was the diverse leadership team and the diverse governing body that we had recruited. We were aligned in our values and unified in our approach, which is often half of the battle in embedding DEI in a school context.

THE IDEA

It was at the gate one morning on duty that Bennie, my then Deputy Headteacher, made a throwaway comment about her frustrations around having to cut herself into quarters to attend multiple grassroots events due to her intersectional identity. I agreed that it seemed unfair that she should have to give up four Saturdays to attend four events when I could give one weekend to attend one event. It is ironic that she cannot remember this conversation, but it had a profound impact on me, as it made me check my privilege as a cishet, able-bodied white woman. I began to mull ideas over in my head... Anyone who knows me, will know that I am a fixer and a problem-solver. Although intersectionality is a complex concept and a multi-layered problem, for me the solution to Bennie's problem was obvious. We would hold an event and invite the other networks to contribute so that we would all be under one roof and could make connections, plus attend workshops across the different strands. The delegates could thus choose to pick a linear path across the schedule, or cross-traverse through different lanes. Ultimately, Bennie, like anyone with an intersectional identity, is one person, who needed one event.

THE INAUGURAL EVENT

We had become quite openly critical of events with tokenistic representation on their line-up (regularly all the keynotes are white straight men and there is one person of colour discussing a niche theme such as radicalisation or FGM in a workshop in the graveyard shift) so we were adamant we would model a truly diverse event with diverse panels that modelled the possibilities of how to curate a great line-up. Thus #DiverseEd was born as an annual event.

I can still remember our first event as clearly as it was yesterday. January 2018 saw 200+ educators travel to Didcot, South Oxfordshire, from across the country. The schedule had keynotes, panels and workshops from all of the grassroots groups and other organisations we had connected with. *The Greatest Showman* had been the film of the previous year and the *This is Me!* song from the soundtrack, performed by Keala Settle, was blasted through our school hall as everyone took their seats. There was an energy and an excitement in our brand-new school building that something important was happening. The day went by in a blur, but the feedback that stayed with me are the series of tweets celebrating: 'This is what a diverse panel looks like!' Bennie closed the event with a cracking keynote entitled: 'Don't tuck in my labels'. You can read her follow-up blog 'Don't tuck in your labels' on our Diverse Educators' website.

THE IMPACT

The event galvanised a group of people who wanted to connect ideas, people and policies to work holistically and in an intersectional way to create a DEI strategy. We received updates of what the attendees had initiated as a result of attending. One such example is from the Sarah Bonnell School – a carload of their middle leaders had driven up together from East London – on their return journey they plotted how they were going to disseminate their shared learning with their colleagues and launch a DiverseEd group at their school. Meanwhile, back in the day job of leading a start-up secondary school, with diverse visible role models teaching, leading and governing our school, we attracted diverse educators and diverse families in a region that is not very diverse. When we opened our sibling primary school a year later, our reputation for our commitment to DEI had grown and diverse children were in the majority, instead of being in the minority. We did not think we were doing anything groundbreaking, a lot of the decisions we made were common sense, but they were intentional. DEI were values that were embedded in the heart of our school's culture and ethos. From our uniform policy, to our toilet and changing room policy, to our catering policy, to our best practice for classroom displays and assemblies, we wove DEI as a golden thread through every discussion we had. It was also central in our CPD offer. Bennie was leading Curriculum Development at the secondary school and she worked with our teachers and middle leaders to diversify their subject knowledge and their schemes of work. You can read about some of the work she embedded in her book: *The Little Guide for Teachers: Diversity in Schools* (2020).

THE CHALLENGE (S)

My Dad tells me that being in the Daily Mail means that I must be doing something right... On the Friday of May half-term (2018) when I emerged from a spa day and turned my phone on to hundreds of voicemails, text messages, WhatsApp messages and twitter notifications, I did not know what had happened. Alas, an aggrieved parent who had contested our diverse food policy in our school had gone to the local press and the Oxford Mail schools' desk was clearly quiet as they ran a piece that went viral. In the course of a few days the local piece went regional and then national, and we had the BBC camped outside our school trying to get someone to go on record about our controversial policies. I could cope with the mainstream media, but it was the social media campaigns that got very personal. Thousands of hateful comments were posted in local Facebook groups and at the bottom of the articles. And then the hand-penned hate mail and death threats began to arrive. All of this because we had a Halal kitchen and there was a lack of understanding about what this meant. Amjad Ali, founder of BAMEed, was our Assistant Headteacher and SENCO, and he carried the weight of being a visible Muslim role model who constantly challenged misconceptions about his faith. Our Trust wanted me to let it wash away, to take it quietly, to let something else happen to take the spotlight off of me/ us, but one of our behaviour mantras was: 'Be an upstander, not a bystander.' We as a staff intentionally practised what we preached, and I personally have never been one to let bullies get away with poor behaviour. I knew that I needed to be strong and to challenge it for my own integrity, for my team, for my students and for the families who were behind us. Thus, I penned a blog called: *The Trolls Under the Bridge* (2018) which went viral that rationalised some of the decisions we had made in long form rather than in tweets which can quickly be taken out of context.

THE PANDEMIC

Fast-forward a few years and I resigned from headship to work independently and focus on my areas of passion including Diversity, Equity and Inclusion, Coaching and Mentoring, Mental Health and Wellbeing. The idea was to spend six months establishing myself as a leadership development consultant, coach and facilitator before deciding how to develop #DiverseEd further. But then the world as we knew it exploded, we experienced the global pandemic of Covid-19 and we went into lockdown. Whilst we were all stuck in our houses and glued to social media, George Floyd was murdered. Police brutality and racism are not new phenomena, but something shifted in the global consciousness. No one could ignore, nor deny what happened, as it was on every news channel and every social media platform. It was a reality check for the world and thus sparked a resurgence of the Black Lives Matters campaign. I wrote to a few of the national education papers to see if I could write an article about it and I was told it was not a UK issue, it was a US issue. This angered me at the denial of the reality for many people in the UK. Emotions were high and people of colour from my network were sharing how psychologically and physically unsafe they were feeling. I pinged from one conversation to another with friends, former colleagues and my network who were reeling. In my circles, there was a renewed sense of agency that we needed to collectively do something about it so a group of us co-organised a virtual safe space for women of colour to come together to share how they were feeling and over a thousand people registered to attend.

THE DEI LEADER

In July we saw a flurry of commitments and statements from national organisations with lots of great intentions about how they were going to create a DEI strategy for their school/ trust. We also saw a flurry of tweets and I received a multitude of direct messages on Twitter from people in our network who had been asked to be the DEI leader in their context. There were mixed emotions – educators who aspired to be leaders were grateful for the opportunity but there was frustration that they were only becoming visible because they had a protected characteristic in their identity. Moreover, they were being asked to take on an important whole school remit, for no extra time and no extra money. I had a conversation with Angie Browne about it as we move in similar circles and have had a similar career journey, both being English teachers who were brought up in the West Country, who have led schools as Headteachers but who have also led a school's DEI strategy before it was en vogue to do so. We decided to create a safe space for those who were leaning into this precarious role. Thus the DEI Leaders Programme was conceived – ten sessions over ten months with a group of twenty colleagues in a group-coaching style approach to support them in doing the inner work in order to show up confidently and competently to do the outer work. One year on and we have supported fifteen cohorts of cross-sector, cross-phase and international DEI Leaders.

THE NEW CHAPTER

Each conversation I had, each blog I read, each event I attended during Summer 2020 made me realise there was a massive gap for signposting DEI services to schools. I reflected on the scenario of being a headteacher, in a rural part of the shires, not from a diverse background, who was not on social media and who had not been exposed to people with diverse identities nor the breadth and depth of the issues being discussed and explored. I mused on what would be a useful asset to add value to the school system and this is where the thinking behind the Diverse Educators website came from. A website to serve as a directory for schools, to signpost them out to the individuals, organisations and charities working and having impact in this space. A resource that was structured around the Equality Act (2010) and organised around the nine protected characteristics so that as and when a school identified a gap in their provision and a blind spot in their CPD, they could source support. The Diverse Educators website launched on 1st September 2020, with fifty organisations listed in the DEI Directory – one year on we now have 110. The website has grown to meet the needs of the educators and the organisations in our network as requests for training, support and resources have come in. The academic year of 2020-21 saw us flipping our face-to-face event to virtual events, where our reach increased exponentially from 200 to 13,500 attendees. Our annual event became a quarterly event to build momentum across the year.

THE COLLABORATIVE PARTNERS

All of this was made possible by our partners who sponsored the launch of the Diverse Educators website and the virtual events throughout 2020-21. The Alliance for Learning (a Teaching School Alliance), The Global Equality Collective (an app), The Carnegie School of Education (Leeds Beckett University), Lyfta (a virtual global storytelling platform) and Teacheroo (a virtual staffroom) all agreed to work with us in our first year to support our work. We are extremely grateful for their generosity and support in bringing to life our vision. You can find out more about the work that each partner does in our DEI Directory on our website. Connecting and collaborating is how our community started and how it has and will continue to grow. We strive to create coherence and cohesion, whilst building confidence and competence. In the 2020-21 academic year we have created a number of spaces and opportunities to bring different national stakeholder together including:

- A national quarterly Diversity Roundtable;
- A half-termly Diversity in ITTE meet up;
- A series of webcasts exploring Diverse Governance.

We have also worked with a number of networks, teaching school alliances, training providers, trusts, unions and localities to curate strands of DEI activity including: AET, Bowden Education, the National Association of School-based Teacher Training, the NEU, the Oxfordshire Teaching School Alliance, Summit Learning Trust and Whole Education.

THE FUTURE

So, what is on the horizon for us?

- Growing the #DiverseEd blog to amplify more voices, share best practice and celebrate the lived experience of our community.
- Developing our Diversifying the Curriculum resource bank and holding our inaugural annual conference.
- Expanding our bank of DEI toolkits to support self-directed learning.
- Returning to face-to-face #DiverseEd events in the Spring, but continuing some virtual events too to harness the impact of hybrid formats.
- Publishing the #DiverseEd book.
- Launching the #DiverseEd podcast, book club and Twitter chat.
- Holding the Diverse Educators' Annual Awards.

Ultimately, we want to support everyone in our network to move from intention to action, to move from individual to collective agency, to affect systemic change when it comes to activating our DEI commitment within our schools, trusts and localities. We want to support in sustaining momentum, keeping DEI on the agenda and ensuring that we see tangible impact.

KEY TAKEAWAYS

- Remember that diversity is a marathon not a sprint, and we need to move from intention to action.
- Consider your sphere of influence and how you can affect change and have impact in your context.
- Reflect on how you can be an inclusive ally to challenge behaviours and practices that are not inclusive.

KEY QUESTIONS

- How truly inclusive is your school and how do you know this? (i.e. are you asking the right questions and listening to the right people?)

- How diverse is your network and how can you disrupt any groupthink tendencies? (i.e. are you in a bubble and how can you pop it for yourself and others?)
- How equitable are the policies and the practices in your school/ trust? (i.e. who has power/ privilege and who is under-represented and being marginalised?)

COMMITMENT TO THE MANIFESTO

- I believe that every school needs to appoint and to remunerate a DEI Leader to drive the DEI strategy and to embed it across the whole school to create sustainable cultural change and legacy.

THE STORY OF A BOOK

BENNIE KARA

THE PROPOSAL

Hannah and I like to set ourselves impossible tasks. This one, curating a book structured around the nine protected characteristics in the Equality Act 2010, with a broad spread of voices, was another of those tasks. How do we put together a book that encompasses the enormity of experiences of those with one or more protected characteristics in education? How do we ensure that everyone is heard who needs to be heard? And crucially, can we do this in a way that is useful?

In August 2020, we decided to finally write the book proposal that we had been discussing for a few years. The timing felt right to formalise the conversations we were having about DEI. We were quite clear when we contacted our preferred publisher, The University of Buckingham Press, how we wanted to structure the book around the Equality Act (2010) to speak directly to the current landscape, the changes to legislation and the activity across the sector.

Thus the book is structured around the protected characteristics with a chapter each exploring: Age; Disability; Gender Reassignment; Maternity and Pregnancy; Marriage and Civil Partnership; Race; Religion and Belief; Sex; Sexual Orientation and Intersectionality. Each chapter has an editor who is either an expert in the field or who has lived experience, and they have worked with their team of ten contributors to capture the breadth and the depth of the issues we need to be aware of.

The original idea for this book was that educators across the profession – and by educators, we mean anyone working in or adjacent to schools across the phases – would be able to pick up this book, open it at any section and learn something useful about diversity, equity and inclusion in any or all of the protected characteristics. Throughout the process of collating content, we have tried to stay as true to this aim as possible. We wanted the book to interweave personal and professional narratives, whilst being framed in theory, to respond to arguments with academic referencing to anchor the subject which can be criticised for being too soft, too 'woke' and too political. We were also clear that we wanted the collective voice to be solutions-focused and to include: practice, pedagogy, people management and policy, hence each submission has clear takeaway learning and questions to reflect on. Each contributor to this co-created book has shared their commitment to diversity, equity and inclusion.

We debated the title of the book across many virtual meetings. One word just kept coming up in our description of the end-point of the book. *Manifesto* a set of ideas that could form the basis for the way things are done in our schools when it comes to diversity, equity and inclusion. The questions around this word reverberated for us – would people assume the book was aimed at politicians and not teachers? Eventually, we drew the title in by considering the articles: 'a' and 'the'. We settled on 'A Manifesto'. In a book about diversity of experiences, we knew that the ideas expressed in our book were just a small snapshot of ideas about identity. We wanted people to read the book and walk away with the foundations of DEI forming in their heads, so that they could go on to formulate what worked in their schools and in their settings.

The chapters that follow are the thoughts and feelings of educators, of those who have committed in some way, shape or form to furthering knowledge, whether that is in school or out of school. They bring with them their stories. As chapter contributors Nick Kitchener-Bentley and Jac Bastian both tell us: stories are fundamental to building empathetic, collaborative societies.

THE LIVED EXPERIENCE

We wanted to balance research-informed information with personal and lived experiences – some of our chapters are fully referenced and some have no references. When we talk about protected characteristics, we have to be able to turn both to the literature on the topic and to the varied and wonderful interpretation of identity that exists in our authors. Lived experience is a vital part of this document, simply because 'It's being experienced makes a special impression that gives it lasting importance.' (Gadamer, 2004). As we do not have the capacity to experience all, we rely on the narratives of lived experiences of others to formulate a reality. While someone else's lived experience may not ring true for all, it allows for a construction-mode of thinking: when we read someone's story, we have to work out how it fits with what we know, what we have known, and what we need to know.

Diversity, equity and inclusion in schools is a growing endeavour in schools. This is not to say that teachers before us have not engaged in the topic – it is clear that today's teachers are standing on the shoulders of giants in the quest to create equitable societies. There are calls to quantify diversity, equity and inclusion to 'prove' that it has an impact on children and young people. This is understandable; if we are to spend our limited time and resources on this area, then surely we should know what impact the work is having?

THE DATA

In our book, we reference statistics that demonstrate the impact of *not* doing the work. They are easily found in university application rates, in employment statistics, in student voice questionnaires. There is, undoubtedly, work to be done in gathering the empirical evidence on the impact of diversity, equity and inclusion on outcomes, on destinations and on employment figures. We welcome all and any attempts to gather this data; however, we know that it may not be possible to accurately extract the statistical impact of this wonderfully human-centred work.

We asked our authors to show us the landscape of each protected characteristic, to set the scene for readers who may or may not be aware of the issues surrounding a particular characteristic. So, there is an attempt to build a picture of the world our authors have inhabited both as educators and as children in education. There are references to legislation, to policy, to funding, to workforce data and to student voice, captured by organisations working in the field. As the field itself is enormous, even in a book this large in scope, we could not hope to include all of the data you might need. So, at the end of each author's chapter, there is a set of key questions that place the responsibility to find out more back in your hands.

THE CONTRIBUTORS

Even in asking for volunteers to put themselves forward to write a chapter, we found that there were more questions than answers. Our networks were solid – full of people from all walks of life, full of people who had a range of lived experiences, full of people of diverse identities. We sent out the call – come and write about the protected characteristics as relevant to schools – and waited for the floodgates to open. Despite the fact that we had hundreds of expressions of interest, we noticed that there were significant groups within those protected characteristics entirely under-represented in the submissions. We noted a lack of men in particular, and within that, a lack of men of colour. While there are no official statistics available on who takes up the diversity and inclusion gauntlet at schools, our experience at Diverse Educators shows that women – and with that, white, cishet women – form a large share of our audience and our participants at conferences and at training sessions.

So, the questions remained: why were we not hearing from men? Do men not engage in work on diversity, equity and inclusion? We did not have an answer other than to adjust the way in which we recruited writers. We spoke to our contacts, we mined people's address books – we convinced, we reassured. It was not enough to just ask people generally to get involved. We had to dig into our networks and nudge people. We had to ask them to bring the wisdom to the page that they had clearly demonstrated in their careers.

The fact we had to work hard to ensure diversity of experience and identity in our writers in itself is not a surprise. One of the accusations levelled at panel events, at conferences, at meetings is the lack of representation from minority groups. Organisers often think that telling everyone they are looking for diversity of representation is enough: 'We asked people and no one came forward from that group' is the response to criticism. One of the things that we have always said is that inclusion is not a passive process. The responsibility to have a representative field in your endeavour is yours and it is proactive.

In any case, we are incredibly proud of our authors. It is not easy to lay yourself open in a book – especially if you have not 'come out' as having a protected characteristic before. You will read their pain, their resilience, their sorrows and their joy all so that you can see them in the children, the young adults and the colleagues you work with.

THE EDITORIAL DECISIONS – LANGUAGE, STYLE, FREEDOMS

Language forms an unalienable thread throughout the chapters. What we choose to call ourselves, what others choose to call us – so much of these considerations are steeped in our view of the world, or lived experience – and indeed, in how society views those with protected characteristics. From pronouns to racial descriptors, from acronyms to titles, from technical terms to reclaimed language – all of the nuances of the words of diversity, equity and inclusion exist in this book.

One of the things you will notice about the chapters is that there is a different approach to language in each one, even within each protected characteristic. We have not attempted to standardise the acronyms that our writers have chosen to use, unless they are factually incorrect. The best example of this is our Sexuality writers referring to LGBTQIA+ identities in their chapters. Some have used LGBT, some LGBT+ and some have used more of the identity markers in the acronym. The only editorial decision was to ensure that the T in the acronym was always included: the removal of the T in LGBT is exclusive and does not sit with our values at Diverse Educators.

Capitalisation of descriptors of identity have also not been standardised. We realised that the view on whether 'B/black' should have a capital letter or not is varied and couched in people's personal choices, political leanings and priorities. So, where our authors chose to use the descriptor, unless there was a compelling reason to capitalise, we left it to the author's discretion.

As ever, where 'reclaimed' language has been used, it is within the context of analysis, or as a personal choice by someone of that protected characteristic grouping. It is unavoidable, when talking about the protected characteristics, to recount words that have traditionally been – and still are – used as slurs, particularly when recalling moments of pain. There is no asterisking out of these words. Our authors' content choices here are their own within the context of their story.

One further point on language: throughout the book there are references to 'diversity'. There are arguments out there that calling this work 'diversity-centred' somehow softens the impact of the work being done – that the work should be 'decolonisation' focused, as that is more challenging to the status quo. Our work is unashamedly intersectional, with a firm recognition that we must tackle structural prejudice in all its forms.

THE ROLE MODELS AND ALLIES

Another golden thread is the necessity and power of representation in the education system. One of the clearest messages we are hearing through the chapters that follow is the importance of seeing and being seen in all your forms. Of course, this raises a question as to the role of people who do not classify themselves as having a protected characteristic. Can you create a diverse, equitable and inclusive environment in your classroom if you do not hold a protected characteristic? Quite simply, of course you can.

While our students deserve to have role models that suit their identity, educators who model allyship in all its forms are also necessary in our schools. What better time than now for demonstrating your commitment to a fairer and more just society? In reading this book, you are actively making a choice on the road to allyship. Perhaps at the end of it, you will find yourself exploring what it means to be a reflective ally, who does not place themself at the centre of the discourse, who actively listens, who is always learning. For our students, with or without protected characteristics, you are providing the safest of spaces for them to be authentic, to explore and develop as young people.

THE COLLECTIVE VOICE

It is always worth remembering that while this book is written collectively by people who define themselves as having one or more protected characteristics, it is not their sole responsibility to carry the weight of diversity, equity and inclusion in schools and beyond. Indeed, one thing our diverse educators often relay to us is the heaviness of the pioneer role – the visible role model, making oneself vulnerable by raising a head above the proverbial parapet. To ensure that the workload of creating a fair society, a just society, and an inclusive society, we must have allies.

You are on this journey with us. Thank you for taking the time and energy to do this heavy lifting.

KEY TAKEAWAYS

- This book is for a wide range of educators working both in and out of schools and it can be used to form the basis of your thoughts on diversity, equity and inclusion.
- Our writers share their stories so that you can build your own views on the protected characteristics.
- Language is important – it outlines the political, and the personal, in diversity, equity and inclusion work.

KEY QUESTIONS

- How can you use this book to drive diversity, equity and inclusion in our schools?
- Where are your gaps when it comes to the protected characteristics?

- What is the 'burning need' in your establishment that has to be addressed when it comes to the protected characteristics?

COMMITMENT TO THE MANIFESTO

- We need to ensure that our stories are heard outside of diversity, equity and inclusion circles so that there can be meaningful structural change – and my pledge is to keep calling people in to help them hear our stories.

REFERENCES

BAMEed, available at: https://www.diverseeducators.co.uk/bameed/

Conscious Being: https://www.diverseeducators.co.uk/conscious-being/

DfE
https://www.gov.uk/guidance/equality-and-diversity-funding-for-school-led-projects#:~:text=Since%202014%2C%20the%20Department%20for,by%20the%20Equality%20Act%202010%2C

DisabilityEd
https://www.diverseeducators.co.uk/disabilityeduk/

Edurio EDI Report
https://www.diverseeducators.co.uk/the-edurio-edi-report/

Featherstone, K. and Porritt, V. (eds.) (2020) *Being 10% Braver*, Sage Publications Ltd

Flexible Teacher Talent
https://www.diverseeducators.co.uk/flexible-teacher-talent/

Gadamer, H.G. (2004). *Truth and method*, London: Continuum Publishing Group, p53

Kara, B. (2020) *Don't Tuck in Your Labels* (Diverse Educators). Available at https://www.diverseeducators.co.uk/dont-tuck-in-your-labels/

Kara, B. (2020) *A Little Guide for Teachers: Diversity in Schools*, SAGE Publications Ltd

LGBTed
https://www.diverseeducators.co.uk/lgbted/

Lyfta
https://www.diverseeducators.co.uk/lyfta/

Maternity CPD
https://www.diverseeducators.co.uk/the-mtpt-project/

Mindful Equity
https://www.diverseeducators.co.uk/mindful-equity-uk/

Statement of Intent
https://www.diverseeducators.co.uk/our-statement-of-intent/

Tomlinson-Gray, D. (2020), *Big Gay Adventures in Education, Routledge.*
Wilson, H. (2018), *The Trolls Under the Bridge.* Available at
https://thehopefulheadteacher.blog/2018/06/03/
the-trolls-under-the-bridge-leadership-resilience/

Wilson, H. (2020) *Tips for Teaching Diversity, Equity and Inclusion* (Innovate My School).
Available at
https://www.innovatemyschool.com/ideas/tips-for-making-your-school-truly-
modern

Wilson, H. (2018), *There's No Point Paying Lip Service* (Teach Wire). Available at
https://www.teachwire.net/news/theres-no-point-paying-lip-service-to-diversity-
and-equality-it-needs-to-be-at-the-core-of-everything-a-school-does-and-is

Wilson, H. (2017), *Diverse Dreams* (TEDxNorwichED). Available at
https://www.youtube.com/watch?v=gMKBH9okWy4

Wilson, H. (2021), *Dear Secretary of State* (Diverse Educators). Available at
https://www.ucet.ac.uk/13094/diverse-educators-dear-secretary-of-state

WomenEd
https://www.diverseeducators.co.uk/womened-england/

CHAPTER 1: AGE

CHAPTER EDITOR: **KATIE WALDEGRAVE**

CHAPTER CONTRIBUTORS

1. Patrick Thomson – **Towards age-inclusive, sustainable careers in the education sector**
2. Ian Hunter – **Valuing Age Diversity in Schools**
3. Jo Brighouse – **The Crime of Miss Jean Brodie: Why are experienced teachers no longer valued?**
4. Nicky Bright – **Menopause and Schools**
5. Leila MacTavish and Isabel Instone – **The potential benefits of age-inclusivity**
6. Richard Lewis – **Age and teachers: challenges and opportunities**
7. Hugh Ogilvie – **Experience and resilience create the counterbalance to imposter syndrome**
8. Jane Clewlow – **Stage Not Age: Ageism in Schools**
9. Tulika Samal – **Knowledge transfer: Shifting the Focus So Differences Become Strengths through Mentorship**
10. Savitri Patel – **Story Book Villains: Where are the Positive Older Role Models in the English Literature Curriculum?**

BIOGRAPHIES

Katie Waldegrave is co-founder of Now Teach, a charity helping experienced career-changers to retrain as teachers. Previously she co-founded First Story, the creative writing charity for students in low-income communities. She began her working life as a history teacher and is committed to improving equity in education (and, on the side, to writing).

Hugh Ogilvie is a teacher of English and Drama, covering all secondary key stages, with a particular interest in A level Literature and continually developing pedagogy and practice, allied to an undimmed passion for lifelong learning and positive relationships between staff and students.

Ian Hunter is Chief Executive of the Knowledge Schools Trust in London. He was a late entrant to the world of education, having had prior careers in global businesses and consultancies. He completed a MEd degree in Educational Leadership as part of his 're-training'. He has employed Now Teach teachers since 2018 and particularly values the diversity and difference that they bring to both the classroom and staffroom.

Jane Clewlow has worked in educational leadership for over twenty years, leading teaching, learning and staff development in schools spanning London, Salford, Manchester and Dubai. She has undertaken a variety of roles including: Head of English, Head of Year, Assistant Headteacher and Deputy Headteacher.

Jo Brighouse is an experienced primary teacher in the Midlands. She is a former *TES* columnist and writes under a pseudonym.

Leila MacTavish is the Head of Ark Teacher Training. She previously worked as the Vice Principal of the City of London Academy, Highbury Grove, and the Head of Initial Teacher Education for Future Academies. Leila is a trustee of Untold and the Charities Advisory Trust and a governor at Ark Brunel Primary Academy.

Isabel Instone is the secondary curriculum lead for Ark Teacher Training. She trained to teach with Teach First and has held a number of teaching roles in London, including Head of Science at Reach Academy, Feltham, before joining Ark Teacher Training as a professional tutor and Science Subject Lead.

Nicky Bright spent thirty years in education, eight as Head and former Chair of the Girls' Schools Association's Professional Development Committee. Nicky runs Bright Lead Ltd. A leadership development coach and facilitator, Nicky serves and enables leaders and their teams to be their 'best selves' and raises awareness of the impact of the menopause.

Patrick Thomson leads the age-friendly employers' programme at the Centre for Ageing Better. Patrick works closely with employers, recruiters, and intermediaries to bring about behaviour change within organisations to maximise the benefits of the ageing workforce. As a former member of the Government Social Research Unit he commissioned and managed projects for the Department for Work and Pensions' ageing society strategy, leading to the evidence base for the removal of the Default Retirement Age.

Richard Lewis is currently a History teacher in an inner London secondary school teaching years 7 to 13. He currently holds the title 'the oldest NQT in Westminster.' Prior to teaching Richard was a banker and an international management consultant developing teams across national and corporate cultures.

Savitri Patel works as a Programme Manager for Now Teach, supporting career-changers to retrain and remain as teachers. Prior to that, she was an English teacher and Head of Media Studies and spent five years as Learning Projects Manager at a London theatre.

Tulika Samal is originally from India and has over fifteen years of experience as an educator in varied roles that include, but are not limited to, the Principal of a residential school, Vice Principal, Headmistress and Junior High Math teacher in Phoenix, AZ, USA. Tulika is the Co-Founder of Eddoxa, an education consultancy excelling in providing various services to schools.

THE PROTECTED CHARACTERISTIC OF AGE: INTRODUCTION

KATIE WALDEGRAVE

INTRODUCTION

Ageism: discrimination or unfair treatment based on a person's age

In his 2021 book, *Extra Life*, science writer Stephen Johnson sets himself a thought experiment: what if there was a newspaper which was published only once every century? What would the headlines be? Almost certainly, something along the lines of 'Average human lifespan doubles.' Our species has pulled off an astonishing achievement.

The story of our altered life expectancy is a fascinating one. The impact of that story plays out in every part of our lives. I had twins in 2016 in the UK; there is more chance that both will live to 100 than that both do not. They will think about education, careers, love, leisure, retirement, health and relationships in ways which are completely different to that of my grandmother, born in 1911 with a life expectancy of fifty-eight.

It often seems that we have not quite kept up with the news. Data collection still captures the experience of people in age brackets spanning decades and then sticks 'sixty plus' on the end, neglecting to realise that this is 23% of the UK population. It is no longer realistic, or desirable, to expect that we will all work until sixty-something and retire. My children will be working into their eighties and this is to be celebrated – but it will take some thought.

DEFINITIONS AND TERMINOLOGY

Every few months a version of the same article appears about ageism experienced by older teachers. There is a strong sense amongst the contributors to this chapter that we do not value our ageing workforce. Some countries are better at it than others. But like most problems, the practical manifestation is money. Older teachers can be replaced with cheaper young ones. They may not be quite as good, but they will put up with more hours and in the end it more or less balances out – and balances the books.

We are not serving our students, nor any of our teachers with the system we currently have. This is not a problem limited to the education sector. Patrick Thompson, of The Centre for Ageing Better, outlines the problem of ageism powerfully:

The National Barometer of Prejudice and Discrimination, shows 26% of people said that they had experienced discrimination based on age in the last year, a higher proportion than any other protected characteristic, including gender, race, or disability.

But it is particularly acute in education.

The effect of a relatively young workforce is not good for that workforce. When I started teaching I endlessly worked beyond midnight only to wake at 5.30am and start all over again. Now I have three children, more responsibilities and a slightly thicker skin, I simply would not and could not do it. In 2016 I set up an organisation called Now Teach, which brings older career changers into teaching. One of the things they are often valued for is holding their boundaries. When I was considering my career progression, my family and whether/how to apply for leadership roles, it might have been useful to speak to more people who had faced those same questions. Perhaps I would not be one of the thousands of teachers, particularly women, who drop out of the profession without really intending to.

Most of all, it does not benefit the students. If you are ageist – that is to say, have negative expectations of older age – as a child, then you will experience a worse older age. Study after study has shown us our life expectancy, health and happiness will all be worse. As teachers we know this: our students fulfil the expectations we put on them. It is incumbent on us for their sake, if for no other reason, that we eliminate ageism from schools. The only sure-fire way of doing this is to ensure the teaching population of any school is age diverse. The more the generations mix, the better off we all are.

LANDSCAPE

Scientists predict that some of the five-year-olds in my twins' class might live until the 2130s. To equip them for that future, they need things people of all ages can offer. The importance of exams, the vagaries of family life, the anger of adolescents, all appear different to us when we have seen it all before. Schools must hang on to these different perspectives. Not least because ageing is going to be a very inequitable conundrum.

People in the poorest parts of the UK live ten years less than people in the wealthiest. Even more worryingly, people in the poorest areas not only have shorter lives, but they spend far less of those years healthy. Currently, the rich-poor gap in the UK's healthy working life is nineteen years; that is to say, a healthy woman born in Nottingham has a healthy life expectancy of fifty-three compared to seventy-two years in Wokingham. This maps directly on to the educational attainments and life chances; we all know the link between poverty and chances of success. This pattern repeats the world over. Globally, too, there is a clear link between schools in low-income areas and young teachers. These are the very children who most need to have a healthy attitude to ageing – and a responsible relationship with their future selves.

VOICES IN OUR CHAPTER IN DIVERSE EDUCATORS – A MANIFESTO

The contributors to this chapter have seen ageism in myriad forms in schools. **Patrick Thompson** opens this chapter by outlining the problem of ageism powerfully. **Ian Hunter** and **Jo Brighouse** show us the view from their perspectives as CEO of Knowledge Schools Trust MAT and an experienced classroom teacher respectively. **Nicky Bright**, founder of Bright Lead with thirty years in education, outlines the imperative for schools to do more around the menopause. **Leila MacTavish**, Head of Ark Teacher Training outlines with **Isabel Instone**, Secondary Curriculum Lead for Ark Teacher Training, some challenges and solutions to ageism within ITT while **Richard Lewis** and **Hugh Ogilvie**, both later entrants to teaching, cover the challenges older trainees can face – and the riches they bring. **Jane Clewlow**, who has been in education leadership roles for the past twenty years, gives us a portrait of how ageism can affect all teachers. **Tulika Samal**, Co-Founder of Eddoxa, an education consultancy in India, describes the value to schools of intergenerational mentoring, while **Savitri Patel**, Programme Manager at Now Teach, looks at lessons learned from other curriculum campaigns, such as anti-racism, asking whether the curriculum itself is ageist.

These contributors can see what is often wrong. But ultimately they are hopeful. They can see what needs to be made right and offer schools and school leaders practical solutions to make it so.

There are other contenders for the headline of the century: 'Earth's surface temperature increases by 1°C'; 'Vaccines and antibiotics save millions'; 'population quadruples'; 'Sharp decline in percentage living in poverty'; 'World loses forested land the size of USA' – one could go on and on, but many of these advances and retreats are intrinsically tied. As we live longer, get healthier and many get wealthier, global inequality, global warming and the existential questions of our species rise.

The good news is that, as the longevity expert and author Marc Freedman puts it, 'Older people are the earth's only growing natural resource.' If we can recast our relationship to age and ageing, we stand a chance of solving many of the most intractable problems we have.

CONCLUSION

Education is, of course, where it all begins. We need the next generation well-prepared for the world they will inherit and for the lives they will lead in it. We need them prepared for their own longer lives. More widely we need to value our ageing workforce. Ageism is a peculiarly internalised '-ism'; we need to stop discriminating against our own future selves. We need to stop seeing the fact that we are living longer as a problem. It is the greatest gift we have been given. Our young people need to see this, and for them to see it, we all need to change our attitudes towards the astonishing human successes which have got us to the point where my youngest child, born in 2019, could well have grandchildren who are born in the 23rd century.

COMMITMENT TO THE MANIFESTO

Know that ageism is a strongly internalised prejudice whose object, uniquely, is our future selves. Intergenerational organisations are strong organisations. We owe it to our young people, who will live longer lives than any generation yet, to eradicate ageism in schools.

REFERENCES

Freedman, M. and Conley, C. (2020). *How to live forever : the enduring power of connecting the generations.* New York : PublicAffairs.

Gratton, L. and Scott, A. (2016) *The 100-year life: living and working in an age of longevity.* London: Bloomsbury Information.

Officer, A., Thiyagarajan, J. A., Schneiders, M. L., Nash, P, and de la Fuente-Núñez, V. (2020).' Ageism, Healthy Life Expectancy and Population Ageing: How Are They Related?' *International journal of environmental research and public health, 17*(9), 3159. https://doi.org/10.3390/ijerph17093159

Vaupel, J.W., Villavicencio, F., Bergeron-Boucher, M. (2021). 'Demographic perspectives on the rise of longevity.' *Proceedings of the National Academy of Sciences,* Mar 2021, 118 (9) e2019536118; DOI: 10.1073/pnas.2019536118

TOWARDS AGE-INCLUSIVE, SUSTAINABLE CAREERS IN THE EDUCATION SECTOR

PATRICK THOMSON

INTRODUCTION

Our workforce and our society are ageing, with one in three workers already aged fifty or over in the UK. More of us will need or want to work for longer, and yet there are structural barriers in many workplaces, and attitudinal barriers in society that mean that many of us are pushed out of work earlier than we might want to. This is a loss to both individuals and the education sector alike. We know that multigenerational teams improve productivity, help workforce planning, retain valuable skills and expertise and yet too many people are not valued.

INCREASED AGE-DIVERSITY IS AN OPPORTUNITY FOR DIFFERENT GENERATIONS AND THEIR EMPLOYERS

Despite widely held misconceptions about intergenerational conflict, different generations want largely the same things from work. The factors that make work fulfilling for older workers are largely the same as for any other age. Older workers look for employment that is personally meaningful, flexible, intellectually stimulating, sociable and age-inclusive. However, some factors become more important with age, in particular support to manage health needs and caring responsibilities (Marvell & Cox, 2016).

Although what older workers want is not substantially different from other ages, the support and access to opportunities they receive is often different. Older workers say that they would benefit from more access to flexible working, opportunities for training and progression and support for long-term health conditions (Thomson, 2018). Not everyone experiences this though, with one in ten workers aged fifty to sixty-nine reporting low job satisfaction, and one in three reporting a lack of control at work (State of Ageing 2020).

Being in good-quality work in your fifties and sixties can be one of the best indicators for how you will experience later life and retirement. Good-quality work is also key to retaining people in any job for longer. Pay is a key part of this, but it is not the only factor as we know that retired people miss the social aspects of work more than anything else (Ageing Better, Ipsos Mori, 2015).

Analysis of international data showed that older workers are just as productive at work as any other age group. Perhaps more importantly, having a worker over fifty in a team is associated with increased productivity of co-workers around them, particularly younger colleagues. These spill-over effects boost productivity in three ways: lower job turnover, their greater management experience and their greater general work experience (OECD, 2020).

Too many people experience ageism in society and the workplace:

Ageism is the most widely experienced form of discrimination in the UK. The National Barometer of Prejudice and Discrimination shows 26% of people said that they had experienced discrimination based on age in the last year, a higher proportion than any other protected characteristic, including gender, race, or disability. Despite its prevalence, the majority of people (54%) view age discrimination as 'not at all' or only 'slightly' serious. People underestimate the frequency and seriousness of discrimination in terms of age, and in many respects age remains a 'forgotten' characteristic in terms of diversity and inclusion. Jokes, comments and stereotypes about age in the workplace are acceptable in a way that would not be tolerated for any other characteristic in a modern workplace (EHRC,2018).

THE EDUCATION SECTOR IS PARTICULARLY IMPACTED

Education is ranked higher than any other major sector in terms of how it will be impacted by the ageing workforce. Not only are a high proportion of the workforce (37%) aged over fifty, numbering more than 1.2m workers, but they also saw a large fall in employment between the ages of 45-49 and 60-64 of 53% (CIPD / ILC-UK, 2015). This suggests that there is both a retention and sustainability issue in terms of supporting older workers in the education sector. Pension arrangements may play a factor in pulling people towards retirement, but stress, ageism, or a poor work/life balance may also push people out of work.

Education also has a higher-than-average proportion of women working in the sector. This matters when combined with age for a number of reasons. Few workplaces have support or policies for the menopause. While both men and women are carers, middle-aged women do a disproportionate amount of unpaid caring, and many are 'sandwich' carers for younger or older relatives, as well as partners. Without proper support or flexibility from employers, what might start as a short-term crisis can lead to people leaving employment in the long term.

Research by Birmingham University shows that two-thirds of UK adults can expect to be unpaid carers at some point in their lives. While half of men become carers by the age of fifty-seven, for women this comes earlier in their lives and careers, with half of women becoming carers by the age of forty-six (Zhang & Bennett, 2019). The impact on your working life between being a carer in your mid-forties and mid-fifties is stark. In a sector that focuses on knowledge transfer and learning, it is worrying that the most experienced part of the workforce is exiting earlier than in other sectors. With many experienced teachers leaving the workforce the sector could struggle to fill the gaps.

WE NEED TO CHANGE OUR THINKING ABOUT WORK AND CAREERS AS MORE OF US LIVE A HUNDRED-YEAR LIFE

For many, 2021 will be a tipping point. One in eight older workers have changed their retirement plans as a result of the pandemic (Crawford and Karjalainen, 2020). We need opportunities to change jobs no matter what our age, whether to progress, take on new challenges, or balance work with other needs. People need to move – up, down or sideways – based on where they are in their life or their career, but they are often stuck because they are seen as too experienced, set in their ways, or lacking potential. This is why organisations such as Now Teach are essential in showing a path that people in mid-life can follow in teaching. Innovative new approaches such as the 'Mid-life MOT' could be one way that the education sector can attract, retain and reinvigorate people in mid-life and beyond (Centre for Ageing Better, 2018).

CONCLUSION

With more of us living a 'hundred-year life' (Gratton and Scott, 2018) it is in all of our interests to make sure that we can move and change jobs free of bias at any point of our working lives. For education to be a thriving and inclusive sector we need to include people of all ages.

KEY TAKEAWAYS

- Education is ranked first out of eighteen sectors by the CIPD in terms of the impact of an ageing workforce.
- More of us will need or want to work for longer, and yet there are structural barriers in many workplaces, and attitudinal barriers in society that mean that many of us are pushed out of work earlier than we might want to.
- According to the Equalities and Human Rights Commission ageism is the most widely experienced form of discrimination in the UK and it is also the one that is likely to be taken the least seriously.
- Flexible working is the number one workplace practice the over-fifties say would support them to work for longer.

KEY QUESTIONS

- As an employer do you know the age profile of your workforce, the average age of exit and whether you can prevent people leaving earlier than they might want to?

- Is age part of your workplace DEI strategy?
- Are your flexible working, carers, and recruitment policy and practices designed with older workers or job applicants in mind?
- What support, progression, learning or development opportunities do you provide and target at older workers?

COMMITMENT TO THE MANIFESTO

Commit to becoming an age-friendly employer, and take action on the Centre for Ageing Better's five steps.

REFERENCES

Abrams, D., Swift, H. and Houston D. (2018). Equality and Human Rights Commission. *Developing a national barometer of prejudice and discrimination in Britain*. Available at: https://www.equalityhumanrights.com/sites/default/files/national-barometer-of-prejudice-and-discrimination-in-britain.pdf (accessed May 2021)

Centre for Ageing Better (2020). *Doddery but dear? Examining age-related stereotypes*. Available at: https://www.ageing-better.org.uk/ publications/doddery-dear-examining-age-related-stereotypes (accessed 24 May 2021)

Centre for Ageing Better (2021). *Too Much Experience*. Available at: https://www.ageing-better.org.uk/sites/default/files/2021-02/too-much-experience.pdf

Centre for Ageing Better (2021). *Work, State of Ageing in 2020*. Available at: https://www.ageing-better.org.uk/work-state-ageing-2020 (accessed 24 May 2021)

Centre for Ageing Better and Aviva and Mercer et al. (2018). 'Developing the mid-life MOT.' Available at: https://www.ageing-better.org.uk/sites/default/files/2018-10/Developing-the-Mid-life-MOT-report.pdf (accessed May 2021)

Centre for Ageing Better and Ipsos Mori (2015). *Later Life in 2015*. Available at: https://laterlife.ageing-better.org.uk/ (accessed May 2021)

Crawford, R., and Karjalainen, H. (2020), Institute for Fiscal Studies. '*The coronavirus pandemic and older workers.*' Available at: https://www.ifs.org.uk/publications/15040 (accessed May 25 2021)

Gratton, L. and Scott, A. (2016) *The 100 year Life, Living and Working in an Age of Longevity,* London: Bloomsbury Information.

Marvell, R. and Cox, A. (2016) *Fulfilling work: What do older workers value about work and why?* Centre for Ageing Better and IES. Available at: www.ageing-better.org.

uk/publications/ fulfilling-work-what-do-older-workers-value-about-work-and-why (accessed 24 May 2021)

OECD (2020). *Promoting an Age-Inclusive Workforce.* Available at: https://www. employment-studies.co.uk/system/files/resources/files/Promoting%20an%20Age-Inclusive%20Workforce%20Living%2C%20Learning%20and%20Earning%20Longer. pdf (accessed 24 May 2021)

CIPD and ILC (2015). *Avoiding the demographic crunch: Labour supply and the ageing workforce.* Available at: https://www.cipd.co.uk/Images/avoiding-the-demographic-crunch-labour-supply-and-ageing-workforce_tcm18-10235.pdf (accessed May 2021)

Thomson, P. (2018). *A silver lining for the UK economy? The intergenerational case for supporting longer working lives.* Intergenerational Commission

Timewise and Centre for Ageing Better (2020) *Inclusivity through flexibility – How flexible working can support a thriving, age-inclusive workplace.* Available at: https://ageing-better.org.uk/sites/default/files/2020-09/Timewise-Flex-Working-full-report.pdf

YouGov / Department of Work and Pensions (2015). *Attitudes of the over 50s to Fuller Working Lives.* Available at: https://www.gov.uk/government/publications/attitudes-of-the-over-50s-to-fuller-working-lives (accessed May 2021)

Zhang, Y. and Bennett, M. (2019). *Will I care? The likelihood of being a carer in adult life.* University of Birmingham. Available at: https://research.birmingham.ac.uk/portal/en/publications/will-i-care-the-likelihood-of-being-a-carer-in-adult-life(79e288e1-d44d-4847-abb7-cb9711a784de)/export.html

VALUING AGE DIVERSITY IN SCHOOLS

IAN HUNTER

INTRODUCTION

Ageism in schools and education is a surprisingly under-researched area. The most cited research, via Google Scholar, references a publication from 2001. This clearly presents a plum research opportunity for the ambitious academic or budding PhD student. However, whilst academic research may be light on the ground, other data and anecdotal accounts indicate that ageism is an increasing issue in schools. In October 2020 the OECD released a report that indicated that since 2005 the average age of teachers had fallen dramatically; UK has more than twice the proportion of teachers aged under thirty than other developed countries and nearly one in three primary school teachers (31%) are aged thirty or under. Could ageism in teaching be to blame or are there other economic and cultural factors in play?

ENCOUNTERING AGEISM

In my role as chief executive of a multi-academy trust, I am aware that I could indeed be the parent of a significant majority of my employees, such is the average age gap between myself and many teaching staff. As I have grown older I have become more aware of age and the limitations that it can impose on career opportunities. I was a late career entrant to education having spent thirty plus years in business and consulting. I was used to working with multi-generational teams but, even so, was horrified to discover that I had taken my A levels at the same time as the parent of one of my Deputy Heads. Postings online indicate that more mature teachers report difficulties in getting appointed beyond the age of forty. Indeed, teachers who are in their fifties report many examples of conscious and unconscious ageism. One long-serving English teacher believes that the most prevalent type of ageism is driven by economic factors. 'About six years ago I asked a Deputy Head at an Independent School to review my application, as I was looking for a new job, and finding I was not getting as far as an interview stage for roles where I felt I definitely fitted what they were looking for.' The Deputy Head advised that her application was well-written and persuasive but that she was too expensive to be appointed.

As such she was experiencing an age apartheid driven by increasingly tight budgets. Possibly it was less a cultural bias against age but more that younger teachers, whose experience might be less but still judged 'good enough', were preferred as they could be appointed lower down the pay scale.

Information collated by the National Education Union (NEU) suggests middle-aged teachers, and especially women, are over-represented in capability procedures in schools. This seemed to be part of a national pattern and the NEU argued that some academy chains were driven by a culture aimed at weeding out expensive prior experience and knowledge which might not be seen to be in line with the management and curricular ethos of those chains. Two teachers I spoke to anecdotally believed that schools are often reluctant to interview anyone who has celebrated birthdays past thirty, which is a pretty radical redefinition of what constitutes 'age' discrimination.

VALUING THE OLDER EMPLOYEE

Broadly speaking, older teachers do not feel that their knowledge based on long experience is equally valued across schools. Interestingly, all but one of the staff I spoke to felt they had not overtly experienced ageism in their teaching careers. Schools who have an age-diverse teaching staff may have a recruitment advantage when it comes to attracting well-qualified returners and career transferees from organisations such as Now Teach. One former professional service firm partner, who career switched to teaching, said that, 'Even though I was fifty-three when I started training, one of the key attractions of joining my school was that it had an age-diverse teaching staff and seemed to be an environment where age appeared to be immaterial to professional relationships'.

GAINING ACCEPTANCE AS A LATE CAREER ENTRANT

The challenge of winning over much younger but more experienced colleagues is recognised by late entrants to the profession. 'I had steeled myself to a default position of humility as there is nothing worse than "outsiders" assuming they can come into any profession and succeed simply because they have succeeded somewhere else,' said a former business consulting partner. Of course, one of the joys of teaching as a second career is the opportunity to work on equal terms with younger colleagues. A fifty- year-old NQT reported that: 'My experience has been that you are accepted based on your commitment to the job, and improving professional standards, rather than anything else. I have also found that age seems not to affect the quality of feedback received from much younger heads of department.'

All of the older teachers contacted reported that the training and feedback they received was invariably direct, focussed, insightful and constructive even though in many cases it was delivered by someone twenty years their junior.

Another late career entrant observed that 'one of the advantages of experience, especially in teaching history, politics and economics, is that you have experienced much of it first-hand!' The extensive cultural capital that age and experience bring is extremely valuable in preparing and delivering lessons and in providing personal context to many subject areas. Older but new entrant teachers are often self-reflective enough to differentiate between the consequences of ageism and inexperience in how they are treated. 'I have been one of the least experienced members of staff in my department and I have not expected to be treated as anything other than a novice,' as one forty-eight-year-old NQT put it.

One factor is that new teachers in their late forties or fifties frequently regard themselves as being post-career. They have already had rewarding and successful careers and climbed the ladder in other organisations and do not have the thirst for promotion beyond being an outstanding classroom teacher. Furthermore, they do not want to hinder the promotion of younger colleagues who do still have something to prove and want to progress to senior leadership roles. However, the fact that Headteachers and SLT members are less likely to seek the views and learnings from other professions, perhaps underscores their belief that 'business experience' only applies to the non-teaching operational aspects of leading a school and has nothing to inform the core pastoral and academic capabilities in the school. Given the profusion of preparation in the business professions that are given for managerial and leadership development this seems like a missed opportunity.

INDIRECT AGEISM

Perhaps a clear example of age not being considered sufficiently was in the return to school after lockdown. Many older teachers were self-evidently in higher risk age groups, where the impact of Covid might be more serious, than for a teacher in their twenties. Older teachers have sometimes been left feeling that school leaders could have been more empathetic for those more at risk with stricter application of covid precautions. This is not necessarily ageist, of course, but may reflect that younger SLT members do not always appreciate the concerns of older colleagues. It is obvious that the pay and progression system in many schools risks creating a financial bias against more experienced and older teachers. With budgets under pressure, schools have increasingly large financial incentives to replace a long-serving teacher with someone younger, less experienced and who commands less salary. Possibly this might be better termed 'experiencism.'

One big issue is the culture of schools being very hierarchical compared to other organisations. This is not directly an ageism point, but it means that a school may miss out on the opportunity to tap into experience. One teacher commented that: 'I notice that even when we have departmental time scheduled, we rarely if ever meet to discuss how we can improve.'

CONCLUSION

Schools have much to ponder and improve in how they recruit, develop and manage older teachers and support staff. Do schools actually value the diversity of the age and experience mix and what steps can they take to preserve it? No school can operate effectively with an over-reliance on trainees and NQTs to make the budget. School and MAT leadership teams need to recognise and leverage the wide range of experience of older hires and use that to enhance the running of school operations. Recognising that ageism or 'experienceism' can manifest itself in many ways and with unforeseen consequences is an important insight. In many instances not being 25-35 but having a more seasoned view of the world can be a major plus.

KEY TAKEAWAYS

- MATs must consider whether their financial and/ or management models make them more likely to be ageist.
- Intergenerational relationships benefit all.
- The UK has amongst the youngest teaching populations in the world.

KEY QUESTIONS

- Does your school/MAT have a policy on ageism?
- How do you take full benefit of the lived experience of older teachers?
- Do you think SLT recognises the concerns of older colleagues?

COMMITMENT TO THE MANIFESTO

Acknowledge that ageism may come as much from financial and management systems as it does from individual attitudes and prejudices.

REFERENCES

Busby, E. (2019). UK Teachers are younger and paid less than in any other developed country, report finds, *The Independent*, 10 September. Available at: https://www.independent.co.uk/news/education/education-news/oecd-study-uk-teachers-britain-youngest-pay-salaries-countries-a9099216.html (Accessed 20 April 2021)

National Education Union (2021). *Capability Procedure*. Available at https://neu.org.uk/advice/capability-procedure (Accessed 1 July 2021).

THE CRIME OF MISS JEAN BRODIE: WHY ARE EXPERIENCED TEACHERS NO LONGER VALUED?

JO BRIGHOUSE

INTRODUCTION

What is life like in schools for an older teacher? I do not mean a Headteacher or SLT – just your standard, everyday classroom teacher with several decades of experience under their belt. You would think such experience would reap certain benefits – increased confidence, a level of job security, respect and support from those above them. This would not always be a correct assumption to make.

WHY HAVE EXPERIENCED TEACHERS BECOME A 'PROBLEM'?

For certain school leaders, experienced classroom teachers pose something of a problem. For one thing, they are hard on the budget. Costing thousands of pounds more than an NQT, experience has also given them convictions and opinions which make them less malleable than career starters. Such teachers can be viewed as a problem to be solved: an immovable object blocking a space that could be better filled by a bright young thing more likely to carry out all leadership requests with uncritical obedience. Experienced teachers working in these school cultures are likely to feel – at best – unappreciated and, at worst, actively targeted and aggressively managed out. All of which seems illogical in a climate where nearly one in five teachers quits after just a year in the classroom and less than 70 % of new starters are still in the job after five years. (DfE, School Workforce in England, 2019).

With so many new teachers leaving the job, surely we should be doing everything we can to appreciate those who actively choose to stick at the chalkface? But are we? UK teachers are currently younger and less well-paid than in any other developed country (Busby, The Independent, 2019

Nearly one in three primary teachers are aged thirty or under and the percentage of teachers aged between fifty and sixty fell from 21.7 % in 2010, to 15.6 % in 2016 (Whittaker, Schools' Week, 2019) which raises the question of where are they going and why?

AGEISM IN ACTION

The hard truth is that some school management teams are blatantly ageist. Under certain school leaders, teachers with years of experience and a solid track record of raising standards can find themselves reassessed overnight and found wanting. They will have their data plotted against impossible targets and their subsequent failure to meet these held over them.

They are sidelined and dismissed in meetings while younger, cheaper teachers are singled out for public praise. They find themselves moved into smaller classrooms and into year groups they do not want to teach. They have curriculum areas they are passionate about taken away from them. They are forced to change the way they plan and teach, crossing i's and dotting t's in a one-size-fits-all approach that completely ignores the individual needs of the staff and benefits no one. Sometimes they are told point blank that their status on the upper pay scale is crippling the budget and 'damaging' the school. At some point along the line, it is very likely that the experienced teacher will give up the ghost and leave. There will be no talk of ageism or 'being managed out'. Even if they could summon the reserves of energy and confidence needed to challenge this, it is still all too easy for school leaders to come up with a plethora of reasons why their treatment of staff does not constitute ageism. After all, nobody is perfect. If you are a headteacher intent on finding flaws in someone's teaching, there is a good chance you will find them.

And what then? The school fills the gap with an NQT and the teacher either quits the profession or dusts themselves down and goes in search of a school that will pay something close to their former pay scale (in no other profession do people routinely accept a cut in pay for doing the job they were already doing). For schools who favour this management style, it is no longer uncommon to have every classroom occupied by teachers with less than five years' experience. I once left a school where there were more NQTs than there were experienced teachers to mentor them.

WHY YOU SHOULD CELEBRATE YOUR MR CHIPS

Of course, the biggest losers are the children. Experienced teachers who choose to stay in the classroom are not celebrated nearly enough. This is a job where to have 'been there, done that' means a great deal. While it may be increasingly common for school leaders to see the experienced classroom teacher as a budget-gobbling dinosaur, to many within the school they are nothing short of a lifeline:

- They are the official (and often unofficial) mentor for younger staff, the go-to teacher for parents in times of trouble, the listening ear for everyone from cleaner to headteacher and the dependable pair of hands in times of crisis.
- They have seen every teaching fad going. From thinking hats to brain gym, through the 'VAK years' and the paperwork avalanche that was APP, they have survived the rise and fall of countless new initiatives that were going to

revolutionise the profession. Their curriculum expertise will be partly borne out of trial and error. They know what works and what does not. And while it obviously does not always follow that 'experienced means better', you simply do not last in teaching these days if you are not doing something right.

But beyond the academic results, experienced classroom teachers bring something to a school that is unquantifiable. Creating a genuine sense of belonging and shared ethos within a school community is not something that can be rushed. It takes time to build up and it will not happen if the adults in the building are constantly changing. There is a reason why retirement celebrations for teachers who have spent decades in one school are so heartfelt. A longstanding classroom teacher is a physical embodiment of a school's ethos. The school's history and traditions are interwoven with their own career. They are the reason former pupils come back to visit, they are trusted by parents (some of whom they may have taught) and they are probably the only person in the building who can locate the megaphone from last year's sports day and who knows what is kept in that weird cupboard under the stage.

PLAY THE LONG GAME

Schools which champion young, inexpensive teachers while nudging older, more expensive staff towards the exit, are short-sighted. Even looked at purely from a money-saving perspective, filling a school with cheaper staff will not keep the budget down in the long run. On top of the NQT cover and CPD costs, these are salaries which will only go up year on year while the salary of experienced teachers may start high but is not going anywhere even as their experience builds.

CONCLUSION

But you cannot always blame the schools. The system they operate within is becoming heavily weighted against the classroom stalwarts. Budget cuts have bitten so deeply that many heads simply have no choice but to employ cheaper staff and so the cycle continues.

KEY TAKEAWAYS

- Experienced teachers bring more to a school than just classroom expertise.
- School budgets make it very difficult to employ very experienced staff who want to remain in the classroom.
- Ageism is quietly present in many schools but is rarely challenged and discussed.

KEY QUESTIONS

- Is your staff management tailored to bring out each individual teacher's strengths and experience? Do you consider the CPD needs of experienced teachers?
- How do you show older, more experienced classroom teachers in your school that their work is valued?
- Is your rhetoric about staff ageist? Do you talk about teachers being 'energetic' and 'enthusiastic' or 'set in their ways'?

COMMITMENT TO THE MANIFESTO

Ensure that all experienced class teachers feel publicly and privately valued.

REFERENCES

Busby, E. (2019) 'UK Teachers are younger and paid less than in any other developed country, report finds', *The Independent*, 10 September. Available at: https://www.independent.co.uk/news/education/education-news/oecd-study-uk-teachers-britain-youngest-pay-salaries-countries-a9099216.html (site accessed 20 April 2021)

The UK Government, (25th June 2020, updated 26th November 2020) Explore Education Statistics. *School Workforce in England, Reporting Year 2019*. Available at: https://explore-education-statistics.service.gov.uk/find-statistics/school-workforce-in-england (site accessed 20 April 2021)

Whittaker, F. (2019) 'Forced out: The experienced teachers losing their livelihoods as schools cut costs'. *Schools Week,* 28 April. Available at: https://schoolsweek.co.uk/forced-out-the-experienced-teachers-losing-their-livelihoods-as-schools-cut-costs/) (site accessed 20 April 2021)

MENOPAUSE AND SCHOOLS

NICKY BRIGHT

INTRODUCTION

Menopause is not an issue affecting women in isolation, this affects workplaces, communities and families in equal measure. Everyone knows, or will know, someone who may be going through the menopause whether that is a mother, aunt, wife or colleague at work, and so proper understanding of this stage of life is crucial. This is the fastest growing demographic in the workplace, with significantly more women in leadership positions than in the past, and so it is vital that employers encourage open discussions to ensure they get the right support in place to fulfil their legal and moral duties. With approximately forty different possible symptoms, each woman's experience is unique, which makes a 'one-size-fits-all' approach to support impossible. Supporting these, often highly experienced staff, in the right way for them, can also help stem the loss of valuable skills from the profession and so starting the conversation has never been more important.

THE MENOPAUSE: WHAT IS IT AND WHAT ARE THE PRACTICAL IMPACTS?

Twenty-five percent of women going through menopause have considered leaving work, and around 10% do actually give up work altogether (Wellbeing of Women Survey 2016). With women dominating the teaching profession, this is a retention issue which must be more effectively addressed than it is currently. It is not only an issue for governors and senior leaders in schools, an increasing number of whom fall into this demographic, but for every line manager, indeed every person in our school communities.

Given there are more than forty symptoms associated with the menopause, experienced by each woman in a unique combination, perhaps it should be no surprise that many women do not recognise the signs of reaching this stage in life. I did not. Menopause was relegated to the cursory mention in my school of 'and then, when you stop ovulating, your periods stop', as the focus of understanding our cycles was on 'how not to get pregnant'. A taboo subject for many years, only recently being more widely talked about, it is no wonder many women themselves are ignorant of the impacts of the menopause and the support available to them.

The menopause occurs when the ovaries no longer produce eggs and the levels of estrogen, progesterone and testosterone fall. During the perimenopause, the levels of these hormones fluctuate greatly, often leading to symptoms of the menopause occurring. For some women, symptoms only occur for a few months whereas other women experience symptoms for many months or years before their periods stop. The average age of the menopause in the UK is fifty-one years, and symptoms often start at around forty-five years of age. Younger women may experience premature menopause or surgical menopause, for various medical or surgical reasons.

Most people know about night sweats and hot flushes, and can imagine the impact this might have upon a woman's ability to work. Brain fog and memory issues can be particularly debilitating in the workplace. But many do not realise that dry eyes, itchy skin or loss of confidence, to name just a few, may also be part of the package. With nests emptying and the pressures of elderly parents, the sometimes associated low moods, lack of sleep, irritability or debilitating anxiety can often easily be explained away. And, as menopause does not currently form part of the compulsory education for GPs, often 'support' comes in the form of antidepressants, or other medication, rather than the often more appropriate HRT which, in its various more modern iterations, is considered suitable for far more women than was previously possible and with positive preventative effects, such as reducing the risk of osteoporosis. Sadly, outdated perceptions and a lack of education mean many women 'soldier on' not realising they could be supported more effectively.

Often women themselves are completely unaware that their symptoms are related to menopause, as indeed was I. Even so, a CIPD survey found that 59% of working women between the ages of forty-five and fifty-five who were experiencing menopause symptoms said it had a negative impact on them at work (CIPD 2019). Women over fifty are the fastest growing demographic in the workplace and currently constitute around one in eight of the British workforce . By 2022 it is forecast that around one in six will be women over fifty (Department for Work and Pensions 2015). Whether the pandemic will have impacted these figures remains to be seen. All this has implications for school leadership teams, and for governors supporting leaders. School leaders need to look after themselves as well as their colleagues.

WHAT CAN BE DONE FOR TEACHERS AND LEADERS AS EMPLOYEES?

We make adjustments for, and are sympathetic to, new parents in a way that we are not currently for menopausal women, when both groups may suffer from sleep deprivation and a substantial change in their self-perception and identity. Menopausal women can too often be seen as 'cranky', 'difficult' or even laughable (Les Dawson has a lot to answer for), even though they may be struggling silently, trying to 'manage themselves' and how they feel at this disconcerting stage of life.

Reasonable adjustments should be made in terms of both Equalities Act and Health & Safety at Work Act responsibilities. The CIPD and NEU both have excellent menopause toolkits which can be a first stop for governors and leadership teams when considering their responsibilities, including posters, checklists and sample policies. Ensuring awareness is raised among the community is the first step to ensuring empathetic and supportive conversations which will provide women with the adjustments appropriate to their unique combination of symptoms and a poster might make all the difference.

Many schools have maternity and paternity policies, very few have menopause policies. Putting one in place can provide several opportunities for menopause to be mentioned in staff meetings, which will in itself make this taboo more acceptable by raising a conversation. Involving the community in commenting upon the draft goes a step further. For some women a fan might help them have control over their environment and make all the difference, particularly in modern air-conditioned buildings, for others it will be being able to keep a stock of sanitary products easily accessible in the bathrooms, or having a working shower with storage to enable a change of clothing after having been drenched in sweat. Some schools may consider more flexible working possibilities for colleagues, for example either being able to come in later some days of the week if sleep is an issue, or being able to leave earlier if the colleague has been up since the early hours of the morning. Many women though do not want to work flexibly or reduce their hours, they simply want support to enable them to continue as before.

WHAT CAN BE DONE TO IMPROVE EDUCATION FOR YOUNG PEOPLE?

We owe it to our young people to ensure their menopausal teachers have support, so they can continue to be as effective as possible when working with the young people they are responsible for. Our young people also have mothers and grandmothers, aunts, friends' mothers, teachers and employers, and they deserve to have a better understanding in preparation for their later years, as partners and colleagues if not for themselves. The 2020 Relationships and Sex Education (RSE) regulations require that menopause is covered, and it is important it is dealt with carefully, not glossed over.

CONCLUSION

Simple awareness that we are all facing challenges, so that we can be empathetic to others and kind to ourselves, is a first step. When I talked in assembly about 'wonky hormones' not just being the preserve of the teenager, some girls apparently told their tutor, 'So that is what is up with my Mum!' I hope that, as a result of awareness raising, women of future generations will realise what is happening to them, in the way I did not.

KEY TAKEAWAYS

- Menopausal women are the fastest growing demographic in the workplace and their needs are often ignored or overlooked as the combination of over forty symptoms is unique to each individual, leading many women to leave the profession earlier than they might otherwise had they been given appropriate support.
- After decades of stigma and a lack of education or conversation around the menopause, menopausal women themselves often do not realise their symptoms are related to the menopause and that they can be supported.
- Schools need to go further than they do currently to support menopausal women, raising awareness with students, staff, leaders and governors, enabling empathetic conversations to happen leading to supportive action.

KEY QUESTIONS

- How far have you considered supporting menopausal women in your school?
- Have you considered implementing a menopause policy in order to raise the debate and reduce barriers to menopause awareness?
- How can you engage your community to raise menopause awareness?

COMMITMENT TO THE MANIFESTO

Raise awareness among students, teachers, leaders and governors of the impact of the menopause upon women in schools, and the reasonable adjustments that can be made, to create an inclusive environment supporting the retention of menopausal women.

REFERENCES

Wellbeing of Women Survey (2016). Available at https://www.itv.com/news/2016-11-23/quarter-of-women-going-through-menopause-considered-leaving-work/ and https://www.aviva.co.uk/business/business-perspectives/featured-articles-hub/about-the-menopause/ (accessed 19 May 2021).

Newson Health Limited (2020). *What is the Menopause?* Available at: https://d2931px9t312xa.cloudfront.net/menopausedoctor/files/information/518/What%20is%20the%20Menopause%20v21-03.pdf) (accessed 19 May 2021).

CIPD (2019) *Majority of working women experiencing the menopause say it has a negative impact on them at work.* Available at: https://www.cipd.co.uk/about/media/press/menopause-at-work (accessed 19 May 2021)

Department for Work and Pensions (2015) *Employment statistics for workers aged 50 and over, by 5-year age bands and gender.* Available at: https://assets.publishing.

service.gov.uk/government/uploads/system/uploads/attachment_data/file/568240/ employment-stats-workers-aged-50-and-over-1984-2015.pdf (accessed 19 May 2021).

CIPD (2019) *CIPD Let's Talk Menopause Toolkits*. Available at: https://www.cipd.co.uk/ knowledge/culture/well-being/menopause (accessed 19 May 2021).

NEU (2019) *NEU Menopause Toolkit*. Available at: https://neu.org.uk/menopause (accessed 19 May 2021).

Department for Education (2020) *Relationships Education, Relationships and Sex Education (RSE) and Health Education regulations*. Available at: https://www.gov. uk/government/publications/relationships-education-relationships-and-sex-education-rse-and-health-education (accessed 19 May 2021).

The Wellbeing of Women Survey 2016 was carried out in 2016 with ITV for a TV programme they ran:
https://www.itv.com/news/2016-11-23/quarter-of-women-consider-leaving-work-because-of-the-menopause
https://menopauseintheworkplace.co.uk/articles/menopause-and-work-its-important/ https://menopausesupport.co.uk/?page_id=71mention

Harris, C." (2019).*1/4 of women have considered leaving their job because of the menopause*. Health Awareness. Available at: https://www.healthawareness.co.uk/ menopause/1-4-of-women-have-considered-leaving-their-job-because-of-the-menopause/

Aviva   https://www.aviva.co.uk/business/business-perspectives/ featured-articles-hub/about-the-menopause/

THE POTENTIAL BENEFITS OF AGE-INCLUSIVITY

LEILA MACTAVISH AND ISABEL INSTONE

INTRODUCTION

Diversity within schools and initial teacher training organisations has positive impacts for both social cohesion and in providing visible role models for pupils (DfE, 2019). When considering age-diversity, we can also recognise the value of life experience, good work habits and maturity.

Beyond the soft skills associated with greater life experience, what about the impact of age-diversity on pupil progress? It has long been known that teacher quality is the biggest indicator of pupil academic success and that time spent in the classroom has a significant impact on teacher quality (Allen and Sims, 2018). All the more reason to ensure that schools are age-inclusive organisations; that they can retain teachers who have developed expertise over years spent in the classroom and that they can attract career-changers with life experience and good work habits. Going further, we find that older teachers can perform the role of the 'canary in the coalmine'; when organisations ensure their structures and practices are age-inclusive, all teachers benefit.

WHY HAS AGE-INCLUSIVITY BEEN ELUSIVE?

Schools have failed to be age-inclusive employers. There are two reasons for this. The first being that schools do not always adapt to the lives of teachers as they get older; teaching is seen the purview of the young and energetic (DfE, 2019). Secondly, career-changers have been less successful than their younger peers on teacher training courses (Wilkins, 2017). Despite often being motivated by the moral purpose of education, and with many career changers having experience in high-calibre jobs, which should have developed their resilience, older entrants have repeatedly failed to become teachers. Many find it difficult to adapt and embrace their new identity, exacerbated by financial and familial pressures (Lee, 2011). Like all new teachers, career-changers struggle with the challenges of behaviour management. Initial teacher training courses have been inflexible and excessively bureaucratic and colleagues have found mentoring older entrants to the profession, who can sometimes be critical, challenging (Wilkins, 2017). But some organisations are beginning to buck the trend.

ARK TEACHER TRAINING AND NOW TEACH – A CASE STUDY OF INCIDENTAL SUCCESS

Ark Teacher Training (ATT) is a school-based initial teacher training programme. Each year, ATT trains a number of Now Teach trainees, career-changers who complete a compressed course over a four-day week. ATT made a number of changes to its programme in the academic year 2020/21. Many of these were unrelated to considerations around age-inclusivity but had a positive impact on outcomes and wellbeing of the Now Teach cohort.

The Covid-19 pandemic forced ATT to reconsider the delivery of its training, which changed from lengthy in-person sessions to front-loaded preparation work completed at the convenience of the trainee, followed by short, intensive, live, virtual sessions.

> The 'front-loading' of content into the independent preparation with the live sessions being devoted to complex concepts and live practice and feedback feels very natural and efficient; I love being able to spend as long as I want to on each non-live session and having them to refer to as a resource. The online delivery has really been thought through and has not hindered our learning at all.
>
> *Joanna Young, Now Teach ATT trainee,*
> *Ark Greenwich Free School*

In light of the pandemic, ATT started its course with a 'call to arms', connecting trainees to Ark's central mission to ensure *every child receives a quality education and is able to go on to the university or career of their choice*, because teachers who they have a moral 'calling' are more willing to manage conflicting personal and professional demands (Lee, 2011).

Training in the early part of the year focussed on repeatedly practising behaviour management strategies, addressing the issue that poor behaviour is one of the biggest factors in teachers leaving the profession (DfE, 2019). ATT also used a highly structured instructional coaching model which ensured that mentors and mentees were clear about their roles and that career-changers received high quality feedback. Early in the academic year, Ark gave all trainees offers of employment for the following year, reducing the anxiety of participants. This was particularly for older trainees who were more likely to have financial and family commitments (Lee, 2011).

ATT also made some specific changes for its Now Teach trainees. Now Teachers were given a dedicated tutor who was able to adapt the curriculum to their needs, for example providing additional time for critical discussion of theory.

> Many of the career trainees we work with have plenty of experience with further education – many have completed masters, some PhDs. Therefore, they often like to focus on critiquing the educational literature in greater depth than a core group of 'younger' trainees might. Additionally, my experience suggests that the career changer cohort likes to feel 'heard' in discussions so it is important to give them space to have their thoughts and ideas listened to.
> *Clare Smith, ATT Tutor for Now Teachers*

They also received pastoral support, often related to caring responsibilities. Finally, ATT encouraged Now Teachers to take the QTS-only route to lighten their workload which was particularly beneficial given their compressed course.

ATT's programme changes resulted in all trainees making better progress, but the Now Teach cohort have gone from making slower progress than their younger counterparts to excelling in many areas. When assessed for behaviour management, the latest cohort of ATT Now Teachers showed a significant improvement on the previous year, and were ahead of the rest of the ATT cohort:

	2019	2020	Variance
Now Teachers	48%	73%	+25%
Rest of ATT cohort	65%	69%	+4%
Variance	-17%	+4%	+21%

The drop-out rate for Now Teachers has plummeted and school leadership have shared the valuable contribution this group make:

> Our experience has been that career changers can bring a wealth of experience from industry and this really benefits our students. They also bring a sense of perspective and transferable skills which have been developed from working in other fields.
> *Rhys Spiers, Principal, Ark Greenwich Free School*

SUPPORTING CAREER CHANGERS HAS A POSITIVE IMPACT FOR ALL TRAINEES

Just as Quality First teaching strategies, designed to benefit those with special educational needs, enable all students to make faster progress, adaptations made to schools and training programmes that disproportionately benefit career-changers, will help teachers and trainees of all ages.

THE HAPPY BY-PRODUCT OF AGE INCLUSIVITY

Age inclusivity can have positive impacts on school organisations and pupils' educational outcomes. It can also address one of the biggest challenges faced by the UK education system: the recruitment and retention crisis (DfE, 2019). Not only has teacher recruitment failed to meet recruitment targets for many years (Carr, 2019), but research from Becky Allen and Sam Sims (2019) shows that 40% of new teachers are no longer working in publicly-funded schools five years later.

Where schools and initial teacher training providers actively seek to hire career-changers, they gain access to a pool of teachers that has historically not been utilised. Where schools and initial teacher training providers reflect on their structures and systems to better support their newly recruited age-diverse workforce, for example introducing flexible or part-time working and reducing time spent on onerous administrative tasks, they can also address factors that have historically driven experienced teachers out of the workforce as their lives change (DfE, 2019), and in so doing retain staff with years of experience, who are known to have the most positive impact on pupils.

KEY TAKEAWAYS

- Age-inclusive practices benefit the whole school community.
- Age is a protected characteristic, but structures and practices prevent schools from being age-inclusive organisations.
- School recruitment and retention challenges demand that schools actively seek to recruit and retain a workforce that is age-diverse.

KEY QUESTIONS

- How age-diverse is your organisation?
- What aspects of your school culture promote age inclusivity and how can you amplify and embed these?
- How can you ensure that staff training and development are structured, flexible, impactful and do not create unnecessary workload?

COMMITMENT TO THE MANIFESTO

Age inclusivity benefits school communities. Structures and practices that allow career-changers to thrive will support all staff and must be at the centre of our institutional planning.

REFERENCES

Allen, R. and Sims, S. (2018) *The Teacher Gap*, Routledge

Carr, J. (2019). 'Government misses secondary teacher training target for seventh year in a row.' *Schools Week,* 28.11.19. Available at: https://schoolsweek.co.uk/government-misses-secondary-teacher-training-target-for-seventh-year-in-row/ *accessed: 1.4.21*

Department for Education (2019) *Teacher recruitment and retention strategy*

Lee, D. (2011). Changing Course: Reflections of Second-Career Teachers. *Current Issues in Education*, 14(2), pp.1-19.

Wilkins, C. (2017). 'Elite' career-changers and their experience of initial teacher education. *Journal of Education for Teaching*, 43(2), pp.171-90.

AGE AND TEACHERS: CHALLENGES AND OPPORTUNITIES

RICHARD LEWIS

INTRODUCTION

Age in teaching has come very much to the fore as the Government has been keen to make up declining teacher numbers and to fill significant gaps, especially in science and maths. The changing working environment has also encouraged people in late careers to decide to try teaching as a profession. This has brought both older men and women with no teaching, but some with considerable management experience, into the profession for the first time. This section explores how age impacts the older newcomer to teaching and to what extent age impacts their chosen new career. This section is based on a series of interviews with a small cross-section of colleagues about how age impacts teamwork in schools.

DOES AN AGE-HOMOGENOUS TEAM WORK BETTER THAN ONE WITH AGE DIVERSITY?

This piece has been written with the benefit of interviews with younger colleagues, to see how they react to working with or managing someone who might be older than their parents. Almost resoundingly, the answer comes back – 'Age scarcely matters at all.' Funnily enough, that is exactly how it feels on the other side of the equation from the point of view of an over-sixty-five-year-old. Younger and more senior colleagues have given nothing but wise advice with no hint of eye-rolling or sense that, 'If only this person were thirty years younger, we would not be having this conversation...' This small-scale research is born from countless academic papers proving that, more important than age, people are people, they need time to work each other out (*American Psychologist,* 2018). All teams take time to form and create a bond and teaching is no different in that respect to other organisations (Volini et al., 2020).

IF AGE DOES NOT MATTER WHAT DOES?

Emotional intelligence is vital to effective team functioning in education (Jada et al., 2016). When asked if age was a distinguishing factor in teamwork those interviewed, in one form of words or another, identified emotional intelligence as being the deciding factor as to whether a person fitted in or could be integrated or managed easily. This finding is borne out by academic research. This works for the person being managed as well. Working in a low-ego environment, where neither those leading nor those being led allow their ego to override others helps to ensure that trust is built, work is delivered on time and a good working spirit is achieved. An environment where people genuinely listen to each other and allow others to be heard and reach shared decisions, makes for successful teams. This is more than a platitudinous summing of some accepted norm. People who are open and reflective do make better team managers and better teammates. Emotional intelligence is not age-related.

OVERCOMING THE CHALLENGES

A critical factor in creating an intergenerational workforce is how the organisation deals with the challenges of experience and expectation. A new, older, trainee coming from a very different sector work environment may bring with them a range of preconceptions about their new work, which are misplaced. New young teachers and older experienced teachers may hold damaging preconceptions about one another.

Expectations can be a limiting factor on both sides of this debate. For mentors of older trainees, the interviews reveal that when they work with a much older person, there is the thought that: 'This person is very experienced, they will just be able to get on and do this…'. This perhaps reflects a momentary amnesia about quite how hard becoming a teacher was for them in the early years and their expectation of age gets the better of their experience.

For the older newcomer to teaching, as they start their new career, they simply do not understand quite how different teaching is from virtually any other profession and hence how much they have to learn to master the process. Older newcomers to the profession may have excellent subject knowledge, in which they feel secure and, therefore, seek refuge. However, they soon learn that subject knowledge is only a fraction of the skills required to teach. The sooner they recognise their limitations, the faster they can adapt and learn. Different generations have vast amounts to learn from one another, but it is crucial to acknowledge that it may not simply happen without articulating what can be tricky.

HOW TO HARNESS THE STRENGTHS OF THE OLDER TEACHER

There are two examples which might be usefully considered here. The first is parental engagement. While your students are a diverse group of individuals with hugely varied home experiences and teaching them is quite unlike bringing up your own children, there is nonetheless benefit to be gained as an older person. Having seen children (your own or other people's) through GCSE and A-Level and into university, the older teacher has really useful experience to draw on. This is especially true in secondary school since UK teachers are amongst the youngest in the world.

The second aspect is what might be called 'behaviour and life guidance'. Teaching is all about relationships. When the number of years spent in relating to adults and children is on the side of the older teacher, they are often asked to help to take the heat out of situations and avoid confrontation. Bringing coaching experience, learned over decades (in school or other careers), can really help mid-teen students feel respected and find their route to more settled behaviour. The older teacher is well positioned to develop this nurturing growth relationship with teenagers – and indeed with their parents.

AGEISM IN RECRUITMENT

Is it easy to get a job if you are over sixty? It is hard to tell whether teaching is inherently more ageist than the rest of society, but NASUWT is one of many organisations to point out that there certainly is a problem (2019). The interviews conducted for this work indicated that while there is no official bias against age, in reality when faced with a pile of applications for a job, it is likely that when offering interviews these will be given to a thirty-year-old rather than a sixty-year-old. The problem for schools is that there are a range of 'truisms', which need to be faced. For example, 'Teaching is a young person's profession, it requires energy and drive' or 'Older teachers are more expensive, they are bad for the budget.' Without interviewing someone, no school can know the difference between an energetic sixty- year-old and a lethargic thirty-five-year-old or know that a sixty-year-old teacher with four years' teaching experience is quite a cheap catch. While no one will admit it, questions are raised about an older person's drive, energy levels and commitment, in a way that would not be asked of a younger person. Age really does matter when a candidate is trying to get through the door. Limited evidence suggests that if an older candidate can sit at the interview table and express themselves, then there is a chance of being employed. Thoughts about whether an older person can be easily integrated into a team or will be relaxed about being managed by someone half their age are always there as an unconscious or even conscious thought. Teachers, like most managers, will tend to take the path which superficially offers fewer challenges. After all, the job is hard enough as it is.

KEY TAKEAWAYS

- Age has little impact on either new entrants or those who have to manage them.
- Emotional intelligence, the capacity to be aware of, control, and express one's emotions, and to handle interpersonal relationships judiciously and empathetically, is very important for both sides of the issue.
- School senior leadership teams need to be more aware of the benefits of employing the older, less experienced teacher.

KEY QUESTIONS

- To what extent do school management teams really consider how to fully use the broader skills that the older newcomer to teaching brings to the school?
- Does the school have a culture in which negative stereotypes of youth or age are challenged?
- Does the school's commitment to diversity in recruitment extend to ageism?

COMMITMENT TO THE MANIFESTO

Commit to including an older teacher in job interviews/ shortlist panels.

REFERENCES

Special Issue – 'The Science of Teamwork', *American Psychologist,* Vol.73 Issue 4, May-June 2018.

Volini, E., Schwarz, J. and Mallon, D. et al. (2020). 'The post generational workforce.' *Deloitte Insights,* May 2020.

Jada, U., Jena,L.K. and Pattnaik, R. (2016) 'Emotional Intelligence, Diversity, and Organizational Performance: Linkages and Theoretical Approaches for an Emerging Field.' *Jindal Journal of Business Research* 3(1&2):1-12, May 2016

NASUWT (2019) *Older Teachers Face Discrimination Again.* Available at: http://www.agediscrimination.info/news/2019/7/24/older-teachers-face-age-discrimination-claims-nasuwt-again (accessed 1 July 2021)

EXPERIENCE AND RESILIENCE CREATE THE COUNTERBALANCE TO IMPOSTER SYNDROME

HUGH OGILVIE

INTRODUCTION

Changing career, at any stage in life, comes down to perceptions: of the person creating and making the change, then of those around them and how they might view that shift in emphasis, focus and direction. These perceptions might persist and make the career-changer appear set adrift, slightly rudderless, suffering from frequent encounters with the ever-present shadow of imposter syndrome at their shoulder. Yet, potential positives abound: real world experiences coupled with a different, well-rounded, holistic perspective, cultivated from years working within a different sector, offer up variety and knowledge which can impact directly upon students within a wider pastoral role.

INEXPERIENCE FOR THE EXPERIENCED

Experience is paramount, or so it seems. The older trainee teacher ought to be brimming with confidence, ready to amaze willing students with the bounty of their knowledge. Yet, this is not always the case; for everyone at least. In the arena of the classroom, the sword is double-edged – 'mistemper'd' even, to quote the Bard himself. Fledgling teachers emerge, fully-formed, skills honed at the coalface of another respectable profession with a possibly naive belief that no real barriers exist and the students will just eagerly listen and learn. That's before factoring differentiation, pace and assessment into the equation; and it's a most complicated equation, a veritable balancing act, encompassed within a journey from 'established expert' to 'novice' then – over time – back to expert again. In some cases mature students are less likely to achieve QTS status than their younger counterparts and up to two and a half times more likely to withdraw than trainees aged under twenty-five (Hobson et al., 2009.)

The discipline is chosen: English. The trainee studied it at A level and adored it.

Yet, the inspiration came from their teachers, who cared deeply about their subject and made their students feel that ambition was not a dirty word. In the interview, the panel were impressed by their 'love of learning' and 'desire to make a difference'. Research reveals that most teachers' career decisions are driven by altruism and intrinsic rewards from the experience of being a classroom practitioner (Wilkins and Comber, 2015).

At the police station and the court, they listened: the police officers (sometimes), the magistrates, the judge, the prosecutor. And they responded with courtesy and equanimity. In the classroom, there is a different level of expectation which takes the willing trainee by surprise. Why would the students not want to listen, have their heads filled with knowledge? Reality becomes a hard taskmaster. At this point, the now achingly familiar feeling kicks in and will not release itself, like an obstructive, heavy weight bearing down on your conscience and confidence. However, positive previous professional experience coupled with 'real-world' experiences help, over time, to provide a sense of resilience to help overcome challenges as they arise in the day to day (Wilkins and Comber, 2009).

THE CURSE OF IMPOSTER SYNDROME

Where does this mismatch come from? Over twenty years' experience working in teams, working alone, developing a reputation and feeling generally respected can come crashing down, so easily. A once seemingly solid ego falls away, looks for support and all the advice sounds foreign; then the ego needs to practise, continuously, to build itself back up to a level of competence. Being articulate is not enough. Every move / moment in the classroom must comply with the Teacher Standards, every idea and thought cross-referenced and explained within a meticulously prepared lesson plan to be handed to a mentor and observer. Scrutiny is at previously unheard of levels; the pressure starts to ratchet up. The precipice is moving ever closer.

At this point, support counts and it is given, willingly. The knowledge is present but knowing how to apply it has undergone a form of betrayal. Self-doubt starts to creep into focus. First placement bleeds into second placement and the labels are sticking: 'support plan' and 'cause for concern' double down into an all-consuming sense of inadequacy; that feeling of being an outsider, looking in on the 'experts' in the classroom, prevails. Even so, the transition from expert to novice to expert is made possible via a reframing of an existing professional identity to help create a more stable and sustainable teacher identity (Wilkins and Comber, 2009).

Over time and with the power of mentoring and suggestion, a mature trainee can start to emerge from their shell, start to find confidence in small, yet slowly increasing increments towards a plateau of competency, where the primary feeling of inadequacy is supplanted by one of growth, of variegation, stretching tentatively upwards. The autumn and winter months of malcontent somehow transform into an ability to 'do it right'. The trainee even feels confident enough to introduce anecdotes from their own experiences, their previous career, their likes and dislikes.

The mismatch between how one appears, how one feels and how others perceive a 'young' (yet 'experienced') teacher starts to become less pronounced, less worrisome. Age is now a potential advantage, rather than a hindrance, an upward trajectory from bare competence to potentially instructive, with the ability to become an agent for change (Wilkins and Comber, 2009).

EXPERIENCE OFFERS OPPORTUNITIES

The path from trainee to NQT is not paved with gold or any precious metal, for that matter. However, when a school accepts a new teacher and that teacher finds a place and a space to call their own, then the gradual transformation can start to take place: from seed, to root, to flower, to self-seeding and so on. Resilience takes up residence, the experience of the bigger, outside world starts to occupy the older, newer teacher's headspace more and more and it becomes clear that the 'offer' is richer than first thought. This teacher introduces anecdotes from their previous career and the joins are now glued up, the imparting of knowledge becomes more seamless. The transition from failing in the classroom because doing the teaching is difficult *and* new, mature teachers find it hard to cope, is now more manageable and resides within the memory of continuous teaching experience. This is clearly linked to prior experience, skills and personal qualities which invariably help to balance out those initial feelings of inadequacy (Kaldi and Griffiths,2013).

CONCLUSION

Reflection is the watchword now. It allows for contemplation, revision, expansion, a new, more forceful and confident language. The voice of experience can now be heard more clearly.

KEY QUESTIONS

- Is relative age, coupled with the feeling of being a novice again, a contributing factor when deciding upon whether a person is competent and willing to enter the teaching profession?
- What resources are on offer for mature trainee teachers to provide clear structure when starting out?
- What opportunities are there for including the practical aspects of previous professional experience within PSHE and other aspects of the curriculum?

KEY TAKEAWAYS

- Mid-life career-changers need support, sometimes more than they think and the ITT providers realise, especially with planning, schemes of work and delivery of content.

- Previous, even extensive experience of interacting with young people, does not guarantee immediate engagement within a classroom setting.
- Give new, 'older' teachers time to establish themselves, so they can develop into a valuable resource for the whole school community.

COMMITMENT TO THE MANIFESTO

ITT providers can offer appropriate support for career-changers when entering the profession and take full advantage of their transferable skills.

REFERENCES

Kaldi, S. and Griffiths, V. (2013) 'Mature student experiences in teacher education: widening participation in Greece and England.' *Journal of Further and Higher Education*, 37:4, 552-573, DOI: 10.1080/0309877X.2011.645468/

Hobson, A.J., Giannakaki, M.S. and Chambers, G.N. (2009). 'Who withdraws from initial teacher preparation programmes and why?', *Educational Research*, 51:3, 321-40, DOI: 10.1080/00131880903156906

Wilkins, C. and Comber, C. (2015) 'Elite career-changers in the teaching profession,' *British Educational Research Journal*, 41:6, 1010-1030, DOI: 10.1002/berj.3183

STAGE NOT AGE: AGEISM IN SCHOOLS

JANE CLEWLOW

INTRODUCTION

AGEISM (noun): prejudice or discrimination on the grounds of a person's age (OUP).

Ageism is most commonly depicted as affecting older individuals; however, there is much evidence that ageism (or reverse ageism as it is often called) affects younger people too. In fact, our educational institutions often embody ageism throughout the whole spectrum: older individuals, middle-aged individuals and younger individuals each denied opportunities, treated as lesser or ignored completely because of their years. In this chapter we will explore, in the style of Shakespeare's Seven Ages of [Wo]Man, how this discrimination and stereotyping occurs and what we can do to confront and eradicate the issue; as the WHO says we need to 'enhance empathy, dispel misconceptions about different age groups and reduce prejudice.'

AGEISM EXPERIENCED BY OLDER COLLEAGUES

Let us turn first to the 'lean and slippered pantaloon', the man or woman with 'spectacles on nose' teaching our pupils. They are often seen as too old to be promoted; too old to learn new skills; unable or unwilling to 'keep up with the times.' Prejudice against people based around their age, like many other forms of prejudice, is inherent; there are many negative stereotypes of older people present in all forms of media and social media and those stereotypes are rife within education. With the average age of teachers falling – the UK has twice the number of teachers under thirty than other developed countries and in 2019 only 2.6% of the UK teaching population were over sixty – supporting those at the opposite end of the age range is all the more important.

Take Barbara, still teaching and leading at sixty-two, enjoying the challenges of her inner-city school where she has taught for the best part of forty years, keen to move to a part-time and flexible mode of working to enable her to support her aging mother for one morning or afternoon per week. Let us see what happens to her when a new headteacher takes over and notes that Barbara is not quite as strategic as her younger senior colleagues, she is not quite as adept with technology, she is not quite as forward-thinking, not aware of the latest educational 'best-practice.' There has been a historical lack of CPD for Barbara, and many others like her. Does the headteacher invest time in Barbara to bring her up to speed? Is there a plan made to educate her about the newest pedagogical thinking? Are her forty years of experience harnessed, respected and utilised? Seldom is the answer yes. What often happens in this case is what many of us have seen time and time again. Barbara is marginalised, her request for part-time or flexible working seen as further evidence of her ineptitude in her role (Gov.uk 2020). It is not long before Barbara's days are numbered and she is left feeling like, in the words of Eric Clapton, she has 'been on the road too long and moving in the wrong direction.' Her vast experience is lost to the cruelty of ageism.

THE LOST POTENTIAL OF POST-NATAL WOMEN

Let us turn next to the recently 'round-bellied' post-natal women, full of 'wise saws' and 'modern instances.' Unlike Barbara, they are much more likely to be closer to the 'cutting edge' of educational best practice. The average age for pregnancy in the UK is 29.6 (UK Parliament); many of these are teachers: recently graduated from their teaching qualifications, rich with knowledge and skills, adept practitioners in their field. They are also new mothers – nine months of carrying their babies, often nine to twelve months at home away from the chalk-face of education. Many of these outstanding professionals choose not to return to the chalk-face, not to return to a job they initially saw as a vocation because they cannot juggle the demands of motherhood with the demands of teaching. Between the years 2008 and 2012 more than a quarter of the teachers who left the profession were women aged 30-39 (Patel, 2016). The constant reforms and changes in education often mean that catching up after a year away can feel like an insurmountable challenge. A challenge that many teachers choose not to take up. This is a different form of ageism, this is ageism linked to gender and motherhood.

Flexible working and part-time working are still all too uncommon in education. As a deputy head aged twenty-nine, I was fortunate to work with four successive heads who believed in me and my abilities and supported me via a part-time working option which enabled me to continue in my role as a senior leader whilst also having a day a week, later a day a fortnight, to be a mum. That day gave me many things over the eleven years I had it: initially it was a day where I attended playgroups with other similarly-aged mums, swapping stories and getting support; later it became the day I could walk the children to school. It was also a day where I could catch up with the humdrum of motherhood: food shopping, house cleaning, ticking off the jobs on the to-do list as well as a day to catch my teacher-breath. Many Fridays 'off' have been spent poured-over a laptop reading emails, writing policies, catching up on the week gone by and preparing for the week ahead. I will be forever grateful to those headteachers who entrusted me to continue to do a good job for the children in my care whilst working flexibly to support my own. How many more people can say the same?

AGEISM EXPERIENCED BY YOUNG LEADERS

We now approach the 'soldier' seeking the 'bubble reputation' who often finds they are in the 'cannon's mouth' so to speak, whether that be the mouth of leading in some of our more challenging schools or the mouth of educational ageism. These are our young leaders. The ones who are head teachers in their late twenties and early thirties, the heads of department at twenty-two, the executive heads on the right side of forty. There is a belief, in some sections of our educational world, that our younger leaders are not experienced enough, are not knowledgeable enough, and have not earned their metaphorical stripes.

Take Stuart, with a first-class honours degree in maths, a Teach First and Future Leaders graduate, promoted quickly to head of department, next to assistant head and then onto deputy headship. All by the time he is thirty-three. Is he more or less ready for headship than a fifty-three-year-old with the same career pathway? The only difference being that the fifty-three-year-old has spent longer within each stage.

There is an old, and frustrating, idea that progression through the ranks of education is linear: five years or so as an NQT, another five years with a TLR of one type or another, a further five to ten years at middle leadership level and then, and only then, would one be ready for the dizzying heights of senior leadership, let along headship. Of course, being time-served comes with the benefit of a broader range of experiences but that does not always go hand-in-hand with excellent leadership. How many leaders have you met who are older but definitely not wiser? Who no longer seeks the 'bubble reputation' but would never dream of permitting the young soldiers amongst us to do so either? If Stuart is the best person for the job, the right fit for the school in question, then it should be stage not age that triumphs.

AGEISM EXPERIENCED BY PUPILS

Finally, we come to the 'whining schoolboy' who we often find, as Shakespeare did, 'creeping unwillingly to school.' But what if we do not find this? What if we find the jubilant schoolboy, running excitedly to school where he is able to demonstrate knowledge and skill in his subjects that belie his year group? What happens when we find ourselves faced with a Year 7 boy who is capable of taking his GCSEs almost immediately upon joining his secondary school? Or the Year 9 girl, so skilled in her subjects that she is scoring full-marks on GCSE papers at the end of Year 8? What happens with these pupils?

Years ago now, David Marley presented at the Specialist Schools and Academies Trust conference, and focussed on the whole notion of 'stage not age.' He spoke to his audience about teaching pupils in mixed age groups so as to ensure maximum engagement and maximum progress in order to maximise outcomes – not only in the short-term currency of GCSEs and A-Levels but in the long-term currency of life chances (*TES*, 2007). That was back in 2007, arguably (apart from our technology) classrooms and age-focussed education across the world have not changed much since then, and probably not much since the Victorian period (FEE 2019).

CONCLUSION

Life is not experienced in year groups, jobs are not done in Key Stages and friends are not limited to those the same age as us. Challenging conventions is key here to ensure that we are limiting the ones who 'creep unwillingly' to school by providing a bespoke, broad and balanced curriculum which enables all pupils to progress at the rate appropriate to them.

KEY TAKEAWAYS

- Bespoke CPD should be offered with regularity to all colleagues, irrespective of years in the profession.
- Flexible working models should be looked at for all teaching roles.
- Age should never feature in a recruitment process.
- Pupils should be allowed to progress at the rate right for them.

KEY QUESTIONS

- How are older colleagues supported and developed within your school?
- How flexible are your roles (including part-time, later start times, earlier finish times)?
- How does your recruitment process ensure that age is not a considered factor?
- How is your curriculum and timetable structured to enable children to progress at the rate that is right for them?

COMMITMENT TO THE MANIFESTO

Banish all forms of ageism from our education system.

REFERENCES

Oxford English Dictionary: https://languages.oup.com/research/oxford-english-dictionary/

Shakespeare, W., *As You Like It*, Act 2 Scene 7

Busby, E. (2019). 'UK Teachers are younger and paid less than in any other developed country, report finds.' *The Independent*, 10 September. Available at: https://www.independent.co.uk/news/education/education-news/

oecd-study-uk-teachers-britain-youngest-pay-salaries-countries-a9099216.html (site accessed 20 April 2021)

School Workforce in England (2020). Available at: https://explore-education-statistics.service.gov.uk/find-statistics/school-workforce-in-england

Flexible working in schools (2017). Available at: https://www.gov.uk/government/publications/flexible-working-in-schools/flexible-working-in-schools--2 (Accessed 1st July 2021).

Flexible Working Practice, Factsheets (2021) CIPD. Available at: https://www.cipd.co.uk/knowledge/fundamentals/relations/flexible-working/factsheet#gref. (Accessed 1 July 2021).

Have kids, settle down – UK Parliament Available at: https://www.cipd.co.uk/knowledge/fundamentals/relations/flexible-working/factsheet#gref. Accessed 1 July 2021.

Patel, G. (2016) 'Hello Baby, Goodbye Teaching.' *The Guardian*, 17 March, 2016. Available at:https://www.theguardian.com/teacher-network/2016/mar/17/teaching-how-to-get-mums-back-into-classroom. (Accessed 1 July 2021).

Building a fair education for all, Teach First. Available at: https://www.teachfirst.org.uk/. (Accessed 1 July 2021).

Future Leaders Programme. Available at: https://www.gov.uk/guidance/join-the-future-leaders-programme-to-help-you-progress-to-headship#:~:text=have%20qualified%20teaching%20status%20or,next%20role%20in%20your%20career (Accessed 1 July 2021).

Marley, D. (2007) 'Stage, not age, is key to better learning, specialist schools told'. *Tes News*, 23 November 2007.

Schools Are Outdated. It's Time For Reform (2021) Foundation for Economic Education. Available at: https://fee.org/articles/schools-are-outdated-its-time-for-reform/ (Accessed 1 July 2021).

KNOWLEDGE TRANSFER: SHIFTING THE FOCUS SO DIFFERENCES BECOME STRENGTHS THROUGH MENTORSHIP

TULIKA SAMAL

INTRODUCTION

Age is a number and not a credential. Five different generations are working in the workplace. Knowing how to tap into their talents, skills, and strengths, and making communication easier can be challenging. Statements such as 'He is too old to learn a computer program' or 'She is too young to lead a team" diminish the value and qualifications of the people involved.

CHALLENGE AND OPPORTUNITY

Enhancing knowledge transfer and sharing across age-diverse organisations has been proven to improve workers' efficiency and eventually the organisation's success. Knowledge transfer between younger and older employees can be valuable as they benefit from each other's diverse knowledge. However, age diversity can also impede knowledge transfer as individuals have a natural tendency to prefer interactions with peers that are similar to them.

There is no denying that differences exist in the experiences, styles, and perspectives of people from different generations. Although these differences can sometimes be a source of conflict, these same differences can also become a source of strength when addressed and managed effectively by HR and the leaders. That is why we need to focus on two aspects of knowledge sharing:

- Leadership's role
- Mentoring programs to boost knowledge and skill transfer.

LEADERSHIP ROLE

Knowledge sharing is ultimately a human process that requires dynamic interaction and good relationships between employees. It is therefore important for the leaders to understand what drives this process in a multi-generational workforce. When I first started my career as a teacher what bothered me most was the lack of leader's involvement in decision making about the various roles assigned to the teachers that were not based on skill but on age (seniority level).

The leaders of age-diverse schools must have two goals to make the transfer of knowledge happen. The first goal for the leaders is to examine how selected individual characteristics influence the decision to share knowledge with co-workers. The second goal is to evaluate whether employees are satisfied with the amount of knowledge that is transferred from their mentors.

Knowing and understanding the employees' perceived satisfaction with the depth and intensity of knowledge sharing can help leaders to develop formal programmes, which facilitate interactions, stimulate knowledge sharing, and increase the frequency of collaborations among generationally diverse employees.

According to van den Hooff and de Ridder (Research Gate), knowledge sharing involves either actively communicating to others what one knows, or actively consulting others in order to learn what they know. As per Szulanski knowledge sharing is a communication of shared understanding of knowledge as defined in an integrated knowledge management system.

Whether an employee decides to help co-workers by sharing their own expertise may depend primarily:
- on his/her desire and the want to do so i.e., willingness and motivation.
- on the nature of the working relationship i.e., communication and collaboration.

WILLINGNESS AND MOTIVATION

The existence of inter-generational differences among workers has posed great challenges to managers in effectively managing their employees' motivation.

COMMUNICATION AND COLLABORATION

The quality of interpersonal communication between employees greatly impacts knowledge sharing. Communication styles within teams also contribute to knowledge sharing. Communication styles may be different between people of very different ages. Leaders have a role to play in articulating both the potential and the challenges and setting up formal mechanisms to get the most out of their employees in terms of knowledge transfer.

MENTORING PROGRAMS TO BOOST KNOWLEDGE AND SKILL TRANSFER

Mentoring programs can be one of these key mechanisms to support and facilitate the knowledge transfer among young and older workers. Mentoring can also facilitate sharing knowledge across generations with the goal of mutual learning and competence development. It is a two-way exchange of knowledge, skills, and beliefs.

In such a mentoring relationship both employees learn about the perspectives and experiences of each other's generation.

Mentoring is a method by which organisations can establish a workplace that appreciates and embraces employee differences. The mentoring programs seek to diversify the workplace by:

- Helping employees improve upon skills they have already shown an aptitude for.
- Matching employees with mentors who can help them learn in a style that is best suited for their needs.
- Spreading knowledge throughout the organization so that more employees learn a wider array of skills.

During my initial days teaching in the USA, I struggled due to the differences in culture and classroom practices between the USA and India. I was on the verge of quitting until my coach paired me up with a colleague, who was younger to me not just in age but in experience as well. My struggles diminished due to the mentoring and real-time experience I was getting from my mentor.

Mentoring has been found to be highly appreciated in the sphere of knowledge transfer and especially across multi-generational work groups.

Mentoring has flexibility, it can happen in so many ways and under lots of different circumstances. Mentoring is people-centred and provides a feedback system to enhance learning. Setting up a mentoring programme carefully gives clear expectations and guidelines. Here are the steps for building a mentorship programme in your workplace:

1. Define and align goals with the organisation's vision.
2. Identify the participants – mentors and mentees.
3. Promote the mentoring program.
4. Build the pool of mentors.
5. Match the mentee and mentors.
6. Train the mentors and mentees to help them understand their role and objectives.

Those organisations which have really focussed on age-diverse mentoring have seen impressive results. This is an area in which teaching could benefit from looking to the outside world – projects such as Encore.org in the United States, The Intergenerational Mentoring Network in Glasgow and those of many corporations. The tech industry has been particularly good in pairing experienced executives with younger colleagues to the mutual benefit of both.

CONCLUSION

Knowledge sharing between the different generations at work is essential for an organisation's survival. Yet, given the generational diversity of employees, the unique characteristics of each generation may impede the effectiveness of the sharing process. Companies which recognise the benefits of a diverse workforce are utilising an assortment of knowledge management strategies to share knowledge from experts in the baby boomer cohort to members of Generation Y. While a variety of knowledge management strategies have been successfully implemented, companies should design knowledge-sharing strategies conducive to multi-generational workforce dynamics keeping in mind the generational diversity. One such strategy is mentoring. Indeed, we find that the level of knowledge shared through cross-generational mentoring relationships is below that desired. In order to benefit from the demonstrated employees' eagerness to learn as well as generational diversity, organisations need to implement formal mechanisms through which knowledge sharing occurs.

KEY TAKEAWAYS

- Emphasis on augmenting knowledge transfer in age diverse organisations or schools.
- Internships for workers of all ages and mentoring programs can boost knowledge and skill transfer.
- Shift the focus to employees' abilities, skills, experiences and knowledge so that their differences become strengths.

KEY QUESTIONS

- How can we ensure that people of all ages are given a fair chance of knowledge sharing in our schools?
- What can organisations / schools do to support mentoring from an employee's perspective?
- How can schools learn from outside education about the benefits of intergenerational mentoring?

COMMITMENT TO THE MANIFESTO

Consider setting up an intergenerational mentoring project in your setting to ensure optimal sharing of knowledge and experience for the benefit of your students.

REFERENCES

Gassam, J. (2019). 'The Key to Diversity is Mentorship.' *Forbes*. Available at: https://www.forbes.com/sites/janicegassam/2019/09/26/the-key-to-diversity-and-inclusion-is-mentorship/?sh=1d6be5877fbd (accessed March 2021)

Manfredi, S. (2008). *Developing Good Practice in managing age diversity in the Higher Education Sector: AN Evidence Based Approach*. (Report for Center for Diversity Policy Research and Policy Research and Practice, Oxford Brookes University).

https://www.researchgate.net/publication/220363314_Knowledge_sharing (accessed March 2021)

Savage, C. (2011). *'Generations on the move: 3 ways to ensure Knowledge Transfer.* Available at: https://www.vantageleadership.com/our-blog/generations-move-3-ways-ensure-knowledge-transfer (accessed March 2021)

STORY BOOK VILLAINS: WHEREARE THE POSITIVE OLDER ROLE MODELS IN THE ENGLISH LITERATURE CURRICULUM?

SAVITRI PATEL

INTRODUCTION

We know that the content of a curriculum communicates implicit messages. In the case of the English curriculum, with its focus on the powerful medium of stories, these messages can be particularly profound and lasting. Conflict, misunderstanding or even neglect makes for better drama – but is this at the expense of positive older role models being present in the English curriculum? And if so, what does the frequent representation of older characters as selfish, clueless, absent, bigoted, war-mongering or eccentric do for young people's perception of the generations that came before?

THE GENERATION GAP

For many English teachers, a love of reading goes with the territory. A passion for literature and a wish to share the texts that inspire and move you is what takes many of us back to the classroom. There is also an awareness that the books we encountered in school – even those we loved – may not resonate with today's students. Great work is being done in many classrooms (and on many a teacher's laptop, late into the night) to acknowledge and redress past oversights, mistakes or deliberate exclusions.

One stigma so deeply ingrained and internalised that it is often invisible, however – and where visible, often defended – is ageism.

In 2018, before the upheaval of the global pandemic – but with issues such as Brexit, 'cancel culture' and the shift of the word 'woke' into mainstream discourse – the generation gap was back on the media agenda (Delaney, 2018). In one form or another, however, it had never left the English Literature GCSE curriculum.

As with attempts to analyse class, age is a tricky thing to pin down. On the one hand, older people are often grouped together as homogenous (e.g. 'Boomers' or

'60+' in surveys); on the other hand, people do not tend to self-identify as 'old'. Age can be as much a matter of perception as of fact (YouGov, 2018). Experiences of ageing and those older than you are widely divergent – based on income, location, and culture (WHO, 2021).

Surveyed in 2018 by the Royal Society for Public Health (RSPH, 2018), 44% of 18-24-year-olds agreed that 'In elections, most older people just vote for their own selfish interests rather than the wellbeing of the younger generation and society as a whole.' For over 65s, this figure was just 14%. A quarter of 18-34- year-olds believe it is normal to be unhappy and depressed when you are old. Children as young as six can show an awareness of ageist stereotypes, and the majority of children display overwhelmingly negative attitudes to the notion of getting older.

Why does that matter?

Unlike most protected characteristics, age is not hard and fast. We will all find ourselves crossing into new categories – whether imposed by society or ourselves. Self-image is a key determinant in our experiences of aging. Those with a negative attitude towards it tend to have worse outcomes. Thus, role models and representation are important.

While the RSPH found that 64% of people don't have a single friend thirty or more years older or younger than them, empathy and co-operation between generations is essential: whether to address the world's great challenges or simply to succeed in the workplace. What representations of aging or of relationships between older and younger people are explored in the English Literature curriculum? And what messages are today's students unwittingly absorbing about how they will be seen and valued in their turn, as they grow old in the world they inherit?

THE ENGLISH LITERATURE GCSE CURRICULUM

The range of textual options necessitates a superficial skim read at best, but a first glance does not reveal any obvious examples of positive representation.

SHAKESPEARE

With *King Lear* kept to Key Stage 5, Shakespearean characters encountered up to Key Stage 4 are usually 'older' rather than 'old'. In a schedule so packed some schools cannot even study the whole text, it is unlikely every teacher makes time to encourage students to re-examine older secondary characters and build empathy – for example by considering the impact of marriage at thirteen on characters beyond Juliet, or the rights and wrongs of Juliet's Nurse taking orders from a teenager.

Students tend to empathise with Shylock in *The Merchant of Venice* at once, unlike the play's original audience, but it would take a teacher with specific interest to focus for long on the breakdown of his relationship with his daughter as an example of transgenerational racial trauma. A potentially touching story of intergenerational love (platonic or otherwise) between Antonio and Bassanio in the same play is only part of the backdrop. *The Tempest* and *Much Ado About Nothing* both feature the kind of bullying, authoritarian fathers that it is understandable to disobey and quite hard to respect, while a tender reference to a parent in *Macbeth* comes only incidentally, when Lady Macbeth states that it is the resemblance to her father that stops her stabbing the sleeping Duncan herself.

19TH CENTURY NOVELS

A quick canter through the Victorian options offers: *The Strange Case of Dr. Jekyll and Mr. Hyde* (Stephenson, 1886) – middle-aged hubris and hypocrisy; *A Christmas Carol* (Dickens, 1843) – a miser who is redeemed after a misspent lifetime; *Great Expectations* (Dickens, 1861) – a twisted, vindictive spinster who blights the lives of the young people she manipulates; *Jane Eyre* (Bronte, 1847) a terrible foster mother and a mixed bag of teachers; *Frankenstein* (Shelley, 1818) – a 'father' who rejects his 'child' completely; *Pride and Prejudice* (Austen, 1813) – an older generation at best lovably silly and at worst imperious, overbearing or dangerously neglectful; *Silas Marner* (Eliot, 1861) – perhaps the brightest spot in terms of representation: a reclusive misanthrope restored to humanity through his devotion to the baby he takes in.

MODERN DRAMA AND PROSE TEXTS

The most commonly used play-texts include *An Inspector Calls* (Priestley, 1945) – no one comes out of this well, but at least the younger members of the family feel some guilt; *Blood Brothers* (Russell, 1983) – the mistakes of the older generation unravel the lives of the children they love; *The History Boys* (Bennett, 2004) – teachers who have a lot of knowledge but are not much better adjusted than their students; *The Curious Incident of the Dog in the Night-Time* (Haddon, 2003) – parents trying their best but getting it very wrong for much of the time; *Hobson's Choice* (Brighouse, 1916) – a dominating drunk father whose smarter daughter first gets the better of him and then rescues him from penury.

Some modern texts, as well as having increased racial diversity, do show parents in a more sympathetic light. *Refugee Boy* (Zephaniah, 2001) shows parents doing their best; *Boys Don't Cry* (Blackman, 2010) shows a father who is ultimately supportive of his son's 'mistake'. And of course, presenting adults as fallible human beings is not necessarily bad. *Lord of the Flies* (Golding, 1954) perhaps suggests that things can go quite seriously wrong without older, wiser people in charge... though the tears of relief when the grown-up rescuers arrive in a passing warship suggest perhaps it is more a case of the devil you know. However, more politically-minded young people may be quick to identify a possible parable about who suffers most under an oppressive status quo in *Never Let Me Go* (Ishiguro, 2005).

CONCLUSION

Stories are open to interpretation, but finding positive representations in the curriculum as it stands would take some work. While it is possible for this to be done by an individual teacher in their classroom, is there awareness of the benefits of doing so? Or, with teachers as liable to ageism as anyone else – and the average age of the profession currently fifth youngest in the world at thirty-nine, – is there any impetus actively to promote positive representation of a group wide enough to include the holders of power as well as the marginalised? (OECD, 2018).

KEY TAKEAWAYS

- The UK's English Literature curriculum as it stands does not actively promote positive depictions of old age or older people.
- Negative attitudes towards aging have a negative impact on individuals and their experiences of aging.
- Teachers should consider their own attitudes towards aging, and where conscious or unconscious bias may impact how they encourage students to interpret characters.

KEY QUESTIONS

- How far have you considered your own views on aging and intergenerational conflict?
- What are the main barriers to promoting positive depictions of aging in your classroom?
- How can you engage students in understanding the importance of representations of age and older people?

COMMITMENT TO THE MANIFESTO

Acknowledge ageism as damaging for young people as well as old, and challenge representations within the curriculum which present a limited or one-sided view of older people.

REFERENCES

Austen, J. (1813) *Pride and Prejudice*. London: T Egerton.

Bennett, A. (2004) *The History Boys* (Royal National Theatre, London. 18 May)

Blackman, M. (2010) *Boys Don't Cry*. London: Penguin Random House Children's UK.

Brighouse, H. (1915) *Hobson's Choice* (Princess Theatre, New York. 2 November)

Bronte, C. (1847) *Jane Eyre*. London: Smith, Elder & Co.

Delaney, B (2018.) 'The generation gap is back – but not as we know it.' *The Guardian,*

14 April, 2018 https://www.theguardian.com/commentisfree/2018/apr/14/the-generation-gap-is-back-but-not-as-we-know-it (accessed on 4 July 2021)

Dickens, C. (1843). *A Christmas Carol*. London: Chapman & Hall.

Dickens, C. (1861). *Great Expectations*. London: Chapman & Hall.

Eliot, G. (1861). *Silas Marner*. Edinburgh: William Blackwood and Sons.

Golding, W. (1954) *Lord of the Flies*. London: Faber and Faber.

Haddon, M. (2003) *The Curious Incident of the Dog in the Night-Time*. London: Jonathan Cape.

Ishiguro, K. (2005) *Never Let Me Go*. London: Faber and Faber.

Organisation for Economic Co-operation and Development (2018) *Results from Teaching and Learning International Survey (TALIS)*. Available at https://www.oecd.org/education/talis/TALIS2018_CN_ENG.pdf (accessed 4 July 2021)

Priestley, J.B. (1945). *An Inspector Calls* (Leningrad Comedy Theatre, Moscow. 6 July)

Royal Society for Public Health (2018). *That Age Old Question*. Available at https://www.rsph.org.uk/static/uploaded/a01e3aa7-9356-40bc-99c81b14dd904a41.pdf (accessed 4 July 2021)

Russell, W. (1983.) *Blood Brothers* (Liverpool Playhouse, Liverpool. 8 January)

Shakespeare, W. (1604-6) *King Lear*

Shakespeare, W. (1595) *Romeo and Juliet*

Shakespeare, W. (1596-7) *The Merchant of Venice*

Shakespeare, W. (1610-11) The Tempest

Shakespeare, W. (1598-9) *Much Ado About Nothing*

Shakespeare, W. (1606) *Macbeth*

Shelley, M. (1818) *Frankenstein*. London: Lackington, Hughes, Harding, Mavor and Jones.

Stephenson, R.L. (1886) *The Strange Case of Dr. Jekyll and Mr. Hyde*. London: Longmans, Green & Co.

World Health Organisation (2021) *Global report on ageism*. Available at https://www.un.org/development/desa/dspd/wp-content/uploads/sites/22/2021/03/9789240016866-eng.pdf (accessed 4 July 2021)

YouGov (2018) *How young are "young people"? And at what age does a person become "old"?* Available at https://yougov.co.uk/topics/politics/articles-reports/2018/03/06/how-young-are-young-people-and-what-age-does-perso (accessed 4 July 2021)

Zephaniah, B. (2001) *Refugee Boy*. London: Bloomsbury Publishing.

CHAPTER 2: DISABILITY

CHAPTER EDITOR: RUTH GOLDING

CHAPTER CONTRIBUTORS

1. George Fielding – **Stunned into silence: towards an education without judgement**
2. Artemi Sakellariadis – **Extending our welcome, transforming our schools**
3. Lena Carter – **To diagnose or not to diagnose? That is the question!**
4. James Hollinsley – **Disability and Mental Health**
5. Julie Cassiano – **Creating a school culture which includes staff who are disabled with mental health illness – Running on Empty to Having a full tank.**
6. Anya Diaz-Cebreiro – **Living Your Best Life: A call for better pastoral care for disabled students**
7. Rebecca West – **Sex, Sex, Sex – Making sex and relationships education inclusive.**
8. Elizabeth Wright – **Why the Hell Does Disability Representation Matter?**
9. Laura McConnell – **The Hidden Autistic Workforce**
10. Caroline Powell – **Empowering disabled people in education settings**

BIOGRAPHIES

Ruth Golding is a disabled leader who is committed to making education equitable for all. Other roles she undertakes include Vice Chair of Governors, National Leader for @WomenEdEngland and as a founder of @DisabilityEdUK.

Anya Diaz-Cebreiro is Head of Diversity and Inclusion, Housemistress and teacher of Spanish, German and Italian at a school in Oxfordshire. Anya has a passion for diversity and inclusion and seeks to bridge the gap between pastoral care and diversity.

Artemi Sakellariadis is a teacher who taught in special schools for many years before devoting her time and energy to the development of more inclusive education. She is currently Director of the Centre for Studies on Inclusive Education (CSIE, www.csie.org.uk) and Honorary Research Associate at the University of Bristol.

Caroline Powell is Joint Head of English in a Secondary School and Sixth Form College. She gained an MEd in Researching Practice from the University of Cambridge. Caroline uses her experiences of chronic life-threatening illnesses to support others: her volunteer work includes caring for children with disabilities and acting as 'Students with Disabilities Officer' during her undergraduate degree.

Elizabeth Wright is an editor, consultant, speaker, and disability activist. She brings forth all of her life experience as a disabled woman to challenge people around disability, representation, and inclusion.

George Fielding mentored 500+ young wheelchair users in his teens, then became the youngest ever recipient of the British Medal in 2014 for services to young disabled people and their families (aged nineteen) and the youngest director of a social care provider in 2017 (aged twenty-two).

James Hollinsley is Executive Head Teacher of Longwood and Waltham Holy Cross Primary Academies (NET Academies Trust). He is a former lead SEND professional for a local authority, qualified SENCO and holds an MA in Specific Learning Difficulties (SpLD/SEND). James is the founder of AllSupportEd, focusing on mental health in schools.

Julie Cassiano has been working within the teaching profession for just over ten years. She started teaching as a GTP teacher. Julie has experience of working for three local authorities in England (London, Leicester and Northampton). She recently began her headship journey in January 2021. She is currently completing an MSc in Educational Leadership. Julie is passionate about ethical leadership, and diversity, equity and inclusive practice.

Laura McConnell is a writer, speaker, broadcaster, and teacher in an ASN primary school. As an adult, Laura was diagnosed with ADHD, Autism, and PTSD and reflects on her experience in her writing. Laura presents 'Representation Matters' on Teacher Hug Radio every Saturday, interviewing well known guests from the disability community.

Lena Carter has been teaching and working in education since 1992. Early in her career, she also trained in Dramatherapy and Counselling Skills. She has held a range of middle and senior leadership roles and had significant experience of timetabling, curriculum design and tracking and monitoring. She writes and speaks extensively on a range of issues related to inclusion and equity.

Rebecca West (MA) is a late career changer coming to teaching in her early thirties; after a successful career she was looking for something more inspiring. As an ADHD learner, she found her passion lay in SEND teaching and she currently works with ASD students. She has written on this topic for the *TES* and continues to pursue her research studying for her MEd on inclusive practice in Aberdeen. Beckie (she/her), who identifies as a lesbian, has a passion for ensuring students receive inclusive sex and relationships education which is adapted to suit all neurodiversities.

THE PROTECTED CHARACTERISTIC OF DISABILITY: INTRODUCTION

RUTH GOLDING

INTRODUCTION

Disability is as varied as the individuals who identify as disabled. This section relates to disability as identified in the Equality Act 2010. It includes physical disability, neurodiversity, psychological disabilities, learning disability, sensory disability and chronic illness. This definition pertains to approximately one fifth of the UK population (Office of National Statistics, 2019). You will read in this chapter that despite the large numbers of disabled people in society, disability is often misunderstood, overlooked and ignored. In this part of the book we aim to place disabled identities firmly on the equality, diversity and inclusion map and we ask all educators and social policy makers to ensure that all education settings within a wider society are accessible and welcoming to anyone disabled.

All of the authors of the disability chapters subscribe to the social model of disability. This means that society disables them. Every chapter talks about accommodations or reasonable adjustments in one way or another. A reasonable adjustment is any change to the environment or to school or working practices to support a disabled person. To hold the view that it is your right to grant or deny reasonable adjustments is ableist; reasonable adjustments are human rights to help disabled people to not only survive, but thrive. If you educate or work with disabled people (and you do), ask them how you can meet their needs and what else you can do.

DEFINITIONS AND TERMINOLOGY

You may not be aware that the social model of disability is the one of the reasons that many people use identity first when describing themselves as disabled, for example 'disabled school leader'. This is a conscious choice to support the idea that society is the disabling factor in people's lives and that they have embraced their disabled identity. Identity-first language is on the increase as it establishes disabled identities as part of society. Person-first language, for example 'person with a disability', aims to recognise the individual and not a disability. However, person-first has been falling out of favour over the past few years and you are much more likely to hear identity-first language from disabled people. Therefore, it is important that if you are not disabled, you listen to how a disabled person describes themself and use this.

Another concept that is gaining traction is the word 'ableism'. Put simply, ableism means that you favour and value people who are not disabled over those that are. If you are ableist you hold prejudicial views about disabled people's capabilities in society, and consider disabled people as having lower status than those who are not disabled. Like many other inequalities in society, ableism is structural and requires attitude and behaviour shifts of epic proportions to undo it. Everyday ableism is pervasive, and harmful to disabled people. There is ableism in every area of education and what the authors of these chapters have presented you with are ways of confronting your own ableist thinking so that you consider new perspectives on disability. It is not unheard of for educators to talk of disabled students as 'refusing' to attend a class, indeed comments like 'picking and choosing' lessons is commonplace in schools, on social media and beyond. All of these phrases come from an ableist perspective which does not understand that reasonable adjustments are not used to get out of lessons, but to manage a condition or disability that can, at times, be overwhelming. The same goes for colleagues who need reasonable adjustments. If you are suspicious as to whether they need reasonable adjustments, or if you are questioning why additional support is given, then you are holding an ableist perspective. It is crucial that you actively confront the ableism that you have internalised, because ableism is rife and no one is immune. Firstly, you must accept that you are ableist, then you need to learn from the chapters ahead, and as you become conscious of your thoughts, language, feelings and behaviours towards disability you are on the way to being an effective ally.

LANDSCAPE

As there is extensive ableism in society, you will not be surprised to read that disabled people without observably physical differences (or with hidden disabilities) feel more safe and secure in society (especially in the workplace) when they remain in the 'disability closet'. The term was first used by Olney and Brockman in their 2003 research into perceptions of disability. The aim of the chapters that you will read is to increase understanding, access and support for disabled people, so that disabled people can confidently leave the 'disability closet' and take their rightful place in society as people with disabled identities.

Prior to the 1990s, the approach to disability was through the medical model. This model views the individual as a problem to be solved. Many disabled people were 'treated' in residential hospitals and residential homes. Disability segregation was commonplace and disabled identities were even more stigmatised than they are now. The NHS and Community Care Act 1990 was pivotal in ending much of the segregation of disabled people and the Disability Discrimination Act 1995 instigated a change in attitudes, and increased rights for disabled people in employment, goods and services including schools. The Equality Act 2010 states that all public services have a duty not only to accommodate disabled people, but also to take actions to advance equality. If you were to be asked: 'What is the disability demographic of your setting?' would you know? Would you be able to explain the attendance and behaviour data of disabled students? 0.5% of the workforce are disabled (DfE 2016) in contrast to 20% of the population of the UK. This suggests many people working in education could be disabled and hiding in the 'disability closet' for fear of negativity and institutional ableism. Disabled students receive half of all the permanent exclusions in England. These statistics alongside the chapters you are about to read will provide you with compelling evidence that there is still a long way to go in disability equality. Your knowledge and understanding of disability is as important as the legislation that is in place to prevent disability discrimination. By understanding disability, you will contribute to greater access and representation in the setting you work in. By creating these chapters, the authors give you practical ways that you can improve disability equality and they urge everyone to come together in disability allyship.

VOICES IN OUR CHAPTER IN DIVERSE EDUCATORS – A MANIFESTO

The chapter in this section takes you through a learning journey from being a student in school, through to working in education. This journey that you will be taken on is punctuated with reminders of your legal duties and other responsibilities towards the students that you teach and the people that you work with. The powerful opening Chapter 1 is **George Fielding**, who adds to the school exclusion discourse by giving you an insight into the traumatising impact of school rules for autistic children and young people. Chapter 2 is written by **Artemi Sakellariadis,** who expertly sets out the legal duties to follow, in order to transform education through accessibility, support and advocacy. In Chapter 3 we move on to **Lena Carter** who makes an important contribution to the debate about whether children and adults should get a diagnosis so that their needs are officially recognised. **James Hollingsley,** in Chapter 4, offers a sobering and unique discussion that considers the impact of disability on mental health and considers how schools can reduce the impact of poor mental health by supporting personal and social agency. This leads on to Chapter 5 by **Julie Cassiano** who brings intensely personal and lived experiences that asks leaders in education to make their settings accessible and flexible for colleagues with mental health illnesses. **Anya Diaz-Cebreiro** continues the discourse around accessibility and Chapter 6 takes a creative look at the pastoral system in secondary schools. She describes how to support the development of well-rounded disabled people. The theme of disabled identities continues into Chapter 7 with **Rebecca West** who focuses on the SRHE curriculum; in this chapter she supports the reader to stop seeing disabled people as one-dimensional beings and instead view them as multifaceted identities who have love and relationship needs. Moving on to Chapter 8, **Elizabeth Wright** raises awareness of the way the media socialises us into ableism; she makes the case for more disabled people in education settings. The penultimate chapter in this section is Chapter 9 by **Laura McConnell**, who shares her passion for improving the experiences of disabled adults in the workforce from the perspective of autistic teachers. Finally, **Caroline Powell** closes the disability section in Chapter 10. This chapter calls the reader to action, to increase empowerment, and makes the suggestion that by becoming anti-ableist the reader will support disabled equality in education and beyond.

CONCLUSION

These creative and energetic authors provide you with insight into disability. They challenge you to address disability prejudice, improve disability equality and become a disability ally and anti-ableist activist.

COMMITMENT TO THE MANIFESTO

Value disabled people, redefine disability, make life and work accessible.

REFERENCES

DfE (2017), *School workforce in England:* November 2016

National Audit Office (2019), *Support for pupils with special educational needs.*

Office of National Statistics (2019), https://www.ons.gov.uk/peoplepopulationandcommunity/healthandsocialcare/disability/bulletins/disabilityandemploymentuk/2019, [accessed May 2019]

Olney , M.F. and Brockman, K.F (2003),.'Out of the Disability Closet: Strategic use of perception management by select university students with disabilities.' *Disability and Society* Vol 1 (2003), Routledge

STUNNED INTO SILENCE: TOWARDS AN EDUCATION WITHOUT JUDGEMENT

GEORGE FIELDING

'What's the use of two strong legs if you only run away?
....the finest voice if you've nothing good to say.
...strength and muscle if you push and shove?
...ears if you can't hear those you love?'

– Si Khan

No work of art evokes the sense of unease that envelops me when writing about education like Si Kahn's song *What You Do with What You've Got* as it strikes at the heart of the fallacy within 'the system'. 'What's the use...?' was the prefix to the majority of questions I asked as a student. However, answers were not forthcoming. Whether it was the queries that were the issue, or my interlocutors, remains a mystery. This chapter uses first-hand experience to explore the psychological and emotional effects of not fitting into school.

The uniform masks the problem, and the bruises. In no other context is the maxim 'first impressions count' more potent than in a school. One judgement often sets your course, the sum of your achievements, 'shown and told' by whether 'the uniform' fits, can be afforded or looks appropriate upon your person. Adam is better than Eve because he has a cap and it fits; Eve cannot 'brush up' well because there is no food at home, let alone deodorant, a bottle of shampoo and shoe polish. Joseph Rowntree Foundation's findings are arresting because they ring true. There are 4.2 million disabled people living in poverty, which is 29% of all people living in poverty. The impact of difference is deep, political and gendered too. The Office for National Statistics estimates that women with disabilities are more than twice as likely to experience domestic abuse than their non-disabled peers, a shocking stat that many say is conservative – in quantity and cause. Life reflects school, and it is harder for students who do not fit into the institution that is also their refuge.

The Children's Society suggests that 23% of parents say that their child must go to school in wrong, ill-fitting or dirty uniform. One in eight families miss out on food in order to cover the cost (averaging £340 per uniform) and that 500,000 students have been sent home as a 'reward' for their (unsatisfactory) efforts. The Trussell Trust states that people would rather stop buying toiletries before they use food banks. The irony remains that it is termed a school uniform for a reason. The Academy wants pupils to be recognisably 'one', distinguishable outside of the gates but indistinguishable inside of them, given that students have all submitted themselves to the same rules, codes of practice and behaviour, 'the treadmill of the mainstream.' Within school a governing body insidiously governs students' bodies and minds aiming to mass-produce the same itemised, monetised and categorised product – do we consent? Many disabled students look different, think differently and behave differently and their very presence in school puts them in conflict with their peers, the staff and system right from the start. To date, five decades later, too few have heeded Mario Savio's anguished call and 'put bodies upon the gears' of the machine (Savio, 1964). What is the cost of our dither and delay?

There is something deeply Kafkaesque about education for any pupil with additional needs. Autistic students can find themselves in the position of 'criminals' for daring to be different. From the perspective of the student, they might require a little support to access a fair trial in this environment. School is a bureaucratic and painstaking process for students, your value being demonstrated through 'showing your workings' and having your name ticked off of the register. Everybody else seems to be in positions of authority except you, although you are the one in the spotlight. They 'throw the book at you' (metaphorically speaking). If you are autistic this environment is overwhelming and anxiety-provoking and not a place to thrive. Instead, it can turn the purest of people into individuals labelled as 'naughty', 'troublesome' and a problem to be solved. The solution is exclusion in a variety of ways.

'The first cut is the deepest' – Cat Stevens

There are 1.2 million disabled students and 23% of these have speech, language, and communication needs (Department for Education, 2020).

The Department of Education's estimated statistics paint an uncomfortably dark picture. Students with disabilities are not at their desk as the bell sounds, the verdict is that they are disruptive: 4,500 pupils with a statutory right to special needs support are awaiting suitable provision or being home-schooled. The permanent exclusion rate for pupils with SEND with an EHC plan is 0.16%, and for those without one 0.34%. This is six times higher than for non-disabled individuals, which poses the questions, how inclusive are schools, and what happens next?

Once excluded, the judiciary system often takes over: while only around 1% of the population is autistic, an estimated 9% of the prison population is autistic (Young et al., 2015). The Equality and Human Rights Commission wrote in a damning report that 'the existing framework to provide adjustments to secure effective participation for disabled defendants and accused people is inadequate and that legal professionals do not consistently have the guidance or training they need to be able to recognise impairments, their impact, or how adjustments can be made.' This demonstrates that it is not just schools but the 'system' that is inaccessible.

The point is not that schools are prisons; however, schools do dehumanise. They use codes and practices as a supposedly legitimate and powerful means to strip people of their individuality, rendering those who do not understand the purpose of the rules, to feel that they do not fit. These students are voiceless and without defence. A stuttering apology is what can be heard most frequently from the mouths of young people with disabilities, which is ironic given that an apology originally meant defence (see Plato, *The Apology*, circa 399 BCE). Disengagement is never a child's fault; silence is not the sound of a free agent. Muteness is the product of hurt and it is deafening in its disapproval. There have to be better experiences at school for disabled students.

'Don't confront me with my failures, I have not forgotten them.' Jackson Browne

I gave up on schooling before it gave up on me, seeing the institution's value solely in its proximity to the train station, the tracks leading to a better life. I physically could not do homework and my thought processes led me to marking my teacher's work! My favourite day at school was the one after I interviewed Ed Balls, then Shadow Secretary of State for Education, who inspired me to continue campaigning for change as Whizz-Kidz's Chair of The Board of Young Trustees (a position I held until 2017). Campaigning is the art of catharsis. For most activists it is a necessary form of healing and repossession. Would civil disobedience exist in a truly inclusive society? If we equitably recognised the value of everybody's truth, whistleblowing would be a redundant practice.

Organise! Make a placard with Pritt Stick, cardboard and crayons! Mario would insist!

Feeling targeted and tasered, incapable of expressing anything of note, observant but unconscious, the coping mechanism is to force yourself undercover(s), in the embryonic position, night after night asking yourself: have I developed at all? Is that why they are examining me: in order to highlight all of my faults that I am fully cognisant of already? These thoughts are in my mind and that of autistic students. We understand emotions, and simply feel them intensely.

'I tell you what freedom is. No fear.' Nina Simone

KEY TAKEAWAYS

- Listen to and act upon the needs and voices of disabled students.
- Reasonable adjustments are a civil right. Do not punish or exclude, find alternatives.
- Sign/support the Cultural Inclusion Manifesto.

KEY QUESTIONS

- Has your setting planned proactively reasonable adjustments around attendance, behaviour, uniform policies, and curriculum for disabled students?
- Have you sat down with disabled students and gathered their views on life at school?
- Is your training led by disabled adults who have been through the school system?

COMMITMENT TO THE MANIFESTO

Classrooms not courtrooms. Disabled students not criminals. Inclusion not exclusion.

REFERENCES

Equality and Human Rights Commission (2020). *Inclusive Justice: a system designed for all*. [Accessed: 10 May 2021]

BBC News, (2021) *Disability and Domestic Abuse: 'No-one knows what is happening behind those walls'* [Accessed 8 May 2021]

Cultural Inclusion Manifesto (2018): https://culturalinclusion.uk/ (Accessed 10 May 2021)

Joseph Rowntree Foundation (2016). *Disability and Poverty: why disability must be at the centre of disability reduction*. [Accessed 10 May 2021]

Plato (circa 399 BCE). *The Apology.* Encyclopaedia.com. [Accessed 9 May 2021]

Public Campaign. For the Arts (2021). *Gavin Williamson – stop the 50% funding cut to the arts subjects in Higher Education* (Accessed 8 May 2021)

Savio, M. (1964). *Bodies Upon the Gears* YouTube www.youtube.com/watch?v=xz7KLSOJaTE [Accessed: 12 May 2021]

The Children's Society (2021), *Cut the Cost of School Uniforms* (Accessed 10 May 2021)

Young, S. et al. (2015) 'Neurodevelopmental disorders in prison inmates: comorbidity and combined associations with psychiatric symptoms and behavioural disturbance.' *National Library of Medicine.*

EXTENDING OUR WELCOME, TRANSFORMING OUR SCHOOLS

ARTEMI SAKELLARIADIS

'Any fool can know. The point is to understand.' Albert Einstein

This chapter is a call to transform schools on the grounds of human rights. It invites us to reflect on how we treat disabled people and explores:

- inconsistencies in the implementation of law and policy,
- established practices which are incompatible with disabled children's rights,
- perceptions of disability and the impact of stereotypes on children's life chances.

NATIONAL LAWS

The Human Rights Act 1998 brings the European Convention on Human Rights into UK law and asserts people's fundamental rights and freedoms. It lists sixteen basic rights, including the right to an effective education.

The Equality Act 2010 protects people from unfair treatment and includes disability. It also places a duty on all public service providers, including schools, to make reasonable adjustments in response to people's impairments. This is an **anticipatory** duty: organisations must not wait until a disabled person arrives before transforming their cultures, policies and practices. The aim is to ensure no disabled person misses out or is disadvantaged.

Part III of the Children and Families Act 2014 concerns the education of children and young people identified as having special educational needs or disabilities (SEND). It confirms every child's right to a mainstream education, as long as this is consistent with their parents' wishes, the efficient education of other children, the efficient use of resources, and that the education offered is appropriate to the child's needs. The last three conditions are often cited as reasons why a child cannot be included in a particular school, even though these issues largely depend on the way teaching and learning are organised in school.

The SEND Code of Practice explicitly states in paragraph 1.26 that the UK Government is committed to inclusive education and that the law presumes that **all** children and young people will be educated in a mainstream school (Department of Education and Department of Health, 2015, p. 25, emphasis added).

INTERNATIONAL LAWS

The UN Convention on the Rights of the Child (1990) protects all children (0 – 18) from discrimination (Article 2) and states that all decisions should be in the child's best interests (Article 3), aiming for the child's optimal development (Article 6) and taking into consideration the views of the child (Article 12). Article 23 confirms that disabled children have all rights in the Convention and Articles 28 and 29 that every child has a right to an education which develops their personality, talents and abilities fully.

The Committee on the Rights of the Child has issued a number of General Comments (documents clarifying the meaning of the Convention). General Comment no. 9 (2006, on the rights of disabled children) states that disabled children are still facing barriers to the full enjoyment of their rights, that the barrier is not the disability but a combination of social, cultural, attitudinal and physical obstacles which disabled children encounter, and that 'inclusive education should be the goal.'

The UN Convention on the Rights of Persons with Disabilities (2008) states that all disabled children and young people should participate in the state education system and that this should be 'an inclusive education system at all levels'. General Comment no. 4 (2016) clarifies that inclusion necessitates 'systemic reform' involving changes in content, methods, approaches, structures and strategies in education, so that all pupils can have an equitable and participatory learning experience.

PUTTING LAWS INTO PRACTICE

It follows from all the above that the legal imperative for including disabled children in ordinary schools is clear and undeniable. To achieve this, it is essential that examples of effective inclusion are shared widely and that educators are better prepared and better supported to work with disabled pupils.

At school children learn more about themselves and others, develop their sense of identity and belonging, and can make life-long friends. All children should have these opportunities together and learn from, and about, one another.

Some people argue that disabled children should not be included in local schools because teachers may not have the training, experience or time to respond to their needs. Initial teacher education and continued professional development can, indeed, be improved, as can practical support to make inclusion effective. As for evaluating what time is considered well-spent and what not, we may need to pay closer attention to who is valued and on what grounds.

Judith Snow, Canadian disability rights advocate, describes her experience of having a classmate who was an Olympic diver (2001, pp. 53-4). She lists the support offered when this other girl had to miss school for training or competitions and compares it to her own experience of missing school for medical appointments. She concludes that adults seemed to find it exciting to support an Olympic diver to achieve in sport, and a burden to support a disabled child to attend their local school.

Recent evidence suggests a twofold benefit of supporting disabled children's learning and development in ordinary schools: it leads to improved educational outcomes for disabled and non-disabled children, and better supports the social and emotional development of **every** child (Hehir et al., 2016).

In England the picture is patchy. Latest figures show an almost tenfold difference between the local authorities which send the highest and the lowest proportions of children to special schools (Black and Norwich, 2019).

There is much that schools, other settings, or individual educators can do to honour disabled people's rights and help align education practice with education law. If nothing else, it helps to make disability visible, treat it as an ordinary part of life and ensure our language and interactions reflect this. Here are some suggestions from CSIE's equality toolkit (2016) and online Knowledge Box (2020):

- Positively represent disabled people.
- Ask 'How can we ...?' (rather than 'Can we ...?').
- Research how to make inclusion effective.
- Consistently challenge disablist bullying, prejudice or harassment.
- Help disabled children get a stronger sense of belonging in school.
- Ensure disabled people are treated in ways which confirm they are valued and respected.

CONCLUSION

The education system needs to transform, by working within the law, so that schools are better equipped and better supported to include disabled pupils. A widespread assumption that separate special schools are usually preferable is out of sync with the law, and inconsistent with contemporary values of disability equality and human rights. This chapter invites readers to contribute to become agents of change in their own setting or sphere of influence.

KEY TAKEAWAYS

- National and international laws call for a transformation in education, so that disabled children can be routinely included in ordinary schools.
- There are likely to be more similarities than differences between any two people. We must not let one striking difference overshadow many similarities.
- We are all of equal value, by virtue of being human, and should all know not to judge a book by its cover.

KEY QUESTIONS

- On what grounds is it acceptable to exclude disabled children from their local community?
- If we do not question the futility of stereotypes about beauty or intelligence, where does that leave those of us who do not have what society values?
- Are you, or your school, working in ways which breach disabled children's rights?

COMMITMENT TO THE MANIFESTO

Education practices need to be brought in line with education law as a matter of urgency. This is a call to action to challenge inequitable practices and develop more inclusive settings.

REFERENCES

Black, A. and Norwich, B. (2019) *Contrasting Responses to Diversity: School Placement Trends 2014–2017 for all Local Authorities in England*. Centre for Studies on Inclusive Education (CSIE) Available at: www.csie.org.uk/resources/free.shtml#trends2019 (accessed April 2021).

Children and Families Act (2014) Available at: https://www.legislation.gov.uk/ukpga/2014/6/contents/enacted (Accessed April 2021).

Committee on the Rights of the Child (2006) CRC/C/GC/9 *General Comment no. 9* (2006) The Rights of Children with Disabilities. Available at: http://www.csie.org.uk/inclusion/GeneralComment9_Sept2006.pdf (accessed April 2021).

Committee on the Rights of Persons with Disabilities (2016) CRPD/C/GC/4 *General Comment no. 4* (2016) on the right to inclusive education. Available at: https://tbinternet.ohchr.org/_layouts/treatybodyexternal/Download.aspx?symbolno=CRPD/C/GC/4&Lang=en (accessed April 2021).

CSIE staff and associates (2016) *Equality: Making It Happen – A Guide to Help Schools Ensure Everyone is Safe, Included and Learning*. Bristol: Centre for Studies on Inclusive Education (CSIE).

Department for Education and Department of Health (2015) *Special Educational Needs and Disability Code of Practice: 0 to 25 years*. Available at: https://www.gov.uk/government/publications/send-code-of-practice-0-to-25 (Accessed April 2021).

Equality Act (2010) Available at: www.legislation.gov.uk/ukpga/2010/15/contents (accessed April 2021).

Hehir, T. et al. (2016). *A Summary of the Evidence on Inclusive Education*. Available at: https://alana.org.br/wp-content/uploads/2016/12/A_Summary_of_the_evidence_on_inclusive_education.pdf (accessed April 2021).

Human Rights Act (1998) Available at: https://www.legislation.gov.uk/ukpga/1998/42/contents (accessed April 2021).

Knowledge Box on Disabled Children's Rights in Education (2020). Available upon free registration at: https://dlot.eu/course/index.php?categoryid=22 (Accessed April 2021).

Snow, J. (2001) 'Dreaming, speaking and creating: What I know about community', in *Great Questions: Writings of Judith Snow*. Available at: https://resources.depaul.edu/abcd-institute/publications/Documents/Judith_book_1.1%20copy.pdf (accessed April 2021).

TO DIAGNOSE, OR NOT TO DIAGNOSE? THAT IS THE QUESTION!

LENA CARTER

In this reflection, we examine the question of whether the formal diagnosis of a disability (or impairment that has a 'substantial' and 'long-term' negative effect on a child's ability to do normal daily activities) for a child of school age is necessary or desirable.

I am writing this piece as a teacher and school leader who has been a champion for inclusion and the rights of disabled children since I qualified as a teacher in 1992. I am also disabled myself, following a late diagnosis of ADHD last December, at the age of fifty-one.

CHILDREN'S RIGHTS

The United Nations Convention on the Rights of the Child (UNCRC) has fifty-four articles that cover all aspects of a child's life and set out the civil, political, economic, social and cultural rights to which all children everywhere are entitled. Every child has rights, whatever their ethnicity, gender, religion, language, abilities, or any other status. (UNICEF, 2021)

Teachers, along with all adults, are duty bearers under the UNCRC. Within this role, each teacher has a duty to ensure that each child learns and thrives within the learning environment that they design and to ensure that the individual needs of all children are addressed.

INCLUSION AND EXCLUSION

True inclusion in schools ensures that all pupils are given personalised support, regardless of diagnosis or labels. In Scotland, it is stated in Statutory Guidance on legislation:

> Generally, it is preferable to ensure that support is
> provided as early as possible, in ways that are well

integrated within everyday practice and do not single out the child requiring additional support. Some children, young people and families will find terms such as dyslexia or autism spectrum disorder useful in helping them explain and understand any difficulties being experienced. Others may experience such terms as limiting and stigmatising. Generally, children and young people are keen to be seen as being no different to their peers.

(Scottish Government, 2017)

Diagnosis or no diagnosis, schools and education staff in Scotland are required to look at the child, not the label, and to ensure that barriers are reduced, and needs are addressed.

Occasionally, however, we need to remind schools and staff of their duties relating to legislation around additional support (or special educational needs) or equalities. The Technical Guidance for schools on the 2010 Equality Act (Equality and Human Rights Commission 2014) should be mandatory reading for all of those working in education. In it, for example, there is excellent exemplification of the need for reasonable adjustments to systems and policies to ensure that pupils with disabilities do not fall foul of discriminatory exclusion policies. How many headteachers and staff working in education are even aware of this document and its implications? Given the disproportionate numbers of exclusions involving pupils with disabilities or additional needs, it is important that they do.

Anyone working in education has a duty to ensure that their professional learning and understanding allows them to do their job in a way that is inclusive of all children. It is not acceptable to say 'I am not a specialist' and leave all the work around teaching and supporting pupils with additional needs to a small, segregated group of teachers.

CULTURE AND VALUES

Good schools ensure a 'quality of knowing' amongst all adults who work with children. They use all the information, data and intelligence they can gather to ensure that they respond to and meet the needs of the actual child in front of them, rather than some generalised concept of 'a child at that age and stage' or 'a child with that diagnosis'.

Of course, this quality of knowing can only exist where values-based relationships are at the heart of school culture. School leaders must prioritise time and space for quality relationships to form and for adults to see and hear all pupils, regardless of the pace, volume and style of their voices. This is not easy in a world where there is pressure to judge and assess children using a narrow range of measures that put financial efficiency and ease ahead of integrity. It is always useful to return to the words of Biesta (2008): 'The danger here is that we end up valuing what is measured, rather than measuring what we value'.

IS A DIAGNOSIS REQUIRED?

If schools are working in the ways that best practice, guidance and legislation advocate, we might come to the conclusion that diagnosis is almost unnecessary. If Child A knows that he has ADHD, his parents know it and all in the school community know it and are ensuring that Child A is thriving, what benefit might be gained through official diagnosis from a specialist?

I would argue that there are absolutely occasions when a diagnosis can be of benefit.

I was diagnosed with ADHD at the age of fifty-one. Up until that point, I had lived and worked, on the whole, within settings where the systems and working relationships I had meant that I thrived. I had suspected for many years that perhaps my brain worked differently to those of others but because I was functioning well and relatively successful in all parts of my life, I had never felt the need to seek further clarification or a diagnosis. That changed in 2020 when the perfect storm of the COVID-19 pandemic, the perimenopause and changes in my workplace led to me feeling de-skilled and misunderstood. As the result of a diagnosis, I have managed to gain a much better understanding of myself and my situation and I now have a clear definition of the reasonable adjustments of which others need to take account, in order to allow me to achieve my potential.

This leads to the two reasons why I assert that a diagnosis for Pupil A, who is still at school, is advisable. Firstly, although a good school may reduce barriers to Pupil A's engagement and success and enable him to thrive and shine, there may come a time when he is in a potentially less inclusive and positive environment. A diagnosis and a clear statement of the reasonable adjustments that will help him can be crucial in ensuring that the transition from school into the post-school world is positive.

Secondly, a diagnosis of ADHD may lead to a child being prescribed medication. This can significantly help some, although not all, children to overcome some of the challenges associated with ADHD such as physical and mental restlessness, sleep issues and emotional dysregulation. A pill is not the answer but can help as part of a range of strategies that lead to a solution which facilitates a successful and joyful life.

Similarly, then, with a diagnosis; it will never tell the whole story of an individual child or explain everything about their individual qualities, gifts and potential challenges but may be a helpful part of the index.

KEY TAKEAWAYS

- Diagnosis of a disability or condition is not always required to ensure that a child can thrive at school but may be of benefit.

- All teachers have the responsibility to develop a 'Quality of Knowing' in relation to each and every child.
- Diagnosis may ensure that the post-school journey of a child is as smooth as it can be.

KEY QUESTIONS

- Are you aware of your duties in relation to supporting and addressing the needs of all children under the UNCRC and legislation, regardless of any formal diagnosis?
- Do you take responsibility for your learning about disability, barriers to inclusion and how to address them?
- Does your setting allow the time and space to ensure that there is a Quality of Knowing of every child, who they are and who they have the potential and ambition to be?

COMMITMENT TO THE MANIFESTO

See and know the child before you. Use all of the intelligence and information that you can to learn about what will help every child in your setting to learn and thrive. You have the power to both create and break down barriers; learn, be aware and choose wisely.

REFERENCES

Biesta, G. (2008) *Good education in an age of measurement: on the need to reconnect with the question of purpose in education*. Published online: 2 December 2008 © Springer Science + Business Media, LLC 2008.

Equality and Human Rights Commission (2014) *Technical Guidance for Schools in Scotland*. Available at: https://www.equalityhumanrights.com/sites/default/files/equalityact2010-technicalguidance-schoolsinscotland-2015_0.pdf (accessed May 2021)

Scottish Government (2017) *Additional support for learning: statutory guidance 2017, section 25*. Available at: https://www.gov.scot/publications/supporting-childrens-learning-statutory-guidance-education-additional-support-learning-scotland (accessed May 2021)

UNICEF (ND) *A summary of the UN Convention on the Rights of the Child*. Available at: https://www.unicef.org.uk/what-we-do/un-convention-child-rights (accessed May 2021)

DISABILITY AND MENTAL HEALTH

JAMES HOLLINSLEY

INTRODUCTION

People with disabilities have a higher mortality rate than the national median (LeDeR review, 2018). Research by SCOPE in 2014 shows that two-thirds of the British public admit that they feel uncomfortable talking to disabled people. This awkwardness often stems from a fear of seeming patronising or saying the wrong thing, or a lack of life experiences with individuals with disabilities. The underlying exclusion and surrounding stigma towards the disabled population is directly causing poor mental health and reducing life outcomes.

In this chapter, you will learn about the current mental health crisis for disabled people, why schools are the main catalysts for future change and why school leaders need to do more. It focuses on the proactive celebration of disabilities through a range of mediums, the importance of social inclusion and how this can potentially impact on better mental health.

Over the course of seventeen years, I have become increasingly aware of the importance of inclusive school environments. Those with disabilities are at more risk in not thriving at an earlier age – the impact of this extends beyond that of the school years.

HEALTH MATTERS

It has been shown that there are direct correlations between social interaction and mental health (Ono et al., 2011, pp.246-9). The better our interactions and the more frequently we have these, the more likely we are to have better mental health, less stress, and a stronger sense of belonging. When reflecting on learning disabilities and autistic spectrum conditions (ASC), we can also see positive correlations in this area:

- In 2018, the Learning Disabilities Mortality Review (LeDeR) found that the median age of death for those with learning disabilities was sixty for men (national median eighty-three) and fifty-nine for women (national median eighty-six).

- The average life expectancy of a man with autism (no learning disability) in the UK is between fifty-four and fifty-eight. Those with ASC and a learning disability have an average life expectancy of thirty-nine.

LONELINESS AND SOCIAL AGENCY

Under The Equality Act 2010, schools have particular obligations in their duty to make 'reasonable adjustments' to place disabled pupils on a more equal platform to those without disabilities. When doing so, schools will often look at the 'education' provision – in many ways rightly so. However, it is not widespread practice that schools will place an equal or greater concentration on friendships and social development/interaction as they do academic standards and coverage/structure of the curriculum – for the many, this works. We do however know that there is a growing issue in schools in the UK, regarding loneliness and the lack of social agency for disabled pupils.

In schools, nationally, there is a large focus on curriculum content. We ask about the retention of knowledge and parents ask the common question 'What did you learn today?' For those with disabilities, this is still relevant, but we need to also be asking ourselves and seeking the answers to the following questions for pupils with disabilities with as much gravitas:

- Are they playing with anyone?
- Who is talking to them in the dining hall? What is the quality of their daily peer-peer dialogue?
- Are they involved with social activities outside of school with their peers? How socially included are they?
- How are their social interactions initiated?

Research by the University of Virginia (Narr et al., 2017) found that strong, intimate teenage friendships can help foster long-term mental health. The success of true social inclusion therefore runs deep into the ethos and constructs of every single school and its ability to support all pupils to feel included within lessons, playgrounds, and social circles.

CURRICULUM CONTENT

Many people refer to the Paralympics as providing positive awareness of disabilities and providing role models for all. However as highlighted by Kirakosyan and Junior (2018) if this is highly promoted and not balanced with the achievements of regular disabled people, it can send out messages to the disabled community that every disabled person should overcome their impairment or must strive to do similar.

Self-stigma for disabled pupils, through feeling shame either by social exclusion or through lack of appropriate curricular content in its widest forms, is something that all schools need to seriously consider and actively tackle. A recent study by Silvan-Ferrero,

Recio, Molero and Nouvilas-Palleja (2020) triangulated the negative association between internalised stigma and quality of life in people with physical disability.

REASONABLE ADJUSTMENTS TO SUPPORT DISABILITY AND MENTAL HEALTH

To further develop and establish the best school climate for pupils with disabilities to socially thrive and have more positive wellbeing, some of the ideas below may benefit schools.

Baseline students' social agency – Monitor selected individuals from afar. Are they included within conversations? Are they playing with anyone? What is the quality of their relationships?

Be proactive in establishing and extending friendship circles – Sometimes children need help in making friendships. A small nudge here, a quiet word there and at times formal social interventions are needed.

Build resilience specific to the disability. Think carefully about the dialogue around the child. Are all adults using positive language about their specific needs and championing what they can do? Teach them to know, champion and love themselves.

High quality staff-pupil relationships – For those experiencing stress or frustration, the relationships with the adults in school is paramount.

Celebrate differences – Use high quality texts to explore and celebrate all differences within society and the school. Create opportunities for high-quality discussion.

Give time to talk – some pupils may benefit from having a series of high-quality 1:1 sessions with a member of staff that they trust.

Positive self-identification – Build a positive disabled identity with the child. Celebrate and champion what they feel they are best at. Help them to accept and think about what they may find difficult.

Celebrate the individual – Highlight disabled children's talents, encourage other children to see them in a positive light to raise their social status.

Healthy life habits –Support disabled children in establishing a healthy mindset to holistic wellness: nutrition, sleeping and exercise.

Support the parents and carers – Have regular discussions with parents. Open a parent support group for children with disabilities.

KEY TAKEAWAYS

- Schools need a wide, positive exposure of people with disabilities through staff employment, visitors, resources, and curriculum content so that disability is viewed as part of life.
- Focus on the social agency and belonging of disabled pupils by building on their sense of self.
- View mental health as an area of need for disabled students, whether this is around self-esteem, anxious feelings or lack of confidence there will be a hidden impact of disability that needs addressing.

KEY QUESTIONS

- What are the current mental health presentations of your disabled pupils in schools?
- How far are pupils with disabilities socially included and accepted with their peers?
- How is your school increasing/improving the voice, representation, and social confidence of people with disabilities?

COMMITMENT TO THE MANIFESTO

Raise the importance of social agency in school, to support social inclusion, to improve long-term mental health and to reduce stigma for those with disabilities.

REFERENCES

Cassidy, S., Bradley, P., Robinson, J., Allison, C., McHugh, M., Baron-Cohen, S. (2014). 'Suicidal ideation and suicide plans or attempts in adults with Asperger's syndrome attending a specialist diagnostic clinic: a clinical cohort study'. *Lancet Psychiatry* 2014; 1: 142–7.

Cooper, S., Smiley, E., Morrison, J., Williamson, A. and Allan, L. (2007). 'Mental ill-health in adults with intellectual disabilities: Prevalence and associated factors.' *The British Journal of Psychiatry*, 190, 27-35.

Equality Act 2010. https://www.legislation.gov.uk/ukpga/2010/15/contents

Hirvikoski, T., Mittendorfer-Rutz, E., Boman, M., Larsson, H., Lichtenstein, P. and Bölte, S. (2015) 'Premature mortality in autism spectrum disorder.' *The British Journal of Psychiatry*: 208; 3: 232-8.

Kirakosyan, L. and Junior, M. (2018) 'Exploring the social legacy of Paralympic games for disabled people'. *Brazilian Journal of Education, Technology and Sport* 2018; 11: 136-47.

Narr, R., Allen, J., Tan, J. and Loeb, E. (2017). 'Close Friendship Strength and Broader Peer Group Desirability as Differential Predictors of Adult Mental Health.' *Child Development*, 2017; DOI: 10.1111/cdev.12905

NHS. 2018. *Learning Disabilities Mortality Review*. London: NHS.

Office for National Statistics. 2021. *Outcomes for disabled people in the UK: 2020* London: ONS.

Ono, E., Nozawa, T., Ogata, T., Motohashi, M., Higo, N., Koayashi, T., Ishikawa, K., Ara, K., Yano, A. and Miyake, Y. (2011) 'Relationship between social interaction and mental health.' *2011 IEEE/SICE International Symposium on System Integration (SII)*, Kyoto, Japan, 2011: 246-9.

Sakyi, K., Surkan, P., Fombonne, E., Chollet, A. and Melchior, M. (2015) 'Childhood friendships and psychological difficulties in young adulthood: an 18-year follow-up study.' *European Child Adolescent Psychiatry*. 2015 Jul; 24; 7: 815–26.

Silvan-Ferrero P., Recio, P., Molero, F. and Nouvilas-Palleja, E. (2020) 'Psychological Quality of Life in People with Physical Disability: The Effect of Internalized Stigma, Collective Action and Resilience.' *International Journal of Environmental Research and Public Health*. 17; 5.

Ware, H., Singal, N. and Groce, N. (2021). 'The work lives of disabled teachers: revisiting inclusive education in English schools.' *Disability and Society*: 23 Feb 2021.

CREATING A SCHOOL CULTURE WHICH INCLUDES STAFF WHO ARE DISABLED WITH MENTAL HEALTH ILLNESS – RUNNING ON EMPTY TO HAVING A FULL TANK

JULIE CASSIANO

> Data shows 23% of teachers are on medication and 12% have sought counselling to help deal with work stress. The 'shocking' impact of the Covid pandemic on teacher mental health has been revealed
>
> (NASUWT in Speck, 2021)

The statistics above highlight a growing need for school leaders to educate themselves on employee mental health illness so that they can mitigate the risk of serious illness and create a mental health-friendly culture for all staff.

This chapter aims to educate school staff/leaders on how to create a working environment for those diagnosed with a mental health illness.

MY CONTEXT

I was raised in a socially deprived area in London. My parents struggled financially over the years which led to them developing a dependency on alcohol. My parents' continuous focus on their financial difficulties led to unintentional neglect. By the age of eighteen, I had accumulated five Adverse Childhood Experiences (ACES).

> Adverse Childhood Experiences (ACEs) are stressful or traumatic events experienced before the age of 18 years...Exposure to these adversities in childhood, without the buffering protection of a caregiver, may lead to changes in children's developing brains resulting in a dysregulation of the stress response, impairment of executive functioning
> (Koita et al., 2018. p2).

At the age of nineteen, I was clearly on track to follow my statistical pathway. I suffered a mental health breakdown which led to suicidal thoughts; I required treatment for five years.

WHAT DO SCHOOLS NEED TO CONSIDER?

In 2010, after graduating, I took up the post of class teacher in a primary school. I soon learnt that having a diverse, representative staff body of all protected characteristics enables a school to have a greater understanding of the community it serves. My lived experience of childhood trauma and mental health meant I had an advantage when supporting families who were experiencing similar difficulties. I am also highly competent at managing children experiencing 'crisis behaviour'.

The headteachers who served at this school were compassionate, ethical leaders who created a non-bullying, inclusive culture. I considered I benefited from the following:

- Discriminatory behaviours were challenged.
- Empathy was modelled by the headteachers/senior leaders.
- A non-fear culture around absence was established.
- Counselling/psychotherapy was available to staff and students.
- Supervision was available for safeguarding leaders (DSLs).
- Bereavements were managed sensitively, and differentiated approaches were offered (thinking contextually).
- A flexible working policy was introduced.
- Flexibility around PPA time was supported (work from home or school).
- The leadership team always found time to highly praise staff.
- Professional development opportunities were exciting – growth was encouraged.
- External accountability remained the responsibility of the senior leadership team.

A colleague I supported, who was diagnosed with Bipolar Disorder, asked me how, with my condition, had I been able to progress so quickly from an NQT to Assistant Headteacher whilst also being a mother to a child under five. I was able to list the above. During this employment, my illness was never considered a hindrance, in fact, the culture of the school meant my symptoms were never exacerbated. I would even put forward that my workplace improved my symptoms as I felt a strong sense of purpose, I had autonomy within my role and felt a sense of belonging. I later learnt about Self-Determination Theory (SDT). Without knowing the theory, leaders at this school implemented a leadership model incorporating three fundamental factors: competence, autonomy, and a connection/belonging to the environment, which mitigates the risk of exacerbating existing mental health illness symptoms. In addition, it reduces the risk of developing new cases.

Gagne and Deci (2005) conclude in their research that: 'Self-determination Theory...provides a fuller and more useful approach to understanding the motivational bases for effective organisational behaviour.'

ILL NOT INADEQUATE

Professionals and relatives have discouraged me from sharing my condition widely. In their defence, they are trying to protect me, but unfortunately, this repeated message only reinforces the stigma creating an unimaginable hurt.

Considering this in the workplace is immensely important. Employees who are suffering from a mental health condition will feel this burden. They will feel isolated and have shame causing a reluctance to share.

> The stigma associated with mental health conditions (MHCs) is an emergent concern in the workplace and is now increasingly being challenged by anti-discrimination legislation, as well as disability, mental health promotion and anti-stigma campaigns.
>
> (Mindful Employer, 2016; Time to Change, 2014 in Elraz, 2018 p723).

I have learnt that the torment in silence is detrimental to the condition and increases the uncomfortable symptoms, creating a feeling of self-loathing and for some creates a prolonged battle with imposter syndrome.

BEING AN ALLY IN LEADERSHIP

Angela Browne (author of *Ethical Leadership: Lighting the Way*), leads a social network group for female leaders. Within the network she advocates the importance of sharing our stories (being an ally to yourself).

As a Headteacher, I follow through with all I have learnt from other leaders mentioned but having lived experience, I also offer and encourage leaders to do or not do the following:

- Have a considerably basic understanding of what Cognitive Behaviour Management (CBM) is and what it involves.
- Never doubt or question the authenticity of a lived experience.
- Do NOT try to become their GP and ensure members of staff in school do not offer medical advice.
- Promote a culture of care and support whilst leaving medical professionals to discuss medication, therapy and possible absence required.

- Show you believe your employee can make a full recovery during an episode – you will never know how much this means to them.
- Listen attentively, let them educate you about how the illness presents for them.
- Know your employee may feel anxious about their relationship with you once they have shared their illness with you.
- Aim to set up regular review meetings to check in. This will enable you and the employee to build a positive, trusting relationship.
- Let them own their illness and inform you of their needs. Do NOT make suggestions as this can offend.
- Make it known how you adhere to confidentiality policies. Inform them that information will only be shared on a need-to-know basis (share which person this may be with).
- Encourage building a work toolkit (their reasonable adjustments) with them. Some HR companies offer a template.
- If a staff member is absent ensure you arrange Keep in Touch (KIT) calls that are disconnected from the absent management process.
- Ask about any lifestyle changes they are engaging in (take an interest).

YOU CAN LIVE WITH A MENTAL HEALTH ILLNESS AND WORK IN SCHOOLS

Schools need to be aware of their duty to staff with mental health illness under the Equality Act 2010. They need to plan and prepare for re-occurrences of episodes and give their staff members personal agency around managing their condition independently.

I am living proof that you can survive with a mental health illness and remain in education if the culture is right. If you have been diagnosed with a mental health illness and consider leaving, please ensure you consider the strengths you have first, work closely with the senior leadership team to take ownership of your illness. You will have allies. Ensure you have found your toolkit that works for you and go to it when needed.

KEY TAKEAWAYS

- Discrimination and prejudiced behaviours cause mental health difficulties. Consider intersectionality.
- Research the work of Deci and Ryan's (1985) Self Determination Theory and studies into neuroplasticity to understand how these improve motivation and wellbeing in the workplace.
- Discuss with your senior leadership team how to create a safe working culture for those with a mental health illness.

KEY QUESTIONS

- What is the mental health profile of staff in your school?
- Considering your recruitment process, how do you welcome and encourage applications from disabled candidates disclosing mental health conditions?
- How can you challenge mental health 'microaggressions' being used in your school, thus protecting the dignity of those disabled with mental health?

COMMITMENT TO THE MANIFESTO

A school is designed to fulfil human and societal ambitions. Be committed to social justice and creating a world everyone can fit into safely without prejudice.

REFERENCES

Gagne, M and Deci, E. (2014). 'The History of Self-Determination Theory in Psychology and Management' in Gagne, M., *The Oxford Handbook of Work Engagement, motivation, and Self-Determination Theory*. Oxford: Oxford University Press

Koita K., Long, D., Hessler, D., Benson, M., Daley, K., Bucci, M., et al. (2018) *Development and implementation of a pediatric adverse childhood experiences (ACEs) and other determinants of health questionnaire in the pediatric medical home: A pilot study.* PLoS One: 13(12) pp 1-16

Speck, D. (2021). 'One in 50 teachers 'has self-harmed' amid Covid stress.' *TES: UK* https://www.tes.com/news/one-50-teachers-has-self-harmed-amid-covid-stress [Accessed: 3rd April 2021]

Tough, P. (2013). *How Children Succeed. Grit, Curiosity, and the Hidden Power of Character.* UK: Random House Group

LIVING YOUR BEST LIFE: A CALL FOR BETTER PASTORAL CARE FOR DISABLED STUDENTS

ANYA DIAZ-CEBREIRO

SYNOPSIS

Schools are a microcosm of life and to children and adolescents, school represents life; it is where friendships are made and broken, where sexuality is explored, where talents and passions are found and where pupils equip themselves for life beyond a school building. There are various barriers that the disabled child or young person (CYP) may face, but with excellence in Special Education Needs and Disabilities (SEND) regular and relevant training for teachers and proactive reasonable adjustments in place, disabled students can live their best lives.

PASTORAL CARE AND DEVELOPMENT

Pastoral care is everyone's responsibility, all educators in school act 'in loco parentis' which means that school staff are equally responsible for both academic and personal development of young people as their parents/carers. If the pastoral care for students is not made a priority for school improvement planning, schools fail to develop the whole child. The disabled student can be viewed as only the responsibility of SEND departments. Limited school resources can lead to academic subjects taking precedence and the personal, social, emotional development (PSED) curriculum is narrowed to such an extent, many children do not experience all the lessons they should.

In the rush of the academic year and the race to finish a syllabus, it can be forgotten that classrooms also serve as 'a critical dimension of child development' (Hutchinson, 2021).

> *The Impact of early cognitive and non-cognitive skills on later outcomes* states that 'many important later life outcomes such as participation in post-16 education, adult employment and wages, involvement with crime

and adult health status depend on personal, social and emotional development.'

(Carneiro, Crawford and Goodman, 2007).

For both disabled and non-disabled students, a lack of engagement in PSED and a lack of effective pastoral systems that support PSED could mean involvement in crime, truancy, absenteeism and exclusion from school (Ojewunmi, 2019). This is not just a school issue however, as future impacts could incur costs for both the school and for wider society (Carneiro, Crawford, & Goodman, 2007). Hutchinson identifies in her study 'Identifying pupils with special education needs and disabilities', the importance of personal, social and emotional development. She argues that 'a greater whole school focus on social, emotional and mental health (SEMH) could assist in both prevention and early identification of difficulties' (Hutchinson, 2021). Therefore, it makes both economic and social sense that all leadership teams, multi-academy trusts and local authorities build strong SEND-focused pastoral systems in their schools.

BRIDGING SOCIAL, EMOTIONAL AND MENTAL HEALTH GAPS

In the last few years, we have seen more attention being given to mental health, but with PSED being primarily addressed in personal, social, health and citizenship education (PSHCE) lessons, the message can be lost in the day-to-day life at school. Students therefore miss out on the holistic nature that pastoral care is meant to give in supporting wellbeing, and this can manifest in low self-esteem, emotionally based school absences and a lack of resilience. There are ways to ensure access.

Change the culture: Start by educating staff. This means that effective and specific continuing professional learning (CPL) is needed. Leaders should monitor staff knowledge of students and keep up to date with changes in pastoral approaches. This can be supported by performance management objectives that include pastoral goals. Empowering staff to consider themselves as pastoral workers who support disabled CYP, schools can include these values on job descriptions, ensuring that this culture continues with every new person that is hired.

Strategically plan pastoral care: Pastoral care is a key feature of school improvement to support disabled CYP. This needs to be developed at whole school and departmental levels. Whole school targets that are reviewed and published allow for greater accountability. Before implementing any pastoral intervention use the Education Endowment Foundations (EEF) Implementation Plans (2018) to support this.

Work together: It is essential that staff work together with SEND teams to provide appropriate support, and not to undermine any work being done by specialists. A

'Plan, Do, Review' cycle that involves key people will ensure everyone is working for a child or young person.

Increase accountability: It is essential that pastoral outcomes have the same accountability as academic outcomes. Using resources such as Social, Emotional and Mental Health (SEMH) surveys or Performance Assessment of Self-care Skills (PASS) assessments students can monitor students' emotional and social wellbeing and provide valuable data to schools to inform planning, whether whole school or for the individual child.

Macro and micro transition planning: Transitions occur in daily life and can be challenging for some CYP. Micro transitions refer to daily occurrences, such as going from lesson to lesson, travelling to and from school and changes in staff. Macro transitioning can include occurrences such as changing school, moving from primary to secondary school, or secondary school to college. We need to explain both terms and explain good practice in these areas. This is an expansive area and should be allocated due thought, time, and planning. Staff should regularly assess how micro and macro transitions may affect the disabled CYP. For micro transitions, this could include meeting daily with the child and helping plan the day. For macro transitions, this could include setting up meetings with a prospective student with disabilities and having introductory meetings with staff and introducing them to the new space.

Building an inclusive culture: By educating staff and including pastoral care specifically for disabled CYP, the beginnings of a fully inclusive culture can be built. Pastoral care can continue to support an inclusive culture, with an awareness of reasonable adjustments that is communicated to all staff and students. Embedding pastoral care focussed on PSED will provide the school community with greater empathy and empowerment, and, in turn, help reduce bullying and help build a greater sense of self.

FINAL THOUGHTS

My own experience of living with neurodiversity at school and higher education, as well as being an educator, has allowed me to see the value of pastoral care from multiple viewpoints. As a student struggling with academia, pastoral care could have provided an essential focus on socialising and organisational skills and helped with reinforcing skills learned in the limited time I was allocated to spend with specialised SEND teachers. It also could have helped me prepare more effectively for micro and macro transitions in both my personal and educational life. As an educator, I see how tutors and teaching staff can help with screening CYP, identifying changing needs and supporting SEND departments in their mission to develop the whole child. With severe underfunding in some SEND departments, and governmental cuts to education, schools should be turning to pre-existing pastoral care systems that can act as a supportive structure in educating CYP. Pastoral care should be seen as a valuable, if not essential, asset to a system struggling to support disabled and non-disabled CYP. By working the pastoral system and training staff effectively, we can ensure that everyone gets the diagnosis they need.

KEY TAKEAWAYS

- Education settings have a responsibility to ensure there is equal focus on both the academic and the pastoral by actively considering the 'hidden curriculum'.
- Disabled students face more challenges in their personal, social, and emotional development and this needs to be addressed.
- Reasonable adjustments should be reflected in whole-school strategic planning.

KEY QUESTIONS

- What do you know about the personal, social, and emotional development of the CYP in your setting?
- What plans are in place to support the social and emotional development of disabled students, and have reasonable adjustments been identified?
- What actions can you take to improve the pastoral system and support all students to live their best life?

COMMITMENT TO THE MANIFESTO

Be responsible for developing the 'whole' child through inclusive teams that monitor, advocate for and meet the personal and social development needs of all students.

REFERENCES

Department of Education, 2015. *Special educational needs and disability code of practice: 0 to 25 years Statutory guidance for organisations which work with and support children and young people who have special educational needs or disabilities.*

Education Endowment Foundation, 2018 *What Works in Education: A School's Guide to Implementation. A Guidance Report*

Goodman, A., Crawford, C. and Carneiro, P. (2007). *The Impact of Early Cognitive and Non-Cognitive Skills on Later Outcomes.* [eBook] Centre for the Economics of Education. Available at: <http://eprints.lse.ac.uk/19375/1/The_Impact_of_Early_Cognitive_and_Non-Cognitive_Skills_on_Later_Outcomes.pdf> [Accessed 23 March 2021].

Hutchinson, J. (2021). *Identifying pupils with special education needs and disabilities.*

[online] Available at: <Identifying pupils with special educational needs and disabilities – Education Policy Institute (epi.org.uk)> [Accessed 23 March 2021].

Ojewunmi, B., 2019. *Pastoral care: a whole-school approach to creating the ethos of wellbeing that culminates in better engagement and improved academic achievement of learners.* [Blog] British Educational Research Association. Available at: <https://www.bera.ac.uk/blog/pastoral-care-a-whole-school-approach-to-creating-the-ethos-of-wellbeing-that-culminates-in-better-engagement-and-improved-academic-achievement-of-learners> [Accessed 13 April 2021].

SEX, SEX, SEX – MAKING SEX AND RELATIONSHIPS EDUCATION INCLUSIVE

REBECCA WEST

Compulsory Sex and Relationships (SRE) is now statutory in England and this new framework has posed many challenges for schools. Debates over LGBTQ+ families and understanding consent have raged on the pavements outside schools and in the media. However, there is another debate which is rarely featured in the news, the importance of the inclusivity of this curriculum for students with disabilities and learning difficulties.

Relationship ableism has littered our media and society for generations – discussions of sterilisation and eugenics around learning disabilities the 1980s, and more recently the most popular dating programme for people with disabilities in the UK was branded *The Undateables*. These microaggressions highlight the unconscious bias which occurs in this area of sexuality and disability.

Historically, in research around disability and sexuality, there have been difficulties in obtaining ethical approval due to debates around participants' ability to give fully informed consent. This is replicated in schools where concerned educators fear the repercussions from parents (Alexander and Gomez, 2017). However, there can also be unconscious biases within us as educators and it requires open conversations about the diversity of needs when planning SRE (Turner and Crane, 2016). This chapter aims to provide guidance on how to make the statutory curriculum accessible for all.

KNOW THE STUDENTS

Teachers spend lots of time with their students both during their learning and in pastoral interactions between learning, they are the experts when it comes to their students. However, SRE is a difficult judgement as a class teacher as it is often a subject that has no comparison in the national curriculum.

Turner and Crane (2016) carried out research into young adults with intellectual disabilities and sexual relationships. The research revealed that there were intrinsic difficulties when planning a curriculum around the sexual and non-sexual aspects of relationships and these groups can end up being excluded. They concluded that if you don't ask disabled students what they need in the curriculum, if their experiences are not investigated, the planning falls short of its aim. Loomes (2019) explains this is a key problem with the understanding and development of effective curriculums for girls with autism and the curriculum must be adapted to meet their needs.

ADAPTING THE CURRICULUM TO MEET NEEDS

Paramount to all-inclusive educational needs is the correct communication. Students must have access to their own alternative communication method preloaded with terminology and vocabulary to allow for full accessibility with visuals and opportunities for pre-teaching planned in. It is essential that educators research specific disabilities and seek specialist advice where necessary.

When teaching disabled students, preparations like this should apply to all curriculum subjects. However, there are potentially unique adjustments for SRE which can only be discovered through one-to-one discussion with the student and their family. For example, the need to see concrete examples of human body parts, or recognition of the anxiety SRE can create for individuals, therefore requiring one on one teaching.

Common adjustments which are required when considering the needs of SEND pupils are:

- Using visual supports to support communication needs.
- Reinforcing concepts through repetition, overlearning and addressing misconceptions.
- Developing concrete resources; websites such as *www.supportedloving.com* have full anatomically correct dolls that are suitable for this.
- Explicitly teaching important elements of the course prior to starting the SRE programme. Examples include for girls the concept of wet and dry to support the use of sanitary wear.
- Lessons that explicitly teach emotions and feelings. For example, how it feels to fancy someone as opposed to liking them by explaining the body's response to emotions.

THE NEED FOR HIGH-QUALITY PROFESSIONAL LEARNING FOR EDUCATORS

Although SRE is notoriously an area of education where parents of all children can have concerns (Shipley, 2015), conversely it is a topic in which, even though sensitive, there is little training in initial teacher training programmes (Ninomiya, 2010). This results in teachers who are anxious about delivering SRE which impacts student engagement and progress. Research has found that the level of anxiety a practitioner has when delivering SRE can directly affect the student's feelings on the topic. Therefore, training staff well gives them the confidence to deliver which in turn improves student confidence within relationships (Alldred et al., 2003).

The Sex Education Forum have recognised this is an area of improvement and Paul Bray, the founder of INSIGHT, has worked with them to put together courses to provide CPD. Statistically students with learning disabilities are most vulnerable to risk (Williams, 2015) and there are safeguarding urgencies that mean providing well-informed lessons could reduce the likelihood of students experiencing trauma in later life.

LEARNING THROUGH LIFE EXPERIENCE: SEX AND RELATIONSHIPS EDUCATION IN EVERYDAY LIFE

The 'hidden curriculum' is the unwritten rules and social behaviours learned from being in school. When staff discuss the relationship, nuances brought up in other areas of the curriculum such as English and History with SEND students these hidden social expectations can go from implicit to explicit for students.

Good curriculum design in the most inclusive schools will use the curriculum to break down stigma. High profile cases of institutional racism have led to a movement to decolonise the curriculum. To continue this process the next step is to further diversify by moving on to LGBTQ+ learning, particularly for disabled students. It goes without saying that all LGBTQ+ students need to see themselves throughout the curriculum, yet SEND students still lack visibility in many educational environments. Educators need to ensure we see people with disabilities in loving relationships and family groups throughout the curriculum. One method of doing this would be books which represent loving relationships between young people with disabilities.

MAKING A CHANGE

There is now a recognition that 'If you can see it, you can be it' which has adorned many a twitter handle during the last eighteen months. My challenge to everyone would be that we must make sure that when we say this, we have ensured that our day-to-day activities live and breathe it. The books our students read, the history they learn and the discussions they have should support them to see themselves as active participants in the world we live in.

As educators, we must challenge ourselves when teaching SRE and deliver this essential learning in a way which is accessible to every child. COVID-19 reinforced more than ever before that connection and belonging is essential for human survival; it is our responsibility to equip every student with the ability to access this through the relationships they form.

KEY TAKEAWAYS

- Include all key stakeholders in making the right adaptations for the student including the student themselves.
- Give your teachers good SRE training and make them confident practitioners.
- Include visible depictions of loving relationships for people with different disabilities.

KEY QUESTIONS

- How have you addressed the needs of students with SEND within your new SRE policy?
- Do your teachers feel confident to support every child in their classroom to develop healthy and happy loving relationships?
- How are you ensuring that every child in your school can see themselves within the curriculum in the context of a healthy loving relationship?

COMMITMENT TO THE MANIFESTO

All humans deserve the right to loving respectful relationships, so all educators have the responsibility to deliver the education for all students to access them.

REFERENCES

Alexander, N. and Taylor Gomez, M. (2017) 'Pleasure, Sex, Prohibition, Intellectual Disability and dangerous ideas.' In: *Reproductive Health Matters Disability and Sexuality: Claiming sexual and reproductive rights* 25 (50) https://doi.org/10.1080/096 88080.2017.1331690 (accessed January 2020)

Alldred, P., David, M. E. and Smith, P. (2003) 'Teachers' views of teaching sex education: pedagogy and models of delivery.' In: *Journal of Educational Enquiry*. 4 (1) pp 80-96.

Williams, R. (2015). 'Pupils with learning difficulties are being denied their right to sex education,' *The Guardian,* 23 March 2015.

Loomes, G. (2019) 'Help us make our own way. Talking to autistic girls and women about adolescence and sexuality.' In: Carpenter, B., Happe, F. and Egerton, J. (2019) *Girls and Autism: Educational, Family and Personal Perspectives* (1st Ed, 82-94) Routledge: Abingdon.

Renold, E. and McGeeney, E. (2017) *Informing the Future of the Sex and Relationships Education Curriculum in Wales.* Wales: Cardiff University. https://orca.cf.ac.uk/id/ eprint/107648 (accessed July 2020)

Ninomiya, M. M. (2010) 'Sexual Health Education in Newfoundland and Labrador Schools: Junior High Schools teachers' experience, coverage of topics, comfort levels and views on professional practice.' *The Canadian Journal of Human Sexuality*. SIECCAN, the Sex Information and Education Council of Canada. 19 (1-2), pp 15–26.

Shipley, H. (2016). *Teaching Sexuality: Sexuality education and Religion in Canada, Palgrave Handbook of Sexuality Education*, Palgrave.

Turner, G. and Crane, B. (2016) 'Pleasure is Paramount: Adults with intellectual disabilities discuss Sensuality and Intimacy,' *Sexualities*, 19 (5-6): 677-697: Sage. https://doi.org/10.1177/1363460715620573 (accessed January 2020)

Ullman, J. (2015) *Free2Be? Exploring the schooling experiences of Australia's Sexuality and Gender Diverse Secondary Students*. https://doi/org/10.4225/35/5aa0636045a3a (accessed February 2020)

WHY THE HELL DOES DISABILITY REPRESENTATION MATTER?

ELIZABETH WRIGHT

INTRODUCTION

Being the only child with a physical disability at my school, I never saw any teachers or children that looked like me. I never saw disability represented in the curriculum. I never saw anyone like me succeeding. Disability representation matters, and whilst there have been improvements in representation, there are massive gaps, particularly in education. With over a billion disabled people worldwide, disability is the largest protected characteristic group: we need representation. Here we look at what disability representation is, why it is so important, and what steps we can take to ensure that disability is represented in education.

WHAT IS DISABILITY REPRESENTATION?

According to the disability charity Scope (2020), as of 2019, there are approximately 14.1 million disabled people living in the UK. Out of this 14.1 million people identifying as disabled, 8% are children, meaning that there are over a million disabled children that are potentially in our education system as of today. And whilst much focus is placed on inclusion and access for disabled children in schools, one aspect of inclusion is clearly missing – disability representation. But what is disability representation and why is it important?

Disability is often stereotyped into particular narratives and tropes that are harmful towards the disabled community and misleading of the disability lived experience. Mostly these tropes play out across the media, i.e., movies, news, books, etc. These media tropes include *the villain, the superhero, the victim,* amongst others (Aruma, 2020). For example, in the film *The Witches* the Grand High Witch is limb different and represents *the villain*, and in *Daredevil,* Daredevil himself is blind and represents the inspirational *superhero*.

These tropes are problematic when they become the general representation of disability, including in schools. These representations contribute to ableism and discrimination that can negatively impact a disabled person every day of their life through micro-aggressions and inaccessibility. Which is why we need to be mindful of not falling back on these tropes when we represent disability in our curriculums and schools.

WHY IS DISABILITY REPRESENTATION IMPORTANT?

A few years ago I did a talk at a primary school for parents. A school with a significant amount of disabled students, the headteacher felt that some of the parents were struggling. My story as a Paralympic medalist was intended to give the parents some hope. It was not the parents that really needed the hope though. After my talk I spoke to a pupil, Emily. Like me, Emily is limb different, and when I spoke to her she was crying. Similar to my own experience at school, Emily had never seen anyone with a disability succeeding in life. Her non-disabled peers would talk about what they wanted to do when they grew up. Emily felt that she didn't have much of a future to dream of. My story was the representation she needed to understand that she could be included in society, and have a future that actually meant something. Authentic, positive disability representation in our schools can change not only perspectives, but also the lives of disabled children.

Representation shouldn't be a one-off, a single talk, a momentary awareness of a characteristic. Representation is important because for children like Emily, she cannot be what she cannot see. Academic Laura Thomas states that: 'Our children's early experiences... shape what they imagine to be possible for people who look like them, live where they live, or come from where they come from. Simply put, kids determine what they can be based on the examples around them.' (2016) Representation shouldn't be a revolutionary act or something that is difficult to achieve. Representation should be drawn from the richness of the world around us, drawing on what it means to be human. Disability is an integral part of this.

HOW CAN WE BRING MORE DISABILITY REPRESENTATION INTO SCHOOLS?

Disability representation must go beyond being seen as a revolutionary act to something that all schools actively work at. When this happens significant change can occur. Here are two examples of schools that have made a conscious choice to actively build on their disability awareness and representation.

Head of PSHEE at Queen Mary's Grammar School in Walsall, Sophie McPhee has actively worked over the past twelve months towards a balanced PSHEE curriculum that authentically represents disability. Sophie's own learning experiences influenced the introduction of disability awareness and representation in the PSHEE curriculum. 'After watching some disability awareness workshops in February 2020, I realised that we needed to add disability awareness into our PSHEE curriculum. Like many non-disabled people, I realised that disability was something I did not think much about, didn't know much about, and was scared of getting wrong.'

Sophie grew her awareness of the spectrum of disability, in all of its complexity and depth – including invisible and cognitive disabilities, neurodivergence and mental health. As a disability ally she ensures that her students' awareness of negative disability representation is creating a change in their language, attitudes, and inclusion of disability.

Sophie created a plan to increase disability representation in her curriculum, showing what is possible for teachers to educate themselves about disability and share their knowledge. 'I have made this lesson a permanent fixture in our Diversity & Discrimination topic – our pupils go on to work in medicine, architecture and engineering... it is essential that our future leaders in society are mindful of the needs of all in their work, rather than disabled people having to put up with an ableist society not built with them in mind.'

Sophie's students are young adults, but what about ways we can increase representation for younger children?

Annelouise Jordan from King's Infant School in Madrid has been introducing disability representation to her young pupils through the books and resources they bring into the school. As a school they are aware of lacking representation across all protected characteristics, and though they are a relatively small school, they have actively channelled resources to remedy this. Annelouise says that they 'acknowledge and understand what disability representation means to our children, families and community. By investing in books and resources for our children we make disability visible and our targeted training for staff creates an environment where stereotypes can be challenged with increased confidence.'

Annelouise has taken the overwhelm out of increasing disability representation in school. By being open and honest about their purpose, the school is not afraid to ask for help and recommendations from disability consultants and activists. This creates a culture of learning and growth around a protected characteristic too often ignored.

CONCLUSION

US disability civil rights activist Judith Heumann in her memoir (2021) talks about her systemic exclusion from education, both as a student and a teacher. Exclusion that is globally experienced and felt by disabled people, even today. Heumann (2021, p103) writes, 'We were a people who were generally invisible in the daily life of society... If you didn't see us in school, because we weren't allowed in; or your place of employment... on your form of public transport... or in restaurants or theatres... then where in your everyday life would you have seen us?'

Disability discrimination still continues today in many guises and this is why representation in education matters. Representation shows disabled students that they are just like their non-disabled peers, with dreams and hopes and wishes. Inclusion and accessibility are more than the practicalities of installing ramps and providing hearing loops. Without seeing disability in the classroom, we fail to see it as part of the very rich human experience.

KEY TAKEAWAYS

- When creating more disability representation in your classroom/school include examples of visible and invisible disabilities.
- Increase representation through the media you use in your school. For example, does your library have a wide variety of books by disabled authors or representation of disability?
- By including disability representation, you are shifting the narrative of what disability is. This helps to build a deeper understanding of disability, leading to more inclusion, access and policy change.

KEY QUESTIONS

- What disability representation do you have in your school already and what does it look like?
- How can you include authentic disability representation in your curriculum that is not reflective of the negative tropes discussed in this chapter?
- Does your staff and wider school community represent disability at a community level?

COMMITMENT TO THE MANIFESTO

Representation of disability matters more than you think. Representation goes beyond the media we see. Representation is who teaches you, who you read and learn about and who you aspire to be.

REFERENCES

Aruma (2020) *Disability stereotypes in the media*. Available at: https://www.aruma.com.au/about-us/blog/run-forest-run-disability-stereotypes-in-the-media/ (accessed 03 April 2021).

Heumann, J. (2021) *Being Heumann – an unrepentant memoir of a disability rights activist*. Boston: Beacon Press.

Scope (2020) *Disability Facts and Figures*. Available at: https://www.scope.org.uk/media/disability-facts-figures/ (accessed 03 April 2021).

Thomas, L. (2016) *Why Representation Matters*. Available at: https://www.edutopia.org/blog/why-representation-matters-laura-thomas (accessed 28 March 2021).

THE HIDDEN AUTISTIC WORKFORCE

LAURA MCCONNELL

It is impossible to know how many Autistic teachers there are in the UK as no data is collected to ascertain the statistics, but there are Autistic teachers. Several projects are interested in the needs of the Autistic education workforce including 'The Autistic Teachers' Project' at University College London (UCL) and the 'Autistic Teachers' Support Group'. Evidence from the accounts of Autistic teachers in both forums describe several challenges, including barriers to disclosing Autism and discriminatory practices after disclosure. This section explores these barriers and practices and highlights what school leaders can do to support Autistic teachers.

In the UK, it is estimated that around 700,000 people have an Autism diagnosis (British Medical Association, 2020). Autistic people can be diagnosed from early childhood to their more senior years, and at any point in between. This range of experience can affect how an Autistic person feels about their Autism; they could be comfortable with their Autistic identity, know a lot about what works for them and the support they need. Or the diagnosis may be new, so they are still processing what this means for them.

Autistic teachers have this range of experience too, which means that not only will they experience Autism differently to each other, they will experience being an Autistic teacher differently too. However, there are several commonalities in the barriers to disclosure and in discrimination Autistic teachers face after disclosing.

BARRIERS TO DISCLOSURE

One common barrier to disclosure of Autism is because the diagnosis is new, and the individual is still trying to process it themselves. They may not have told their family and friends yet, so they do not feel it is appropriate to tell their place of work. An Autistic teacher who does not disclose their Autism to leaders immediately is not being dishonest, they are taking time to process their diagnosis, and often assessing if the school culture is safe to disclose in.

School culture appears to be one of the most referenced barriers to disclosure. Part of this relates to the way that Autistic children are spoken about in school. Staff members questioning an Autism diagnosis: 'I've heard other teachers say that Autism is an excuse that middle-class parents use because they can't accept their children are quirky' (Autistic Teacher A, 2021). Doubting the existence of Autism: 'A very vocal colleague is always telling the staffroom that there are more Autistic people now than there were in the past and that it is because doctors are over-medicalising and labelling children' (Autistic Teacher B, 2021). Or direct complaints made about the Autistic child by staff: 'We shouldn't be taking these sorts of kids, they set a bad example and they're better off in a special school.' (Wood, 2020).

If Autism, and Autistic children in the school, are talked about in a disparaging manner, it puts an Autistic member of staff in a very awkward position. How will staff react to their disclosure and will they be judged on similar terms?

Fear that disclosing Autism, or any disability, will halt career progression is another common barrier to disclosing in the workplace.

ARE THESE FEARS UNFOUNDED?

While several Autistic teachers report positive experiences of disclosure, with supportive leaders who have engaged with appropriate training and opened a dialogue with them to put adjustments in place, several teachers from the Autistic Teachers' Support group have described being overmanaged, their diagnosis being doubted by leaders or being told that they do not seem disabled enough for adjustments.

The Westminster AchieveAbility Commission (WAC) on neurodivergence and recruitment has reported that these fears are not unfounded, and they are not uncommon. Their report identifies that there needs to be management training on what disclosure means and that disclosure can lead to discrimination which in turn leads to a spiral of stress, and in some cases bullying. The report identifies that the Equality Act 2010 is not being implemented adequately and that Reasonable Adjustments are often poorly conceived and focus on the individual rather than on the systematic barriers presented by the organization. It also identified that, 'A lack of awareness and understanding among managers often leads to treating neurodivergent employees as the problem, rather than recognising the barriers presented by the work systems and culture.' (WAC, 2018)

Additionally, The Institute of Leadership and Management reported that 25% of people they surveyed said they would not employ an Autistic person and 50% said they would not employ a neurodivergent person overall (Institute of Leadership & Management, 2020).

While these reports are not specific to the education sector, to date there has been no similar research carried out that is education-specific, but they do indicate wider societal attitudes that are in line with the lived experiences of Autistic teachers in both projects.

HOW CAN LEADERS SUPPORT AUTISTIC STAFF?

It is important that there is a culture in schools that allows staff to feel safe to disclose Autism, or any hidden disability, without fear of judgement or discrimination. It is clear from the accounts that Autistic teachers have given that the way children are spoken of in school is a barrier to disclosure. That is not only problematic for the Autistic teachers, but it is unprofessional practice in the school. Rather than letting this practice go unchecked to allow staff the space to vent, school leaders should communicate professional expectations clearly.

As evidence from the WAC report shows, there is a need for greater understanding of disability in general, including the Equality Act 2010 and employer obligations within that, particularly that reasonable adjustments are for the teacher and not the school.

Ideally, disability training that includes unconscious bias training should be a standard facet of all leadership training provided by local authorities, trusts or universities. However, seeking out that training would be a positive step for school leaders who recognise it as one of their development needs, and this can be accessed through Access to Work in partnership with the employee. Access to Work is a government scheme that the employee can apply for to help where the employer cannot support with reasonable adjustments. Before applying, the employer should put all reasonable adjustments in place, but workplace coaching that includes advice to employers is certainly available to eligible candidates.

An inclusive school culture where difference is valued and celebrated, in addition to supportive leadership structures, will help break down the barriers to disclosure for Autistic teachers.

KEY TAKEAWAYS

- Autistic teachers may be at different points in their diagnosis journey, so may need ongoing support in the form of reasonable adjustments.
- It is important for leadership training in the education sector to involve disability training including unconscious bias training.
- Access to Work is a key government agency that school leaders should be aware of.

KEY QUESTIONS

- How can we make schools a safe environment for Autistic staff to disclose?
- How can school leaders support Autistic staff who do disclose?
- What part does school culture play in disability discrimination?

COMMITMENT TO THE MANIFESTO

There are Autistic teachers in our education workforce that are hidden. They are hidden because school culture and fear of discrimination prevents them from disclosing. In a sector that is supposed to be caring, we must care for all of our teachers too.

REFERENCES

The Autistic Teachers' Facebook Closed Group (2021), Anonymous accounts from Autistic Teachers A and B.

AchieveAbility, (2018). WAC report is released presentation at BDA conference [online] Available at: https://www.achieveability.org.uk/main/policy/wac-report-is-released-and-presentation-at-bda-conference-2018 [Accessed 1st March 2021].

British Medical Association, (2020) *Autism spectrum disorder*. [online] Available at: https://www.bma.org.uk/what-we-do/population-health/child-health/autism-spectrum-disorder#:~:text=It%20is%20estimated%20that%20around,have%20a%20diagnosis%20of%20autism. [Accessed 1st March 2021].

Dyslexia Scotland, (2018) WAC Media Release. [online] Available at: https://www.dyslexiascotland.org.uk/sites/default/files/library/WCMediaReleaseJan2018.pdf [Accessed 1st March 2021].

The Institute of Leadership and Management, (2020) *Workplace Neurodiversity: the power of difference* [online] Available at: https://www.institutelm.com/resourceLibrary/workplace-neurodiversity-the-power-of-difference.html [Accessed 1st March 2021].

Wood, Dr. R. (2020) *Autism and employment: facilitating the inclusion of autistic school staff.* NAHT News

EMPOWERING DISABLED PEOPLE IN EDUCATION SETTINGS

CAROLINE POWELL

Ableism is pervasive throughout our society and within our education system. We must challenge this through promoting wellbeing and inclusion in our settings. We should strive to represent disabled people in our communities and curriculum and ensure that these representations celebrate disabled people, whilst also conveying the realities of being disabled. We must ensure our own community and policies are anti-ableist and equip our learners to be anti-ableist. These strategies can help us to empower the disabled people within our settings and instill a sense of disability 'pride' rather than 'stigma'.

INTERNALISED ABLEISM

What do you think of when you hear the word 'disabled'? To me, it evokes images of fragility and suffering. It connotes inability. I was born disabled yet identifying as such makes me squirm. More widely, 'Disability' is a protected characteristic still shrouded in stigma and shame. These are all huge problems.

I have the privilege of being able to hide my illnesses for most of the time. When I do not have a feeding tube or IV line prominently displayed, I can pass as healthy. But my motivation for doing so is often to ease the discomfort of *other* people and to manage the way that *others* perceive me. Difficult as it is to confront, I have internalised a lot of ableism. As an otherwise happy and confident teacher, denying this influential part of my identity sends a poor message to the next generation of disabled people. My own prejudice needs challenging.

As educators, we have both the opportunity and responsibility to address these biases. It starts with admitting our own. We educators must resist external and internalised ableism, and empower students and staff to be themselves, unapologetically.

In this chapter, I outline strategies that your education settings can implement in order to enable the inclusion, agency and success of people with disabilities in your community.

PROMOTE INCLUSION AND WELLBEING FOR ALL!

Sources of discomfort for many disabled people include having to ask for help and appearing different, negative, or needy. A commitment to establishing an inclusive ethos within your setting will help support your whole community and mitigate discomfort for those requiring additional support. Creating opportunities to discuss and enhance wellbeing for everyone may also lessen the 'taboo' of discussing physical and mental health.

Considerate language use is an important part of such conversations: listen to the labels and terminology people use to describe themselves and respond accordingly. For example, some people value 'person-first' language (e.g., people with disabilities), while others prefer 'identity-first' language (e.g., disabled person). Identity-first is increasingly popular in the United Kingdom and some groups have a clear preference for identity-first language, such as the Autistic and Deaf communities (FutureLearn, 2019). Be sensitive to these distinctions so that disabled people can maintain agency over their own identity. We are often dehumanised and judged by our limitations, so having control over the labels assigned to us is important.

It is also crucial to embed a culture in which self-care and compassion for others are encouraged. Let us all learn from the Covid-19 pandemic and never again drag ourselves to school with infectious bugs; normalise recovering from illness and supporting colleagues in doing so.

PRACTICAL SUGGESTIONS

- Ensure each student/staff member has a positive professional relationship with the teacher/line manager appointed to support them. These appointed leaders should provide frequent opportunities to discuss wellbeing with their student/staff members in confidence. Proactively listen and respond to any concerns or issues and arrange reasonable adjustments as appropriate.
- Encourage and normalise learning/working from home when infectious and taking time off school/work when unwell.
- Re-think and rewrite student and staff attendance policies. Consider dealing with all attendance issues privately and scrapping public awards for 100% attendance. Abolish 'sick day' limits for staff.
- Maintain systems for facilitating remote and accessible learning. For example, upload resources on to online platforms so that students with disabilities can access them. Allow teachers to work from home when it is medically indicated.
- Frequently check in on disabled people. Provide them opportunities to truly discuss their wellbeing and the support they may require.
- Explicitly put wellbeing on the agenda for form time and meetings.

REALISTIC AND POSITIVE REPRESENTATIONS OF DISABILITY

We need disabled leaders and positive role models. Otherwise, we perpetuate the narratives of limitation and inability to our students and staff. But we must be careful with how we present the stories and experiences of the disabled people we promote: wholly positive or negative representations of disability are disingenuous and invalidate the lived experiences of disabled people. Nuance is necessary.

In particular, avoid the toxic habit of presenting disabilities as needing to be 'overcome,' as this erases the experience of disability and portrays it as negative. Similarly, avoid simply telling 'victim' and 'single-story narratives' (Kara, 2020, p.56) about the struggles of being disabled. Honest, realistic and balanced portrayals of disability are important.

The best representation of disability that I have witnessed is watching CBeebies with my toddler. The 'CBeebies model' (as I like to call it) is to present disabilities, illnesses and impairments as the normal experiences that they are. They make disabled children visible without focusing on their differences, and they place the audience in the position of 'learner'. Spend a few hours watching CBeebies and you will learn a range of words and phrases in Makaton. Whole shows are conducted in British Sign Language (BSL) and stories are told from the perspective of neurodiverse characters. You will see a range of children with disabilities and learning difficulties, without their additional needs ever being pointed out or dwelt upon. Everybody benefits from this. It is a joy to experience, and we should strive to embrace a similar ethos in education settings.

PRACTICAL SUGGESTIONS

- Position students as teachers, and staff as leaders. Learn from their skills. For example, can a deaf student who uses BSL teach the class how to sign a word/term? What can we learn from a chronically ill teacher about managing wellbeing?
- Consider how to represent disabled people in your displays, extra-curricular activities, lesson resources and curriculum.
- Where it is appropriate and you feel comfortable, consider sharing any experiences you have had with disabilities, illnesses and impairments with your students and colleagues.

ACTIVE ANTI-ABLEISM

Disabled people are constantly fighting to prove assumptions of our capabilities wrong, not least to ourselves. We need teachers and role models to have high expectations of us so that we can excel, like our peers. We do not want to be patronised or limited.

Active anti-ableism is necessary to foster a culture where disabled people can thrive. There is still a lot of work to do in this region: ableist slurs and idioms are still common, disabled people are labelled 'inspiring' for their mere continued existence, disabled people's needs are frequently questioned, and there is a bizarre phenomenon of disbelieving the achievements of people with disabilities. (See the conspiracy theory among young people in which Helen Keller's ability to write books was called into question, on the account that she was deaf and blind (Cosslett, 2021)). We need to fight these attitudes and assumptions just as fiercely as we fight other prejudices.

PRACTICAL SUGGESTIONS

- Celebrate disabled people's achievements throughout history and in popular culture.
- Read and explore literature by and about disabled people.
- Encourage and facilitate participation and success from disabled students and staff.
- Challenge ableism when you encounter it and teach others to do the same.

CONCLUSION

Disability is an essential part of our identity: the adaptations we make, the coping mechanisms we develop and what we can and cannot do are central to who we are. The obvious irony of ableism is that disabilities often catalyse strength and resilience. There is much to be proud of and a lot you can learn from us. Help us fight the stigma. Amplify our voices and share our disability pride.

KEY TAKEAWAYS

- Promote a culture of wellbeing and inclusion for all students and staff by reviewing all systems and structures that could be ableist.
- Ensure your representations of disability are a balance of realistic and positive.
- Encourage anti-ableism among your community and ensure it is reflected throughout your policies.

KEY QUESTIONS

- Does everyone in your setting feel comfortable asking for reasonable adjustments, and are additional needs met?
- Do you visibly represent a range of disabled experiences with nuance?
- Are ableist attitudes and biases actively prevented and challenged in your setting, and allyship actively encouraged?

COMMITMENT TO THE MANIFESTO

Foster a community that challenges ableism whilst empowering and celebrating disabled people.

REFERENCES

Cosslett, R. (2021) 'Helen Keller: why is a TikTok conspiracy theory undermining her story?', *The Guardian*, 7 January 2021. Available at: https://www.theguardian.com/books/2021/jan/07/helen-keller-why-is-a-tiktok-conspiracy-theory-undermining-her-story (accessed 21st March 2021)

FutureLearn (2019) *Person-first or identity-first?* Available at: https://www.futurelearn.com/info/courses/inclusive-education/0/steps/69339#:~:text=Identity%2Dfirst%20language%20is%20often,is%20not%20commonly%20in%20use (accessed 28th March 2021)

Kara, B. (2021) *Diversity in schools*. London: SAGE.

CHAPTER 3: GENDER REASSIGNMENT

CHAPTER EDITOR: HARRY SCANTLEBURY

CHAPTER CONTRIBUTORS

1. Tasha Fletcher – **Transgender Advocacy Fundamentals: Rocking the boat (the good ship Gender)**
2. Kip Webb-Heller – **Exorcising the ghost of Section 28: Education not Indoctrination**
3. Kate Hollinshead – **Freedom to Be: Embedding Transgender Equality into Primary School Teaching and Learning**
4. Dylan Ahmed – **Bringing them in from the cold: Empowering and understanding transgender and gender diverse students**
5. Chara Aramis – **'Out of place': Supporting and Celebrating Trans and Non-binary Staff**
6. Jami Edwards-Clarke – **We all belong here: making transgender and gender-diverse students feel at home in their school environment**
7. EJ-Francis Caris-Hamer – **Beyond binary boxes: Challenging the status-quo**
8. Cal Horton – **Being an Ally: Supporting trans pupils in early years, primary and secondary schools**
9. Matthew Savage – **If we are forced to live in the shadows, how will we ever be able to shine?**
10. Kit Rackley – **The power and pitfalls of visibility privilege: a personal perspective**

BIOGRAPHIES

Harry Scantlebury is an Assistant Principal for Teaching and Learning, and a teacher of English at a secondary school in West Sussex. He has an MA in Twentieth Century English Literature from the University of Sussex, where he focussed academically on Sexual Dissidence and Cultural Change (Queer studies).

Cal Horton is a PhD researcher focusing on the experiences of trans children and an advisor to All About Trans and the Trans Learning Project.

Chara Aramis (they/them) is a non-binary early-career teacher and blogger. They have written a master's thesis on gender stereotyping in primary schools, presented at the University of Birmingham ROLES Conference in 2017 and facilitated round table discussions at the Centre for LGBTQ Inclusion in Education Conference in 2019.

Dylan Ahmed is a student and aspiring PE teacher who draws on his own experiences as a transgender male to advocate for better support and inclusion of gender-diverse children within schools. He is eager to continuously challenge the cisnormative and heteronormative ideals that are often present in school environments.

Mx EJ-Francis Caris-Hamer is a PhD student at the University of Essex within the Department of Sociology. Ze have worked within the education sector for seventeen years, working in both 11-19 and Higher Education. Their work focuses on queer inclusion within education, gender, and the new RSE curriculum.

Jami Edwards-Clarke is the Director of Diversity and Inclusion, alongside her PE teaching and housemistress role at an independent school in West Sussex. She recently received the BSA outstanding INDEX (Inclusion and Diversity) leadership award and was a finalist at the Queer Student Awards leader of the year.

Kate Hollinshead has an MA (Distinction) in Managing Equality and Diversity and is co-founder and director of EqualiTeach CIC. She has been working in equality for eleven years, delivering consultancy services and training to adults and students in a wide variety of education settings and organisations.

Kip Webb-Heller is a newly-qualified Early Years teacher, who is also trans, non-binary, queer and Jewish. They are motivated by inclusion and creating an accepting and nurturing environment for children to grow. They live in East Sussex with their partner and two rescue dogs.

Kit Rackley taught high-school Geography for thirteen years but continues to work in education including providing teacher CPD and student workshops as a freelance educator, maintaining a close connection to teacher networks, training providers and professional associations. Kit is a trans non-binary person and uses 'they/them' pronouns.

Matthew Savage is the former Principal of an award-winning international school and now also an Associate Consultant with LSC Education, Matthew is the proud father of two queer transgender adult children, and founder of #themonalisaeffect®, training schools worldwide to maximise the wellbeing, belonging and learning of each individual student, enabling everyone to thrive.

Tasha Fletcher is a lead primary teacher in KS1, a mum of two boys, a Women & Teen Girls Confidence Transformation Life Coach, a Designated Safeguarding Officer and an ELT Materials writer. With a specialisation in Early Childhood and Psychology, she has more than sixteen years of experience in young learner education, starting in pre-primary and primary in Trinidad & Tobago (Caribbean) before specialising in TEFL to young learners. She has lived and worked in nine countries across the world, working in teaching, teacher training, assessment and educational development. When she is not teaching, she enjoys spending time with her family playing football, basketball and nature walks.

THE PROTECTED CHARACTERISTIC OF GENDER REASSIGNMENT: INTRODUCTION

HARRY SCANTLEBURY

INTRODUCTION

It is Sports Day, probably 1996, but I am not participating. Instead, I am lying at the side of the track, pulling daisies from the ground like I am picking at a scab. I am not listed for a single event. My name is not on any team sheet. I feature nowhere in the day. The shell-suited thighs of the Head of PE swish past, to tend to the other girls: longer; leaner; neater, more convenient. I go home and draw myself in a new body.

Fast-forward three years and I am walking across the school campus with my best friend. We have started – with a flash of fake ID – visiting gay bars, and we are effervescent with the thrill of it all. With new swagger in our gait, we deliberately pass by a small office at the corner of the science block, turning to try and find, through the window, the eyes of the teachers on break: women with cropped hair and secrets just like ours. We see them, we know who they are and we are desperate for them to really see us. But, no. Not at the end of the 90s. Not yet. We must walk on, unseen and unknown.

The lived experiences of those who suffered under Section 28 – and its legacy – are better documented now than ever before, and there is much to be celebrated in the way of progress. Since 2005, the organisation Stonewall have been supporting schools nationwide in tackling homophobic discrimination and campaigning for equality, and in 2015 they widened their remit to campaigning for trans equality too. Add to this the 2010 Equality Act, and in the context of where we have been, the progress that has been made, feels nothing short of miraculous. So far, so good then. Well, sort of...

We are at a crucial juncture. Over the last few years, we have seen the rising tide of fear creating division and discord anew, and this time it is the turn of the transgender community to face the firing squad. Today the discourse feels toxic; perspectives perennially polarised and debates increasingly incendiary. Crucially, as the war rages on, across institutionalised platforms of power, educators are left on the front line of classrooms, having received insufficient training and drowning in the demonising rhetoric of the national newspapers.

DEFINITIONS AND TERMINOLOGY

It is widely asserted that in the first five months of 2021, *The Times* published 223 stories about trans people and 'trans issues', without a single one written by a trans person. Truthfully, I have learnt to approach nearly all news platforms with trepidation, expecting to encounter the ubiquitous views of the 'concerned columnist': *Why are more people than ever identifying as transgender*? (hmm...perhaps because the previous generation spent their entire youth under Section 28); *There were no trans people in my school in my day* (no, but do you remember that one kid who was a bit girly? He used to get beaten up quite a lot and later committed suicide.), *Young gay people are being set on a lifelong path of medicalisation* (err, no... and less than 1% of trans people express any regrets about transitioning medically or detransition).

LANDSCAPE

The level of rhetoric, so often personal and pernicious, changes you despite your best efforts. The morning after the dropping of a high-profile tweet, you go out into the world feeling less safe, more scrutinised and more painfully aware of the incongruencies of your own gender presentation. In this increased state of hypervigilance, inevitably the creeping changes to your own behaviour follow: avoidance of eye contact; use of self-service checkouts to negate the need for human interaction, and *no you are not coming out for that after work drink.* The temptation is towards self-protection: to withdraw from society; to isolate; to disengage, but as both a parent and an educator, I know that I have a responsibility to live and participate as fully as I can. It is hard being a visible trans person when visibility means vulnerability, but I will never stop believing in the transformative power of education, and, as such, I am delighted to be involved with **Diverse Educators** and this project.

VOICES IN OUR CHAPTER IN DIVERSE EDUCATORS – A MANIFESTO

This section of the book then, focussing on the protected characteristic of *Gender reassignment*, is home to the voices of ten different writers – most previously unpublished. We have not attempted to align our views and values in order to produce an assimilationist polemic or a didactic treatise. This section of the book is not heavy on telling you what to think or on giving you all the answers (*we do not have them of course*), but it does hand the megaphone to both trans writers and trans allies, and it does offer a range of perspectives that will allow you to open up a conversation in your schools about what it means to be trans inclusive and how you can better support trans and gender diverse individuals.

'**Transgender Advocacy Fundamentals: Rocking the boat (the good ship Gender)**' is authored by **Tasha Fletcher (she/ her)**, and it provides a reflection on gender as a deeply ingrained societal construct before offering insight on some useful terminology, hopefully to empower you to speak up, and ending with a consideration of how children first experience their gender. Following this we have, '**Exorcising the ghost of Section 28: Education not Indoctrination**', which offers, from the lived experience and personal perspective of Early Years educator, **Kip Webb-Heller (they/he)**, some musings on how a greater openness is needed in our schools, and more willingness amongst educators to listen to what children are telling them. For the third piece, '**Freedom to Be: Embedding Transgender Equality into Primary School Teaching and Learning**', by **Kate Hollinshead (she/ her)**, the focus stays on education in a primary setting. It is full of practical, actionable advice for how you can make your classroom more inclusive and avoid practices which uphold rigid gender binaries. **Dylan Ahmed (he/him)**, provides the fourth piece, '**Bringing them in from the cold: Empowering and understanding transgender and gender diverse students**', with a focus on language and how educators must look for opportunities to engage and connect with trans and gender diverse children to provide a sense of belonging. The next contribution is from **Chara Aramis**, and significantly this piece, "**Out of place': Supporting and Celebrating Trans and Non-binary Staff**" shifts the focus away from the support of children, in educational settings, to staff. Chara makes the case that all individuals must be able to bring their whole authentic selves to work. **Jami Edwards-Clarke (she/her)**, in '**We all belong here: making transgender and gender diverse students feel at home in their school environment**', documents the thorough work that she has been doing as Director of Diversity and Inclusion in her educational setting, with some useful behind-the-scenes, strategic insight. Moving on, '**Beyond binary boxes: Challenging the status-quo**', authored by **Mx EJ-Francis Caris-Hamer (ze/ zir)**, is an advocacy piece for re-imagining your education setting, to ensure that all members feel included and engaged. **Cal Horton (they/them)**, our next contributor, in '**Being an Ally: Supporting trans pupils in early years, primary and secondary schools**' comments on what it means to be a trans ally, and makes recommendations for how schools can best support the mental and emotional health of trans pupils. The penultimate piece, '**If we are forced to live in the shadows, how will we ever be able to shine?**', is a personal piece authored by **Matthew Savage (he/him)**, providing insight on what it is to love somebody who is transgender, and to be part of their journey, before advocating for further training in schools, so that all children can thrive. Lastly, **Kit Rackley (they/them)** provides us with the final think-piece of the chapter with, '**The power and pitfalls of visibility privilege: a personal perspective**'. This is a personal reflection on the role and responsibility of trans or gender diverse adults in schools, and it asks leaders in education to consider how these staff members can best be supported.

CONCLUSION

I hope that you find, in our contribution to this debate, a 'golden nugget': something to take back to your school for further advocacy work or implementation. There are many strategies and practices that can be leaned into, but doing one thing really well could make all the difference: allowing students both to find themselves and be themselves in your school. One day, because of something we have done as educators, somebody will not throw that punch, swallow those pills or push that job application to the bottom of the pile. I believe that we evolve towards truth, and away from ignorance, so we must not allow anti-trans legislation (a new kind of Section 28) to creep into our schools.

COMMITMENT TO THE MANIFESTO

In 1987, Margaret Thatcher proclaimed *'Children [...] are being taught that they have an inalienable right to be gay.'* Today, let us stand together and pronounce that **all children must be taught that they have an inalienable right to experience and express their gender safely, surrounded by adults who will see them, include them, respect them, and want to know them as they truly are.**

REFERENCES

Bradlow, J. and Guasp, A. (2020) *Shut Out: The experiences of LGBT young people not in education, training or work.* Published by Stonewall, 2020. Available at: www.stonewall.org.uk

Mermaids' research into newspaper coverage on trans issues (2019). Available at: https://mermaidsuk.org.uk/news/exclusive-mermaids-research-into-newspaper-coverage-on-trans-issues/

School Report: The experiences of lesbian, gay, bi and trans young people in Britain's schools in 2017. Published by Stonewall, 2017. Available at: www.stonewall.org.uk

Thatcher, M. (1987) Speech to Conservative Party Conference. Available at: www.margaretthatcher.org

TRANSGENDER ADVOCACY FUNDAMENTALS: ROCKING THE BOAT (THE GOOD SHIP GENDER)

TASHA FLETCHER

INTRODUCTION

Gender is a foundation upon which people create a social persona, and for many the experience of gender may feel elemental. However, I will argue that gender is far from a congenital reality and suggest that whilst gender identity can, from earliest memory, *seem* innate, the stories that we tell each other about our experiences are largely ostensible.

Instead, these stories are culturally influenced and the stereotypical gender roles we are taught to assume are social constructs governed by societal norms. A 'girl' subjectively experiences her sexed attributes to be female and thus she easily accepts the stories that culture tells her. This indoctrination system is in no small way, part of the bedrock of dominant cultural norms.

ONCE UPON A TIME...

For centuries the stories we have told each other about the performance of gender roles have been narrow and prescriptive, designed to sustain the division of labour and patriarchal structures. In Trinidad & Tobago, for instance, it was taboo until as late as 1974, for a woman to open her own bank account without the expressed authority of a man. Does financial expediency have anything to do with a person's sexed attributes? Of course not, this is just one example, in an ocean of examples, of how women are forced to conform to narrow descriptors of female social performance.

It is trans and intersex outliers who, by their existence, disrupt the system and who offer us living proof against the cultural assumption of any innate single sexed 'essence' that is characteristic of all males or of all females. It is trans and intersex individuals who help us to see what it means to live in a body that is sexed by our culture and not prescribed by a God or by the laws of nature.

Largely, it is believed that the phallus is the locus from which 'maleness' derives, regardless of how one might experience their own body. We witnessed just how flawed this assumption was with the tragic case of Canadian David Reimer, born Bruce Reimer (1965). Reimer was sexed male at birth, but a botched circumcision removed not only his foreskin, but the entire phallus itself. Since there was no longer an acceptably long phallus present, doctors – conflating gender identity with gender role – believed that if Reimer was given vaginoplasty hormones and was socialised as a girl, Reimer would 'be' a girl. As it turned out, Reimer experienced his body as male regardless of what our culture had to say about his lack of sex organ.

FINDING THE RIGHT WORDS

There are a lot of ways that transgender people can describe their identities, and certainly not all terms fit all people. The term, 'transgender' came into common usage during the 1970s, with the earliest known use around 1965, to refer to individuals who went on to have genital reconstructive surgery (1), before becoming more of an umbrella term as early as 1974 (2). Today, it is most commonly used in the media to refer to individuals who have both medically and socially transitioned from the sexed identity assigned to them at birth, to the sexed identity that most closely matches their gender identity; which is to say, the term is most commonly used to identify people who are not 'cisgender'.

'Trans' is an abbreviation, and a shorthand, for 'transgender' and is used as an umbrella term for encompassing a variety of identities, including (but not limited to): people who are intersex; transsexual; cross dressers; drag king/queens; bigender; androgynous; gender non-binary, gender non-conforming, and/ or non-gender individuals.

'Cis' is short for cisgender. The cis- prefix is Latin for 'on the same side (as).' The trans- prefix is Latin for 'on the other side (as).' In other words, cisgender is a term that generally describes non-transgender people and transgender is a term for describing non-cisgender people. In the same way one might say 'trans women' (for transgender woman) one might say 'cis women' (for non-transgender women). Cisgender generally refers to a person who did not have to transition because their gender identity already matched up with the sexed identity that they use. While the cis and trans dichotomy has been used to describe gender behavior since at least 1914, many people are encountering cis as if it were a retronym. Somewhat similarly, ipso (ipsogender) is a term that some intersex people use to note that they identify with the sex they were assigned at birth.

'Transgendered' is not a word generally used within the contemporary trans community, in much the same way that 'homosexualed' is not used in the gay community. Transgender is generally an adjective or a noun, but not a verb. Likewise, transgendering and transgenderism are terms generally only found in anti-trans literature in the same way that homosexualising and homosexualism are generally only found in anti-gay literature.

CHILDREN AND GENDER PERFORMANCE

Largely speaking, trans people who go on to socially and/ or medically transition have, at some stage, suffered profoundly in their subjective experience of their own sexed attributes. Often, they have tried everything they can think of to force their gender identity into being male, if assigned male at birth, or female if assigned female at birth. Unfortunately, it is not uncommon for trans people to experience extreme hardship regarding the process of self-acceptance. Some are lucky enough to be able to rely on economic privilege to insulate them from some of the worst of it. Even so, each trans person knows that they risk everything when telling the truth about their gender identity. As we each live subjectively experienced lives, I would suggest that many trans children think that all other children are also privately struggling with gender in ways that are at least somewhat similar to their own experience.

For a friend of mine, with whom I was and still am very close, he thought everyone must consciously monitor each body movement, each expression and every act of communication so that it would meet the gender expectations assigned to them in the way that he did. We were both in our early teens when he began to realise that not everyone was consciously forcing each social interaction as if they were actors; for them, it seemed that they had internalised the dominant gender norms and were subjectively experiencing gender as being 'natural.' To put it another way, while the children who were boys were male, he was a boy who was consciously aware of being male in the way an actor is: someone who is consciously aware of the role that they are performing. It was not until we were both in our early twenties that he made the following disclosure:

> It had always been like this for me and it was only when my vocabulary expanded to the point that I could begin to contextualise and articulate my experience with nuance that I became truly aware that my experience with gender wasn't like everyone else's.

> J. Smith, Personal Communication, June 15, 2001.

CONCLUSION

Most trans people are hyper-aware of gender roles, stereotypes and the demands of sustaining gender performances. For many, their childhood is experienced as an anthropologist stuck in the wilds of gender, trying to decode the various rituals that gendered people engage in.

KEY TAKEAWAYS

- Sex is the 'classification of people as male, female or intersex, assigned at birth, based on anatomy and biology', while 'gender' is 'the social attributes and opportunities associated with being male and female and the relationships:

between women and men and girls and boys; and between women and between men. These attributes, opportunities and relationships are socially constructed and are learned through socialisation processes'.

- Gender identity is a person's deeply felt internal and individual experience of gender, which may or may not correspond with the sex assigned to them at birth.
- Being trans 'may involve, if freely chosen, modification of bodily appearance or function by medical, surgical or other means and other expressions of gender, including dress, speech and mannerisms', but trans is an umbrella term which exists to allow for divergences of identity; it is not used to create a homogenous group.

KEY QUESTIONS

- In your educational setting, what are some common misconceptions about trans individuals?
- How can educators have a joined-up conversation, using a commonly understood language, about gender identity?
- How can your educational setting best support gender questioning children, to ensure that they are not isolated and unsupported?

COMMITMENT TO THE MANIFESTO

Seek to address discrimination of transgender individuals within your educational setting, in line with the legal rights of transgender children to express their gender identity. Call for more/ better CPD to develop the understanding of staff, and therefore their ability to support individuals who are questioning their gender or experiencing gender dysphoria.

NOTES

(1) When the term transsexual was used in 1965 in this context, transsexual people were seen as very extreme transvestites. However, when the term transgender was proposed as a better term for transsexual, in this 1965 context, it should be noted that it was gender and not sexuality (as in, transsexual) which was the drive behind being transsexual. At that time, the Magnus Hirschfeld trans paradigm held sway in some respects and for Hirschfeld's sexology lexicon, transvestite was an umbrella term inclusive of several types of trans people, including transsexuals.

(2) (In 1974) some of the jargon used took an odd twenty years to become widespread. The first use of the term 'trans.people' (sic) was when Julia Tonner referred to 'the two worlds of the trans.people' (i.e., transsexuals and transvestites). Additionally, there was also talk of transsexuals seeking 'gender alignment' and of 'trans-gender' also used as an umbrella term.

REFERENCES

Colapinto, J.. (2000) *As Nature Made Him: The Boy who was Raised as a Girl.* New York: HarperCollins Publishers.

Demsky, K. (2007) 'How do Americans Approach Gender Transition': *Gendys Journal,* 14, July (2007). Available at http://www.gender.org.uk/ (Accessed: 26 April 2021)

Whittle, S. (2010) 'A brief history of Transgender Issues': *The Guardian*, 2 June)2010. Available at https://www.theguardian.com/ (Accessed: 25 April 2021)

EXORCISING THE GHOST OF SECTION 28: EDUCATION NOT INDOCTRINATION

KIP WEBB-HELLER

INTRODUCTION

Currently, fear and reluctance to discuss gender identity in UK schools abound. Being transgender is often seen as dangerous to children, with some adults concerned that transgender people promoting trans inclusion have an 'agenda'. As a trans non-binary Early Years teacher, lived experience, research and reflections have led me to understand it is imperative that children are taught about diversity. Naturally, this encompasses learning about gender and the vast ways that people experience and embody it. This chapter will explore why learning about gender identity is beneficial for all children and for society at large.

THE PURPOSE OF EDUCATION

What are we educating children for? To top academic leader boards? To be well-rounded individuals? To improve society? The purpose of education is a political issue (Dahlberg and Moss, 2005), with curricula set by the government, but individual teachers and schools also have a role to play, working towards the aims that they prioritise, underpinned by diverse values. Parents, carers and young people have widely differing lives, so they, too, have varied expectations of schools. Education can be extremely personal and extremely political. My belief is that education should prepare children to be a part of the world, in all its diversity. Inclusive education – celebrating and valuing differences – benefits every learner, socially and academically (Rieser, 2010). Education should provide opportunities for children to be curious, to consider other points of view and to be exposed to a variety of role models.

Gender enters the picture when we consider that, to thrive, children need to understand themselves and their world; pupils with greater societal and self-knowledge learn better (Pollard, 2019). Gender is something that every child experiences because we live in a gendered world. Giving young people the opportunity to consider gender diversity builds skills including developing questioning abilities; understanding different communities; creating a positive sense of self, discussing and conversing, and understanding the feelings and needs of others and themselves – all of which are outlined as vital foundations for educational and developmental success by the DfE (2020).

Learning about gender is not simply telling children that some people are transgender. Every child has a relationship to gender that is influenced by myriad factors that schools can choose to suppress or explore. For instance, trans identities are not new, having existed in various cultures for time and memoriam (Oyewumi, 1997; Schuller, 2017). Nor is mainstream society's current view of gender and sex one that has been around for more than a few centuries (Laqueur, 1990; Schuller, 2017). Gender and sex have been regarded in different ways throughout time, often intimately tied to racist and colonial ideology (Snorton, 2017), which is why understanding that gender is as nuanced as people are is not such an 'out there' idea.

The aim of trans-inclusive education is that future generations will grow up with agency over their own identities, bodies and feelings. Creating a learning environment where children understand how to treat others with respect and dignity paves the way for a safer and happier society (Osler and Starkey, 2018).

TAKING A CLEAR STANCE

Whilst views towards trans identities are changing, particularly amongst young people, trans-positive spaces are often sparsely scattered, with opinions varying between schools (Bragg et al, 2018). This is why learning about gender diversity must happen in all schools, led by teachers and embedded in the curriculum (Smith and Chambers, 2010) beyond a one-off Relationships and Sex Education lesson, which pathologises and sexualises trans people unnecessarily (Carlile, 2020).

Teachers in the UK must uphold Fundamental British Values (DfE, 2014) which include respecting individual liberty and promoting tolerance for all. Much like the Early Years Foundation Stage framework (DfE, 2020) outlines, good teaching is underpinned by fostering pupils' sense of self, promoting appreciation for differences, teaching pupils how they can positively affect others and acting democratically (DfE, 2014). The Teachers' Standards (DfE, 2013) specify the importance of dignity and mutual respect, curiosity, and encouraging and modelling positive behaviour in and out of the classroom. We must hold these constitutional cornerstones in mind when deciding our attitude towards trans inclusion.

THE BACKLASH

Being trans is seen as inappropriate for children, yet children are surrounded with examples of being cisgender and are expected to be so. An argument often heard against teaching about gender diversity is that it is dangerous to 'encourage' young people to explore their gender identities because being trans is a trend. Whilst there are more people now identifying as transgender or non-binary, this is because contemporary society's increased awareness and visibility of those who are not cisgender has given language to different identities and ways of expressing gender that have always existed, built on feminist and queer scholarship (Lester, 2017; Bragg et al, 2018).

Children should be enabled to come to understand their own and each other's identities by being equipped with knowledge, compassion and respect. The United Nations Convention on the Rights of the Child (UN, 1992) recognises that as a child grows, they should have increasing respect from adults to make their own choices and are entitled to lawful freedom of expression. It also states that education should develop a child's personality and respect for human rights (UN, 1992). It seems obvious that gender pertains to these vital issues that we must allow children to explore.

Another common belief is that including trans people takes something away from cis people. For example, some believe that using the phrase 'people who menstruate' rather than 'women' when a discussion about periods is being had is motivated by taking away women's womanhood. However, 'people' excludes no one, but if it is assumed that 'women' describes all relevant parties, trans or cis women who do not have periods, or trans men or non-binary people who do, are excluded. There is a danger of overlooking marginalised groups in policies intended to be supportive if we do not choose to be consciously inclusive.

KNOWING IT ALL

Adults do not know everything. No one does. We are all always learning. As a teacher, I try to take this attitude, remaining open to things I find challenging. In my own life, curiosity is what has helped me grow to accept and eventually celebrate my (trans, queer) identity. I had to unlearn my own ideas about gender to live genuinely as myself. Resistance to embracing trans-inclusion in schools can come down to the perception that it is too big a can of worms to open (Carlile, 2020); it is too complex and one must understand all of it to talk about any of it. People feel sure of the simple, received facts that there are (cisgender) men and (cisgender) women and that's the norm (DePalma, 2013). But that is far from the reality of so many people, evidenced throughout history and cultures, despite efforts made to silence these voices. Equally, we should listen to the wisdom that pupils hold. Appreciating and considering students' worldviews and experiences leads to more ethical teaching (Dahlberg and Moss, 2005).

CONCLUSION

I constantly find myself returning to a quote I stumbled across whilst coming out to myself: 'Enlightenment is a destructive process... [it] is the crumbling away of untruth' (Adyashanti, 2010, pp. 136-7). Too often, teachers are propelled by the pressure to impart more and more knowledge into pupils' heads rather than unpick and consider what is already there. I think the profession may well be afraid to let go of some things that feel like hard facts but are actually constructed ideas, such as our current understanding and policing of gender. When the requirement to unlearn damaging viewpoints – in order to survive as a trans person – lies solely at the feet of trans people, it is bittersweet for those who succeed. Self-acceptance has perhaps been accomplished, but the world is now an isolating space because those who have not needed to undergo the same reflections exclude, erase, pathologise, or harm trans people for being who they are. Education is instrumental in changing this for the better.

KEY TAKEAWAYS

- All young people should learn about gender. Supporting pupils to develop self-understanding and confidence are crucial elements of education.
- Questioning received ideas about gender can initiate intersectional conversations about vital aspects of human life that we should embrace, even if we do not know all the answers.
- Educators – as role models – should hold themselves to the highest standards in inclusion, especially if they find certain aspects (such as understanding trans identities) challenging.

KEY QUESTIONS

- To what extent have you considered trans perspectives?
- What are the main barriers to trans-inclusion in your setting?
- What conversations could you have with colleagues to explore the relevance of gender?

COMMITMENT TO THE MANIFESTO

Allow and create opportunities for all pupils to explore gender without judgement or fear.

REFERENCES

Adyashanti (2010) *The End of Your World*. Boulder, USA: Sounds True.

Bragg, S., Renold, E., Ringrose, J. and Jackson, C. (2018) '"More than boy, girl, male, female": exploring young people's views on gender diversity within and beyond school contexts.' *Sex Education* 18(4): 420 –34.

Carlile, A. (2020) 'Teacher experiences of LGBTQ- inclusive education in primary schools serving faith communities in England, UK.' *Pedagogy, Culture & Society*: 28(4): 625-44.

Dahlberg, G. and Moss, P. (2005) *Ethics and Politics in Early Childhood Education*. Abingdon: Routledge.

DePalma, R. (2013) 'Choosing to lose our gender expertise: queering sex/gender in school settings.' *Sex Education*: 13(1): 1-15.

Department for Education (2013) *Teachers' Standards*. London: HMSO.

Department for Education (2014) *Promoting fundamental British values as part of SMSC in schools.* London: HMSO.

Department for Education (2020) *Statutory framework for the early years foundation stage (EYFS reforms early adopter version)*. London: HMSO.

Laqueur, T. (1990) *Making Sex: Body and Gender from the Greeks to Freud*. London: Harvard University Press.

Lester, C. N. (2017) *Trans Like Me*. London: Virago.

Meyer, E. J. and Leonardi, B. (2018) 'Teachers' professional learning to affirm transgender, non-binary, and gender-creative youth: experiences and recommendations from the field.' *Sex Education*: 18(4): 449 – 463.

Osler, A. and Starkey, H. (2018) 'Extending the theory and practice of education for cosmopolitan citizenship'. *Educational Review*: 70(1): 31 – 40.

Oyewùmi, O. (1997) *The Invention of Women*. Minneapolis, USA: University of Minnesota Press.

Pollard, A. (2019) *Reflective Teaching in Schools*. London: Bloomsbury Academic.

Rieser, R. (2016) 'Global approaches to education, disability and human rights: why inclusive education is the way forward'. In: Richards, G. and Armstrong, F. (eds.) *Teaching and Learning in Diverse and Inclusive Classrooms*. Abingdon: Routledge, pp. 153-166.

Schuller, K. (2017) *The Biopolitics of Feeling*. Durham, USA: Duke University Press.

Smith, M. and Chambers, K. (2016) 'Half a million unseen, half a million unheard.' In: Richards, G. and Armstrong, F. (eds) *Teaching and Learning in Diverse and Inclusive Classrooms*. Abingdon: Routledge, pp. 19-29.

Snorton, C. R. (2017) *Black on Both Sides*. Minneapolis, USA: University of Minnesota Press.

UN Commission on Human Rights (1990) *Convention of the Rights of the Child*. E/CN.4/RES/1990/74. Available at: https://downloads.unicef.org.uk/wp-content/uploads/2010/05/UNCRC_united_nations_convention_on_the_rights_of_the_child.pdf (Accessed 11 April 2021).

FREEDOM TO BE: EMBEDDING TRANSGENDER EQUALITY INTO PRIMARY SCHOOL TEACHING AND LEARNING

KATE HOLLINSHEAD

INTRODUCTION

The idea of taking steps to embed transgender equality into teaching and learning at primary school level can be met with fear, concern and avoidance. In an atmosphere of changing statutory duties around Relationships and Sex Education; protests against LGBT+ education outside schools; and misinformation and hate campaigns orchestrated against transgender people on social media sites, advocating for and implementing trans equality in school can feel like a battle. This chapter will focus on debunking some of the more common myths and misconceptions around what transgender equality in primary schools looks like and provide readers with some practical strategies to implement in the classroom, providing a starting point for ensuring all pupils feel free to be themselves in a safe and inclusive learning environment.

CONFRONT MISCONCEPTIONS

My experience of working in the field of equality in education suggests that one of the most common concerns people have about trans-inclusive teaching is the idea that it will involve teaching 'adult issues' to children; that it is not age appropriate in primary schools, and that the resources used will not be suitable. I have spoken with parents who are worried that teaching may include showing images of surgical procedures and explanations of how to transition. This misinformation is often spread between parents and carers on WhatsApp groups or on social networking sites, exacerbating fears further. It is vital that parents and carers are reassured that this is not the case. This type of content would of course fall outside the remit of the primary PSHE and science curriculum. In addition, and often overlooked in this discussion, all teachers have a statutory duty to safeguard young people against harm, which will include inappropriate content.

There also exists the concern that talking to a young person about trans people will make that person themselves 'become transgender.' Not only does this highlight the underlying assumption that being transgender is somehow negative – perhaps showcasing in itself why work on transgender equality is so important – but also outlines a misconception that a person's gender identity can be manipulated by someone else. Gender identity is a deeply felt, psychological identification as a man, women, some other gender or as genderless, not something that can be changed on a whim. In the same way arguments about talking about sexual orientation can 'make someone gay' have historically been levelled as criticism for LGB equality in schools, not least due to Section 28 legislation preventing local authorities from 'promoting homosexuality' between 1988 and 2000, arguments about 'promoting being transgender' are often brought out in opposition to transgender equality.

MEETING STUDENTS WHERE THEY ARE

This brings us onto people's next reason for avoiding trans inclusive education; the assumption that there are no trans children in their classroom, so they do not need to teach about this. It is estimated that 1% of the UK population is transgender (GEO, 2018; Stonewall, 2021), a figure thought to be much lower than the actual transgender population due to limited mechanisms to gain a comprehensive data snapshot and underreporting because of societal stigma and prejudice. Nevertheless, due to increased visibility of trans people in the media recent years, and the resultant increase in conversations about gender identity in the mainstream, children and young people are now living in a world where they are more likely to encounter conversations about trans identities from family, friends or the media, know someone who is trans or see trans characters in TV and film. Some pupils will have transgender or non-binary parents and carers, family members and friends, and some pupils themselves will be transgender. Research suggests that from the time children are able to communicate verbally, children have been reported to express discomfort with their assigned gender identity (Ehrensaft, 2011, Brill & Pepper, 2008 and Vitale, 2001 in Gregor, 2013). In addition, retrospective research by Kennedy and Hellen (2010) highlights that most individuals realise that their gender identity is incongruent with their biological identity before they leave primary school (Gregor, 2013). Trans-inclusive education will help all young people to better understand the world around them and to better understand themselves. Not all children who question their gender identity will be transgender, but by providing an environment where the young person's identity is validated and changes are supported if they come to explore their gender identity further, pupils will feel safe, included and fully able to be themselves.

WHAT CAN TEACHERS DO?

Firstly, it is about being aware of how much the gender binary is relied upon in classroom practice and taking steps to avoid this. It is much more inclusive of gender questioning or non-binary pupils to address the class as 'everyone' or 'year 5' rather than 'boys and girls.' Often the whole class has a name, such as 'Penguins' or 'Monet Class' which is ideal for this (even better if the class is named after an LGBT+ role model!) In addition, avoid grouping or selecting pupils by gender; this is often unnecessary and can make pupils feel uncomfortable. Instead, try separating pupils by surname – those with surnames beginning with the letter A-H in one group and I-Z in another, or creating more imaginative ways to break pupils up into groups. Seating pupils 'boy, girl, boy, girl' can also create a difficult environment for non-binary pupils, as well as perpetuating damaging stereotypes about gender and behavioural expectations.

From the age of two, children are aware of gender (Martin and Ruble, 2004) and from a very early age they can pick up messages about what they can and cannot do as a girl or a boy. It is important that the school does not reinforce these ideas but takes active steps to allow young people to explore what they enjoy and who they are. Ensure that fiction books in the classroom and the school library are not separated by gender, i.e., 'books for boys' and 'books for girls', and that the books do not reinforce gender stereotypes. Choose books that look at how important it is that we are all different and that difference is respected, such as *The Hueys in the New Jumper* by Oliver Jeffries; books that begin to explore gender identity, such as *Red* by Michael Hall and *Alien Nation* by Matty Donaldson, and books that contain trans protagonists, such as *10,000 Dresses* by Marcus Ewert and *George* by Alex Dino.

In addition, dressing up boxes should be combined so that all young people are free to choose the items that they wish to wear and to mix and match outfits if they desire – a police ballerina or a dinosaur princess allow for more creativity and exploration than standard gendered choices! A school may find that despite not gendering activities, some pupils gravitate to particular toys, for example, girls always choosing to play with the kitchen and boys with the tool set. Mixing and matching things in the home corner, for example adding a screwdriver in the kitchen, can encourage children to be more imaginative in their play and try new things. And throughout all subjects, ensure that teaching includes transgender role models. These could include Dr Ronx, a trans non-binary A&E doctor and presenter of CBBC's *Operation Ouch!*; Elliot Page, a trans Canadian actor and producer; or Marsha P Johnson, who was an American LGBT+ rights activist, amongst many others.

CONCLUSION

Do not shy away from the questions young people may have about what it means to be transgender. Answering questions can be tricky, but silencing or ignoring questions can send out the message that it is shameful or negative to be trans. Instead, role model the importance of research by taking questions away to gather accurate information and answer at a later stage. Having a list of responses to frequently asked tricky questions, which has been signed off by senior leadership and disseminated to all staff, can give teachers reassurance that their answer is considered and consistent. Of course, trans-inclusive teaching and learning is just one part of providing truly equal and inclusive spaces for trans people in schools, but it is a vitally important one, and one that all teachers can have a part in changing, regardless of position or power. By making a few key changes to teaching and learning, teachers can have a profound effect on pupils' experiences of the education system and therefore their experiences later in life.

KEY TAKEAWAYS

- Ensure that you are equipped with effective challenges against the most common myths concerning trans-inclusive teaching.
- Avoid any practices which uphold rigid gender binaries.
- Ensure teaching and learning is representative of trans identities.

KEY QUESTIONS

- Do all pupils see themselves reflected in my teaching?
- Does my teaching equip pupils to live in a diverse and global society?
- How do I know what I know? What sources am I using to inform my teaching?

COMMITMENT TO THE MANIFESTO

Challenge yourself to make a few key changes to your teaching and learning practice to ensure all pupils regardless of gender identity feel safe, included and respected.

REFERENCES

EqualiTeach (2020) 'Free to Be: Embedding LGBT+ Equality and Tackling Homophobic, Biphobic and Transphobic Bullying in Primary Schools.' https://equaliteach.co.uk/for-schools/classroom-resources/free-to-be/

Gregor, C. (2013) 'How might parents of pre-pubescent children with gender identity issues understand their experience?' University of East London and Tavistock and Portman Library and Information Service http://repository.tavistockandportman.ac.uk/803/1/Claire_Gregor_Gender_Identity.pdf

Martin, C. and Ruble, D. (2004) 'Children's search for gender cues: Cognitive perspectives on gender development,' *Current Directions in Psychological Science*, 13(2).

Stonewall (2021) *The Truth about Trans* https://www.stonewall.org.uk/truth-about-trans

Government Equalities Office (2018) *Trans People in the UK* https://assets.publishing.service.gov.uk/government/uploads/system/uploads/attachment_data/file/721642/GEO-LGBT-factsheet.pdf

BRINGING THEM IN FROM THE COLD: EMPOWERING AND UNDERSTANDING TRANSGENDER AND GENDER-DIVERSE STUDENTS

DYLAN AHMED

INTRODUCTION

Research tells us that gender-diverse children often go overlooked at school, with the prevailing cisnormative curriculum and the frequent absence of gender-neutral facilities amongst other factors. From the *2017 Stonewall School Report,* we learn that 'three in four LGBT pupils (77%) have never learnt about gender identity and what 'trans' means at school" and that 'seven in ten LGBT pupils (68 %) report that teachers or school staff only "sometimes" or "never" challenge transphobic language when they hear it'. Gender diversity in children tends to be a topic of debate, but there is a failure to understand how to nurture these children in an inclusive and affirming environment in which their wellbeing is considered. In order to engage and empower these individuals, structural changes need to take place within the education system; but where do we start and how do we ensure that we are making effective and well-informed changes rather than tokenistic ones?

BODILY AUTONOMY

Firstly, we must zoom in on the lived experiences of transgender and gender non-conforming students. They continuously experience a school system in which they are not represented and made to feel abnormal. From the beginning of our school experience we become very aware of the labels of male and female that are placed upon us; for the majority of children this is not something which requires a second thought but for those who are uncomfortable with these enforced labels it can cause extreme discomfort and feelings of isolation. Within the school setting, cisnormativity is prevalent and anything which diverts from this is seen as abnormal, therefore making children experiencing gender dysphoria or questioning their gender feel as if they are a taboo. Many gender diverse students find themselves having to resist the pressures of cisnormative ideas in school (McBride, 2021) and ultimately feeling as if they are responsible for breaking institutionalised cisnormativity, when in fact this is not a responsibility which we should be putting on students at all.

More often than not, when children assigned female at birth (AFAB) or assigned male at birth (AMAB) present characteristics stereotypically linked to the opposite sex, they are either discouraged or considered to be going through a phase. Not only does this perpetuate the idea that anatomy dictates characteristics, but it also prevents children from exploring their gender identity as something which they own. Instead, it creates the idea that their gender is something dictated by the society that they are within.

THE CURRICULUM MATTERS

To challenge cisnormativity within schools, we must first identify the different ways in which it is upheld. A big area to tackle is the curriculum, as with many other areas the national curriculum fails to provide informative education on gender diversity and what it means; leaving us to believe that being cisgender is the norm. This not only creates an exclusive environment, but also emphasises the eurocentric nature of our education system. There is a failure to acknowledge how gender diversity in fact exists within many other cultures, such as Two Spirit Native Americans or Hijras in South Asia. It is especially concerning that we are unable to provide inclusive sexual health and relationships education; these lessons near enough always have a completely heteronormative and cisnormative basis, leaving students who do not fit into these labels ill-equipped and having to learn for themselves from unreliable sources.

Having recently experienced the whole secondary school curriculum myself, as a transgender male, I could not account for one time in which I felt represented. The few times that gender diversity did come up within lessons, it was always in the form of a debate over whether differing identities are valid. Rather than informing and engaging students, these lessons were divisive and insensitive. Instead, we need to be able to talk about gender diversity as a matter of fact rather than opinion while still understanding that every individual will have a unique experience of gender. We need to give gender-diverse children the opportunity to see gender diversity in a light where it is not the topic of debate and instead something which can inspire them to be more confident in who they are as a person.

WHAT'S IN A NAME?

Transforming the curriculum will take a lot of informed thought and time, but there are some things which every school can do right now to include gender-diverse pupils. One of my biggest struggles was trying to have my preferred name put on the register; it was a simple thing to do but something that made a huge difference to my emotional state once it was done. Most gender-diverse children will face long waiting lists for medical interventions; many even struggle getting a referral for the waiting list in the first place, making social transition all the more important. To facilitate this process of social transitioning there should be a set process by which students are able to have preferred names and pronouns on record. With waiting lists for the gender identity clinic being around thirty-three to thirty-six months, allowing as much autonomy as possible within a school setting is vital for transitioning students to make them feel validated and respected for who they are.

GENDER EUPHORIA

When thinking about creating an affirmative environment for transgender and gender non-conforming individuals, we should look toward how we can create moments of gender euphoria for them. With an increased risk of transgender and gender non-conforming people developing mental illness in comparison to their cisgender counterparts (Dhejne et al., 2016), it is essential that school is an empowering place for these students where all their emotions (both good and bad) are validated and understood. School is sometimes the only safe space a student will have, so it should be a place in which they are nurtured and able to flourish.

OK GIRLS...AND DYLAN, SORRY

Language used by educators on a daily basis is important to consider; after I came out in year 8, that feeling in the moments where people used my correct name and pronouns far outweighed the moments where they got it wrong. Using gender neutral language can prevent dysphoric experiences for gender diverse students while not singling them out either. Having attended an all girls school myself, one phrase that I heard near enough every day was 'Okay girls... and Dylan, sorry'; this experience emphasised how ingrained it is within many people to assume someone's gender unless they have openly come out to be transgender.

CONCLUSION

We must remember that many students will be in a position where it is impossible for them to come out; whether that be because they have not fully figured out their identity or because of personal reasons. This makes it all the more important to make the whole school environment inclusive of all gender identities, regardless of whether students have come out or not. We need to make every student feel seen even when they are still hiding their true identity. Even the smallest adaptations to our everyday school life could have a hugely positive impact on those who are questioning or exploring their gender identity; we have a duty to nurture and empower these students however we can; you never know how the smallest change could make the biggest impact on a student's wellbeing.

KEY TAKEAWAYS

- Transgender and gender diverse children exist in the margins of our schools.
- Not enough is being done to bring transgender and gender diverse children into the discourse.
- Opportunities are missed every day for adults to make things better for transgender and gender diverse children.

KEY QUESTIONS

- Are you recognising the needs of transgender and gender diverse children in your care?
- Are you working to enable transgender and gender diverse children to join in the conversation, by bringing them in from the cold?
- What small change can you make to help transgender and gender diverse children feel included?

COMMITMENT TO THE MANIFESTO

Look for opportunities to give transgender and gender diverse children a sense of belonging.

REFERENCES

Dhejne, C., Van Vlerken, R., Heylens, G. and Arcelus, J. (2016) 'Mental health and gender dysphoria: A review of the literature', *International Review of Psychiatry*, 28:1, 44-57.

McBride, R.S. and Neary, A. (2021) 'Trans and gender diverse youth resisting cisnormativity in school', *Gender and Education*.

The Stonewall School Report (2017), University of Cambridge

'OUT OF PLACE': SUPPORTING AND CELEBRATING TRANS AND NON-BINARY STAFF

CHARA ARAMIS

INTRODUCTION

Different uniforms, alternating seating plans, 'miss' and 'sir': the school environment is often a binary gendered one. This chapter explores how trans and non-binary staff can be made to feel uncomfortable and unwelcome in this regulated environment, as they face invalidation and discrimination if they are open about their identity, while the alternative means hiding a big part of themselves away, affecting their ability to find satisfaction and success in their job.

THE BINARY WORLD OF SCHOOL

In 2017, a programme aired on BBC2 brought the issue of gender stereotypes in primary school classrooms into the mainstream. *No More Boys and Girls: Can Our Kids Go Gender Free?* (Outline Productions) highlighted the prevalence of gendered practice in primary schools and found ways to challenge and reduce it. Although it made no mention of trans or non-binary people, it did challenge some of the assumptions that may be used to invalidate trans identities and that was enough to draw strong criticism from some quarters, with some going so far as to call it harmful and abusive.

What is clear from watching *No More Boys and Girls* is that the primary classroom environment is a world in which gender is both absolutely binary and clearly delineated. The show identified numerous ways in which girls and boys were explicitly treated differently or separated – and this is without considering any aspects of unconscious bias that might lead to tiny, subtle differences in treatment between them. Teachers may be able to recall numerous similar issues from their own teaching experience, from schools having a head boy and a head girl to alternating boy-girl seating plans. Teachers are expected to conform to and perpetuate appropriate gender roles and are often addressed almost exclusively by gendered titles throughout the school day.

This heavily regulated binary gender model creates a sense that, although we may claim that boys and girls – or men and women – are equals, they are fundamentally different and must follow different paths through life. They make their way through life on tracks that may well be largely parallel but which are nonetheless separate and which, as we often see, tend to diverge in practice. Certainly, as can be seen when individuals are chastised for being 'unmanly' (David Beckham in his sarong, Harry Styles on the recent cover of Vogue), or 'unladylike' (Lady Gaga, Mary Beard, Jo Brand etcetera) and in the prevalence of homophobia, transphobia and cisnormativity (the assumption that all individuals are either boys/men or girls/women and remain so throughout their lives), society deems it unacceptable for these tracks to either cross or merge.

This then leaves certain members of society in a quandary: those who are gender non-conforming; lesbian, gay, or bisexual and, perhaps most of all, those who are trans or non-binary. These are the people who, for any number of reasons, find themselves on or desiring to be on the gender tracks that society does not believe they should be on, and they are often punished for it. The fact that this model is often so strongly enforced in schools, with teachers expected by parents, school leaders and wider society to be the enforcers, means trans and non-binary teachers can struggle to reconcile their identities with their vocation.

TOEING THE LINE

How many trans and non-binary staff members are there in our schools? It is difficult to know; there are no hard and fast population-wide statistics on the matter but Stonewall (*The Truth About Trans*) estimates roughly one percent of the general population are trans or non-binary. The proportion may be similar among teachers and school staff, though it may well be lower due to the issues discussed in this chapter.

The importance that is given to the binary gender system within schools can put a lot of pressure on staff to remain in the closet and not reveal their trans identity when in school, as can social attitudes. Search for 'transgender teacher' online and it does not take long to find the story of Lucy Meadows, the teacher who took her own life after being criticised in the press just for daring to transition at work. In North America, an NPR Ed survey found that more than half of transgender teachers face harassment at work (NPR, 2018), while at home in the UK in 2017, more than one fifth of people believed suitably qualified transgender people probably or definitely should not be employed as primary school teachers (Swales and Attar Taylor, 2017).

Even if trans teachers want to quietly transition and continue living and working 'stealth' – that is, living as their true gender without being open about their transgender history – there are many challenges to face. When applying for jobs, many teaching application forms request previous names, teachers may be outed by previous employers when references are collected and relevant experience (working in Girlguiding, for example) may make it obvious that they previously lived as a different gender. All of these things can make trans teachers feel as though they have to choose between living their truth and pursuing their career: Khayatt and Iskander (2020) describe teachers feeling 'that it would be impossible to be an openly transgender teacher in the classroom' (Khayatt and Iskander 2020: 9) and that their genders were 'out of place in the regulated and regulating space that is the school' (Khayatt and Iskander 2020: 14), with one teacher explicitly told by a supervisor to 'choose between their gender and their chosen profession' (Khayatt and Iskander 2020: 10).

TEACHING FROM THE CLOSET

What does this mean for the teachers who choose the profession and teach either from inside the closet or while 'stealth'? How does teaching in this way, with such a huge part of one's identity hidden away, affect teachers' well-being and performance, when teaching is so much about relationships?

McCarthy (2003) shares the experience of one trans teacher, 'Kelly' (a pseudonym), who felt the judgement of students and staff was like a weight during term time compared to the freedom of the summer holidays, adding that their appearance was not appreciated at school. Some non-binary teachers have said (Khayatt and Iskander, 2020) that their gender caused them to feel vulnerable or in danger at school, while others were gendered inconsistently by colleagues and students, leaving them uncertain whether it was best to correct them or let it go. Meanwhile, Johnson et al. (2020) found that non-binary individuals tend to conceal their identities in order to avoid the risk of invalidation or the burden of explaining themselves to others, with invalidation experiences causing self-doubt, confusion, increased rumination and internalised shame.

These reports suggest many trans and non-binary teachers may spend their day in a state of heightened anxiety or distraction as these thoughts whirl around in their minds and that reflects my personal experience. I know that I have spent a significant amount of time and mental resources worrying about whether I should disclose my gender to my colleagues and if not, how I should ensure it remains hidden – the less safe I have felt, the more pressing the need to hide has seemed and the greater this burden has been.

Indeed, Johnson et al. (2020) discuss minority stress theory, including stressors unique to trans and gender non-conforming people (non-affirmation of gender identity and identity invalidation) which definitely describe many of the experiences of trans and non-binary teachers. They explain that repeated exposure to minority stressors can lead to poor mental health and the Centres for Disease Control and Prevention (2019) note that poor mental health and stress can reduce employees' job performance, productivity, work engagement, and communication among other things. It is likely, then, that teaching from the closet stifles trans and non-binary teachers' potential at work.

Additionally, most teachers understand the importance of relationships with pupils in successful teaching, but teaching from this closet requires shutting part of yourself away and holding those around you at arm's length.

CONCLUSION

Of course, all teaching involves a certain amount of performance – the development of a 'teacher persona' – but this is much more difficult when the foundation of this performance is itself an unstable construction rather than a stable truth. My own observation feedback has more than once advised me to be more outgoing and expressive in the classroom, but how can I do that while anxiously trying to maintain the closet walls at the same time?

KEY TAKEAWAYS

- The school environment reinforces and perpetuates a binary and cisnormative model of gender.
- Trans and non-binary staff members do not feel able to be their authentic selves in school.
- Trans and non-binary teachers are prevented from achieving their full professional potential by the regulating pressures of the school environment.

KEY QUESTIONS

- To what extent is your school safe and welcoming to trans and non-binary individuals?
- What changes can you make to create a more inclusive environment in your school for trans and non-binary staff members?
- How can you encourage understanding and inclusion of trans and non-binary individuals within your school community?

COMMITMENT TO THE MANIFESTO

Ensure schools are safe spaces for trans and non-binary staff members to bring their whole authentic selves to work.

REFERENCES

Centres for Disease Control and Prevention (2019) *Mental Health in the Workplace.* Available at: https://www.cdc.gov/workplacehealthpromotion/tools-resources/workplace-health/mental-health/index.html (accessed 23 March 2021).

Johnson, K.C. et al. (2020) 'Invalidation Experiences Among Non-Binary Adolescents.' *Journal of Sex Research*, 57(2): 222–233. DOI: 10.1080/00224499.2019.1608422.

Khayatt, D. and Iskander, L. (2020) 'Reflecting on 'coming out' in the classroom.' *Teaching Education* 31(1): 6–16. DOI: 10.1080/10476210.2019.1689943.

McCarthy, L. (2003) 'Wearing my identity: A transgender teacher in the classroom'. *Equity and Excellence in Education,* 36(2): 170–83. DOI: 10.1080/10665680303510.

No More Boys And Girls: Can Our Kids Go Gender Free? (2017) BBC2, 16 & 23 August.

NPR (2018) *More Than Half Of Transgender Teachers Surveyed Tell NPR They Are Harassed At Work.* Available at: https://www.npr.org/sections/ed/2018/03/08/575723226/more-than-half-of-transgender-teachers-face-workplace-harassment (accessed 27 February 2021).

Stonewall (no date) *The truth about trans*. Available at: https://www.stonewall.org.uk/truth-about-trans (accessed 8 March 2021).

Swales, K. and Attar Taylor, E. (2017) 'Moral Attitudes: Sex, gender identity and euthanasia.' In: Clery, E., Curtice, J. and Harding, R. (eds.) (2016) *British Social attitudes: the 34th Report*. Available at: http://bsa.natcen.ac.uk/latest-report/british-social-attitudes-34/moral-issues.aspx (accessed 27 February 2021).

WE ALL BELONG HERE: MAKING TRANSGENDER AND GENDER-DIVERSE STUDENTS FEEL AT HOME IN THEIR SCHOOL ENVIRONMENT

JAMI EDWARDS-CLARKE

INTRODUCTION

Most schools across the UK are structured to only recognise binary gender identities and therefore persistently exclude many trans and non-binary students and staff. An obvious example is the existence of single-sex schools, but in co-ed schools the binary language and systems of organisation are ubiquitous. The use of phrases such as 'boys' and girls' or 'ladies and gents', enforce the idea that there are only two genders, thus failing to recognise non-binary, gender non-conforming and intersex people. Those that grew up before and during the days of Section 28 (British law, 1988, that prohibited the promotion of homosexuality by local authorities), when knowledge of LGBTQ+ identities was either lacking or expressly forbidden, carry the scars of having their identities invalidated.

DEVELOPING OUR UNDERSTANDING

Jude Guaitamacchi (public speaker; LGBTQIA+ awareness trainer) works closely with our College and has been a great help in raising awareness of gender diversity. As a trans and non-binary person, Jude can offer their authentic self to help us understand the structures we need to break down. Jude works predominantly on delivering transgender inclusivity sessions to pupils and staff, and had this to say about language:

I believe one of the primary aims should be working towards using inclusive language when referring to pupils. An example of this would be making a concerted effort to apply gender neutral terminology where possible, especially when referring to groups of young people; using terms such as 'folks' or 'people', as well as embedding this language into the wording of any content related to the school: websites, literature, prospectus, social media and event promotion.

To avoid running the risk of 'assuming' a person's gender identity, based on the stereotypical idea of what it means to look 'male' and 'female' or the traditional gendering of a name, we can begin by encouraging and normalising the idea of asking people for pronouns. In schools this could be as simple as an email signature sign off. That way, it gives people the opportunity to embrace their identity in a very easy way. People have often expressed their confusion when it comes to gender neutral pronouns; however, we should challenge this notion by reminding them that, perhaps 'unknowingly' they have been using gender neutral pronouns in the singular sense. For example, if someone were to leave their bag behind in lessons, often our automatic response would be to say, 'someone has left *their* bag behind'. We do this because, not having seen the person, we cannot automatically assign gender to that individual. We should apply the same approach to everybody.

VISIBILITY

As a school we have a collection of proud members of the LGBTQ+ community amongst our staff body and a larger body of wonderful allies. However, we still have a way to go in increasing visibility for our transgender and gender-questioning students – hopefully through diversified curriculum and guest speakers, such as Jude, they will increasingly experience validation. Hearing from past pupils, and guest speakers who identify as a gender other than their ASAB (Assigned Sex at Birth) has been wonderfully received – encouraging both staff and students to feel comfortable acknowledging their true gender identities. We have also had a great response from allies in the community. Many have learned a great deal about appropriate language usage and how to best support friends who are questioning their identity.

UNIFORM

The ability to dress and express yourself is an important part of self-discovery and something which current binary uniform options restrict. We as a school are working hard to update and modernise our uniform, which currently takes a traditional approach of 'girls' in skirts and 'boys' in trousers and ties. An issue a lot of schools are facing is the need to sign off on specific cases for gender-questioning and transgender students. A way to tackle this, and something we are hoping to introduce with a policy change, is to create simple options which any gender can choose to wear. This should reduce some of the anxiety and restriction caused by binary uniform choices. A current problem is the lack of guidance on this from various educational bodies. Greater clarity would help take the pressure off schools, which at the moment are having to make decisions under the pressure of various stakeholders who hold more traditional views.

FACILITIES

When presented with a choice between only male and female toilets, transgender and questioning individuals are often forced into deciding between their personal safety, the comfort of others, and staying true to their identity. Whether trans or questioning students use the toilet of the sex they were assigned at birth or of the gender they most likely identify (assuming this is either male or female), they are forced into an environment, away from the presence of teachers, where they may be challenged by other students. Not only does this present a risk to physical safety, but can be such a daunting experience that many will refrain from using the bathroom altogether.

By ensuring the provision of gender-neutral toilets throughout school grounds, the requirement to choose between male and female toilets is removed. While many schools have a disabled toilet on the premises, clear signposting that disabled toilets are also gender-neutral toilets not only allows the student the knowledge that using that toilet is permitted, but that the school recognises the presence of individuals who may wish to avoid choosing between a male or female toilet. Although a start, the presence of a single toilet is not sufficient to ensure trans students have equal access to bathroom facilities, so gender neutral toilets should be available within a reasonable distance of each school area: sports halls, separate academic blocks, boarding houses.

SAFE SPACE

Another way of increasing support for trans students is ensuring there is a safe space for them, alongside other LGBTQ+ individuals, to use as a place to reflect and take a breather, but also to find strength and support in other individuals, both trans, questioning and allies. A safe space is something we are seeking to introduce in our own school for our READI (Rainbow Education Alliance of Diverse Identities/Individuals) platform. Every student deserves to feel safe and empowered at school; a simple change like this should help work towards that goal.

PARENTS AND CARERS

Our intention as a school is to include a gender and sexuality chapter in our pupil and parent annual handbook that goes out to new joiners. This would demonstrate the values of our institution, but should also provide a plethora of resources, links, testimonials and support for anyone who wishes to learn more and engage in what it truly means to have diversity in education. A difficult position to be in as a school is how best to engage with parents who view gender and sexuality as taboo topics. Our fundamental responsibility as educational professionals is to act in a way that best benefits the child. So what do we do when parents challenge how we choose to celebrate LGBTQ+ History Month or when we support a trans student's name change against their wishes?

Though every student is different they deserve more than to feel like the school is muddling through the 'right' thing to do in terms of supporting their gender-questioning or trans identity. This will undoubtedly come with time and experience within the education sector, but is it fair to make a child wait for better support just because we, as educators, are not fully equipped to best support them? I have faith that my school will act with the best intentions to support a child, but is that enough?

CONCLUSION

One way to reach out to parents is through the delivery of parent-specific talks. It is naïve to think all parents will happily engage in events put on, but instead we're likely to attract parents who are like minded in how they feel LGBTQ+ should be discussed in schools. This is still beneficial for several reasons. Firstly, we are showing, perhaps unapologetically, that as a school body we are determined to focus on these 'tough' topics because it matters. Secondly, mildly supportive parents may become strongly supportive. Thirdly, it provides a more evidence-based influx of knowledge to continue conversations at home (based on students receiving tutorials / information in the school day). It may also then empower individuals to stand up in those conversations they are a part of with the parents who do not agree with the stance a school takes, or the way they handle and support a trans student. It is our responsibility to put the child first – and with parental support that role becomes so much easier.

KEY TAKEAWAYS

- Consider how transgender and non-binary students experience the binary world of school.
- Seek out ways to make school more gender inclusive e.g. uniform policy and/ or gender-neutral toilets.
- Reach out to parents, so that the conversation can continue at home.

KEY QUESTIONS

- How can you evolve your language, the language of your policies, to be less binary?
- Do transgender and non- binary students see themselves in your school/ in your school curriculum?
- Does your school have a gender-neutral uniform and gender-neutral toilet facilities?

COMMITMENT TO THE MANIFESTO

Enact a conscious evolution of your language, so that it is less binary and more inclusive of others.

REFERENCES

Bragg, S., Renold, E., Ringrose, J. and Jackson, C. (2018). "More than boy, girl, male, female': exploring young people's views on gender diversity within and beyond school contexts.' *Sexuality, Society and Learning, 18*(4), 420-34. https://doi.org/10.1080/14681811.2018.1439373

Cerezo, A. and Bergfeld, J. (2013). 'Meaningful LGBTQ Inclusion in Schools: The Importance of Diversity Representation and Counterspaces.' *Journal of LGBTQ Issues in Counseling, 7*(4), 355-71. https://doi.org/10.1080/15538605.2013.839341

Edwards, L., Brown, D. and Smith, L. (2014). "We are getting there slowly': lesbian teacher experiences in the post-Section 28 environment.' *Sport, Education and Society, 21*(3), 299-318. https://doi.org/10.1080/13573322.2014.935317

Slater, J., Jones, C. and Procter, L. (2016). 'School toilets: queer, disabled bodies and gendered lessons of embodiment.' *Gender and Education, 30*(8), 951-65. https://doi.org/10.1080/09540253.2016.1270421

BEYOND BINARY BOXES: CHALLENGING THE STATUS-QUO

EJ-FRANCIS CARIS-HAMER

INTRODUCTION

Within the education centre of adult learning, a member of staff calls out 'Mr Roberts.'

Somewhat awkwardly my wife stood up.

'No, I said Mr Roberts...'

'It says "Mx Caris-Roberts", that's my title, that's my name, that's me.'

What came her way was initially a look of confusion, then a blank stare and finally a deep 'for F+*$'" sake' sigh. Too often, such exchanges occur in all parts of society and there is a 50:50 chance as to whether you will receive curiosity as to what Mx means and a willingness to change the data system to include Mx as did my dental practice, or the response that my wife received because somehow our decision not to be categorised into a gender binary somehow makes it awkward for others.

Today's world shows increasing visibility of people who choose to challenge the hegemonic gender binary some countries have historically enforced (Driver, 2008; Yeadon-Lee, 2016). These alternative genders include people like myself whose sex identity is female, but identifies as gender queer/gender fluid because of a fundamental uncomfortability with the gender binary that is placed upon me by society, and my pronouns are Ze/Zir. There are others e.g., non-binary trans who are not aligned with the sex identity they were assigned at birth, nor the gender binary identity society enforces (Healthline, 2021). It is important to recognise that, along with transgenderism, alternative gender identities form part of minority gender identities. However, such visibilities are not always reflected within the realm of education (Stonewall, 2017). With much research and resources on how important it is to be queer inclusive in education (Dellenty, 2019; Stones and Glazzard, 2019), my PhD research (based upon interviews of forty teachers in various schools across England) seeks to explain why there are still inconsistencies regarding inclusion of queer identities including non-binary. What are the barriers? How can we overcome these to build a meaningful culture of inclusion within education?

BARRIERS TO GENDER DIVERSITY

The first main barrier identified by teacher participants found that there was a general silence and invisibility around non-binary genders. This invisibility is not amongst the students, in fact we could generally argue that students are more accepting of fluid genders, sexual orientation and trans identities today than ever before (Janmaat & Keating, 2019) in comparison to the adults working within the schools. Only 17.5% of the teachers interviewed discussed non-binary identities. Of those who discussed non-binary, one conversation detailed an example of good practice where a theme project for Y9 English was set researching how gender oppression was explored throughout literature and nonfiction, noting that 19th and 20th century texts focused upon binary genders, whereas 21st century texts explore alternative genders; however, the interviewee recognised that not all teachers do this *because that's not in the curriculum.'* (PG, 2020).

Teachers expressed how silence is maintained by creating and reinforcing fixed gender binaries within the everyday school experience. Such microaggression experiences include not acknowledging 'Mx' as a title in the school system, some schools refusing to allow alternative names and pronouns due to a decision that only names from students' birth certificates will be included in school registers, and inadequate space for gender-neutral toilets. It manifests when teachers insist on using a seating plan of boy/girl, boy/girl, PE is still taught as girls' PE and boys' PE rather than allowing a choice regarding what games they prefer. Such microaggressions manifest verbally when teacher participant 19 (P19) admits that he taunts the students he teaches regarding gender identities:

> I did quite a bit of "boys, behave" when, you know, it's a mixed group just to wind them up. I do that to amuse myself more than anything else. *(P19, 2020)*

Another teacher participant conveys how a science teacher states that 'You're born male or female, there is no in-between', (P7, 2020) thus ignoring the fact that sex and gender are both socially constructed as many countries identify more than two sexes and genders (BBC, 2019). Whilst working in the 11-19 education sector I was an openly gay woman in all the schools I taught in. Microaggressions such as 'You look nice today, you look so feminine' made it difficult for me to disclose my non-binary identity. Comments such as these prove both frustrating and powerful in the consequent impact on the self-esteem of the recipient as it reinforces that the term 'look nice' is aligned with when a female presents as feminine. In addition, at times, I felt unaccepted by some senior staff members as an openly gay teacher and thus to add an additional identity that challenges the binary norm felt too much to cope with, consequently and though I feel ashamed to say it, I contributed to the invisibility of alternative gender identities. P13 suggests that schools need a 'cultural reset... [involving]...lots of discussions and facilitated workshops'. All those interviewed asked for multiple differentiated (to maximise engagement) training sessions for all staff members and students to develop a deeper understanding of such identities. Of the forty teachers interviewed, they seldom received any related training and those who had asked for training were often dismissed by senior leaders stating that there was a lack of time in the CPD diary.

Teachers also ask for there to be guidance and policies from the government and senior leaders regarding the inclusion of minority gender identities. My analysis unearthed an appetite for the government to rethink and update the Equality Act 2010 in terms of gender identities. Mermaids UK (2019) suggest that teachers should be teaching about all gender identities under the 'Keeping Children Safe in Education (2021)' guidance in order to help prevent bullying. However, other legal guidance can create confusion depending upon its interpretation:

> We have conflicting advice around our obligations under the Equality Act in terms of gender identity...Stonewall are telling us that it very much is. Whereas other people are telling us that it isn't...so what are our actual, genuine legal obligations here? *(P14, 2020)*.

The Equality Act 2010 states that under the protection of gender re-assignment: 'The person is proposing to undergo, is undergoing or has undergone a process of reassigning the person's sex...' (Legislation, 2021.) However, this is problematic for students within education because it excludes those who are questioning their gender and those who want to challenge the hegemonic gender binaries. The government must realise that questioning one's gender can involve a long process of exploration and self-reflection. For those trans individuals who choose to navigate such medical processes there are long waiting lists for surgery, it is expensive and thus often only the privileged can afford this. In addition, the Government must realise that there are more than two genders and we must not allow institutions to discriminate against those whose identity does not fit within the male/female binary. We all have a human right to work and be educated in an environment that is free from discrimination and legislation must reflect all gender minority identities.

OVERCOMING THE CIS-GENDER NORMATIVITY.

The removal of structural barriers that exist to reinforce the gender binary may include urging school leaders to create a culture of choice, choice regarding what games they would prefer to play in PE with no division on gender binaries, the choice to wear non-binary school uniforms. After all, what purpose does insisting that females wear skirts possibly serve? Many believe that education is a microcosm of society in which equal opportunities should be part of the foundations. However, such a foundation is more frequently spoken about rather than acted upon (Patrick and Sanders, 1994: 118). Staff members are the key actors in creating and maintaining a culture of hegemonic gender binaries that excludes some students because of prejudicial personal beliefs and a lack of understanding and training.

CONCLUSION

Government and teachers must play an integral role in challenging such exclusions in school environments. By working together through collective dialogue and legislation guidance that reflects the society we live in, we can help to prevent negative wellbeing, achievement gaps, and create a supportive, safe environment for all.

KEY TAKEAWAYS

- Let us never underestimate the power of the language we choose to use – often what may seem like small steps or gestures can make a huge difference in making people feel included and valued.
- Educators demonstrate an appetite to celebrate a culture of gender diversity, but they lack the guidance and training on how to achieve this in their day-to-day teaching within schools.
- The personal is still political! Therefore, we need to support and campaign to update the Equality Act 2010.

KEY QUESTIONS

- How often in a given week do you make assumptions about people's gender identities?
- What do you see as the main barriers to creating a positive environment for those students who have alternative gender identities?
- Where could you make alternative genders visible and create choice in your education institution?

COMMITMENT TO THE MANIFESTO

Do not rely on outdated legislation and syllabuses to provide inclusion of gender minority groups. Instead, you must consider what is required for your education community to ensure *all* members feel included and engaged.

REFERENCES

BBC (2019) *Germany Adopts Intersex Identity into Law*. Available: https://www.bbc.co.uk/news/world-europe-46727611 (Accessed: 3 April 2021).

Dellenty, S. (2019) *Celebrating Difference: A whole-school Approach to LGBT+ Inclusion*. London: Bloomsbury Education.

DofE (2020) *Department of Education, Keeping Children Safe in Education 2020 (Statutory Guidance for Schools and Colleges)*. Available at: https://assets.publishing.service.gov.uk/government/uploads/system/uploads/attachment_data/file/954314/

Keeping_children_safe_in_education_2020_-_Update_-_January_2021.pdf (Accessed 2 April 2021)

Driver, S. (2008) *Queer Youth Subcultures: Temporalities and subculture lives*. New York: SUNY Press.

Gov.UK (2021a) *Equality Act 2010: Guidance*. Available at: https://www.gov.uk/guidance/equality-act-2010-guidance#overview (Accessed 30 March 2021).

Healthline (2021) *Non-binary. What does it mean?* Available: https://www.healthline.com/health/transgender/nonbinary#trans-andnonbinary-identities (Accessed: 31/3/2021).

Higa, D., Hoppe, M.J., Lindhorst, T., Mincer, S., Beadnell, B., Morrison, D.M., Wells, E.A., Tod, A. and Mountz, S. (2014). 'Negative and positive factors associated with the well-being of Lesbian, Gay, Bisexual, Transgender, Queer and Questioning (LGBTQ) Youth.' *Youth Soc*. 46(5): 663-87.

Janmaat, J.G. and Keating, A. (2019) 'Are today's youth more tolerant? Trends in tolerance among young people in Britain'. *Ethnicities*. 19(1): 44-65.

Kosciw, J.G., Palmer, N.A. and Kull, R. M. (2015) 'Reflecting resiliency: Openness about sexual orientation and/or gender Identity and its relationship to wellbeing and educational outcomes for LGBT students.' *American Journal of Community Psychology*. 55:167-78.

Legislation (2021) *The Equality Act, 2010 Legislation*. Available: https://www.legislation.gov.uk/ukpga/2010/15/contents (Accessed: 31 March2021).

Mermaids UK (2019) *Trans Inclusion Schools Toolkit: Supporting trans, non-binary and gender questioning children and young people in Brighton and Hove educational settings*. Available: www.mermaidsuk.org.uk/wp-content/uploads/2019/12/AllsortsYouthProject-Trans-Inclusion-Schools-Sept-18.pdf (Accessed: 1 April 2021).

Patrick, P. and Sanders, S.A.L. (1994) 'Lesbian and Gay Issues in the Curriculum'. In Epstein (1994) (ed) *'Challenging Lesbian and Gay Inequalities in Education'*. Buckingham: Open University Press.

Stonewall (2020) *Shut Out: The experiences of LGBT young people not in education training or work*. Available: www.stonewall.org.uk/system/files/shut-out-2020.pdf Accessed: 31 March 2021.

Stones, S. and Glazzard, J. (2019) *Perspectives and Research on LGBTQ+ Inclusion in Education*. Norfolk: Witley Press Limited.

Stonewall (2017) *Stonewall School Report 2017*. Available at: www.stonewall.org.uk/system/files/the-school-report-2017.pdf (Accessed 31 March 2021).

Timmerman, G. (2003) 'Sexual Harassment of Adolescence Perpetuated by Teachers and by Peers: An exploration of the dynamics of power, culture, and gender in secondary schools.' *Sex roles*. 48(5): 231-44.

Yeadon-Lee, T. (2016) 'What's the story?' Exploring online narratives of non-binary gender identities. *The International Journal of Interdisciplinary Social and Community Studies*. 11(2): 19-34.

BEING AN ALLY: SUPPORTING TRANS PUPILS IN EARLY YEARS, PRIMARY AND SECONDARY SCHOOLS

CAL HORTON

INTRODUCTION

Individual teachers and members of staff can make a profound difference to a trans child's experience at school. Trans and non-binary pupils can find immense value in a teacher who celebrates rather than problematises gender diversity, who recognises the vulnerabilities of trans-minority pupils and who proactively takes steps to ensure trans pupils are safe and supported. Many schools and individual teachers are already doing this, prioritising inclusion and trans positivity and safeguarding trans children's right to an equitable educational experience. Emotional care is critical, providing an educational environment that protects trans pupils' mental and emotional health, recognising the impact of gender minority stress and taking action to ensure school is a validating and affirming space. Teacher allies can play an important role, advocating for systemic change to create trans-positive schools that are welcoming for trans children of all ages. Throughout this piece I refer to the views of a number of transgender and non-binary pupils (taken from my PhD research) – their names and details are anonymised to safeguard their right to privacy.

ADVOCACY AND EQUAL RIGHTS

Trans children continue to face exclusion, discrimination and even segregation in our schools. Too often trans pupils shoulder the burden of negotiating their own inclusion, with trans children (or supportive families) needing to assert their rights (Horton, 2020). Teacher allies can play an important role in ensuring that trans children are aware of their rights, to ensure that child-centred discussions on inclusion are framed against a clear commitment to trans children's right to education with dignity, with equality, with physical and emotional safety. Some trans children find their schools under-prepared to welcome trans pupils, with teachers and staff on a learning curve on gender diversity and trans inclusion (Bartholomaeus and Riggs,

2017). In these situations, trans children can find themselves surrounded by adults with limited understanding or areas of misunderstanding or prejudice. In these situations, trans children can be faced with the overwhelming prospect of educating their own teachers, of correcting mis-information, defending their own rights and challenging trans-negativity. One non-binary pupil shared advice for other trans children, emphasising that it is not their job to educate their own teachers. A teacher ally can play an important role in protecting trans pupils from being left to educate their own teachers – advocating for staff education, demonstrating trans positivity, and taking forward (to senior management or beyond) any ongoing areas of concern – rather than leaving vulnerable children to fend for themselves.

TRANS POSITIVITY AND INCLUSION

Many schools remain under-prepared to effectively welcome trans pupils, with trans identities erased or invalidated at school (McBride and Neary, 2021). Invisibility, exclusion from the curriculum, and explicit or implicit delegitimization promotes shame and stigma. However, trans pupils report that even simple gestures of affirmation can make a significant difference to how included and welcome they feel at school. This can be particularly important in early years, primary and the lower years of secondary, where trans pupils continue to navigate systems where trans identities are completely erased (Neary, 2021). Parents of trans children reference a number of simple changes that can enable trans pupils to feel validated at school, from normalisation of words like trans and cis, to ensuring inclusive PHSE (referring to 'most girls' in primary education on bodies), to inclusion of trans role models or books with trans-positive representation. One trans pupil found validation even in small gestures, like a teacher including a trans flag as a question in an informal class quiz.

EMOTIONAL CARE

For too many trans children, school remains an unsafe space (Bradlow et al., 2017). One pupil described their school as having extremely low expectations for in-school emotional safety, expecting the pupil to tolerate and withstand persistent microaggressions and invalidation from staff, syllabus and peers. The pupil in this instance did not withstand this pressure, suffering mental health consequences and leaving mainstream education. School teachers and leaders need to recognise the emotional strain trans pupils face, even in schools without extremes of abuse or harassment (Miller, 2016). Schools exercising a duty of care to trans pupils need to proactively address and minimise the persistent stress placed on trans pupils, instead of waiting until serious repercussions like mental health impacts or school avoidance highlight the impact of chronic stress.

BEING A TRUSTED ALLY

Even just one trusted, trans-positive teacher is known to make a significant difference to trans pupils' experience at school (Ullman, 2017). One non-binary pupil mentioned that they have learnt to assume all staff members are transphobic, whether unintentionally or otherwise. They were not alone in referencing a series of negative school experiences (often of teacher inaction or teacher minimisation of ongoing microaggressions) that led them to lose trust that staff would understand or take action to enable them to thrive at school. A trans pupil contrasted two differing primary school experiences: in one school there was no safe and trans-positive staff member to turn to, leaving her alone to navigate cisnormative systems and transphobic microaggressions. In another school she noted the positive impacts of having a trusted staff member, a teacher who was well-informed and trans positive, who listened, who cared, who understood the stresses and pressures of being a trans-minority pupil, who took each incident seriously and ensured each issue was proactively addressed. For this pupil, that one teacher's care, understanding and action transformed her primary school into a safe and welcoming space.

KEY TAKEAWAYS

- Trans pupils continue to encounter cisnormativity and minority stress at schools.
- Schools can do more to ensure trans pupils receive an equitable education, in an environment that is trans-positive and welcoming.
- Teacher allies can play a vital role in building schools that are emotionally safe for trans pupils.

KEY QUESTIONS

- How are you supporting the mental and emotional health of your trans pupils, recognising the toll of each encounter with microaggressions, ignorance or exclusion?
- How are you standing up for trans children, ensuring their rights to equitable opportunities to thrive are upheld, ensuring they do not carry the burden of advocating for their own inclusion?
- How are you normalising trans-positivity in your school, building an environment where trans pupils can grow up self-confident, without shame or stigma?

COMMITMENT TO THE MANIFESTO

Stand up for trans-equality through being a visible and active ally for trans children across early years, primary and secondary education.

REFERENCES

Bartholomaeus, C., Riggs, D.W. (2017). *Transgender people and education*. Palgrave Macmillan, New York.

Bradlow, J., Bartram, F., Guasp, A. and Jadva, V. (2017). *The School Report 2017*. Stonewall, London, UK.

Horton, C. (2020). *Thriving or Surviving? Raising Our Ambition for Trans Children in Primary and Secondary Schools*. Front. Sociol. 5. https://doi.org/10.3389/fsoc.2020.00067

McBride, R.S. and Neary, A. (2021). 'Trans and gender diverse youth resisting cisnormativity in school.' *Gender and Education,* 1–18. https://doi.org/10.1080/09540253.2021.1884201

Miller, S.J. (Ed.) (2016) *Teaching, Affirming, and Recognizing Trans and Gender Creative Youth: A Queer Literacy Framework*. Palgrave Macmillan US, New York. https://doi.org/10.1057/978-1-137-56766-6

Neary, A. (2021) 'Trans children and the necessity to complicate gender in primary schools.' *Gender and Education* 0, 1–17. https://doi.org/10.1080/09540253.2021.1884200

Ullman, J., (2017) 'Teacher positivity towards gender diversity: exploring relationships and school outcomes for transgender and gender-diverse students.' *Sex Education* 17, 276-89. https://doi.org/10.1080/14681811.2016.1273104

IF WE ARE FORCED TO LIVE IN THE SHADOWS, HOW WILL WE EVER BE ABLE TO SHINE?

MATTHEW SAVAGE

INTRODUCTION

This was going to be 'Jack's Story', the remarkable journey of my son from traumatised transgender teen to self-actualised adult male, but I realised it is not my story to tell. And it is not just Jack's story anyway: it is also the story of his transgender sister, and of us, their parents; the story, by privileged (and presumptuous) proxy, of thousands of transgender, non-binary and gender non-conforming teens across this rainbow world (Blad, 2017); and the story of how schools across the world can a) embrace and celebrate; b) pretend to meet and recognise; or c) quietly or blatantly disregard – the need and right of every single child to belong and thrive, regardless of their identity. Therefore, like so many stories, this has so many protagonists and narrators, and my authorship is Barthesian in its demise (Barthes, 1968).

JACK'S STORY

However, Jack's story is a good starting point: I know it better daily, and through a unique lens (Transformers Youth Group, 2015). Born AFAB (Assigned Female At Birth) in 2001, he started to question his gender identity from the onset of puberty at age ten. However, despite obvious signs, our obliviousness to which shames us still, he did not come out to us as a gay, transgender male until fifteen. By this time, we were living in Jordan, with its complex, contradictory and uncomfortable relationship with gender and sexuality, and he attended the school of which I was Principal. Seemingly inevitable exclusion, isolation and ignominy quickly closed in, and soon he was a school refuser, teaching *himself*, in those moments when curiosity trumped despair, from a darkened bedroom – not a cocoon, safe and nourishing, but a cage made by many – his mental health rapidly spiralling to severe self-harm and suicidality.

Eventually, we made the overdue decision for him to return with my wife to the UK, before my contract finished. Upon first footfall 'home', albeit far less rainbow-paved than he had imagined and hoped, a new journey began, first with the legal adoption of his new name. Able to eschew the Tavistock's expert but hamstrung provision (Care Quality Commission, 2021), we then registered him with a private gender clinic: he has been on testosterone since January 2020 and underwent top surgery in August 2021. After years outside education, he graduated with distinction from an Art Foundation course. Challenges have continued to assail his daily life, from showering and binding to social anxiety, and the estrangement from his maternal grandmother whose love proved conditional, but his new chapter brims with hope and opportunity, and a bright, bountiful future beckons. Interestingly, he told me this year that his trans identity is now but a tiny fraction of who he is.

THE DILEMMA CUL-DE-SAC

A Jordanian friend and mentor, and bold LGBTQ+ ally and activist, advised me that stories such as Jack's were one thing, but the trans kid in Ma'an or Mafraq 'coming out' could have even fatal consequences, in a country where honour killings still seem to play out with impunity despite the relentless campaign to outlaw them (Husseini, 2020). This highlighted to me a dangerous spotlight of which we must be aware as international educators in host countries where characteristics protected elsewhere are without any legal protection. However, it is also a spotlight from whose glare many an international school, leadership team or governing body, willingly hides, despite their power and privilege to play a bold role in forging a safer and fairer world. Look at most international schools' Guiding Statements: they refer to 'inclusivity', 'belonging' or every child being able to 'thrive'. However, if such inclusivity is conditional, is it inclusivity at all? And how can any child possibly 'thrive' or 'belong' if they are wearing the clothes, metaphorically or literally, of an identity which they do not yet know, doubt, or know not to be their own?

So often we find ourselves in a dilemma cul-de-sac, as binary as gender identity and expression fundamentally are not. Internationally, do we publicly, loudly and indiscriminately wave our rainbow flags from every local platform? Or do we hide from either sociocultural prejudice or local, legislative spotlights, pretending that curiosity about, exploration of, and transition to different gender identities simply do not exist? Meanwhile, how many young people will grow to hate, and hurt, themselves and their bodies, or worse (The Trevor Project, 2020)? And despite the palpable and exciting steps made in schools in the UK in the past decade, can we safely say that every trans teen feels safe, celebrated and able to thrive in their school here on British soil (Hall, 2015)?

(TRANS)INCLUSIVITY IN SCHOOLS

The best inclusive practice benefits not just its target audience but every single student: that is what makes it inclusive. This is also the case for trans-inclusivity in schools, for which I offer but a handful of tips:

- Ensure your Guiding Statements, the DNA of your school, prioritise unconditional inclusivity and #WellbeingFirst, since these till a soil in which every identity can safely grow.
- Set aside meaningful time for expert training in gender and sexuality for all your staff. *The Genderbread Person* (2017) is a great starting point for all ages, and the Yogyakarta Principles (Carpenter et al., 2017) are particularly suited to staff and older students.
- The best schools have a Board completely aligned with their Guiding Statements; in which case, make sure they are also fully and expertly trained, as they may be your forcefield should controversy ever arise.
- Like Andrew Moffat (2021) has done so adeptly, help your students ensure there are 'No Outsiders'. Society has *never* been slow to introduce gender and sexuality into even our youngest children's lives, but to perpetuate the myth of a binary borders on indoctrination.
- Ensure every policy stratum is trans-inclusive (Stonewall, 2019) – as is enshrined, after all and for now, in British law (Equality Act, 2010), in order that we can move beyond mere accommodation to actual adaptation in each and every school.
- Unless we teach them that difference is wrong, children and young people embrace and celebrate it (Dellenty, 2019). I have seen vibrant allyship and Pride societies and programmes, even in schools operating in the most complex of sociocultural contexts. Use this.
- If you feel the need for a uniform at all, please make it gender-neutral, just as you should any dress code for your staff. This is such a simple step, but its impact is immense.
- The language through which we learn and teach, read and communicate, is still systemically gendered, and silent semiotics of cisnormativity abound throughout both campus and curriculum. We need to address these structures, and consciously redistribute their power from oppressor to oppressed (Freire, 1996).
- We all have the right to be called by the name and pronouns we choose. If this changes for one of our students, even several times, we must keep up, and it is not difficult to do so. The hurt and harm to a trans student of our using, verbally or in writing, dead names or pronouns, can be deadening and deep.
- I admit to being bemused by how hot a topic non-gendered bathrooms has become. However, there is guidance aplenty on this issue in schools (Lucas, 2020; Gingell and Beal, 2018), as there is on changing rooms. Every child deserves to feel safe in these vulnerable places, and trans kids are in greater jeopardy than most.
- Finally, every (trans) kid needs a champion too (TED Talk, 2013), and informed and expert trans- inclusive school counsellors can be a lifeline, but even a rainbow badge worn by individual members of staff, or peer counsellors, signifying their allyship and advocacy, can be equally life-saving.

CONCLUSION

I wrote recently of gender identity with reference to the Doctor's explanation of the Tardis' domain: 'A big ball of wibbly-wobbly, timey-wimey stuff' (Savage, 2021). Perhaps this is what makes it so scary and alien to some, but, to me, it is what makes it so magical. As for our schools, just like the conditionality of Jack's grandmother's love made it essentially loveless, so is conditional inclusivity essentially exclusive. With exclusivity inevitably comes shadows; and if we, like Jack, are forced to live in the shadows, how will we ever be able to shine?

KEY TAKEAWAYS

- Address the language and silent semiotics of cisnormativity.
- Ensure that your school is unconditionally inclusive.
- Set aside meaningful time for expert staff training.

KEY QUESTIONS

- How trans-inclusive is your school right now, and, more importantly, how do you know?
- What simple steps could you implement immediately to render your inclusivity unconditionally inclusive?
- Which organisations or resources might be most useful in training each of your stakeholders on this critical topic?

COMMITMENT TO THE MANIFESTO

Every transgender, non-binary and gender non-conforming child and young person has the inalienable right to belong and to thrive, within school and beyond.

REFERENCES

Barthes, R. (1968). *The Death of the Author*. 1st ed. University Handout.

Blad, E. (2017). 'How Many Transgender Children Are There?', *Education Week*. [online] Available at: <https://www.edweek.org/leadership/how-many-transgender-children-are-there/2017/03> [Accessed 30 April 2021].

Brighton College, 2020. *Uniform Policy 2021*. [online] Available at: <https://www.brightoncollege.org.uk/media/3825/brighton-college-uniform-policy-2020-21.pdf> [Accessed 30 April 2021].

Care Quality Commission, 2021. *Gender identity services Inspection report*. [online] Available at: <https://api.cqc.org.uk/public/v1/reports/7ecf93b7-2b14-45ea-a317-53b6f4804c24?20210301173155> [Accessed 30 April 2021].

Carpenter, M., Julia, E., Grinspan, M., Kara, S. and Narrain, A. (2021). *Additional principles and state obligations on the application of international human rights law in relation to sexual orientation, gender identity, gender expression and sex characteristics to complement The Yogyakarta Principles As adopted on 10 November 2017, Geneva.* [online] Available at: <http://yogyakartaprinciples.org/wp-content/uploads/2017/11/A5_yogyakartaWEB-2.pdf> [Accessed 30 April 2021].

Dellenty, S. (2019). *Celebrating Difference: A whole-school Approach to LGBT+ Inclusion.* London: Bloomsbury.

Equality Act 2010, Part 2, Chapter 1, Section 7 (2010) Available at: https://www.legislation.gov.uk/ukpga/2010/15/pdfs/ukpga_20100015_en.pdf

Freire, P.(1996). *The Pedagogy of the Oppressed.* New revised ed. London: Penguin

The Genderbread Person, (2017). *An Adorable, Accessible Way to Explain a Complicated Concept: The Genderbread Person.* [online] Available at: <https://www.genderbread.org> [Accessed 30 April 2021].

Gingell, R. and Beal, S. (2018). *Trans Inclusion Schools Toolkit.* [online] Brighton & Hove City Council and Allsorts Youth Project. Available at: <https://www.theproudtrust.org/wp-content/uploads/download-manager-files/allsorts_Trans%20Inclusion%20Schools%20Toolkit_Sept_2018_V3.pdf> [Accessed 30 April 2021].

Hall, F. (2015). *Getting Started: A toolkit for preventing and tackling homophobic, biphobic and transphobic bullying in secondary schools.* [online] Stonewall. Available at: <https://www.stonewall.org.uk/system/files/getting_started_-_a_toolkit_for_secondary_schools.pdf> [Accessed 30 April 2021].

Husseini, R. (2020). 'Rising against so called Honor Killings in Jordan.' [Blog] *The Wilson Center,* Available at: <https://www.wilsoncenter.org/blog-post/rising-against-so-called-honor-killings-jordan> [Accessed 30 April 2021].

Lucas, (2020). 'Gender-neutral toilets: above all, keep children safe.' [online] *Tes News.* Available at: <https://www.tes.com/news/gender-neutral-toilets-above-all-keep-children-safe> [Accessed 30 April 2021].

Moffat, A. (2021). 'Preparing children for life in modern Britain'. [online] *No Outsiders.* Available at: <https://no-outsiders.com> [Accessed 30 April 2021].

Savage, M. (2021). *Gender is "wibbly-wobbly" and "timey-wimey", and gloriously so.* [Blog] Available at: <https://www.diverseeducators.co.uk/gender-is-wibbly-wobbly-and-timey-wimey-and-gloriously-so/> [Accessed 30 April 2021].

Stonewall (2019). *Next Steps in Inclusive Education: Celebrating Difference and Developing Understanding.* [online] Stonewall, pp.22-7. Available at: <https://www.stonewall.org.uk/system/files/next_steps_in_inclusive_education.pdf> [Accessed 30 April 2021].

TED Talk (2013). *Rita Pierson: Every Kid needs a Champion.* [video] Available at: <http://www.ted.com/talks/rita_pierson_every_kid_needs_a_champion/transcript?language=en> [Accessed 30 April 2021].

Transformers Youth Group (2015). *A Journey without a Map: being a parent of a trans child.* [online] Allsorts Youth Project. Available at: <https://outreachyouth.org.uk/wp-content/uploads/2016/04/AllsortsYouthProject-A-Journey-WIthout-A-Map.pdf> [Accessed 30 April 2021].

The Trevor Project (2020). *National Survey on LGBTQ Youth Mental Health 2020.* [online] New York. Available at: <https://www.thetrevorproject.org/survey-2020/> [Accessed 30 April 2021].

THE POWER AND PITFALLS OF VISIBILITY PRIVILEGE: A PERSONAL PERSPECTIVE

KIT RACKLEY

INTRODUCTION

I have become increasingly resolute and affirmed about my transgender identity, as time has gone on. But this identity, no matter how core and pivotal it is to my being, will likely never surpass my identity as an educator. While I have since left the chalkface itself, I am still an active member of the teaching community and now I perform several different roles that stretch nationwide. With this prominence comes enhanced visibility, something which I try to embrace. This chapter takes a reflective approach, sharing my experiences as a transgender educator, of what I call 'visibility privilege' and the power and pitfalls that come with this.

CONTEXT: MY JOURNEY

I spent thirteen years teaching in a secondary school in rural Norfolk. Over that period, I was what I come to now recognise as 'questioning my gender'. I had a strong rapport with the young people that I taught. I seemed to be one of those approachable teachers, who the students would come to for more than just their Geography homework woes. But why me? That is a question I have revisited time and time again. After teaching, I took a year out, living and working in places like San Francisco and California. I was able to discover more about my identity and begin to experiment with different ways of expressing my gender. When that year came to an end and I returned to the UK, I ramped up my freelancing education work, continued running teaching CPD and worked as an education officer for a non-profit organisation in the climate science sector. I also came out as trans and started to socially transition.

THE PRIVILEGE OF VISIBILITY

I continue to come back to that 'Why me?' question, and increasingly the one word that springs to mind is visibility. Pre-transition, as a classroom teacher, I was 'quirky', somewhat flamboyant in my expression and a little unorthodox. To what extent did that endear me to students who felt out of place themselves? Curious, I recently asked this of an ex-student who told me: '[you were] unafraid to convulse away from the social norms and still presented yourself as thriving because of it – the positivity you brought to yourself was something I would guess many young queer people connected with' [verbat.].

No longer being at the chalkface myself is arguably a privilege that allows me to be a visible trans educator (I opine why that might be in the next section). My personal circumstances have suited someone who is visibly trans. Visibility is exceptionally important not just to my well-being, but also for the well-being of those who cannot or struggle to be visible for whatever reason. I am altruistic by nature and I feel that also has lent itself well to being visible for not just the trans community but also members of the teaching community, something I am still very much a part of.

For instance, a teacher who works at an all-girls school contacted me on the back of some freelance work. They were anxious to support a student who had come out as a trans boy. We talked about pronouns, and their connection with the student in question, and I ended the conversation by telling the teacher that they are 'awesome' and doing a great job to support that student. On another occasion, an ex-student got in touch to say that a member of their extended family had come out as transgender and some relatives were at first not very accepting. However, their stance has continued to soften since hearing about my transition. According to the ex-student, those family members had realised that if someone such as a teacher they respected in their community was transgender, then perhaps it was not a fad or problem after all. This is just one example of many. For anyone out there who is visible and being their genuine selves, they probably do not realise they are probably changing at least one person's life for the better just by being who they are. What a precious thing for someone who is transgender in their identity, but a teacher in their soul.

THE VISIBILITY PARADOX

In 2018, the Government Equalities Office stated bluntly that they 'do not know' how many transgender people there are in the United Kingdom, as 'no robust data on the UK trans population exists.' They tentatively estimate approximately 200,000-500,000, which would work out 0.3-0.7 % of the UK population based on the latest information (ONS, 2021a). That is no small number, and therefore trans and gender non-conforming educators are more common than most people think. With that in mind, there is an apparent lack of 'good news' stories or role models in the teaching profession. Until data from the recent 2021 UK Census is available, in which sexual and gender identities were collected for the very first time (ONS, 2021b), then we are not going to know for certain how many trans educators there are. Indeed, the anonymity of the census could provide a breakthrough in recognising the number of gender non-conforming people in any profession, not just teaching.

So why do we still not have many 'out and proud' transgender teachers in the classroom? Why is this the case despite so much progress being made with the human and civil rights of LGBTQ+ communities, including trans youth? Gilbert & Grey (2020) suggests one factor is the contradiction between the growing culture making schooling more inclusive for young queer and trans students, and the lack of welcome for queer and trans teacher candidates into the teaching profession and their own classrooms. In addition, quite often 'moral panic' occurs over educational initiatives such as 'No Outsiders', spurred on by outrage from prominent players in the popular press (Morgan and Taylor, 2019). And when the suicide of Lucy Meadows in 2013 is one of the more prominent stories of a transgender teacher, then it may make one stop and think whether 'coming out' while working as a teacher is worth it. When I combine these points with my own experiences, I understand the situation to be what is called the visibility paradox.

One of my less favourable experiences can provide an example of the visibility paradox. A year into the start of socially transitioning and presenting publicly in alignment with my gender identity, I was attending a network meeting of teachers across the region hosted at a school. The meeting started during lunchtime and I was escorted to the classroom by some wonderful students, enjoying a chat along the way. It is important to note here, that I was familiar with the school and know that several of its students have felt very supported with regards to their own LGBTQ+ identity – thanks to the affirming culture generated by the school and its staff. The following day, I was contacted by a member of the school's senior leadership team to say that there had been an incident where staff caught some students being offensive about my appearance. I was surprised but appreciative of the sentiment to involve me in potential next steps to deal with the behaviour, but despite my response being swift, there was little-follow up in a timely manner. It did make me think about a couple of things. If those students were being offensive towards one of their peers, would the matter have been dealt with more swiftly and robustly? Also, why should the burden of this behaviour incident be placed on someone by a school they did not work at? Would they have asked this of a cisgender guest who was mocked for their appearance?

CONCLUSION

Being altruistic in nature, I have a strong desire to be visible, especially for those who cannot be or do not feel ready to be themselves. But often it falls on me to provide the 'trans perspective', usually unsolicited, whether it be out of personal curiosity or input into a project or initiative.

KEY TAKEAWAYS

- A trans teacher who is supported and given the agency to be themselves will organically be a source of comfort for students who feel they may be gender nonconforming themselves.

- There is a disparity between trans youth and staff feeling supported in schools.
- Trans staff may be caught in the 'visibility paradox' where their visibility may lead them to be co-opted unsolicited for opinion or participation in issues related to their identity.

KEY QUESTIONS

- What other examples can you give where young people's aspirations are raised when they see a role model or example of someone who is 'like them'?
- What is your school's policy on dealing with members of the school community who engage in abusive behaviour towards a member of staff? Would that policy hold up to scrutiny if the victim was trans?
- Can you name at least two organisations who can work with your school with trans issues, e.g. to support dealing with an incident or run a celebratory event?

COMMITMENT TO THE MANIFESTO

Provide the same high level of safety and safeguarding for members of staff who are transgender as you would your students, allowing those staff to thrive in the safe learning environment that they wish to help create.

REFERENCES

Gilbert, J. and Gray, E.M., (2020). 'Unhappy Histories: Welcoming LGBTIQ+ Teachers into the Profession.' *Teaching Education*. 31 (1): 1-5

Government Equalities Office (2018) *Factsheet: Trans people in the UK*. Available at: www.gov.uk/government/consultations/reform-of-the-gender-recognition-act-2004 (Accessed 30 March 2021).

Morgan, E. and Taylor, Y. (2019) 'Dangerous Education: The Occupational Hazards of Teaching Transgender', *Sociology*, 53(1), pp. 19–35

Office for National Statistics ONS (2021a) *Overview of the UK population: January 2021*. Available at: www.ons.gov.uk/peoplepopulationandcommunity/populationandmigration/populationestimates/articles/overviewoftheukpopulation/january2021 (accessed 30 March 2021).

Office for National Statistics ONS (2021b) *Sex and gender identity question development for Census 2021*. Available at: www.ons.gov.uk/census/censustransformationprogramme/questiondevelopment/sexandgenderidentityquestiondevelopmentforcensus2021 (Accessed 14 February 2021).

CHAPTER 4: MARRIAGE AND CIVIL PARTNERSHIP

CHAPTER EDITOR: JACKIE HILL

CHAPTER CONTRIBUTORS

1. Kiran Satti – **Marriage – The Fairytale?**
2. Claire Price – **Marriage is a Feminist Issue**
3. Jessica Austin-Burdett – **Mr vs Ms, Miss, Mrs or Mx**
4. Lois Nethersell-Webb – **"Miss, What About Same-Sex Marriage back then?"**
5. Hayle Chalke-Davies – **Marriage Equality in the Shadow of Section 28**
6. Rebecca Bothwell O'Hearn – **Real Families, Real Curriculum**
7. Amanda Carter-Philpott – **Commitment, Choices and Courageous Conversations**
8. James and Kate Pope – **Leaders in Education as Parents**
9. Sarah Mullin – **More Than Just a Wife: Supporting Women Leaders in Education**
10. Sadie Hollins and Laura Davies – **Gay, Married and Teaching International**ly

BIOGRAPHIES

Jackie Hill is an experienced teacher/ educator with a particular interest in partnership development and professional learning. She is a Founding Fellow of The Chartered College of Teaching, Network Leader for WomenEdNW and co-founder / strategic leader for WomenEdNI. Her career began in Further Education (Northern Ireland), then switched to secondary MFL (Stockport), followed by a move to TDA and subsequent roles related to teacher recruitment, training and professional development, including Director for School Partnership at Tes Institute. She is passionate about helping schools to become more diverse, inclusive and equitable places for staff, students and their families.

Amanda Carter-Philpott is a Disability /diversity activist/campaigner/ public speaker, writer, blogger, trainer, passionate believer in inclusion and advocate for social justice which is at the core of her business model as a director of Pandora Inc CIC, which stands for: Promoting Achievement Nurturing Diversity Openly Respecting Ability. A voice for the voiceless.

Bex Bothwell- O'Hearn is a History and Politics secondary teacher with responsibility for A-Level History. She has worked in education for ten years in both a pastoral and academic capacity. Bex is currently leading work on Diversifying the Curriculum at her school. Bex is passionate about ensuring that all students see themselves reflected in the curriculum and using the power of student voice to help shape policies, practice and the curriculum.

Claire Price is a feminist school leader. She is a passionate advocate of social justice; this extends to the belief that experienced school leaders should support other women to reach their ambitions. Claire is National Leader for WomenEd, an experienced coach and mentor, and mum to four children.

Hayle Chalke-Davies taught Philosophy and Ethics in a secondary school for ten years prior to moving to the charity sector to work as the Education Officer for Teachers and Schools at Amnesty International UK. They are passionate about teacher training, wellbeing and diversity and recognise the power that LGBTQ+ educators can have in enabling all young people to flourish.

James Pope, formerly a headteacher and executive headteacher, is currently Director of InspirEducate and founder of the HeadsUp4HTs network, Executive Leadership Consultant to Whole Education and Advisory Board member of CollectivED at Leeds Beckett University. **Kate Pope** is Assistant Headteacher at a large secondary school in the South West.

Jessica Austin-Burdett is an experienced art and design teacher with a passion for creativity and cross- curricular unison, holding a variety of educational positions over the years. An experienced mentor who's always learning Jessica completed an MA in education whilst having her first child and has presented at many events.

Kiran Satti is a primary teacher and English Leader, supporting reading across a Trust of primaries. She is part of WomenEd, curating discussions @WomenEdBookClub. Kiran reviews books @TinyOwl and Just Imagine, where she has contributed to their Take One Book project. Kiran speaks at edu-events about empowering fiction, diversity and kindness.

Lois Nethersell-Webb is Diversity, Equity and Inclusion Lead and Assistant Head of Humanities at a Norfolk secondary school where she also leads on diversity and inclusion. She trained as a History teacher at the University of East Anglia and has a particular passion for teaching social changes in the 1900s.

Dr Sadie Hollins is the Head of Sixth Form at a British International School in Chiang Mai, Thailand. Prior to working in international education she worked as a HE lecturer and researcher focusing sociological issues in sport. She is the creator of the WISEducation blog. **Laura Davies** is the Head of Physical Education at a

British International School in Chiang Mai, Thailand. She has a particular interest in inclusion, and is currently pursuing a doctorate focusing on international school provision for students with SEND. Laura's other passions include travelling, rescuing animals and riding motorbikes.

Sarah Mullin is a Deputy Headteacher and Doctor of Education student. She is the author of the number 1 best-selling book *What They Didn't Teach Me on My PGCE*. Sarah is the recipient of the 'Contribution to Education of the Year' award and she has been named a 'Rising Star' in education and academia. Sarah is also the founder of #EduTeacherTips, a YouTube channel for teachers, by teachers.

THE PROTECTED CHARACTERISTIC OF MARRIAGE AND CIVIL PARTNERSHIPS: INTRODUCTION

JACKIE HILL

INTRODUCTION

'In nine days I'm going to get married…'

In schools, positive relationships play such an important role in the success and wellbeing of students and those who teach them (Roffey, 2012). They are also essential for a happy and successful adult life so students 'need to acquire the knowledge to make informed decisions about their wellbeing, health and relationships' (DfE 2019).

Marriages and Civil Partnerships are the legal ways that couples can formalise their relationship. They can overlap with other protected characteristics – sexual orientation, gender re-assignment, sex, religion or belief and race, and laws such as The Human Rights Act 1998 and The European Convention on Human Rights in supporting, for example, rights to a private life and to marry. It is vital that schools – teachers, senior leaders and governors have a secure understanding of the range of associated issues, plus appropriate policies and practices in place to ensure all students and staff can thrive and feel they 'belong'.

Misconceptions begin at an early age. My grandson, Oliver, demonstrated this recently:

Oliver (age three):   'In 9 days I'm going to get married…'
Mummy: 'Who to?'
Oliver: 'To you!'
Mummy: 'I'm already married to Mammy.'
Oliver: 'Hmmm who could I marry…?'

Relationships Education has to start early, with families of different shapes and sizes represented across the curriculum – in this chapter the writers provide great insights and suggestions for this. Teachers also need to be trained and supported to be able to address difficult questions and situations – what if it were a fifteen-year-old pupil saying: 'In nine days I'm going to get married…'?

DEFINITIONS AND TERMINOLOGY

'Marriage is a sentence, not a word.'

One of my literacy students thought this 'definition' was hilarious. For some, it is not funny. Others, including opponents and supporters of same-sex marriage, disagree vigorously about what is meant by 'marriage' and who 'owns' it (Everitt , 2012).

The Equality Act (2010) makes it unlawful to discriminate against or treat someone unfairly because they are married or in a civil partnership. Neither is 'defined' in the Act. It is taken to broadly cover people, same-sex and opposite-sex, who are married in a legally recognised union, or in a legally recognised and registered civil partnership. It applies only at **work**. Outside the workplace it is not unlawful discrimination (Citizens Advice, 2021).

As employers, schools need to ensure terms and conditions of employment do not disadvantage or exclude people because of their 'marital' status – or indeed perceptions of their capacity and priorities arising from stereotypical assumptions. This can be a particular issue for women. Within this chapter, contributors share their experiences and suggestions on how schools could provide more supportive and fertile environments to develop and benefit from the talents of 'married' staff. Civil partnerships do not come with the same traditional and religious connotations, but the rights and obligations are almost identical to those of marriage. For details on differences, see the Government Equalities Office's table (2019).

LANDSCAPE

While the legislation does not cover people not in a legally recognised union (for example those living together, those who are engaged, divorced, widowed or single), schools do have a responsibility to cover all. By the time pupils are at secondary school, they should know that 'marriage represents a formal and legally recognised commitment of two people to each other', and that there are 'different types of committed, stable relationships' (DfE, 2019). All families should experience the same positive environment, level of support, opportunities and visibility across the curriculum. These include single parent families, those with two or more parents (including step-parents), same-sex parents, opposite-sex parents, families headed by grandparents, adoptive parents, and foster parents/carers. There will be those happily married or in a civil partnership, others who are in or have emerged from abusive relationships, some who have divorced or separated, those who have blended families and others who have rejected any form of marriage or 'legalised coupling'. The contributors to this chapter present a range of perspectives to challenge teachers to think about who is in your lesson and senior leaders to think about the staff and families in your school community.

Inter-faith, inter-racial and cross-cultural marriages can provide additional challenges, including disapproval from families and communities, associations of betrayal and shame, and the potential for honour-based violence (HBV) or abuse (HBA). HBV/HBA is not an attribute of any specific culture, faith or religion (Manjoo

, 2018). 'Arranged marriages' are common within some communities (including Romany Gypsies and Irish Travellers). According to Pande (2021) some young British Indians are embracing modern arranged marriages which 'involve a variety of matchmaking practices ...to suit modern identities and ambitions'. It is important to make the distinction between 'arranged' and 'forced' marriages (which are illegal). Shams Uddin (2006) outlines these in his paper on *Arranged marriage: a dilemma for young British Asians*. Schools have a responsibility to educate and safeguard their students to ensure they all understand that, while marriage is an important relationship choice for many, it must be freely entered into (DfE, 2019 p27).

> 'You established peaceful relationships, trading relationships, mutual obligations with others by marrying them (Coontz , 2006)

The institution of marriage is thousands of years old but marrying for love is a relatively recent concept from the nineteenth century (Coontz, 2006). Change has been slow but since the middle of the twentieth century, it has been much faster and more widespread. International research (Ortiz-Ospina and Roser, 2020) shows that marriages are becoming less common, people are marrying later, unmarried couples are increasingly choosing to live together, and we are seeing a 'decoupling' of parenthood and marriage. Same-sex marriage has become possible in many countries but despite positive trends, much remains to be done to improve the rights of LGBTQ+ people.

The introduction of Section 28 of the Local Government Act (1988) prohibited 'promoting' homosexuality content in schools and, although it was repealed in 2003, its effects have been long-reaching. In this chapter, you will find more information, insights and perspectives on this, along with very practical suggestions on how to ensure schools are inclusive and welcoming for LGBTQ+ families. Keeping up to date with changes is vital. They do not happen at the same pace internationally, or even within the UK, but changes are happening. The 'biggest changes to the marriage registration system since 1837' came in 2021 with the inclusion of mothers' names in marriage certificates! (Wright, 2021). Further changes are likely – for example, campaigners want to ban under-18 marriages or 'child marriage by parental consent'. Charities claim it contributes to sexual violence and domestic abuse (Price, 2021). All these issues illustrate why the compulsory introduction of Relationships Education in primary schools and Relationships and Sex Education (RSE) in secondary schools (DfE, 2019) is so important.

VOICES IN OUR CHAPTER IN DIVERSE EDUCATORS – A MANIFESTO

The chapter begins with 'Marriage – The Fairy Tale?'- **Kiran Satti** focuses on the limiting impact of the archetypal 'Disney princess' character and the power of stories to dismantle and re-imagine an equitable 'happily ever after'. In 'Marriage is a Feminist Issue', **Claire Price** moves from the fairy tale to the patriarchal nature of marriage, and shows lone parenting can be a very positive choice. **Jessica Austin-Burdett** delves deeper into the history of marriage as an unequal institution, in which women can lose their identity in 'Mr vs Ms, Miss, Mrs or Mx'. In 'Miss, what about same sex marriage back then?' **Lois Nethersell-Webb** looks at how teachers can adapt and respond effectively when asked impromptu questions in lessons about the history of same-sex marriage. **Hayle Chalke-Davies** follows this with 'Marriage Equality in the Shadow of Section 28', and highlights the importance of a more inclusive learning curriculum and effective LGBTQ+ teacher training. **Bex Bothwell-O'Hearn**, in 'Real Families, Real Curriculum,' focuses on how schools can diversify the curriculum and represent real diverse families, including adoptive families, through enlisting students' help. In 'Commitment, Choices and Courageous Conversations,' **Amanda Carter-Philpott** challenges lack of representation plus misinformation and misunderstanding of marriage, civil partnership and disability. **James and Kate Pope**, as a married couple, share their experiences in 'Leaders in Education as Parents,' advocating more flexible cultures in schools to recognise the diversity of personal and professional drivers of working parents. In 'More than just a wife: supporting women leaders in education', **Sarah Mullin** focuses on enabling more women to progress to leadership, the importance of diverse role models for students and the benefits of having a spouse's support. To finish, **Sadie Hollins and Laura Davies** share their experiences as spouses working within an international school context in 'Gay, married and teaching internationally', providing great insights and practical advice for other couples.

CONCLUSION

It's not just the person you are marrying...

When preparing for this manifesto, I wrote a blog (Hill, 2021) following this loaded statement from Oprah Winfrey. I would like to thank those who responded, particularly Amanda Murphy, Parm Plummer, Alex Purdie, Patrick Ottley-O'Connor and Chris Reddy – your insights have been invaluable. I am particularly grateful to those I am unable to name who were willing to share painful experiences – your bravery and wisdom are powerful. I have learned the range of issues associated with marriage and civil partnerships is immense and impacts differently on every family, adult and child. Within this chapter you will find a wealth of knowledge, lived experiences, insights, ideas and inspiration, so I invite you to dive in!

COMMITMENT TO THE MANIFESTO

For students: schools should ensure that Relationships education is delivered fully and effectively for all, embracing diverse families; for staff, schools should have appropriate policies and flexible working practices in place to support all to thrive professionally, regardless of 'marital status'.

REFERENCES

Citizens Advice (2021) *Marriage and Civil Partnership Discrimination*. Available at: https://www.citizensadvice.org.uk/law-and-courts/discrimination/protected-characteristics/marriage-and-civil-partnership-discrimination/

Coontz, S. (2006) *Marriage, a History: How love conquered marriage.* Penguin Books.

Department for Education (2019) *Relationships Education, Relationships and Sex Education (RSE) and Health Education: Statutory Guidance.* Available at: https://www.gov.uk/government/publications/relationships-education-relationships-and-sex-education-rse-and-health-education

Equality Act (2010) Available at: https://www.legislation.gov.uk/ukpga/2010/15 (accessed July 2021)

European Convention on Human Rights (2010), Council of Europe. Available at: https://www.echr.coe.int/documents/convention_eng.pdf

Everitt, L., (2012) 'Ten key moments in the history of marriage.' *BBC News Magazine.* Available at: https://www.bbc.co.uk/news/magazine-17351133

Government Equality Office (2019) *Marriage and Civil Partnerships in England and Wales* (2019) Available at: https://www.gov.uk/government/publications/marriage-and-civil-partnership-in-england-and-wales (accessed July 2021)

Hill, J., (2021) 'You're not just marrying the person...' In *DiverseEducators.* Available at: https://www.diverseeducators.co.uk/youre-not-just-marrying-the-person/

Human Rights Act (1998) UK. Available at: https://www.legislation.gov.uk/ukpga/1998/42 (accessed July 2021)

Local Government Act (1988) Available at: https://www.legislation.gov.uk/ukpga/1988/9/section/28/enacted

Manjoo, C. (2018) *'Shame' and 'Honour': Comparison of the prevalence of 'honour'-based abuse/violence in Northern Ireland and the rest of the United Kingdom.* Queen's University Belfast

Ortiz-Ospina, E. and Roser, M. (2020) *Marriages and Divorces.* Available at: https://ourworldindata.org/marriages-and-divorces

Pande, R. (2021) *Young British Indians are embracing arranged marriage – just not in the traditional sense.* Available at: https://theconversation.com/young-british-indians-are-embracing-arranged-marriage-just-not-in-the-traditional-sense-159511

Price, E. (2021) *Under-18 marriages 'thriving' in UK and should be banned, say charities.* Available at: https://www.bbc.co.uk/news/uk-56982309

Roffey, S. (ed) 2012 *Positive Relationships: Evidence Based Practice Across the World.* Springer

Shams Uddin, M. (2006) *Arranged Marriage: a dilemma for young British Asians.* Available at: https://diversityhealthcare.imedpub.com/arranged-marriage-a-dilemma-for-young-british-asians.php?aid=2406

Wright, K. (2021) *Marriage certificate to include mothers' names in England and Wales.* Available at: https://www.bbc.co.uk/news/uk-56975357

MARRIAGE – THE FAIRY TALE?

KIRAN SATTI

INTRODUCTION

Once upon a time... An archetypal story opening that promises a sense of security in the knowing that there will be a happily ever after. Yorke (2013) illustrates there is an intentionality with archetypal stories with the introduction of the central character, whereby we experience, empathise and in some cases, internalise the story. In this chapter, we will focus on the archetypal character, the Disney Princess, who has come to reflect the story society has been telling young girls and women – marriage is the happily ever after – the equilibrium to our story arc; or is it? Using Torodov's Theory of Narrative (1969) to frame and dismantle the Disney-esque story arc, I will explore how we as educators can recognise the limiting impact and ultimately disrupt the archetypal story arc to reimagine and restore the power of stories – to authenticate human truths, not societal structures.

EQUILIBRIUM – SOCIETY'S STORY OF STATUS QUO

The beginning – a character's life is normal – everything is as it should be.

Rippon (2019) chronicles the gendered assertions within historic scientific inquiry that privileged men such as Darwin, suggesting that unmarried women were a threat to society and the status quo. Dating back to and from the 19th century, women's marital status equated to societal status, closely aligning to Darwin's theory of sexual selectivity. It can be argued that the science of this time was used to prove the importance of the patriarchal structures, dependent on privileging male power – in public and intellectual spaces. Moving forward to 1937, Disney's *Snow White* seemed to embody, encapsulate and promote certain gendered norms related to perfection, beauty and femininity – superficial submissions to the male gaze permeating through the patriarchal structures erected in the 19th century.

Equilibrium: Marriage is the happily-ever-after. Helpless and powerless women need men to survive in society.

DISEQUILIBRIUM – DISRUPTING THE DOMINANT

An event disrupts the equilibrium.

Even though questioning a common belief may be argued as beneficial to many, those that benefit from the status quo will challenge the questioning by subverting. For instance, literary heroines that questioned or subverted the patriarchal framework in the 19th century were othered or ultimately deemed 'mad' in literature and denied any sort of happy ending, such as Antoinette in Jane Eyre; portrayed as the madwoman in the attic – helpless. Silencing the central character's voice is a theme that emerges in Disney films, which artfully weaves through to sustain the dominant norm, your happiness is dependent on a man because they equate to happily-ever-after. Ariel's choice (1989) to give up her voice to be with a man from land permeates the idea that women's voices are of less value, in comparison to their appearance and beauty. This is emphasised once again in *Mulan* (1998) – a strong leading lady who showcases courage, heroism and loyalty, however, is still othered and silenced because she is a woman.

Disequilibrium: Why are women persistently silenced?

ACKNOWLEDGEMENT – RECOGNISING THE IMPACT

Recognising the event has disturbed the equilibrium.

Developing a critical eye is essential to question the perceptions of truths we are enveloped in – societal and cultural as well as our own experiences. As educators, are we aware of the impact that certain societal constructs and dominant norms may have in and around the classroom? #MeToo, #NotAllMen, Sarah Everard – these are the conversations that echo around our classrooms and educational settings. How as educators can we disrupt the emerging story arc depicting women in the real world as seemingly powerless and voiceless, and so perpetuating the privilege of male power, rooted in 19th century patriarchy?

CONVERSATIONS IN THE CLASSROOM – WHEN YOU THINK OF THE TERM 'GIRL' – WHAT DO YOU THINK OF?

As part of my work for International Day of the Girl, 2017, I posed this question to my Year 5 class at the time. The initial responses concerned me as an educator because from my perception and interpretation of initial responses, they were describing a two-dimensional caricature of a Disney Princess – make-up, wedding, dolls, dress, perfect. After questioning their thinking, the dialogic space that emerged enabled the children to question their own assumptions about gender – adapting, assimilating, embracing, challenging enabled them to shift their mindset. After thirty minutes of discussion, the children offered a myriad of responses to the same question, which included confident, caring, hero, brave, compassionate, strong-minded, determined and happy.

SOLVING – RE-IMAGINING

Repairing the disruption's damage

Fairy tales are not fixed and neither are children's minds. Girls' and boys' brains develop in response to their experiences and so experience shapes our brains (Rycroft-Smith, 2019). This concept is defined as neuroplasticity. Rippon (2019) further develops this concept by illustrating the brain as moldable plastic, therefore, the brain is not a fixed entity (Rippon, 2019).

So, can the concept of neuroplasticity frame our teaching?

Joel and Vikhansi (2019, p 146) suggest 'one way to expose a common belief as a stereotype rather than a truth about the world is to provide counter-examples'. Merida (2012) is the first Disney Princess who is re-writing the archetypal story arc – happily ever after does not equate to marriage. Anna redefines the power of true love – grounded in sisterhood and sacrifice in *Frozen* (2013). Elsa's happily ever after in *Frozen 2* (2019) signals self-fulfilment comes from within. *Moana* (2016) saves Te Fiti and her island by following the voice from within.

Solving: Rewriting the story arc. Helplessness is now heroism. Voiceless is now vocalising your truth, purpose and passion.

EQUILIBRIUM – REWRITING THE STORY

Restoration – renewed – re-equilibrium

Diversifying the narrative in our classrooms is essential to enable impactful and constant renewal of archetypal narratives. For example, Robert Munsch's much loved *Paper Bag Princess* (1980) sees Elizabeth bravely outwit the dragon to save Prince Ronald. However, Ronald is not accepting of Elizabeth's appearance and is dismissive of her courage and character. Consequently, Elizabeth decides to save herself and skip into the sunset. *Interstellar Cinderella* is another example of a reimagined fairy tale, further dismantling the idea that 'happily ever after' means marriage. After helping the prince fix his space vehicle, he offers her marriage as a thank you. Interstellar Cinderella chooses her dream job instead, following her passion – possibly her true love.

KEY TAKEAWAYS

- As educators, we must be aware of societal constructs that we may unintentionally perpetuate and so limit learners' perceptions of themselves.

- Fairy tales are not fixed – neither are learners' minds. Neuroplasticity can be used as a teaching tool.
- Equilibrium – every story we share as educators starts with equity and equality weaves through the happily-ever-after.

KEY QUESTIONS

- What if marriage was not the happily-ever-after?
- Do you have fairy tales that subvert the archetypal story arc in your classroom?
- What is the impact of sharing a re-imagined fairy tale?

COMMITMENT TO THE MANIFESTO

Share stories that curate curiosity, not conventionality. Think 'What If...?'

REFERENCES

MacKay, C, (2016) *Disney Princesses: The Evolution from Maidens to Heroes* (2019.) Available at https://medium.com/@17MacKayCa/disney-princesses-the-evolution-from-maidens-to-heroes-9f6280d77c42 (accessed 2nd May 2021)

Joel, D. and Vikhanski, V. (2019) *Gender Mosaic: Beyond the Myth of the Male and Female Brain.* London: Endeavour

Munsch, R. (1980) *The Paper Bag Princess*. Annick Press

Rippon, G. (2020) *The Gendered Brain: The new neuroscience that shatters the myth of the female brain.* London: Penguin Random House UK

Rycroft-Smith, L. (2020) *The Equal Classroom: Life Changing Thinking About Gender.* Oxon: Routledge

Todorov's Narrative Theory (2013). Available at https://www.slideshare.net/Katrinabrookes/todorovs-narrative-theory-24244633 (Accessed 2nd May 2021)

Yorke, J. (2013) *Into the Woods: How Stories Work and Why We Tell Them.* London: Penguin Books

MARRIAGE IS A FEMINIST ISSUE

CLAIRE PRICE

INTRODUCTION

Marriage, like any other state-sanctioned relationship, is characterised by power; and as such, those who benefit most promote this as being the natural order of things. Marriage continues to disadvantage women, through loss of identity, through loss of earnings, through increased responsibility for unpaid work in the home. Marriage is normative, and even after the Marriage (Same Sex Couples) Act of 2013, it continues to be heteronormative, packaging LGBT+ relationships in the domestic patriarchal sphere. All of this impacts on children and young people. Diverse educators will be aware that not all families are safe and will seek to promote positive relationships and lifestyles over structures.

MARRIAGE: PATRIARCHY IN A SHEEP'S CLOTHING?

Marriage is every girl's dream, or so the fairy tales tell us. And whilst being married is an ongoing state, getting married is seen as an end goal for too many girls. Self-efficacy and self-worth for girls and women are made to be inextricably tied up with being linked to another human being. Schools promote this in their choice of literature, in their curriculum and in the hidden curriculum often without thought. Traditional weddings involve a woman being given by one man to another, at which point the woman loses her father's identity and becomes known as her husband's property. It is only women that are known by their relationship to their marital status, Mrs or Miss. And even the title Ms, the direct equivalent to Mr, is too often taken as a proxy for being divorced. Women conventionally take their partner's last name. It is accidental that the addition of a possessive apostrophe reflects a woman's position once she becomes known as Mr's.

Childbirth, the physical domain of women, is made subsidiary within marriage. Most families still follow the tradition of using the father's family name for their child. Women perform the bulk of the childcare and unpaid work in the home. They are more likely to work part-time than men, and this limits promotion possibilities and their pay. Brynin's (2017) research into the gender pay gap showed that, by the age of forty, married women are paid less than single women; the 'child rearing penalty'. Married men, on the other hand, whatever their parental status, out-earn single men in every age bracket. *The British Social Attitudes Report* (2021) showed that people are four times more likely to disapprove of women with young children working full-time than men.

Covid 19 has exposed the inequality in society. It is well-trailed that women took on the burden of childcare and home-schooling through the pandemic. An Office for National Statistics (ONS) analysis published in March 2021 showed that, in the same household, women were more likely to be furloughed than men; more likely to homeschool their children than men and engaged in more unpaid housework than men, even whilst both partners were in lockdown at home. (Great Britain, Office for National Statistics, 2021).

A FAIRY TALE ENDING?

Marriage is not a benign state, it is highly controlled and highly legislated. Rape in marriage has only been a crime since 1992. Up until then, in the eyes of the law, by getting married a woman had given her perpetual consent to sexual intercourse, and this could not be rescinded. In a YouGov poll, *Attitudes to Sexual Consent* (2018), a quarter of adult respondents believed that sex without consent in a long-term relationship was not rape. Marriage may still not be a place of safety for women. On average, eighty women a year in the UK are killed by a current or ex-spouse or intimate partner, compared with nine men (Great Britain, Office for National Statistics, 2020). 78% of all homicides in which women are victims occur in or around their home (Great Britain, Office for National Statistics, 2020). Men who kill their partners often get more lenient sentences leading Harriet Harman to comment: 'It must be perverse that you get a discount on your sentence if your victim is your wife, when you're killing somebody who should be able to trust you, and should be able to be safe in her own home.' (in Topping, 2021)

Offences against women and children are hugely under-reported. Despite this, there were 2024 Honour Based Abuse offences, including forced marriage, physical abuse, emotional abuse, imprisonment, killing, rape, acid attacks or abduction recorded in England and Wales in 2019-20. (Great Britain, Home Office, 2021). In 2019 there were 1355 cases relating to forced marriage (Great Britain, Home Office, 2020 p.3). Child abuse is notoriously difficult to measure, with many cases remaining hidden. In the year ending March 2019, 227,530 child offences had been recorded by the police. There were 55,080 children on a Child Protection Plan and a further 54,380 looked after by their local authority because of experience or risk of abuse in their home.

Family life itself is not always safe for women and girls.

GROWING UP IN A SINGLE PARENT HOUSEHOLD

For many young people, their lived experience is defined by others by what they do not have, rather than what they do. In 2020 there were 2.9million lone parent families which account for 14.7 % of all family types in the UK. (Great Britain, Office for National Statistics, 2020). For the children in these families, the lack of one parent at home is often used to infer educational underachievement, poor moral development, poor mental health, lower aspirations and engagement in criminality. This projection of children's future is not positive and may be counter to their experiences of traumatic family life before they became part of a single parent household. Societal beliefs that two parents are always better than one is not supported by the research. Harkness, Gregg and Fernandez-Salgado (2019) used three longitudinal studies to look at the impact on cognitive development for children living in single-mother families and found that it was poverty not family structure that impacted on children's development. Despite this, the narrative for young people raised by a single parent, and particularly those from black and black Caribbean backgrounds, is bleak.

KEY TAKEAWAYS

- Not all young people's experiences of a traditional family life are positive. Be vigilant that for some children the very fact of living in a two-adult home has been traumatic or dangerous. Be inclusive in how you speak about all family types.
- Lone parenting can be a very positive choice. Use examples, read books, celebrate successful children from one-parent households.
- Promote positive self-esteem and self-worth derived from the individual and not in relation to desired female behaviours for all young people. This could be lifesaving.

KEY QUESTIONS

- Revisit your curriculum. Is it diverse in how it represents all families, and can all children see themselves reflected in it?
- Is your school ethos and culture alive to the harm that can be caused through the promotion of marriage as an ideated lifestyle? How inclusive is your language around this?
- Does your school build a culture of celebration of young people living independent and successful lives to help inoculate them against pressures of marriage?

COMMITMENT TO THE MANIFESTO

Reflect diverse relationship structures in all their forms. Commit to articulating the harm that can be derived in relationships to give young people the tools to seek alternative structures and means of support.

REFERENCES

British Social Attitudes Survey (2020). Available at: https://natcen.ac.uk/our-research/research/british-social-attitudes/ (accessed 28 March 2021)

Brynin, M. (2019) 'The Gender Pay Gap.' *Equality and Human Rights Commission Research Reports 109*

Great Britain, Office for National Statistics (2020) *Child abuse in England and Wales.* Available at: https://www.ons.gov.uk/peoplepopulationandcommunity/crimeandjustice/bulletins/childabuseinenglandandwales/march2020 (accessed 28 March 2021)

Great Britain, Home Office (2020) *Forced Marriage Unit Statistics.* Available at https://assets.publishing.service.gov.uk/government/uploads/system/uploads/attachment_data/file/894428/Forced_Marriage_Unit_statistics_2019 (accessed on 28 March 2021)

Great Britain, Office for National Statistics (2020) *Families and Households in the UK 2020.* Available at: https://www.ons.gov.uk/peoplepopulationandcommunity/birthsdeathsandmarriages/families/bulletins/familiesandhouseholds/2020 (accessed 28 March 2021)

Great Britain, Office for National Statistics, (2020) *Homicide in England and Wales.* Available at https://www.ons.gov.uk/peoplepopulationandcommunity/crimeandjustice/articles/homicideinenglandandwales/yearendingmarch2020 (accessed 28 March 2021)

Great Britain, Home Office, (2020) *Statistics on so-called honour-based abuse offences recorded by the police.* Available at: https://www.gov.uk/government/statistics/statistics-on-so-called-honour-based-abuse-offences-england-and-wales-2019-to-2020/statistics-on-so-called-honour-based-abuse-offences-recorded-by-the-police (accessed 28 March 2021)

Great Britain, Office for National Statistics, (2021) *Coronavirus and the different effects on men and women in the UK, March 2020 to February 2021.* Available at: https://www.ons.gov.uk/peoplepopulationandcommunity/healthandsocialcare/conditionsanddiseases/articles/coronaviruscovid19andthedifferenteffectsonmenand-womenintheukmarch2020tofebruary2021/2021-03-10 (accessed on 28 March 2021)

Harkness, S., Gregg, P. and Fernandez-Salgado, M. (2020) 'The Rise in Single☐Mother Families and Children's Cognitive Development: Evidence From Three British Birth Cohorts.' *Child Development* Volume 91, Issue 5, pages 1762-85

Marriage (Same Sex Couples) Act (2013). Available at: https://www.legislation.gov.uk/ukpga/2013/30/contents Accessed 13 May 2021.

Topping, A. (2021) *Calls for a review of five-year jail term for man who strangled wife in Wales.* The Guardian, London 19 February 2021. Available at: https://www.theguardian.com/uk-news/2021/feb/19/calls-review-five-year-jail-term-man-strangled-wife-wales-anthony-williams (accessed 28 March 2021).

YouGov (2018) *Public's Attitudes to Sexual Consent.* Available at: https://yougov.co.uk/topics/resources/articles-reports/2018/12/01/publics-attitudes-sexual-consent

MR VS MS, MISS, MRS OR MX

JESSICA AUSTIN-BURDETT

INTRODUCTION

Until the Sex Disqualification Removal Act was passed in the UK in 1919, I would have had to leave the teaching profession if I got married. Marriage bars in the UK meant that it was almost impossible for a woman to work as a married teacher until 1944. As I grew up, I was societally groomed to believe marriage was a desirable goal. Despite feminism being a powerful force in the 1980s, there was no real question of whether marriage was a good goal to aim for, or if there were alternatives to it. Feminists have been objecting to marriage for centuries. For the anarchist Emma Goldman, marriage was an insurance policy that a woman, 'pays for with her name, her privacy, her self-respect, her very life', one that 'condemns her to life-long dependency, to parasitism, to complete uselessness, individual as well as social'(Goldman, 1914).

On joining my current school, I realised I had automatically been designated a 'Mrs' title. I had it changed to 'Ms'. It made me wonder, why are there so many title options for a woman but only 'Mr' for a man. In all the schools where I have worked, students have addressed teachers as 'Miss' or 'Sir'. I have seen some schools actively change this to 'teacher' or another term that is not gender-specific, which is an interesting approach.

HOW DOES THE CHOICE OF A PREFIX DEFINE US OR CREATE ISSUES WE HAD NOT FORESEEN?

Patel (1979) emphasises that language defines us because it is 'a reflection of the condition of society – like everything else' so when societal conditions change so too should the language used to describe them and the roles of those within. Schools can be progressive places, but they are also one of the few places where Mr, Ms, Miss and Mrs are routinely used. For many educators, this poses challenges, but also opportunities for learning, education and affirmation. Many teachers agree that we teach beyond our subject specialisms and have holistic views, therefore explorations of issues relating to identity, labelling, stereotypes and societal norms and expectations are areas that offer important learning points. Chambers (2017) states, 'Historically, marriage has been a deeply unequal institution. Each of the three aspects of state recognition have been used in ways that instigate and perpetuate a variety of hierarchies, most consistently based on gender but also on race, religion, sexuality and class.' Sociological research shows continuing associations between marriage and gender inequality: married women do more housework than both married men and unmarried women; married women are unhappier than married men; marriage renders women more vulnerable to domestic violence. Marriage remains a powerful pull towards patriarchy. Elevating marriage as the relationship form of unique value denies respect and recognition to the unmarried, whether single or partnered, and contributes towards the stigmatisation of unmarried people (particularly women) and their children.

In a modern society like that in the UK, benefitting from advances such as mechanisation and birth control, the male advantage has become questionable and less relevant. The terms we use still generate the stereotypical roles of man and wife which emphasises man as breadwinner and woman as homemaker. Baker (2010) writes at length on how the suffix of 'ess' generally relates to subjugation and worse. However, he also recognises that the terms are now less widely used. The nouns and pronouns we prescribe emphasise gender inequality, though recently there has been more tendency to use one noun to describe the same role for both sexes. Should the exploration of the use of the terms Ms, Miss, Mrs or Mx also be explored in terms of this further connotation?

A LOSS OF IDENTITY

Nugent (2010) explains that a woman's surname change signals how women's identities are altered by marriage, whereas men's identities remain largely the same. As long as women are subjected to societal pressure to change their surname, the practical and professional costs to name change are disproportionately borne by women, as are the psychological costs of losing an individual identity.

The story of the painter Isabel Rawsthorne highlights how talented women have often missed out on the recognition they deserved. She married three times and took a different name each time rendering her oeuvre apparently unrecognised as a product of one person. Other stories of women whose work has been subsumed by their male counterparts need to be highlighted – this can be used in so many contexts to stimulate debate and critical inquiry. As well as marital subjugation there is also the Matilda effect (Rossiter, 1993) which describes examples of women's achievements being appropriated by the men they worked with.

EXPLORING THESE ISSUES IN YOUR CURRICULUM DESIGN

Moving schools recently gave me the challenge of auditing and redesigning the curriculum delivery with a new team, challenging them on decisions taken and how they framed learning and the creation of role models or stereotypes. We could see that too many male role models were being used, leading to the inference that men are the great makers of Art and Design. We have now included the work of a diverse range of artists and makers which offers opportunities to develop critical thinking skills, open up debate and stimulate deep conversations and discussions.

CONCLUSION

The current assimilation of a woman's identity represented by the taking of her husband's name represents a much deeper issue related to equality, equity, feminism and fairness; questioning and analysing this gives the students the power to see how this could be changed and rethought. If we are educating young people to see equality as fundamentally important then discussions around marriage, the titles apportioned to married people, how married women are lessened in their societal positions in relation to men, and the history of marriage as a contract of ownership need to be explicitly woven into the learning experiences we provide.

KEY TAKEAWAYS

- The terms used about and by women to denote their marital status are very loaded, and intertwined with the history of marriage – this should be highlighted in any curriculum area where relevant.
- Women's achievements are often undermined or appropriated by their husbands, or their efforts are lost to history because of name changes due to marriage. We should try harder to highlight this and these women's achievements in our learning environments.
- Many of the normalised terms used to refer to teachers are no longer fit for purpose – governing bodies and school leaders need to explore more effective and equal terminology.

KEY QUESTIONS

- How is marriage and civil partnership treated in your classroom discussions around contributions to the world?
- Do you enable the children you teach to think critically and question their assumptions about marriage, civil partnerships, relationships, gender equality? How do you model this? How can you plan for questions that stimulate critical thinking?
- Have you explored the wives' roles in the lives of key male protagonists in your subject area – what contribution did they make that may have been overlooked?
- Are there relevant role models you could research that would challenge normative thinking about marriage, assumed roles and celebrating forgotten or unheard voices?

COMMITMENT TO THE MANIFESTO

To generate learning experiences that facilitate courageous conversations about marriage and the labelling of women, and how the experience of marriage can lead to a woman's achievements being subsumed.

REFERENCES

Baker, P. (2010) 'Will *Ms* ever be as frequent as *Mr*? A corpus-based comparison of gendered terms across four diachronic corpora of British English.' *Gender and Language* 4.1: 125-9

Chambers, C. (2017) *Against marriage: An Egalitarian Defence of the Marriage-Free State.* Oxford University Press. Available at: https://aeon.co/essays/why-marriage-is-both-anachronistic-and-discriminatory (accessed March 2021)

Goldman, E. (1914) *Marriage and Love.* Available at: https://www.marxists.org/reference/archive/goldman/works/1914/marriage-love.htm (accessed March 2021)

Kesslen, B. (2019) 'Ms., Mr. or Mx.? Nonbinary teachers embrace gender-neutral honorific.' *NBC News*, 20 January 2019. Available at: https://www.nbcnews.com/feature/nbc-out/ms-mr-or-mx-nonbinary-teachers-embrace-gender-neutral-honorific-n960456 (accessed March 2021)

McClintock, E.A. (2018) Should Marriage Still Involve Changing a Woman's Name? *Psychology Today*.. Available at: https://www.psychologytoday.com/gb/blog/it-s-man-s-and-woman-s-world/201809/should-marriage-still-involve-changing-womans-name (accessed March 2021)

Nugent, C. (2010) 'Children's Surnames, Moral Dilemmas: Accounting for the Predominance of Fathers' Surnames for Children.' *Gender and Society*, vol. 24, no. 4, pp. 499-525.

Patel, Z. (1979) 'Call Us Ms', *Ufahamu: A Journal of African Studies*, 9(2) pp 78-85 0041-5715 Available at: https://escholarship.org/uc/item/6xt2r5bk (accessed June 2021)

Rossiter, M.W. (1993) 'The Matthew Matilda Effect in Science.' *Social Studies of Science*, vol. 23, no.2 pp. 325–41. JSTOR Available at: www.jstor.org/stable/285482 (accessed March 2021)

Thorpe, V. (2021). 'What's in a surname? The female artists lost to history because they got married.' *The Guardian,* 13 February 2021. Available at: https://www.theguardian.com/artanddesign/2021/feb/13/whats-in-a-surname-the-female-artists-lost-to-history-because-they-got-married? (accessed February 2021)

'MISS, WHAT ABOUT SAME-SEX MARRIAGE BACK THEN?'

LOIS NETHERSELL-WEBB

INTRODUCTION

Every educator has experienced situations where a student asks a question in a lesson that, whilst linked to the topic, might deviate the discussion away from the intended knowledge and outcomes. We make judgments about those questions we deem irrelevant or wish not to tackle, those we give a brief answer to and those we use to facilitate further discussion. The times we allow the lesson to take a different route can provide some of the most purposeful and inspiring learning experiences for the young people in our charge. How would you respond when asked a question about same-sex marriage in your lesson?

THE LESSON

Teaching a switched-on year nine class is a dream: the focus, the understanding and the inquisitive minds create a wonderful atmosphere in the classroom. During a history lesson about the position of women in the early 20th century students discussed the historical traditions of marriage and their patriarchal origins: they were thinking hard. One student raised his hand and asked 'Miss, what about same sex marriage back then?' In this situation a teacher has two options:

1. Answer the question with a brief and simple 'they were not allowed back then' to ensure an answer was given without deviating from the lesson plan.
2. Answer the question in more depth, enabling students to draw on their own knowledge and experiences to facilitate broader learning and encourage deeper thinking.

In *The Learning Rainforest: Great Teaching in Real Classrooms*, Tom Sherrington (2017) discusses the concept of Mode A and Mode B teaching. Mode A teaching consists of teacher-led instructions, pre-planned tasks and feedback to ensure students have acquired the knowledge they need to progress their learning. Mode

B teaching develops a student's ability to question, debate and sculpt the learning of the lessons. When posed the question regarding same-sex marriage, many educators may have chosen option one: to remain in Mode A teaching. The question was not relevant to the lesson objectives and a more in-depth answer might have slowed down the anticipated progress of expected knowledge acquisition. Maybe some educators wouldn't have the proficiency to explain when same sex marriage was introduced and why, until 2014, these unions were not allowed in Britain, or to answer subsequent questions so a shorter, more succinct reply reduces the chance of a teacher feeling out of depth. When posed the question 'Miss, what about same sex marriage back then?' I made the decision to exit Mode A teaching and enter Mode B.

All of those reasons are justifiable but, unfortunately, draw attention to the wider problem of the purpose of education. Is education about factual recall, making sufficient progress against numerical targets and qualifications or is it about instilling a lifelong love of learning in an environment where students feel confident to ask questions and know that these questions will be answered? In *The Teaching Delusion,* Bruce Robertson (2020) discusses how an education system focused on examinations and preparing young people for future employment 'is to gloss over the excitement, wonder and enthusiasm which can come from learning for learning's sake'. The students in the year nine class had a richer experience in that lesson because of the question that was asked and the subsequent discussions regarding when same-sex marriage was introduced in different countries, starting with the Netherlands in 2001, why legalisation of these unions took so long and why the majority of countries in the world do not permit or recognise gay and lesbian weddings.

THE RELATIONSHIPS

The relationship between a teacher and their class is central to ensuring students feel comfortable and confident to ask questions about marriage or any of the protected characteristics. In *The Hidden Lives of Learners*, Graham Nuthall (2007) identifies three worlds that students inhabit: the public world of the classroom, the semi-private world of their peer relationships and the private world of their own mind. In the lesson the student made a connection in the private world of their mind between the historical topic of women's rights in the early 1900s and LGBTQ+ rights today.

If the relationships between that student and his peers, as well as that student and myself, as his teacher, were not strong those thoughts would have remained unspoken and therefore his question unanswered. Sherrington (2017, p.142) states how we must remember we are teaching our subjects to 'individuals with whom we need to foster relationships if we are going to cohabit our learning spaces happily'. It is debatable whether the student would have asked the question about same sex marriage in every classroom of the school; did they feel more comfortable asking me the question because I am open about my marriage to a woman and lead on diversity and inclusion?

THE KNOWLEDGE

When asked questions about marriage, particularly same-sex marriage, or any of the protected characteristics, some educators may opt for a swift response that does not open the door for broader conversations due to a lack of knowledge and understanding: this should not be the case. It is every teacher's duty to be aware of the society in which they teach; a student's question on marriage might not be able to be answered immediately, but the conversation can have just as much power in a subsequent lesson once an educator has taken the time to develop their own knowledge. A student's ability to have their question answered should not be the luck of the draw, depending on which teacher they have in front of them.

CONCLUSION

Teachers must also be prepared to plan opportunities for same sex relationships to be naturally and organically discussed in their classrooms. In Maths, scenario-based questions should regularly focus on same-sex couples. When teaching about the culture of different countries, language teachers could consider marriage laws in those areas. In Art, depictions of marriages and families must be inclusive. In PE theory, acceptance of same-sex relationships can be discussed as a potential barrier to participation. Creating natural opportunities for same sex relationships to be seen in lessons will, in turn, give students confidence to ask further questions.

KEY TAKEAWAYS

- Training must ensure all staff, no matter their role, have knowledge of the same sex marriage laws in the country in which they teach to ensure they can confidently answer student questions.
- It is okay not to know the answer and to convey this to students but, if this is the case, staff must know where the answers can be found through being signposted to colleagues or resources where they can acquire the knowledge they need.
- Learning environments must ensure that students feel confident when asking questions about same sex marriage and, in turn, all protected characteristics.

KEY QUESTIONS

- Are staff in your school adequately trained to answer students' questions about same sex marriage and its historical context?
- Do the relationships between staff and students in your school allow students to ask questions about same sex marriages and their place in society?

- Are staff in your school empowered to bring their own lived experiences of marriage into their teaching?

COMMITMENT TO THE MANIFESTO

Staff must be given confidence by school leaders to deviate from the lesson plan when students show an interest in and ask questions about same sex marriages.

REFERENCES

Nuthall, G. (2007) *The Hidden Lives of Learners*. NZCER Press

Robertson, B. (2020) The *Teaching Delusion: Why teaching in our schools isn't good enough (and how we can make it better)*. John Catt Educational Ltd.
Sherrington, T. (2017) *The Learning Rainforest: Great Teaching in Real Classrooms*. John Catt Educational Ltd

MARRIAGE EQUALITY IN THE SHADOW OF SECTION 28

HAYLE CHALKE-DAVIES

INTRODUCTION

The way that we discuss marriage in the classroom is deeply heteronormative and because of this many Lesbian, Gay, Bisexual and Transgender (LGBT+) educators may not feel able to share that they are married or in a civil partnership. This chapter will explore the steps that all teachers can take to build more inclusive learning spaces and teach more diverse curriculums that recognise all LGBT+ identities, including those in civil partnerships and marriages. It will also reflect on what teachers can do to overcome the lasting impact that Section 28 (Local Government Act, 1988) has had on our schools so that all young people can thrive.

LGBTQ+ RIGHTS IN SCHOOLS

The statistics around LGBT+ young people in UK schools are worrying with Stonewall's School Report (2017) showing that 86 % of LGBT+ young people hear the word 'gay' used negatively within their schools. Alongside this, two in five LGBT+ pupils are never taught about LGBT issues and 45% of those experiencing homophobic bullying do not tell anyone that bullying is taking place (Stonewall, 2017). These statistics are unfortunately not surprising and show the lasting impact that Section 28, the law prohibiting local authorities from promoting homosexuality or the teaching of the acceptability of homosexuality as a 'pretend family relationship' (Local Government Act, 1988) still has in our schools despite its repeal.

Having grown up under Section 28 and taught for ten years in secondary schools I have seen the negative impact that Section 28's legacy and the heteronormative curriculum are having on students and staff. Beginning my teaching career before equal marriage was legal also created fewer opportunities to discuss LGBT+ rights in the classroom. Therefore, although it was normal practice for heterosexual colleagues to mention their spouses it took me much longer to feel comfortable talking about my wife. This was largely due to the homophobic abuse that I received at school which was not unusual given that 44% of teachers have been the target of homophobic language from pupils (Stonewall, 2014) and also because the heteronormative curriculum stops many LGBT+ staff from speaking about their relationships.

In the light of this, it is not surprising that more than half of LGBT+ pupils report not having an adult to talk to about being LGBT+ (Stonewall, 2017) making it vitally important for all teachers to build safe spaces and inclusive curriculums for their students. A good place to start is to ensure that LGBT+ relationships, including civil partnerships and marriage, are normalised within our classrooms and school communities. It is also important for LGBT+ staff to have allies in their schools who commit to actively challenging discrimination and promoting equal rights to enable LGBT+ students and staff to be their authentic selves. This would lead to more inclusive schools that teach young people about rights-respecting behaviour and celebrate diversity which would arguably significantly improve the school environment for all students.

LGBT+ INCLUSIVE RSE

One obvious place to embed teaching about LGBT+ Marriage, Civil Partnerships and families is in the new statutory Relationships and Sex Education (RSE) curriculum. This includes exploring different families in age-appropriate ways within primary schools (Department for Education, 2020a) to allow children with LGBT+ parents to be represented in the curriculum. At secondary school, including LGBT+ communities when teaching about sexuality, sexual health, and healthy relationships (Department for Education, 2020b) would also help to combat the fact that only 20 % of LGBT+ young people learn about safe sex for LGBT+ people and 13 % about healthy LGBT+ relationships (Stonewall, 2020). The Department for Education (DfE) also makes it clear that LGBT+ content should be integrated into the RSE curriculum and not delivered as stand-alone units (DfE, 2020). Arguably ensuring that RSE is taught well would thus enable LGBT+ students to flourish as they see more diverse relationships being celebrated within their schools.

LGBTQ+ INCLUSIVE CURRICULUMS:

Teaching about LGBT+ marriage and civil partnerships should however not just take place in RSE as it can be embedded across the curriculum. This could include using key marriage and civil partnerships data to explore statistics in Maths or learning about diverse sportspeople in PE. More diverse families can also be celebrated in the books we use, displays we make and resources that we create to ensure that all students are taught lessons that are representative of their reality.

Throughout my career I have tried to ensure that my teaching has been inclusive and that we have celebrated LGBT+ rights throughout the year and not just during LGBT+ History Month. This effort was rewarded by my students when equal marriage became legal in England in 2013, who baked me a rainbow cake to celebrate and thank me for creating a safe space for the LGBT+ community. The way that we discuss marriage in the classroom is however still deeply heteronormative and changing this will allow more LGBT+ married educators to feel comfortable being out in their schools. All teachers must however commit to making this change as it is not just LGBT+ educators who should be creating more inclusive learning spaces if we want all young people to thrive.

LGBTQ+ INCLUSIVE TEACHER TRAINING

One way to ensure that teachers feel more confident when discussing LGBT+ rights, including equal marriage and civil partnership, is to ensure that training is available to help them develop more inclusive practice. There is clearly an issue with training around LGBT+ rights with 86 % of primary school teachers and 80 % of secondary school teachers having no specific training to combat homophobic bullying (Stonewall, 2017) and only 20 % of teachers stating they are extremely confident delivering LGBT+ inclusive RSE (Sex Education Forum, 2018). Therefore, although excellent LGBT+ inclusive teacher training does exist, more needs to be done to ensure that all teachers have the confidence and skills to teach more inclusively. By ensuring that LGBT+ rights, including equal marriage and civil partnership, are explored in teacher training it may also help to support teachers to challenge homophobic bullying which has a significant impact on LGBT+ young people's schoolwork (Stonewall, 2017). By opening up space in our classrooms to celebrate a diverse range of relationships and families we thus give young people the skills and understanding to thrive in our diverse world and bring about a more positive and meaningful approach to teaching LGBT+ rights in the UK.

KEY TAKEAWAYS

- Celebrate diverse families, including those in civil partnerships and marriages, throughout the school year.
- Ensure that you teach LGBT+ inclusive sex and relationships education, including exploring safe sex from a variety of sexualities.
- Be a safe space for your LGBT+ students and colleagues when they need support.

KEY QUESTIONS

- Does your curriculum and school celebrate diverse relationships and not simply reinforce heteronormative assumptions?
- How can you meaningfully explore LGBT+ rights within your classroom, school and wider community?
- What needs to change to make your context a safer space for LGBT+ young people and staff?

COMMITMENT TO THE MANIFESTO

Create inclusive, rights respecting spaces in your school for all students, including those who are LGBT+, to ensure that they are represented within the curriculum and empowered to thrive.

REFERENCES

Department for Education (2020a) *Relationships and sex (RSE) and health education: Introduction to requirements.* Available at: https://www.gov.uk/government/publications/relationships-education-relationships-and-sex-education-rse-and-health-education/introduction-to-requirements (accessed 30 March 2021).

Department for Education (2020b) *Relationships Education, Relationships and Sex Education (RSE) and Health Education: Statutory Guidance for governing bodies, proprietors, head teachers, principals, senior leadership teams and teachers.* Available at: https://assets.publishing.service.gov.uk/government/uploads/system/uploads/attachment_data/file/908013/Relationships_Education__Relationships_and_Sex_Education__RSE__and_Health_Education.pdf (accessed 30 March 2021).

Local Government Act (1988). Available at: https://www.legislation.gov.uk/ukpga/1988/9/section/28/enacted

Sex Education Forum (2018) *Statutory RSE: Are teachers in England prepared?* Available at: https://www.sexeducationforum.org.uk/sites/default/files/field/attachment/Statutory%20RSE%20-%20are%20teachers%20in%20England%20prepared.pdf (accessed 30 March 2021).

Stonewall (2014) *The Teacher Report: Homophobic Bullying in Britain's Schools.* Available at: https://www.stonewall.org.uk/system/files/teachers_report_2014.pdf (accessed 30 March 2021).

Stonewall (2017) *School Report: The experiences of lesbian, gay, bi and trans young people in Britain's schools in 2017.* Available at: https://www.stonewall.org.uk/system/files/the_school_report_2017.pdf (accessed 30 March 2021).

Stonewall (2020) *LGBT-Inclusive RSHE: Putting it into Practice A guide for schools.* Available at: https://www.stonewall.org.uk/sites/default/files/putting_it_into_practice.pdf (accessed 30 March 2021).

REAL FAMILIES, REAL CURRICULUM

BEX BOTHWELL O'HEARN

INTRODUCTION

As the only openly gay girl in high school, I quickly realised that my place in the world was going to be compromised. The lack of gay role models in school emphasised that I was 'different' and my sexuality would inevitably mean I would never fall in love and have a family. Fast-forward and I now find myself navigating even greater challenges. Three important life events have spurred me on to change the narrative. Becoming a teacher, entering into a same-sex marriage and adopting our daughter, have made me examine the experience of relationships and families within the school curriculum. When my daughter goes to school, will she see herself and her same-sex married, adoptive parents reflected or will history repeat itself, leaving her feeling like the younger me?

REAL FAMILIES

In 2020, the Department for Education reported that one in six adoptions in England were to same-sex couples. This was welcome news to my wife and me, making us feel like our family was not so 'different' after all. If more families are looking like mine, then my daughter might be able to identify with others and share lived experiences, creating a sense of belonging. For children in our classrooms who have same sex parents, 'this is the reality of their everyday lives.' (Dellenty, 2019, p. 149). I want our daughter's reality to be recognised, her family to be included and her to feel proud of having two adoptive mums. To ensure that, she must see real families represented all throughout her educational journey, the earlier the better. Dellenty reminds us, 'If they (children) arrive at nursery and see no validation of their lives, the "othering" and sense of shame have already begun". (Dellenty, 2019, pp. 149-50).

My daughter's nursery reacted positively by purchasing and reading a book with same-sex parents to all of the children. However, our initial elation at this was followed by questions about whether these resources should have already been in place? As Barnes and Carlile argue, 'It's the invisibility of LGBT+ people and issues that makes our children think there is something wrong in talking about them' (Barnes & Carlile, 2018, p. 65). It is crucial that as educators, we all equip ourselves with tools to teach all children about the diverse nature of relationships and families, no matter what their own set-up is.

Teaching about diverse, varied families and cultural differences should be 'non-negotiable from the outset' (Dellenty, 2019, p. 149). If the latest government figures show that same-sex, adoptive families are rising, schools and the curriculum need to be ready to educate young people about them. Stonewall's 'Different Families' study (Stonewall, 2010) revealed the lived experiences of children with gay or lesbian parents, saying that, 'Lesbian, gay or bisexual people or families are never mentioned in schools and they find this difficult and it makes them feel invisible.' In addition, 'lots of young people don't know that families can have two mums or two dads and this means many of the children and young people we spoke to had to answer lots of questions from their friends, even when they were as young as four.' (Stonewall, 2010). The children interviewed explained the impact of different families not being represented, or taught in school, claiming 'the job of explaining gay people always falls to them.' (Stonewall, 2010). Whilst it is crucial that we give children the chance to talk openly about their family, it is down to schools to lead and commit to 'usualising' (Sanders, 2016) same-sex marriage and adoption. If we leave this for young people to have to constantly explain, we are inferring that their family does not belong.

REAL CURRICULUM

In England during the 1990s, schools were prevented by Section 28 of the 1988 Local Government Act (UK Government, 1988) from discussion of LGBTQ content. Despite being repealed in 2003, the hangover of Section 28 is still felt today so my priority as an educator is to diversify the curriculum. I realised it was not enough for me to just be a gay out teacher – I needed a proper audit of my privileges, bias and knowledge of protected characteristics. This led to the setting up of a student Diversity and Community Group. Hearing their own lived experiences, it became clear that our school had to act. One student explained, 'It feels wrong that how I choose to live my life cannot be represented in class but other people can because it's socially acceptable.' This was corroborated by another student who claimed, 'I see myself reflected in the curriculum but not everyone does.' In a history lesson, one student stated, 'I cannot relate to any figures we learn about. They are very different to the people who are around us.' Clearly a review of the curriculum was needed. Were we neglecting certain narratives? Was our curriculum even relevant? What impact might this have on our children?

Schools serious about diversifying their curriculum and representing real families must put students at the heart of this and listen to their lived experiences. Listening to our Diversity and Community Group led to some early changes, including consistent embedding of the LGBTQ content into the history curriculum plus a complete revamp of how relationships are taught in PSHEE. Students produced an LGBTQ+ Language Toolkit to equip staff with the terminology to talk confidently about relationships. However, whilst enlisting students to help diversify the curriculum is powerful, they need to see educators doing the majority of the work. Our school now has a staff group dedicated to diversifying the curriculum, responding directly to issues raised by student voices. This has become a significant part of performance management and our School Improvement Plan, making staff accountable.

Whilst current Government guidance on Relationships and Sex Education and Health Education (RSE) expects 'all pupils to have been taught LGBT content at a timely point as part of this area of the curriculum' (Department for Education, 2019, p. 15), it does not go far enough. It states that the teaching of LGBT content should be 'sensitive and age-appropriate in approach and content' (Department for Education, 2019, p. 15), language reminiscent of Section 28 and the stigma around LGBTQ relationships. Nevertheless, the guidance does advise that all primary-aged children must be taught about different family types including LGBT and adoptive families.

CONCLUSION

Without a curriculum that teaches about different relationships and families, we risk children from diverse families continuing to feel neglected. Embedding their realities into the whole school curriculum will enable students to feel reflected and celebrated, giving them and their peers the opportunity to truly thrive in the diverse, global future that awaits them.

KEY TAKEAWAYS

- Real families and relationships should be fully integrated into the curriculum.
- It is our duty as educators to always present real families, not just when those families are in front of us.
- Schools must listen to and act upon student voice and lived experiences to bring about curriculum change.

KEY QUESTIONS

- How often do you listen to student voices and lived experiences?
- Where in your curriculum can you ensure better representation of same-sex marriage and adoptive families?
- Does your institution provide quality staff training when it comes to all protected characteristics?

COMMITMENT TO THE MANIFESTO

Create a curriculum that includes diverse, real families based on lived experiences.

REFERENCES

Barnes, D.E. and Carlile, D.A. (2018) *How to Transform Your School into an LGBT+ Friendly Place: A Practical Guide for Nursery, Primary and Secondary Teachers.* London: Jessica Kingsley Publishers.

Dellenty, S. (2019) *Celebrating Difference: A whole-school approach to LGBT+ inclusion.* London: Bloom.

Department for Education (2020) *Children looked after in England including adoption: 2019 to 2020.* Available at: https://www.gov.uk/government/statistics/ children-looked-after-in-england-including-adoption-2019-to-2020

Department for Education (2019) *Relationships Education, Relationships and Sex Education (RSE) and Health Education: Statutory Guidance*
Available at:
https://www.gov.uk/government/publications/
relationships-education-relationships-and-sex-education-rse-and-health-education

Sanders, S. (2016). *Up close and personal with Sue Sanders, founder of LGBT History Month.* [Online]
Available at:
https://wearefamilymagazine.co.uk/up-close-and-
personal-with-sue-sanders-founder-of-lgbt-history-month/
[Accessed 15 May 2021].

Stonewall, 2010. *Different Families: The experiences of children with lesbian and gay parents.* Available at: https://www.stonewall.org.uk/resources/different-families-2010 (accessed June 2021)

UK Government, 1988. *Legislation.* Available at:
https://www.legislation.gov.uk/ukpga/1988/9/section/28/enacted
[Accessed 15 May 2021].

COMMITMENT, CHOICES AND COURAGEOUS CONVERSATIONS

AMANDA CARTER-PHILPOTT

INTRODUCTION

It is more than ten years since the Equality Act 2010 came into force. Yet, it is clear that our society along with many others globally continues to believe in the medical model of disability and the assumption that disabled people are less than everyone else and therefore ineligible for the opportunities that for others are an inalienable right. This damaging belief continues to impede the effective participation of disabled people despite the increased visibility of disabled people through self-advocacy movements and the development of the social model of disability. Nowhere is this more prominent than in discussion about the patriarchal constructs of marriage, civil partnership and indeed relationships in general.

I want to explore the reasons why this is still happening in the 21st century and why it continues to be reflected in apparently enlightened environments such as the classroom. I will explore the realities and challenges disabled people face and how these are compounded by particular social and cultural expectations. I will include the impact of all this on ourselves and our families (Rioux and Bach, 1994). I will cover the following areas:

a. Context
b. Language
c. Representation
d. Equality Act 2010
e. The reality

I will conclude with key messages and questions for you to consider and take into your schools for the development of learning on the topic of marriage and civil partnership. These will be solution-focused.

CONTEXT

Whilst exploring issues of marriage and partnership for this chapter I have been concerned by the lack of substantive research into this area in relation to disabled people. What I have found can basically be split into two camps:

I.   legal, political, jargonistic discussion largely by those who are not disabled;
II.   nice, sanitised and therefore 'safe' discussion about the issue (Champaign, 2014).

What both have in common is the silent but lethal overriding message that disabled people should not really be involved in relationships other than those directly relating to their disability and definitely not intimate relationships. Both also lack any meaningful evaluation of how disabled people are impacted by said research, which then becomes policy and informs practice (Oliver, 2013).

There is a third group, however, and that is those who have lived experience of disability, marriage and civil partnership. I am part of that third group.

LANGUAGE

Historically, the language around disability has been, and largely continues to be, negative. The collective term 'the disabled' is still used a great deal instead of 'disabled people'. This reinforces the idea that disabled people are a homogeneous group. I and many of my peers reject this idea completely. We are individuals who want the same things as everyone else: inclusion, acceptance and a sense of belonging.

REPRESENTATION

Our experiences clearly affect how we present ourselves to others and I know that when I realised there was a downside to having a disability I became guilty of lateral ableism, that is to say I was determined never to have a relationship with another disabled person and distanced myself as far as possible from other disabled people. I spent many years like that pursuing what I considered to be a 'normal' relationship. I even enjoyed being the token disabled person in the room, because I usually was.

This tokenism has been reflected through depictions in TV, film, and theatre. Fortunately, both my attitude and social attitudes have progressed and continue to evolve and yet we are still blighted by the attitude that we are somehow different in a negative way. One only has to look at television programmes like *The Undateables* (2012-2021) to see what I mean. The show explores the realities of looking for love in an image-obsessed world in which first impressions are often used to make snap judgments. I am fully aware that some see such programmes as opening up possibilities for relationships with others but the title itself is abhorrent to me personally.

THE EQUALITY ACT 2010

The Equality Act 2010 outlines the three aims of the general duty to have due regard for equality, across all organisations including educational establishments:

1. Eliminate discrimination, harassment, victimisation and other conduct that is prohibited by the Equality Act 2010.
2. Advance equality of opportunity between people who share a protected characteristic and people who do not share it.
3. Foster good relations across all protected characteristics – between people who share a protected characteristic and people who do not share it.

Specifically, due regard is to be given within organisational life in order to:

1. Remove or minimise disadvantages.
2. Take steps to meet different needs.
3. Encourage participation when it is disproportionately low.

One of the issues with the Equality Act is that it relates only to employment. For example, you can only complain about marriage and civil partnership discrimination at **work**. If you are treated unfairly outside the workplace because you are married or in a civil partnership, it is not unlawful discrimination under the Equality Act. Proving your complaint is also notoriously difficult (Schweik, 2009).

THE REALITY

The reality is that in terms of marriage, civil partnerships and relationships in general, disabled people have the same needs and wants as their non-disabled peers: the need to feel valued, included, nurtured and a sense of belonging (Bourke, 2016). Educational establishments are the ideal environment to plant the seeds of acceptance and celebration of diversity from the earliest ages so that we can answer difficult questions and work through the solutions together in an atmosphere of reciprocal learning and developing understanding. This is a process rather than a single event and hopefully this Manifesto will be a first step towards presenting richer and more accepting relationships for us all. The *Relationships Education, Relationships and Sex Education (RSE) and Health Education guidance* from the Department for Education (DfE 2019) is a comprehensive guide for both staff and parents in how to address relationship and health issues.

KEY TAKEAWAYS

- Create safe informed environments for conducting courageous conversations around the issues mentioned in this chapter.

- Challenge misinformation and misunderstanding of disability issues through curricular exposure.
- Develop an effective evaluation system for analysing impact, incorporating feedback from staff, students/pupils, parents, local community groups and other agencies.

KEY QUESTIONS

- Teachers: How far have you considered disability, marriage and civil partnerships in your PSHE sessions?
- SLT: What are the main barriers to disability awareness/confidence in your institution?
- Governors: How can you consult with and engage the disability community in raising awareness/confidence in your education settings?

COMMITMENT TO THE MANIFESTO

Facilitate forums for courageous conversations with both children, young people and staff in relation to marriage, civil partnerships and disability.

REFERENCES

Bourke, J. (2016). 'Love and limblessness: Male heterosexuality, disability, and the great war.' In: *Journal of War and Culture Studies* Vol 9. No 3, pp3–19. Available at: https://www.tandfonline.com/doi/abs/10.1080/17526272.2015.1106756 (accessed June 2021)

Champaign, I.L. (2014) *Disability histories*. University of Illinois Press pp. 17–36

Oliver, M. (2013). 'The social model of disability: Thirty years on.' In: *Disability & Society* Vol 28 No 7, pp1024–26. Available at: https://www.tandfonline.com/doi/abs/10.10 80/09687599.2013.818773

Rioux, M.H. and Bach, M. (Eds) (1994) *Disability Is Not Measles: New Research Paradigms in Disability* Roeher Inst., North York (Ontario)

Schweik, S.M. (2009) *The ugly laws: Disability in public.* New York University Press

Department for Education (2019) *Relationships Education, Relationships and Sex Education (RSE) and Health Education.* Retrieved from https://www.gov.uk/government/publications/relationships-education-relationships-and-sex-education-rse-and-health-education

The Equality Act (2010) Available at: https://www.gov.uk/guidance/equality-act-2010-guidance (accessed: June 2021)

The Undateables (2012-21) Channel 4. Available at https://www.channel4.com/programmes/the-undateables/ (Accessed June 2021).

LEADERS IN EDUCATION AS PARENTS

JAMES AND KATE POPE

INTRODUCTION

As a husband and wife who both hold leadership positions in educational organisations we present our perspective on balancing the demands of our roles with the demands of family life over the last decade. Our journey in raising a family whilst balancing the demands of work will be one conversant to many families across the UK. As a married couple with a growing family we have faced the thorny issue of whether downshifting or reducing our working hours would obtain a better balance between work and family life. Like so many families we have had to navigate financial considerations, the availability of child-care and employer flexibility in seeking the panacea to support our children whilst also retaining our professional working lives.

PROFESSIONAL ON PARENTAL LEAVE OR PARENT ON PROFESSIONAL LEAVE?

Stepping away from a career after our first baby was a difficult pull for Kate. The 'handing in' of the school laptop created a feeling of disenfranchisement from everything she had worked so hard for in a professional context. Whilst all elements of the bliss of getting to know a new arrival were fully embraced, planning to work a few 'Keeping In Touch' (KIT) days enabled a slice of what felt like normal for her amidst the sea of baby groups and talk of teething. Kate would have loved a CPD opportunity or the ability to have felt connected to her 'work family' via a weekly briefing email. Upon returning to work with our childcare duly arranged, we faced a number of adjustments as working parents – the complexity of the drop off and pick up regime and how we would work the inevitable book, bath, bed routines amongst mounting evening marking and emails.

FINANCIAL CONSIDERATIONS

Returning to work following a short parental leave after baby number two, we felt the financial pressures of having two children under the age of five, both in full-time nursery provision, much more keenly. Whilst there is financial support for families returning to work, we fell short of the threshold for the government schemes being offered. Against the backdrop of it being more financially difficult to raise a family, we did have the right to request flexible working of our employers. However, with James now working in senior leadership and progressing with his career, and Kate now in what was a full-time pastoral role, it did not seem the right time to rock that boat. To all intents and purposes our employers had communicated that the shape of our particular responsibilities were full-time. One key observation is the number of women in particular who have stepped off the career ladder to focus on supporting their families from home, only to find it extremely difficult at a later stage to be recognised and considered for roles within educational leadership where they now felt out of touch.

CAREER CHOICES

This highlights two issues: the numbers of parents who may be put off career progression within education because they are unsure if they will be able to secure future flexible working arrangements in a new role; the stagnant picture this creates in schools (NASUWT, 2016). One reflection is the number of colleagues, particularly women, who have not sought opportunities for career advancement because of concerns about managing their working and personal lives amidst inflexible working arrangements. This is set against the backdrop of another key observation that very few men seek out opportunities for permanent flexible working hours as a result of their changing family dynamic (Working Families Modern Families Index 2019). Of note is the binary nature of these decisions, enforced on families at such a time of change, and the permanence of the routes we are driving skilled and experienced professionals down.

The Office for National Statistics indicates that in a family with three or more children, it is more likely that the father is working full-time and the mother part-time. Over 50% of mothers said that they had made a change to their employment for childcare reasons, compared with 22.4 % of fathers. A key statistic to reflect on within our own family dynamic is that just 36% of mothers elected to retain a full-time career in a family of over three children (ONS Families and the labour market, UK: 2019). For us, the return to work after baby number three exposed different attitudes from friends and family over how we would continue to make it work. James had become a headteacher during Kate's third maternity leave and we discussed Kate being part-time. Kate will say hands down that maintaining a full-time role herself during 'the headship years' were the hardest, most unrelenting long hours with very little space for self-care and less flexibility to dual-parent.

FINDING A WAY THROUGH

We have identified some key enabling factors for successful shared care roles:

- We have worked for fantastic employers. James was able to take his paternity leave in stages for baby number three, to enable his working role to be fulfilled and so that he could spend some time in the family unit. This was only feasible because of his senior leadership role, so it may be challenging for colleagues in other roles to negotiate this flexibility.
- Being on Senior Leadership salaries, we were afforded the privilege of choice. It has not been without sacrifice including working extremely long hours, but nonetheless we both recognise that this is not something regarded as an option by working families on more challenging incomes.
- We have a good support network. Despite one set of grandparents living four hours away, they have been prepared to help when needed. We say resolutely, that without them we could not have done it.
- Having no pre-defined domestic roles has been key to navigating the last few years. Whilst Kate may have absolute domain of the kitchen, James is the master of the recycling. Both have a shared love of a bracing hill walk, a good box set and a decent bottle of red wine. Ultimately we are able to step into each other's 'family shoes' without a mis-step.

KEY TAKEAWAYS

- The debate around flexible working hours needs to be on the agenda at all schools to create a culture where family dynamics can be discussed openly and honestly.
- Open and flexible conversations are needed around the nature of policies at local (school) and national (system) level that consider 'parental' leave systems that encompass more diverse families.
- The notion that all women who go on parental leave or decide to have children have 'checked out' of work is outdated, so now policies need to be adapted to encompass fresh thinking around parental leave and KIT days.

KEY QUESTIONS

- To what extent does your organisation promote flexible working and encourage discussion without bias?
- How do your school policies go beyond the minimum legal requirement to encourage flexible working and how inclusive is the language of your policies?
- How can we better support the careers of parents whilst on parental leave and be more understanding of the rapidly changing family context?

COMMITMENT TO THE MANIFESTO

To create cultures of flexibility, discussion and understanding that recognise the diversity of the personal and professional drivers of working parents.

REFERENCES

NASUWT (2016) *Flexible Working: The Experiences of Teachers*. Available at: www. nasuwt.org.uk/uploads/assets/uploaded/6fd07ce3-6400-4cb2-a8a87b736dc95b3b. pdf (accessed 6th April 2021)

Working Families (2019) *Modern Families Index 2019*. Available at: https://www.workingfamilies.org.uk/wp-content/uploads/2019/02/BH_MFI_ Report_2019_Full-Report_Final.pdf (accessed 2nd April 2021)

ONS Families and the labour market, UK: 2019. Available at: https://www.ons.gov.uk/employmentandlabourmarket/peopleinwork/ employmentandemployeetypes/articles/familiesandthelabourmarketengland/2019 (accessed 2nd April 2021)

MORE THAN JUST A WIFE: SUPPORTING WOMEN LEADERS IN EDUCATION

SARAH MULLIN

INTRODUCTION

> *'A girl has the power to go forward in her life. And she's not only a mother, she's not only a sister, she's not only a wife. But a girl...should have an identity. She should be recognised and she has equal rights as a boy.'*
>
> – Malala Yousafzai

Gender representation, in addition to other forms of diversity, is essential for society to thrive. Despite research highlighting the benefits that women bring to leadership positions both in organisations and society as a whole, gender inequality is still prevalent within the top Fortune 500 companies (Florentine, 2018), medicine (Soklaridis et al, 2017) and in education (Fuller and Berry, 2019; Fuller, 2017). Despite the advantages of having a diverse workforce, many organisations report difficulties in attracting and retaining women leaders. It is important, therefore, that we consider how women, whatever their marital status, can be supported to become educational leaders, so that they can become the change we wish to see in society.

PAY, PROGRESSION AND REPRESENTATION

In the education sector, issues concerning pay, career progression and representation are inextricably linked. Despite the teaching workforce being predominantly female, just 38% of secondary school headteachers are women. In the primary sector, men in senior leadership positions are represented at a ratio of almost 2:1 compared to their overall representation in the workforce (DODS D&I, 2020). The gender pay gap in education is just as concerning, with women earning almost £3000 less than their male colleagues, a gap which widens further in headship (NEU, 2018). On average, female headteachers under forty earn £5700 less than male headteachers, rising to £11,300 pay difference for headteachers in their fifties and £13,500 in their sixties (NEU, 2018).

Fuller (2017) suggests that personal, organisational and societal matters contribute towards this social injustice. She argues that the careers of women are disproportionately 'interrupted and disrupted' in comparison to men (Fuller, 2017). In a survey on teachers' workload conducted by the National Education Union, it was found that career breaks and part-time working contracts had a detrimental impact on the salary and career progression of women educators (NEU, 2018). It is therefore essential that conditions are created which allow women to balance their competing personal and professional roles so that gender disparity in educational leadership can be addressed.

LOVE, MARRIAGE AND LEADERSHIP

Partners play an important role in supporting women to achieve their career aspirations. Whilst marriage and cohabitation are generally considered positive life transitions which facilitate personal growth (Soulsby and Bennett, 2015; Burke, 2006), sometimes individuals can experience a loss of identity as they evolve into their respective roles in marriage. Spouses are essential in encouraging their partners to embrace life opportunities (Feeny, 2019). However, it is equally important that each partner prioritises their own happiness and wellbeing so that they can realise their potential, maintaining a personal identity in the marriage. Long gone are the days where women were expected to give up their careers when they wed. However, for women who are mothers, we find ourselves living in a society which expects women to work as though they do not have children and raise children as though they do not work. This paradox has been further amplified by the challenging times we find ourselves living in. Whilst we are all navigating the devastating impact of Covid-19, society's biases, inequalities and injustices mean that we are each experiencing the global pandemic differently. Recent research suggests that women had taken on disproportionate amounts of childcare, household and other caring responsibilities in addition to their paid work, negatively impacting their ability to carry out their employment in the ways they had previously (Power, 2020). It is important, therefore, that partners have open discussions about their personal, professional and domestic responsibilities so that inequality is not further perpetuated.

PREPARING GIRLS AND YOUNG WOMEN TO BECOME LEADERS

For years, girls have outperformed boys academically from primary school through to GCSE (Allen-Kinross, 2019), yet girls may lack the confidence to believe in themselves and their future potential. We can help girls to be aware that having feelings of self-doubt is normal; imposter syndrome can affect anyone at any time right through to adulthood. We can empower girls to embrace and celebrate their positive qualities which will be beneficial in their future personal and professional roles (Mullin and Outhwaite, 2020). We can celebrate the multifarious roles that women leaders possess: women can be mothers and partners in addition to being leaders. We can encourage conversations about the possibilities of flexible working patterns and teach them how to be assertive and confident so that they are able to make the future life choices which are right for them. As educators, we can inform children about inspirational women from diverse backgrounds in a range of careers so that they have positive role models to look up to.

KEY TAKEAWAYS

- In the education sector, women are vastly underrepresented in secondary school leadership. Issues concerning pay and career progression adversely affect women.
- Spouses play an important role in encouraging their partners to embrace life opportunities.
- It is important that children have a diverse range of inspirational role models that represent them so that they have people they can aspire to be like.

KEY QUESTIONS

- How can we further encourage boys and men to be allies so that girls and women are supported to become leaders?
- What can the education sector do to recruit women into leadership positions?
- What are the conditions necessary to ensure women stay in the jobs they love to do?

COMMITMENT TO THE MANIFESTO

It is important for children and young people to see women and underrepresented groups more equitably distributed in leadership positions so that they have role models who represent them. We must create the conditions which will enable women to fulfil their ambitions because they are, after all, more than just a wife.

REFERENCES

Allen-Kinross, P. (2019) 'GCSE results 2019: Girls still lead the way over boys'. *Schools Week.* Available at: https://schoolsweek.co.uk/gcse-results-2019-girls-still-lead-the-way-over-boys/ (Accessed: 17th May 2021).

DODS Diversity and Inclusion (2021). *Leading by Example: Where are the Female Leaders in Education?* [online] Available at: <https://www.dodsdiversity.com/news/view,leading-by-example-where-are-the-female-leaders-in-education_206.htm> [Accessed 15 May 2021].

Feeney, B.C. (2004) 'A secure base: Responsive support of goal strivings and exploration in adult intimate relationships.' *Journal of Personality and Social Psychology.* 87:631–48. Available at: http://dx.doi.org/10.1037/0022-3514.87.5.631.

Florentine, S. (2018) *Women still underrepresented in Fortune 500 leadership roles.* Available at: https://www.cio.com/article/3302376/women-still-underrepresented-in-fortune-500-leadership-roles.html (Accessed: 7th October 2020).

Fuller, K. (2017) 'Gendered educational leadership: beneath the monoglossic façade.' *Gender and Education,* 26(4): 321-37.

Fuller, K. and Berry, J. (2019) *#WomenEd: A movement for women leaders in education.* Nottingham: University of Nottingham.

Goryunova, E., Scribner, R.T. and Madsen, S.R. (2017) 'The current status of women leaders worldwide.' In S. R. Madsen (Ed.), *Handbook of research on gender and leadership* (pp. 3–23). Cheltenham, England: Edward Elgar Publishing.

Madsen, S. and Andrade, M. (2018) 'Unconscious Gender Bias: Implications for Women's Leadership Development.' *Journal of Leadership Studies.* 12. 10.1002/jls.21566

Mullin, S. (2021) *Women in education: risks and opportunities post pandemic.* [online] Education Support UK. Available at: https://www.educationsupport.org.uk/blogs/women-education-risks-and-opportunities-post-pandemic

Mullin, S. and Outhwaite, D. (2020) 'You Can't Be What You Can't See: Growing Future Leaders in Education.' *Engage Magazine,* issue 21, p9.

National Education Union (2018) *Gender Pay Gap.* Available at: https://neu.org.uk/policy/gender-pay-gap

National Education Union (2018) *Teachers and Workload.* Available at: https://neu.org.uk/media/3136/view

Power, K. (2020) 'The COVID-19 pandemic has increased the care burden of women and families.' *Sustainability: Science, Practice and Policy,* 16:1, 67-73, DOI: 10.1080/15487733.2020.1776561

Soklaridis, S., Kuper, A., Whitehead, C. et al. (2017) 'Gender bias in hospital leadership: a qualitative study on the experiences of women CEOs.' *Journal of Health Organization and Management,* Vol. 31 No. 2, pp. 253-68. Available at: https://doi.org/10.1108/JHOM-12-2016-0243

Soulsby, L.K., Bennett, K.M., 'When Two Become One: Exploring Identity in Marriage and Cohabitation.' *Journal of Family Issues.* 2017;38(3):358-380. DOI:10.1177/0192513X15598547

GAY, MARRIED AND TEACHING INTERNATIONALLY

SADIE HOLLINS & LAURA DAVIES

INTRODUCTION

On paper, the idea of living and working abroad with your spouse seems like a dream come true. At least it did for us. And so it was that we first decided to make the move to live internationally together. We were excited for the opportunities, both personal and professional, this new challenge would present. For Laura, hired as a PE teacher at a British international school, the advantages of working overseas were vast – small classes, well-behaved students and respectful parents, the low cost of living, the chance to travel, easily, and affordably.

In this section, we will share the important factors we had to consider when choosing which country to work in, our experiences in practice once we moved there, and practical advice for other gay couples considering a similar move.

LIVING AND WORKING IN THAILAND

Thailand became our country of choice for many reasons; the warmer climate, the travel opportunities, the greater quality of life, and its seemingly accepting nature of LGBT+ persons. In many ways Thailand has, as Beech (2020) writes, been 'a rare bastion in Asia for gay, lesbian, bisexual and transgender people'. When we began considering our move overseas, it was always a conscious decision to move somewhere we could live openly as a gay, married couple. Several countries, many popular with expatriate teachers, were struck from our list due to their anti-LGBT+ laws. In our previous visit to Thailand we had never experienced any hostility or discrimination due to our sexuality – and indeed, just last year, a draft bill that would allow same-sex unions to experience many of the same benefits as those of heterosexual marriages was passed by the Thai Cabinet (Tanakasempipat, 2020).

Whilst this is a positive step, the difficulty that we faced when we moved to Thailand was that same-sex marriage certificates from other countries are not recognised when it comes to issuing spousal visas. As such, Sadie also had to find work in order to be legally allowed to stay in the country. The reality was that being a trailing spouse was not so simple – many of the jobs that she took did not afford the same benefits as working at an international school. She had to work longer hours, with substantially less time off, and less than half of the pay of Laura's teaching position. Struggling through this process, we watched on enviously as heterosexual couples in the same situation (one teacher, plus one trailing spouse) were able to easily apply for and receive spousal visas, enabling them to remain in the country legally without working, and negating any worry about how they could remain together if work was not readily available.

For us, the initial disparity between our pay and opportunities could not have been more different. Throw in the lack of legal protection and rights because of our sexuality, and there were certainly times when we considered giving it all up. It was not until Sadie was eventually able to secure a job at the same international school, that we finally felt able to live (happily!) internationally.

LGBT+ EDUCATORS IN INTERNATIONAL EDUCATION

At the time of writing this chapter in May 2021, there is a growing body of work being produced on LGBT+ inclusion in education, that has set out specifically to amplify the voices of LGBT+ educators (Tomlinson-Gray, 2021; Lee, C. 2020; Dellenty, S. 2019). On social media, movements such as #LGBTed, and Facebook groups for LGBT+ educators, have rapidly increased in popularity. These platforms are incredibly important, yet we have discovered a distinct lack of research and written experiences from LGBT+ teachers working internationally. This is further complicated given that many international schools are rooted in cultures that may have very different value systems to the countries in which their curriculums originated. Such schools are not homogenous bodies – they are subject to different regulatory organisations, are often more heavily influenced by the parent population they serve, and without doubt are impacted by a number of external factors including the culture, religion, and politics of the country in which they are based. All of these factors significantly impact upon the experiences of teachers, and that is before taking into account the level of acceptance of LGBT+ persons by wider society. A male colleague of ours who is also in a same-sex relationship, shared with us during the writing of this chapter that he had similarly chosen not to take job offers in some countries because of their anti-LGBT+ legislation. In this respect, he echoed our own thoughts when he said: 'I want to be able to be myself and not have to hide my relationship if I am going to be living somewhere long-term.'

CONCLUSION

International schools offer so many fantastic benefits but sometimes it can feel that as a gay (and married) teacher, you can be entering a situation with very little guidance, particularly from the schools in which you are going to work. It is often a case of 'seeing how things go' and hoping to identify and network with other gay teachers upon arrival. This is something that gay teachers must be proactive about, as it will not be provided as part of any support or training offered to teachers. Whilst the welcome packs provided by your new school may include information for families, and those travelling with young children, they are unlikely to offer any information about living and working in a country from an LGBT+ perspective. It is therefore our personal opinion that international schools could do more to support teachers with a non-teaching 'trailing spouse', and more specifically gay teaching couples. For LGBT+ educators, it is not as simple as turning up and having everything taken care of. The legalities of visas, health insurance, even living together as a couple in a countries where gay marriage is not legally recognised, must all be taken into account by those wishing to make a move.

KEY TAKEAWAYS

- Do your own research about the country you are applying to! It is particularly important to find out the existing laws on same-sex marriage or partnerships in any countries you are considering. Find out if your union will be legally recognised and (if not) the implications of this for both you and your spouse.
- Many LGBT+ educators do choose to work in countries with anti-LGBT+ laws and policies. We are not saying you cannot or should not do this but consider carefully how prepared you are to go 'back in the closet'. Reach out to other LGBT+ educators working internationally. Find out about their experiences, and any difficulties they have had, so that you know what issues you may face.
- Always be open with the school. Consider if you really want to work somewhere that will not be supportive of your identity and relationships.

KEY QUESTIONS

- To what extent are you honest with LGBT+ educators (particularly those in marriages or civil partnerships) about the context they will be entering when they accept a job at your school?
- To what degree have you considered how you can best support LGBT+ staff, their partners and families?
- What are the main barriers to supporting LGBT+ inclusion in your school (taking into account the culture in which you are situated)?

COMMITMENT TO THE MANIFESTO

Within your international context, actively consider how to create safe environments for the LGBT+ educators and students at your school.

REFERENCES

Beech, H (2020). 'Thailand Moves to Legalize Same-Sex Unions, a Rare Step in Asia.' New York Times. Available at https://www.nytimes.com/2020/07/09/world/asia/thailand-same-sex-unions.html (accessed 21 March 2021).

Dellenty, S. (2019) *Celebrating Difference: A whole-school approach to LGBT+ inclusion*. London: Bloomsbury Education.

Lee, C. (Ed) (2020) *Courage in the Classroom: LGBT Teachers Share Their Stories.* Woodbridge: John Catt Educational Ltd.

Tanakasempipat, P. (2020) *Thai cabinet backs bill allowing same-sex unions*. Available at https://www.reuters.com/article/us-thailand-lgbt-idUSKBN2491W4 (accessed 16th May 2021)

Tomlinson-Gray, D. (Ed) (2021) *Big Gay Adventures in Education: Supporting LGBT+ Visibility and Inclusion in Schools*. Oxford: Routledge.

CHAPTER 5: PREGNANCY AND MATERNITY

CHAPTER EDITORS: VICKY AND ALEX FOX

CHAPTER CONTRIBUTORS

1. Cleo de Jong – **Equitable Expectations: Navigating the Teacher-Parent Journey**
2. Mags Gee – **Supporting staff during parental leave: a guide for line managers**
3. Julie Waddington – **Returning from parental leave: being seen, heard and professionally developed**
4. Kirsty Colburn-Hayes – **Maternity, Mummy and Middle Leadership: Aspiring For More**
5. Lucy Starbuck Braidley – **Family Friendly Leadership: exploring career path support for teaching mothers**
6. Claire Neaves – **Beyond Maternity: Recognising the Diversity of Parenthood**
7. Ruth Kennell – **Being an adoptive parent and teacher: a perspective from both sides.**
8. Mark Chatley – **An IVF journey: the challenges and how to support staff**
9. Nadine Bernard – **Multiply and Thrive! The benefits of pregnancy and maternity and how it can set you on the path to becoming an even better educator and leader**
10. Chris Reddy – **Partnerships through pregnancy: Dialing up the empathy in a policy-driven world**

BIOGRAPHIES

Alex Fox is an Assistant Principal at Dixons Sixth Form College in Bradford. Alex has worked in a range of schools in North and West Yorkshire, teaching History and Politics and balances his time working with looking after his two small children with Vicky Fox. Alex is a passionate advocate for shared parental leave and has worked with the Maternity Teacher/ Paternity Teacher project to share knowledge and practice.

Vicky Fox is an Assistant Headteacher at Skipton Girls' High School in Yorkshire. After having the opportunity to work for the Department for Education on their diversity hubs, Vicky has always been a passionate advocate for diverse representation in the education sector and, as a regional representative for the Maternity Teacher/Paternity Teacher project, champions maternity/paternity teacher rights in schools. She lives with her two children and husband in West Yorkshire, on the same street as her twin sister!

Chris Reddy has fifteen years' pastoral leadership experience within the secondary and sixth form sector. He now works as a coach and founded Bright Leaders to develop leadership skills within young people. He is actively involved within the #WomenEd community as a #heforshe, coaches for the MTPT Project and facilitates sessions for Purposeful Educators.

Claire Neaves is a Bristol-based Special Educational Needs and Disabilities Coordinator and Senior Leader with responsibility for Inclusion and Equalities. She has been teaching for more than a decade across primary and secondary, in mainstream and special. She writes about parenting, identity and authenticity.

Cleo de Jong is an Assistant Headteacher at a secondary school in North-West London. She has been teaching for fifteen years, primarily in diverse West London state schools with a brief stint in the international private sector. She is passionate about creating opportunities for those from financially unstable backgrounds.

Julie Waddington is a proud mum to two primary-aged children, a graduate of geography, Advanced Skills teacher and experienced school improvement partner. She has worked in senior leadership, as a local authority adviser and since 2020 has been Director of School Improvement for the Mercian Trust. She is passionate about staff and student wellbeing and champions a holistic approach to improvement.

Kirsty Colburn-Hayes works as a Head of Faculty for Humanities and MFL in an Academy in Lincolnshire. She is an experienced middle leader as well as a wife and mum of three active children aged ten, eight and four. Always striving to find the balance that works professionally and personally, Kirsty is unashamedly ambitious, feminist, political and passionate about leadership and teaching and learning.

Lucy Starbuck Braidley has over a decade's teaching experience, specialising in leading primary English. She is an active member of the MTPT Project, an organisation which empowers teachers who choose to complete CPD whilst on parental leave. Lucy currently leads nationwide Reading for Enjoyment programmes for The National Literacy Trust.

Mags Gee is a forthright feminist, passionate about creating safe spaces and an open dialogue around mental wellness. She facilitates a coaching circle for her Trust women's network, combining inner-city teaching with wrangling a tiny version of herself, taking on the small task of fixing Science education in the process.

Mark Chatley is Trust Leader at The Coppice Primary Partnership, having previously been Headteacher at Palace Wood Primary School. He is passionate about teacher autonomy and wellbeing and uses research-informed practice to focus on developing his staff.

Nadine Bernard displays her heart for social justice as a passionate Headteacher, and proud wife and mother of three. She excels by embracing challenges, propelling forward with integrity, purpose and clarity. Founder of the leadership programme Aspiring Heads, Nadine is on course to positively impact the landscape of education.

Ruth Kennell is married and lives in Oxfordshire. She has three adopted children. Ruth is a passionate advocate for young people who are fostered or adopted. Ruth runs a charity based in Didcot with her husband, which supports disadvantaged young people, many of whom have suffered trauma and loss.

THE PROTECTED CHARACTERISTIC OF PREGNANCY AND MATERNITY: INTRODUCTION

VICKY AND ALEX FOX

INTRODUCTION

There is a wealth of literature already saturating bookshelves that bemoans the inequalities facing new mothers, mothers returning from maternity leave, mothers taking 'career breaks' to raise children and working mothers facing judgement for choosing office over offspring. In 2019, American publication *Forbes* reported on 'The Motherhood Penalty', a sister term to the enduring 'gender pay gap'. In this article, Shelley Zalis claims that '60% say career opportunities are given to less qualified employees instead of working moms who may be more skilled.' (Zalis, 2019).

Closer to home and more recently, in a report from Alexandra Topping in *The Guardian*, statistics are shared proclaiming it '47% more likely' for mothers 'to have permanently lost their job or quit' since the start of the pandemic (Topping, 2020). The article goes on to explore the affordances of 'flexible working', on which the pandemic has shed light. She quotes Sam Smethers of gender-based charity 'The Fawcett Society', who declares that, after the pandemic forced a shared 'work-care' routine upon us, 'the genie is out of the bottle and there's no going back.' (Smethers in Topping, 2020).

When we delve into this same discourse within the education sector, similar narratives proliferate. And much of the focus remains the same; being a mother in the teaching profession is too hard, too inflexible, and school culture too presenteeist. This must be the reason for the teacher retention crisis. A failure to understand the barriers facing *all parents* in the teaching profession is posing existential questions for the teaching profession and society's capacity to continue educating our young people.

In *TES* in 2020, founder of the 'Maternity Teacher/ Paternity Teacher' (MTPT) network Emma Sheppard questions whether 'teacher training [is] compatible with parenthood', exploring barriers and difficulties like the 'parent-teacher tightrope' and 'the juggling act' (Sheppard, 2020). In the seminal work on the teacher retention crisis, *The Teacher Gap* of 2018, Rebecca Allen and Sam Sims advise educational leaders to 'systematically [remove] any burdens which stand in the way of [...] success' for early career teachers, so that the profession benefits from 'teachers [who] thrive in the classroom', so that 'our children [...] thrive as adults.' (Allen and Sims, 2018).

LANDSCAPE

But is this really happening? Are school leaders and organisations considering the 'burdens' that exist in the teaching profession that turn good teachers away from the profession? Are they doing this for parent-teachers?

According to Kat Knocker and Lindsay Patience, the answer is no. In a 2020 alumni publication from Jesus College, Oxford, Knocker and Patience claim that the teaching profession is one of the least flexible professions with a deeply concerning picture of gendered leadership (Knocker and Patience, 2020). Patience founded 'Flexible Teacher Talent', originally a project aimed at unearthing and going some way to solve the teacher retention crisis through a spotlight on women aged thirty to thirty-nine, who are 'the biggest group leaving the teaching profession after retirees', Patience and co-founder Lucy Rose reveal (Patience and Rose, 2018). Knocker and Patience also claim that 'the education sector has one of the worst median gender pay gaps in the UK at 19.7% (2018)'. They put this down to the cold hard fact that 'in state-funded schools men are disproportionately represented at the top.' They share the harrowing statistic that 'in primary and nursery schools only 14% of all teachers are men, but look to the headteacher level and men make up 27% of headteachers'. They share how, in the secondary phase, '36% of teachers are men but 62% of heads are male'.

But why such a leadership gap?

Knocker and Patience explain how the lack of flexibility in the profession means good female teachers do not stay long. In fact, they go as far to say that 'flexibility is nearly impossible if you are a senior leader' and this is why they are leaving the profession. They go on to query whether the pandemic has afforded us a damascene moment. Since schools have operated so effectively remotely, they question, does the sector now acknowledge that school leaders can work effectively from home? Is it too fantastic to rely upon what is coined in BBC journalist Amol Rajan's post-pandemic book *Rethink*, as a 'much-needed global "reset-moment"' (McCall, 2021)?

And will this make a difference to the leadership gap, the gender pay gap, the teacher retention crisis?

These are big hopes.

We have to try. American schools district leader Michael Hynes demands that educators see it as 'our collective responsibility ... to revolutionize this antiquated system built on old structures and ideologies' (Hynes in Almazol and Tennant, 2020). He calls for an 'entirely different paradigm of physical, mental, and emotional well-being for students and staff'. Flexible working, respectful and compassionate approaches are a must if we want to retain our talented educators.

But how?

Huntington School's John Tomsett talks about 'putting staff first' and practises this mantra in what he calls his 'blueprint school', where he sloughs away presenteeist, inflexible educational ideologies, in favour of prioritising 'professional learning and ... staff workload' (Tomsett, 2020). On top of that, Tomsett's school boasts of 'half [of its] teachers [being] part-time', with only a '7% staff turnover rate' ('Timewise', 2021). And if we are to believe the claims that high teacher turnover and a lack of teacher credibility have the biggest impact upon educational outcomes for children, Tomsett is doing it all right. Tomsett makes this point loud and clear: 'A school which does not prioritise ... staff wellbeing ... is disadvantaging its own students.' (Tomsett, 2020)

In 'Flexing Our Schools', Marsh and Derbyshire rightly clarify that, while '[teaching] is a vocation', this status as lionised martyrdom 'does not grant it permission to be all-consuming' (Marsh and Derbyshire, 2019). People are complex. People have complex lives. People are more than their jobs.

While there are many grains of truth in some of the pretty big claims in what we have thus explored (and this chapter will reinforce some of them), we need to widen this narrative. Look at the margins. And the footnotes. What is still buried behind the shock headlines? Which voices in the parenting education world are we yet to hear from?

VOICES IN OUR CHAPTER IN DIVERSE EDUCATORS – A MANIFESTO

We will hear ten voices from the pregnancy and maternity community within the teaching profession. We start with **Cleo de Jong** who provides us with her personal journey on all things pregnancy and maternity. **Mags Gee** goes on to give advice on different stages in the maternity process for new parents and for schools. Then **Julie Waddington** explores the nuances of maternity/paternity leave – and the impact it can have on career and mental health. Following on, we have **Kirsty Colburn-Hayes** examining the economic impact of parenting. The trajectory of a career when you are a parent is discussed in **Lucy Starbuck Braidley**'s chapter. **Claire Neaves** continues our chapter with a helpful look at the issues surrounding the language of parental leave in the context of gender definitions. We range into the issues surrounding teachers who are adoptive parents in **Ruth Kennell**'s excellent piece. **Mark Chatley**'s highly personal insight into IVF and fertility issues as a teacher provides a starting point for us to understand what our staff might be experiencing. Our penultimate chapter is from **Nadine Bernard**, who points out that new parents have to develop a striking skill set – one that schools need! Finally, **Chris Reddy** rounds our chapter off with solid advice about the role of empathy for our parent-teachers.

Within this diasporic narrative, we hope you find some meaningful or validating messages on flexible working, supporting staff through parental leave, the leadership gap and creative leadership, possibly even some answers or direction.

COMMITMENT TO THE MANIFESTO

The teaching world needs to make some great leaps to respect the heterogenous experiences and identities of teachers, including those seeking, entering and living through parenthood.

REFERENCES

Zalis, S. (2019) 'The Motherhood Penalty: Why We're Losing Our Best Talent To Caregiving.' *Forbes*, 22 February [Online]. Available at: https://www.forbes.com/sites/shelleyzalis/2019/02/22/the-motherhood-penalty-why-were-losing-our-best-talent-to-caregiving/?sh=3451839246e5 (Accessed 12 July 2021).

Topping, A. (2020) 'Covid-19 crisis could set women back decades, experts fear.' *The Guardian*, 29 May [Online]. Available at: https://www.theguardian.com/world/2020/may/29/covid-19-crisis-could-set-women-back-decades-experts-fear (accessed 12 July 2021).

Sheppard, E. (2020) 'Is teacher training compatible with parenthood?', *TES*, 29 October [Online]. Available at: https://www.tes.com/news/teacher-training-compatible-parenthood?amp (accessed 12 July 2021).

Allen, R. and Sims, S. (2018) *The Teacher Gap*. Oxon: Routledge.

Knocker, K and Patience, L. (2020) 'Closing the Gender Pay Gap: Flex and Share.' *Jesus News*, 2020 [Online]. Available at: https://www.alumniweb.ox.ac.uk/jesus/file/JC-News-2020-FINAL.pdf (accessed 12 July 2021).

Patience, L and Rose, L. (2018) 'Flexible Teacher Talent: About us.' *flexibleteachertalent.co.uk* [Online]. Available at: https://flexibleteachertalent.co.uk/about-us (accessed 12 July 2021).

McCall, C. in Rajan, A. (2021) *'Rethink: Leading Voices on Life After Crisis and How We Can Make a Better World'*. London: Ebury.

Hynes, M. in Almazol, K. and Tennant, P. (2021) 'Back to School: Rethinking Education After the Pandemic.' *Markkula Center for Applied Ethics*, 27 April [Online]. Available at: https://www.scu.edu/ethics-spotlight/covid-19-ethics-health-and-moving-forward/back-to-school-rethinking-education-after-the-pandemic/ (accessed 12 July 2021).

Tomsett, J. (2020) 'This much I know about … Putting Staff First.' *johntomsett.com*, 28 February [Online]. Available at https://www.johntomsett.com/2020/02/28/this-much-i-now-about-putting-staff-first/ (accessed 12 July, 2021).

Anonymous. (2021) 'The school where half the teachers are part-time (and how they make it work', *timewise.co.uk* [Online]. Available at: https://timewise.co.uk/article/school-half-teachers-part-time-how-they-make-it-work/ (accessed 12 July, 2021).

Marsh, H. and Derbyshire, C. (2019) *10% Braver: Inspiring Women to Lead Education, Chapter 10: Flexing Our Schools*. London: Sage.

EQUITABLE EXPECTATIONS: NAVIGATING THE TEACHER-PARENT JOURNEY

CLEO DE JONG

Dr Naheed Dosani concisely said, 'Equality is giving everyone a shoe, equity is giving everyone a shoe that fits'. Schools effectively deliver a bespoke curriculum tailored to meet the needs of individual students on a daily basis. The notion that that same level of flexibility be shown to staff is one which is only recently being discussed. Staff come with their own complex needs particularly those navigating their way through parenthood and it is imperative that there is a greater acknowledgement of the adaptability required to allow colleagues to fulfil their roles without compromising their wellbeing. This piece will look to explore ways in which schools can be mindful of the external pressures placed upon teacher-parents in what can be at times a very rigid work environment.

THE FERTILITY JOURNEY:

Working in an extremely challenging school takes its toll on your mental and emotional load in an all-encompassing way. In the early stages of a teaching career, when you have bags of energy and enthusiasm, the ever-changing demands of the job and the adrenalin keep you going. As a young single teacher with few demands on your time, staying late to mark books, receiving email notifications at all hours on your phone and regularly running weekend and half-term intervention classes are all par for the course. Before teacher workload or wellbeing were hot topics of conversation, many found themselves prioritising all things school before giving any consideration to a healthy life balance.

I met my husband at school and shortly after he proposed, I was promoted. After getting married the road to conceiving was not a smooth ride. I was a middle leader of a core department in a school undergoing rapid improvements. Not wanting to show any reduction in my commitment to the role, I continued working at the same pace as always, despite now fitting in hospital appointments in my lunch breaks and receiving at times heart-breaking news before returning to work the next day. Schools are under immense pressure to produce results and this pressure can trickle down to staff. They can be rigid and highly stressful work environments that take little account of personal circumstances.

The stress of trying and failing with different combinations of fertility treatments was compounded by the pressure being placed on me to perform.

And so I made a decision to leave.

Not just the school, but the country.

I loved the school, I loved the role but I did not love the effect it was having on my ability to have some semblance of balance. As people grow, they change. Developments are more obvious and explicit the younger you are but no less significant as life continues to throw challenges your way.

If schools can offer a moving day for the acquisition of a new home, should they not also consider other big life-changing events?

New Zealand has just passed a miscarriage bill allowing parents the time to grieve their loss in an official compassionate way. With a quarter of women experiencing this loss in their lifetime this legislative response is powerful. How an organisation acknowledges and responds to major life events, parenting being one of the most significant, is critical to retaining and developing valued staff.

FIRST-TIME MUM:

Many, if not all, first-time parents are completely naïve to the demands that await them upon the arrival of a child. I assumed that not only would I be able to work at the same rate as before but that I would somehow be able to fit in more. It was with gusto that I applied to take part in an intensive leadership course whilst on maternity leave. Breastfeeding between sessions and bringing a small baby along to the social events felt like I was mastering being able to juggle parenting and maintaining my ambitious drive. Much like the early stages of my career I was running on adrenaline and determination. I embraced the trope of being a strong, limitless woman and so the idea that the change in my circumstance required a change in operation was not something that sat well.

Returning to work following maternity leave is a daunting process but returning to work in a new school brought its own fair share of angst. The toll of having a baby that did not sleep for more than two hours in a row was beginning to show and this was in front of colleagues with no previous experience of my pre-maternal work rate. I was time-poor and tired. I had gone from being able to work as late as was required and be as responsive as necessary to being very protective of my time. Time, which had once been an infinite resource to be flitted away at will, was now incredibly valuable and as such I had to be more considered and critical about how it was being used. Little concession was made for the fact that I was a parent with a child under one, that I was still expressing milk throughout the day or that I could not respond to an email that had been sent at 9:00pm. My commitment to the role was unquestionable but my ability to carry it out in a way that assumed it was the only thing I had to do was an impossible marker to reach.

Recognition of the demands of being a new teacher-parent and the reasonable adjustments that can be made to accommodate an exhausting and strenuous time would go a long way to building discretionary effort when calculations about home-life balance are being made.

A FLEXIBLE APPROACH:

Falling pregnant with my second child did not stop me attending a deputy headteacher interview two weeks before my due date, nor did it affect the impact I was able to have in my current role. What it did do was provoke in me the need to evaluate what my own non-negotiables were as a parent and how I could ensure they were fulfilled with no detriment to the school or my career path.

The morning routine as any parent will testify is one which no matter the amount of forward planning and military time-keeping still requires generous buffers to ensure no parties arrive at their destinations late. The debates over breakfast choices, teeth brushing and numerous outfit changes remain lengthy regardless of their daily repetition.

For the past two years I have benefited from late starts, arriving just as the school day begins with no obligation to be there any earlier. The thirty to forty-five- minute lenience is enormously beneficial to facilitating the start of a more pleasant day. The impact on students is negligible as I arrive before their first lesson has started and the impact on my children is enormous. Instead of a frantic mother desperately cajoling them to keep to time we are able to have conversations over breakfast and set the right tone for the day.

I was also encouraged to take as much time as needed to settle my child in for their first day at school. The expectation was that I would require this and not that I would need to request it. A school culture that thinks ahead to events that parents may need more time to accomplish and then encourages staff to take that time is one which appreciates the value to teacher-parents and aims to reduce any outdated stigma attached to having to balance working at a high performing level with the demands of home life.

As a final observation, in schools in which an empathetic approach is taken and staff roles are viewed holistically and not rigidly there are a multitude of ways in which colleagues can be supported at every stage of the parenting journey. Staff who feel that their specific demands are being tailored to will repay this acknowledgement ten-fold. In an industry in which discretionary effort makes up such a significant portion of effectively carrying out the role, the more leaders can do to build up this reserve the better.

KEY TAKEAWAYS

- The importance of support and care starts before someone is pregnant. Ensure the work environment is conducive to facilitate a mentally healthy and well-balanced lifestyle.

- Becoming a new parent involves a period of adjustment. Recognise this and give colleagues time and flexibility to accommodate their new personal role into their already established professional role.
- Encourage staff to consider how a flexible work arrangement may benefit them so that it is something that is celebrated and not seen as a minimisation of their role.

KEY QUESTIONS

- What systems are in place for teacher-parents to access the support they need? Is this support effectively promoted?
- How does the leadership team reinforce and model the idea that significant life events deserve time?
- How is empathy celebrated? Do all staff have a person they can approach who will respond with empathy and compassion?

MANIFESTO STATEMENT:

Provide parent-teachers with a framework for requesting support which is fully celebrated within the ethos and culture of the school before and throughout the parenting journey begins.

REFERENCES

Twitter (2014) *Equality is giving everyone a shoe, Equity is giving everyone a shoe that fits.* Available at: https://twitter.com/NaheedD/status/451847459242012672 (Accessed 10 February 2021)

The Guardian (2021) *New Zealand brings in bereavement leave for miscarriages and stillbirths.* Available at: https://www.theguardian.com/world/2021/mar/25/new-zealand-miscarriages-stillbirths-bereavement-leave (Accessed 25 March 2021)

SUPPORTING STAFF DURING PARENTAL LEAVE: A GUIDE FOR LINE MANAGERS

MAGS GEE

'27% of teachers leaving the profession in 2013 were women in their thirties' was a headline published by the Department for Education in 2016. It was suggested that for many, their leaving was related to childcare. I know many teachers who left the profession citing the pressure of trying to balance a young family and the never-ending workload that is part-and-parcel of being a teacher as just too much. And although many do step back into the classroom, schools and therefore students lose out on high-quality teaching for a period of time. Recruitment is harder than ever, and schools can pay up to £250 a day to agencies for supply teachers, where the expectations of them is lower, and the quality of education for the children is variable. I will explore how we can better support those returning from parental leave, to minimise this loss.

PREPARING FOR PARENTAL LEAVE

Although I did have colleagues who had recently had children, I felt as though I had to unfairly anticipate what I would need in school during my pregnancy. Something as simple as having a key to access the disabled toilet near our office, instead of having to cross the school during the five-minute break time, would have made that time easier. Having to ask to switch break duty spot, as my position in the canteen meant I got shoved almost constantly by students. Not having a clear date for when my maternity leave would start, so finding out two days before the summer holidays that I did need to come back in for one day in September. I did not realise how vulnerable and isolated I could feel in a building I used to walk through confidently.

As a line manager now, I have an informal checklist to discuss when a member of my team tells me they are pregnant. As well as my spreadsheet of 'things John Lewis says you need but we used this instead and found a good website for that', I check if there is time and ease built into their timetable for toilet breaks, or sitting down as they get closer to their due date! I ask them if there is anything bothering them about their day-to-day that I can support them with, so they don't need to feel like they are asking for too much. I try to avoid sentences that start with 'You must be feeling …' and instead offer 'I felt like this, and did that and it helped. Is there anything similar we can do for you?' so that I do not impose my experience upon them and risk stifling them.

CPD AND CONTACT DURING PARENTAL LEAVE

It is worth having, as part of your parental leave offer, dates in the diary of particular CPD or specific training. Make it very obvious that you do not expect attendance, but some people will really appreciate the thought to include them in whole-school professional development. Again, everyone will approach their time away from school differently. Some may be very excited to spend a period of time not thinking about work, but others may find that they struggle with the feeling of disconnection. Hopefully you will have some idea about their feelings going into it, but do not be afraid to ask if they had any thoughts on how much contact they want during parental leave.

Make them aware of their right to up to ten KIT days, and how these can be a really useful way of easing back into school. Maybe they run an intervention, or deliver a CPD, attend a Year Eleven Leavers Assembly, or simply use the time to meet with colleagues to focus on what they want when they return to work fully. If they organise these for the same day each week leading up to their return, that could be used to settle into childcare, for example.

Showing your staff that you value them and want them to come back is really important. When I raised the issue of a hostile working environment in my final performance review before starting maternity leave, I was told that they probably would have dealt with it 'if you were going to be here next year'. I started doing calculations as to how many days I needed to be back at school before I could leave. Make sure staff know that their place in the team is secure and offer them ways of easing back in using their KIT days.

RETURNING AND RETAINING

Part-time versus full-time is a conversation worth having well. I started a new job having been recruited during my maternity leave, taking on a promotion to manage an entire department and starting my eleven-month-old in childcare full-time. I asked if I could start my job working four days a week, just until Christmas. Although certainly inconvenient for my new school, they valued what I was bringing and gave me the chance to get myself settled in for that first term. I used my Tuesdays to take her swimming, and checked my emails when she napped in the afternoon. It made me feel slightly less guilty about being a working parent, and that I had made the right choice in moving to a school that wanted to support me. If they want to return part-time, consider carefully which classes will be shared and how the workload balances for each teacher.

Do not underestimate your new parents when they return to work. Yes, they may be shattered, yes, they may be struggling, but they will have some new skills they can bring to the mix. Having spent the last four and a half years desperately trying to stop my daredevil daughter leaping to her own destruction, my reflexes are now lightning-fast! I have learned to present a calmer facade under stress, and to make decisions more quickly.

Make sure that meetings and parents' evenings are scheduled in the calendar and shared, preferably before they return. I have no family living close who can step in at short notice, so I shared the list of dates with our childminder months in advance. Having a school calendar that links to email accounts isn't a new idea, yet I do not see it done very much. I link my school email calendar to my phone so I can easily check what events are coming up, and use an A3 wall planner in my office to show likely crunch periods where I may need extra help balancing time.

As we have had to deal with virtual meetings for a decent amount of time, more people have realised that they do not need to be in the same room to be productive. It obviously has benefits, but I would rather a member of my team dial in to a meeting from home having dealt with a childcare emergency, than miss the meeting completely or sit in the room distracted and less productive.

If I were building a school from the ground up, I would make childcare closer and more accessible. An on-site nursery for staff, preferably subsidised, would be an incredible incentive for both current and prospective staff. There is great merit in developing novice teachers, but retaining and attracting experienced staff is essential for this task. If you can give your teachers reason to stay past the seven-year point where they are likely to have become 'expert teachers' (Omar Lopez 1995) then you are creating an environment of excellence where students and staff alike can thrive.

KEY TAKEAWAYS

- Do not let your staff feel that you're writing them off. If they want more or different responsibility on their return, listen to them. Do not assume they do not want to come back, because they will then feel that you do not want them back.
- Be organised yet flexible. Children are unpredictable, so at least if school has events scheduled months in advance, that is one less thing to worry about.
- Investigate the feasibility of on-site childcare to match the days and times that school staff need.

KEY QUESTIONS

- Do you have a checklist of 'tips and tricks' to offer those going through pregnancy and parental leave?
- What barriers are there to offering a Re-Induction Programme to staff returning from parental leave?
- Can non-teaching commitments be moved online to support flexible working? Could CPD be recorded and sent out to be watched after the school run? Could we do online training, instead of prescribed hours in school?

COMMITMENT TO THE MANIFESTO

Create a supportive environment for parent teachers, to boost productivity and overall happiness in schools.

REFERENCES

Dickens, J. (2016). 'Female teachers in their 30s leave classroom at highest rates.' *Schools Week*, 4th March [Online]. Available at https://schoolsweek.co.uk/female-teachers-in-their-30s-leave-classroom-at-highest-rates/ (accessed 26th August 2021).

Education Executive (2018) 'ASCL survey reveals soaring cost of supply teachers.' *Education Executive*, 12th March [Online]. Available at https://edexec.co.uk/ascl-survey-reveals-soaring-cost-of-supply-teachers/ (accessed 26th August 2021)

Lopez, O.S. (1995). 'The effect of the relationship between classroom student diversity and teacher capacity on student performance'. US Department of Education, Education Resources Information Centre.

RETURNING FROM PARENTAL LEAVE: BEING SEEN, HEARD AND PROFESSIONALLY DEVELOPED

JULIE WADDINGTON

Ask any new parent what life is like and they will describe the hardest and most wonderful thing they have ever experienced. Think now of these new parents as teachers and leaders who have always been committed to helping young people through education; yet the ability to juggle being a teacher and a parent is challenging. It is especially difficult for new mothers who have physically and mentally changed due to childbirth and are still placed with the societal expectation that they will be predominantly responsible for childcare. Reconciling these realities with a desire to succeed and progress in a demanding and time-consuming career is tough. Women are woefully underrepresented at the top of their profession. Fuller (2017) suggests that the representation of women in leadership in education will not be in balance until at least 2040. As a profession we need to ascertain why there is a motherhood penalty and how, as school leaders, we can combat this.

PREGNANCY: JOYOUS AND FEARFUL

When I first announced I was pregnant, I was fearful of colleagues' responses. Some acted with surprise and unhelpful phrases like 'Was it planned?' I found myself stating my very much planned for and wanted pregnancy was indeed an accident and joined in with the inconvenience narrative, feeling that I had to falsely act as though having children was an inconvenience and that work was my only priority.

Presenteeism is 'showing up for work when one is ill' (Johns, 2010). Pregnant presenteeism, as discussed by Gatrall (2011), is the determination of pregnant women to rally against the notion that they are always off and instead drag themselves into work when they are actually too ill, resulting in inefficient contributions despite their physical presence. I am guilty of pregnancy presenteeism. Part way through my second trimester in one of my pregnancies I was signed off sick for two weeks as I was simply so poorly and refused to take time off due to fear of being perceived as someone who is 'not resilient' or 'lazy'.

Even though the Equality Act 2010 offers protection to a myriad of protected characteristics, the lack of support in initial early pregnancy stages influences the confidence women feel in raising issues of discrimination in the workplace. When you are pregnant, exhausted and sometimes ill, it is very hard to have the courage and resilience to raise such issues.

BECOMING A MOTHER – CONFLICT AND CHAOS

Most new parents would agree that the arrival of children in life is a joyously chaotic experience. When a woman returns to work after living in the 'new-born fog' they are often judged and categorised by those in school as either 'a career woman' should they go back quickly, or 'not ambitious enough' because they have spent a year on maternity leave. After my second child I returned to work after weeks rather than months, simply because, as the main breadwinner, I had no choice. There was an inner voice reminding me that the longer I was away from my position the more difficult it would be to catch up.

Maternity leave should be celebrated as a transformative event, an opportunity for in-school secondments to facilitate experience and development for others and a chance to mentally, professionally, refresh for the on-leave parent. For some, engaging with professional development when on maternity leave can be a unique opportunity. The Maternity Teacher/Paternity Teacher project supports teachers to use parental leave as a time to engage with personally-chosen CPD. In *Being 10% Braver* (2020) Dalton and Mahil both found a confidence boost could be gained from undertaking CPD in this time. The addition of keeping in touch days can help parents on leave to remain informed about changes and decisions. Carefully planned transitions for new mothers, seconded staff and students can allow for opportunities to flourish and improvements to continue.

RETURNING AFTER MATERNITY LEAVE

A return to work brings about the eternal conflict characterised as mothers' guilt. I absolutely wanted to be at home with my beautiful new baby, but I couldn't. Yet when I was being committed at work, I felt I was having to 'make up' for being off. Despite this, when a colleague would praise my efforts and add 'you are such a career woman', the pain and guilt I would feel would slice through me. Support, understanding and a degree of flexibility in the workplace makes this more bearable, so that you can juggle the conflict and the chaos with a degree of skill. Yet it is so often the case that when women return they are seen in a different light.

This kind of professional marginalisation only reinforces the notion of the motherhood penalty and influences younger teachers in their career to concede that their career will stall or plateau completely if they choose to start a family. For many returning to work there is a keen desire to regain career ground lost and an enthusiasm for doing a good job, doubly motivated by increased responsibilities as a mother. It is also important to role model the ability to juggle motherhood and a career for younger women teachers.

LONG-TERM CONSEQUENCES

The Equality and Human Rights Report of 2015 found that one in five mothers experience harassment or negative comments related to pregnancy: this could mean as many as 100,000 mothers a year.

It is inevitable that someone going on parental leave has an impact on a school. Those desperately chasing Ofsted grades and trying to maximise opportunities for young people are fearful of their often key staff taking leave; indeed '40% of employers say they would avoid hiring a woman of childbearing age' (*The Guardian*: 2014). Whilst their fear is somewhat understandable, discrimination of any kind is never permissible and a better system for all needs to be found so that both parties can view a career break as positive.

Many women, who still bear the burden of childcare, opt for part-time working to be more flexible. However, the cost of childcare in the UK is second only to New Zealand for a working couple (OECD 2021), so returning to work in a full-time capacity is often too costly. Add part-time working to the fact that women often have a career gap when they have children and the gender pay gap is reinforced further, with the biggest gap in the over forties age bracket.

BEING SEEN AND HEARD

If schools make reasonable adjustments and support expectant mothers to avoid the need for 'pregnant presenteeism' we can ensure a happy, dedicated workforce that are committed to the needs of their students. Together members of the profession need to address the motherhood penalty and tackle what is often a system characterised by inequalities. Leaders need to be advocates for mothers and fathers in school. Family friendly schools can be created where presenteeism is not expected, with women feeling empowered and professionally valued whether they work part-time, full-time or take extended leave.

KEY TAKEAWAYS

- If you are a leader with children, make sure you are visible so that others see that it is possible to juggle families and careers.
- See and hear new mothers. Ask them what they need and don't assume they are prioritising one aspect of their life over another – encourage balance.
- Establish a culture of professional development and succession planning. If this is in place any 'gaps' at the top are actually opportunities for secondments.

KEY QUESTIONS

- Why is there still a motherhood penalty in terms of career progression and pay in 2021?
- Why do we value presenteeism so highly when it is not linked to efficiency?
- How do you ensure communication and equality are at the heart of your school ethos?

COMMITMENT TO THE MANIFESTO

Ensure all teachers, including expectant and new mothers and fathers, are seen, heard and developed to support them to do the best for all learners.

REFERENCES

Dalton, H. and Mahil, K. (2020) 'Pregnant and Screwed'. In: Featherstone, K. and Porritt, V. (eds.) (2020) *Being 10% Braver*, Sage Publications Ltd, p.174.

Equality and Human Rights Commission (2015). *Is Britain Fairer? The state of equality and human rights,* 2015.

Fuller, K. (2017) 'Women secondary head teachers in England: Where are they now?' *Management in Education,* 31(2), pp. 54–68. doi: 10.1177/0892020617696625.

Gatrell, C.J. (2011) '"I'm a bad mum": Pregnant presenteeism and poor health at work.' *Social science & medicine, 72*(4), pp.478-85.

Johns, G. (2010) 'Presenteeism in the workplace: A review and research agenda.' *Journal of organizational behavior, 31*(4), pp.519-42.

Kell, E. L. (2016) *Shifting Identities: A Mixed-Methods Study of the Experiences of Teachers who are also Parents.* Other thesis, Middlesex University [Online]. Available at: http://eprints.mdx.ac.uk/20805/1/EKellThesis.pdf (Accessed: 02 February 2021)

Legislation.gov.uk (2010) *Equality Act 2010*. Available at: https://www.legislation.gov.uk/ukpga/2010/15/contents (Accessed: 03 February 2021)

Lincoln, J. (2016). 'The perfect role model doesn't exist – we need visibility and cultural change'. *The Guardian,* 12 January 2016. Available at: https://www.theguardian.com/women-in-leadership/2016/jan/12/the-perfect-role-model-doesnt-exist-we-need-visibility-and-cultural-change (Accessed: 01 February 2021).

OECD (2021), *Net childcare costs (indicator)*. Available at: https://data.oecd.org/benwage/net-childcare-costs.htm. (Accessed 01 March 2021)

The Guardian (2014) *40% of managers avoid hiring younger women to get around maternity leave*. Available at: https://www.theguardian.com/money/2014/aug/12/managers-avoid-hiring-younger-women-maternity-leave (Accessed 02 February 2021)

The Maternity/Paternity teacher Project (2021). Available at: https://www.mtpt.org.uk/ (Accessed 01 February 2021).

Williams, A. (2017). *Working mums Annual Survey 2017.*Available at: https://www.workingmums.co.uk/workingmums-annual-survey-2017. (Accessed: 02 February 2021)

MATERNITY, MUMMY AND MIDDLE LEADERSHIP: ASPIRING FOR MORE

KIRSTY COLBURN-HAYES

Government data shows that in 2019, 75.8% of schoolteachers were women. In every ethnic group, there are more female than male teachers. I am a mum of three, faculty leader of Humanities and MFL and aspiring Assistant Headteacher. The question is often 'How do you do it all?' Does 'having it all' mean family life, friendships or your career have to be sacrificed?

At times it may feel like no roles are completed fully and adequately – 'mum guilt' is commonplace and the struggle for balance is always there. As we are nearly three quarters of the teaching profession, we can have it all. We just need to be braver!

PRE-MOTHERHOOD

I started off as an opinionated teenager from working class roots in Barry Dock, South Wales, with parents who instilled a great work ethic of meritocracy and the belief that anything could be achieved. The odds were stacked against me from the start, considering that 'lower social class groups represent 28% of the total entrants to full time undergraduate study' (Connor et. al 2001). Finishing university as the first and only in a large family, the inspiration for teaching was weak at best. In 2005, my drive was that teaching was one of the higher paid graduate entry jobs and could be transferred anywhere.

My early teaching saw a steep learning curve but I developed a very quick love for the job. As with most new teachers, the days were long and tough. My first school whose demographic and context included the children of BNP and National Front supporters, set my fundamental beliefs in ambition, diversity and equality.

'Brave' was a term used from the beginning, when taking pupils into the town centre to complete questionnaires on racism, getting pupils involved in anti-racism projects and presentations, when calling parents who had refused their child attendance to a Sociology marriage workshop at a mosque. For me, the need to make a difference to working-class children with restricted insight into the world around them was and continues to be a driving force. 'Brave' was how it felt when in the second year of teaching, a post with some responsibility came up in a different setting. I was brave enough.

POST-MOTHERHOOD

However, I needed more courage. Within a year, the biggest challenge was navigating pregnancy. The expectation of continuing to work as before, at the same pace while experiencing first trimester exhaustion was nothing short of horrendous. All of the leaders around me were male. I learned that male leaders in this setting led differently. I had few female leaders as role models. And I had a lack of training. All of this meant that my leadership was ineffective. Leadership was a brave leap and one that I was unprepared for. But juggling new motherhood as a new leader was a bigger challenge, physically, mentally and financially.

Maternity pay did not mitigate for the staggering nursery fees that were needed upon my return to work. On reflection, with the youngest now in school, it is unbelievable that even with two professional pay checks, the total cost in childcare for three children is eye-watering ('Weekly cost of childcare is £210 a week per child on average outside London', (Babycentre, 2018)). Some months, the childcare bill cost double that of the mortgage payment. My husband and I had the conversation about whether it was worth returning to work full-time with childcare costs being so high. As an ambitious young teacher, my thoughts were that stepping out would cost my career at this point. On reflection I realise that I needed to be braver and request a little more flexibility but ultimately I loved my job and it was a known fact in the school I was working that part-time working mothers were not highly regarded.

When returning to school, the shift in priority was soon realised. More flexibility and understanding were needed from my school. The lack of flexibility in some schools is disheartening; teachers are expected to put other people's children before their own and continue to work as before. Parents are very good at prioritising time and jobs, but when the culture of the school does not support working mothers and the senior leadership team are all men or operate in an androcentric way, understanding can be limited. Ambition in new mothers seems to be a dirty word. With new responsibilities and hefty bills to pay the 'brave' re-emerged in the form of taking on another role nearer to home as a middle leader.

Schools that have visible senior leaders with children are attractive. It shows that there is an understanding of female ambition. The journey into leadership is exciting and tough. New challenges while juggling small children can be exhausting but hugely rewarding. The 'brave' decision to leave some afternoons on the bell to collect children should not be seen as a 'brave' decision. It should be the norm for teachers who work their hours around their childcare.

There is a need for flexibility if we want to encourage female leaders in this profession. An example could be providing opportunities for PPA time to be taken at home. Maybe what is needed is a complete culture change around childcare and the teaching profession and at least more support for working parents. Working in a school where this happens provides motivation, a feeling of being valued as a member of the team and people's work ethic becomes more ambitious.

Finding the right fit in a school when you are a parent is vital. Setting your expectations at the outset is important. Think about the culture of the school. Are the senior team looking to see who stays the longest each day, or is wellbeing really being addressed and flexible working welcomed?

My final move came just before lockdown, when two jobs, two schools and lots of after school activities in different places became too difficult to navigate. The need to be together as a family unit was at the top of my priorities. The pull of open space and countryside was needed. Finding a school that would fit the above expectations would be hard. Upon hearing the Regional Director of an academy trust discuss the love of education, drive and ambition they had for their schools and leaders, I made it a personal ambition to work for them. The bonus was also that she is a working mother. Now, finding oneself in a school where leadership is nurtured, wellbeing is at the heart and ambition encouraged is refreshing. Finding that perfect setting to help gain balance sometimes takes more than a few schools but is always achievable.

Being unapologetically ambitious in teaching can be seen as a dirty word for women with children. Ambition is not a dirty word; it is just believing in yourself and your abilities. At the centre of everything are our children and pupils who are watching, being inspired by and learning about how to navigate life, career and parenthood.

KEY TAKEAWAYS

- Put yourself forward, volunteer, get involved. If you want to be noticed for your work or ambition, show how great you are. Be your own cheerleader!
- All teachers are leaders including parents – provide opportunities for this, use your leadership as a stepladder for others.
- Have an open mindset – be reflective about working parents; we are always learning.

KEY QUESTIONS

- Does Senior Leadership support flexible working? Can you see examples of this?
- Are there role models that support strong female leaders?
- Are your family at the heart of your big decisions?

COMMITMENT TO THE MANIFESTO

As strong, empowered leaders, mothers are some of the best decision-makers you could have in leadership in schools. Schools that support, mould and inspire ambitious mothers to become fantastic leaders will receive in return leaders who can juggle, prioritise and make the fabric of a school one that attracts and expects the best.

REFERENCES

Gov.UK (2019) *School Teacher Workforce.* Published 18th February 2021. Available at: https://www.ethnicity-facts-figures.service.gov.uk/workforce-and-business/workforce-diversity/school-teacher-workforce/latest [Accessed March 2021]

Connor H., Dewson S., Tyres, C. and Eccles, J. (2001) *Social Class and Higher Education: Issues Affecting Decisions on Participation by Lower Social Class Groups:* Institute for Employment Studies. Available at:
https://www.researchgate.net/publication/268366216_Social_Class_and_Higher_Education_Issues_Affecting_Decisions_on_Participation_by_Lower_Social_Class_Groups [Accessed March 2021]

DfE. 2015. *Childcare Bill.* The Department for Education. GOV.UK www.gov.uk [Accessed March 2021]

Money Advice Service. *Maternity and paternity rights: childcare costs and options.* Available at:. www.moneyadviceservice.org.uk [Accessed March 2021]

Family and Childcare Trust. *Childcare cost survey 2015* www.familyandchildcaretrust.org[pdf. Accessed March 2021]

FAMILY FRIENDLY LEADERSHIP: EXPLORING CAREER PATH SUPPORT FOR TEACHING MOTHERS

LUCY STARBUCK BRAIDLEY

Despite being a large percentage of the education workforce, women are underrepresented in school leadership and mothers even more so. However, some women are able to overcome the barriers put in their way. This chapter interviews three such women and explores what we can learn from their career paths and personal approaches to leadership. In exploring the commonalities between their stories and leadership practices, it seeks to identify potential avenues for supporting more mothers into leadership roles in the future and identifies the ways in which these family-friendly practices can benefit all staff, not just those with children.

IN WHAT WAYS DOES MOTHERHOOD IMPACT THE CAREER TRAJECTORY OF FEMALE TEACHERS?

A brief summary of existing statistics around teaching and parenthood shows why parenthood is an important factor in teacher retention and career progression. More up to date figures are hard to find but according to figures from 2004, whilst 84% of teachers in the primary sector are female, by the time they reach school leadership, the proportion of females in headship has dwindled to 64% (Coleman, 2005). The impact of parenthood on female career progression in education is further evidenced when comparing male vs female headship and parenthood figures; in Coleman's study 94% of male heads were parents in comparison to only 56% of female heads (Coleman, 2005).

Clearly, parenthood is a key barrier to career progression for women; however, it does not seem to have a similar effect on the careers of male parents. This differing effect has been termed the 'motherhood penalty' (Kell ,2016). In Kell's study, '84% of female focus group participants making explicit references to having suspended or abandoned their career aspirations and 80% of questionnaire respondents citing parenthood as having had a negative impact on their aspirations.' (Kell, 2016 p166).

In Coleman's survey of secondary school headteachers, only ten of the 470 female respondents had a child under five (Coleman, 2003). Kell further indicates that part-time working is not seen as compatible with management-level positions in education (Kell, 2016). This has a limiting effect on the career progression of mothers who may struggle with the workload of senior leadership whilst still being responsible for the lion's share of household duties.

The recent Covid-19 pandemic has only further exacerbated the disparity with studies showing that, across the general workforce, 72% of mothers have had to reduce their working hours due to childcare issues and that 65% of furloughed mothers cited a lack of childcare as the reason for their furlough. (Pregnant Then Screwed, 2021).

WHAT ACTIONS AND SUPPORT ENABLE SUCCESSFUL FEMALE LEADERS TO OVERCOME THE BARRIERS TO BECOMING LEADERS AS PARENT-TEACHERS?

And yet, despite the obstacles in their way, some women do succeed in reaching and thriving in school leadership roles whilst having young children. What follows are the findings of a series of interviews with female school leaders (all of whom have children under the age of thirteen); commonalities between interviewees' career path support have been identified and, importantly, the way in which their experiences shape their own leadership style in order to support others are examined.

All three parent-participants in the interviews developed their skills and mental preparation for leadership through a variety of sources; they actively sought mentoring and coaching throughout their early careers and from those experiences gained encouragement, an opportunity for self-reflection and a mechanism through which to manage feelings of parental guilt. They undertook formal leadership training and used negative experiences of poor leadership as a springboard to improve their own practice.

> 'So in my first job the headteacher was really inspiring and made me want to do it and then she left and was replaced by somebody in my second year by somebody who was really rubbish...and I did think to myself at that very moment, I did think "I could be doing a better job than you – and I know I've only taught for a few years but I just know". (Liz Robinson)

There were also clear practical aspects that needed to be managed in order for balance to be kept and there was a clear acknowledgement that settled homelife enabled them to achieve at work. This included a range of factors: reliable childcare, outsourcing or reorganising of household management duties, setting clear home and work-life boundaries and a reliable network of support from family and friends.

HOW DO FEMALE PARENT-LEADERS APPROACH THE NOTION OF FAMILY FRIENDLINESS IN THEIR SCHOOL?

Strikingly, the leaders interviewed had all put in place many interesting and innovative practices within their schools in order to reduce workload for all and to encourage parent-teachers to stay in the profession.

The leaders interviewed ensured that they modelled sustainable practices from the top down – including setting clear boundaries with home and work-life, coaching and job sharing. They established a coaching culture within their schools and remained dedicated to seeking coaching themselves. Despite having been a head for over twelve years, to Liz Robinson the benefits of monthly coaching sessions were still clear in her mind:

> Well, it's a structured reflection time, isn't it? So it's somebody – if they're good anyway- skillfully helping you navigate that reflection and surface what's challenging for you and reflect on what's going on and why it's challenging and empowering you to think about what you want to do really. (Liz Robinson)

Using this focus on coaching and self-reflection, they created a culture of continuous improvement to enable teachers to feel empowered to continue their professional development and develop the self-recognition and reflection skills that were evident in their own leadership styles.

Two out of three of the headteachers interviewed were leading their schools on a part-time basis. Their presence in itself created a culture accepting of part-time work, which they went beyond by openly promoting the possibility of part-time work within their settings. Even those who worked full-time worked hard to facilitate job shares, including at leadership level:

> I'm a massive, massive advocate of part-time working, although I haven't done that myself, 60% of our classes are taught by job share and 70% of our SLT are part-time. Now what I would say is, it doesn't always work, and there's been times when it hasn't worked but what I've learnt over the years is that it can work if you put in place a very deliberate strategy to make it work. (Interview – Primary Academy Head)

In some aspects, Covid-19 shifted perceptions around working parents with opportunities for flexible working in the general workforce increasing from 64% to 84% throughout the pandemic (Jones 2021), but with mounting pressure to close the post-pandemic attainment gap, whether this translates across into the education sector remains to be seen and it is important that the benefits of offering full career progression opportunities to part-time workers are not lost.

IS RETENTION OF PARENT TEACHERS A WORKLOAD ISSUE?

Managing workload is a key factor in women's self-perception as successful and, as a consequence, managing that workload is key in retaining potential female leaders after they become parents (Caudroit, Boiche, Stephan, Le Scanff et al. 2011). Therefore, although it has implications for all staff, measures that seek to appropriately manage workload and teacher wellbeing should be seen as key to the notion of 'family friendliness'. A range of approaches to this were discussed as part of the interview process; creation of a workload charter or 'myth buster' style document which enabled all staff to work to the same set of guidelines around expectation, ensuring emails were not sent outside of working hours and 'pyjama day' policies to ensure equity between parent and non-parent employees were all recommended.

This idea of parity for parent and non-parent teachers is a key point to end on, because the development of family-friendly working practices should be applied to all members of the workforce, including those without children – meaning that everyone benefits from this shift in school culture. The development of school leadership as a career path that is accessible for people with any outside commitments has a broad appeal – not just for parents – and works towards creating a sustainable future for the education workforce across the board.

KEY TAKEAWAYS

- School leaders are key to the establishment of a family-friendly working culture within schools.
- The development of leadership roles for part-time workers is a key strategy in developing parent-teachers in leadership.
- Coaching and mentoring is key in supporting and sustaining parent leaders and developing the leaders of the future.

KEY QUESTIONS

- How do practices in your school support and develop part-time workers in leadership roles?
- What impact does workload have on retention and development of parent teachers?
- How can you proactively model family friendly working-practices to all staff?

COMMITMENT TO THE MANIFESTO

Challenge the hierarchy between part-time and full-time educators and adopt more flexible approaches to working to maximise a broad range of workplace talent, regardless of gender or status as a parent.

REFERENCES

Caudroit, J., Boiche, J., Stephan, J., Le Scanff, C. and Trouilloud, D. (2011) 'Predictors of work/family interference and leisure-time physical activity among teachers: The role of passion towards work.' *European Journal of Work and Organisational Psychology,* 20:3, 326-44.

Coleman, M. (2003) *Women as Headteachers.* Trentham, Stoke on Trent

Coleman, M. (2005) *Gender and Headship in the 21st Century.* National College for School Leadership.

Jones, R. (2021) *COVID-19 and flexible working: the perspective from working parents and carers.* Available at https://workingfamilies.org.uk/publications/covid-19-and-flexible-working/ (Accessed 22 May2021)

Kell, E. (2016) *Shifting identities: A mixed-methods study of the experiences of teachers who are also parents.* Middlesex University.

Moreau, M., Osgood, J. and Halsall, A. (2007) 'Making sense of the glass ceiling in schools: an exploration of women teachers' discourses.' *Gender and Education,* 19:2, 237-53.

Pregnant then Screwed. (2021) *The True Scale of the Crisis Facing Working Mums.* Available at https://pregnantthenscrewed.com/the-covid-crisis-effect-on-working-mums/ (Accessed 22/5/2021)

BEYOND MATERNITY: RECOGNISING THE DIVERSITY OF PARENTHOOD

CLAIRE NEAVES

Pregnancy and maternity are seen as universal experiences. There is a shared narrative and a common language. We are all experts, in some way. We are parents, step-parents, partners; we are children ourselves. We all know how this works. As teachers, we speak to parents daily and we act in loco parentis. We feel secure in our knowledge that this is within our professional understanding, so meeting the needs of pregnant and parent-teachers should be simple.

Yet the system does not include us all. It is set up to reflect the majority, which works well unless you fall outside of accepted norms.

This section explores the impact this can have.

THE PREGNANT PERSON

Some readers will have already flinched, or scratched their heads at this subheading. Why 'person', in the place of woman?

It is a fact that some people who become pregnant are not women. Non-binary people, transgender men, and those identifying in other ways can and do give birth. Whilst many disagree and believe that only women can become pregnant, a refusal to include transgender and non-binary people in dialogues around pregnancy does not make them disappear. Whilst the overwhelming majority of pregnancies will be women, this is no excuse for excluding everyone who does not identify in this way. As educators, we understand the importance of valuing everyone as individuals and finding ways to include them. This must extend to our staff. We cannot expect those who are not women to feel comfortable with the language of 'maternity' rather than more gender-neutral alternatives.

Assumptions around a pregnant person's relationship circumstances can also be uncomfortable. We work with children on valuing different types of family and being as sensitive as possible around their circumstances. Yet for adults, heteronormative standards and gender stereotypes are pervasive and this is no more evident than when one becomes pregnant. As someone who has spent a long time becoming comfortable with their identity as part of the LGBTQ+ community and being open about this as a teacher, it was difficult to immediately be put back in the role of assumed heterosexual woman with a male partner. Casual mentions of my child's father are well-meaning but misplaced; my son's other parent is non-binary. Further mentions of me having another child assume that I would be in a relationship where I was the only one able to give birth. Yet my chosen partners do not reflect this reality.

We must become more comfortable as educators with not making assumptions. It is easier to clarify than to correct and our language must be more inclusive so as to open up discussion, rather than make marginalised people embarrassed to share our truths.

PARTNERS AND PARENTS

Colleagues affirming our identities and relationships by using the correct language goes some way to building an inclusive organisation. But it is often paperwork where we come unstuck.

Most schools have maternity leave, paternity leave and adoption leave policies. The last should mirror the first and the second is for the non-birthing parent to take a short leave. This results in bizarre situations where women whose female, transgender or non-binary partners have given birth have to take their mislabelled 'paternity' leave. Indeed, the use of language like 'maternity' and 'paternity' also perpetuates gender stereotypes, in that women take the bulk of the leave and men are only afforded a short time with their children. Many would argue that the birthing parent *should* spend more time with the baby in the early days and should, of course, be given due consideration to their recovery from birth. But the reality is that both parents deserve to have time to bond with their child and to choose to return to work when it is right for them. In same-sex relationships, both or neither parents may be nursing the child. In the case of adoption, there is not a parent who will need time to recover from the birth and parents may want to be more flexible with time taken for leave.

Whilst Manchester University's guidance to staff to use 'parent or guardian', rather than 'mother or father' has come under fire from critics, this has been standard practice in schools for decades and there is no reason not to extend this language to staff, to reflect the inclusive approach we take with our students. With shared parental leave now an option for new parents, it is time for school policies to reflect the reality of families and offer more flexible options. Schools continue to offer guidance for maternity and paternity, which not only marginalises those outside of the cisgender, heterosexual norm but also fails to take account of those who are single parents by choice, those supporting partners through fertility treatment or those who are taking on a parenting role outside of a standard relationship set-up.

POLICIES AND PRACTICE

School policies are often written using templates, taking examples from other schools and personalising them as needed. This is a sensible approach, especially where they must be legally compliant. However, this often leaves them too narrow to include the scope of experiences I have described above. The law often fails minorities. See for example, the case of Freddy McConnell, a transgender man who gave birth. He is 'recognised by law as male' (BBC 2019) but listed as his child's mother on the birth certificate.

Schools have a duty to include all staff members in their policies, especially where they fall into groups with a protected characteristic covered by the Equality Act. Pregnancy can be a vulnerable and difficult time for people and the stress of becoming a parent is often exacerbated for those in marginalised groups, as explained above. It should not be left to the individuals in schools to ask for rewording of school policies so that they are included. This should be thought of when policies are written, agreed and reviewed. Given that not all staff may be out at work, it is also inappropriate to base policies on the demographic you *imagine* your staff to have. Start from a place of inclusion and your policies will work for everyone. Put these on your website and you will be more likely to attract a diverse range of staff who will feel safe in your school.

If we are to be proactive in setting up policies to be inclusive, rather than reactive and waiting until individuals ask, how do we go about this?

The obvious answer seems to be using gender-neutral language; this includes everyone. Moves to gender-neutral language are often criticised for 'erasing women'. My answer to that would be to respond that women are people too, but a more pragmatic approach is possible! Brighton and Sussex University Hospital Trust's new guidance outlines a 'gender-additive approach', using 'gender-neutral language alongside the language of womanhood, in order to ensure that everyone is represented and included'. (Green and Riddington 2020, pp13-14). This means that the majority is still recognised but those outside of this are also included; the phrase 'women and birthing people' excludes no one.

KEY TAKEAWAYS

- Not everyone who is pregnant or a parent will feel included under current policies.
- If the system works for the majority, this does not mean it is inclusive and we need to go further.
- Policies and guidance should be flexible to fit personal circumstances; asking for the reverse causes discomfort.

KEY QUESTIONS

- How far have you considered marginalised genders and sexualities in your school policies?

- Are your policies and procedures flexible enough to include everyone?
- How can you work with staff to ensure that your policies work for their circumstances?

COMMITMENT TO THE MANIFESTO

Include everyone in policies and practices relating to pregnancy and parenthood, reviewing them to add inclusive language and remove any unintended misrepresentation.

REFERENCES

BBC (2019) '‹Seahorse› transgender man loses challenge to be named father.' *BBC News*, 25 September [Online]. Available at: https://www.bbc.co.uk/news/uk-49828705 [Accessed 14 March 2021].

Green, H., and Riddington, A. (2020) *Gender Inclusive Language in Perinatal Services: Mission Statement and Rationale*[Online]. Available at: https://www.bsuh.nhs.uk/maternity/wp-content/uploads/sites/7/2021/01/Gender-inclusive-language-in-perinatal-services.pdf [Accessed 14 March 2021]

The University of Manchester (n.d.) *Inclusive Language* [Online]. Available at: https://www.staffnet.manchester.ac.uk/equality-and-diversity/training/inclusive-language/ [Accessed 14 March 2021]

BEING AN ADOPTIVE PARENT AND TEACHER: A PERSPECTIVE FROM BOTH SIDES

RUTH KENNELL

Becoming the parent of an adopted child or children, and being a teacher who has children who have experienced trauma and loss in their classroom, presents many challenges. The average teacher may have little understanding of the undertaking involved in taking adopted children into their home and caring for them as their own; what they will know, however, is what it takes to manage and support such a child in their classroom. It has not been possible to obtain figures for the number of teachers who are adoptive parents even in a vague sense and there appears to be very little research in this area.

This chapter will look at some of the issues and challenges that arise in being teachers at the same time as being parents to adopted children. It will also seek to carve a place for training for staff in schools that is delivered directly from the adoptive parent/teacher's authentic and personal experience.

PARENTS/ TEACHERS IN THE 'NORMAL WAY'

The assumption that many people have is that they will become parents in 'the normal way'. It does not occur to them that they may find themselves parenting the very children who, in their classrooms, can be the most challenging pupils to teach; that they will become the parent who has the teacher on the end of the phone; the parent at the primary school gates that the class teacher seeks out at the end of the day; the parent who starts to feel shame and embarrassment every time they pick their child up; the parent who starts to question the core of what Donald Winnicott calls 'good enough parenting', as their many attempts at good parenting are thwarted. (*The Child, the Family and the Outside World*, 1973.)

Teachers who adopt would benefit from a monthly catch-up session with a trusted colleague to ensure that they are ok and that they are coping with what they are experiencing both at home and in the classroom. That colleague could also be responsible for feeding anything relevant or important through to Senior Management where the adoptive parent/teacher might struggle to communicate.

VULNERABILITY AND COMPASSION – AT HOME AND IN THE STAFF ROOM

Parents/teachers of adopted children instantly become vulnerable. Brené Brown talks about courage, compassion and connection as being the core components of a person being able to feel worthy of love, of showing their vulnerability which in turn will lead to being able to feel love, joy and gratitude (Brené Brown, TED Talk, March 2014). Adopted children are often described as vulnerable in the negative sense: sad, open to negative influences, fragile.

Brené Brown's definition of vulnerability flips this on its head and shows us the compassionate, joyful side of love. In trying to unlock this positive vulnerability, a negative vulnerability for the adoptive parent/teacher may arise, as they are exposed as being parents who cannot control their child, indeed, *parents who cannot parent.* They have unknowingly welcomed trauma and loss into their homes under the illusion that this act of adoption will fulfill their emotional need.

Key areas for schools to consider if they have an adoptive parent/teacher are compassion and understanding of these feelings. One of the most difficult times for me was when my child was suspended from the very school that I taught in. The headteacher showed great compassion and understanding but I was mortified that this was happening right under my professional nose. I had to negotiate the realm of the staffroom with the shame of a suspended child plastered across my forehead. But I was protected and supported by my headteacher. This was, and is, key.

SHAME AND STIGMA FOR THE ADOPTIVE PARENT/TEACHER

This leads us further into the area of shame and stigma. Prior to adopting, it is likely that the adoptive parent/teacher has been through an experience which will have brought up many different emotions; frustration, shame, failure, helplessness. The decision to adopt is often driven by the desire to be like everyone else, to fulfill the maternal/paternal instinct. In attempting to join the ranks of normality, ironically, what ensues is that the teacher/parent Is then set apart through the behaviours and actions of their children as they endeavor to navigate the mainstream education system and the rigors of a society that does not allow for those who start their lives on the back foot. The adoptive parent/teacher has a double-edged sword in that they are expected to manage the children who attend their classes every day and then go home and do the same. Respite in terms of behaviour management and strategy does not occur.

Shame is present at the school gate, on the telephone, at parents' evening.

DISPLACEMENT – THE CLASH OF THE PROFESSIONAL AND THE BACKGROUND OF THE ADOPTED CHILD

Social, environmental and cultural factors have a large part to play in this as many parents who are unable to have children are not conforming to the norm within their family/culture.

Children who are placed for adoption will often come from a background which is steeped in poverty, unemployment and negativity. Children are often placed in middle-class, high-achieving families with parents who are professionals. The incongruity arises as the parents realise that their children are behind at school, behind socially and emotionally, are not meeting the expected milestones and never will. Merging these factors is complex and is fraught with often invisible and unknown difficulties. Reference to Francis Galton's 'nature versus nurture theory' may be relevant and interesting here.

Conversely, the understanding an adoptive/teacher parent can bring to a school is crucial. These parent-teachers have been trained in adoption, they know how the child works and what issues they are facing. These parent-teachers can inform, support and help others to understand. Shame then turns to pride when our adoptive children in our schools achieve those small steps that are crucial to their educational journey.

Schools need to be considerate and aware of these issues. Triggers for adopted children are well hidden and can arise out of seemingly nowhere. Schools need background information if they are to successfully manage a child who has been adopted. The key to success is awareness. Schools need to use their adoptive teacher/parents to inform and support.

EDUCATION

The issues at the heart of adoptive parents/teachers in education are complicated. Current thinking is advancing very fast with the onset of leaders in attachment and trauma informed approaches in schools (Bomber, Hughes, Golding) but it is interesting to compare this to a time when there was no mention or indeed understanding of these approaches.

Has our treatment of adopted children improved as the trauma-informed approach gathers pace? The practices recommended by Hughes and Bomber in *Settling to Learn*, such as PACE, require consistency and patience. A schoolwide approach to using PACE is needed for a child to feel safe and secure at school and for a teacher to feel confident in his/her approach. Dan Hughes recommends that we are 'open and engaged with PACE (*Settling to Learn,* 2013). How do we ensure that *all* staff do this?

TURNING THE ADOPTIVE PARENT/TEACHER INTO SOMETHING USEFUL

New adopters will be unaware of the extent of the time and energy needed to parent adopted children. Personally, I gave up teaching to become an adoptive parent as we adopted three children all at the same time. My husband also came out of the education system (he was a deputy head) because I was unable to manage the children while he was working such long hours. Over time, we have re-engaged in education by opening our own charity, SOFEA, which specifically educates young people who have struggled/do struggle through the education system with a specific, bespoke trauma-informed approach. This is a charity which has had huge success using a therapeutic and trauma-informed approach to education.

I am passionate about using my experience as an adoptive parent/teacher to inform and support professionals in the educational world and can only see this as a positive step in the direction of improving experiences for teachers in the classroom.

KEY TAKEAWAYS

- Develop a trauma-informed approach using the expertise of teachers who have adopted children to train and inform staff and policies.
- Allow flexible/part time working for teachers who have adopted.
- Develop a mentoring/support system where staff can 'offload' on a regular basis.

KEY QUESTIONS

- What can schools learn from having a teacher who is also an adoptive parent?
- How do current practices in your school support children who have suffered trauma and loss and their families?
- What support can schools put in place for teachers who adopt so they can be retained?

COMMITMENT TO THE MANIFESTO

Use adoptive parents who are teachers to train and inform educators thus ensuring the perspective from both sides and enabling a better experience for both the teacher and the child.

REFERENCES

Winnicott, D. (1973) *The Child, the Family and the Outside World*. Penguin, p. 10.

Brown, B. (2014) *The Power of Vulnerability* . Available at https://www.ted.com/talks/brene_brown_the_power_of_vulnerability (Accessed 23 May 2021)

Bomber, L. and Hughes, D. (2013) *Settling to Learn*. Worth Publishing. P.79

AN IVF JOURNEY: THE CHALLENGES AND HOW TO SUPPORT STAFF

MARK CHATLEY

Despite the diversity in the world around us, there can still be a very traditional feel towards some things. Pregnancy, and the journey towards it, still seems to be something that is seen as very traditional. The stereotypical journey to having children would be for a heterosexual couple to marry, have a house and then start a family. This has the potential to present a range of problems and pressures, often unseen by many. There is also a risk that when things appear from the outside to be falling into the stereotypical mould, that unseen challenges can be difficult to address. IVF can be unseen. There are no broken bones in plaster or no bruises to look at. I think if there were then people would perhaps be more wary of what they say. IVF can also be incredibly expensive and there are still no guarantees of success. There can be loss, heartache and despair. This is felt by everyone in the process – men and women alike – and we need to look after both.

It is worth mentioning from the outset that I consider myself incredibly lucky. I know that there are many who continue to have ongoing struggles with pregnancy and starting a family, and that these may not always be overcome. The drive behind me wanting to write this was to share my thoughts and learnings over what is undoubtedly an incredibly complex area and to widen our lens of focus on this in terms of what we can do to support colleagues through any challenges they face.

MY PERSONAL EXPERIENCE

When my wife and I married in 2009, we had the future fairly mapped out. We had the house already and so wanted to start our family. Both of us were young and healthy, had never smoked and did not really drink. It was simple – or so we thought. After a few years, we went to the doctors and were eventually referred to an IVF clinic who diagnosed unexplained infertility.

Over the next eight years, my wife and I went through a few unsuccessful rounds of IVF. These were all challenging in their different ways. Initially, we were incredibly naïve about the whole process and, in some ways, assumed that because of our age and lifestyles, our chances of being successful would be quite high. With each unsuccessful round, new emotions were experienced and in many ways each time became a bit like the first time all over again. Invariably, there was a sinking feeling with each unsuccessful attempt and thoughts often went to alternative futures.

We were incredibly lucky. On our fourth round and after seven and a half years, we had a successful round of IVF. We had two embryos transferred and, initially, both were successful. Unfortunately, one was weaker but the other survived and we were able to extend our family. As a leader I think people look to you to be strong and have all the answers. Showing your vulnerability when you are struggling with something like this is empowering for both you as a leader and those you lead. It also creates an environment of mutual trust, where others will check in with you, but also feel secure in confiding in you. By showing your vulnerability, you can appear more human which opens the doors to many who know you will help them to find solutions.

HOW DOES THIS AFFECT AN EMPLOYEE?

The NHS recognises that around one in seven couples have difficulties conceiving. Based on the sizes of staff in schools, it means that it is likely that it is a potential issue for all schools. As an employee in this situation it can be very challenging. Returning to the stereotypical view, if an employee is recently married, a likely question they will be asked is 'When are you going to have children?' Whilst this can seem innocent, for a colleague where this has not worked for them, it can be tough to hear. The employee is carrying this with them every day and the longer it goes on, the harder it can be for them.

Employees always have things that they bring with them to work and everybody's is different. At different points, these can weigh heavily. For example, one of the hardest parts of the IVF experience for me was the two-week wait – the period between embryo transfer and finding out if it has worked. Unfortunately, people will experience loss at this stage if the embryo transfer is unsuccessful. Very often, this will be without many colleagues knowing what they are going or have gone through – it is likely that the employee may only have confided in a leader and/or a few trusted colleagues. This can make things very hard too for employees as they may feel isolated at work, struggling through the grief and sadness.

WHAT CAN COLLEAGUES DO?

It can be incredibly difficult for colleagues who have not been made aware of the situation. Members of staff going through any kind of 'non-stereotypical' family arrangements may choose to keep their circles small, usually to protect themselves from having similar conversations many times over. So what can colleagues do to support these, often unknown, situations?

As with so many areas of diversity, the first and possibly most powerful thing to do would be to challenge the stereotypes in our society. It is important that our standard responses or 'go-to' colloquial questions are challenged to take account of the variety of circumstances that colleagues may find themselves in. The direct nature of some of the harmless questions can make colleagues feel uneasy or upset despite having the best of intentions. Over time, my wife and I were honest with people about doing IVF and that was probably the best way. It gave people the understanding of where we were and prevented further potentially awkward questions. It would be fantastic to see something in school induction processes, or in staff wellbeing charters that addressed this and to raise awareness of staff to the potential struggles people may be facing.

Always approach situations with an open mind. That is not to say you have to overthink every conversation that you have, but consider the variety of choices or circumstances that people face today. It can be incredibly difficult for colleagues who are experiencing challenging personal times to share what they are going through. It may be that they are willing to open up given the right invitation. It may be that you can offer support and guidance. It may even be that you have been there before and can really empathise with the situation. At that point, show an interest in the colleague personally. Ask them how they are – and then ask them again. Be authentic with your listening and, where appropriate, give them the time to open up. Similarly, if they are not willing to share, do not push, but be available.

WHAT CAN LEADERS DO?

Working in schools can be hard. It can feel like you are performing every day and so when you are carrying other burdens, it makes a hard job even more challenging. For leaders, one of the key roles is to remove the barriers for staff so that they can do their jobs to the best of their ability.

As with all colleagues, leaders need to be aware of the wider picture and challenge traditional stereotypes. It is so important that leaders remain open not only to conversations and requests but also to the different circumstances that they may be presented with. By opening the door, you can build trust with your staff which, in turn, will encourage them to confide in you.

Leaders also need to be accommodating of the logistical challenges that are presented. Staff invariably try to book appointments in holidays or out of hours, but leaders need to be respectful of the need for various appointments. It's important that leaders encourage staff to take the time when they need it, not only for the appointments, but also if the member of staff needs some time. It is an emotional experience and leaders should be looking after the mental health of staff too. For staff, I think the hardest part, especially if you are struggling or feeling uneasy, is asking for help. As a leader, I worked hard to build a culture of trust. By doing this, staff knew that they could come and ask and we would always accommodate. By sharing my own vulnerability and by being open about when I needed time, staff knew that the same would be applied to them. Going further than this, it is important to recognise that these challenges will affect other parts of our work. Leaders need to be understanding of the impact this can have and provide support at work. This may be through reduction in duties, support in planning or even things as simple as regular check-ins. Always remember that we need to be acutely aware of the impact of unseen challenges.

It is a leader's job to make sure that all staff are not made to feel different. It may be that a member of staff feels embarrassed about not 'matching the stereotype'. Leaders need to make sure that everyone in their organisation has access to the same opportunities in whichever form they come. By affording them the time and space, staff members will feel far more comfortable and will repay you in spades.

KEY TAKEAWAYS

- Stereotypes are developed over time, but times are changing and the stereotypes need to change with them if we are to create equality and celebrate diversity.
- Circumstances affect people in so many different ways. No one experience is exactly the same and so bespoke interactions are needed.
- Leaders need to empower their staff, both personally and professionally. Your staff are your greatest asset and supporting them to be happy and successful must be your priority.

KEY QUESTIONS

- How far do you challenge the stereotypes of 'normal' family life?
- In what ways do you support staff with their personal goals as well as their professional ones?
- What would the ideal support look like if you were in a particular situation? What is stopping you from doing it?

COMMITMENT TO THE MANIFESTO

Challenge traditional stereotypes by accepting the differences we face and provide a level of support that allows staff to feel confident and cared for.

REFERENCES

NHS, *How long does it usually take to get pregnant?* Available at: https://www.nhs.uk/pregnancy/trying-for-a-baby/how-long-it-takes-to-get-pregnant/ [accessed June 2021]

MULTIPLY AND THRIVE!

THE BENEFITS OF PREGNANCY AND MATERNITY AND HOW IT CAN SET YOU ON THE PATH TO BECOMING AN EVEN BETTER EDUCATOR AND LEADER

NADINE BERNARD

Pregnancy can be one of the most pleasing moments in time. But, it can often become a limiting reality, stunting opportunities of further professional development and promotion. This notion must be challenged as having babies should not stop an individual from thriving and leading in the workplace. Arguably, it will take longer for a woman to step into leadership roles due to maternity breaks, but should it ever be made impossible or a personal aspiration made dismissible? Could parenting actually be a valuable route to leadership?

THE CURRENT NARRATIVE

Whether you believe in Adam and Eve or the Big Bang, growth of some kind needed to happen in order for the human race to have developed. Having babies has been an integral benefit for all, but seems to have evolved into becoming a stumbling block for many within the education sector and beyond. For new minds to grow, for new inventions to be made, for new buildings to be built, for new ideas to be birthed, the productivity of reproduction is key! So why has it become such a problem? Lived experiences tell us about dismissive employers who suddenly no longer feel an individual is best for a role because they are now pregnant or a parent; employers who are unaccommodating and refuse to explore flexible working options; women who feel overlooked and are not considered for training opportunities.

PARENTHOOD THE ROUTE TO EVEN BETTER LEADERSHIP

The process from pregnancy to birth to parenthood is life-changing. There will naturally be ways of living that will automatically adapt and shift, and this creates many personal learning opportunities which subsequently promotes the chance for growth and development. This must not be overlooked but rather celebrated and appreciated. In fact, a lot can be learnt about better ways to lead in a professional space from the pregnancy and motherhood journey.

Not convinced? Let us explore further.

LEADING HEALTHILY

Pregnancy involves regular health checks for mother and baby. It is also important that the intake of food is well considered and that no meal is missed. How many times do leaders compromise their health for the running of a school? It seems that not having time to eat lunch at work is trending! It apparently means you are working hard (please hear the sarcastic tone). Why is this okay? The physical health of leaders matters too. Let our pregnant staff be our role models in looking after our bodies.

LEADING STEADILY

Imagine the pregnancy waddle. One step at a time, steady and measured steps forward so that balance is not lost and a natural pace to breathing is maintained. This not only supports the weight of the baby but ensures no burn-out. How many leaders carrying the substantial 'weight' of a school move at a steady pace? Accelerating at a fast pace is commonly admired however evidence shows it is unsustainable.

LEADING MENTALLY STABLE

Stress can lead to mental health imbalances and physical health complications. During pregnancy and whilst breastfeeding, stress must be minimised as much as possible in order for the body to maintain good health and for milk production to flourish. However, it is somewhat confusing that it seems to be socially acceptable for anyone who is not pregnant or breastfeeding to be stressed. Mothers have to learn how to minimise stress and this is a great skill to have in leadership. It is okay to put your feet up even if you are not pregnant. A well-balanced mind also reduces the fog that can often distort our thinking. Leadership requires clarity in order for staff and children to flourish.

LEADING FORWARD

From conception, to pregnancy, to birthing plan, to childbirth, to after birth, to feeding, to weaning, to food preparation, to toddler-proofing the house, to childcare arrangements – the list goes on. Looking ahead and planning well is paramount. It is not an easy skill but one that every parent has to develop. It is also an essential core skill for school leaders. For both mothers and leaders, being able to plan ahead takes a multi- layered approach and should be applauded.

LEADING CREATIVELY

Parenthood develops a new way of living. Do babies change your life? Yes, they do, and arguably for the better. Parenthood leads to greater creativity. Before having a completely reliant little human being, the adult is able to generally do what they want, how they want, when they want. Parenthood involves much more consideration and forces individuals to explore new possibilities and new ways of working, for example, working early rather than late. This could mean having a governors meeting at 7am in the morning rather than 6pm in the evening, or even during a school day. Making this shift means the important routines for children are not disturbed. There should be no need to stick to 'what is normally done'. It may be worth looking around the table and assessing the needs for all. Lockdown has provided us with new insights of possibilities that can promote inclusivity for all stakeholders.

LEADING PRODUCTIVELY

One of the most efficient ways of working according to author Brian Tracy is by chunking work into manageable parts and then attuning intense focus to the 'chunk' for a suitable length of time. Once complete, time to 'switch off' is required. How many are guilty of simultaneously focusing on a number of things and then not completing anything at all? Something that could have taken ninety minutes of intense focus has now taken two months! When children are in the equation, there is no room to be wasting time. Time automatically becomes more valuable and precious because you inevitably have less of it to tend to work duties. This in itself can be a blessing because your proficiency within the time you have is used with greater care and attention. Switching off and attending to a baby at the end of a working day with the 'gurgles and coos' can also bring much more joy and personal satisfaction than extending a working day at home each evening.

LEADING WELL-INFORMED

Parenthood comes with many new encounters. These encounters shape new perspectives that can be much more relatable to other parents. Schools are places where parents are key stakeholders and being a leader who is a parent can present as an added bonus due to the shared lived experiences and first-hand knowledge and understanding.

CONCLUSION

The learning journey from pregnancy to parenthood is one that should be highly regarded. The knowledge and skills gained are transferable and complement the role of a leader.

It is immensely important that more time is focused on the benefits of pregnancy and maternity, and the added value a mother can bring to the leadership table.

Mums can lead and they can lead very well! In a predominantly male-led profession it is wise to consciously give greater space for mothers to craft new styles of working that potentially will have long-term benefits for all.

KEY TAKEAWAYS

- Parents have a number of transferable skills that richly complement leadership roles and greater attention should be given to this.
- Pregnancy and maternity births new possibilities for new ways of working and creativity that should be well-considered and embraced.
- Parenting is a valuable experience that should not be hindered but rather celebrated in the working environment.

KEY QUESTIONS

- Are current working practices representative of the needs of the staff?
- How can current leadership expectations be adapted to create a greater balanced approach to embrace the valuable role of parenting?
- How are school budgets supported by the Government to promote effective flexible working practices that strengthen home commitments whilst not compromising the needs of the school?

COMMITMENT TO THE MANIFESTO

Greater consideration must be given to allow parents to 'multiply and thrive' and schools should tap into the huge skills bank that new parents develop.

REFERENCES

Tracey, B. (2003) *Goals! How to get everything you want – Faster than you ever thought possible*: San Francisco: Berrett-Koehler Publishers

PARTNERSHIPS THROUGH PREGNANCY: DIALING UP THE EMPATHY IN A POLICY-DRIVEN WORLD

CHRIS REDDY

Through the Policy Exchange think tank, Jonathan Simons stated 'More than a quarter of working age teachers who leave the profession are women aged 30-39." (Patel GA, 2016).

The emotional impact of parental responsibility and anxiety about returning to work can be huge and can change quite significantly over time. It is important that parents, colleagues and schools consider how emotions and personal circumstances can change pre-, during and post-parental leave.

How does the education system support staff throughout this life cycle?

I want to advocate for how high-quality, empathic partnerships can shape and transform not only the individual experience of parents but also form the fundamentals of inclusive cultures in a school and staff body.

A factor that must be considered and explored is the need to support parents emotionally through all these stages, regardless of their gender identity. This will lead to emotionally strong, loyal and resilient staff. There are many aspects that come into play with regard to returning to work after a period of parental leave, but if schools are to grow a loyal and diverse workforce, there is a need to explore this.

Would schools prosper and flourish if there was a shift to a more compassionate and empathic culture?

How inclusive are schools when it comes to supporting parents through the life cycle of parental leave and in supporting them as they fully transition back to work and beyond?

I want to break down what can be done to facilitate the strengthening of partnerships between institutions and returning parents, focusing mainly on three broad areas: What can schools do? What can colleagues do? And what can individuals do to create their own supportive partnerships to build confidence and positively influence the parental lifecycle?

SCHOOLS: PEOPLE OVER POLICY

Building strong partnerships between school organisations and employees takes more than a written policy in a manual.

It does not start with a system or policy, it starts with a person who believes in something. Policy is the basic minimum expectation. If you are driven by policy, you will only ever meet the minimum expectation. It is actually about the culture and the ethos of the school. (Sarah Haines, Assistant Headteacher & Teaching School Manager at Malmesbury School, Wiltshire)

Creating partnerships that support parents is about having a strong vision with a clear and well-lived culture and ethos. Sarah Haines goes on to say: 'Showing and demonstrating flexible working from the top is empowering for staff in our organisation and Trust'. Malmesbury School, part of The Athelstan Trust, proudly has 60 of its 119 staff working part-time using various flexible working patterns. This is a Trust which truly lives and breathes its ethos, demonstrating flexible working from the CEO through to support staff. Their preference for creating solutions rather than barriers towards flexible working is what enabled them to achieve a 'Flexible Working Ambassador' school status. They promote and support other schools in becoming more flexible and create school to school partnerships to help others recognise the benefits of flexible ways of working, not just related to parenting, pregnancy and parental leave.

COLLEAGUES: ENTERING DISCUSSIONS WITH EARS

Being compassionate means recognising the difficulties we all face, and recognizing that sometimes people just need to be heard. (Simmons, 2019).

To support each other fully and recognise the diverse needs of the workforce, it is important to note that personal experience of parental leave or pregnancy is not essential. What is essential, however, is that colleagues and staff are ready to really listen to their coworkers whilst understanding their individual needs and remembering that every pregnancy is different, as is every experience of parental leave.

The role of the supporting colleague is not to solve problems for parents but to be there to listen, empathise and informally help them to navigate the emotional aspects of their journey. Strong partnerships, whether informal or formal, such as line management or mentoring systems, can be an essential connection built on trust and compassion that underpins the values of the school in which it operates. Empathic partnerships like this can quickly make individuals feel valued and understood.

SELF: PERSONAL CARE AND EMPOWERMENT

With just 28% of women in full-time work three years after childbirth, compared with 90% of new dads (Baska, 2019) and 56% of men who are currently on extended paternity leave reporting feeling anxious about returning to work (CIPD 2020), supportive pregnancy partnerships are essential in addressing these statistics.

The journey of parenting is an ongoing cycle of transition. A cycle that impacts both the family dynamic and the emotions of parents as they drive to excel in their parenting role as well as their professional capacity.

One way to bring a truly empowered and personalised partnership is to explore the work carried out by The MTPT project. The Maternity Teacher/Paternity Teacher Project inspires, empowers and connects teachers choosing to complete continued professional development whilst on parental leave (www.mtpt.org.uk). Through self-selected professional development activities, enriched by transformational coaching, this work supports educational professionals as they transition through maternity or paternity leave and return to work.

Creating strong partnerships that work for parents and schools requires a multifaceted approach to provide solutions for individual needs. There can be no one-size-fits-all approach which is why schools must go beyond policy and lead with empathy.

KEY TAKEAWAYS

- **Schools**: Explore flexible ways of working in your school through creating partnerships with your regional flexible working ambassador school
- **Colleagues:** Enter into formal or informal conversations with staff, ready to listen rather than to respond or leading with your own agenda.
- **Self**: Look to The MTPT Project for transformational coaching, professional development and to engage with an existing group of strong partnerships.

KEY QUESTIONS

- How does your school implement a parental leave policy in a way that is truly inclusive, making parents feel welcome and supported?
- As a colleague, how can you support your peers pre-, during and post-parental leave as they continue through the life cycle of parenthood?
- How can you as a new or experienced parent access empathic and compassionate networks to support you emotionally and practically through this time?

COMMITMENT TO THE MANIFESTO

Facilitate open, compassionate and empathy-led discussions around parental leave to build a loyal and connected workforce.

REFERENCES

Patel, G.A. (2016) 'Hello baby, goodbye teaching: how to get mums back into the classroom,' *The Guardian*, 17 March 2016.

Simmons, A.(2019) *The Compassionate Teacher*. John Catt Educational Limited, pp.206.

Baska, M. (October 2019) *People Management*. Available at: www.peoplemanagement.co.uk/news/articles/women-less-likely-to-be-promoted-after-having-children

CIPD (December 2020) *Managing Extended Paternity Leave Report*, pp.10

CHAPTER 6: RACE

CHAPTER EDITOR: **SUFIAN SADIQ**

CHAPTER CONTRIBUTORS

1. Adrian Mclean – **Dismissed, Discredited, Demonised and Destroyed: The Lived Experience**
2. Albert Adeyemi – **Labelling of black students in schools**
3. Ash Pollard – **Integrating Histories: Emboldening Diversity**
4. Claire Stewart-Hall – **Institutional Racism and Whiteness in Schools**
5. Ebanie Xavier-Cope – **Addressing the issue of a teacher being racially abused by students at school and what support our colleagues can offer us**
6. Jenetta Hurst – **Supporting Black female teachers in the English educational workforce**
7. Jessica Boyd – **Culturally Relevant Pedagogy: Putting Students' Identity at the Centre of Your Classroom Practice**
8. Laura McBean and Dr Shrehan Lynch – **Centralising culture in physical education: A Caribbean perspective**
9. Rhia Gibbs – **The recruitment and retention of Black teachers in the UK**
10. Sharon Porter – **Coaching as a tool for developing anti-racist schools**

BIOGRAPHIES

Sufian Sadiq is the Director of Teaching School at Chiltern Learning Trust, with responsibility for overseeing two regional Hub areas. He is a passionate activist within the educational landscape around equity and inclusion. He is a Fellow and Board Member of the Chartered College of Teaching, as well as a Fellow for the Chartered Institute of Educational Assessors.

Adrian McLean is a former headteacher with 20 years' experience in education. In addition, he is a mentor, coach, public speaker and a Governors for Schools trustee, actively using his platform to drive an increase in the number of people from the protected characteristics, 'usualising' their presence in positions of authority.

Albert Adeyemi is a teacher of PE and Maths in Bedfordshire. Passionate about pastoral care and enhancing outcomes for students from challenging backgrounds, Albert advocates for mentoring as early intervention and alternate provision in schools. Furthering his mission, Albert co-founded GMB Mentoring CIC. providing mentoring services for disadvantaged communities.

Ash Pollard is a history teacher with five years' experience in schools in the UK, Qatar and Kuwait. He has held positions such as Deputy Head of Sixth Form, Head of House and Director of MUN. Ash established the Integrating Histories Facebook group which aims to support CPD and share best practice to create an empowering, representative and inclusive curriculum for all.

Claire Stewart-Hall is a researcher and coach who studies the role race plays in institutions. Her research uses Critical Race Theory to embed anti-racist practice through interrogating whiteness as an ideological framework. Claire is a former school leader who founded Equitable Coaching, which uses coaching to rethink inequity in organisations.

Ebanie Xavier-Cope has been a teacher since 2011, spending the first five years of her career as a secondary music teacher before moving to teach in primary schools. She is currently a middle leader and has had whole school responsibility experience covering performing arts, English and Black History Month.

Jenetta Hurst is a music specialist with fifteen years' experience in secondary school middle and senior leadership. Jenetta's interests are staff development, ITT and teacher induction. Jenetta is an alumnus of UCL Institute of Education (MA Leadership), an Honorary Member of the Birmingham Conservatoire and founder of The Creative-Educator.com.

Jessica Boyd is a music teacher by trade and taught across London for ten years. She co-founded the BAME Network at Teach First and now works in initial teacher training. Currently Director of Participants and Alumni Impact at Teach for All, Jessica supports teachers to refine their equity and inclusion practices.

Laura McBean is a physical educator and doctoral student at the University of East London. Her research focus includes critical whiteness studies in physical education. **Dr Shrehan Lynch** is a Senior Lecturer within Initial Teacher Education at the University of East London. Her research focus includes equitable physical education.

Rhia Gibbs currently teaches Sociology to Years 9 -13 and Criminology to Year 12. She studied Sociology at The University of Birmingham before going onto train as a teacher at the IOE where she completed the PGCE in Social Science. She also has a background in Youth Work. Rhia believes that Black teachers need more representation in the education system at all levels and they need to have a system of support, hence she created Black Teachers Connect. This is aimed at supporting both the recruitment and retention of Black teachers through providing support, training and CPD.

Sharon Porter is an experienced educator and researcher with expertise in Research Methods and Professional Development. She has been a Specialist Leader in Education, Lead Practitioner, and Head of Mathematics in inner city Bristol schools. Through her consultancy Sharon provides coaching and mentoring for educators working in schools, colleges, and universities.

THE PROTECTED CHARACTERISTIC OF RACE: INTRODUCTION

SUFIAN SADIQ

INTRODUCTION

> Racism cannot be defined without first defining race. Among social scientists, 'race' is generally understood as a social construct. Although biologically meaningless when applied to humans … race nevertheless has tremendous significance in structuring social reality. (Clair, M. Denis, J.S. 2015)

The term 'race' has become a powerful root word, from which derives the term 'Racism': at the simplest level *the unfair treatment of people who belong to a different race,* Oxford English Dictionary (2021). It is this that drives the discussions in society whether it is in the terraces of football stadiums or in the corridors of schools, the question of 'us' and 'them' is becoming increasingly more prevalent in society. Differences exist amongst humans, but it is the amplification and degradation of differences, especially those that are visible which affects educators across our sector. A more recent term used in education is 'anti-racism', where the focus has shifted from addressing the issue of racism in schools, to becoming schools that are vocally against it in all its forms.

This chapter provides readers with insights from educators that have not only provided unique perspectives but also a glimpse into the impact race and how it is viewed in society has had on their experiences as an educator.

DEFINITIONS AND TERMINOLOGY

If I look back at my personal journey, it is interesting coming from a community that is a minority but as many young children from minority ethnic backgrounds will have experienced, you do not truly appreciate this when you live in areas within the United Kingdom that have high levels of ethnic minorities concentrated in a particular geographical area. This is also reflected in the way teachers are spread across the UK, with 46% of schools having no BAME staff and 16% of schools in the

UK employing over 20% of BAME staff (UCL 2021). This false illusion creates a sense of safety early on and therefore you do not necessarily develop the resilience that you may need in later life. Many would ask: 'Why is resilience needed when it comes to being a minority?' but sadly as we have seen in recent times, racism is still rife in mainstream society as evidenced in the statistical data which shows a significant year on year increase in reported incidents from 47,548 in 2012 to 76,070 in 2019 (Statista). Therefore, resilience is a key characteristic needed to simply survive and thrive in society, if you are a minority. The abuse you will receive as a young black footballer is distinctly different to that a white footballer may receive, as evidently seen in the cases of Raheem Sterling and more recently with Marcus Rashford and Bukayo Saka. This is even prevalent in the way commentators within sports speak about sports people from minority backgrounds (Campbell and Bebb, 2020).

Entering the teaching profession, I realised early on that although many students looked like me, only a minority of staff truly represented me. The further up you look in an organisational chart, the more unlikely you are to find yourself represented as an educator from a minority background, with only 3% of Headteachers coming from a minority ethnic background (DfE 2018 Statement of Intent on the diversity of the teaching workforce). This lack of representation manifests itself in the decisions being made and the language being used, which whether intentional or not, leads to a fertile culture for discrimination to thrive in. The perspectives of educators cannot be summed up with broad generalisations; some work in diverse communities and schools, where they are represented at a teaching or support staff level, others work in less diverse communities and although they are not represented proportionately, this does not mean they have experienced discrimination due to their race. However, the loneliness is more profound and the stories from BAME professionals are a lot more harrowing than those from further up the food chain. The sector is grappling with the sheer dominance of one race at the very top, which not only fails to represent the diversity that exists amongst people of different racial backgrounds, but also fails to represent a number of other protected characteristics.

LANDSCAPE

In recent times, whether this is through the murder of George Floyd and the subsequent rise in the Black Lives Matter movement, or the debates around the treatment of members of the royal family and popular sporting figures, the debate around race has now taken centre stage. It is the focus of discussion in organisations and schools are desperately looking at inclusive curriculums as a quick fix and solution. The governmental response in the form of the *Commission on Race and Ethnic Disparities Report* (Sewell, 2021), further fuelled the debate through essentially denying the existence of institutional racism. However, what we do know is that the key challenge which cannot be addressed overnight is the lack of diversity at teacher recruitment and the lack of progression into senior leadership of staff currently within the system. These blockages cannot be cleared overnight and require a systemic approach to redressing the balance. The key takeaways and actions recommended by contributors in this chapter provide pragmatic solutions that can be implemented at an organisational level which can make a positive difference. We fully appreciate that the real difference can only come about as a result of policy change in education on a macro scale as opposed to organisational change at micro level within the system.

VOICES IN OUR CHAPTER IN DIVERSE EDUCATORS – A MANIFESTO

In the first chapter, **Adrian McLean** takes us through the four-stage journey many black leaders experience. This starts with micro aggressions and being constantly 'dismissed', this then moves on to being 'discredited' and 'demonised'. Finally, the journey of a leader ends with their career and ambitions being 'Destroyed.' In our second chapter **Albert Adeyemi** looks at the impact of labels and how young black males are currently labelled in society. He explores the impact of labelling and the disadvantages this creates very early on for these students. In our third chapter **Ash Pollard** explores integrating histories, to help bring a sense of diversity in the history we teach. This chapter powerfully identifies existing curriculum opportunities where the diversity has been conveniently forgotten over time. **Claire Stewart-Hall** challenges the whiteness that exists in schools and the concept of institutional racism, something which has become controversial in recent times through governmental published reports denying this is an issue. This chapter looks at the impact of processes, policies and attitudes in organisations. **Ebanie Xavier-Cope,** in her chapter, provides a moving insight into the impact of racism from pupils to staff, something often forgotten when speaking of the issue of race within education. In the sixth chapter **Jenetta Hurst** looks at the stereotypes and challenges faced by black female educators, looking at her own experiences teaching Music and the wider impact on the school community. **Jessica Boyd** looks into culturally relevant pedagogy, focusing on how the educator can allow pupils to maintain their cultural integrity whilst achieving academic success. **Laura McBean and Dr Shrehan Lynch** provide a Caribbean perspective of physical education – they challenge eurocentrism in PE, whilst creating a real sense of understanding around how cultures being embraced at the heart of PE link directly to improved performance and participation. **Rhia Gibbs,** in our ninth chapter, explores the challenges that exist within the recruitment of black teachers into the profession, which consistently fails to reflect the general population and pupil population statistics. This chapter also looks at the impact on the sector as a result of black teachers leaving the profession due to lack of inclusion and opportunities. Our final chapter by **Sharon Porter** looks at how coaching can be used to develop more anti-racist schools, moving people from the manifesto stages to commitment and action to change.

CONCLUSION

Teachers from minority ethnic backgrounds carry the same passion for imparting knowledge, the same ambitions for making a change and progressing within an organisation as their white counterparts. Time has come for us all to ask the difficult question, 'Is our organisation racist?' We can no longer sit back and see this as an issue for those from minority backgrounds, because it is an issue for us all and therefore we either become allies or remain a part of the problem. If we do not show our teachers from minority ethnic backgrounds that they can be leaders of our schools, then we cannot with any integrity say this to our pupils from the same backgrounds in our classes.

COMMITMENT TO THE MANIFESTO

To ensure racism is called out in every educational organisation and a clear commitment to be anti-racists and allies against racism is at the heart of every organisation's commitment moving forward.

REFERENCES

Campbell, P.I. and Bebb, L. (2020). '"He is like a Gazelle (when he runs)": (re) constructing race and nation in match-day commentary at the men's 2018 FIFA World Cup.' *Sport in Society*, pp.1–19.

Clair, M. and Denis, J.S. (2015). 'Sociology of Racism'. *International Encyclopedia of the Social and Behavioral Sciences*, 2nd edition, volume 19. Available at: https://projects. iq.harvard.edu/files/deib-explorer/files/sociology_of_racism.pdf

GOV.UK. (n.d.). *Diversity of the teaching workforce: statement of intent.* [online] Available at:
https://www.gov.uk/government/publications/
diversity-of-the-teaching-workforce-statement-of-intent

Statista. (n.d.). *Racist incidents in England and Wales 2020*. [online] Available at: https://www.statista.com/statistics/624093/racist-incidents-in-england-and-wales-2009-2018/.

Sewell, T. (2021). *Commission on Race and Ethnic Disparities: The Report.* [online]. Available at: https://assets.publishing.service.gov.uk/government/uploads/system/uploads/attachment_data/file/974507/20210331_-_CRED_Report_-_FINAL_-_Web_Accessible.pdf.

UCL (2019). *Retention of teachers from minority ethnic groups in disadvantaged schools.* [online] Institute of Education. Available at: https://www.ucl.ac.uk/ioe/departments-and-centres/centres/centre-teachers-and-teaching-research/retention-teachers-minority-ethnic-groups-disadvantaged-schools [Accessed 30 Jul. 2021].

DISMISSED, DISCREDITED, DEMONISED AND DESTROYED: THE LIVED EXPERIENCE

ADRIAN MCLEAN

INTRODUCTION

People of colour are significantly underrepresented in senior leader and headteacher positions. In this chapter, you will learn how the four-stage process of Dismissing, Discrediting, Demonisation and Destroying (Allen, 2019) maintains the status quo with everyday real-life examples. The chapter concludes with some key takeaways and questions for you to examine its presence in your setting.

THE 4 STAGES

The path to the summit that is senior leadership is not an easy one. It's even trickier when you look at the number of Black males who achieve this feat. Many are called, few are chosen, literally! Getting a seat at the table... a chance to shape the lives of young people and make positive change in our communities has a high degree of difficulty. This tale encompasses fear, frustration and a failure of fairness for people who are melanin-rich. Though it may sound like a cliche, many people of colour experience this negative four-stage process in leadership positions in schools.

FIRST THEY DISMISS YOU

The first step of dismissal is the most obvious and frustrating step. The recipient is made to feel insignificant, like all the brilliance they showed to be appointed to the role is no longer relevant. Their knowledge, ability and most importantly their 'lived' experience is dismissed, brushed to the side as if they do not have what it takes, or their viewpoint is irrelevant. It starts subtly, such as when presenting a strategic plan. When reading the room, you find the body language displayed is closed. Folded arms, smirks, furrowed brows, knowing looks between colleagues and eye-rolling. The presented strategies are shot down as 'previously tried', 'unsuccessful', 'won't work here' or not priorities 'we' want to focus on. Your knowledge and prior experience count for nothing. The desire to keep the status quo remains strong, and that sense of frustration begins to burn inside you.

THEN THEY DISCREDIT YOU

The frustration in you starts to grow from the dismissal of your ideas; strategies that you know work and are evidence-based. Despite the dismissal of key parts of your strategy, you tentatively push on. Your ideas and initiatives are quietly working, gaining momentum. However, something has changed. You feel the eyes start to burn a hole in you. The whispers start. You notice it, and begin to second guess yourself. Am I paranoid? It has begun. Snide remarks are made outside of your presence by senior colleagues, who flatly deny it when you broach the subject. The same colleagues undermine your decisions, processes and systems across the organisation. The scrutiny becomes more intrusive and your work ethic, character, effort, communication, time on site are suddenly called into question. You feel you have to be significantly better than your peers. The walls feel like they are closing in. The whispers get louder, and the silence is deafening when you enter the room. Nobody tells you what is going on... everyone knows but you, as you are being discredited behind your back.

THEN THEY DEMONISE YOU

The inherent lack of fairness begins to eat away at you. You question yourself. Have I got this wrong? Is my self- awareness off? You check yourself. You put more hours in. Your work ethic is through the roof trying to prove your worth, showing your ideas/strategies work. The first two stages get repeated. You are hurting, tired of the snide remarks, the lack of public support from senior colleagues has you feeling like you're suffocating. You get frustrated and speak out assertively, like your colleagues do. KABOOM! Your response is a huge shock to everyone. Your behaviour is deemed unprofessional. Your attitude is called into question. You are demonised for standing your ground. Labelled as argumentative, aggressive, arrogant, intimidating and defiant... rather than enthusiastic, passionate, confident, courageous or sceptical, like your colleagues are when they speak out. Words are powerfully used here to position you in a negative light and paint you to be a monster. The narrative is set. This is the justification required to silence you and move onto the final stage.

FINALLY, THEY DESTROY YOU

Once you have been demonised, the supporters you have are forced to pick a side. Do they stay with you or do they move their support to that of the power base? It no longer is about the ideas/strategy. It is now personal. It is made known that you are 'trouble' and your authority is taken away. The credibility that you had built up with students, staff and parents is systematically eroded. Those whispers you heard previously have become ear-shattering. You are micromanaged, overruled and left powerless to stop the inevitable happening. The inevitable being you cannot continue in this role. You are moved sideways, into another role, or worse, faced with actions to support your 'competency'. Your self-esteem is shredded, leading to your self-belief falling off the cliff. You are made to feel that you have it all wrong and you do not have what it takes to be a senior leader. Many are left scarred by this process and unwilling to put their head above the parapet again. Many observers are put off as they watch what happens.

THE CHALLENGE

It does not have to end this way. This tale has the power to break that concrete ceiling and diminish the dismissal, discrediting, demonising and destroying of talented colleagues of colour. When you know better, you do better. The status quo is not one that promotes a diverse, equitable or inclusive society and that must change. The challenge for all of us is to increase the 'usualisation' (Sanders, 2010) of people in colour in positions of authority. After reading this, you now have the knowledge. It is said that knowledge applied is power. You now have the knowledge to prevent this happening. How will you turn that into power?

KEY TAKEAWAYS

- **Dismiss** – colleagues of colour often have their lived experiences dismissed as trivial or not important/relevant.
- **Discredit** – the 'behind the back' conversations to undermine colleagues' authority and questioning of decision-making is significantly damaging.
- **Demonise** – the choice of language used to describe is deliberately negative in a play to isolate that colleague and silence their voice/influence.
- **Destroy** – colleagues' credibility, competency and character are overtly questioned. Their self-esteem is destroyed, often leading to them leaving the role.

KEY QUESTIONS

- Where have you seen this before? Where have you missed the chance to be an ally?
- How can you be an inclusive ally to prevent this cycle happening in your organisation?
- How prepared am I for the energy/effort required?

COMMITMENT TO THE MANIFESTO

To challenge the use of the four Ds in your context through speaking up and calling out these behaviours.

REFERENCES

Allen, B. (2019). *The Breakfast Club*. [Radio] New York: iHeartMedia. Available at: <https://www.youtube.com/watch?v=gEsMFlh1MLk> [Accessed 6 July 2021].

Sanders, S. (2010) *'Usualising' and 'Actualising.'* http://the-classroom.org.uk

LABELLING OF BLACK STUDENTS IN SCHOOLS

ALBERT ADEYEMI

INTRODUCTION

Troublemaker, aggressive, confrontational, lazy, loud, the list goes on. These are just some of the labels placed on our black students daily within the education system. Often these labels are given by teachers due to prejudice, bias, and stereotypes. In some cases, students are given titles within minutes of meeting teachers, and this label follows them for their entire journey through education. Emdin (2016) depicts how he and other trainee teachers labelled students based on their perception of what students would be like without even meeting them. He described it as a narrative rooted in fear: 'We hyper-analysed everything... Before they even spoke, we read their exchanges with each other and marked them as either teachable or not.'

This rhetoric lends itself to the work of Coard (1971), who makes suggestions that the word 'white' is associated with good and 'black' associated with evil. These findings indicate the bias teachers have when applying labels to students. They are often based on appearance, directly linking the pupil's skin colour to the title given; due to preconceived information that teachers and the education system have regarding students from particular races or ethnic backgrounds. I aim to provide insight into labelling theory and the long-term effects that labelling can have.

SO, WHAT IS LABELLING?

Generally, this involves making a judgement that places students into a broad and simplistic category used to define them. Due to the broadness of labelling, it tends to be inaccurate and restrictive. Becker (1963) suggests that labels are given based on one's feelings and emotions towards an individual or situation, using the example of aggression: what makes a student's behaviour aggressive is not what is done by the individual but instead how a teacher reacts to this behaviour which is labelling the student as aggressive. Other teachers then reinforce the label, arguably their peers, to recognise the student's actions as aggressive. Historically this aggression has been attributed to black students due to the view of black people as more aggressive as physical beings; this is a common misconception seen in sport. Becker's research into labelling theory supports the prejudice and bias approach to labelling in schools with the idea that labels are given due to the child's social factors rather than their actual behaviour. For example, not engaging in lessons is a typical example of being labelled as lazy, whereas the student may lack confidence, understanding, or interest. These labels are usually given due to the teachers' perceptions of how students should contribute to lessons. Anything varying from the teacher's ideals, will receive a 'brand' based on their assumptions rather than fact.

IS IT BECAUSE I'M BLACK?

So why may black pupils get labelled as confrontational whilst other students are considered assertive? Additionally, why may black students be labelled as argumentative, whereas their counterparts may be labelled as passionate? We can relate this to the prejudice against black people in society, the social context influencing how black students are labelled in schools. Research findings published in the *Psychological Science* journal suggests that teachers are likely to respond to students' misbehaviour differently depending on the child's race. Statistics regarding the disproportionate exclusion of black boys in schools compared to their white counterparts supports this – their behaviour results typically in harsher consequences, but why? Eberhardt and Okonofua (2015) found that with just the assumption that students may be black or white, determined by their names, racial stereotypes shaped how the teachers responded to the given scenarios. The stereotype of black students as troublemakers is what led teachers involved in the study to decide on harsher consequences – remember, this is based on simply assuming the child is black by their name. Mclean (2017) carried out interviews on this topic in the UK, which painted a similar narrative. The interviewees expressed beliefs that black students were being labelled because of how they dressed, their friendship groups, but more poignantly because of the colour of their skin. Both findings also identified the results would have further implications beyond the educational setting, indicating that the labels are difficult to discard, so often end up following students beyond their education into society. This becomes a damaging cycle for black students and an indication of structural racism and the schools-to-prisons pipeline – black students, particularly boys, are labelled by police as aggressive and receive harsher consequences. Similarly, black females are labelled as loud and aggressive in the workplace, with white counterparts feeling threatened by their confidence and passion.

WHAT IMPACT CAN LABELLING HAVE?

What is most exciting and pertinent about Becker's work is the idea of self-fulfilling prophecy which highlights the potential effect of labelling for students. He implies that once students are given labels, they begin to internalise this, becoming a self-concept – how that student begins to identify themselves. Students become aware of how they are being labelled in schools by their teachers then start to live up to this expectation. As such, being labelled as defiant may then lead to the student displaying increasingly unruly behaviour. They essentially become the label given to them. As mentioned previously, it is difficult to detach the label from the student as their actions aim to fulfil the label following them beyond the school setting into society. I previously alluded to the inaccuracy of these labels given to the students by teachers; consider how much damage an inaccurate label can do to the lives of a black student.

WORK TEN TIMES HARDER!

There are alternative views to labelling theory and the impact of labels on black students in schools. Margaret Fuller's research (1984) on black girls labelled as 'low achievers' found that they responded to negative labelling by working harder to prove their teachers and school wrong. Research by Gilborn and Youdell (2000) shows that this is not an isolated theme, with teachers tending to have lower expectations for black students than white students. I would argue that this notion of the black child having to work ten times harder is equally damaging and links to structural racism. Black students are expected to be from low economic backgrounds, causing them to be placed in lower-tier sets and have an increased focus on control and punishment as the system expects more disciplinary issues. Why should black students have to work harder than their white counterparts to be deemed successful? The label placed on them was false and aimed to restrict their potential. The concern here is that not all black students can be resilient and work ten times harder; relating to the previously discussed idea of self-fulfilling prophecy, some students will live up to the expectations of failure expected by their teachers. This behavioural response indicates the damage that labelling can cause.

CONCLUSION

Labelling in schools is a complex topic, so admittedly I have only scratched the surface. We could go on to explore the labelling of black hair as unprofessional, not to mention the impact of assessment bias, particularly in light of centre-assessed grades used in response to the pandemic. Here are three things I want you to consider.

KEY TAKEAWAYS

- Racial Literacy training – every school and the initial teacher training provider should partake in equity, diversity and inclusion training.
- Power of positive labelling – schools should be environments where students feel empowered and are supported to overcome barriers and labels placed on them by the wider society.
- Challenge your personal biases and stereotypes. Whether it be race, gender, disability, and the list continue, we all have our own biases, but we need to actively challenge these and not impose them on the young people in our care.

KEY QUESTIONS

- What training does your school offer?
- Could you use positive affirmations to empower ALL students?
- What work have you done to tackle your biases?

COMMITMENT TO THE MANIFESTO

As a practitioner I commit to consciously tackle the negative labelling of students based on my own prejudice, bias or stereotypes and be aware of the long-term implication's labels can have.

REFERENCES

Emdin, C. (2016) *For White Folks Who Teach in the Hood... and the Rest of Y'all Too.* Boston: Beacon Press.

Becker, H. (1963) *Outsiders; studies in the sociology of deviance.* London: Free Press of Glencoe.

Coard, B. (1971). *How the West Indian child is made educationally subnormal in the British school system: the scandal of the black child in schools in Britain.* London: New Beacon for the Caribbean Education and Community Workers' Association.

Okonofua, J. A. and Eberhardt, J. L. (2015) 'Two Strikes: Race and the Disciplining of Young Students.' *Psychological Science* [Online]. 26(5), pp. 617-24. Available from: https://edens.berkeley.edu/PDF/2strikes.pdf

Demie, F. and McLean, C. (2017) *Black Caribbean Underachievement in Schools in England.* London: Schools' Research and Statistics Unit. Available from: https://www.lambeth.gov.uk/rsu/sites/www.lambeth.gov.uk.rsu/files/black_caribbean_underachievement_in_schools_in_england_2017.pdf

Gillborn, D. and Youdell, D. (2000) *Rationing education: Policy, practice, reform and equality.* Buckingham: Open University Press.

Fuller, M. (1984). 'Black Girls in a London Comprehensive School.' In: Hammersley, M. and Woods, P. (eds.) *Life in School. The Sociology of Pupil Subculture.* 1st ed. Milton Keynes: Open University Press.

INTEGRATING HISTORIES: EMBOLDENING DIVERSITY

ASH POLLARD

INTRODUCTION

Integrating Histories aims to develop an inclusive curriculum with empowering, and assertive History for all students. Numerous organisations and historical research shed new light on often-taught topics intending to create a sense of belonging and significant, meaningful social change. There must be collaboration across the curriculum and society as these multifaceted social ills can be tackled by insightful, reflective and diverse teams of organisations that put the worth of individuals at the heart of what they do. Education continues to be the best form of tackling racism, prejudice, and discrimination.

DIVERSITY OF EXPERIENCE

One of the fundamental second-order concepts of teaching History is enabling students to assess the diversity of experience of any period, event, or time. This is introduced to every aspiring educator in their Initial Teacher Education course and is constantly in schemes of work throughout their careers. Recent events that include but are not limited to the murder of George Floyd and the Black Lives Matter Movement have demonstrated that there should be a greater acknowledgement, appreciation, understanding and assessment of the diversity of experience throughout British and global history. Many educators have successfully incorporated diversity into their curriculums from the outset. Still, the work must continue by all so that the first aim of the National Curriculum in England is achieved. The aim is that students are expected to know 'how people's lives have shaped this nation [Britain] and how Britain has influenced and been influenced by the wider world.' The traditional narrative is from a conservative, white, affluent perspective. That needs to be rectified so that the kaleidoscope of experiences can encourage students and society that each person has something to offer.

PURPOSE OF INTEGRATING HISTORIES

History is central to our society and helps promote the development of young people with their sense of identity and citizenship. It is an essential subject for any school. It offers students self-awareness, tolerance, and critical thinking. All educators must strive to provide our students with a History that better reflects the multi-cultural society they experience daily. Therefore, History needs to be representative of and empowering for all. It is crucial to put the agency into the Histories of Black, Asian and Minority Ethnic peoples rather than the victims of History, which is still all too frequent. Queen Nanny of the Maroons, the Tudor trumpeter John Blanke, the Turkish origins of Saint George, the cross-continent trading routes of medieval society. Or the fact that Indian troops conducted the first trench raids in World War One. These all contribute to a vibrant, enabling and empowering History. These scenarios need to be incorporated so that students from underrepresented ethnicities feel valued, a sense of belonging and an agency in their learning. It will also allow students from predominantly white backgrounds to acknowledge, respect and engage with the diverse world around them through education so that society will be better equipped to tackle forms of racism, discrimination and prejudice.

The ongoing work of organisations that are committed to social change and raising attainment for all students has not gone unnoticed. These include:

- The One Bristol Campaign that addresses the marginalised voices that reflect the vibrant people, cultures and ideas that are at the heart of Bristol.
- Diverse Educators on Research into Ethnicity, Gender and Social Mobility.
- The Black Curriculum aims to provide a sense of belonging and identity to young people across the UK.
- Numerous unofficial Facebook groups have a common bond to reflect thoughtfully on the curriculum taught in schools and centres for Higher Education. They share best practices with fellow educators, such as Integrating Histories.

All these grassroots organisations are and will lead to change, and it is pleasing to note that Edexcel has offered a brand-new GCSE: *Migrants in Britain, c. 800-present and Notting Hill, c1948-1970*. All of these organisations recognise that more work needs to be done, and it is encouraging to see how, as a group, educators are coordinating improvements for the greater good.

A WHOLE-SCHOOL APPROACH

To behold natural, effective and perspective-changing education in terms of inclusivity, agency, and race, it is paramount that subjects across the curriculum reflect their students' curricula and educators collaborate with their colleagues across the curriculum and communities. In English Literature, *Lit in Colour* has just been published by Penguin Books, who have partnered with the Runnymede Trust, which aims to boost diversity in the reading lists of students. Across areas of Art, Drama,

Music, Mathematics and Science, there are endless examples of Black, Asian and Minority Ethnic painters, actors, composers, and inventors to enhance the cultural capital. Learning from our diverse group of colleagues across our schools about their expertise and lived experiences will help better reflect our students' education.

A WHOLE-SOCIETY APPROACH

Many individuals, organisations, charities, educators, and businesses continue to promote the public goods of tolerance, diversity, and acknowledgement to tackle the public ills of racism, prejudice, and discrimination. The robust discourse that these campaigners provide is an influential educational tool against the battle of inherited ignorance of our shared histories. More reaffirming teaching and learning have been made through connecting our understanding of History to our local environments with the One Bristol Curriculum creating a safe, enlightened, and purposeful space for Bristolians to engage, acknowledge and be critical of the city's past. The publishing of the *100 Great Black Britons* book and website and the production of the *100 Great Black Britons* website have expanded the visibility of our country's and nation's unique heritage.

There are other projects around the country and worldwide that help to provide agency, empowerment, and accountability within their teachings. It is far better than allowing initiatives like Black History Month to be tokenism; our whole society must strive to make inclusive, empowering, integrated histories a fundamental right for all.

CONCLUSION

The momentum gained from recent tragic events must not be lost or shift focus. The demand and the necessity of social change allow students to undertake a three-dimensional, three-hundred-and-sixty-degree history, three hundred and sixty-five days a year. Such action would have such a profound effect on Black, Asian and Minority Ethnic students and their white counterparts.

KEY TAKEAWAYS

- History needs to be representative of and empowering for all.
- There needs to be a whole-school and whole-society approach to social change and integrating historical teaching.
- Appreciating the diversity of experience helps tackle racism, prejudice and discrimination.

KEY QUESTIONS

- What aspects of your teaching and learning and/ daily life have you altered to be more inclusive of diversity?

- Where are your opportunities for collaboration across your school, business or society?
- How have you educated yourself on this matter and those around you?

COMMITMENT TO THE MANIFESTO

Collaborate to create and embed an empowering and diverse curriculum for all students across our schools.

REFERENCES

National Curriculum for Key Stage 3 and 4,(2013), DFE-00194-2013, Page 1 https://assets.publishing.service.gov.uk/government/uploads/system/uploads/attachment_data/file/239075/SECONDARY_national_curriculum_-_History.pdf

Bernard, I. (2011). *Queen Nanny of the Maroons (? – 1733).* BlackPast.org. https://www.blackpast.org/global-african-history/queen-nanny-maroons-1733/

Kaufmann, M. (2017) *Black Tudors: The Untold Story.* Oneworld.

Rohan, P. (n.d) *From the Middle East to Britain: the migrating legend of Saint George,* https://www.ourmigrationstory.org.uk/oms/the-migration-of-the-legend-of-saint-george?fbclid=IwAR1Vc9tb1Ht-2i7Ifqa2eYV6xb-eAxIFk5PmWwjovBo-c23DrSt4nyBQjUo

Mansson, M.J. (2018) *An Incredibly Detailed Map Of Medieval Trade Routes.*:https://merchantmachine.co.uk/medieval-trade-routes/?fbclid=IwAR0jC0YIHDgChYBTvwSKfoXpJafu9ljh4BhjrRM44Y4FpDw8XPyrxKYOEX8

Imperial War Museum, https://www.iwm.org.uk/history/everything-you-need-to-know-about-trench-raids-in-the-first-world-war

One Bristol Curriculum: https://www.onebristolcurriculum.org.uk/

Diverse Educators: https://www.diverseeducators.co.uk/

The Black Curriculum:: https://theblackcurriculum.com/

Integrating Histories, https://www.facebook.com/groups/integratinghistories/about

Whitburn, R. and Mohamud, A. (2021) *Hodder GCSE (9–1) History for Pearson Edexcel: Migrants in Britain, c. 800–present and Notting Hill c1948–c1970.* ISBN: 9781398336018 Published: 28th October 2021

Lit in Colour, Penguin Books and the Runnymede Trust, https://www.penguin.co.uk/campaigns/lit-in-colour.html

INSTITUTIONAL RACISM AND WHITENESS IN SCHOOLS

CLAIRE STEWART-HALL

INTRODUCTION

Macpherson's (1999) definition of institutional racism constructed ways to recognize how the murder and multiple injustices against Stephen Lawrence and the Lawrence family happened. By using legal purposes, institutions can locate, name and challenge racism, recognizing how organizations can unify and group affiliates to discriminate around race. The Equality Act (2010) and The Public Sector Equality Duty (PSED) (2011) further underline the responsibilities of leaders 'to foster relationships between people from different racial backgrounds.' Schools face a crossroads: no longer able to ignore race; opportunities are offered to develop strategic leadership of anti-racism and what this looks like in practice.

WHAT IS INSTITUTIONAL RACISM?

Macpherson (1999) defines institutional racism as:

> The collective failure to provide an appropriate and professional service to people because of their colour, culture or ethnic origin. It can be seen or detected in processes, attitudes and behaviour, which amount to discrimination through unwitting prejudice, ignorance, thoughtlessness and racist stereotyping, which disadvantage minority ethnic people. (paragraph 6.34)

> Every institution must assess its policies and the outcomes of its policies and practices to ensure that no segment of our communities is disadvantaged. (paragraph 46.27) Macpherson (1999)

Schools are fast-paced organizations where the 'processes, attitudes and behaviours' of children and staff are increasingly surveilled.

The 'collective' approach to school challenges is often reinforced, valorised and normalized as a vehicle to generate ethos, success and rewards: year, house, subject, class teams, all featuring heavily in schools. The requirement to assimilate and group-affiliate through processes such as uniform, Trust-branding, colour-coding and team-building all suggest a regularly process-orientated environment. Macpherson identifies how institutional racism occurs and is grown in dynamic with and amongst people through 'processes' and signals a need to look carefully at how institutional racism is cultivated, not behind our backs outside of school gates, but through 'unwitting' implementation of such processes.

WHITENESS RE-CENTRES

The dynamic nature of racism means it can reposition and recreate itself (Gillborn, 2008). *The Commission on Race and Ethnic Disparities: The Report* (2021) is an excellent example of transferring around institutional racism. Published by the British Government, the report attempts to invalidate and deny institutional racism as a cause of inequality by redirecting attention away from structures towards individuals' perceived failures. Black and Brown people become positioned as self-limiting and self-defining, responsible for determining their futures as if racism has not existed or prevented. Disparities between different ethnically categorised groups are underlined, such as family structure or educational outcomes.

Black Asian and Minority Ethnic (BAME) groups become divided, their statistical successes or failures binarised and interrogated, linked to ethnic categorization. This positioning of the 'problem of race' back into categories is an active denial of people's lived experiences of racism. Moreover, it enables a distancing of any structural cause, strategically avoiding discussion of Whiteness and its ability to manifest, uphold and underpin racism within institutions. It is iterative of the shifting dynamic problem of racism itself.

The Commission on Race and Ethnic Disparities: The Report (2021) was arguably a governmental attempt to ignite 'Interest Divergence' (Thompson-Dorsey and Venzant Chambers, 2014) away from shared international condemnation of #BlackLivesMatter (#BLM) following the murder of George Floyd in 2020.

INTEREST CONVERGENCE-DIVERGENCE-RETRENCHMENT

In his seminal work on interest convergence, Bell (1980) observed more sweeping social change around race equality often coincides with temporary self-interest of elite Whites, citing examples such as the desegregation in American schools. Such 'convergence,' Bell argues, means change contributing to racial equity happens where the benefit is seen to serve greater White majority interest, but ultimately, systems of racism remain intact.

Building on this concept and Harris's *Whiteness as Property* (1993), Thompson-Dorsey et al. (2014) observed cycles of Convergence-Divergence-Retrenchment (known as 'Cedar' or C-D-R). They found that following periods of temporary convergence, as seen in the communal outrage of #BLM, there follows a period of 'divergence'. These actions are followed by further retrenchment for minoritised groups, often resulting in a reversal of policy and additional removal of rights, making it worse than before. Because of structural advantage, Whiteness can re-centre (Frankenberg, 1993; Lander, 2012). The broader structures of Whiteness enabling and maintaining social norms of racism acquiesce temporal allowance without disturbing systems of racism and notably 'property', such as institutional power, remains with White majorities (Harris, 1993).

This #BLM period might be described as a concurrent awakening for some people racialized as White to bear unavoidable witness to institutionalized racism and its resulting inhumanity; an exciting time therefore for the Government to publish their report using colour-blindness ideology as a lens through which to view, evaluate, even celebrate race equality in the U.K.

For many schools, such events have brought institutionalized racism into sharp focus. Macpherson's definition offers school leaders the opportunity to use their agency to notice and interrupt social norms of racism. Some are, arguably, in a period of concurrent regeneration, providing gateways for the institutional transformation of how racial identity is learned and celebrated in schools. A shared belief that anti-racist positions safeguard everyone and create healthier and safer places for staff to teach, families to be and children to learn is needed. There is a growing acceptance that colour-blindness prevents teams racialised as White from connecting with race as an area of professional learning and noticing racism.

The PSED (2011) and The Equality Act (2010) state statutory public duties of school staff to safeguard Black and Brown staff, children and families from any racism hidden and embedded in schools and, significantly, through staff attitudes, such as 'unwitting prejudice,' 'ignorance' and 'thoughtlessness' and 'racist stereotypes'. This frame helps notice the potential for 'collective' damage inflicted by micro and macro acts of racism and positions schools as owners of this responsibility.

EXAMINING THE IMPACT OF PROCESSES, POLICIES, ATTITUDES

Macpherson's definition leads us to consider and question how school cultures (re)create racism not only in corridors but, critically, in classrooms. There is a need to problematize and question pedagogies, explore teachers' professional identity and ask why curricula privilege some stories whilst marginalising others. Like other safeguarding elements, racism has a shifting, dynamic nature embedded in social relationships and communication. Racism's ability to re-invent and reposition demands strategic, agile leadership approaches to safeguard our children from experiencing racism.

Some school leaders accept how colour-blindness contributes to complicit silence and discomfort felt when teachers racialise White talk about race in their practice. It is worth remembering the White men who attacked and murdered Stephen Lawrence in 1993 because he was Black – and they all were once boys who attended schools. We must not forget the heavy calling on educators to interrupt and educate children racialized as White who are exposed to entrenched racism to safeguard them from committing such brutal and inhumane acts.

CONCLUSION

It cannot and will not be enough to decolonise the curriculum; schools must be attentive, active, and determined to communicate what anti-racism is, questioning how and why racism continues by preparing staff to disrupt its presence in schools. To stop divergence and end retrenchment, we must examine and heal the damage that has been done by looking forensically at how all race identities are socialized, constructed, and stereotyped. As well as how a majority workforce (DfE, 2020) has been racialised and associated with Whiteness contributes to racism.

'Processes, attitudes and behaviours', Macpherson (1999) notes, are not race-neutral. Thus the *way* we do things, *the method*, must be problematized and interrogated to 'guard' and 'examine' (paragraph 46.27) *and prevent* impact on people's lives.

We will explore race identities, preserve schools, and stop oppressive cycles by noticing race and racism rather than ignoring it and addressing yawning professional gaps.

KEY TAKEAWAYS

- Racism remains a safeguarding risk to all children.
- Whiteness recentres itself, so there must be strategy around institutionalised racism.
- We must address our profession's legacy gap when confronting racism.

KEY QUESTIONS

- How can processes be developed to notice the role majority whiteness has?
- How can we develop strategic approaches to evaluating implications of 'race' on pedagogy, teaching, governance, behaviour, adult curriculum, hidden curriculum, community relations and spiritual learning?
- How can we develop racial literacy as part of our professional toolkit?

COMMITMENT TO THE MANIFESTO

Notice how Whiteness is recentring and interrupt patterns of convergence-divergence-retrenchment.

REFERENCES

Bell, D.A. (1980) 'Brown v. Board of Education and the Interest-Convergence Dilemma.' *Harvard Law Review*, vol. 93: 3 pp.518-33

Frankenberg, R. (1993) *White Women, Race Matters: the Social Construction of Whiteness*, Routledge, London.

Gillborn, D. (2008) 'Coincidence or conspiracy? Whiteness, policy and the persistence of the Black/White achievement gap', *Educational Review*, 60:3, 229-48.

Harris, C. (1993), 'Whiteness as property', *Harvard Law Review*, Vol. 106 No. 8, pp. 1709-91.

H.M. Government, *Commission on Race and Ethnic Disparities: The Report* (2021). Available online: https://assets.publishing.service.gov.uk/government/uploads/system/uploads/attachment_data/file/974507/20210331_-_CRED_Report_-_FINAL_-_Web_Accessible.pdf (accessed 14 May 2021).

Smith, H.J. & Lander, V. (2012). 'Collusion or collision: effects of teacher ethnicity in the teaching of critical whiteness', *Race, Ethnicity and Education,* vol. 15: 3, pp.331-51.

Macpherson, W. (1999) *The Stephen Lawrence Inquiry: Report* (London: Home Office)

The Equality Act, 2010. Available online: http://www.opsi.gov.uk/acts/acts2010/ukpga-20100015-en-1 (accessed 14 May 2021).

The Public Sector Equality Duty (2011) Available online: https://www.gov.uk/government/publications/public-sector-equality-duty (accessed 14 May 2021).

Thompson Dorsey, D. and Venzant Chambers, T. (2014) 'Growing C-D-R (Cedar): working the intersections of interest convergence and whiteness as property in the affirmative action legal debate.' *Race Ethnicity and Education*, 17:1, 56-87

U.K. Government (2020). *School Workforce in England: Reporting Year 2019*. Available online: https://exploreeducation-statistics.service.gov.uk/ find-statistics/school-workforce-in England (accessed 14 May 2021).

ADDRESSING THE ISSUE OF A TEACHER BEING RACIALLY ABUSED BY STUDENTS AT SCHOOL AND WHAT SUPPORT OUR COLLEAGUES CAN OFFER US

EBANIE XAVIER-COPE

INTRODUCTION

Having been a teacher since 2011, I sometimes wonder if I would recommend this profession to others because it has been an arduous journey as a black woman working in white-majority schools. However, there have been few black teachers and students who look like me. I have not experienced many openly apparent racist incidents, but there is one that will always stick in my mind.

WHAT IS RACISM?

Racism is the prejudice, discrimination, or antagonism directed against someone of a different race based on the belief that race is superior. It is spoken about daily but is it ever indeed addressed? There are usually discussions on racism between pupils and institutional racism, but has anyone thought about addressing the issue when students have racially abused the teacher. What is being done to tackle racism in our schools? What is being done to support students and staff who experience racism whilst in an educational setting?

I remember having a conversation with someone from a different ethnic background, and them telling me that they do not see colour; they know the person. Whilst I appreciate what they were trying to say, I can assure you that everyone sees colour. What would be nice is if there was more honesty about the fact that we all see colour and become allies and support networks for when the colour of our skin is used against us.

MY PERSONAL EXPERIENCE

Before teaching in primary schools, I was a secondary school music teacher. I was working in a school where the students struggled to pronounce my full name, so they called me Miss Cope. This school had over 1200 students, and less than 3% of the students were from a black background. I went to cover a year 11 ICT lesson. I walked into the lesson, and the students were getting on with their work. During the class, I heard monkey noises but dismissed them because I thought I had to be hearing things. I listened to the same noises again, so I walked around the room. Whilst walking around the room, I overheard some of the year 11 students laughing. The bell rang to signal the end of the lesson, and the students left.

One of the girls in the lesson was also in my tutor group. We began talking about the ICT lesson and I told her that I thought I heard monkey noises. She responded that I did hear monkey noises, and those students do it to the maths teacher (a black male) all of the time, and he does nothing about it. Over the next few days, I heard that the students were laughing and talking about the incident. They kept on referring to me as that teacher, to which my student responded with, 'Her name is Miss Cope.' Their response was, 'More like Miss Coon!'

There was a battle for the school to do anything about it. The girl in my tutor group was asked to write a statement about what had happened. She did, and the staff members left it open on their desks when they talked to the other students involved in the racist incident. The student who wrote the statement then became very worried that she could now become a target.

Their parents were called in for a meeting, which I was not informed about or invited to attend. The students were excluded for a few days and then put in isolation. They lost their sixth form place and were not allowed to follow their year 11 prom. I never received an apology for how this incident was dealt with, not from the racist students nor the administration.

I felt that the school was too lenient but learnt that across the UK in the academic years 2018 to 2019, fifteen permanent exclusions (0.2%) were due to racist abuse. For temporary exclusions, 4,889 (1.1%) were due to racist abuse. Both of these rates have remained roughly steady since 2014/15.

THE RESULTING IMPACT IT HAS ON TEACHERS

When schools choose not to take these types of racial incidents seriously, they need to think about their impact on their teachers. It can be challenging to get over an incident like this, and it can have lasting effects as the scars can be challenging to heal because you have been attacked based on something you cannot change – your skin colour. Teachers may begin to feel that their feelings do not matter, and they have no right to feel this way. There may be times when they question their abilities as a teacher and assess their career path based on the demographics of a school and its surrounding communities. They may limit their aspirations for fear of working in a predominantly white school and not receiving the support.

Recently there have been many newspaper articles about racism in schools. One noted that whenever a black teacher questions sanctions against the student(s) in question, we are made to feel like we are the problem.

DATA

According to the 2019 research conducted by the government, 0.9% of the teacher workforce are Black African, 1.1% are Black Caribbean, and 0.3% are Black Other. The most dominant race of the teacher workforce, with 85.7%, is White British. According to these same statistics, 800 deputy and assistant headteachers in the country identify as either Black African, Black Caribbean or Black Other. Once again, White British dominate this area with 41,800 deputy and assistant headteachers in the country. Finally, out of all of the schools in England, 0.2% of headteachers are Black African, 0.7% (around 200) are Black Caribbean, and 0.1% identify as Black Other. Once again, the dominant race of headteachers in the country is White British with 92.7%.

What do you think this data says about our country and helping non-White British teachers progress within their careers? Do you not believe that a straightforward way to tackle racism in schools is to have more diverse leadership teams across the country, showing students that with hard work, they can progress?

Remember the famous quote by Marie Wilson, Founding President of The White House Project, You can't be what you can't see.' Seeing more diverse leadership teams in schools will also help tackle racism within education by more teachers in different positions addressing the problem and not leaving it to the teacher who has been racially abused to resolve.

ALLIES AND SUPPORT

Let us go back to the conversation with someone from a different ethnic group who does not see colour – everyone sees colour. It is a part of our identity. It is who we are. If people say that you do not see colour, they do not see me, and they do not see themselves. Instead of making others feel good with those comments, it would be more appreciated if we had allies or support for when staff members are treated differently because of their skin tone. To be an ally, you could call out racism and prejudice when you see it, listen to our experiences and understand your privilege. That would be the first step in making us feel supported in our journey as we progress in our careers.

CONCLUSION

A fundamental way to combat racism in schools is to have a more ethnically diverse workforce across the school, as reports show that a diverse staff team impacts the environment for pupils and staff. According to the data mentioned previously, this is not currently happening enough, and educational establishments are still white, especially at the leadership level. Diversity should be celebrated and discussed in schools, not just on occasions such as Black History Month. Throughout the year children need to be educated to understand the multicultural heritage in Britain and the positive impact this has had on society. A more inclusive curriculum would help combat this problem as children will be taught using a curriculum that represents their current society.

Understandably, some may feel uncomfortable discussing racism and race, but if anything is to change, then these discussions need to be had. It is up to us to help to educate the next generation. No one is born racist; racism is learnt.

KEY TAKEAWAYS

- Any form of racism should be addressed as soon as possible.
- Racism is for everyone to tackle and not only for black individuals and organisations.
- Offer support to those who have been racially abused, even if it feels a little uncomfortable.

KEY QUESTIONS

- Is enough being done within schools to tackle the issue?
- What can be done to enable more non-white members of staff to progress into senior leadership positions successfully?
- How can schools engage the families and their local community in order to enable them to realise there is a problem?

COMMITMENT TO THE MANIFESTO

Create safe spaces for these topics to be discussed and the effects it has on the individuals without fear or repercussions. Be supportive, be understanding, be an ally.

REFERENCES

Barrier's Report: *The impact of racism on Black teachers*. https://neu.org.uk/barriers-report-impact-racism-black-teachers (May 2021)

Commission on Race and Ethnic Disparities: The Report (2021) pp. 76-7. Available at: https://assets.publishing.service.gov.uk/government/uploads/system/uploads/attachment_data/file/974507/20210331_-_CRED_Report_-_FINAL_-_Web_Accessible.pdf (accessed April 2021).

Guardian Newspaper (2021) https://www.theguardian.com/education/2021/mar/24/systemic-racism-teachers-speak-out-about-discrimination-in-uk-schools (accessed April 2021).

School Teacher Workforce – Published 21st February 2021 https://www.ethnicity-facts-figures.service.gov.uk/workforce-and-business/workforce-diversity/school-teacher-workforce/latest (accessed April 2021)

[1] Color Oxford Dictionary and Thesaurus and Wordpower Guide (2003) p. 498.

[2] Commission on Race and Ethnic Disparities: The Report (2021) pp. 76-7.

[3] Guardian Newspaper (2021) https://www.theguardian.com/education/2021/mar/24/systemic-racism-teachers-speak-out-about-discrimination-in-uk-schools (April 2021)

[4] School Teacher Workforce – Published 21st February 2021 https://www.ethnicity-facts-figures.service.gov.uk/workforce-and-business/workforce-diversity/school-teacher-workforce/latest (April 2021)

[5] Barrier's Report: The impact of racism on black teachers. https://neu.org.uk/barriers-report-impact-racism-black-teachers (May 2021)

SUPPORTING BLACK FEMALE TEACHERS IN THE ENGLISH EDUCATIONAL WORKFORCE

JENETTA HURST

INTRODUCTION

This chapter identifies the challenges faced by some Black female teachers as documented in the literature on education, from personal experience and gleaned from experiences shared anecdotally, highlighting the stereotypes and barriers to remaining within the profession. While positionality must be considered when looking at the observations presented, shared lived experience is valuable and informs the recommendations. This chapter will provide suggestions for school communities and, more specifically, school leaders and governors on how they might support Black female teachers in the hope of improved retention and sustained progression, creating a more diverse workforce to benefit all learners.

It would be prudent of school leaders and governors to act upon and train all members of the school community on the racial bias and stereotypes experienced by some Black women in the English educational workforce, as identified by Ellemers et al. (2012) (cited in Bailey-Morrisey and Race, 2019, p128). Raising awareness of the support that is beneficial to Black female teachers (Farinde, Allen and Lewis, 2016, p120) and of their experiences of the glass ceiling that exists concerning progression once qualified will go some way to making progress in this area (Farinde et al., 2016, p122).

WHAT SUPPORT IS NEEDED?

In light of the statistical evidence of Black female teachers disproportionately failing to progress to senior positions (Gov.UK; Earley , 2013, p41), school leaders have a responsibility to meet the nuanced needs of Black women in the English educational workforce. In a time where the very existence of institutional racism is being downplayed at a governmental level, increased diversity amongst governing bodies will be instrumental in understanding and supporting Black teachers, pupils, families and employees.

Sufficient support should be provided for colleagues who report racism in the workplace and for those who experience race-based trauma (Kinouani 2021), through the provision of safe spaces for colleagues to discuss these incidents and the encouragement of networks for Black female teachers, either within the school or across groups of schools. Whilst Black female teachers may not view themselves as victims, the combined effect of these actions is a more positive experience for this intersectional group, with all stakeholders benefiting from broader input into the school community.

EXPLORING THE LITERATURE ON BLACK FEMALE TEACHERS

When facing racial microaggression, Black women may experience being viewed through a lens of distrust. The need to continually demonstrate exceptional professionalism levels and be proven trustworthy and competent without receiving constructive support becomes physically and mentally exhausting. Black women become more at risk of leaving the profession early, sometimes failing to make it through Initial Teacher Training (ITT) programmes or Induction periods (Farinde et al., 2016, p121; Bailey-Morrissey and Race, 2019, p128).

The impact on the wider school community may include feelings of disempowerment amongst these colleagues, lack of progression to more senior roles and the loss of positive role models for all children and particularly Black children. Maylor (2009, p18) has argued that not all Black teachers see themselves as role models for Black children and as such, we must be mindful of the additional pressures on Black teachers of taking up the assumed position of role model to Black children in schools. In the accompaniment to the second edition of Bernard Coard's (1971) seminal text *How the West Indian Child is Made Educationally Subnormal in the British School System*, Diane Abbott MP in Richardson (2001) concluded:

'The 1985 Swann Report point(s) out: "Teachers' attitudes towards and expectations of West Indian pupils may be subconsciously influenced by stereotyped, negative or patronising views of their abilities and potential, which may prove a self-fulfilling prophecy and can be seen as a form of unintentional racism."

Some thirty-six years later, we see similar stereotypical views perpetuated of Black Caribbean children in the government's *Commission on Race and Ethnic Disparities* (gov. UK, 2021 p69), with possible explanations for underachievement within this group identified as being a lack of motivation and optimism of the pupils, racial bias from teachers and within the curriculum.

If indeed this is the case, then in 2021, children who do not see themselves reflected in the school's staffing at all levels may be deprived of an opportunity to develop their aspirations. An American study of twelve Black female teachers' intentions to remain in the classroom as K-12 teachers by Farinde et al. (2016) focused on three predominant themes impacting their decisions: administrative support, salary and teacher advancement. Key findings of the study identified a lack of support and the experience of 'top-down models', 'oppression' and 'a climate of intimidation' as reasons for Black females leaving the profession (Farinde et al., 2016, p120). Salary is not often deemed to influence job satisfaction; several participants cited the pursuance of increased financial security and limited options due to the glass ceiling experienced, despite working towards post-baccalaureate degrees (Farinde et al., 2016, p121 – 2).

Bailey-Morrisey and Race (2019) address the lived experiences of Black women leaders in English schools, highlighting the 'double jeopardy' (Berdahl and Moore, 2006 in Bailey et al., p135) of challenging the perceptions and preconceived ideas of what leaders look like and how they behave. Bush (2019, p95-6) presents five implications for school leaders in supporting the development of all staff, including under-represented groups. Bush's (2019, p95-6) recommendations on training for school governors and increased community engagement are essential for encouraging the retention and progression of teachers.

THE EXPERIENCE OF WORKING AS A BLACK FEMALE TEACHER

As a Black female teacher, you are likely to see others promoted sooner or faster; you may see people who have similar or less experience earmarked for promotion and new roles created for teachers who fit in. Fit is, of course, essential, and one might say that they would rather be where they are wanted and their expertise valued, than not. This is a story of several Black female teachers who have shared experiences over the years. We see this narrative reported in national newspapers, highlighted on local and national news items, and it is now time for a change.

CONCLUSION

To ensure that more Black female teachers can thrive, survive and progress within the workforce, school leaders can both embed and embody policies that support those teachers. Indeed, not only in word but also diversifying governing bodies and offering bespoke mentoring at crucial transition points, including ITT, induction, promotion to middle and senior leadership, and headship. The creation of professional networks for Black female teachers, training all staff on the protected characteristics and discrimination law and ensuring that good teachers are recruited across all ethnic groups.

KEY QUESTIONS

- How can school leaders, governing bodies, local authorities, and multi-academy trust leaders demonstrate their commitment to challenging Black female teachers' disadvantages?
- How can the government address the recruitment and retention of Black female teachers?
- How can schools be held to account over the retention and equitable promotion of Black female teachers?

KEY TAKEAWAYS

- Offer bespoke training at key professional transition points.
- Ensure that good teachers are recruited across all ethnic groups.
- Diversify school governing bodies.

COMMITMENT TO THE MANIFESTO

Take positive action at a leadership and governance level to counteract the racial bias and stereotypes experienced by Black women in the English educational workforce.

REFERENCES

Abbot, D. (2005). 'Teachers are failing Black boys.' In: Richardson, B. (ed) *Tell it Like it Is: How our schools fail Black children.* London: Bookmarks Publications, pp.108-10.

Bailey-Morrissey, C and Race, R. (2019). 'The lived experiences of black women leaders: Barriers to progression'. In: Miller, P. and Callender, C. (eds.) *Race, Education and Educational Leadership in England: An Integrated Analysis.* London: Bloomsbury Publishing, pp.121–36.

Bush, T. (2019). 'Talent, determination and resilience: Leadership accession and enactment for black, Asian and minority ethnic leaders'. In: Miller, P. and Callender, C. (eds.) *Race, Education and Educational Leadership in England: An Integrated Analysis.* London: Bloomsbury Publishing, pp.81-96.

Earley, P. (2013). *Exploring the School Leadership Landscape.* London: Bloomsbury Academic, pp.41

Farinde A.A., Allen, A. and Lewis, C.W. (2016) 'Retaining Black Teachers: An Examination of Black Female Teachers' Intentions to Remain in K-12 Classrooms'. USA: Routledge. *Excellence in Education* 49(1): 115–27.

Maylor, U. (2009). "They do not relate to Black people like us". Black teachers as role models for Black pupils.' *Journal of Education Policy.* 24(1): 1–21.

https://www.ethnicity-facts-figures.service.gov.uk/workforce-and-business/workforce-diversity/school-teacher-workforce/latest#by-ethnicity-and-gender-headteachers-only (accessed 14 April 2021).

https://assets.publishing.service.gov.uk/government/uploads/system/uploads/attachment_data/file/974507/20210331_-_CRED_Report_-_FINAL_-_Web_Accessible.pdf (accessed 14 April 2021).

Kinouani, G. 01.03.21, Race Reflections At Work: The Podcast Episode 1, 4'51" – 5'05" (accessed 4 April 2021)

CULTURALLY RELEVANT PEDAGOGY: PUTTING STUDENTS' IDENTITY AT THE CENTRE OF YOUR CLASSROOM PRACTICE

JESSICA BOYD

INTRODUCTION

> *We must teach the way students learn, rather than expecting them to learn the way we teach.* – Pedro Noguera.

Culturally Relevant Pedagogy is a teaching method that challenges us to ground our classrooms in critical thinking, educational equity and social justice. It is a practice that deliberately empowers students to maintain their cultural integrity while still being academically successful. Based on a study conducted in the 1990s, Culturally Relevant Pedagogy is anchored on three key teacher actions; academic success, cultural competency and sociopolitical consciousness.

I think we teach children to hate themselves. Not directly but in the invisible messaging of our day school culture. It could be that language is wrong, or an accent is terrible (not different, just bad), or the way hair is covered is incorrect, or the way hair grows out of one's head is 'unprofessional' and therefore also is wrong. However, it seeps through that we are all too often unaware and complicit in contributing to shoving children into conformity. That enables them to fit within the dominant culture as much as possible without disturbing the status quo.

CULTURALLY RELEVANT PEDAGOGY

Over time, we could be in danger of teaching children to be a shell of who they are. Indirectly via school norms, we are hypothetically saying, *'Yes you have value but only if you act a particular way (usually middle class, white, cis, heterosexual, protestant, male). This mould is at the centre and that is where success lies, so the closer you can get to this centre then the closer you are on the road to success. Every step you are away from that the further away from success you are. So the better you can lie about who you really are, the more permissive we (the system) will be in giving you access to that success.'* If our identities are formed by how other people see us, then over time, the most important message that a minority student hears i they know or understand is not relevant or valued in school.

They then carry around that picture of themselves, slowly tolerating the idea that they are not equal to others, and just like that, we have all contributed to inequity. It is terrifyingly easy. So how do we start to move away from this messaging? We begin by taking a hard look at how we teach teaching, and then teaching it.

In the early 1990s Dr Gloria Ladson-Billings, an American teacher, educator and professor in Urban Education conducted a fascinating study that set out to drive pedagogical change. Instead of reiterating familiar questions about the problems, challenges, and barriers for students and teachers in urban classrooms, she instead asked what was going right in these spaces. This study examined the daily practices of eight 'good' teachers. They recorded everything they did from their small interactions with students, curriculum design, lesson planning, lesson delivery, classroom management, and connections with their local community. After lengthy interviews and observations, common patterns and trends emerged based on the three domains. The following teacher actions were presented: academic success, cultural competence and sociopolitical consciousness. Ladson-Billings coined these findings as 'Culturally Relevant Pedagogy'.

ACADEMIC SUCCESS

Teachers from this study demanded, reinforced and nurtured academic excellence in all of their students. Their students pursued clear goals and teachers were regularly explicit about the link between students' academic success (grasping literacy, numeracy, technological, social and political skills) and the reality of them becoming active participants in democracy. Their academic achievement was measured through a variety of means to avoid testing bias. These teachers would think deeply and critically about what they taught, how they taught it and why they were teaching it, made evident by their learners' knowledge and how to best teach them in their context. An example of this was one teacher (a white woman) who recognised that the black boys in her class held most of the social power. Instead of labelling the boys as loud or disruptive, the teacher challenged the boys to demonstrate academic ability by drawing on issues and ideas that they found meaningful. As the boys showed educational leadership, other students saw this as a positive trait and began to copy. This teacher intentionally found ways to value their abilities, interests and skills and channelled these characteristics accordingly. Ladson-Billings affirms this by noting that the trick of culturally relevant teaching is to get students to 'choose' academic success.

CULTURAL COMPETENCE

Secondly, Culturally Relevant Pedagogy requires students to maintain cultural integrity. Ladson-Billings explains that instead of 'acting white' culturally relevant teachers utilise students' culture as a vehicle for learning, directing them not to switch off who they are to be successful. The study found that these teachers actively developed their own and their students' cultural competence through ongoing reflections and conversations about their identity, culture, biases, and privilege to assess and strengthen their instructional practice critically. The teachers took responsibility for learning about their students' community. Students were frequently encouraged to recognise and honour their own cultural beliefs and norms while also accessing and learning about the wider world. There was a prioritisation for creating a community of learners, building relationships with and amongst students that centre care, trust, student voice and agency, ensuring that students feel a sense of belonging, connectedness and value.

SOCIO-POLITICAL CONSCIOUSNESS

In these classrooms, teachers actively cultivated both their own and their students' socio-political consciousness. Beyond academic achievement and cultural competence, there were different expectations that students engaged with the world and others critically, including the morals and values held within school, society at large and institutions that perpetuate social inequities. Teachers took responsibility for learning about political issues in both the local community and nationally and incorporated equity into the required curriculum. For example, several teachers from this study had out- of-date textbooks to use in lessons. Rather than making a complaint about being under resourced, they, together with their students, would critique the knowledge presented and explore counterarguments. They would also always discuss the inequitable funding that prevented them from learning from the same texts as more affluent schools. Encouraged to advocate for themselves regularly, students would collectively write letters to local newspapers informing the community of their situation and raising awareness of the inequity they faced. In one classroom, a group of students were dubbed 'community problem-solving' by a local newspaper. This kind of social activism was deliberately planned into the curriculum by the teachers, thoughtfully preparing students for active citizenship.

CONCLUSION

Over twenty years later, Culturally Relevant Pedagogy is widely known amongst educators in the United States. It has also naturally forgone several iterations, namely culturally *sustaining* pedagogy and culturally *responsive* pedagogy. I am also sure that similar practices exist in the UK (but they are not yet celebrated in mainstream teacher talk). Our biggest challenge in implementing this type of pedagogy into teacher training is that we need to commit to maintaining such authentic and organic practice after 'doing the work'. Beyond this study and application of its principles, static and fixed interpretation of what it meant to be culturally relevant also surfaced. Teachers who initially engaged with this teaching model became stuck in minimal and superficial notions of culture. My dream is for Culturally Relevant Pedagogy to become the new talk of the town. However, I worry that after a while, cultural competency can easily slip into just a display board with lots of flags and the word 'hello' in multiple languages. Academic success can be reduced to merely passing tests, and socio-political consciousness can be lumped into PSHE or even fall off the radar entirely.

KEY TAKEAWAYS

- Students value themselves based on what and how they are taught.
- A strong understanding of a student's identity, community and culture are vital in bringing about their success.
- Teachers must practise cultural competency and socio-political consciousness to dismantle inequality.

KEY QUESTIONS

- What do I know about my students, their culture and community?
- What am I actively doing to dismantle the inequity that my students face?

COMMITMENT TO THE MANIFESTO

Engage with culturally relevant pedagogy as a vehicle to dismantle educational inequity.

REFERENCES

Ladson-Billings, G.J. (1995). 'But that's just good teaching! The case for culturally relevant pedagogy.' *Theory Into Practice*, 34 (3) 159-65.

Ladson-Billings, G.J. (1995). 'Toward a theory of culturally relevant pedagogy'. *American Education Research Journal*, 35, 465-91.

Paris, D and Alim, S. (eds.) (2017). *Culturally Sustaining Pedagogies: Teaching and Learning for Justice in a Changing World*. Teachers College Press. New York.

Paris, D. (2012). 'Culturally sustaining pedagogy: A needed change in stance, terminology, and practice'. *Educational Researcher, 41*(3), 93–7.

Gay, G. (2010). *Culturally Responsive Teaching: Theory Research and Practice*. Teacher College Press. New York.

CENTRALISING CULTURE IN PHYSICAL EDUCATION: A CARIBBEAN PERSPECTIVE

LAURA MCBEAN AND DR SHREHAN LYNCH

INTRODUCTION

Physical education (PE) and its wider contribution to social justice issues are well established within the PE research community. Arguably, as a marginalised subject within education, this contribution is often missed in practice, where sport, fitness and regulation of the body are heralded as its purpose. As members of this community, we are concerned that this Eurocentric approach marginalises many of the students that we serve. In this chapter, we seek to challenge this by centring on Caribbean culture to provide practical examples of a more equitable approach to PE.

EUROCENTRISM IN PE

Historically and characteristically, PE has been used to standardise bodies through obedient and docile means focused on student discipline (Culp 2017). Such a 'Eurocentric approach' to regulating individual bodies in England has notoriously excluded black people and black culture(s). The physical education national curriculum reflects a sport-focused, traditionally-orientated, competitive ideal for students. We argue that such a goal-driven curriculum centralises whiteness due to its hyper-focus on surveillance of the body. And neoliberal models of what a 'perfect body' looks like are represented by Eurocentric activities such as football, rugby, gymnastics, athletics, cricket, and rounders, repeated yearly, also the implementation of direct instruction and command-style teaching. We are not alone in our arguments surrounding the discipline. Several educationalists have highlighted the need to reform the hegemonic Eurocentric PE and suggest approaches that do not perpetuate racism, elitism, individualism and dehumanisation within the domain. (Culp, 2020, 2021; Lynch, Sutherland, and Walton-Fisette, 2020).

A Eurocentric curriculum is problematic in England (and globally) because our communities are diverse in both bodies and thought. By dominating the curriculum with Eurocentric approaches, certain cultures become educationally marginalised. Specifically, our current form of recycling the same curriculum sports/activities is a form of social and cultural reproduction, shaping the future of our society. Ultimately, whiteness (as an ideology) has been normalised in physical education, and we would like to re-centre the educational purpose of the discipline, using our spaces in an emancipatory and liberation-focused way and advocating for pro-blackness rather than anti-blackness. We suggest using PE as a space to celebrate students' cultures in various movement forms, recognising that culture and education are 'transmitted by a group's core values, beliefs, attitudes, type of communication, and linguistic styles' (Culp, 2013, p. 35). And bringing culture into the classroom means going beyond non-traditional, non-Eurocentric activities such as Peteca (Brazil), La Gallinita Ciega (Mexico), and Ki-o-Rahi (New Zealand) (Lynch and Curtner-Smith, 2019).

Of course, just changing our sporting/activity does not make our curriculum diverse and our efforts should be seen as a holistic approach, combining anti-racist pedagogical approaches and a decolonising philosophy towards education. We need spaces to work through our pedagogy, curriculum and assessment methods, which takes courage on our part, but we feel it is our moral obligation to centralise students' cultures in teaching spaces, and we share in this chapter just one example of what centralising culture could include.

EXPERIENCING CULTURE: OUR THOUGHTS

Laura recognises that she has been very fortunate to have travelled home to Jamaica from a young age. It was nothing like she had imagined it to be, a land that holds so much history, yet none of it formed in her 'formal' education. Instead, she learnt about her culture through her grandparents and family traditions. Trips 'home' for Laura have helped her navigate her identity and everything that comes with being a Black woman in England. Laura views culture as hard to express as it is individually interpreted, and therefore we should all be allowed to access our cultures and others through our education.

Shrehan has felt that her culture has been ignored for twenty-five years of her life, and consequently, she feels immense guilt for keeping her Palestinian heritage silent. In the last six years, after enormous identity work and historical work, she has questioned whether her culture was 'silenced' by the white ideologies that she grew up around. Shrehan now proudly identifies as a British-Palestinian woman, mixed race; however, she recognises the benefits of systemic privilege as she can pass as a white woman. Shrehan views culture as a complex phenomenon; however, she feels it is heavily interrelated with our identity and that our cultures should be celebrated in positive ways.

CENTRALISING CULTURE WITHIN PE

There is a togetherness about the culture of Jamaica; cooking, eating and dancing, to name a few practices often done in collaboration. 'Out of Many One People'; the motto on the Jamaican coat of arms could be seen to reflect this. Through an English-Jamaican lens, thoughts on a Caribbean culture in PE first presented the 'norms' linked to the culture, i.e., Jerk chicken, Bob Marley, Usain Bolt. Food, music and athletics have undoubtedly helped to bring Jamaica to the attention of a global stage, and they deserve their recognition. However, we advocate for a shift in thinking from such stereotypes; in PE, stereotypes are realised through articulations such as the 'Black body being most suited towards running rather than swimming'. Culp (2013, p.36) states: 'Cultural negotiation is a means of communication and instruction that strives toward a progressive, equitable, and thriving environment for participants'.

In essence, for thriving environments to occur, cultural competence is required for our pedagogy and should not be viewed as a tokenistic attempt to be equitable.

The chosen activities have sought to present what this negotiation *could* look like by utilising various activities (see Table 1).

Table 1. Practical examples of fusing Caribbean culture

Activity one: Map it out

Task:	Orienteering session using dingbats in place of words to name locations within Jamaica, such as the three counties and fourteen parishes.
Challenge:	With further clues, get students to place them correctly on the map of the island.
Skills:	Teamwork, problem-solving.
Cross-curricular:	History – the link between colonialism and the names of places, e.g., Surrey is a county in Jamaica.

Activity two: Dance it out

Task:	Students create their ring dance in small groups – 12:07 – 14:03 in video (https://www.youtube.com/watch?v=vOux_Y6tFgU&t=108)
Challenge:	Increase the group size, increasing the difficulty and encouraging leadership as each group can teach their dance to the rest of the class.
Skills:	Creativity, teamwork, leadership.
Cross-curricular:	History – a fusion of cultures resulting from slavery, e.g., traditional folklore dances have origins in Africa, Maypole dance has roots in Europe.

Activity three: Dance it out Pt 2

Task:	Students learn some of the most popular dance moves of Jamaican origin.
Challenge:	Student leaders learn the dance moves and teach them to their peers.
Skills:	Leadership, memory, creativity.
Example dance moves by artist Elephant Man:	Pon di River, Pon di bank Signal di plane Crazy hype (https://www.youtube.com/watch?v=jJ1Mz0itsec).

Activity four: Black Women in sport

Task:	Critical discussion centred on women in sport using Jamaican athletes and centred around women accepting themselves/their bodies.
Challenge:	Students to think in-depth about swimming and black culture.
Athlete examples:	Alia Atkinson (swimming) Shelly-Ann Fraser-Pryce (sprinting) Stefanie Taylor (cricket)
Skills:	Critical thinking, self-love.
Cross-curricular:	All subjects, through developing a critical eye and building self-confidence.

Activity five: Cook in together

Task:	To recreate the national dish of Jamaica, Ackee and Saltfish (fish can be removed).
Challenge:	Students can link this dish to understanding nutrition and the benefits of fresh rather than processed foods.
Skills:	Teamwork, following instructions, cooking skills, safety in the kitchen.
Cross-curricular:	Nutrition, Food technology

Please note that these ideas aim to stimulate your thinking and require research and input from students to develop further.

POSSIBLE COUNTER-ARGUMENTS

As the authors of this chapter, we recognise the importance of a critical perspective when curating our pedagogies and, therefore, expect and welcome counter-perspectives to our work; the challenge is necessary for growth. The first counter-consideration is that we have moved from one approach to another; we ask you to take this as *one* example. We believe curricula should be developed contextually and *with* students. Tokenism is an area of concern; to prevent this, we encourage student input and culture weaving into our everyday practices avoiding standalone lessons.

It is also debatable if these activities will help to develop our future generation of Olympians. We seek to challenge this view by creating equitable experiences in PE that places **education,** not **products**, at the centre. Lastly, such a curriculum as the one presented requires in-depth research and knowledge. Thus, teachers should heavily research the culture and speak to community members (elders) to give culturally sensitive ideas.

CONCLUSION

The ultimate goal of education for all subject areas should be social betterment for all cultures and communities. The purpose of the Caribbean curriculum is to (re)centre marginalised communities, voices and cultures within the mainstream Eurocentric provision for students in PE. It is a process, one that is part of re-envisioning a further education for our young people. However, it is filled with possibility and hope. To do it justice, consider the holistic approach to reimagining your curriculum, pedagogies and assessment offers.

KEY TAKEAWAYS

- Know your students: likes, dislikes, contextual information, prior learning and experiences.
- Share your curriculum ideas with students and negotiate delivery.
- Avoid tokenism; implementing a 'one off' unit does not make your curriculum non-Eurocentric .

KEY QUESTIONS

- What are the various student cultures in your class, and how can you improve your cultural fluency?
- What pedagogies and knowledge areas can you draw upon for support?
- How can you expand your knowledge of discipline-specific examples and appropriate pedagogies for your students?

COMMITMENT TO THE MANIFESTO

Revision of the PE curriculum; moving away from a focus on sport and competition to focus on movement, joy, and culture celebrations.

REFERENCES

Culp, B. (2013). 'Eliminating barriers to physical activity: Using cultural negotiation and competence.' *Strategies, 26*(3), 35-40.

Culp, B. (2017). '"Illegitimate" Bodies in Legitimate Times: Life, Liberty, and the Pursuit of Movement': *National Association for Kinesiology in Higher Education*, 26th Delphine Hanna Commemorative Lecture 2017. *Quest, 69*(2), 143-56.

Culp, B. (2020). 'Physical Education and Anti-Blackness.' *Journal of Physical Education, Recreation & Dance,* 91(9), 3-5.

Culp, B. (2021). 'Everyone Matters: Eliminating Dehumanising Practices in Physical Education.' *Journal of Physical Education, Recreation & Dance, 92*(1), 19-26.

Lynch, S. and Curtner-Smith, M. (2019). '"You have to find your slant, your groove:" One physical education teacher's efforts to employ transformative pedagogy.' *Physical Education and Sport Pedagogy, 24*(4), 359-72.

Lynch, S., Sutherland, S. and Walton-Fisette, J. (2020). 'The A–Z of Social Justice Physical Education: Part 1'. *Journal of Physical Education, Recreation & Dance, 91*(4), 8-13.

THE RECRUITMENT AND RETENTION OF BLACK TEACHERS IN THE UK

RHIA GIBBS

INTRODUCTION

Black teachers in the UK make up a minority of the teacher workforce. There has been some research around the recruitment and retention of Black teachers. Still, today we do not have a great picture. If the education system is to become truly inclusive, how can this be done without looking at the lack of recruitment and retention of Black teachers? It cannot. This chapter will cover the present recruitment and retention of Black teachers and the underlying challenges that prevent Black educators from entering and remaining in the system, and how to address them.

THE CURRENT PICTURE

The narrative around race in the UK has changed over the past ten years. We are told that the UK is not 'institutionally racist' (CRED, 2021). But when we look deeply into our institutions, a different story is told. When Black African/Caribbean men and women decide to enter the education system as a teacher, many do not know that statistically, they are to be considered a rarity. They also do not realise that statistically, they will be much more likely to leave the profession earlier than their white counterparts (Basit et al., 2006). At every level of education, Black teachers, particularly those from Africa and the Caribbean, are underrepresented.

This notion is not a new conversation. The government has emphasised and continuously urged the need for minority ethnic teachers (DES, 1985). Unfortunately, that need continues. Black teachers in the UK make up around 2.5% of the UK teacher workforce compared to white teachers, who make up 85.7% of the teacher workforce (DfE, 2020). Directly looking at this, some may argue that these statistics reflect the national population, with Black people making up around 3% of the UK population. However, 33.9% of primary school children are from an ethnic minority background, and 32.3% of ethnic minority students are in secondary schools (DfE, 2021). To engage with this issue, it has to be clear that there are disparities between the diversity of the teacher workforce and our student body. Teachers do not represent their students, and this can cause massive problems.

Figures from UCAS show that in 2020 teacher training applications rose by 16.7% in England and Wales. When we delve further into the statistics, there are stark differences in the acceptance rates amongst ethnic groups. White trainees have an acceptance rate of 71.8%; Black trainees have an acceptance rate of 48%. These figures are startling and emphasize the need to look into the issues around the recruitment and retention of Black teachers in the UK. The difficulty is that some of the research uses the terms 'BAME' or 'BME'. However, researchers recognize the problems in homogenising the experiences of ethnic groups and how this can cause issues in really understanding the root cause of the issues at hand (Tereshchenko et al., 2020).

RECRUITMENT

The current picture of the recruitment of Black teachers looks bleak despite the push towards a diverse teacher workforce (DfE, 2018). Much of the focus tends to be looking at treating the symptoms without treating the cause. The lived experience of many Black people has a direct impact on why Black teachers are much less likely to enter the teaching profession. Black Caribbean children are five times more likely to be excluded from school in some parts of the UK. This problem has been ongoing, but it may also shed light on the direct issues we are now facing with the recruitment of Black teachers.

Frequently, Black students' school experiences are fueled with feelings of isolation, teacher labelling and racism. The education system does not always value its Black students as it should, and as a result, they are left resenting their educational experience. Because of the scarcity of Black teachers in the system, Black pupils are less likely to be taught by one throughout their school careers.

The problem here is twofold. Black students are marginalised because returning to the education system as teachers would be a disservice. Their experiences of racism and unfair labelling as students means that they can pre-empt the experiences of Black teachers, which makes this career path less appealing; a possible explanation as to why we have so few Black teachers. In the same instance, the lack of representation of Black teachers during schooling means that Black people are less likely to aspire to teach. You cannot be what you cannot see, and the direct impact of this is now showing. Tackling the retention of Black teachers must go beyond initial teacher training down to the experiences of the students themselves. These issues are systemic and often go unchallenged. Early intervention is required to observe real progress.

RETENTION

Recruitment is one issue, but retention is a much larger issue. Black teachers are more likely to leave the profession (Basit et al., 2006). Tereshchenko et al. (2020)

cited several reasons as to why Black teachers go. From the lack of progression to racism in the workplace, these factors drive Black teachers out of the system.

Imagine a young Black teacher excelling in their career and being offered a promotion. But then imagine being offered three times less than the current person who holds that position, that individual being someone white. These experiences are not one-off experiences and happen more than we recognise. Now put yourself in their shoes. That teacher feels undervalued, and as a result, they walk away from the profession into a career that values them. These barriers to progression often result in Black teachers leaving teaching altogether.

Another emerging issue around the retention of Black teachers is the idea they are suffering from burnout at a much quicker rate than their white counterparts. The issue starts with cultural assumptions around how Black teachers build relationships with students, especially those from ethnic minorities. They are often given more complicated groups in terms of behaviour. Thus Black teachers are usually viewed as a figure for discipline but this can also hinder career progression as Black teachers become pigeonholed into more pastoral roles in a school.

EXCELLENCE DOES NOT EXIST WITHOUT DIVERSITY

Every school wants to be excellent. But you cannot be excellent without diversity. When George Floyd was killed in May 2020, there was a recognition that the education system needed to become a truly diverse and inclusive space. Conversations around anti-racism, tackling unconscious bias and decolonising the curriculum have taken place. But what about the workforce? Often these conversations are overlooked. Diversity in a staff body provides richness to schools. It allows them to see themselves in their teachers and gives hope for what they can achieve. It offers new ways of thinking, new ideas and new talent to staff, and it helps us achieve what we want with education – to create a better world with great citizens. But merely just hiring more Black teachers will not solve the problems around recruitment and retention. If Black teachers are to genuinely thrive in their careers, not just survive, fundamental change is needed.

CONCLUSION

Some suggested actions you can take:

1. Create safe spaces for your Black teachers – these locations have a lot of power, and it is important not to underestimate them. The power of these spaces should not be undermined; these spaces mean that fewer Black teachers leave.
2. Consider the working environment for Black teachers. Is this a school in which they can excel in their career, or is it space where they will feel invisible and undermined?
3. Reflect on your staff body. Does everyone have a voice? Are teachers of colour heard? Does anyone represent the students?

You will not be able to make these changes overnight but being committed and taking the first step is what matters.

KEY TAKEAWAYS

- The teacher workforce in the UK lacks diversity.
- Recruitment of Black teachers is pointless without tackling retention issues.
- Excellence can't be achieved without diversity.

KEY QUESTIONS

- Have you created safe spaces for your Black teachers?
- Consider the environment you are recruiting Black teachers into. Is this a school in which they can excel in their career or is it a space where they will feel invisible?
- Do all staff have a voice? Are teachers of colour heard?

COMMITMENT TO THE MANIFESTO

You will not be able to make these changes overnight but being committed and taking the first step is what matters.

REFERENCES

Basit, T. N. Roberts, L., McNamara, O., Carrington, B., Maguire, M. and Woodrow, D. (2006). 'Did they jump or were they pushed: reasons why minority ethnic trainees withdraw from initial teacher training courses.' *British Educational Research Journal*, 32 (3), 387–410

Commission on Race and Ethnic Disparities. (2021). *Commission on Race and Ethnic Disparities: The Report.* Available at: https://assets.publishing.service.gov.uk/government/uploads/system/uploads/attachment_data/file/974507/20210331_-_CRED_Report_-_FINAL_-_Web_Accessible.pdf (Accessed 3rd April 2021)

Department of Education and Science. (1985). *Education for all: Final Report of the Committee of Inquiry into Children's Education from Ethnic Minority Groups* (London, HMSO).

DfE. (2018). *Diversity of the teaching workforce: statement of intent.* London: DfE. Available at: https://www.gov.uk/government/publications/diversity-of-the-teaching-workforce-statement-of-intent (Accessed 1st April 2021)

DfE. (2020). *School workforce in England*. Available at: https://explore-education-statistics.service.gov.uk/find-statistics/school-workforce-in-england (Accessed 1st April 2021)

DfE (2021) *Schools, pupils and their characteristics – The academic year 2019/2020*. Available at: https://explore-education-statistics.service.gov.uk/find-statistics/school-pupils-and-their-characteristics (Accessed 1st April 2021)

Tereshchenko, A., Mills, M., Bradbury, A. (2020). *Making progress? Employment and retention of BAME teachers in England*. UCL Institute of Education: London, UK.

UCAS. (2020). *UCAS Teacher Training End of Cycle 2020 Data Resources*. Available at: https://www.ucas.com/data-and-analysis/ucas-teacher-training-releases/ucas-teacher-training-end-cycle-2020-data-resources (Accessed 3rd April 2021)

COACHING AS A TOOL FOR DEVELOPING ANTI-RACIST SCHOOLS

SHARON PORTER

INTRODUCTION

In the United States, coaching and therapy are viewed as interchangeable, with therapy being a widely accepted practice. In the United Kingdom, the connection between therapy and coaching is also prevalent. The concept of coaching as a tool to *'fix you'* and the association with deficit models of development does not appear to make it an attractive approach. The following is an exploration of anti-racism coaching as a tool for development for all staff.

SENIOR LEADERS & EXECUTIVES

Coaching has been a luxury for the elite in education, with many organisations '... providing mentoring/coaching to promote white males [*which*] forms part of the organisational culture...' (Showunmi, 2018, p. 11). There is value in coaching, but understanding how coaching can be used beyond developing strategic capability needs to be explored. When addressing issues of race, it is impossible to meet all staff needs with sweeping presentations and reading materials; therefore, approaches to Learning & Development (L&D) need updating.

By adding coaching to the suite of L&D tools, the door to addressing issues of race across the education sector can be opened. When leaders develop a better understanding of issues linked to race, their duty to share this knowledge whilst supporting others in experiencing this transformation enables positive change. Such practices and conversations become the norm and not just a tick box exercise to help individual progression. However, where staff want to progress, they should not feel like they have to become 'clones' (Lumby and Coleman, 2007) or 'bleach' their identities to fit in (Showunmi, 2018).

Research has shown the effectiveness of a combination of approaches to L&D in leadership (Bush et al., 2005) and personalised coaching providing alternative coping mechanisms in corporate leadership (Holder, Jackson and Ponterotto, 2015). The latter has not been fully explored in education, but giving coaching to understand race issues from all perspectives is essential.

It is beneficial for leaders from *all* ethnic groups to explore their experiences of race, how their presence impacts others in their organisations, and coach (*not mentor*) or obtain coaching for their team members. When leaders are comfortable talking about issues of race, this subject will be likely to surface regularly on meeting agendas and school improvement plans.

EDUCATORS

Professional development sessions may include discussions on '*hot topics*'[1], but educators are not explicitly provided with coaching to develop their understanding of issues of race. Those responsible for mentoring new and experienced educators may not address issues of race because they consider it outside of their remit, not relevant in their school setting, or think it is being covered elsewhere.

Research on race equality issues has found there is a lack of training for mentors and recommend: 'University training for mentors who support student teachers in school also needs to integrate race equality issues.' (Lander, 2011, p. 365). Lander highlights the lack of research conducted in the secondary phase relating to this phenomenon, suggesting a gap. Equally, there is a lack of research involving Black Initial Teacher Trainees (ITTs) and an understanding of how to deal with issues of race in schools; there are limited role models to provide support from an experiential perspective. More recently, Brownsford (2019) found that White ITTs were:

'...unconfident in teaching children from BAME groups or backgrounds.' (Brownsword, 2019, p. 3)

To build confidence and dispel ambiguous beliefs about race, the appointment of a dedicated coach responsible for the development of all staff would be a logical step. As a result, instructors may adopt an anti-racist perspective, which will be echoed across the school and community. This could lead to educators embracing an anti-racist mindset that becomes mirrored across the school and broader community.

WHY USE COACHING TO ADDRESS ISSUES OF RACE?

Learning and development come in many guises across the education sector, so when educators learn and talk about race, approaches generally adopted involve presentations, seminars, and workshops. These one-off events will not change the current position in education. Nor will these approaches address the discomfort experienced by many who feel (*and are*) less informed about issues of race and culture. Using coaching to explore the problems of race furnishes educators with the opportunity to unpick how their values and beliefs are formed and identify ways of making changes.

Stokes and Jolly (2018) stress the importance of coaching to develop executives' ability to have difficult conversations. So, one questions why this is not filtering through to all staff, especially when guidance is available (Lofthouse, Leat and Towler, 2010; Lofthouse and Whiteside, 2020). At some point in all educators' careers, difficult conversations will occur, making coaching an essential tool for developing skills to talk about issues of race. This is necessary for new and existing educators, support staff, leaders, and the wider community.

POLICY – INCORPORATING COACHING INTO SCHOOLS' PROGRAMMES OF PROFESSIONAL DEVELOPMENT.

Coaching is an approach that provides a space to reflect, review options, develop thinking about values and beliefs, and have ideas challenged in a safe environment. This would seem an ideal developmental approach for making organisational change at all levels. Coaching *is* personalised and complements other approaches to L&D, therefore making it a golden thread connecting teaching, learning, communication, relationship building, and personal development in schools.

Evidence shows that educators who experience coaching perform better in their day-to-day roles and have better relationships with colleagues and students (Robertson, 2008; Baglyos, 2017). Furthermore, by creating a policy that ensures issues of race are discussed in safe forums and personal coaching spaces, organisational change can occur with greater ease.

The Global Framework for Coaching in Education (Campbell and van Nieuwerburgh, 2018) enables leaders to assess where coaching is currently being used and where it may need to be applied. The framework focuses on four areas:

- Educational Leadership
- Professional Practice
- Community Engagement
- Student Success and Well-Being

Incorporating a model that has been created for use in education supports other approaches to L&D and builds credibility.

CONCLUSION

In developing educators' understanding of race and creating anti-racist schools, there continues to be opportunities for growth. This growth will inevitably occur at various stages of an educator's journey and can be supported through coaching. With educators having different backgrounds, variable knowledge of other cultures, and differing requirements for professional development, it is important that coaching is personalised when addressing issues of race. Campbell and van Nieuwerburgh (2018) discuss the increasing popularity of coaching in educational establishments worldwide and provide a model that incorporates coaching.

Application of *The Global Framework for Coaching in Education* (2018, pp. 5–11) to school development plans will provide leaders with the opportunity to build confident teams that are open to discuss issues of race (and other matters of concern) in a professional, balanced, and considered way.

KEY TAKEAWAYS

- Coaching is for all, not just leadership teams.
- Training is required to support the development of educators who are 'uncomfortable' or 'unfamiliar' with teaching students from BAME backgrounds.

KEY QUESTIONS

- What are the barriers to setting up a coaching programme that develops a better understanding of issues of race?
- When books are not enough, where do staff find out how to develop their understanding of race?

COMMITMENT TO THE MANIFESTO

Incorporate *The Global Framework for Coaching in Education* into development plans (Campbell and van Nieuwerburgh, 2018)

REFERENCES

Baglyos, G. (2017) *The Impact Of Racial Equity Coaching On White Educators' Personal Growth And Professional Practice*. Hamline University. Available at: https://digitalcommons.hamline.edu/hse_all/4281 (Accessed: 4 May 2021).

Brownsword, S. (2019) *Preparing primary trainee teachers to teach children from Black, Asian and other minority ethnic (BAME) backgrounds or groups: participation, experiences and perceptions of trainee teachers*. Available at: https://ueaeprints.uea.ac.uk/id/eprint/70107/1/SBrownsword_Preparing_primary_trainee_teachers_to_teach_children_from_BAME_Backgrounds_FINAL.pdf (Accessed: 8 April 2021).

Bush, T. et al. (2005) *Black and minority ethnic leaders Final Report to the National College for School Leadership*. Available at: http://citeseerx.ist.psu.edu/viewdoc/download?doi=10.1.1.550.244&rep=rep1&type=pdf (Accessed: 11 November 2018).

Campbell, J. and van Nieuwerburgh, C. (2018) *The Leader's Guide to Coaching in Schools*. London, UK: SAGE Publications Sage UK: London, England.

Holder, A. M. B., Jackson, M. A. and Ponterotto, J. G. (2015) 'Racial Microaggression Experiences and Coping Strategies of Black Women in Corporate Leadership', *Qualitative Psychology*, 2(2), pp. 164–80. DOI: 10.1037/qup0000024.

Lander, V. (2011) 'Race, culture and all that: An exploration of the perspectives of White secondary student teachers about race equality issues in their initial teacher education.' *Race Ethnicity and Education*, 14(3), pp. 351–364. DOI: 10.1080/13613324.2010.543389.

Lofthouse, R., Leat, D. and Towler, C. (2010). 'Coaching for teaching and learning: a practical guide for schools.' *CfBT Education Trust*, (April), pp. 1–37.

Lofthouse, R. and Whiteside, R. (2020) *Sustaining a Vital Profession*. Carnegie Education. https://www.leedsbeckett.ac.uk/blogs/carnegie-education/2020/01/htcoaching/

Lumby, J. and Coleman, M. (2007) 'Leadership Theory and Diversity: Critiquing theory.' in *Leadership and Diversity: Challenging Theory and Practice in Education*. Sage Publications, pp. 68–84.

Robertson, J. (2008) 'The 3R ' s for coaching learning relationships.' *Professional Development Today*, 11(2), pp. 42–7.

Showunmi, V. (2018) 'Black and White Women's Leadership: Privilege, Power, and Prejudice in School and Society', in Brooks, J. S. and Theoharis, G. (eds) (2019) *Whiteucation: Privilege, Power, and Prejudice in School and Society*, Routledge

[1] Black Lives Matter Movement, HALO code, Digital Divide

[2] i.e., Teaching & Learning, CPD, Professional Development

CHAPTER 7: RELIGION AND BELIEF

CHAPTER EDITOR: **DAVID HERMITT**

CHAPTER CONTRIBUTORS

1. Dr. Phillip Smith – **Motivation, Faith, Belief and Spiritual Values: Black Male Leaders and Spirituality in Leadership**
2. Jacqueline M Newsome – **'When worlds collide': Leading a multi-faith school**
3. Esther Cummins – **Christian values – it's who I am**
4. Aysha Khanom – **The Power of Interfaith and Dialogue/Religious Literacy**
5. Orla McKeating – **Religion and Mental Health**
6. George White – **LGBT Inclusion in Catholic Schools**
7. Elizabeth Walsh-Iheoma – **Embracing the Least**
8. Anjum Peerbacos – **'You look like a Nun'**
9. Nasra Barre – **What's that on your head?**
10. Allison Zionts – **What did you hear about me? Being an openly Jewish teacher as a student resource**

BIOGRAPHIES

David Hermitt is a former Chief Executive of a large 3-19 multi-academy trust in Cheshire. He completed thirty-three years as a teacher (seventeen as a secondary headteacher) before becoming a consultant, author and speaker. David has been a strong advocate for racial justice and inclusion. He is currently a doctoral student at Keele University, Anti-racist Schools Associate of Leeds Beckett University, Chair of the Chester Diocesan Safeguarding Advisory Panel and is an independent school leadership consultant.

Allison Zionts (she/her) is a secondary school teacher in a girls' school in London and a PhD student at Goldsmiths, University of London, studying inclusive spaces for LGBTQ+ students in single-sex schools. She is a trustee of KeshetUK, the Jewish LGBT+ charity, and a staff governor for her school, and runs her school's LGBTQ+ clubs.

Anjum Peerbacos is an experienced teacher who has taught in schools in London for twenty years. Anjum has also been involved in advising the Chinese Government on implementing creativity and alternative curriculums for students across the ability spectrum. Her experience has spanned from teaching children from underprivileged backgrounds to placing them at Oxbridge and Russell Group universities. Anjum has developed and delivered materials for schools to use on Islamophobia.

Aysha Khanom is the founder of The Race Trust and Wisdom Against Racism, which focuses their work on Racial Literacy for students and teachers, and mentoring Black, Asian, and White students with a focus on identity and improving educational engagement. Aysha has over ten years' experience as a teacher and currently leads the Religion department in a high school in Manchester.

Elizabeth Walsh-Iheoma leads with passion and purpose. She is a leader who shares her ethics and values with the teams she leads and models how to use diversity constructively. She has delivered diversity workshops to a wide range of organisations and has a desire to see organisations and communities transform to places where employees can flourish and thrive and make meaningful contributions in their workplace, thus leaving a better world for the next generation.

Esther Cummins is a Course Director at Leeds Beckett University, where she uses her experience as an Inclusion Manager and as an Assistant Principal to develop and teach inclusive practice for students. Esther is studying for a PhD at the University of Manchester, researching values and ethos in faith settings.

George White is a transgender and Catholic teacher of Religious Education at a Catholic secondary school in Leicester. He holds a BA in Philosophy & Theology from Heythrop College, an MA in Global Ethics and Human Values from King's College London and a PGCE in Secondary Religious Studies from the University of Cambridge.

Jacqueline M Newsome is a serving headteacher at an urban multicultural secondary school in the West Midlands and is a current doctoral student at the University of Birmingham. She has been recognised nationally as an outstanding practitioner, having achieved Advanced Skills Teacher status. She is a Specialist Leader in Education (Behaviour and Attendance) and a Local Leader of Education.

Nasra Barre is a primary school teacher based in Northamptonshire. She trained at the Institute of Education at UCL. Nasra leads a phonics programme and is passionate about teaching and learning. She has a purpose and drive for providing a holistic education for children, creating opportunities for all and is an advocate for inclusive allyship.

Orla McKeating is an entrepreneur, writer, coach and motivational speaker from Belfast, Northern Ireland. Orla founded *Still I Rise – Diversity Story Telling for Kids* in 2019 in order to share stories with young children with true representation and role models, stories that celebrate different types of families and people, and promote emotional and mental well-being as well as kindness and acceptance for our little humans to make an impact as our next generation on our beautiful planet. She is an internationally accredited life coach trainee specialising in BAME women, and wants to see more diversity in leadership positions, reaching goals and more diverse role models. Orla works with women to fight bias, build self-confidence and belief to move forward with integrity and vision, on a professional and personal level.

Dr. Phillip A. Smith is a Research Fellow with the Edmund W. Gordon Institute for Urban and Minority Education (IUME) at Teachers College, Columbia University, U.S.A, where he also completed his Ph.D. in Education Leadership. His research interests include education leadership and policy studies, critical race theory and Black education leadership, with a focus on Black men and the principalship. His award-winning dissertation entitled, *Leading While Black and Male: A Phenomenology of Black Male School Leaders,* examined how the racial identities and lived experiences of Black male K-12 public and independent school leaders informed their professional lives and leadership. Dr. Smith has over thirty-five years' experience working across the range of education: early years – secondary (PK-12) education, community, further, higher, and adult education both in the UK and the US

THE PROTECTED CHARACTERISTIC OF RELIGION AND BELIEF

DAVID HERMITT

INTRODUCTION

Policy makers and school leaders are faced with the practicalities of balancing religion and belief in schools. Studies show that 85% of the world subscribe to some form of belief system The three main world religions are Christianity (31%), Islam (25%) and Hinduism (15%) but according to researchers by 2035 the number of babies born to Muslims is expected to modestly exceed births to Christians (Pew Research Centre, 2017). Religious belief will continue to be a feature of UK schooling and in the future many children in our schools will increasingly come from a range of religious backgrounds.

In the UK, the Human Rights Act 1998 enshrines the national commitment. This creates a framework for balancing the religious rights and perspectives of different children. Religion and Belief are protected characteristics in the Equality Act 2010; everyone has the freedom to choose to believe in a religion or not to. Children from all faith communities come together to learn in a typical UK school. One of the core benefits of religion in schools rests in the fact that all the major world religions promote humanitarian aid and charitable giving. This provides a way of unifying the belief systems of children and supports a narrative which supports tolerance in our school communities.

This chapter provides some practical ways to help policy makers and school leaders navigate their responsibilities in a changing world.

DEFINITIONS AND TERMINOLOGY

Whatever you personally believe, spirituality is not confined to the development of religious beliefs or denominations. It can be the expression of empathy, self-awareness, devotion, and tolerance. Spirituality includes nurturing these attitudes, the spirit of each child by allowing them to develop these qualities for themselves. It is one aspect of cultivating humanity.

A lack of humanity amongst a school community may be seen as a good indicator of a lack of spiritual awareness. Incidents of physical aggression, racism, sexism and other forms of abuse illustrate wider issues. The spiritual health of a school community is the responsibility of those who lead. This spiritual health cannot be assessed in any straightforward way. For those leaders and teachers who wish to make improvements in schools, there is often conflict in balancing the views of all faith groups and the increasing number who say they have no religious belief. However, most stakeholders will support a focus on what they deem to be humanitarianism or spiritual development.

Many teachers are ill-prepared to discharge their responsibilities towards children with religious beliefs. For teachers, knowing enough about world religions is essential. For example, showing a cartoon of the Prophet Mohammed (pbuh) can result in a religious outcry from children and parents. Forcing children to pray to a God that they do not recognise is disrespectful and acts of worship need to be carefully worded.

LANDSCAPE

The Education Act 1944 requires schools to '...promote the spiritual...development of pupils at the school and of society'. If schools ignore this and the Equality Act 2010, they risk expensive prosecution and damaged reputations.

There are checks and balances that ensure that schools are taking this matter seriously, for example, through school inspection frameworks. The Education Inspection Framework makes it clear that schools will be judged for what they do in this area by school inspectors. This is not just a priority for faith schools who have their own framework of Section 48 outside Ofsted. This is something that all schools need to tackle to ensure they secure a favourable Ofsted grading. Government-funded schools must also follow the Public Sector Equality Duty (Public Sector Equality Duty 2021). Schools must all consider how they will ensure that religion and belief are carefully considered and constantly under review. The 'do nothing' option is not available.

Schools face the challenge of creating a shared culture that allows everyone in school to feel that having faith or no religion are both valid positions to hold. It must not be forgotten that moving between those two statuses – of having faith and having none – can also be transformative in a person's life. Currently, there is no shared framework that everyone agrees upon for assessing and monitoring the spiritual health of a school.

The Equality Act provides a potential framework to audit the school response to spiritual development, religion and belief. It is a starting point that allows schools to consider their response to this protected characteristic. By looking at the treatment of different religious perspectives, we can make a valuable start to a journey of culture change. We can go beyond what takes place in Religious Education lessons, to look at the overall ethos and culture of the school. We can involve everyone in our community by talking openly about religion and belief.

VOICES IN OUR CHAPTER IN DIVERSE EDUCATORS – A MANIFESTO

Our authors are unpicking what religion and belief means for you in school. They are asking questions about how we can focus on spiritual development and what this means for those in leadership. There are three sections to this chapter.

The first section looks at the culture of leadership when it comes to faith. **Phillip Smith** brings to bear his transatlantic experience to help us to see how leaders can develop their schools in terms of religion and belief. **Jacqueline Newsome** follows on with a UK perspective. **Esther Cummins** looks at Christian values whilst **Aysha Khanom** looks at interfaith dialogue and how to work across more than one faith.

The second section looks at feelings of belonging. With large numbers of children in our schools having religious affiliations it is important to think about their needs. This supports safeguarding and our health and safety obligations. **Orla McKeating**, **George White** and **Elizabeth Walsh-Iheoma** tackle potentially controversial issues with a clear focus on pupils feeling like they belong.

Finally, our curriculum can be enhanced by making religious differences visible as a catalyst for learning. **Anjum Peerbacos** and **Nasra Barre** discuss wearing attire that signifies their faith whilst **Alison Zionts** considers how Jewish staff can be a useful resource for schools. They encourage us to look at ways we can encourage people to express their religious differences and still be included.

CONCLUSION

In writing all these chapters, all our authors have considered the major world religions and those who have no religion or perspectives that are different to their own. This critical approach ensured all leaders can draw upon their work. We have sought out unifying principles across all faiths.

We have done this because tackling this is not just for those who claim to have a religion or belief. It is the law. We must make every effort to ensure that we do not discriminate between our fellow humans based on their religion or belief.

COMMITMENT TO THE MANIFESTO

Spirituality is one of the fundamental experiences of life that covers all humanity as evidenced by the large numbers worldwide who ascribe to the major world religions; it should not be ignored in school. It is the responsibility of everyone to follow the law and ensure that members of our school community are not discriminated against, to make our schools welcoming places for people of all faiths or none. This chapter provides you with some tools to do this.

REFERENCES

https://www.theguardian.com/news/2018/aug/27/religion-why-is-faith-growing-and-what-happens-next [accessed April 2021]

The Changing Global Religious Landscape | Pew Research Center (pewforum.org)

https://www.ons.gov.uk/peoplepopulationandcommunity/populationandmigration/populationestimates/articles/researchreportonpopulationestimatesbyethnicgroupandreligion/2019-12-04 [accessed April 2021]

https://www.equalityhumanrights.com/en/publication-download/measurement-framework-equality-and-human-rights [accessed Jan 2021]

https://www.equalityhumanrights.com/en/advice-and-guidance/public-sector-equality-duty [accessed February 2021]

MOTIVATION, FAITH, BELIEF AND SPIRITUAL VALUES: BLACK MALE LEADERS AND SPIRITUALITY IN LEADERSHIP

PHILLIP SMITH

Now faith is the substance of things hoped for, the evidence of things not seen.
(Hebrews 11:1, New King James Version)

This chapter explores the phenomenon of spirituality in leadership. The chapter draws on the results of a previously conducted research study [The London Study] exploring the leadership and leadership development of male senior leaders of African-Caribbean heritage in secondary schools in London, England – in particular, how these leaders describe, experience and understand the utility of faith and spiritual values as part of leadership (Smith, 2012). The chapter concludes that for African-Caribbean heritage school leaders in particular, and also for leaders from other racial and gendered groups, spirituality in leadership constitutes a ministry or calling, and informs leadership philosophies and engagement with a school's community to create a connection that raises mutual levels of motivation, action, and care.

THE EQUALITY ACT 2010: RELIGION OR BELIEF

The Equality Act 2010 (The Act), identifies the presence or absence of 'religion or belief' within a person's described identity as one of nine characteristics through which individuals are protected from discrimination, harassment, or victimisation. The other eight protected characteristics are: age; disability; gender reassignment; marriage and civil partnership; pregnancy and maternity; race; sex; and sexual orientation. On the protected characteristic of religion or belief, as applicable to schools, the Act allows for exemptions to the admissions criteria, provision of education, curriculum, and collective worship for schools with a religious character serving pupils with a designated religious affiliation. However, no school, denominational or non-denominational, is permitted to discriminate against any individual (pupil or adult) on the grounds of that individual's religion or belief, or any other protected characteristic.

LEADERSHIP THROUGH FAITH, SPIRITUALITY, SPIRITUAL VALUES AND PRACTICE

The concept of spirituality is very distinct to and differs from religion in that 'religion is an institutionalized space where spirituality may be nurtured and celebrated (Dantley, 2010, p. 214). In the same way that spirituality may or may not be 'nurtured and celebrated' within a religious tradition (Dantley, 2010, p.214), as the Equality Act 2010 outlines, 'belief' may be religious or philosophical. These are important distinctions in understanding the notion of spirituality in leadership for as Reave (2005) asserts:

'In the case of effective leadership, we shall find that spirituality expresses itself not so much in words or preaching, but in the embodiment of spiritual values such as integrity, and in the demonstration of spiritual behaviour such as expressing caring and concern. (p.656-7).

There is an increasing body of scholarship exploring the role of faith, spirituality, spiritual values, attitudes, and behaviours as core motivating [enabling] attributes of effective leadership and particularly in defining race-conscious, culturally sensitive paradigms of school leadership (Dantley, 2010; Lomotey, 2019; Smith, 2019; Smith, Francis and Harper, 2015). Noteworthy examples of leaders who exemplified spirituality in leadership are Dr. Martin Luther King Jr. and Nelson Mandela, individuals whose respective leadership stances were committed to civil-rights activism, action-oriented social justice, liberation, equity and care.

Smith (2019) examines the personal and professional experiences, philosophies and praxis of Black male public and independent school leaders in the USA. The study explores the range of strategies these leaders developed that enabled them to navigate the systemic layers of racism, power, post-racial and colour-blind ideologies, and workplace organizational structures that both maintain and perpetuate racial inequities across the education system. This in-depth phenomenological study provides descriptions as well as a synthesis of the essence of 'leading while Black and male' through co-constructed themes to include the leadership philosophies, influences, and values that inform leadership as ministry. On leadership as ministry, Smith asserts:

Leadership as ministry, exemplified through faith, spirituality, a sense of moral purpose, and action-oriented social justice, are foundational to the leadership philosophy and influences (ministry) of Black male school building-level leaders. For many of these leaders, spirituality has guided and informed their practice and acted as a motivating influence behind their leadership. (Smith, 2019, p.222)

The concept of transformational leadership is closely aligned to the attributes of spiritual values, beliefs, behaviours and practices associated with spiritual leadership and leadership as ministry. Transformational leaders are 'leaders who inspire followers to transcend their own self-interests and who are capable of having a profound and extraordinary effect on followers' (Robbins, Judge, Miller and Waters-Marsh, 2008, p.699). These leaders ignite a belief and motivation in their followers synonymous with the Bible definition of 'faith' (Hebrews chapter 11, verse 1) as outlined in the opening of this chapter. Indeed, Dantley (2010) proffers that 'principals who are transformative leaders are those who allow their spiritual selves to assist them in the execution of their leadership responsibilities.' (p.215).

THE LONDON STUDY

The London Study, a qualitative research study, using a questionnaire and in-depth phenomenological interviews, explored the range of strategies that inform the promotion prospects, career success, and encounters in the headship of eight African-Caribbean male secondary school leaders in London. Participating leaders were employed in a headteacher, deputy or assistant head position within mixed secondary maintained schools or academies of differing sizes across Greater London, which sometimes included a sixth-form provision for sixteen to eighteen--year-old students. All were nationally recognized for their leadership and management. The leaders described their experiences, understanding and perceptions of inhibitors and enablers to their leadership and leadership development.

For the majority of participating African-Caribbean secondary school leaders, leadership was positively influenced and motivated by a sense of a spiritual-centered moral purpose and commitment to providing an equitable education for students, families and communities. Faith as an attribute of spirituality — a belief in God or Supreme Being — was also identified as a culturally prominent and enabling influence in participants' leadership philosophies and approach, with almost one-third identifying faith and belief in God as key influencing factors. One African-Caribbean leader, headteacher Harrison Reid (pseudonym), an educator of thirty-three years, with fourteen years' experience in a senior leadership position, described his faith thus: 'I have a strong faith in God. Not that I would say that I was a practicing Christian but within myself it is something that I can draw on.' (Smith, 2012; Smith, Francis and Harper, 2015, p.84).

IMPLICATIONS FOR POLICY, PRACTICE AND LEADERSHIP DEVELOPMENT

Leadership paradigms that are cognisant of and responsive to the motivating influences of faith, belief and spiritual values have much applicability to the fields of education policy, practice and leadership development. Spirituality in leadership in education encompasses a leadership philosophy and influence that is motivated by faith, spirituality, and evidenced through ethical behaviour, values and care. For the African-Caribbean leader, work is viewed as a vocation, spiritual calling or ministry and engenders race-centered, culturally sensitive, sensemaking, and understandings of action-oriented social justice, liberation, and care in support of students, teachers, and the wider school community.

KEY TAKEAWAYS

- The concept of spirituality or belief is distinct and different to that of religion.
- Spirituality in leadership views leadership as a vocation, calling or ministry.
- Spirituality in leadership or leadership as ministry constitutes culturally sensitive approaches to transformational leadership.

KEY QUESTIONS

- What are the differences and similarities between the attributes of transformational leadership and spirituality in leadership?
- In what ways may school leadership be viewed as a ministry or calling?
- How many leaders utilise the obligations for schools as set out in the Equality Act 2010 through their demonstration of a model of spirituality in school leadership?

COMMITMENT TO THE MANIFESTO

Incorporate the concept of spirituality in school leadership in the formulation and design of culturally sensitive leadership and leadership development opportunities for Black, African, African-Caribbean heritage educational leaders in particular, and for all leaders broadly.

REFERENCES

Dantley, M.E. (2010) 'Successful leadership in urban schools: Principals and critical spirituality, a new approach to reform.' *The Journal of Negro Education* 79(3): 214-19.

Equality Act 2010 c.15. https://www.legislation.gov.uk/ukpga/2010/15/data.pdf

Fry, L.W. (2003) 'Toward a theory of spiritual leadership'. *The Leadership Quarterly,* 14(6): 693-727. doi:10.1016/j.leaqua.2003.09.001

Lomotey, K., (2019)' Research on the leadership of Black women principals: Implications for Black students.' *Education Researcher,* 48(6): 336–348. https://doi.org/10.3102/0013189X19858619

Reave, L. (2005) 'Spiritual values and practices related to leadership effectiveness.' *The Leadership Quarterly* 16(5): 655-687.

Robbins, S.P., Judge, T.A., Millett, B, and Waters-Marsh, T. (2008). *Organizational behaviour*. Pearson Education, Australia.

Smith, P.A. (2012) *Succession planning in London secondary schools: Implications for male African-Caribbean leaders*. MBA (Public Services) Dissertation, University of Warwick, Coventry, UK.

Smith, P.A. (2019) *Leading while Black and male: A phenomenology of Black male school leadership.* Doctoral Dissertation, Teachers College, Columbia university, New York, NY. https://doi.org/10.7916/d8–kc0x–w079

Smith, P.A., Francis, D.G. and Harper, A. (2015) 'Reframing transformational leadership for education and nation building in the Caribbean.' *Caribbean Educational Research Journal,* 3(2): 76–89.

'WHEN WORLDS COLLIDE' – LEADING A MULTI-FAITH SCHOOL

JACQUELINE M NEWSOME

As the UK becomes more diverse in terms of its religious identity, school leaders are faced with the challenge of fulfilling the requirements of the Equality Act 2010 to advance equality of opportunity and foster good relations. This chapter explores the tension that exists when accommodating sometimes competing demands and how schools can use the curriculum commitment to deliver compulsory religious education to create ideology spaces for debate and better understanding.

Schools are a reflection of the increasing religious diversity within the UK population. A microcosm of society but with each member connected to one another by the school's own culture, ethos and shared values, schools are uniquely placed to foster interfaith dialogue and promote mutual understanding and tolerance. Unfortunately, this ideal is not always attained. In the shared social space that is a school

'interethnic and interreligious friendships and conflicts coexist' (Santagati, 2020) and school leaders often have to navigate the complexities of accommodating an individual's right to religious expression and celebrating diversity while ensuring they are compliant with equalities legislation.

LEGAL CONSIDERATIONS

The Equality Act 2010 introduced a single Public Sector Equality Duty (PSED). Sometimes referred to as the 'general duty', it applies to public bodies, including maintained schools and academies, and extends to certain protected characteristics – race, disability, sex, age, religion or belief, sexual orientation, pregnancy and maternity and gender reassignment. In fulfilling this duty, schools are required to have *due regard* to the need to:

- Eliminate discrimination and other conduct that is prohibited by the Act,
- Advance equality of opportunity between people who share a protected characteristic and people who do not share it,

- Foster good relations across all characteristics – between people who share a protected characteristic and people who do not share it.

Pupils (and staff) also have the right to manifest a religion or belief, under Article 9 of the Human Rights Act 1998. *Article 9* Freedom of thought, conscience, and religion states that:

> Everyone has the right to freedom of thought, conscience, and religion; this right includes freedom to change his religion or belief and freedom, either alone or in community with others and in public or private, to manifest his religion or belief, in worship, teaching, practice and observance.

By explicitly recognising various religious celebrations, inclusion in school curriculum, uniform and pastoral policies and practices, school leaders can go some way to promoting understanding and tackling prejudice. As OFSTED assess a school's compliance with these legal duties, school leaders are ever-cognisant of these issues.

CHALLENGES FOR SCHOOL LEADERS

The right to manifest a religion or belief does not mean that you can do this necessarily at all times, places or in a particular manner. School leaders must balance the rights of individual pupils against the best interests of the school community as a whole and this can pose practical dilemmas (Russo, 2015). For example:

- How do you reconcile the requirement for the initiated Sikh child to wear a Kirpan in line with religious requirements when the school's stance is one of no weapons on school grounds?
- Consider the Rastafarian child whose dreadlocks are an integral expression of their faith but the child is at odds with a school's uniform policy regarding length of hair – do you operate one rule for one and not the other?
- What should the school leader do when they receive a request to provide the facilities to pray and observe Wudhu in a non-faith school when teaching space is at a premium?
- How does the school leader ensure equality for the LGBT child while dealing with the damage to its reputation and image when sections of the local faith community who oppose the teaching of relationships and sex education are at the front gates?

Although legal advisors may give their expertise (and there are several good resources in these areas that offer guidance), it is the school leader and the governing authority of the school that have to ultimately resolve these issues knowing that not all members of the school community will be satisfied.

Another area that school leaders need to be mindful of is faith-based conflict between pupils. In 2008, a UK bullying prevention charity conducted an interfaith survey of over 1000 pupils and their findings make for uncomfortable reading. Where bullying is defined as 'being taunted, excluded, or abused physically, emotionally or verbally on the grounds of your religious beliefs, affiliation to a given religion, perceived religious identity, or sectarian view by others, including those of other religious groups or belief systems' (BeatBullying, 2008, p.3), they reported that one in four young people who practise a religion reported faith-based bullying (p. 11). The duty of the school to promote community cohesion may also be being undermined with faith seemingly an indicator of friendship groups with 19.1% choosing friends of the same religious or faith backgrounds (BeatBullying, 2008, p. 9). Although only a snapshot survey, observations of peer interactions on any typical school playgrounds seem to support this claim.

In UK schools, religious education is still compulsory. Despite the rise in secularisation and prevalence of a non-religious worldview, it still has a role in helping pupils 'learn about the beliefs, teachings and practices of the great religious traditions of the world (Grimmitt, 1987, pp. 225-6). There is an opportunity for religious education to be more than the mere gaining of knowledge and understanding. White (2004) argues that it should be used to create an opportunity to engage with the religious world view in a critical way, examining religious claims and exploring the negative aspects of religion (p. 162). For example, it has been argued that 'fear and anxiety about the Muslim other' in Britain has led to fundamental British values being promoted in schools as distinct from the values of Islam (Crawford, 2017, p.199). Schools are uniquely placed to challenge this and constructively debate erroneous ideology. It should be noted that the school leader who sanctions the exploration of ideology, gives space for informed debate within their school and allows teachers to develop curricular material that enhance the agreed syllabus, is a courageous one. The advantages are evident, but the potential ideological pitfalls are great.

IMPLICATIONS FOR POLICY AND PRACTICE

Developing young people into citizens who are both well-informed and tolerant of a range of religious and non-religious world views starts with the recognition that the process of getting there involves reconciling competing views and needs. Schools that foster mutual respect will have anti-bullying policies that acknowledge and address faith-based bullying. They will also seek support from a range of religious communities whilst preserving the ethos and culture of their school. Schools must go beyond legal compliance to a duty or an article of the Human Rights act and commit to developing its workforce and enhancing its religious education curriculum provision to allow room for critical engagement with religion and belief.

KEY TAKEAWAYS

- The right to manifest a religion or belief in school must be balanced against the best interests of the whole school community.
- Anticipate and address faith-based conflict between pupils.
- Be deliberate in creating space within the current curriculum constraints for dialogue, to explore ideology and all aspects of religious and non- religious world views.

KEY QUESTIONS:

- How will you ensure that your teachers are equipped to deal with religious issues?
- In what ways can your current inclusive practice be improved so that religious diversity is celebrated and not tokenistic?
- Does your RE curriculum help pupils learn about religion or from religion?

COMMITMENT TO THE MANIFESTO

To make schools a place of genuine interfaith dialogue and practice that promotes mutual understanding and respect for all world views.

REFERENCES

BeatBullying (2008) *Interfaith report*. Available at: file:///C:/Users/User/Downloads/InterfaithReport.pdf

Crawford, C. (2017) 'Promoting 'fundamental British values' in schools: a critical race perspective.' *Curriculum Perspectives*, 37 (2) pp: 197-204.

Grimmitt, M. (1987) *Religious education and human development: The relationship between studying religions and personal, social and moral education.* Great Wakering, Essex: McCrimmons.

Russo, C. J. (2015) "Religious Freedom in Education: A Fundamental Human Right." *Religion and Education*, 42 (1) pp. 17-33

Santagati, M. (2020) 'Religious Conflicts in Multi-Cultural Schools: a Generational Divide between Students and Adults. *Migrants and Religion: Paths, issues, and Lenses,* Leiden, The Netherlands: Brill, pp. 715 -53

White, J. (2004) "Should religious education be a compulsory school subject?' *British Journal of Religious Education*, 26 (2), pp. 151-64

CHRISTIAN VALUES – IT'S WHO I AM.

ESTHER CUMMINS

INTRODUCTION

The acceptance or rejection of religion informs an individual's values, actions and identity. Religious beliefs are complex, and schools cannot simplify religion to application forms. There are significant differences within and between religions. This chapter explores the problems with ignoring these differences, using Bourdieu's thinking tool of cultural capital to understand how practitioners can create more inclusive spaces in their schools. Here the term 'religion' means any and no religion, as outlined in the Equality Act 2010.

CHRISTIANITY AS AN IDENTITY

I am a Christian, but my church leader does not wear special clothes and we do not meet in a building with a steeple. I am confident in discussing my faith but I am always reluctant to answer the question: 'Are you religious?'. My averseness to the question may not be unusual; a 2011 survey found that 60% of participants identified with a religion, but only 29% said they were 'religious' (Humanists UK, 2021).

I am nervous that someone will think that I am 'that sort' of Christian, projecting their ideas regarding judgmentalism or 'happy clappy' songs. The degrees of commitment to religion impact daily life in schools. For some practitioners, Christianity is part of their tradition and heritage, affecting key life events. Others use their faith to make daily decisions in the classroom and significant life choices about employment. This variation in the expressions of belief is not distinct to Christians but true for all religions.

The hesitations and complexities relating to religious identities will be present in every school community. Hemming and Hailwood (2018) contest that religious pluralism impacts school life through access, recognition and accommodation, and identity and belonging. School leaders need to examine the balance of power within the school; which religious beliefs, values and actions are more acceptable to stakeholders?

BUT RELIGIONS ARE ALL THE SAME, AREN'T THEY?

For many Christians, the values of community, love, forgiveness and service stem from their beliefs about the Trinity (God as both one person and as three beings). It is through this understanding of God that many Christians view the world. Non-faith schools commonly may adopt similar values for ethos statements but not hold the same beliefs. Furthermore, if society assumes that all religions are identical, individuals may feel ignored or belittled.

Elton-Chalcraft and Cammack (2019) point to the different private and professional effects of faith on Christian teachers' actions in the Indian education system. The significant distinctions within religions mean that school practitioners must not assume that all faiths produce the same set of beliefs and values. Every individual will make conscious and unconscious life choices concerning what they believe and value, even if they do not verbalise these beliefs to other people.

CULTURAL CAPITAL AND CHRISTIANITY

Bourdieu's (1977) idea of cultural capital helps critique the dynamic of power within society and educational settings. His identification of cultural capital as the 'objectified state' (what we see) and the 'embodied state' (dispositions and attitudes) facilitate recognition of why people feel that they belong more in specific communities. Religion often has an objectified form of cultural capital, such as owning a Bible or cross necklace. Within a school context, some settings accept or even promote the objectified form. An Anglican school may require a Bible in every classroom, or a Catholic school may expect each teacher to have rosary beads. Outsiders have 'clues' to another person's religion.

Anyone who prefers not to say what their religious views are may not exhibit cultural capital explicitly. Instead, it is more likely that they display certain traits in the 'embodied state'. For many Christians, it is the understanding of Jesus that shapes their dispositions. They may show the Biblical characteristics of 'love, joy, peace, patience, kindness, goodness, faithfulness, gentleness, and self-control' (Galatians 5:22-23). In a crisis, Christians may choose to pray or meditate on Bible verses. A person may choose to respond in these ways privately, without naming their religion. This capital is more nuanced and may not give an outsider an indication of the beliefs behind the actions.

THE SPACE TO BE A CHRISTIAN

There is a danger that some individuals may have the 'wrong' capital; their objects or dispositions may gain acceptance into some social circles but exclude them from school spaces. Students may meet in a Christian Union and some faith schools may start staff meetings with prayers, whilst in some non-faith schools there may not be a clear space to pray. There are three apparent answers; that you choose a space that correlates with your own beliefs and values, that no one discusses religion, or educational settings are for people of 'all faiths and none'.

The first approach is problematic because of the diversity within each faith group. Within a Christian school, stakeholders need to be careful not to invalidate a person's cultural capital because of differences that highlight 'otherness', such as if a child or adult commonly uses a Catholic or Protestant ending of the Lord's Prayer. There are many different translations of the Bible and individuals may not be familiar with the one heard in collective worship. The disparities tip the power balance and, in turn, prevent the acceptance and belonging of stakeholders who have any other religion.

A common alternative is that students and staff do not discuss religion beyond the RE classroom. This approach places power on those stakeholders who reject or do not discuss their religion. If there is no commonly held understanding of faith, it may be common to schedule school events for Sunday mornings; this automatically creates an 'othering' of Christians who may choose between a school event or attending church. More contentious issues include banning the wearing of a cross necklace or excluding Jesus from Christmas celebrations. Each example suggests that an individual's religious belief is 'wrong' and does not lead to an inclusive approach.

Schools often adopt an inclusive statement saying they welcome students and staff of all faiths and none. This third approach does not mean that the experience of the individual is positive. There is a danger of tokenism. For Christian pupils, this may lead to schools ignoring significant life events such as confirmation, baptism or first communion (denomination dependent). People only value the events in other spaces; thus, the child does not have the power to express their religious identity.

MOVING FORWARD

It is essential to look at which cultural capital stakeholders validate within settings and how stakeholders express different faiths. I use my Christian lens to view the world, inform my values and act accordingly. Each of us has religious beliefs. If we do not recognise the impact of beliefs on an individual's actions, we do not create inclusive environments where each person's cultural capital is acknowledged, valued and celebrated.

KEY TAKEAWAYS

- Religious beliefs inform values, which inform actions.
- Religions are not all the same; there are differences within each religion and denomination.
- There are spaces in which it is difficult to express religion.

KEY QUESTIONS

- How is religion expressed in your school?
- Who is being 'othered' in your school community because of their religion?
- How can you support religious expression for all your community members?

COMMITMENT TO THE MANIFESTO

Challenge assumptions of religion, including expressions of faith.

REFERENCES

Bourdieu, P. (1977) *Outline of a theory of practice*. Cambridge: Cambridge University Press.

Elton-Chalcraft, S. and Cammack, P. (2019) 'Christian values in education: teachers in India narrate the impact of their faith and values on practice.' *Journal of Beliefs and Values* 41(3): 284-304. Available at: http://insight.cumbria.ac.uk/id/eprint/5064/

Equality Act 2010, c. 15 Available at: https://www.legislation.gov.uk/ukpga/2010/15/section/10 (Accessed 31 March 2021)

Galatians 5:22-23, *Holy Bible: New Living Translation*.

Hemming, P.J. and Hailwood, E. (2018) 'Religious Citizenship in Schools in England and Wales: Responses to Growing Diversity', in Peterson, A., Stahl, G. and Soong, H. (eds.), *The Palgrave Handbook of Citizenship and Education*. Cham: Palgrave Macmillan. https://doi.org/10.1007/978-3-319-67905-1_44-1. Available at: https://cris.brighton.ac.uk/ws/files/12643030/Hemming_Hailwood2018CHPpostprint.pdf (accessed 30 March 2021).

Humanists UK (2021) *Religion and belief: some surveys and statistics*. Available at: https://humanism.org.uk/campaigns/religion-and-belief-some-surveys-and-statistics/ (accessed 30 March 2021).

THE POWER OF INTERFAITH AND DIALOGUE/RELIGIOUS LITERACY

AYSHA KHANOM

INTRODUCTION

Google the word 'religion', you will find images often dominated with themes surrounding 'control' and 'power'. Religion has always carried negative baggage related to violence, division and indoctrination. Seldom do we see images or themes around cohesion and mutuality, or not enough of it. Too often, this is then carried into adult life to continue this cycle. Thus, it is important for us as teachers to address the positive aspects of religion in the classroom, to highlight that religion has been a great force and driver for positive social change – on a micro and macro level. Religion has been a truly *powerful force* for the most part of human history. Religion taps into an enormous urge in human nature to follow a higher power and serve something *greater than oneself*. A message of peace and love towards others is at the heart of all the major world religions. For millions of human beings, God is where you turn in joy or sorrow, and religion is what comes to mind when you think about who you are.

RELIGION IS ALWAYS RELEVANT

Religion is here to stay; ignoring it will not make it disappear. The ongoing conflict between Palestine and Israel and how this rippled into schools and classrooms this year, the debate and controversy over the cartoons in the school in Batley which divided the education community, demonstrates how important and pertinent it is to cultivate religious literacy.

Religion is power, it offers clarity and opportunity for regular self-development and mindfulness. It promotes accountability and is beneficial to society. For those who attend religious gatherings, the main believers are invited to share, to love, to care and to forgive. The existential reality goes beyond material gains but is the community and relationships. There is no denying that religion has and will continue to provide an appropriate disguise and induce hateful actions, and is exploited by the power-hungry, but in fact, this demonstrates more about the nature of human beings, than it does about religion.

In the haste to revoke all association with hateful acts and religion, many have lost sight of the power and contribution of religion today, and in the past. In many ways, religion is wounded by its own triumph. Holy texts and teachings have been scrutinised meticulously for centuries, yet still hold the faith of billions. It is arguably no different to the 'isms' such as socialism, nationalism or communism which carry their own controversies. Religion is governed by humans, who are capable of both good and evil.

SACRED CANOPY

The term 'sacred canopy' was coined by Peter Berger (1987), who wrote a book of the same name. The idea of a sacred canopy is that the worldview of a group of people, nation, or culture is shaped by a certain set of common assumptions which give order and meaning to life.

Religion has a love-hate relationship with the world and religiosity has swept the world and then plummeted, although the 20th century proved God was not dead. Reasons have been advanced for this wave of religiosity sweeping the world. But one overwhelming factor contributed to it: the grand failure of secular atheism foisted onto the 20th century by 19th-century modernists who sought to accommodate religion to contemporary thought. Author Gilles Kepel (1993) observed:

> A new religious approach took shape, aimed no longer at adapting to secular values but at recovering a sacred foundation for the organization of society—by changing society if necessary. Expressed in a multitude of ways, this approach advocated moving on from a modernism that had failed, attributing its setbacks and dead ends to separation from God.' (*Revenge of God,* (1993) p54).

This demonstrates how and why religious literacy is ever-important. Religion is woven into everyday life and has been the driver of social change. Religion has triumphed in times of social and economic deprivation.

It is therefore important to understand the contribution of religion in the classroom and how religion is interwoven in the very fabric of social change and become part of healthy discussion and debate.

IMPORTANCE OF INTERFAITH

The Greeks introduced the idea that individuals are not intelligent on their own, that it is only by reasoning together that they are able to uncover the truth for themselves (Scott, 2009). So, it is important that students leave school with a good level of religious literacy. Religious literacy is not monolithic, it is an ongoing journey, one which requires understanding varying worldviews.

Religious literacy helps students understand the worldview of others and helps them understand their own. At its most basic level, interfaith dialogue involves people of different religious faiths coming together to have a conversation. 'Conversation' in this sense has an expansive definition and is not limited to verbal exchange alone. In his seminal work, Sociologist Robert Bellah (1985) placed conversation at the very heart of civilization, defining cultures as 'dramatic conversations about things that matter to their participants.' (Bellah, 1985) Language allows a form of release that nothing else can match, then why not model it in our classrooms?

True tolerance is contingent not only upon gaining a more sophisticated view of other groups, but also of gaining a similarly complex view of one's own. Interfaith dialogue and understanding are great platforms and methods to demonstrate how we can mutually understand differences and respect them, while we maintain our own views. As students enter a matrix of ideologies, it is important they have the skills to navigate and form their own 'sacred canopy'.

MY EXPERIENCES

Religion played an important part in my life from when I decided to explore various religions and came to a better understanding of my own. It shapes the fabric of my life and is the driver behind most of my good actions and this very contribution.

I came to understand the value of understanding other faiths during my post as an Interfaith Project Manager, commissioned to integrate a small community. There was a time where funding was allocated to local community groups to help promote cohesion and understanding in the wake of terrorist attacks and to combat hate crime. We held exhibitions, debates, Jacob's joint-style get-togethers and community Iftars. We learnt the power of food in addressing difficult conversations and topics. Eventually, our events were attended by hundreds, and these continue to happen each year, fifteen years on.

Every religion carries a theme of peace and goodness. Every year, I hold a 'random acts of kindness' week during interfaith week as everyone has something to offer, followed by topical discussions delivered by speakers of various faiths. Students' complete acts of kindness at home and around school and teachers begin the ripple by being kind to each other.

KEY TAKEAWAYS

Religion is ever-important and relevant. Students should be equipped with good levels of religious literacy to process events in the social and political world.

Interfaith dialogue promotes and models understanding and the positive force of religion. It demonstrates how a personal and intimate belief system which may contradict another, can be respected and mutual ground can be celebrated.

In a world where differences and disputes are rife, teachers are ever-needed to teach and model respectful discussions.

KEY QUESTIONS

- How do you model good interfaith dialogue in schools?
- How is your RE curriculum shaped to help students build their own 'sacred canopy'?
- How do we take into account the views of those with no faith?

COMMITMENT TO THE MANIFESTO

Build an RE curriculum that promotes understanding and positive forces of religion and belief systems through curricula and key events, ensuring that students leave school with confident levels of religious literacy, with the ability to think critically and analyse religion.

REFERENCES

Berger, P. (1900) *Sacred Canopy: Elements of a Sociological Theory of Religion*. Open road media.

Gilles, K.. (1993) *The Revenge of God.* Pennsylvania State University Press

Bellah, R.N. (1985). *Habits of the Heart: Individualism and Commitment in American Life*. Berkeley, CA: University of California Press.

The Power of Dialogue blog. Available at. http://scott.london/articles/ondialogue.html

RELIGION AND MENTAL HEALTH

ORLA MCKEATING

INTRODUCTION

Religion. A word that carries conflict, pain and trauma but a word that has brought a sense of hope and community throughout times of political violence, particularly throughout the thirty years of the Troubles in Northern Ireland and the aftermath right up to today.

Northern Irish society during these times was split in two. This separated politics, residential areas, opinions and education. Having a segregated system in critical learning years and vital development stages facilitated learning about other cultures, practices and beliefs through the media alone. And while the media can be a powerful learning tool, it can amplify common stereotypes created by society. For example, Muslims are terrorists, Black men are a threat and women are less than. Feeding into this narrative is damaging to children's development, critical thinking, awareness and social understanding. Without daily learning, conversations and practice, our younger generation may accept what society teaches them about groups that are perceived as different.

Religious division has had a huge effect on the mental health of Northern Ireland, given that Northern Ireland has the highest recorded rate of PTSD of any studied country in the world (Ulster University Study, 2011) and continues to have the highest suicide rate in the UK according to official government figures. Frederick Douglass, social reformer, abolitionist and international human rights champion who had strong links with Ireland said, 'It is easier to build strong children, than repair broken men.' There is a strong argument that what we are doing is not working to build strong children.

SEGREGATION

Segregation has always existed within the education system in Northern Ireland with mainly Protestant state schools and Catholic schools run by the church. Along with residential and social segregation, this means that an alarming majority of young children in Northern Ireland do not have the opportunity to develop healthy friendships with someone from a different creed between the ages of four and eighteen. In 1998 the Good Friday Agreement promised a more peaceful and together Northern Ireland; however, despite widespread agreement on the need for integrated education and the reformation after the agreement in other institutions including the civil service, the police and the parliament, today 93% of children in Northern Ireland attend either a Protestant or a Catholic school (*The Growth of Integrated Education since the Good Friday Agreement.* Integrated Education Northern Ireland).

Our young people have been left behind. The 'ceasefire babies' who were promised a life of common understanding, hope and inclusion are now having their own children, who continue with segregation in their daily life with a big impact on socialisation in later life.

Having spent my own school years in the 1980s and 1990s in Catholic schools in Belfast, the majority of people had never met someone of a different faith. This fostered misunderstanding, fear and common misconceptions about the 'other'. The experience of living in a very international environment in mainland Europe following this meant I saw first-hand the impact of societal integration on the skills that are required later in life which I missed out on and re-learnt – including communication, a deeper desire to learn, the acceptance of different viewpoints and the ability to work towards consensus. There was mostly a respect for disagreement and a need to find solutions through seeking common ground.

What if we implemented policies where we were all integrated, where there was a curriculum learning about history and background of all cultures, creeds and ethnicities, with learning tools that showed different family structures, non-white heroes, those who lived with disabilities, how to navigate emotions, that we cannot be good at everything, where definition of self is not measured on academia but measured on emotional intelligence, resilience, compassion and applying these to tasks at hand?

MENTAL HEALTH

Mental health is the single largest single cause of ill health and disability in Northern Ireland (DHSSPS, 2015) There have been more deaths by suicide in Northern Ireland than deaths during the political violence between 1969 and 1997 and there is 25% more mental health illness in Northern Ireland than in England (www.changeyourmindni.org). Our country is on its knees and we need to come together to make change. In Northern Ireland, stigma is still a major deterrent to seeking help for mental illness. Research found that internalised stigma (holding stigmatised views about oneself), and treatment stigma (stigma associated with seeking or receiving treatment for mental illness), were the main factors in not seeking help (Betts and Thompson, 2017). And how do we reduce stigma? By having conversations. By raising awareness. By showing compassion. And by educating.

We need to integrate mental health practices into our curriculum to learn about thoughts, feelings and behaviour and to foster an understanding of coping mechanisms and building positive relationships with peers and adults. These skills improve academic performance, can be preventative in mental health issues in later life and schools play an important role in setting the emotional foundations for a healthy future generation.

Learning and practising skills, including self-management, self and social awareness, relationships skills and responsible decision-making, have proved to help children identify and manage feelings, resolve conflict, manage and overcome difficulties and recognise and grow into balanced, thriving adults (Collaborative for Academics, Social, and Emotional Learning, 2006). For example, taking sixty seconds to pause and breathe can lower cortisol levels, reduce anxiety and hyperactivity and promote fuller concentration and healthier lives. (Nestor, 2020). Incorporating short mindful exercises into the already heavy curriculum can result in improved attention, emotional regulation, better compassion skills and reduced stress and anxiety.

So, would implementing a more inclusive curriculum and introducing a deeper understanding of mental well-being into teacher training build a more positive outlook for the future of schooling?

INCLUSIVE CURRICULUM & REPRESENTATION

To move towards a healthier and more wholesome future, it is important to look at the representation in the education system. Are our leaders, learning tools and stories reflective of true society? And if not, what impact could this have on our children?

Representation is important for all children to see themselves in learning tools, books and have role models in the home, school and around them. This builds confidence and teaches empathy, allows connections and inspires and creates impact allowing young people to realise their own potential. The mirrors and windows concept (Style, 1987) allows children to see their own reflection in books and learning tools to nurture their own culture and identity and offer views into someone else's experience, allowing children to find their place in the world and have healthy relationships and a general well-being.

When we cannot see ourselves in the world around us this creates limited beliefs, a fixed mindset on what is achievable and increases othering. It is important to consider perspectives in all academic and learning areas on materials that use data, conversations, models, theories and historical context that is inclusive to all groups of society. Allowing reading tools for children to be diverse improves experience, builds authentic relationships, skills and attainments for all students. When there is a lack of representation in books, this can nurture ignorance, prejudice and racism as their interpretation of the world is limited.

In order to allow for all children to participate fully and achieve at equal rates and effect lasting and positive views, promote acceptance, tolerance and minimise discrimination we need to change the current model.

KEY TAKEAWAYS

- A segregated education system does not foster common understanding, tolerance or equality.
- The mental health rate has declined, and suicide rates increased and while there are other factors to consider, the education system is not beneficial to this.
- The lack of representation and inclusion within the curriculum has maintained a fixed mentality, halted intellectual curiosity and challenges the basic human right of equity for all people.

KEY QUESTIONS

- How can we implement an authentic approach to mental and emotional well-being within the school system?
- How can we positively change views, reduce discrimination and empower our future generation through learning?
- How do we break the generational cycle of trauma to allow for a thriving future?

COMMITMENT TO THE MANIFESTO

Create a more inclusive approach to education where all are valued, respected and have equal opportunity to thrive as well as build a thriving nation.

REFERENCES

Betts, J .and Thompson, J. (2017) *Mental Health in Northern Ireland: Overview, Strategies, Policies, Care Pathways, CAMHS and Barriers to Accessing Services*, 2017

'The Growth of Integrated Education since the Good Friday Agreement'. *Integrated Education Northern Ireland.* Retrieved 23 June 2020.

Delivering Excellence, Achieving Recovery, A professional framework for the mental health nursing profession in N.I. DHSSPS 2015, p10.

www.changeyourminni.org

Collaborative for Academics, Social, and Emotional Learning (CASEL), 2006.

Nestor, J. (2020) *Breath: The New Science of a Lost Art,* Penguin Life Style, E. (1987) *The National SEED Project* 1987

Ulster University Study, 2011

LGBT INCLUSION IN CATHOLIC SCHOOLS

GEORGE WHITE

WHY IS LGBT+ INCLUSION NECESSARY IN CATHOLIC SCHOOLS?

In Catholic schools in the USA, LGBT staff can be removed from their roles if their identity becomes known. In early 2021 in the UK, we have seen relationships and sex education guidance published for use in traditional Catholic schools, detailing men as 'initiators' and women as 'receivers' in sexual relationships. In addition, there have been recent efforts from the Catholic Education Service to ensure that homophobic and biphobic bullying have no place in Catholic schools (CES, 2018). Without embedding LGBT inclusion more widely in Catholic school life, I would argue that such efforts cannot fully support those who are to be protected by the Equality Act 2010 particularly those who are part of the LGBT community and a religious one. There is often a lot of disparity when discussing these two aspects in particular in the context of modern life. Fr James Martin SJ suggests that the starting point is for the Catholic Church to listen to the lived experience of LGBT people (Martin SJ, 2017).

BEING BOTH: CATHOLIC AND TRANSGENDER

I am a Catholic and transgender teacher of Religious Education (RE) in a Catholic school where I have had many positive and some negative experiences that have led me to question how we might make Catholic schools more inclusive for the LGBT community.

Despite not coming from a religious family, I have always been in Catholic education. Despite being born female, I always knew there was something different about me. I was lost for most of my time in school as I was navigating my way with a problem I did not know how to describe or who to tell about it. The school I attended was a Catholic School in Leicester; many different religions, ethnicities and cultures were present in the school community. However, there were no visible signs or support for openly LGBT staff or pupils. I started secondary school in 2004; Section 28 had only been repealed one year earlier. I became disruptive but I had some teachers who never lost faith in me. I decided that I wanted to be fully part of this community so I changed my behaviour, became a Catholic and was hopeful for a future career in teaching. I was baptised in the school chapel at the age of sixteen and chose some of my most inspiring teachers to be my baptismal sponsors, some of whom are now my colleagues.

I continued to study RE whilst exploring my faith and my gender identity. In the midst of what I would describe as an existential crisis where I believed I had to choose between the two, I started teaching at a well-known Catholic girls' school in West London as Miss White. In my first year, two of our pupils came out as transgender. Our headteacher wrote a letter that went out to parents stating that the school recognised their dignity and supported them by using their chosen name and pronouns (*Catholic Herald,* 2017). Some parents did not welcome this; one even removed their daughter from the school. National Catholic media published the letter and this led to the school facing a backlash because they had decided to support the decision of our transgender pupils (The Christian Institute, 2017). It would have been a big fight if I were to stay there and transition, especially as a teacher of RE where the expectation is that you are a 'practising Catholic'. For lots of people who did not support the school (and the transgender pupils' decision) there was an assumption that you cannot be both a faithful Catholic and LGBT or supportive of LGBT people.

I came to an interview at the secondary school I attended as a child where we spoke openly about transition and what that would mean for time off for appointments and surgeries which has been honoured ever since. I had started the process of hormone replacement therapy to trigger male puberty only one month prior to accepting this role. Inevitably, pupils and staff were going to have questions. I wanted to have open dialogue but the interviewers advised me to shut down any conversations brewing, as teachers did not have to answer questions about their personal life. I was supposed to be seen as a normal appointment to a job but without the openness, it felt as though my identity had to be kept secret and as a result, any transphobic comments were not dealt with in the same way other discriminatory remarks were. For many people in the school community, I am the first openly transgender person they have met and for some, perhaps the first LGBT Catholic. The more open I have been with the pupils, the more respectful and educated they have become about LGBT and faith identities and issues. The more open I have been with staff, the more confident they have been in understanding appropriate behaviour and challenging discrimination.

PRACTICAL NEXT STEPS TO IMPROVE LGBT + INCLUSION IN CATHOLIC SCHOOLS

To improve, I believe we must stop talking about LGBT people as 'the other'. It is common that Religious Education teachers in Catholic schools are asked how they would respond to a question on homosexuality from a pupil in their interview for the job. The expected response is that the candidate will not publicly deviate from church teaching. Other aspects of modern life that may conflict with church teaching are not questioned in this way; abortion, divorce, IVF, female ordination, who can receive the Eucharist and so on. These questions, in my opinion, need to be reconsidered as they give an impression that we must be silent on LGBT issues and that is not explicitly the same for all 'difficult' topics within RE or the wider school life nor does it respect the importance of conscience.

Also, a document approved by many dioceses outlines which candidates constitute 'a practising Catholic' for certain school roles. It suggests several violations which deem a person unworthy of applying for a particular role as a practising Catholic; same sex relationships being implicitly referred to as just one of them (Diocese of Nottingham, 2019). This document simply does not reflect the lived reality of many schools in the UK, there are many teachers in the roles who do not fit the criteria and have to remain secretive about it. There are many who have been overlooked from promotion to such roles based on this list of requirements. The document seems to forget that the leaders Jesus chose were not perfect and that he was aware of that. I think it is important we remember that humility when selecting suitable candidates for roles within Catholic Education. The document, in outlining the details of what makes an 'official' practising Catholic, suggests that some of the people listed do not meet the conditions of being a practising Catholic, yet they are present in our community. In fact, they are not just present, but actively participating and doing an excellent job.

This idyllic view of what constitutes a practising Catholic is great in theory – but it does not accurately reflect the people working and living in its institutions. As Pope Francis puts it: 'The Church does not exist to condemn people but to bring about an encounter with the visceral love of God's mercy.' For the Church to offer God's mercy it must 'go outside and look for people where they live, where they suffer and where they hope.' The enemy of mercifulness is self-righteousness, the disease of religious folk 'who live attached to the letter of the law but who neglect love ...who only know how to close doors and draw boundaries'; their approach, sadly, is 'repeated throughout the long history of the Church' (Pope Francis, 2016). Taking this message from Pope Francis on board would give the bridge-building process between faith institutions and LGBT people a much more stable foundation.

I understand that there is fear around leaders discussing LGBT rights in the context of education but choosing to remain silent about us does a great disservice to both LGBT and non-LGBT people. There is no conflict between church teaching and respecting the human dignity of each person, supporting them pastorally and visibly reaching out to them. There are several examples of the Pope reaching out to the LGBT community and he continues to stress the importance of the individual's conscience in decision-making, both of which are things that can be emanated by wider society. For example, he has given funds to a struggling transgender community showing that he is both listening and supporting the LGBT community (*The Tablet*, 2020). Learning about others is one of the ways in which Catholic schools embody the call to love one's neighbour and that is a gospel value that is at the heart of Catholic Education.

KEY TAKEAWAYS

- Being Catholic and supporting LGBT students and staff are not mutually exclusive.
- We have Catholic role models who practise acceptance within the faith.
- Transgender staff and students have a place in Catholic schools which remember the teachings of the Bible.

KEY QUESTIONS

- What is currently in place to support LGBT staff/pupils feel comfortable in sharing their experiences in Catholic schools and how can you better facilitate the 'listening' process?
- How can a Catholic school promote the dignity of **all** people without exclusion in policies and practices?
- In understanding the Equality Act 2010, how will you challenge individual or institutional religious freedom when they/it begins to actively discriminate against LGBT people in your educational context?

COMMITMENT TO THE MANIFESTO

To make schools a place of genuine interfaith dialogue and practice that promotes mutual understanding and respect for all world views.

REFERENCES

Catholic Education Service (2018) *Made in God's Image: Challenging homophobic and biphobic bullying in Catholic Schools.* Available at: https://www.catholiceducation.org.uk/images/CES-Project_Homophobic-Bullying-Booklet_JUN18_PROOF-9.pdf (last accessed 6th June 2021)

Martin, J. (2017) *Building A Bridge: How the Catholic Church and LGBT community can enter into a relationship of respect, compassion and sensitivity.* San Francisco: HarperOne.

Catholic Herald (staff writers) (2017) 'School: use transgender "preferred pronouns"', *Catholic Herald,* 5th October 2017

The Christian Institute (2017) *Girls face 'confusion' over trans policy at RC school.* Available at: https://www.christian.org.uk/news/girls-face-confusion-trans-policy-rc-school/ (last accessed 6th June 2021)

Diocese of Nottingham (2019) *Definition of a Practising Catholic.* Available at https://www.dioceseofnottingham.uk/application/files/5915/5266/8243/Definition_of_a_Practising_Catholic_-_January_2019.pdf (last accessed 6th June 2021)

Pope Francis (2016) *The Name Of God Is Mercy.* Bluebird (English translation).

Cairns, M. (2020) 'Pope Gifts Funds to Transgender Community.' *The Tablet,* 1st May 2020

EMBRACING THE LEAST

ELIZABETH WALSH-IHEOMA

INTRODUCTION

Christianity originated with the ministry of Jesus, who was described as 'homoousion to Patria' – *of the same essence or substance of God.* It has been argued by some male theologians and Biblical feminists that Jesus's maleness has been used as an excuse and a vehicle to prevent the progress of women taking up leadership positions within some Christian churches and has been used to keep 'women in their place'. In this chapter you will learn how some feminists have addressed this imbalance and how the concept of embracing the weak or the least by liberating the oppressed should be at the heart of the Christian message and should be the Christian's mission, because Christ is a Saviour for all humanity.

IS JESUS'S MALENESS A BARRIER TO WOMEN'S SALVATION?

God became incarnate in the man Jesus. He was a Jewish teacher and healer who proclaimed the imminent kingdom of God and was crucified in Jerusalem in the Roman province of Judea but resurrected on the third day. In short, God entered human history through Jesus Christ and achieved our salvation.

Jesus's impact after death has been unparalleled. Perhaps the most profound behaviour demonstrated by Jesus was his inclusivity in his treatment of women. This is what drew people, particularly women, to him. He was born in a patriarchal society, where men dominate women. The norm existed in men undervaluing women thus supporting oppressive practices and structures for women. It could be said that Jesus was maladjusted to his present (Russell, 1982).

Jacquelyn Grant (1989) asserts that as a direct challenge to this, 'feminists have developed a feminist Christology which articulates the meaning of the gospel of Jesus Christ for women today and promotes liberation of women from oppressive structures which have negated their humanity'. Biblical feminists and liberationist feminism work towards the same goals in challenging the theological community to look at women's experiences in relation to theology and Christology.

The key goal of feminist theology is to show how traditional male-articulated

Christologies have been used to 'keep women in their place'. They use the very instrument that has been used against them – the Bible – and have made it the basis of their egalitarian discussions. Paul Jewett (1975) writing in *Man as Male and Female* affirms that Jesus was revolutionary in how he related to women in that 'he treated women as fully human, equal to men in every aspect; no word of depreciation about women as such is ever found on his lips'. Jesus did not see women as the opposite sex, he saw them as the neighbouring sex. His treatment of women inverted the belief that women were second-class citizens. Judaism was unusual in teaching that women as well as men fully bear the image of God. We read in the Bible (Genesis) and in the Torah (bereishit):

> So God created man in His own image; in the image of God
> He created him; male and female He created them" (Gen.
> 1:26, 27, NKJV).

WHO ARE THE LEAST?

Jacquelyn Grant (1989) in her book *White Women's Christ and Black Women's Jesus* sees that the solution must emerge out of the condition of the least and identifies such people as those whose oppression is a tri-dimensional reality of race/sex/class. She asserts that Black women's faith experience is different to that of White women and this needs to be recognised. Grant (1989) identifies the poor Black American woman as being the least in modern American society as they are most often on the bottom of the social and economic ladder due to the impact of classism. Alice Walker introduces the term 'womanist' to distinguish feminists of colour. A womanist just means *being* and *acting* out who you are – being authentic. Womanist theology draws upon the life and experiences of some Black women who have created meaningful interpretations of the Christian faith.

Grant's rationale in identifying the American Black woman as the least in that they are exposed to the tri-dimensional oppression of race/sex/class, means they share in a reality of a broader community. They share race suffering with Black men; with White women and other third-world women, they are victims of sexism; and they share experiences with both poor Blacks and Whites. To speak of Black women's tri-dimensional reality, therefore is not to speak of Black women exclusively, for there is an implied universality which connects them with others.

Christ represents a threefold significance: first he identifies with the 'little' people, these were the women, the poor, the lame, the outcasts; second, he affirms the basic humanity of these, the 'least'; and thirdly, he inspires active hope in the struggle for resurrected liberated existence. Letty Russell (1982) in her book *Becoming Human* asserts we should look for a clue to the meaning of our humanity among the losers of society as we have a great deal in common with such people.

GOD – A PROJECTION OF MAN

In contrast to Christianity, atheism is the denial of the existence of God. According to the Annual Population Survey, between 2012 and 2018 there was a slight decline in people professing Christianity as a religion but there was an increase in people professing no religion.

Hans Kung (1980) proposes that theology and atheism are close to one another – if there are atheists who become theologians then there are theologians that are atheists. In the nineteenth century, atheism became more widespread among the educated classes following the French Enlightenment and increasing secularisation of society brought on by the advancement of modern science and democracy which was pitted against the belief in God.

Two prominent atheists of the nineteenth century, Ludwig Feuerbach and Friedrich Nietzsche, promoted an atheism that threatened belief in God. Ludwig Feuerbach (1841), in the *Essence of Christianity (Das Wesen des Christentums)* saw God as nothing but a projection of man and sought to affirm the real nature of man by restoring the true divine that theism took away. There is a direct relationship between our perception of Jesus Christ and our perception of ourselves. Friedrich Nietzsche(1882) writing in *The Gay Scientist (Die Fröhlich Wissenschaft)* declared *'There is no God. I do not believe in any God'*. This declaration was aimed at those whom he coined 'superficial atheists', thus calling on them to embrace a passionate atheism. If one was going to be atheist, then one needed to bear the vast consequences of the 'murder of God'.

Feminist theologians argue that generic language is in fact no more than male language which represents a male perspective. Man has, in fact, projected himself as the subject with the authority to say who Jesus Christ is for us (men and women) yesterday, today and tomorrow. This then could equate to a form of forced atheism.

Similarly, we could argue that when discussing religion and faith in schools, using exclusively masculine language that makes the male perspective the normative and keeps many women in the margins, where their contributions are negated, can be akin to 'murdering God' on their behalf or driving some women (and men) towards a superficial form of atheism. Atheism should be a choice. Just as Christianity should be an informed choice. This choice can be supported by disrupting the hegemony of using exclusive male language that marginalises women.

Freeing humans from bondage was Jesus's definition of his ministry. This meant that Jesus identified with the lowly of his day. He was born in a lowly manager and lived a life embracing the least and the weak and died for those who loved him as well as those who hated him, thus turning human values upside down (Niebuhr 1932). The least are those people who have water to give but offer what they have. Jesus declared: 'Truly I tell you, whatever you did for one of the least of these brothers and sisters of mine, you did for me'. (Matt. 25:40)

KEY TAKEAWAYS

- The significance of Christ is not his maleness but his humanity.
- We should teach that men and women were created to complement each other.
- Embracing the least requires our students to identify those who experience tri-dimensional oppressions of race/class/sexism; working to affirm the basic humanity of these.

KEY QUESTIONS

- If Christ is among the least, then who are they?
- What does Christ mean in a society in which class distinctions are increasing?
- Does the style of leadership and basic structure in your school or institution ensure the continuation of a privileged class?

COMMITMENT TO THE MANIFESTO

Promote a liberating Christology by challenging oppressive distorted Biblical interpretations through curricular exposure.

REFERENCES

Grant, J. (1989), *White Women's Christ and Black Women's Jesus: Feminist Christology and Womanist Response,* Atlanta, Georgia: Scholars Press

Kung, H. (1980) *Does God Exist? (Existiert Gott?)* London: SCM Ltd

Niebuhr, R. (1932), *Moral Man and Immoral Society: A Study in Ethics and Politics.* Louisville, Kentucky: Westminster John Knox Press

Russell, L. (1982), *Becoming Human.* The Westminster Press: Philadelphia

'YOU LOOK LIKE A NUN'

ANJUM PEERBACOS

'There is no beauty better than intellect' Muhammed (peace be upon him)

Teaching is often considered a vocation; as people, we are intrinsically tied to what we do. I always considered teaching a way in which I could impart and share the knowledge that I have, however small, with others and I have been fortunate enough to have had a career spanning over twenty years which has enabled that.

GROWING UP MUSLIM IN THE UK – PRE-BREXIT

My journey with faith began as an early teenager having visited an Islamic youth camp over the summer holidays as a thirteen-year-old. It was set in a gorgeous place up in the Highlands for a week, away from family and friends, and in the most scenic surroundings. One of the conditions of the camp was that if you were a girl, you would wear a hijab or headscarf during the activities as well as for prayer. It became a part of your attire during the course of the week and when I came home I felt like this was something that I wanted to continue, it felt like it was a part of me. This was at the time when very few Muslim women would have worn the hijab; I think I was incredibly resolute in what I wanted to do at a very young age, and was aware that I wanted to practise my faith demonstrably.

MY SPIRITUAL JOURNEY

The real journey began on my return back to normal life at home, starting a new academic year in September as it was in late August that I returned from this trip. I remember lots of curiosity from girls who were in my class. Out of curiosity I was asked about it; I gave my reasons and they were received well. I was left to carry on as I felt comfortable. One negative comment really struck a chord with me and that has stayed with me so many years later was when one boy called me a 'tea towel head' as he was running past with his friends. The irony was that he was also a Muslim, and it was as though he was attempting to gain some credence with his white friends at the time. I always found solace and comfort in prayer which is still a great comfort to me, so I feel the connection I had as a teenager has stayed with me and has become even stronger as an adult.

THE TEACHING JOURNEY BEGINS

When I started my teaching career, my schools were in a demographic where the children looked like me. I always taught in inner-city London schools, where the intake of students was diverse. I met children like myself, with parents from all over the world and so there were many Muslim children in the schools I taught in. My faith didn't really register until I started working in a Catholic secondary school. At my previous schools, even though the students looked like me, the staff body didn't. When I kindly declined to go to the local pub on a Friday evening after school, rumours began circulating that I was antisocial, or snobbish. It became glaringly obvious that although the staff taught a largely Muslim population, they were unaware of the practices of Muslims. This itself is a concern, surely you should be aware of your demographics and their religious and cultural practices?

The truth is that I'd never thought about applying to work in a Catholic school, but it was time to move on to pastures new. I mentioned it to a friend who knew a school that was looking to appoint an English teacher and I was happy to go there for an interview. My friend told me it was a Catholic school and I assumed that they would want to appoint somebody who was a practising Catholic. This was not the case and I went for the interview and met the headteacher. In a nutshell, I was offered a job and I accepted thinking that I would do it for a year and then move on. I started my sixth year in September 2020 and have no intention of leaving.

THE REALISATION

In my first year at the Catholic school, I took a day off to celebrate Eid. On my return to school the next day a student had asked me about my health and I said 'I'm fine thanks' and he responded by saying 'But you weren't here yesterday, Miss'.

I said: 'I wasn't ill, I was celebrating Eid.'

'Oh, so you're Muslim?'

'Yes.' Clearly the headscarf was not enough of a clue.

'But you're not like those Muslims we see on TV...'

And for me this was an awakening, this young man had a very misconstrued notion of what Muslims were like and how they were portrayed in mainstream media.

> **(God) has established for you (The Arabs) the same religion enjoined on Noah, on Abraham, on Moses and on Jesus, the Quran says, (42:13)**

I suggested we organise an assembly-style gathering of the year group (Year 9), as they were studying Islam. I started with a presentation about the Abrahamic faiths, discussing the similarities of the three faiths. These being the oneness of God, the prophets Adam,

Noah, Abraham, Moses, and Christ. Charity is also a fundamental aspect of Catholicism and Islam, and the amount of fundraising/ charitable activities at my school are absolutely phenomenal and a real testament to the entire community. It is such a fantastic ethos and culture, a true understanding of what you can do to help others less fortunate.

After my presentation, all students were given opportunities to ask questions anonymously or openly. My caveat was that no question was too stupid, and if I did not know the answer then I would endeavour to find out. I answered questions for over an hour and I could have gone on for longer. What I found interesting was that although we lived in London, possibly the most diverse city in the world, these students would not have spoken to a Muslim (in particular, a Muslim woman) to ask questions or have a conversation. There are a million Muslims in London; however, had I not been in this school at this time, these questions would have been left largely unanswered, or worse still, their notions of Muslims would have been solely formed by the portrayal in mainstream media.

I wrote a piece for *TES* in an attempt to share my experience and hoped that it could help others. When my current headteacher read the article above she didn't respond immediately, and I thought the worst. I wanted to let her know that I had taken some steps to educate our young people about Islam. The following week my headteacher asked me if I would like to have a prayer room on-site. The students had asked how I completed my prayers during the day and I had said that I prayed when I got home. As a person and a headteacher she valued my faith as much as her own and has since provided me with the facility for me to pray during the school day – I am grateful for that space to this day. This headteacher has also recognised the value of the Q&A sessions and has since invited members of staff to attend the sessions with the young people, to ensure that if there was something that adults in our community wanted to learn or know, then they could too.

The learning for me continues every day. However, one moment stands out for me among them all. A jaw-dropping moment was when I attended a mass and everyone turned to each other at the end and said 'Peace be with you.' I nearly fell off my chair! In Islam our salutation and greeting to all is 'Peace be with you' – I just didn't know, thus demonstrating my own ignorance of the Catholic faith.

'Whoever kills an innocent life it is as if he has killed all of humanity' (5:32)

I have also been asked to speak at staff inset sessions regarding the perceptions around Muslims and in particular Muslim women, to challenge misconceptions. It was following this that several members of staff approached me regarding the comments that they had heard from students regarding Muslims and misconceptions. As mentioned previously in this chapter, The Equality Act 2010 states that the presence of religion or belief within a person's described identity are protected from discrimination, harassment or victimisation. Unfortunately, this has not been the case in our society. Post-Brexit Britain has not been kind to me and many Muslims, especially Muslim women. We saw an increase of 700% in religious hate crime post the Christchurch attack that predominantly targeted Muslims. As

Muslim women are often more visibly Muslim, they are often the target of these horrendous attacks. It all comes back to education for me and I am trying to dispel misconceptions about Muslims on a daily basis, and in particular about Muslim women. This quote above from the Quran has become crucial for me in our current political climate. Always trying to make a small difference within circles of influence I have to teach people that Islam is a religion of peace and not war.

One day I happened to be wearing a black dress and one of the teachers said: 'You look like a nun'. I was rather taken aback at first but was not offended. A nun is someone who is devoted to God and their faith. I think that if it was a compliment, I will take it as such.

KEY TAKEAWAYS

'Allah is the best of planners' (8: 30)

- As teachers we are all leaders. For the young people in front of you every day you are leading the way, shining the light; be that light.
- Take the leap of faith; if you do not feel that your school values and appreciates you, then move on. Do not settle for less.
- Step out of your comfort zone, I did and it is probably the best career move I ever made.

KEY QUESTIONS

- Have you been accepted and appreciated through integration or assimilation?
- Are you appreciated and valued in your current setting?
- Could you voice any concerns regarding your identity and beliefs where you currently are?

COMMITMENT TO THE MANIFESTO

To incorporate the concept of faith and moral purpose in the privilege that is my vocation as a teacher and as a leader, in every capacity. To facilitate and always develop opportunities for all stakeholders, in particular for all those that are children of immigrants.

REFERENCES

Ali, K. (2019), *The Guardian*: https://www.theguardian.com/commentisfree/2021/mar/16/the-christchurch-massacre-continues-to-haunt-muslims-across-the-world-online-and-offline

Dodd, V. (2019), *The Guardian*: https://www.theguardian.com/society/2019/mar/22/anti-muslim-hate-crimes-soar-in-uk-after-christchurch-shootings

WHAT'S THAT ON YOUR HEAD?

NASRA BARRE

INTRODUCTION

The term 'hijab' directly translates to *cover* and can be more accurately described as a set of codes that epitomises morality, modesty, and privacy. These sets of codes are practised by many people of faith, as well as people of non-religious beliefs. Most citizens in the Western world associate the term hijab with the headpiece alone, which is commonly associated with and worn by Muslim women. However, there is a lot more to the hijab than a piece of scarf placed on your head. In this section, you will gain an insight into how a visible difference can contribute to and generate discrimination in society, within education and the impact and effectiveness of intercultural education that ultimately prepares young, minority citizens to thrive in a diverse society.

THE HIJAB AND ME

A question that many ask is, 'What's that on your head?' For many Muslim women, it is a symbol of faith that presents a part of them to the world by default. Like many women who wear the hijab, it is a personal and special journey that connects them spiritually to their religion. As mentioned above, the hijab is more than the headscarf itself; it is also the modesty in one's character and an amalgamation of how people of a Muslim faith represent themselves through their behaviour, speech, and the way they treat others. The hijab is a way of life that is followed by Muslims. The headscarf is one of many variations of the hijab, which Muslim women use (who also choose to wear or not wear) across the globe for religious reasons and can be worn in many ways. The versatility and creativity many of these women express when they wear their hijab is admirable.

Wearing the hijab is personal, yet it is often the first and most visible thing people see about hijab-wearing Muslim women. Personally, it symbolises and serves as a reminder of who I am. Some would say that they feel 'lucky' to live in a society that allows them the power to choose to wear something that outwardly represents morality, modesty, and pride in being a Muslim woman. In the United Kingdom (UK),

The Equality Act 2010 protects anyone who chooses to represent their religion or belief. There is a sense of empowerment in having the control to choose how I show myself and what I want the world to see.

Nonetheless, this admiration has its barriers. Since the attacks on the 11th of September 2001, there have been negative repercussions for (headscarf-wearing) Muslims. The positive and empowering effect of this head covering became a struggle for many. Crime rates were soaring not only against visibly Muslim women but also for anyone who was perceived as a minority with a head covering. It was reported that men and women of the Sikh faith were also targeted because of stereotyping and preconceived notions (Ahluwalia and Pellettiere, 2010). Within the Sikh faith, men and women use a special head covering, which is unique and important to their Sikh identity. This obvious visibility across religions and various cultures has created an assumption that negatively impacts a wider population of people who wear a head covering. This raises the importance of talking about an issue and educating society by being a catalyst for learning. This is vital for change, starting with us, and our young people.

CAN YOU UPHOLD BRITISH VALUES?

As a Muslim, British values are welcomed; I recognise and promote them as being integral to living in an increasingly diverse society. It is unfortunate, however, that as many as 55% believe that there is a fundamental clash between Islam and British values and that they are therefore not compatible (IPSOS, 2018). With over three million Muslims living in the UK according to the 2011 census (ONS, 2018), half of whom are British born, why is this figure so high?

Predominantly speaking, British values are ideals that many Muslims can support and accept, as they are also synonymous with Islamic teachings. The subject is disputed through the media. Lots of negative notions stem from inaccurate representation and misinformation to society. The impact this creates, especially to those that are visibly Muslim, can be damaging, and with Islamophobia simmering, prejudice and hate crimes are rising to their highest levels since records began.

Can you uphold British values? This was a question that I was once asked at an interview for a primary teaching post. As you can imagine, there was disbelief and shock after this. Why was I being asked this? Was this because they could see I was a Muslim? Growing up in society as visibly Muslim, I have always lived on edge, wondering if others are judging me because of the piece of material on my head and questioning whether I should fill or skip the question around religion on job applications, especially with more recent media coverage on 'Islamic' attacks. They are not Islamic, might I add. That said, the negative connotations of the religion and the hijab should never restrict one's goals in life. Growing up as a child in Britain and choosing to wear the hijab held so many mixed emotions: admiring the women in my family and knowing the backlash this could have from the wider world.

Questions around the hijab are always welcomed; it is empowering knowing that my hijab serves as a constant motivator to break the associated stereotypes through conversations, however I possibly can. Nonetheless, during that interview, I found myself speaking to someone who already held preconceived notions about what Islam was. Research states that many Muslim women feel that wearing the headscarf at work is an additional visual marker of perceived difference and leads to experiences of further discrimination (Everett et al. 2015).

THERE IS POWER IN VISIBILITY

Representation in all aspects of life is important, as it reduces marginalisation. As a hijab-wearing Muslim primary school teacher in a Church of England and majority white school, I have seen first-hand the surprise on minority ethnic pupils' faces when they first see me, as well as their parents on the playground during drop-off and pick-up. This restores faith in some families that their children will feel valued, listened to and part of an inclusive school environment with high ambitions for all. Maintaining high expectations for all pupils, especially marginalised groups like hijab-wearing girls, is equally as important.

The education system is the earliest and most significant mainstream social institution in which young Muslim pupils encounter wider society. With many Muslim pupils attending state schools, it is even more vital for educators to understand the basic beliefs, practices and cultural norms that are predominant in the Muslim community. Educators who can meet the needs of their pupils through understanding and acceptance are ultimately able to provide a welcoming school experience for all children. For children of a minority community, finding commonalities in an educator that looks like them can provide them with newfound ambitious fire. Knowing that others who 'look' like them are in positions that they do not usually see can positively influence a pupil. There is this famous quote: 'You can't be what you can't see', by Marian Wright Edelman. However, many people who are in stages where they have made achievements, are in positions in which they have not seen a minority like them before. It is possible to be what you cannot see – it is just ten times harder for you than your majority peers.

While the visibility of being Muslim has its battles in wider society, in the education system and as a leader, it can automatically assist in tackling attitudes of Islamophobia and underachievement among minority pupils with other educators. A visible presence creates a culture of openness and trust between teachers and pupils based on educators understanding, valuing, and listening to all.

KEY TAKEAWAYS

- The hijab is a spiritual journey, and it is also described as a way of life that is followed by Muslims.
- Pre-empt the barriers that a visible difference can have and allow for a society that is a catalyst for learning.
- Diverse representation is valuable in all spaces to dismantle false narratives.

KEY QUESTIONS

- How can you advocate for and ensure diverse representation within your school and staffing body?
- In what ways may schools ensure marginalised groups feel a sense of belonging?
- How do we create respectful spaces which tackle discrimination and empowers all through learning?

COMMITMENT TO THE MANIFESTO

Embrace and value any visible difference, and to allow for a culture of openness and equity in and around the school, staffing and pupils.

REFERENCES

Ahluwalia, M. and Pellettiere, L. (2010) 'Sikh Men Post 9/11: Misidentification, Discrimination, and Coping.' *Asian American Journal of Psychology* (1)4: 303-14.

Everett, J., Schellhaas, F., Earp, B., Ando, V., Memarzia, J., Parise, C., Fell, B. and Hewstone, J. (2015) 'Covered in stigma? The impact of differing levels of Islamic head-covering on explicit and implicit biases toward Muslim women.' *Journal of Applied Science Psychology* (45)2): 90-104.

IPSOS (2018) *A review of survey research on Muslims in Britain*. Available at: https://www.ipsos.com/sites/default/files/ct/publication/documents/2018-03/a-review-of-survey-research-on-muslims-in-great-britain-ipsos-mori_0.pdf (accessed 04 April 2021).

Office for National Statistics (2018) *Muslim population in the UK*. Available at: https://www.ons.gov.uk/aboutus/transparencyandgovernance/freedomofinformationfoi/muslimpopulationintheuk/ (accessed 04 April 2021).

WHAT DID YOU HEAR ABOUT ME? BEING AN OPENLY JEWISH TEACHER AS A STUDENT RESOURCE

ALLISON ZIONTS

INTRODUCTION

Teachers hold simultaneously multiple roles within schools: as an expert in their field, one who provides feedback and guidance, in *loco parentis*, and as a role model. Teachers who are from minority religious or ethnic groups have the additional pressure of being living resources, representing their people. As a Jewish teacher, I have become a living resource when students study the Holocaust or read books with Jewish characters, and they need to see what a contemporary Jewish person can be like. Being this resource has impacted my relationship with students and colleagues and has taught me about the importance of nurturing authenticity in teaching.

BEING UNIQUE

For two weeks a year, students walk past my classroom, poke their head in, and then start whispering. This happens like clockwork: the first week is after the Holocaust Memorial Day assembly in January, and the second is when the Year 9 English lessons are reading *The Merchant of Venice* in May. The first time this happened, I was confused, asking myself if it was fair that as a contemporary Jewish woman, that I was a stand-in for the history and culture they were exploring in their other subjects. I became conscious of how they began to analyse my actions and words in light of what they had been learning about. Students would question me about my own experiences with loss during the Holocaust and antisemitism living in London.

Being an openly Jewish teacher in schools with little or no visible Jewish presence can be a challenge. Beyond the logistical considerations of time off for holidays or having to explain rituals and practices, teachers and educational staff from a minority religion or background can become inadvertent emissaries for their people. Our days are spent not only performing our roles as teachers, but also having to be aware that we may be the only contemporary and tangible representation of our culture or religious people for thousands of students. While during the day-to-day, our professionalism and manners will reflect positively and show that individuals from different religions and ethnic minorities can contribute equally to a multicultural British society, this openness can make us more vulnerable to challenging conversations or stereotypes.

AUTHENTIC RESOURCE

Within academic writing, this openness is referred to as being 'authentic' (Laursen, in Beijaards et al., 2005). Authentic teaching is not about just being oneself, as teachers need to maintain their boundaries of professionalism and remain apolitical within their teaching spaces. This model requires teachers to explore how they can be open enough about their personal characteristics and find ways to use these characteristics to build bridges and form relationships (De Bruyckere and Kirschner, 2016). As with many aspects of teaching practices, there is no roadmap for how a teacher can become an authentic teacher, nor is there a guidance as to when a teacher is sufficiently authentic or has overstepped (Bialystok, 2015). This falls within the boundaries of professionalism and school policy, but also requires the staff members to feel confident within themselves and safe in their spaces to be open and share.

Religious Studies departments often employ authentic resources in their pedagogy; this can include having staff and students bring in objects of religious value from their homes or reading directly from core texts. Field trips to holy sites and religious buildings are a vital way in which students develop an understanding of how contemporary religious people practise (Rigel and Kindermann, 2016). Guest speakers, including members of the clergy, can also be brought in so students can ask questions to deepen their understanding of how these figures and concepts, sometimes so abstract on the page, can be tangible. Having these authentic resources, as either objects or people, allows students to develop a more nuanced understanding of situations and religious groups.

Staff cannot be forced into sharing their identities or stories with students; for a number of reasons – they may not feel safe doing so, or it does not suit their style of teaching. However, creating a culture within the school where staff do feel comfortable in sharing themselves authentically is an investment the school leadership can make in order to provide students with regular experiences to enrich their education and cultural capital. Living within contemporary British society, students are surrounded by millions of people who are similar and dissimilar to them in myriad ways, and being authentic is one way to expose students to a wider range of characteristics within a controlled and safe space.

INCORPORATING LIVING RESOURCES INTO YOUR CLASSROOM

Rather than being brought in, having teachers willing to act as authentic resources can be a vital tool for students to reconcile with what they have been taught about a people and how they can be in reality. However, in having teachers become this bridge, it opens them up to being treated differently by the students. Similar to the example in the introduction, as students read *The Merchant of Venice* and learn about the stereotypes of Jewish people in fourteenth-century Italy, they question whether these stereotypes apply to their Jewish teacher in twenty-first century England. This could cause discomfort for those staff members, who now need to contend with an altered perception that students have of them due to a text they are studying.

One of the methods of reducing such discomfort for staff can be mapping the curriculum across a wide range of protected characteristics and having this be the starting point for a discussion around representation within schools. Using this model, for five years I have been invited to speak to the English classes while they are reading *The Merchant of Venice* to answer questions they have about being Jewish today and my own experiences with antisemitism. This not only suited the needs of the English department that students develop an understanding of the context of the book, but it allowed students to ask questions about what it is like being a Jewish person today. While I make it clear that I cannot answer for all Jews, they can begin to put together a richer picture of how these abstract characters may live their lives. In doing this, I remember the value in having a Buddhist teacher present and answering questions when I read Hermann Hesse's *Siddhartha*, and being able to regularly refer to my teacher's mannerisms and ways of life in light of what they taught us about their Buddhist practices. Not only did I feel closer to that teacher, knowing more of their philosophy and experiences in the world, but I was able to engage with Hesse's text to a much deeper level.

CONCLUSION

Inviting staff to act as living, authentic resources is not something which schools can embrace lightly. It involves vulnerability on behalf of the staff member being introduced and a clear set of boundaries from both the school and the staff member about what can be shared. It provides outsiders with an insight into one's life and experiences and can change the relationship between staff and students. In my case, because of my clear boundaries and reflecting on what I would share beforehand, these relationships improved, and I have never felt vulnerable or unsafe because of what I have shared; however, it is important that any member of staff taking part in being a living resource reflects on their boundaries and practise setting them.

KEY TAKEAWAYS

- It can be challenging to be the sole representation of a religious group within a school setting.
- Using a model of authentic or living resources can allow students to engage more deeply with a topic.
- The curriculum may be outdated in both its representation of people from a religious minority and how people from those religious groups live their lives in the UK today.

KEY QUESTIONS

- At which points in your curriculum could you invite 'living resources' as guest speakers?
- How can you develop a culture of safety within your department or school so staff can feel comfortable being 'living resources'?
- Do you have representation within your curriculum of contemporary people from various religious groups, or is your representation restricted to negative examples or outdated?

COMMITMENT TO THE MANIFESTO

Create a culture within your school where staff (and students!) can be comfortable speaking up as an authentic, living resource.

REFERENCES

Bialystok, L. (2015) 'Should teachers be authentic?', *Ethics and Education*, 10(3), pp. 313-26.

De Bruyckere, P. and Kirschner, P. (2016) 'Authentic teachers: Student criteria perceiving authenticity of teachers', *Cogent Education*, 3(1), p. 1247609.

Laursen, P. (2005) 'The Authentic Teacher', in Beijaard, D., Meijer, P. and Morine-Dershimer, G. (eds.) *Teacher Professional Development in Changing Conditions*. Rotterdam: Springer, pp. 199-212.

Riegel, U. and Kindermann, K. (2016) 'Why leave the classroom? How field trips to the church affect cognitive learning outcomes', *Learning and Instruction*, 41, pp. 106-14.

CHAPTER 8: SEX

CHAPTER EDITOR: RACHEL ELGY

CHAPTER CONTRIBUTORS

1. Virginia Mendez – **Gender Stereotypes in the Early Years: A Self-Fulfilling Prophecy**
2. Annelouise Jordan – **Gender Stereotypes, Empowerment and Consent in the Early Years**
3. Jeremy Davies – **Why Do So Few Men Work in Early Years Education in the UK?**
4. Yamina Bibi – **Womanhood and Motherhood in Education**
5. Alexander Purdie – **The Strength of Women**
6. Anita Fiddes – **Sport: Are We Still Fighting for Gender Equality?**
7. Lindsay Patience and Lucy Rose – **Flexible Working and the Gender Pay Gap in the Education Sector**
8. Ninna Makrinov – **Organisational Interventions to Address the Gender Pay Gap**
9. Patrick Ottley-O'Connor – **Becoming an Ally for Women as a HeForShe Advocate**
10. Diana Osagie – **The Conquering**

BIOGRAPHIES

Rachel Elgy is Business Development Manager at EqualiTeach. She has an MA in Gender Without Borders from Kingston University, throughout which she explored intersectionality, considering the multifaceted ways that individuals may experience prejudice. She takes steps to advance equality wherever possible and is a fellow of Clore Social Leadership's Emerging Leaders programme.

Alex Purdie is an experienced middle leader in a large comprehensive school in the North West. He is passionate about Teaching and Learning, Inclusion (LGBT+ lead), staff wellbeing and a huge advocate for Food & Design education. Alex is currently completing his NPQSL on Parental Engagement and aspires to be a Headteacher.

Anita Fiddes is a Head of Physical Education, a PE PGCE Tutor and a football fanatic.

Anita has battled against pre-conceived notions of women in sport since the day she first kicked a ball. Throughout her career Anita has championed girls' participation and acceptance in all areas of the sporting world.

Annelouise Jordan is Deputy Headteacher of a British school in Spain. Her extensive experience of working and leading in education spans eleven years and she holds a Masters of Education. Annelouise is a passionate educator who strives to ensure all children have equal access to a curriculum that is representative of them and ethical by design.

Diana Osagie has twenty-one years' experience leading secondary education, including six as a successful secondary head; Diana is resilient and skilled in urban leadership in challenging circumstances. Diana founded The Academy of Women's Leadership, specialising in creating women who thrive with deep confidence at the leadership table.

Dr Jeremy Davies leads the MITEY (Men In The Early Years) campaign and is Head of Communications at the Fatherhood Institute. He was Co-Investigator on the GenderEYE study, Deputy Chair of DFE's Gender Diversity Task and Finish Group and a Fawcett Society Gender Stereotypes in Early Childhood Commissioner.

Lindsay Patience and Lucy Rose are co-founders of Flexible Teacher Talent, an organisation which campaigns for better flexible working in the education sector, supports individuals looking to work flexibly and help schools to improve their culture of flexible working. They both work flexibly in schools.

Ninna Makrinov is an organisational psychologist, trainer and coach. She currently supports the skills development of Higher Education students at the University of Warwick and is Chair of Governors at Water Mill Primary School. Ninna defines herself as a white fat immigrant woman and is passionate about education, mental health and equality.

Patrick Ottley-O'Connor is an Executive Headteacher, leadership development consultant and coach. He has been a senior leader for over twenty-five years, including seventeen years as a headteacher in secondary, primary and special schools. Patrick coaches many aspiring, new and experienced leaders, headteachers and CEOs, both in the UK and internationally.

Virginia Mendez is a multilingual children's author, public speaker and co-founder of The Feminist Shop. She has a degree in Law and a master's in Business. After starting her career in corporate, she now pursues her passion of spreading awareness and understanding of feminism through her website, her books, talks and workshops, both in schools and businesses.

Yamina Bibi is an Assistant Headteacher in an East London Secondary School. As an English teacher, experienced mentor and coach and senior leader, Yamina is invested in the development of all staff from support staff to senior leaders. Yamina is also a WomenEd Network Lead and committed to ensuring equity, diversity and inclusive practice is embedded in all spheres of the education sector so that everyone is represented and celebrated.

THE PROTECTED CHARACTERISTIC OF SEX: INTRODUCTION

RACHEL ELGY

INTRODUCTION

Sex as a protected characteristic is under incredible scrutiny in public discourse, caught up in a heated debate about transgender rights and women's rights (Humphery, 2020). This book is inclusive of people of all sexes and genders, and this chapter will explore the inequalities based on these characteristics that we see in the field of education (the barriers faced by trans and non-binary people are explored in Chapter 3). Some of the experiences and perspectives shared may resonate with your own lived experience, however some may be introducing a new point of view or may challenge your assumptions, and either way will provide insights and solutions to tackling gender inequality in education.

DEFINITIONS AND TERMINOLOGY

It is important to clarify the terminology that will be used in this chapter. The protected characteristic as it appears in the Equality Act 2010 is 'sex' and that is defined within the Act as 'to mean being a man or a woman' (Gov UK, 2010). But what does it mean to be a man or to be a woman? Where does the term 'gender' fit in?

The definition of sex is biological. Previously believed to be a strict binary of male or female, biological sex can now be understood as a spectrum (EqualiTeach, 2019). Someone who is biologically male will have male internal and external sex organs, XY chromosomes and a typically 'male' balance of hormones. Someone who is biologically female will have female internal and external sex organs, XX chromosomes and a typically 'female' balance of hormones. Beyond these two binaries, we know that approximately 1.7% of the UK population is Intersex, with a mixture of sex organs and/or chromosomes and/or an atypical balance of hormones (UN, 2021). Understanding sex as a spectrum recognises that each of us is biologically unique in our make-up.

Biology is important when it comes to things such as healthcare, to ensure that we are receiving the most suitable treatment for our body, and to understand various biological processes related to sex organs, chromosomes or hormones, such as the menopause. In *Invisible Women*, Caroline Criado-Perez wrote about the significant data gaps in areas such as healthcare and safety, where medicines have been predominantly tested on male bodies, and car crash test dummies are based on typically male physiques (Criado-Perez, 2019). However, when discussing equality and discrimination, we are very often actually talking about gender rather than biological sex. Gender is a social construct which sets expectations of the types of behaviour, roles, skills and attributes a person will have based on their biological sex (EqualiTeach, 2019). The construct of gender is what tells us what it means to be a man or a woman, and again it has historically operated in a way that enforced a binary: someone is either a man and they will be strong, unemotional, logical, authoritative and will go to work to support their family; or they are a woman and they will be highly emotional, empathetic, timid and will stay at home to clean the house, raise the children and cook the dinner. These binaries might sound antiquated, but sadly, as this chapter will demonstrate, their impact is still very much being felt.

Understanding both sex and gender as a spectrum requires from us a greater nuance in recognising the barriers that different people face, and it gives us a route through which to tackle inequality in an intersectional and fully inclusive way. In this introduction, I will not define gender identity and reassignment, as that is covered by Harry Scantlebury in Chapter 3.

LANDSCAPE THE IMPACT OF GENDER

When we recognise gender as an external societal structure, we can begin to see how many aspects of inequality stem from these ideas and assumptions: crash test dummies modelled on male bodies because men are assumed to be the ones driving to work (or driving anywhere); harassment and abuse catalysed by the pressure placed on men to be tough, dominating and part of the 'locker-room banter'; and glass ceilings held up by assumptions that women will be more interested in having children or caring for family members than building a career. Cordelia Fine explains the plasticity of human brains, using the example of taxi drivers in London having an enlarged hippocampus – the part of our brain used for memory – to highlight this. In essence, we can use this example to highlight the ways in which our skills, interests and abilities develop over time based on what we spend our time doing, learning and practising, not based on our biological sex (Fine, 2010).

Whilst this book allows us to zoom in to particular issues faced within each characteristic, Chapter Ten is an essential reminder that all of these inequalities are intersectional. Exploring and challenging ideas of gender cannot be done without recognising the ways in which women of colour and trans women are often excluded from traditional ideas of femininity and womanhood (Mohdin, 2018; Grover, 2020); without seeing the ways in which non-disabled women are over-sexualised whilst disabled women are often seen as being inherently non-sexual (Addlakha et al, 2017); without seeing the heteronormative framing of a woman based on her relationship with men: as someone's daughter or someone's wife; or without recognising the often-seen ageism that limits a woman's career in ways that men do not experience to the same extent (Solomon, 2020).

LANDSCAPE UNPICKING GENDER INEQUALITY

Despite the title of this chapter, and indeed the name of the protected characteristic being sex, this chapter is unpicking gender as well; looking at the inequalities women and men face within the education sector, exploring where these inequalities come from, and how we can continue working to overcome them.

At the time of writing there has been a much-needed focus and discussion in the national media about the urgent and serious issue of sexual harassment in schools (BBC, 2021) with the experiences of many young women shared on 'Everyone's Invited'- an online platform for anonymously sharing experiences of sexual assault or harassment in schools – and Ofsted's review highlighting that sexual harassment is so pervasive in schools that it is commonplace, and therefore, rarely reported or challenged (Gov UK, 2021).

Allport's research into the steps towards genocide provides a useful explanation of the ways in which seemingly small or subtle behaviours can pave the way for a dangerous culture of prejudice, leading to overt acts of discrimination which can become more extreme over time (Allport, 1954). In the context of gender equality, we can adapt Allport's scale of prejudice and discrimination into a pyramid where the bottom rung demonstrates the harmful implications of gender stereotypes, which pave the way for a culture of misogyny, harassment and an unequal distribution of power throughout society, which leads to systemic discrimination and furthermore at the top of the pyramid to distressing acts such as rape or assault. By challenging those 'lower-level' behaviours, tackling stereotypes and questioning the status quo, we remove the conditions for the rest of the pyramid to thrive (Allport, 1954).

VOICES IN OUR CHAPTER IN DIVERSE EDUCATORS – A MANIFESTO

In this chapter we will first hear from **Virginia Mendez**, followed by **Annelouise Jordan**, who between them provide a comprehensive understanding of how gender stereotypes manifest in the early years and consider ways that we can begin to unpick these in our schools and indeed our personal lives. Staying in the early years, **Jeremy Davies** questions why so few men work in this field, recognising some of the harmful assumptions that are an underlying cause of this disparity. **Yamina Bibi** takes us through the many ways in which women's lives and decisions are scrutinised, and the effect this can have on them and their careers. **Alexander Purdie** shares his own insight into becoming more aware of these barriers that women face and encourages us to consider the significance of women as role models for all young people. Moving to focus on some specific barriers to equality, **Anita Fiddes** shares her experience of opening up sport to women and girls, **Lindsay Patience** and **Lucy Rose** share insights on the gender pay gap and flexible working, and **Ninna**

Makrinov looks at the various organisational changes that can pave the way for greater gender equality. To finish, **Patrick Ottley O'Connor** gives a rallying cry for men to join the #HeForShe movement, and **Diana Osagie** empowers us all to tackle the glass ceilings we may create for ourselves through our own thought patterns. The underlying thread that connects them all is the way that society's understanding and expectations of what it means to be a man or to be a woman hurts us all.

CONCLUSION

May the voices of these contributors encourage you to seek out and listen to more women with varying and diverse identities about their experiences, to challenge your own assumptions about men, women and even yourself, and to light a fire in your stomach that urges you to create a future for young people that allows them to aspire, to dream, to change and to achieve, free from societal constraints imposed by their sex or gender.

COMMITMENT TO THE MANIFESTO

To create inclusive and empowering education settings in which staff and young people can aspire and achieve free from societal constraints imposed by their sex or gender.

REFERENCES

Addlakha, R., Price, J. & Heidari, S. (2017) 'Disability and sexuality: claiming sexual and reproductive rights', *Reproductive Health Matters*, 25:50, 4-9. Available at https://www.tandfonline.com/doi/full/10.1080/09688080.2017.1336375 [Accessed 28 June 2021]

Allport, G. (1954) *The Nature of Prejudice*. New York: Perseus Books

BBC. (2021) *School abuse: 'Rape culture' warning as 8,000 report incidents.* Available at https://www.bbc.co.uk/news/uk-56558487 [Accessed 28 June 2021]

Criado-Perez, C. (2019). *Invisible women: data bias in a world designed for men*, London: Chatto & Windus

EqualiTeach. (2019). *Outside the Box: Embedding Gender Equality and Tackling Sexism and Sexual Harassment in Schools*. Available at https://equaliteach.co.uk/outside-the-box/ [Accessed 28 June 2021]

Fine, C. (2010) *Delusions of Gender: the Real Science behind Sex Differences.* London: Icon Books

UK Government (2010). *The Equality Act 2010*, available at https://www.legislation.gov.uk/ukpga/2010/15/notes/division/3/2/1/8 [accessed 25 June 2021]

UK Government (2021). *Ofsted: culture change needed to tackle 'normalised' sexual harassment in schools and colleges.* Available at: https://www.gov.uk/government/news/ofsted-culture-change-needed-to-tackle-normalised-sexual-harassment-in-schools-and-colleges [Accessed 28 June 2021]

Grover, A. (2020). *Straddling the line between gender and sex: How racism, misogyny, and transphobia intertwine to define notions of womanhood in the world of elite sports* in LSE Blogs. Available at https://blogs.lse.ac.uk/gender/2020/12/07/straddling-the-line-between-gender-and-sex-how-racism-misogyny-and-transphobia-intertwine-to-define-notions-of-womanhood-in-the-world-of-elite-sports/ [Accessed 28 June 2021]

Humphery, K. (2020). 'Trans rights have been pitted against feminism but we're not enemies' in *The Guardian*, 7th July 2020. Available at: https://www.theguardian.com/commentisfree/2020/jul/07/trans-rights-have-been-pitted-against-feminism-but-were-not-enemies [Accessed 28 June 2021]

Mohdin, A. (2018). 'For black women, femininity and feminism are not mutually exclusive', in *Quart.*, Available at https://qz.com/quartzy/1158081/for-black-women-femininity-and-feminism-are-not-mutually-exclusive/ [Accessed 28 June 2021]

Solomon, M. (2020) 'Working Women's Double Dose Of Discrimination: Gender And Ageism' in *Forbes,* Available at https://www.forbes.com/sites/ellevate/2020/11/02/working-womens-double-dose-of-discrimination-gender--ageism/?sh=6c0f3b351d19 [Accessed 28 June 2021]

UN Human Rights Office of the High Commissioner. (2021) *Intersex People.* Available at https://www.ohchr.org/EN/Issues/LGBTI/Pages/IntersexPeople.aspx [Accessed 28 June 2021]

GENDER STEREOTYPES IN THE EARLY YEARS: A SELF-FULFILLING PROPHECY

VIRGINIA MENDEZ

INTRODUCTION

Women and men are different, because they live a different life from the moment that they are born that inevitably makes them become different. The disparity in the expectations, messages, as well as the way they see themselves represented in the world from childhood plays a huge role in those differences. This piece covers the prevalence of gender stereotypes in the early years, where they are and their impact.

Our brains adapt, change and learn. We have all learnt a skill or learnt to like new flavours, but part of society still assumes that girls are born already liking unicorns while boys are naturally predisposed to love dinosaurs. What if those presumptions, those stereotypes, mattered more than we think? The capacity of our brains to be malleable is called neuroplasticity and it illustrates that the way we interact with the world, and the way society interacts with us, has an effect on our brain, and not the other way around. So, by creating completely different experiences for boys and girls from the moment they are born we are completing a self-fulfilling prophecy.

Stereotypes can be useful. They indicate general expectations about members of particular social groups; we use them to make sense of the world. In the case of gender there is an even bigger impact because it is one of the things that we first notice about people. We implicitly cluster unknown individuals by their gender, even if it has no informational value. We say 'I spoke with a woman' instead of 'I spoke with a person' even when it adds nothing to the context. Gender stereotypes, like any other stereotypes, exaggerate and oversimplify reality. But by doing so, they reinforce beliefs and justify the social implications of gender for role differentiation and social inequality. These beliefs and ideas are present in many of the things that help us discover the world around us and tell us what our place in it is.

CHILDREN'S BOOKS

Following the unspoken but very much real rule of thumb: masculine characters are mainstream, feminine characters are niche. In the most popular books, the ones aimed for every child, the main characters and leaders are boys, men or male animals, and so are the villains (Grindel, 2018). Women, girls and female animals are usually supporting characters, and often portrayed as carers (mothers, teachers, nurses). We find a lot of severe stereotyping in the illustrations as well.

FILMS AND TV SHOWS

Male characters are depicted as strong, emotionally restrained, risk-taking leaders (who also get to be funny), while females are agreeable, virtuous, demure, and primarily concerned with their physical appearance (and much more likely to be shown crying). *CBeebies* is the kids' specific channel for the BBC, and in a weekday morning most of the shows are male-dominated (*Bing, Hey Duggee, Go Jetters, Peter Rabbit*...) It is only after two hours that you get eleven minutes of a female lead character in *Bitz and Bob*. Boys are the norm, girls the variation. Boys are given full personalities while the isolated girls in the stories are defined by the fact that they are girls, with over-stereotyped features, skills and interests.

CLOTHES

If we move on to clothes it is easy to think about the obvious pink and blue, which is a quite recent (from the 40s) but widespread gender code, but sadly the deeper we go the worse it gets.

- **Slogans and designs:** The slogans and motifs aimed at boys focus on action, skill, aspirations and taking risks rather than the beauty-focused, flowers and pets in girls' clothing.
- **Shape:** Girls' clothes have no pockets, they are narrower and more revealing, more concerned with following adult trends than with comfort and active lifestyles, while boys have more space in the knees and arms, welcoming activity.
- **Material:** In the girls' section, tulle, or fluffy fabrics ask to be touched, and this is the effect the garment will have, which means that from a very young age, girls will be used to being caressed more than their male peers; whilst boys' clothes are made of higher quality and more durable material. The fabrics are thicker, sturdier, and longer wearing. The clothing is less flimsy and is warmer.

The way we dress girls passes the clear message that being beautiful is more important than being comfortable, reaffirming the idea that has been repeated to them from other channels. Boys are encouraged to go further than that.

TOYS

Marketing, by accentuating stereotypes, plays a huge role in the way toys will be preferred by a child based solely on their gender. When toys are presented in gendered boxes, even novel toys, kids will gravitate towards the ones aimed at their gender (*Let Toys Be Toys*, 2017). What is important to know is that more mixing happens when the toys come with ungendered boxes, or even more interestingly, when they do not feel that their choices are policed. This shows that the real preference of children is not to belong to the group that has been heavily imposed on them, rather a natural preference for certain activities or games. All this, as well as differences in use of language, expectations and boundary- setting creates a completely different reality for kids based on their gender. Masculinity is presented as wild, aggressive and tough and it has been proven that rigid ideas of what it means to be a boy feed the later urgent problem of abuse, sexist language and sexual harassment that is so prevalent in schools (Promundo Global, 2017). The very real problem of toxic masculinity starts much earlier than we think, and it is wrongly associated with hormones or natural instincts.

CONCLUSION

We are telling children, indirectly through all the things that we put them in front of, that boys' stories are the ones that really matter, that girls' narratives and interests are not good enough. We teach boys to be proudly wild, to roar and lead, to attack. We teach girls to romanticise and seek that in boys. We show them masculine role models that use violence to right wrongs and tell them that girls are side characters to accentuate them, admire them and care for them. There is so much effort made, at the moment, to empower girls, but we will only be able to move forward when, at the same time, we redefine masculinity and establish a real balance and equality between femininity and masculinity, right from that twenty-week scan that separates our journeys.

KEY TAKEAWAYS

- Gender stereotypes are a self-fulfilling prophecy: by living different lives we become different people.
- We find stereotypes everywhere from the earliest years – books, TV shows, clothes and toys, all repeating the same narrative.
- The messages that these stereotypes subliminally send are very damaging and need to be corrected from the root in the search for equality.

KEY QUESTIONS

- Are we thinking enough about the subliminal messages that mundane things send to children?

- Are we using those stereotypes to start conversations that encourage critical thinking?
- Would we feel comfortable reversing the gender in books/films? Letting everyone wear the same clothes? Playing with the same toys? Why or why not?

COMMITMENT TO THE MANIFESTO

Be aware of and challenge gender stereotypes in the classroom and actively teach kids to spot and question those around them.

REFERENCES

CBC Radio, The Current (2018). *Can gender-specific toys affect a child's development? Researchers weigh in.* Available at https://www.cbc.ca/radio/thecurrent/the-current-for-december-18-2017-1.4451239/can-gender-specific-toys-affect-a-child-s-development-researchers-weigh-in-1.4451295 (accessed 26 April 2021)

Let Toys Be Toys (2017) *Who's in the picture? Gender stereotypes and toy catalogues.* Available at http://lettoysbetoys.org.uk/wp-content/uploads/2012/12/LetToysBeToys-Catalogues-report-Dec17.pdf (accessed 10 June 2021)

Promundo Global (2017). *The Man Box Key Findings.* Available at https://promundoglobal.org/wp-content/uploads/2017/03/TheManBox-KeyFindings-EN-Final-29.03.2017-POSTPRINT.v3-web.pdf (accessed 26 April 2021)

Grindel, S. (2018) *The Gender Gap in Children's Books is The Real Monster In The Room.* In: Romper. Available at: https://www.romper.com/p/the-gender-gap-in-childrens-books-is-the-real-monster-in-the-room-12576548 (accessed 26 April 2021).

GENDER STEREOTYPES, EMPOWERMENT AND CONSENT IN THE EARLY YEARS

ANNELOUISE JORDAN

INTRODUCTION

It could be said that the #MeToo movement catapulted us towards a more ethical society that started to believe the narratives of women and girls. However, the idea that change has come unfortunately does not reflect the current reality. Statistics on sexual violence continue to shock with around 20% of UK women admitting to being sexually assaulted at some point in their lives since the age of sixteen (Crime Survey for England and Wales, 2017), and one in five US women having experienced rape or attempted rape (The National Intimate Partner and Sexual Violence Survey, 2015). There is still much to be done on breaking down gender stereotypes, and empowering young people to say 'No!' and be listened to. Margaret Mead's work has been admired across the world. Her social experiments got people talking about stereotypes and brought forward the debate that children were who they were and thought the way they did because of the adults surrounding them. Her earliest work on gender stereotypes analysed a range of cultures and was able to show the world of the kind, nurturing men of the Arapesh tribe and the violent aggressive women of the Mundugumor (Mead, 1935). Now, over 80 years later we still engage in such debates.

As educators, we need to understand our own roles in this. What we do in the early years of children's lives will determine their future. What role do we want them to play? And, most importantly, what role do *they* want to play? No-one should be telling them otherwise. Change needs to happen in order to educate our children about gender stereotypes and give them a voice to choose their own path.

GENDER ROLES IN NURSERY RHYMES

Tommy is a thumb and the doctor is a man! OK, so it is not necessary to change every nursery rhyme and eliminate all the male characters but we do need to be aware of these micro stereotypes. If these are the only songs children will hear then it is time to have a look at some other options. Looking at stories and songs with a careful eye is necessary as educators, carers and parents, since they include details of society that a young brain is not able to dissect or interpret. Children ingest and retain the information that is given to them. So, changing the doctor in the rhyme 'Miss Polly' to 'she/her' or 'they/their' is easy to do and it instantly challenges the stereotype of men being doctors and authority figures.

An example of another nursery rhyme that has a range of issues and even early toxic masculinity embedded within it is 'Georgie Porgie':

> Georgie Porgie, pudding and pie,
> Kissed the girls and made them cry,
> When the boys came out to play,
> Georgie Porgie ran away.

Georgie liked to kiss girls and saw them as objects of desire. He ran away afterwards, which shows that he knew what he was doing was wrong. And what did the girls do? Cry! They did not fight back or go and find help, they cried. The subliminal message this rhyme tells girls is that when a boy wants to kiss them they should let him even if they find it distressing, and they should not find help nor stand up for themselves either. What *Georgie Porgie* delivers is the statement that the authority figures are the 'boys' giving the impression that girls can't stand up to Georgie even if they wanted to, and have to wait to be 'saved'. This rhyme says nothing about consent or that girls have the right to defend themselves. It is also teaching boys that they can do what they want to girls with impunity. *Georgie Porgie* teaches boys that it is 'normal' for girls to cry when you try to kiss them, but that it is best not to get caught. Dr Cook (2019) wrote a fantastic and informative article on nursery rhymes and what they would look like if the narrative was flipped to challenge stereotypes.

TEACH THEM CONSENT

Children are able to understand what consent is. Articles 12 and 13 of the United Nations Conventions on the Rights of a Child (2005) specifically gives that power of opinion and freedom of expression to the child. It is the most widely ratified human rights document which demands the rights of every child. By empowering girls to say no and ensuring boys listen we could have a generation of people who will not be held back because of their gender. We do not want more Georgie Porgies running around the playground trying to kiss girls or objectifying them for their own gain. If we do this from a young age boys will grow up to be respectful of girls, to seek consent and to respect boundaries. Equally, girls will grow up seeing themselves as strong, independent people who have the right to stand up and be seen and heard. Let us teach them how to say no and how to make a choice that is right for them.

CHANGING CLOTHES/NAPPIES

When we change a child's clothes, check if they have had a toilet accident or change their nappy, the first thing to do is let them know what we are going to do. Then notice their body language: how are they feeling about you doing this? Really stop and listen to them. If they freeze, shake their head or start to cry, comfort and listen. Check if there is someone else they are more comfortable with who could do it; maybe they have not built up that trust with you yet and that's important. Do not force it and do it anyway with the flying thought of 'What do they know, they are only babies?'

GIVING THEM A CUDDLE

Charging in there with a massive cuddle on the first day of school could be hard to receive for some children. Give them time and space to cry with you nearby, or to come to you for a cuddle if and when they want to. Culture is a confounding factor here. Different cultures soothe children in a variety of ways and this has to be respected at every level of education, especially in the early years. For example, for a child from an Eastern Asian family, cuddles and kisses may be reserved only for those closest to them, whereas many Spanish people will revel in kissing and hugging people they have just met. Knowing this is the first step to giving them the power back.

BODY PART EXPLORATION

Giving children the biological names of their body parts is vital in early development. It empowers the child to not only know what their own parts are called but also their functions and, most importantly, their privacy. When a child knows the reason they have a penis or a vagina/vulva they will know to stand up for themselves if it is used against them later in life. This is not to say that young children need to know that they are sexual organs, but they need to know it is where they do their 'wee wees' from and that it is an area just for them and it doesn't belong to anyone else. Then they have it ingrained that having a vagina does not stop them from achieving their goals in life as it is just another part of their body that belongs to them and has its own function.

CONCLUSION

Taking a look at the early years classroom and thinking about the stories we tell and the songs we sing will ensure the success of empowerment in young children of all genders. We want children to know what is right and what is wrong and we want to expel the myths surrounding gender stereotypes. This can and should be done through teaching consent, respecting privacy and listening to the experiences of others.

KEY TAKEAWAYS

- Children are competent individuals who are able to understand themselves as people and who they are.
- Adults have a profound impact on how children see themselves and the role they have in society.
- Changing the narrative and opening up discussions with children will provide them with a way to empower themselves.

KEY QUESTIONS

- How much time do you dedicate to planning conversations about gender stereotypes with young children?
- What changes will you make to challenge gender stereotypes directly in your educational settings?
- How will you reach out to the school community to continue challenging these stereotypes and bring about wider change to benefit young girls in finding their voice?

COMMITMENT TO THE MANIFESTO

Empower our children to say 'No!' and create a space of mutual respect and acceptance to eliminate toxic masculinity.

REFERENCES

Cook, B. (2019) *Nursery Rhymes: A Perfect Example Of The Perpetuation of Sexism in Society* https://drbcook.medium.com/nursery-rhymes-a-perfect-example-of-the-perpetuation-of-sexism-in-society-b9647ef46392 (Accessed March 2021)

Mead, M. (1935) *Sex and Temperament In Three Primitive Societies*, Harper Perennial

The United Nations Convention on the Rights of the Children (2005) https://www.unicef.org/child-rights-convention/convention-text (Accessed May 2021)

WHY DO SO FEW MEN WORK IN EARLY YEARS EDUCATION IN THE UK?

JEREMY DAVIES

INTRODUCTION

The number of men who work in early years education in the UK is tiny. Why, after decades of progress towards gender equality on so many fronts in British society, does this sector remain so female-dominated? What is being done to increase the gender diversity of the workforce? This chapter explores the challenges involved in recruiting and retaining male staff, considers some beacons of best practice, and highlights why stronger action at government and local levels is needed to give low male representation in early years education the attention it deserves.

The UK's early years education sector has one of the most gender-imbalanced workforces in the world. Only 3% of staff working in early years education in England are male; in Scotland it is 4%. Gender diversity in the sector has barely improved in the last quarter of a century (in 1998 the figure was 2%) (MITEY, 2021).

It might be tempting to assume the lack of men in early years education results from men not wanting to work in 'caring' jobs. But men make up 15% of the UK's primary school workforce, 14% of social workers and 11% of nurses (MITEY, 2021), and early years workforces in some other countries are considerably more mixed: Norway has 9% men, and Germany 7%, for example (Emilsen and Rohrmann, 2021). Why should the lack of gender diversity in UK early years education be so extreme?

Low pay is often cited, and salaries certainly do make it harder to 'sell' early years education as a career. The average early years wage is just £7.42 per hour; not much higher than the average wage in retail, which is £7.02 (Social Mobility Commission, 2020). But not all men need 'breadwinner' salaries, and lots of men – especially younger ones – can be found doing various low-paid jobs such as kitchen assistants, supermarket shelf-stackers, bar staff and waiters.

SO, PAY APART, WHAT ELSE STANDS IN THE WAY OF CHANGE?

Despite decades of legal and social change aimed at reducing gender inequality, boys and men in the UK still live in a society that tells them looking after babies and young children is women's work. Early years employers are not reaching out to male applicants or developing programmes to make it easier for men to access job opportunities. Schools and job centres routinely suggest early years careers to girls and women, but rarely, if ever, to boys and men – and any males that do show an interest in such work are likely to be greeted with anything from raised eyebrows to outright disgust.

Male early years educators are routinely stereotyped, challenged and assumed to be gay and/or a paedophile because of their job choice. It is common for parents to object to their children being looked after (and more specifically, having their nappies changed) by male staff – and some managers accede to such objections, rather than face losing a paying client. A recent study (GenderEYE, 2020) found that 51% of male early years practitioners have considered leaving the sector due to concerns around allegations of sexual abuse. Safeguarding must, without question, be providers' main priority, but this suggests there is also a need to protect male staff from negative, gender-based beliefs and assumptions (and to accept that historically, both female and male staff have perpetrated abuse against young children).

It is unsurprising that very little is being done to challenge this, given the messages that come from those 'at the top'. Just four years ago the then Tory leadership hopeful Andrea Leadsom MP told *The Times*: 'Let us face it, most of us do not employ men as nannies... Now you can call that sexist, I call that cautious and very sensible when you look at the stats. Your odds are stacked against you if you employ a man. We know paedophiles are attracted to working with children. I am sorry but they are the facts'. Ms Leadsom's leadership bid hit the buffers not long after making this controversial statement, but she was not sacked from the Cabinet (Chandler, 2016), has held several ministerial posts since then and recently chaired the government's Early Years Healthy Development Review (Gov UK, 2021).

Apart from in the early 2000s when the then-government set a (soon-to-be-abandoned) target of 6%, there have been no targets, incentives or inspection frameworks around early years workforce diversity – nor a well-funded, male-inclusive national early years recruitment campaign. Indeed, despite many initiatives aimed at improving women's access to STEM careers, the government has a patchy record of even *counting* how many men work in early years education, with figures on early years workforce gender diversity being published literally as a footnote (Gov UK, 2019).

When governments *have* shown an interest – as when the Department for Education mentioned the lack of gender diversity in its 2017 early years workforce strategy (Gov UK, 2017) – they have tended to do so in ways that seek to essentialise gender difference (for example using a narrative that we need more men in early years to solve the 'problem' of underperforming boys) rather than to create a more representative, inclusive workforce. A recent study – the biggest ever conducted in the UK – found that only 14% of early years providers had implemented strategies to improve male recruitment (GenderEYE, 2020). So the lack of men remains a largely unaddressed problem.

In the last few years there have been some encouraging signs of change, including:

- A series of national conferences organised by individuals and groups with an interest in this area, in Southampton (2016), Bradford (2017), Bristol (2018) and London (2019);
- Lobbying and local actions by a small number of innovators, including David Wright, owner of PaintPots Nurseries in Southampton; June O'Sullivan, CEO of London Early Years Foundation; and local groups such as Bristol Men in Early Years Network;
- A programme coordinated by the Scottish Funding Council, working with several FE colleges in Scotland to attract more men to early years courses, and ongoing male-only courses coordinated by Men in Childcare and funded by the Scottish Government and City of Edinburgh Council;
- MITEY (Men In The Early Years), a national campaign/network set up by the Fatherhood Institute in 2017 – which received support from the Department for Education in 2018-19 to run a conference and produce 'how-to' guides and case studies – and which has, since 2020, been working with Kids Planet Day Nurseries to develop a male apprenticeship programme in Manchester, funded by Greater Manchester Combined Authority.

But all these initiatives remain the exception rather than the rule, and lack of serious investment limits their ability to widen their reach and embed new approaches across the early years sector.

High-quality, affordable early years education plays a vital role in the UK economy and makes a huge contribution to children's outcomes. There is much work to be done to raise its status and provide salaries to match. But even as things stand, early years educators report higher happiness levels than the total working population (Social Mobility Commission, 2020). It is way beyond time that we enabled men as well as women to share the challenges – and joys – of this vital work.

CONCLUSION

The solutions are not complicated, but they need effort. We need early years and teacher training colleges, early years providers, careers advisers and others to take seriously the lack of male participation in this workforce and commit to changing things. And we need the Government to back them with a well-funded national recruitment campaign.

KEY TAKEAWAYS

- The UK's early years education workforce is almost entirely female, and very few early years provider organisations take specific action to build and maintain gender-diverse staff teams.
- Gender stereotyping and workplace discrimination, including around male educators' provision of intimate care to young children, are common.
- There are no Government-led targets, incentives or campaigns to improve

the gender diversity of the early years' workforce, and Ofsted does not consider this in its inspections of settings.

KEY QUESTIONS

- What are you doing to improve the gender diversity of your workforce?
- What rationale do you have for greater gender diversification?
- How do you communicate these actions and rationale to parents?

COMMITMENT TO THE MANIFESTO

Take the lack of gender diversity in the early years' workforce seriously, and develop male-inclusive training programmes and recruitment methods to address it, involving actions at national, local and individual provider level.

REFERENCES

Chandler, M. (2016) , 'Theresa May under pressure to sack Andrea Leadsom over 'stupid' paedophile comments', *The Standard.* Available at https://www.standard.co.uk/news/politics/theresa-may-under-pressure-to-sack-andrea-leadsom-over-stupid-paedophile-comments-a3297091.html (Accessed 10 June 2021)

GenderEYE, 2020, *Gender diversification of the early years' workforce: recruiting and supporting male practitioners.* Available at https://gendereye.files.wordpress.com/2020/10/gendereye-final-end-of-project-report-28-oct.pdf (Accessed 10 June 2021)

UK Government (2021), *The best start for life: a vision for the 1,001 critical days.* Available at https://www.gov.uk/government/publications/the-best-start-for-life-a-vision-for-the-1001-critical-days (Accessed 10 June 2021)

UK Government, (2019), *Providers' finances: Evidence from the Survey of Childcare and Early Years Providers 2018. Research report*, p29. Available at https://assets.publishing.service.gov.uk/government/uploads/system/uploads/attachment_data/file/911666/Frontier_-_SCEYP_2018_Finance_Report_v2.pdf (Accessed 10 June 2021)

UK Government, (2017) *Early years workforce strategy.* Available at https://www.gov.uk/government/publications/early-years-workforce-strategy (Accessed 10 June 2021)

MITEY (Men in the Early Years), 2021, *Why we do it*, available at https://miteyuk.org/why-we-do-it/ (accessed 10 June 2021)

Personal communications from Professor Kari Emilsen (Norway) and Dr Tim Rohrmann (Germany) 2021

Social Mobility Commission (2020) *The stability of the early years' workforce in England: an examination of national, regional and organisational barriers*. Available online: https://assets.publishing.service.gov.uk/government/uploads/system/uploads/attachment_data/file/906906/The_stability_of_the_early_years_workforce_in_England.pdf

WOMANHOOD AND MOTHERHOOD IN EDUCATION

YAMINA BIBI

INTRODUCTION

It seems to me that our society is obsessed with women and their choices. From the choices we make about the way we dress and look to our career choices and even to our choices around having children. These decisions are scrutinised at every level by family, friends, colleagues, peers and even MPs. Whatever the choices and decisions, some made for us rather than by us, we seem to be criticised and penalised unfairly. In this piece we will be reminded of the gender biases that permeate our workplaces affecting women, particularly parent-teachers. We will consider how far motherhood within education is compatible with current policies and practice and share some suggestions for next steps to improve the experience of working mothers and women in general.

UNDER THE MICROSCOPE

Even in a society that claims to be forward-thinking and equal, we find bias and prejudice against women ingrained within every aspect of our lives. I grew up in a culture where a woman's path seemed straightforward to many: education, work (maybe), marriage, children, homemaker. If a woman chose to work, it was expected that it would be a career that was deemed to be 'compatible' with family life, allowing a woman to be in employment while also being the main caregiver. If a woman chose this, some may suggest that she was less committed to her career because of her focus on family life and therefore may pay a 'motherhood tax'– a penalty paid by working mothers which impacts on their salaries and career. These gender norms and societal expectations also meant that women like me, who married in their late 20s while successfully pursuing a career may be deemed 'too career-minded' and perhaps even selfish.

Before I married in 2016, I would be bombarded with questions asking whether I wanted to get married or not. Was I only focused on my career rather than my family? Was I forgetting that there was more to life than just teaching and climbing the leadership ladder? When (not if) I did marry, would I still want to be a leader in a school? Wasn't it true that in my culture, when women married, they would not want to work and would instead prefer to stay at home looking after their husbands and children?

The questions about my decisions and choices did not stop after I married but instead became centred around children. I was once asked whether my body clock concerned me because I was in my thirties and still had no children. Another time a colleague asked 'If you had children, you would not want to be a senior leader, would you?' Unfortunately, these questions, assumptions and biases were not just from family and friends but also from colleagues and leaders in school too. These questions opened my eyes to what I had not noticed before. Women, regardless of our circumstances, were disadvantaged in school settings, particularly in leadership roles.

THE MOTHERHOOD TAX

I looked to my own Senior Leadership Team (SLT) at the time and found that, despite the SLT being equal in terms of gender, out of all the senior female leaders we had, only one was a parent while many of the male senior leaders were parents. For a workforce where 75.8% of teachers identify as female (DFE, 2021), how could this be the case?

Simons (2016) noted that 'around 6,000 teachers a year – 27% of all leavers in total – are women aged 30–39 (who make up around 23% of the profession overall)...the obvious conclusion to be drawn here is that this is maternity related.' Simons further cites a report (NFER, 2015) outlining that 14% of all leavers who cited caregiving or were economically inactive people 'predominantly, we assume, mothers – do not come back into teaching.'

As a school leader who currently falls under this age bracket, it is worrying to learn this fact as it suggests that teaching is not seen as compatible with family life. Alternatively, could it be argued that it is not that teaching as a profession is incompatible with family life but rather that assumptions and biases about women in the workplace are pushing mothers out?

THE WOMANHOOD TAX

In seeking to better understand the experiences of women in the teaching profession, I started to speak to female teachers and leaders from a range of backgrounds and at different stages of their career and lives. Some I spoke to felt that they had a better chance of becoming a senior leader if they did not have children or delayed having children. One teacher recalled being told they would be an investment because they were unlikely to go 'off and have babies' as they were unmarried. A few women I spoke to felt that school leaders did not understand specific issues affecting women like them such as the mental wellbeing of women returning from maternity leave or how to support women going through fertility treatments or the menopause. Others felt overlooked for promotions because they were parent teachers and colleagues had questioned their commitment to the school or job.

These conversations seem to reiterate the findings of the McKinsey *Women in the Workplace Report* (McKinsey and Company, 2020) where mothers 'are more than twice as likely as fathers to worry that their performance is being judged negatively because of caregiving responsibilities. They are also far more likely to feel uncomfortable sharing work-life challenges—or that they are a parent at all—with colleagues.' (McKinsey and Company, 2020). This suggests that there is a motherhood tax within school settings which actively impacts women's careers and confidence. Furthermore, while women may be perceived negatively as parent teachers in some workplaces, men with children seem to be viewed favourably.

What are we as school leaders and governors doing to dismantle and address this bias and prejudice in the workplace? I would argue not enough. The culture, policies and systems within our schools do not support women in the way they need to in order to retain them. In fact, some even inhibit women.

How many mothers do we have on our SLT who can lend their voices and experiences in order to ensure practices empower mothers at all levels in the organisation? In addition, looking at our medical leave policies, we need to examine how far they enable equity amongst all. Do they take into account women going through fertility treatment? Do school policies reflect the wellbeing of women who have had miscarriages? How well do our policies support women going through the menopause?

HOW CAN SCHOOL LEADERS SUPPORT WOMEN TO THRIVE?

In conjunction with scrutinising and amending school policies, women should have opportunities to openly discuss the issues that may be affecting them. I advocate for a coaching entitlement within schools for all but particularly women who have returned from maternity leave or who are seeking promotions. The WomenEd community and Maternity Teacher Paternity Teacher Project (MTPT) can support schools with this. Another suggestion may be for senior leaders to have dedicated drop-in mornings where staff can speak to them about what is going well and any issues and concerns they may have. In one school I worked in, the Headteacher had twice weekly drop-ins where any member of staff could speak to her about anything. As a caregiver, having the option of the drop-ins meant that I could speak directly to my Headteacher about the support I required.

CONCLUSION

In a workforce that is predominately female, we cannot afford to be a sector that is seen as incompatible with work-life harmony. We have an opportunity to reset norms by continuing to challenge biases that undermine the place of women in the profession, whether they have children or not. This can only happen if we create spaces and opportunities for women to feel secure and safe with their choices.

KEY TAKEAWAYS

- Senior Leadership Teams and governing bodies should create safe spaces and forums for women to share their experiences within the organisation.
- All organisations should make coaching an entitlement for all, including women returning from maternity leave.
- Flexible working at senior leadership level should be offered to retain experienced working mothers, who may otherwise see the profession as incompatible with family life.

KEY QUESTIONS

- How far have you considered the voices of women at different stages of their career in creating policies to ensure that there is no 'motherhood tax'?
- Do your medical leave policies support women in different circumstances and do you monitor its effective implementation?
- What entitlement is in place for mothers in different roles and responsibilities across the school and how have school leaders been trained in ensuring this entitlement?

COMMITMENT TO THE MANIFESTO

Create and monitor the implementation of medical policies which explicitly outline support and provision for women and ensure equity for all.

REFERENCES

BBC (2020) *Covid has a devastating impact on gender equality*. Available at: https://www.bbc.co.uk/news/business-55002687 (accessed 8 May 2021).

Coury, S., Huang, J., Kuman, A. et al. (2020). *Women in the Workplace*. McKinsey and Company. Available at: https://www.mckinsey.com/featured-insights/diversity-and-inclusion/women-in-the-workplace (accessed 8 April 2021).

Criado-Perez, C. (2020) *Invisible Women: Exposing Data Bias in a World Designed for Men*, London: Vintage.

Department for Education. (2020). *School Teacher Workforce*. Available at: https://explore-education-statistics.service.gov.uk/find-statistics/school-workforce-in-england (accessed 8 April 2021).

NfER, 'Should I Stay or Should I Go? NfER Analysis of Teachers Joining and Leaving the Profession', November 2015 in Simons, J. (2016) *Let's Talk About Flex in The Importance of Teaching: a collection of essays on recruitment and retention*. Available at: https://policyexchange.org.uk/publication/

the-importance-of-teachers-a-collection-of-essays-on-teacher-recruitment-and-retention/ (accessed 12 May 2021).

Simons, J. (2016) *Let's Talk About Flex in The Importance of Teaching: a collection of essays on recruitment and retention*. Available at: https://policyexchange.org.uk/publication/the-importance-of-teachers-a-collection-of-essays-on-teacher-recruitment-and-retention/ (accessed 12 May 2021).

UN Women Headquarters (2020) *UN Policy Brief: The Impact of Covid-19 on Women*. Available at: https://www.unwomen.org/en/digital-library/publications/2020/04/policy-brief-the-impact-of-covid-19-on-women (accessed 5 April 2021).

Worth, J., Bamford, S. and Durbin, B. (2015). *Should I Stay or Should I Go? NFER Analysis of Teachers Joining and Leaving the Profession*. Slough: NFER. Available at: https://www.nfer.ac.uk/publications/lfsa01/lfsa01.pdf (accessed 12 May 2021).

THE STRENGTH OF WOMEN

ALEXANDER PURDIE

INTRODUCTION

Over time the role of women in society has changed dramatically and rightfully so, however can the same be said for men's perspectives towards women? Social expectations from previous decades encouraged women to stay in the home, now that women can choose how to live their professional lives as they wish, are women trying to break down the glass ceiling in education? It is time that all men recognise the inequality that exists and become effective allies.

BIRTH TO TWENTY

Let us set the scene. He lived with his two older sisters and mum, had two aunties, a nan, his grandad died when young. A majority female friendship group and all female teachers until secondary school. He was surrounded by women. This was normal and he loved it. Kelly (2020) argues that 'Boys who are exposed to women role models... don't question that girls are their equals, for it is obvious to them that within women is not just beauty, but strength, power, and incredible intelligence.' It is interesting to consider that men and boys who are surrounded by strong women may be unaware of the barriers that women face every day; however, by not recognising these barriers boys and men are not seeing the impact they can have as allies.

TWENTY TO TWENTY-SIX

Jump forward to 2010 and he started to notice that not all women were as confident as the women in his family. A conversation was had with another inspirational woman saying she was not going to apply for a job due to the fact her male colleague would get it as 'a woman would never get that job.' No one challenged this at the time, but it planted a seed in his head. How many other professional women have thought the same and why? He started to witness more and more women second-guess themselves and for reasons that most men would not.

Gender inequality had never affected him personally and after wanting to find more evidence the enter button on the laptop was pressed and it was there in black and white. It ignited a fire in his stomach to change this. Inequality was common, and in many sectors, but surely not education? In 2019 75.8% of schoolteachers were women (Gov UK, 2021), so if the majority of the sector are women, how many are senior leaders? 38% of headteachers are women (DODS, 2020). The reasons why women do not have the same opportunities compared to their male colleagues will vary but it is doubtful that men have the same barriers. Increasing visibility is key to fixing the problem. Woudstra (2021) states 'Regardless of how many scientific studies are cited, it's hard for men to imagine women would be good CEOs if they don't see many of them.' It is a bold statement, but men created this inequality, the least men can do is to be an effective ally in repairing it. If women were encouraged and empowered to take leadership roles it would allow women to have that confidence and become each other's role models, which will result in more and more women being '10 % braver' (Porritt V, Featherstone K, 2019).

TWENTY-SIX TO THIRTY-TWO

The hero in his life, his mum, always told her children that 'you have a voice; an opinion and it should be heard'. Education is key to forming opinions and facts need to be ascertained alongside lived experiences so that a positive impact can be had. When he secured a Teaching and Learning Responsibility, the team discussed how to encourage more girls to choose Design & Technology at KS4. They worked hard to create an inclusive culture in the team and implemented some simple but effective changes such as badges and renaming classrooms.

Jill Berry, who has written books such as *Making the Leap* (2016) led a session in January 2017, where she introduced WomenEd and after more research HeForShe entered his life. HeForShe is just one way that men can show support and strive for gender equality. Men are a significant part of the solution to this and need to take this seriously to make a difference. He began his allyship by participating on podcasts, attending WomenEd events, celebrating International Women's Day, and supporting female colleagues with personal and professional opportunities.

We generally want the same thing in our lives – equality. We need to continue investigating other countries that are more passionate about gender equality as research claims they are more positive places to live. The Global Gender Gap Report (2020) has concluded that 'it will take 257 years for women to have the same economic opportunities as men, though many countries have made strides in providing opportunities for women in other areas, like politics and education.' Sounds positive, but 'Western countries regressed in their rankings, including Australia, the UK, and the US.'

There have been many positive strides in the right direction for gender equality, but more can and will be done. Women deserve the same opportunities as men, so he pledged to continue to purposefully use his gender privilege to empower, encourage and support all women.

CONCLUSION

Our own perspectives are incredibly important and powerful when we are addressing inequalities. Gorse (2021) says she has had the privilege of working with some incredible men, who truly understand the problems that women face – but these men are all too rare. To any man reading this: believe there is a problem. You may not think there is if you are surrounded by brilliant women, so please ask questions, and have these vital conversations. This is just the start of what you can do to help and support the women in your life. Enjoy the change you will see.

KEY TAKEAWAYS

- Inequality exists everywhere, even if you did not see it before. Do the research and find ways to address it.
- Attend a WomenEd event.
- Embrace the change of your own perception over time.

KEY QUESTIONS

- What is your perspective on gender equality?
- What have you done to try and support women in your life or workplace?
- Find the research focusing on the struggle for men. There is none and therefore this section is important to move society forward.

COMMITMENT TO THE MANIFESTO

A drive to increase the quantity of women in middle and senior leadership roles by developing strategies based on empowerment and encouragement.

REFERENCES

Berry, J. (2016) *Making The Leap: Moving from deputy to head*. Crownhouse Publishers.

CIPD (2021) *Gender equality at work*. Available at: https://www.cipd.co.uk/news-views/viewpoint/gender-equality-work#gref (accessed 24 March 2021).

Ethnicity Facts and Figures (2021) *School Teacher Workforce*. Available at: https://www.ethnicity-facts-figures.service.gov.uk/workforce-and-business/workforce-diversity/school-teacher-workforce/latest (accessed 20 March 2021).

DODS Diversity & Inclusion (2020) *Leading by Example: Where are the Female Leaders in Education?* (2020). Available at: https://www.dodsdiversity.com/news/view,leading-by-example-where-are-the-female-leaders-in-education_206.htm (accessed 19 March 2021)

Gorse, S. (2021) *How can we help more women to become school leaders?* Available at: https://www.tes.com/news/how-can-we-help-more-women-become-school-leaders (accessed 1 April 2021).

Gov UK (2021) *School Teacher Workforce.* Available at: https://www.ethnicity-facts-figures.service.gov.uk/workforce-and-business/workforce-diversity/school-teacher-workforce/latest (accessed...)

Kelly, N. (2020) *Why Women Role Models Matter for Girls and Boys.* Available at: https://www.lottie.com/blogs/childhood/why-women-role-models-matter-for-girls-and-boys (accessed 13 May 2021).

https://womened.org. (accessed 11 May 2021).

https://www.heforshe.org/en (accessed 11 May 2021).

https://www.internationalwomensday.com (accessed 11 May 2021).

Porritt, V. and Featherstone, K. (2019) *10% Braver: Inspiring Women to Lead Education.* Sage Publishing.

World Economic Report (2020) *Global Gender Gap report (2020) Insight report.* Available at: http://www3.weforum.org/docs/WEF_GGGR_2020.pdf (accessed: 14 May 2021).

Woudstra, I. (2021) *Role Models Are Key In Gender Diversity – Especially In Tech & Engineering.* Available at: https://shecancode.io/blog/role-models-are-key-in-gender-diversity-especially-in-tech-engineering (accessed 13 May 2021).

SPORT: ARE WE STILL FIGHTING FOR GENDER EQUALITY?

ANITA FIDDES

INTRODUCTION

We are in the 21st century but what are the views on gender in the sporting domain? Why is it that girls in secondary school still have the perception that being involved in sport and physical activity is wrong? Why is it that boys feel that participating in dance and gymnastics is not for them? Is this issue a nature or nurture debate or is there something so deeply rooted in society that we are still facing these issues? What is it that you are doing in order to make sport truly for all, or are you unsure on what to do?

Growing up loving sport and in particular football in the 1990s made me an easy target for those who questioned my femininity and sexual orientation. The fascination over sexuality linked to the sport I enjoy only made me focus on being the best I could at it. Travis Scheadler and Audrey Wagstaff, Ph.D., MJE wrote an article for *The Sport Journal* which stated that 'If a woman dares to participate in a masculine sport, their sexuality is immediately questioned.' Views I have been on the receiving end of: 'female, PE teacher, play football = lesbian'.

In 2000 I completed my dissertation on the language used in the media for female sports stars – their focus was always on body type and their family life before their sporting abilities, along with smaller articles in comparison to their male counterparts. No wonder society has preconceived notions regarding gender stereotyping in sport and this brings us to the age-old debate of nature vs nurture. Volt Athletics posted a blog in 2019 that stated 'Athleticism requires *both* nature and nurture. We tend to think of things as black or white, but often it is really a shade of grey.'

It is this shade of grey that needs to be taken forward and celebrated; it is looking at giving children options to be who and what they want to be without fearing retribution and isolation. But how can we, as a collective, do this?

BREAKING DOWN STEREOTYPES IN SCHOOLS

Throughout my teaching I have focused on giving students these options and breaking down the gender stereotyping that is associated with sport. I started by changing the dialogue around sport – netball being for girls, football for boys? Not in my department, I want you to try everything and decide for yourself what you enjoy. Boys were put into netball for one of their GCSE sports, some of their grades were better in comparison to their basketball. Girls were put in for football, some of their grades were better in comparison to their netball. They played, and enjoyed, these sports and appreciated the athleticism that was required to play them.

How else can gender stereotyping be broken down? By reinforcing the narrative with constant examples of people who are successful in those sports that you are breaking down the barriers in. Words are there but seeing is believing! Female rugby and football coaches with male dance teachers are used to deliver extra-curricular clubs, competitions were entered throughout the academic years for both genders in all sports. Resulting outcomes saw students enjoying and playing sports they thought they would not – but I am STILL asked if I am the Head of PE and in charge of the male teachers! Why would this still be the case?

The NEU published a report, *Breaking the Mould,* based on research conducted in five primary schools on students' perceptions of 'Boys' things' and 'Girls' things'. The section on sport and playtime highlighted key points that determine the views on gender and sport from a young age. 'The pitch was often an almost all-male preserve and, when girls did play, they were often on the fringes', and 'Girls felt they were being actively excluded with boys refusing to pass the ball to them.' Schools reported that they 'faced challenges around boys dominating some areas of the playground and, in particular, any area designated for team games'.

The views on dance are also noted to be gendered. Primary students commented that 'boys would look silly dancing' but noticed the fact that 'synchronised swimming was not open to men in the Olympics'. This research shows that the notion of gender in sport is being set from a young age and by the time students arrive at secondary school there are years of ingrained gender stereotyping in relation to sport and physical activity (NEU, 2019).

CHANGE IS COMING

It feels like we are fighting a losing battle, why should we continue? Let us consider the changes that are happening slowly worldwide and the impact it has on our battle:
- Female sports reporters on primetime TV
- Top male gymnastics performers
- Female referees / umpires / officials
- Male dance groups
- Female Muslim athletes participating in the Olympics
- The London 2012 Olympic Games had the same number of events for male and female athletes

CONCLUSION

The work that is happening at an international level is filtering through the system – the shift in attitudes is happening as you read this and the work being completed in schools by dedicated teachers, support staff and coaches is making this change happen. If we stop now those changes will not continue – the evidence that primary-aged children still see gender stereotyping in sport should be willing us all to ensure the stereotypes are broken down. Use your local football / rugby clubs – some have funding to support the clubs in schools, look for groups run by a range of people – showcase their skills. Without role models in everyday life our children just have words; open the door for them and see where it can take them.

KEY TAKEAWAYS

- There are options for all genders in sport, someone just needs to look for them and continually promote the freedom for all approaches.
- Breaking down barriers is never going to go away unless we step up and do it.
- There is always support in PE departments for those who want to look for clubs outside of school hours.

KEY QUESTIONS

- Do you automatically assume what the sports students want to do based on their gender?
- Have you opened the door to trying sports regardless of gender?
- Are you making your voice heard that sport is for all?

COMMITMENT TO THE MANIFESTO

Consider how inclusive your sports curriculum is and ensure that you intentionally challenge gendered sports, behaviour and language that excludes individuals.

REFERENCES

Eisenmann, J. (2019), 'The Nature-Nurture Debate in Sports: Are Athletes Born or Built?; [Blog] *Volt Athletics*. Available at: https://blog.voltathletics.com/home/2019/11/7/the-nature-nurture-debate-in-sports-are-athletes-born-or-built [Accessed 25 June 2021]

NEU (2019), *Breaking the Mould* [online] Available at: https://neu.org.uk/breaking-mould [Accessed 25 June 2021]

Scheadler, T. and Wagstaff, A. (2020), 'Exposure to Women's Sports: Changing Attitudes Toward Female Athletes'. *The Sport Journal*, 41(2). Available at: https://thesportjournal.org/article/exposure-to-womens-sports-changing-attitudes-toward-female-athletes/ [Accessed 25 June 2021]

FLEXIBLE WORKING AND THE GENDER PAY GAP IN THE EDUCATION SECTOR

LINDSAY PATIENCE AND LUCY ROSE

INTRODUCTION

Limited flexible working opportunities in the education sector, particularly at leadership level, contribute to the significant gender pay gap in the sector. Providing more flexible working and better supporting those who are already working flexibly in schools would help retain women in the sector, allow them to progress and help to balance caring responsibilities more generally. Flexible working has many benefits and improving diversity and gender balance in school leadership is just one of them. Getting flexible working right is crucial for narrowing the gender pay gap in schools.

THE GENDER PAY GAP

Women earn less than men over the course of their careers; this happens due to complex, often interrelated reasons. Unequal pay, when women are paid less than men for doing the exact same work, is illegal but the gender pay gap is not the same as unequal pay; it reflects inequalities and discrimination in society and the labour market.

The education sector's gender pay gap is shocking. We have one of the worst median gender pay gaps in the UK at 20% (Wisniewska, Ehrenberg-Shannon and Gordon, 2020). Education is third in the UK league table of sectors with the largest gender pay gaps, with only construction and finance companies above them. In state-funded primary and nursery schools only 14% of all teachers are men but 27% of headteachers. In secondary schools 36% of teachers are men but 62% of heads are male (DFE, 2019). There is clearly an issue here, and with a role to play in education for setting the scene for young people in terms of career aspirations and model of family life. It is vital that we do better.

FLEXIBLE WORKING

Aside from outright discrimination, two of the main reasons cited for the existence of gender pay gaps are differences in caring responsibilities and more women in 'low-skilled' and low-paid work. Improvements in flexible working opportunities in schools could address both issues. The education sector has a long way to go on flexible working. 28% of female teachers work part-time, compared with 40% of all female employees in the UK. For men, it is 8% compared to 12% nationally (Carr, 2020).

Flexible working in schools is not just working part-time. There are a wide variety of ways that schools can introduce flexible working practices. This might be job shares, allowing staff to work from home in their non-contact time, condensed hours where lessons are timetabled in a way that reduces the requirements for time on-site, later starts, earlier finishes or time off to be taken when needed. Of course, you would still always be there for your lessons and meetings and there are some aspects of timetabling and maintaining consistency in relationships that mean it may require careful planning, but it can work.

There is a perception that teaching and school leadership is a great career for women and mothers – long holidays, finishing at 3.30pm, a sector dominated by females. However, it remains relatively difficult to secure part-time roles as a classroom teacher and even trickier if you are a senior leader. Jobs are not commonly advertised flexibly and success rate of flexible working requests are poor (in 2016, 100% of flexible working requests made by leaders in the NASUWT union were rejected) (NASUWT,2016).

Other sectors often see more flexibility the more senior you are but in teaching this is not seen to be the case; Headteachers and other senior leaders must apparently be on site at all times. The Covid-19 situation has led to many schools having to operate remotely with minimal numbers of staff and students on site so maybe this will help to promote the idea that school leaders can work effectively from home.

HOW FLEXIBLE WORKING CAN HELP ADDRESS GENDER PAY GAPS

Encouraging flexible working for women and men can help to combat the gender pay gap in a number of ways. More flexibility in senior roles and flexibility for everyone, male and female, at all stages of the organisation, allows progression for those seeking to work flexibly. Whether through choice or societal pressure and expectation, women still take on more caring responsibilities and as such are more likely to request flexible working. Women are still more likely to be primary caregivers, for children (64% of mothers are the primary carer for their children) and for elderly relatives (50% of women will have caring responsibilities for sick or elderly relatives by the age of 46). (Carers UK, 2019).

So long as the majority of caring responsibilities are still taken on by women in our society, we must accept that failing to offer flexible working disproportionately affects women. In too many cases, women's options are reduced due to their caring responsibilities. If the only two options are to work full-time or not at all, then we will haemorrhage effective, experienced women from the profession. Around 6,000 female teachers thirty to thirty-nine leave the profession each year (that is 27% of leavers when this demographic makes up 23% of the profession). (DfE, 2019).

If some flexibility is offered to allow women to work alongside their caring responsibilities but it is done begrudgingly and not managed well, then there is still an issue. For example, if pay is reduced to 80% and you are only expected to be in school four days a week but your responsibilities and workload remain similar to what they were when you were full-time then of course this is unmanageable and unfair. There will be burnout and claims that flexible working does not work. However, in reality, there is a growing body of evidence that well-managed, proactive, positive flexible working can be successful in all school contexts and at all levels.

Improved flexible working opportunities for senior leaders in schools would help to address the gender imbalance in school leadership, allowing more women to progress to, and remain in leadership roles. But remember, flexible working in schools allows men to work flexibly too. This means they can contribute more to caring responsibilities and bring into balance the societal differences in who cares for children or elderly or ill relatives.

THE FUTURE

The more that schools and individuals see successful flexible working, the more widespread the practice will become. If men and women can work flexibly at all levels in education then it will not be seen as such a barrier to progression. Women will be more represented in senior roles and it will not be the case that mums can only work as part-time classroom teachers no matter what their previous level of experience or potential.

KEY TAKEAWAYS

- The education sector is lagging behind other sectors in regard to flexible working;
- Better flexible working opportunities, particularly in leadership roles would improve the significant gender pay gap in the education sector;
- The more common flexible working becomes in schools, the more evidence there will be that it can be successful and the more widespread it will become.

KEY QUESTIONS

- What more can we do as individuals and organisations to promote flexible working and support those working flexibly?
- What are the wider benefits of flexible working to organisations beyond the benefits to individuals?
- Are there any roles in school which cannot be done flexibly? How can your role or the roles in your school be designed to allow more flexibility?

COMMITMENT TO THE MANIFESTO

Flexible working should be available for everyone; male or female, teacher or school leader, primary or secondary, mainstream, special school or alternative provision.

REFERENCES

Carers UK (2019) *Will I care? The likelihood of being a carer in adult life*. Available at: https://www.carersuk.org/component/cck/?task=download&file=policy_file&id=6871 (accessed 3 May 2021).

Carr, J. (2020) '£500k to boost flexible working and drive staff retention.' *Schools Week*, 17 October, 2020. Available at: https://schoolsweek.co.uk/500k-to-boost-flexible-working-and-drive-staff-retention (accessed 3 May 2021).

DfE (2019) Department for Education, *School workforce in England: November 2018*. Available at: www.gov.uk/government/statistics/school-workforce-in-england-november-2018 (accessed 3 May 2021).

NASUWT (2016) *Flexible Working: The Experience of Teachers*. Available at: https://www.nasuwt.org.uk/uploads/assets/uploaded/6fd07ce3-6400-4cb2-a8a87b736dc95b3b.pdf (accessed 3 May 2021).

Wisniewska, A., Ehrenberg-Shannon, B. and Gordon, S. (2020), 'Gender Pay Gap: how women are short-changed in the UK', *The Financial Times*, 25 September, 2020. Available at: https://ig.ft.com/gender-pay-gap-UK/ (accessed 3 May 2021).

Further Reading:

Sharp, C., Smith, R., Worth, J. et al. (2019) *Part-time teaching and flexible working in secondary schools.* Slough: NFER. Available at: www.nfer.ac.uk/part-time-teaching-and-flexible-working-in-secondary-schools (accessed 3 May 2021).

Timewise (2013), *The flexibility trap*. Available at: https://timewise.co.uk/wp-content/uploads/2019/06/Flexibility-Trap-Research-2013.pdf (accessed 3 May 2021).

Timewise (2017) *Flexible working: A talent imperative*. Available at: https://timewise.co.uk/wp-content/uploads/2019/06/Flexible_working_Talent_Imperative.pdf (accessed 3 May 2021).

CooperGibson Research (2019) *Exploring flexible working practice in schools. Literature review*. Available at:
https://assets.publishing.service.gov.uk/government/uploads/system/
(accessed 3 May 2021).

CooperGibson Research (2020) *Exploring flexible working practice in schools – final report*. Available at: https://assets.publishing.service.gov.uk/government/uploads/system/uploads/attachment_data/file/938537/Exploring_flexible_working_practice_in_schools_-_final_report.pdf (accessed 3 May 2021).

McKinsey (2020) *Women in the Workplace 2020* . Available at: https://www.mckinsey.com/featured-insights/diversity-and-inclusion/women-in-the-workplace# (accessed 3 May 2021).

ORGANISATIONAL INTERVENTIONS TO ADDRESS THE GENDER PAY GAP

NINNA MAKRINOV

INTRODUCTION

Education is widely seen as a female-dominated field; this is particularly the case in primary schools. Because of this, female leaders are visible. However, the gender pay gap continues to exist. Supporting women to develop their leadership potential is a great first step, but it will not breach the gap. Schools, colleges, universities and others in the sector should focus on evidence-based organisational interventions. There is a need for systemic societal change: a revaluation and recognition of care and feminist leadership.

IS THERE A GENDER PAY GAP IN EDUCATION?

The answer to this question is a resounding yes. The gender pay gap in the sector was 13.1% in 2020 (Clark, 2020). This means that on average women earn 86.9p for every pound men earn. For a more detailed account, Porritt (2019) presents an undeniable case. In summary, education is a sector where women are visible and active. However, there are more women working in primary than secondary schools; men are overrepresented in leadership positions. Some of the reasons that explain the gap are the underrepresentation of women in leadership, unconscious bias towards women, lower likelihood of women negotiating starting salaries, lower bonus pay for women and the effects of breaks in women's careers (generally associated with care responsibilities).

In 2019 female classroom teachers were paid £900 less per year on average than their male counterparts. Headteachers' average salary was £8,492 less per year for females than males. (Department for Education, 2020). Female leaders also tend to work in lower paid, smaller primary schools. Women's representation is lower in Further and Higher Education. In universities, 'women make up 55% of the total staff population, but only 29% of Vice-Chancellors and 37% of senior leadership teams.' (Hewitt, 2020)

To fully understand pay differentials, it is also important to take into account intersectionality, in particular as it relates to disability, LGBTQ+ and race. These are discussed in other sections of this book, so this chapter has taken a traditional approach to analysing the gender pay gap, while recognising that gender is fluid and non-binary.

COMMON APPROACHES TO TACKLE CHANGE

The first step to solving a problem is to know it exists. In this respect, clear measures of the gender pay gap are an important starting point. In the UK, organisations with over 250 employees are required by law to publicly report their gender pay gap data, including an action plan to address it (Government Equalities Office, 2020). Smaller organisations can report voluntarily, although this is less common. Since reporting was introduced, the gender pay gap has reduced by 1.6% (Blundell, 2021). This may not be as positive as it seems. In his analysis, Blundell concluded that this reduction was mainly due to a reduction in male wages. He also reports that women are likely to accept lower salaries to work in organisations with a lower pay gap. It is possible that both these factors contribute to further differentiation of roles within sectors.

Another common approach has been to support female development. Peer support and encouragement can help women take the leap into leadership positions and encourage them to negotiate their salaries. Many women have felt empowered by participating in these kinds of activities, as proven by the popularity of the #WomenEd movement (Wilson, 2019). From an organisational perspective, however, there is little evidence that offering training for diversity has a long-term impact (Bezrukova et al., 2016). Two risks of taking this approach as a solution to addressing the gender pay gap are:

- Providing training for women is an easy solution: employers might feel they have done their part by having provided training. It is not, however, women's lack of training that defines the gender pay gap (Joshi et al., 2021).
- Women as the problem: in many cases, individual interventions assume women must change. Their individual behaviour determines their lack of progression. It is clear that this is not the case. Structural issues need to be addressed, as the gender pay gap demonstrates structural inequalities related to our patriarchal society.

EVIDENCE-BASED ORGANISATIONAL CHANGE

To move forward effectively in reducing the gender pay gap, organisations should focus on evidence-based interventions. The guidance on 'Actions to close the gender pay gap' by the UK Government Equality Office (2017) can be a good starting point. Ensure there are senior leaders who have a responsibility for diversity and inclusion; you might want to consider this role for a member of the governing body. Some key actions for organisations include:

KNOW YOUR GAP:

- If your organisation has under 250 employees, report your gender gap voluntarily.
- Use the 'Think Business, Think Equality' self-assessment tool to help you think about your processes and actions (Close the Gap SCIO, n.d.).
- Work with relevant trade unions, who have been supporting gender equality. Trade union participation can enhance professional development opportunities for staff (Bradley et al., 2004).

RECRUITMENT AND SELECTION:

- General good practice: include more than one woman in shortlists; integrate tasks in your selection process, rather than only interviews; use structured interview questions, with clear marking criteria.
- Show salary ranges and keep to these. If the salary is negotiable, state this. Women are likely to offer to work for less and men to negotiate up, but this disappears when explicitly mentioning that pay is negotiable (Leibbrandt and List, 2015).
- Be open in offering opportunities for staff to return to education or to full-time employment. The biggest predictor of the gender pay gap is working experience, in particular differences in full-time employment (Costa Dias et al., 2021).

PROGRESSION & CAREER DEVELOPMENT:

- Be transparent on promotion, rewards and pay practices. This is particularly important when bonuses are offered, as there is a bigger gender pay gap in bonuses than in base pay.
- Offer mentorship and coaching. Encourage your staff to participate in networking opportunities as part of their career development plan.

WORKLOAD AND WORK-LIFE BALANCE:

- Offer opportunities for flexible work that are open to all. This is covered in detail in another chapter of this book. Ensuring flexible work opportunities for leadership positions is very important, as women are more likely to look for positions that are compatible with family life (Damelang and Ebensperger, 2020, Petrongolo and Ronchi, 2020).
- Provide practical support to all staff with childcare responsibilities: Women are more likely to leave their profession due to care responsibilities. Childcare responsibilities have a larger negative effect on women's careers (Cortés and Pan, 2020). Fathers tend to earn more (Cukrowska-Torzewska and Lovasz, 2020), maybe due to the perception of men as providers. Consider for example facilitating shared parental leave, financial aids or in-house

childcare. Be aware, however, that parental leave and childcare subsidies have been shown to have little impact (Kleven et al., 2020).

- Ensure manageable workloads: Those working in education will know about the long hours many dedicate to their roles. This is considered normal, something that those who join the sector are aware of and cannot change. For some, it is considered part of the 'calling' to academia or teaching. Women are more likely to have dual workloads, as they take on care responsibilities. Reducing workload so work is completed in a typical full-time week can ensure everyone can progress, while enhancing wellbeing.
- Support your governors: One common restriction for women to participate in governance is that they need to look after children. Consider flexibility in meeting times, allowing online participation and offering childcare options for your governors.

A CHANGE IN CULTURE

It is important to move beyond trying to change women. To achieve full equality in education it is important that society re-values care responsibilities, both at work and at home. As the COVID-19 pandemic has clearly demonstrated, we cannot subsist without those who take on the responsibility for educating our future generations. This is not only a role for women, but for all. Real gender equality will not only provide better opportunities for women, but also open options for more men to participate in care related activities.

CONCLUSION

It is also important that we not only focus on the participation of women in leadership, but rather on feminist leadership. This is an approach that embraces leadership that is participatory, caring, critical, and focused on anti-oppression (Strachan, 1999). It recognises that leadership is not about an individual leader but about the collective role of the education community. It can take different characteristics, as it reflects the true values of those who participate in the leadership process. Taking this approach will allow us to question ideas of what leadership is and what leaders look like. As demonstrated by feminist movements such as #WomenEd (Wilson, 2019), small actions can lead to global reactions.

KEY TAKEAWAYS

- There is a gender pay gap in education, despite the participation of strong women.
- Organisational interventions should be evidence-based. Taking an organisation-wide approach to gender equality empowers women by recognising they do not need to change; the system does.

- In the long term, the aim is a change in culture so caring roles, such as teaching, are revalued and feminist approaches to leadership are recognised.

KEY QUESTIONS

- What can you do today to improve gender equality? Are you able to provide evidence for your actions?
- How do you recognise your own leadership?
- How do you empower others to grow?

COMMITMENT TO THE MANIFESTO

Commit to organisational change and evidence based organisational interventions for gender equality, empowering everyone to flourish.

REFERENCES

Bezrukova, K., Spell, C., Perry, J. et al. (2016) 'A meta-analytical integration of over 40 years of research on diversity training evaluation.' *Psychological Bulletin* 142(11): 1227-74.

Blundell, J. (2021) *Wage responses to gender pay gap reporting requirements*. Available at: https://cep.lse.ac.uk/pubs/download/dp1750.pdf (accessed 14 April).

Bradley, H., Healy, G. and Mukherjee, N. (2004) 'Union influence on career development –bringing in gender and ethnicity.' *Career Development International* 9(1): 74-88.

Clark, D. (2020) *Difference between men and women's average hourly earnings in full-time employment in the United Kingdom (UK) in 2020, by industry sector*. Available at: https://www.statista.com/statistics/760342/gender-pay-gap-difference-in-male-and-female-full-time-hourly-earnings-uk-united-kingdom/ (accessed 14 April).

Cortés, P. and Pan, J. (2020) *Children and the remaining gender gaps in the labor market*. NBER Working Paper Series.

Costa Dias, M., Joyce, R. and Parodi, F. (2021) 'The gender pay gap in the UK: children and experience in work.' *Oxford Review of Economic Policy* 36(4): 855-81.

Cukrowska-Torzewska, E. and Lovasz, A. (2020) 'The role of parenthood in shaping the gender wage gap – A comparative analysis of 26 European countries.' *Social Science Research* 85: 102355.

Damelang, A. and Ebensperger, S. (2020) 'Gender composition of occupations and occupational characteristics: Explaining their true relationship by using longitudinal data.' *Social Science Research* 86: 102394.

Department for Education (2020) *School workforce in England: November 2019.* Available at: https://www.gov.uk/government/statistics/school-workforce-in-england-november-2019 (accessed 13 April).

Government Equalities Office (2017). *Reducing the gender pay gap and improving gender equality in organisations: Evidence-based actions for employers.*

Government Equalities Office (2020) *Gender pay gap reporting.* Available at: https://www.gov.uk/government/collections/gender-pay-gap-reporting (accessed 14 April). Hewitt, R. (2020) *Mind the gap: gender differences in higher education.* Available at: https://www.hepi.ac.uk/2020/03/07/mind-the-gap-gender-differences-in-higher-education/ (accessed 13 April).

Joshi, H., Bryson, A., Wilkinson, D., et al. (2021) 'The gender gap in wages over the life course: Evidence from a British cohort born in 1958.' *Gender, Work & Organization* 28(1): 397-415.

Kleven, H., Landais, C., Posch J., et al. (2020) *Do family policies reduce gender inequality? Evidence from 60 years of policy experimentation.* NBER Working Paper Series.

Leibbrandt, A. and List, J.A. (2015) 'Do women avoid salary negotiations? Evidence from a large-scale natural field experiment.' *Management Science* 61(9): 2016-24.

Petrongolo, B. and Ronchi, M. (2020) 'Gender gaps and the structure of local labor markets.' *Labour Economics* 64: 101819.

Porritt, V. (2019) 'What price equality? The gender pay gap.' In: Porritt, V. and Featherstone, K. (eds.) *10% braver: inspiring women to lead in education.* London: SAGE Publications Ltd., pp.135-40.

Close the Gap SCIO (n.d.) *Think business, think equality.* Available at:https://www.thinkbusinessthinkequality.org.uk/.

Strachan, J. (1999) 'Feminist educational leadership: locating the concepts in practice.' *Gender and Education* 11(3): 309-322.

Wilson, H. (2019) #WomenEd: our story and our values. In Porritt, V. and Featherstone, K. (eds.) *10% braver: inspiring women to lead in education.* London: SAGE Publications Ltd., pp.1-13.

BECOMING AN ALLY FOR WOMEN AS A HEFORSHE ADVOCATE

PATRICK OTTLEY-O'CONNOR

INTRODUCTION

I regard myself to be an ally for women and have for much of my adult life actively promoted a culture of inclusion and equality through my intentional, positive and conscious efforts to benefit women. In short, I believe if I am not part of the solution, then I am part of the problem!

In September 2014 the HeForShe movement was launched by the United Nations as a global solidarity movement for gender equality. It was launched at the United Nations on 20 September 2014, by UN Secretary-General Ban Ki-moon and UN Women Global Goodwill Ambassador Emma Watson to engage men and boys as advocates and agents of change for the achievement of gender equality and women's rights. The campaign currently has 1.2 billion HeForShe commitments, including over two million online pledges, and encourages men and boys to speak out and take action against inequalities faced by women and girls.

HeForShe resonates with the desire of many boys and men to understand and support gender equality. It is an invitation for men and people of all genders to stand in solidarity with women. Like two million others, I pledged my commitment and decided to stop merely cheering from the sidelines, instead volunteering, coaching, mentoring and supporting women whenever needed.

The creation of WomenEd provided a perfect vehicle for me to work alongside women in education as a HeForShe ally and take action to support meaningful change in my community. This was not always the case! We are all products of our upbringing. Although I was brought up in a home full of love and kindness, it was also rich in the gender stereotypes and biases typical of a childhood in the 1960s and 1970s.

BUILDING ALLYSHIP

The evolution of any allyship with women can be a lengthy process of building relationships based on trust, consistency, and accountability with women. It can provide great opportunities for personal growth and learning, whilst building confidence in others. Allyship should not be self-defined and allies should continually strive to ensure that their work and efforts are recognised and welcomed by those that they seek to ally with. As a young teacher, I did not recognise my privilege and was openly told in 1989 after my first promotion to Head of Year, that the school needed a 'strong man' for the role. At the time, I took that as a compliment and played out the stereotypical role of a male saviour! It was not until I was a twenty-eight-year-old Assistant Headteacher that I first publicly called out sexist, racist and homophobic behaviour in the staff room with a group of men. I felt complicit listening to their discriminatory 'banter' and decided I needed to live my principles. I simply explained that their comments were inappropriate and offensive to everyone, including me as a straight, white man. I lost many of those 'friends', but instantly gained the respect of other colleagues and walked a foot taller after being true to my emerging beliefs and moral purpose. During the ensuing leadership years, I developed my own values-based vision for equality, inclusion and diversity, shaped by the strong women role models that surrounded me. As a Headteacher I have had the privilege of using my allyship within my school communities and since 2011 onto Twitter and beyond!

Gender equality is an issue of human rights; consequently, it should be as big an issue for men as it is for women. It is the responsibility of all genders. Whenever men talk at conferences and events or write publicly about allyship as HeForShe, they should reach out to women, such as the members of the WomenEd community, for support, inspiration and grounding. To date, my support of HeForShe and the notion of promoting and encouraging allyship from others has always been welcomed, but importantly shaped by the women I strive to ally with. In my experience, women will provide advice on what they want from an ally and will often signpost a range of other resources and/or viewpoints.

To be an effective ally, words and actions must be in sync. As such, allies must hold themselves accountable and encourage others to challenge them when they make mistakes, including apologising and reworking approaches towards allyship as needs change. Why not pledge to WomenEd to actively model and promote the HeForShe movement and help recruit more men to join the journey towards equality and equity for women in education? This could help focus on personal unconscious bias and attitudes and behaviours to women, leading to more personal challenge, learning and growth.

Here are a few every day actions to become an active HeForShe ally:

- lift women up by advocating and amplifying their voices, actions and achievements;
- share equitable and accessible talent growth opportunities and experiences with women;
- invite and welcome women venting without viewing it as a personal attack;
- recognise and acknowledge the systemic inequalities faced by women;
- be aware of gendered terms, and use more inclusive language;

- believe the experiences of women;
- 'call out' inappropriate behaviour towards women;
- importantly, listen, support, self-reflect and change.

BECOMING AWARE OF GENDER INEQUALITY

Johnson and Smith (2021) suggest that lack of gender equality awareness from men can prevent even well-intentioned allies from making a positive difference and becoming effective advocates. The review goes on to say that if men ask questions of female colleagues and engage in generous listening then they are more likely to become situationally aware allies. When combined with men challenging unacceptable language and behaviour towards women this can create even stronger allyship in action. Allies should regularly talk loudly and proudly about their HeForShe allyship and actively create a culture of care that embraces equality, inclusion and diversity, providing multiple opportunities for women's voices to be listened to and importantly be heard. Women in my schools tell me that they are encouraged, engaged and empowered with equitable CPD/career opportunities and experiences. Equally, women need to be comfortable raising issues without a fear of backlash or risk of jeopardising professional relationships. Leaders should make a continual investment of time in supporting others and champion women from the education community to support career growth. Words without actions are detrimental and work against changing the culture.

There are some intentional, positive and conscious efforts that a HeForShe ally can take to start to address the inequalities, such as, including unconscious bias training as a regular feature of CPD, whilst understanding that unconscious, unchecked bias will not be fixed after one session. Treat this as a growing process, with continual challenge of ourselves and peers.

There is a great untapped reservoir of talented women seeking opportunities in schools with the right ethos. To attract and retain women, leaders should review and adapt recruitment methods, including: partnering with organisations which actively push for equality; reaching out to women for their honest feedback on where they would look for roles and listen to the people you are trying to reach; using conferences, training events and social media to publicise roles; speaking openly about support of women in education; and following an array of voices on social media, including the voices and opinions of women.

CONCLUSION

Learning, growth and addressing personal bias will not happen without being open to challenge. A true HeForShe ally must regularly listen to those around them, adapt their thinking, continually revisit and rework what they believe to be correct and become more comfortable feeling uncomfortable.

KEY TAKEAWAYS

- Words without actions are detrimental and work against changing the culture as a HeForShe ally.
- Your allyship should not be self-defined, so strive to ensure that your work and efforts are informed, recognised and welcomed by those that you seek to ally with.
- Model the behaviours that you want to see as a HeForShe ally

KEY QUESTIONS

- What uncomfortable conversations do you need to have with yourself about your unconscious bias towards women?
- What do you need to do to understand the systematic and societal issues which may have played in your 'lucky' career?
- How will you learn and grow to allow you to support, champion and amplify the voices and success of women?

COMMITMENT TO THE MANIFESTO

Encourage, engage and empower boys and men to use their allyship with women by becoming HeForShe advocates.

REFERENCES

Johnson, W.B. and Smith, D.G. (2021) 'Male Allyship Is About Paying Attention '. *Harvard Business Review*, 10 February 2021

United Nations Global Solidarity Movement for Gender Equality (2021). Available at https://www.heforshe.org/en (accessed 20 May 2021)

WomenEd is a global grassroots movement which connects aspiring and existing women leaders in education and gives women leaders a voice in education (2021). Available at https://womened.org/ (accessed 20 May 2021)

THE CONQUERING

DIANA OSAGIE

INTRODUCTION

Women are competent. Women are qualified. They are eligible to sit at the leadership table of our nation's schools, but there is a gap that needs to be addressed *between leadership competence and leadership confidence.* Until this is done, schools will continue to see phenomenal female talent walk out the door. (

Qualifications for leadership are essential – NPQs, MA, PhD – all encourage the holder to swim in the depths of academic leadership and develop the necessary leadership muscle. Qualifications increase gravitas and give permission for the leader to knock on the door of promotion. Then the internal voice begins to speak and the glass ceiling that lives within the female leader seeks to have its dominion. Where are the remedies that conquer the internal glass ceiling?

THE GLASS CEILING

Marilyn Loden first coined the phrase 'glass ceiling' while speaking as a panellist at the 1978 Women's Exposition in New York. This sharp focus against societal norms of accepted gender roles in the workplace came in the midst of a conversation where the discussion centred on how women, and their self-image, were to blame for their lack of advancement in the workforce (*Washington Post,* 2018). It became popular as a concept in the 1980s and it describes invisible obstacles so subtle that they are transparent as glass, yet so strong that it makes the higher levels of leadership impossible for women to access. A commission from the US Department of Labour (1991) defined the glass ceiling as artificial barriers that are based on bias in attitudes of individuals and organisations, and that prevent the advancement of individuals into management positions they qualify for. The glass ceiling disregards merit and achievement, by reinforcing barriers that are discriminatory in nature. *Now imagine this scenario coming from within the leader herself.*

Equally important barriers to women's advancement are not external, but internal. It is challenging to navigate the realities of the workplace and learn the necessary skills of self-advocacy, networking, and political savvy without first tackling the limiting beliefs that affect self-confidence and self-worth (Marcus, 2013). On paper the evidence is irrefutable. The woman looks at herself with the workplace lens and sees years of experience that have proved profitable to the organisation. Impact and desirable outcomes litter her CV demonstrating quality leadership that is sought after. The woman takes a second look at herself through the lens of academia. Again, she sees a valuable leadership journey, one where the evidence points to a leader qualified to speak with a masterful approach on many areas of the educational landscape. Finally, she tries to visualise herself operating in the higher echelons of leadership. Perhaps as the Headteacher, with the entire school community weighing her every word, or as the CEO of the multi-academy trust, responsible for millions of pounds and the strategic lead for the entire system. It is here that the papers detailing qualifications and experience count for nothing, if her internal limiting beliefs express themselves forcefully:

- Internal bias against what she can do. The unconscious internal reinforcing of societal myths regarding women in the workplace.
- Internal attitudes that limit her potential. Attitudes originating from others who have whispered or said unequivocally this is what someone like you can do, this is how far someone like you can go. Attitudes that dial down the volume of internal authority.
- Internal narratives that set up a model of self-discrimination. Internal answers that say NO, (for whatever reason) you are not ready, eligible, able, suitable, or desirable for that role. Remain here under the glass ceiling where it is safe.

THE PICTURE OF LEADERSHIP

So, we have a national picture where women make up a high proportion of the teaching workforce (particularly in primary schools), but are under-represented at leadership positions. The proportion of women is highest amongst classroom teachers and middle leaders, and *lowest for senior leaders and headteachers*. There is a smaller difference between roles in primary schools, where women made up 85% of the workforce in 2016 compared with 73% of headteachers, than in secondary schools, where women made up 62% of the workforce compared with 38% of headteachers. Analysis found that there was a significant effect for gender, with more men on average progressing to both first leadership and headteacher roles within the first years than women (DfES 2018).

CONCLUSION

The picture of school leadership in the UK is skewered. It shows how we consistently relinquish the strategic advantage of female leadership around our tables of power and influence. It shows an acceptance of glass ceilings wherever or however they manifest themselves and it lies within the grasp of female leaders to conquer the internal narrative that limits their natural and deserved progression into leadership.

The diminishing of strategic diversity, as too few women sit comfortably at the leadership table is an outcome that affects us all. Younger women have fewer role models than their male counterparts; seeing someone like you in authority in your profession is a powerful unspoken encouragement. The advantage of female difference, female perspective and strength is lost to many organisations who choose to fill their top leadership roles with a continued male dominant narrative.

KEY TAKEAWAYS

- **Limiting beliefs about yourself** that make you feel like you cannot do something because something is inherently wrong with you. This is also true if you examine the beliefs you hold about others. Do you have limiting beliefs about others that are inherent in the way you think?
- **Limiting beliefs about the world** that make you feel like you cannot do something because no one will let you.
- **Limiting beliefs about life** that make you feel like you cannot do something because it is too difficult. Is it just too complicated to be an ally to someone whose pathway is not as straight as yours?

KEY QUESTIONS

- Ask yourself, 'What if I am wrong?' Generally, limiting beliefs lose their power as soon as we consider that they may not be true.
- Ask yourself, 'How is this belief serving me?' We like to imagine ourselves as the victims of our own limiting beliefs, but the truth is that we adopt these beliefs because they serve us in some way. Generally, we hold onto limiting beliefs for the same reasons — to protect ourselves from struggle and failure.
- Create alternative beliefs. Come up with ways in which you may be wrong. There is nothing stopping you other than your own mind. What are the alternatives to your internal assumptions?

COMMITMENT TO THE MANIFESTO

Intentionally choose to relinquish the role of being your own internal enemy, refuse to be confined by your perceptions, make room for a change in your understanding of what is true or false.

REFERENCES

DFES (2018) *School leadership in England 2010 to 2016: characteristics and trends.* Available at:
https://assets.publishing.service.gov.uk/government/uploads/system/uploads/attachment_data/file/725118/Leadership_Analysis_2018.pdf (Accessed April 2021.)

Marcus, B. (2013) *Shattering The Internal Glass Ceiling To Thrive In The External World*. Available at: https://www.forbes.com/sites/bonniemarcus/2015/02/23/shattering-the-internal-glass-ceiling-to-thrive-in-the-external-world/?sh=5e3f378524b4 Accessed April 2021

Vargas, T. (2018), 'She coined the term 'glass ceiling.' She fears it will outlive her.' *The Washington Post*, 1 March 2018 (Accessed April 2021.)

U.S. Department of Labour (1991), *A Report on the Glass Ceiling Initiative.* 1-25.

CHAPTER 9: SEXUAL ORIENTATION

CHAPTER EDITOR: JONATHAN GLAZZARD

CHAPTER CONTRIBUTORS

1. Amy Ferguson – **Your Teacher Identity**
2. Andrew Moffat – **No Outsiders – Everyone different, everyone welcome**
3. Daniel Tomlinson-Gray – **Why Schools Need Funding For LGBT+ Work Now More Than Ever**
4. Shaun Dellenty – **Schools Supporting Some Diverse Children or All Diverse Children?**
5. Carly Hind – **The Remarkable Power of Positive LGBTQ+ Representation in Schools**
6. Jac Bastian – **The Power of Personal Stories**
7. Lisa Jordan – **Educators Need to Become Effective LGBT+ Role Models: Disrupting Heteronormativity and Developing Authentic Relationships**
8. Mahlon Evans-Sinclair – **Sexuality, Blackness and Masculinity**
9. Mayur Gupta – **What If I Don't Want To Be A Celebrity Blogger When I Grow Up? Preparing LGBT+ Students for Professional Careers**
10. Nick Bentley – **Shared Narratives: How Stories and Collaboration can Empower LGBTQ+ Communities in Education**

BIOGRAPHIES

Professor Jonathan Glazzard's research focuses on mental health, wellbeing and inclusion in education. He is a qualitative researcher and uses a broad range of approaches, including narrative methodology, visual/participatory methods and more traditional interviews and focus groups. Jonathan's recent projects include exploration of headteacher resilience, teacher and child mental health and the experiences of teachers who identify as LGBTQ+. Jonathan is a co-convenor of the British Educational Research Association (BERA) Special Interest Group, Mental Health and Wellbeing in Education. He is also a member of the Excellence in International Transitions Research which is led by Professor Divya Jindal-Snape. Jonathan is deeply committed to research which advances social justice. He has published widely on aspects of inclusion and social justice for marginalised groups and individuals and he is deeply committed to research which improves the lives of individuals and research-informed teaching.

Amy Ferguson is a Deputy Headteacher at an independent special school for young people with SEMH/ASC/ADHD. Amy has been a teacher of Dance and Drama for eleven years and has a range of experience as both a pastoral and curriculum leader.

Andrew Moffat is a class teacher and PD lead in a primary school multi-academy trust in Birmingham. He is the author of *No Outsiders: Everyone different, everyone welcome* and CEO of the No Outsiders charity. In 2017 he was awarded an MBE for equality and diversity in education and in 2019 he was listed as a top 10 finalist in the Varkey Foundation Global Teacher Prize.

Carly Hind is a secondary school teacher and member of the LGBTQ+ community, who advocates for a more inclusive world for her students. She co-founded Dual Frequency, a social justice teaching resource website that supports educators and schools to embed equality, diversity and inclusion into all aspects of school life.

Daniel Tomlinson-Gray is a secondary school teacher with more than twelve years of experience who has also worked in school leadership. He is co-founder and director of LGBTed, working with teachers and schools to increase visibility of authentic LGBT+ role models and advocate for positive change in the education system.

Jac Bastian is committed to empowering students, staff and the whole school community to create inclusive schools. He has worked at Diversity Role Models for over four years and has trained thousands of teachers, delivered workshops to students at every phase and created a host of teaching resources on LGBT+ inclusion.

Lisa Jordan is a Teaching, Learning and Assessment Data and Performance Manager across the FE colleges at Luminate Education Group and chair of the staff LGBT+ Network. With a background in pastoral care, mentoring, coaching and learning support, Lisa holds an MA in Education and BA in Fine Art and Mathematics.

Mahlon Evans-Sinclair has extensive experience in learning, development and inclusion. He incorporates concepts of equity and diversity into both content and application of curricula developed for Teacher Training and Development courses in the UK and internationally. Mahlon is concerned with empowering marginalised people and hosts the podcast, *Educating While Black*.

Mayur Gupta is the CEO and Founder of Career Accelerator, which provides support for young people from diverse backgrounds who want to access careers in the digital sector, through employer support led by top tech firms. Mayur also volunteers for Stonewall, Out in Tech and the Bisi Alimi foundation.

Nick Kitchener-Bentley is a Lead Practitioner, and a Drama and Nurture Group teacher at a secondary school in East London. He is a member of the LGBTed Steering Group and has completed a Masters in Teaching and a PGCE in Secondary: English with Drama at the UCL Institute of Education.

Shaun Dellenty authored *Celebrating Difference – A Whole School Approach to LGBT+ Inclusion* (Bloomsbury) and is an award-winning educator and global advocate for inclusive education, with a strong focus around LGBT+ identities. Featured on the Global Diversity List 2020, Pink List and designated a 'Point of Light' by the UK Prime Minister.

THE PROTECTED CHARACTERISTIC OF SEXUALITY: INTRODUCTION

JONATHAN GLAZZARD

INTRODUCTION

The Public Sector Duty of the Equality Act (2010) came into force on 5th April 2011. It requires public bodies including schools, colleges and universities to have due regard to the need to eliminate discrimination, advance equality of opportunity and foster good relations between those with and without protected characteristics. The Equality Act makes it illegal to discriminate against individuals on the basis of nine 'protected characteristics' which include sexual orientation, sex and gender reassignment. Schools must comply with the Equality Act by ensuring that LGBTQ+ students and staff do not experience either direct or indirect discrimination.

In 2017 the UK Prime Minister at the time, Theresa May, attended the Pink News Awards. In her keynote address she emphasised the importance of protecting the human rights of the LGBTQ+ community. She demonstrated a commitment to eradicating homophobic, biphobic and transphobic bullying in schools and to providing children and young people with inclusive relationships and sex education. She stated that:

Homophobia, biphobia and transphobia have still not been defeated and they must be. Bullying in schools and on social media is still a daily reality for young LGBTQ+ people, and that has to stop. Trans people still face indignities and prejudice when they deserve understanding and respect... being trans is not an illness and it shouldn't be treated as such.

Of course, 2017 marked fifty years following the partial decriminalisation of homosexuality through the 1967 Sexual Offences Act. Theresa May's stance in 2017 was a stark contrast to Section 28 in 1988 which was introduced by the former Conservative Prime Minister, Margaret Thatcher. Section 28 was a controversial piece of legislation. It stated that local authorities 'shall not intentionally promote homosexuality or publish material with the intention of promoting homosexuality or promote the teaching in any maintained school of the acceptability of homosexuality as a pretended family relationship'. It silenced schools from discussing homosexuality and forced LGBTQ+ teachers further into the closet. It was eventually repealed in

2003. Several chapters acknowledge this historical context and it is important never to forget it.

Research suggests that LGBTQ+ young people experience higher rates of depression, anxiety and self-harm compared to their heterosexual peers (Goldbach and Gibbs, 2017). Evidence also indicates that they are more likely to attempt suicide (Marshal et al., 2011) and experience eating disorders (Austin et al, 2013).

Minority stress theory (Meyer, 2003) considers how stress can affect the mental health outcomes in individuals with a minority status. The theory suggests that individuals with a minority status experience two additional stressors above the general stressors that all people are exposed to:

- General stressors: These are stressors which result from environmental circumstances. They could include family factors such as parental conflict, parental separation, abuse and neglect and community-related factors such as social deprivation.
- Distal stressors: These are stressors which arise from the experience of prejudice, discrimination and violence because of one's minority status.
- Proximal stressors: These are stressors which arise from the expectations of rejection, prejudice, discrimination and violence. That is, an individual with a minority status does not have to actually experience distal stressors, but the anticipation that they might encounter these stressors in different social and environmental contexts can result in internalised stress. For example, they may anticipate that they will encounter prejudice if they disclose their sexual orientation or gender identity. This can lead to students concealing their identities and internalised homophobia.

Negative experiences when disclosing their identities (distal stressors) may increase expectations of further rejection (proximal stressors) in different contexts (Goldbach and Gibbs, 2017). Additionally, concealing one's identity due to fear of rejection (proximal stressors) can reduce the likelihood of experiencing prejudice, discrimination and violence (distal stressor) (Goldbach and Gibbs, 2017) but increase internal psychological distress. Thus, the stressors are inter-related and bi-directional. Research indicates that stigmatising experiences during adolescence can reduce academic achievement and result in negative outcomes later in life (Radowsky and Siegel, 1997). Adolescence is also a critical time during which young people explore their sexual orientation and gender identities, thus integrating this into the curriculum is crucial to help young people make sense of their feelings.

Meyer's theory assumes that the stressors can be moderated by social support systems that are specifically established to foster both group solidarity and positively affirm minority identities. Many schools now provide 'safe spaces' for students who identify as LGBTQ+ to meet informally and effect positive change and some of the chapters specifically address this. Such groups enable students to provide each other with mutual support and advice. Some groups also adopt a proactive approach to LGBTQ+ inclusion within the school by developing initiatives to embed LGBTQ+

inclusion across the whole school. Providing opportunities for LGBTQ+ students to meet as a group can enhance social connectivity, reduce internalised stigma and increase resilience. However, there is also a risk that separating out one group of students in this way can also result in internal exclusion through the creation of an 'othered' group. One way of addressing this is to allow membership of the group to non-LGBTQ+ allies who are deeply committed to LGBTQ+ inclusion and again some of the chapters address this.

We cannot be complacent. Although the UK has made significant strides forward over the last decade, the 2017 Stonewall report demonstrated that homophobic, biphobic and transphobic bullying is still prevalent within schools. The key findings were alarming:

- Nearly half of lesbian, gay, bi and transgender students (45 %) – including 64 % of transgender students – are bullied for being LGBTQ+ at school.
- The majority of LGBTQ+ students – 86 % – regularly hear phrases such as 'that's so gay' or 'you're so gay' in school.
- Nearly one in ten transgender students (9 %) are subjected to death threats at school.
- Nearly seven in ten LGBTQ+ students (68 %) report that teachers or school staff only 'sometimes' or 'never' challenge homophobic, biphobic and transphobic language when they hear it.
- Two in five LGBTQ+ students (40 %) are never taught anything about LGBTQ+ issues at school.
- Around three in four LGBTQ+ students (77 %) have never learnt about gender identity and what 'transgender' means at school.
- More than half of LGBTQ+ students (53 %) say that there isn't an adult at school they can talk to about being LGBTQ+.

(Bradlow et al., 2017)

VOICES IN OUR CHAPTER IN DIVERSE EDUCATORS – A MANIFESTO

The chapters that follow present a strong case for educating all young people about LGBTQ+ identities by providing a curriculum which makes visible and positively affirms LGBTQ+ identities. All authors support an affirmation model of inclusion which views diversity as a positive and enriching characteristic which validates different identities. Chapters cover a broad range of phases of education; **Amy Ferguson** takes a personal approach and **Andrew Moffat's** chapter demonstrates how easy it is to address diversity and inclusion with very young children using story books. **Daniel Tomlinson-Gray** emphasises the need to 'usualise' LGBTQ+ identities and the importance of LGBTQ+ teachers being their authentic selves in schools. **Shaun Dellenty** presents a compelling case for courageous and compassionate leadership in schools and challenges educators to adopt this approach. **Carly Hind** emphasises the importance of a whole school approach to LGBTQ+ inclusion and the necessity to work in partnership with students. **Jac Bastian** presents a strong rationale for the use of storytelling as a tool to highlight the impact of prejudice and discrimination. **Lisa Jordan** illuminates the powerful effect that LGBTQ+ teachers as role models have on students. **Mahlon Sinclair-Evans** explores the intersections between gender, race and sexuality. **Mayur Gupta** provides us with numerous practical examples of how the curriculum can raise young people's long-term aspirations by making links to successful people in the world of business. Finally, **Nick Bentley** discusses the role of student collaboration in establishing LGBTQ+ student groups. The articles are refreshing, energising and offer us hope that education can help to create a more inclusive society in the future.

CONCLUSION

Within the chapters, there is recognition that implementing LGBTQ+ inclusion is not always straightforward, but it is the right thing to do. By demonstrating a firm commitment to LGBTQ+ inclusion and therefore social justice, educators make a significant contribution to the development of a socially inclusive society. Nothing is more important than that and we hope you find the chapters stimulating and thought-provoking.

COMMITMENT TO THE MANIFESTO

We need to examine the role of LGBTQ+ staff in providing positive role models for our students that we mitigate for the stressors evident when we are in a minority. Schools can, and should, be proactive in supporting our LGBTQ+ students through training, the curriculum and conversation.

REFERENCES

Austin, S. B., Nelson, L. A., Birkett, M. A., Calzo, J. P. and Everett, B. (2013), 'Eating disorder symptoms and obesity at the intersections of gender, ethnicity, and sexual orientation in US high school students.' *American Journal of Public Health*, 103, (2), 16–22.

Bradlow, J., Bartram, F., Guasp, A., and Jadva, V. (2017), *School Report: The experiences of lesbian, gay, bi and trans young people in Britain's schools in 2017*. Stonewall.

Goldbach, J.T., and Gibbs, J.J. (2017), 'A developmentally informed adaptation of minority stress for sexual minority adolescents.' *Journal of Adolescence*, 55, 36–50.

Marshal, M. P., Dietz, L. J., Friedman, M. S., Stall, R., Smith, H. A., McGinley, J., et al. (2011), 'Suicidality and depression disparities between sexual minority and heterosexual youth: A meta-analytic review.' *Journal of Adolescent Health*, 49, (2), 115–23.

Radkowsky, M., and Siegel, L. J. (1997), 'The gay adolescent: Stressors, adaptations, and psychosocial interventions.' *Clinical Psychology Review*, 17, (2), 191–216.

YOUR TEACHER IDENTITY

AMY FERGUSON

Your teacher identity is something that is dynamic and will continue to change throughout your career. Your own experiences of education and the teachers you have met will shape your view of the profession and your teacher identity. Knowing how much to 'give' of yourself in the classroom is part of the challenge of establishing your teacher identity.

How do you want others to perceive you as a teacher? When children go home and describe their new teacher, what do you want them to say about you?

I want them not only say "I am safe and supported in Ms Ferguson's classroom" but really believe it – that they are free to be themselves in my classroom and that they are encouraged to do their work to the best of their ability.

Consider what you believe the purpose of school to be and how would this manifest in your identity as a teacher. If you have a clear understanding of your own passions and beliefs and how these align with your views and understanding of education; you will no doubt have a well-formed sense of personal identity and are more likely to be ready to form your teacher identity.

Are there certain aspects of yourself you wish to keep hidden? If there are, then you need to ask yourself why you are choosing to hide it. Section 28 forced LGBTQAI+ teachers and young people into hiding.

Section 28 of the Local Government Act was enacted in May 1998 and it was brought in to "prohibit the promotion of homosexuality" by local authorities. In practice, the clause meant that teachers were forbidden from discussing same-sex relationships with young people. Section 28 was a backwards step for inclusivity after endeavours made by the British LGBT+ movement since the decriminalisation of male homosexuality in 1967. The clause unquestionably played a huge part in homophobia and bullying remaining largely unchallenged in schools, until November 2003 when it was eventually repealed. Those of us who came of age during this time are still living with the hangover from it. Section 28 left us feeling that schools are not an appropriate context to discuss LGBTQAI+ people and relationships. However, schools decide the kind of society, the kind of world that we live in, schools transform children into citizens of the world, schools are where we can start the conversation or change the narrative.

The idea of announcing that you are part of the LGBTQAI+ community during a school assembly may be terrifying. Some people are extroverts, some people are introverts. There are people who choose not to talk about their lives or feelings because they don't want to, and that is ok. There are other ways of being a visible LGBTQAI+ role model in your school. The relationships we have with the young people in our classrooms impacts not only the engagement in the subject and perhaps results but also and most importantly, these relationships have a lasting impact on how the young people see themselves and how they see themselves in the world.

Being visible, authentic and willing to bring your whole self to the workplace is about getting to a space where you have the freedom to be authentic and vulnerable and also the freedom to choose what you reveal about yourself. This is where you need to make sure that your values and the things that are important to you align with the ethos and vision of the school that you work in.

When you join a new school, you must explore the policies and think how you will fit your style and personality to the ethos and values of the school. And where you have had to, and feel comfortable to, adapted your teacher identity and style to suit the school.

But the real magic, has happens in schools where your values and things that are important to you fit with the vision, ethos and values of the school. That is where have you will feel the most comfortable to be your authentic self and we know that people perform better when they can be themselves, and when this happens everybody benefits.

Being part of the LGBTQAI+ community is part of your identity and this is something that you might bring into your teacher identity and talk about openly with young people to improve LGBTQ+ inclusion in schools. By being your authentic self in the classroom will have an impact on the young people you teach.

Research has shown that teachers who show willingness to share details of their life, display elements of their humanity by telling personal stories, making jokes and admitting mistakes help students achieve higher levels of learning and deeper understanding. This is research from California State university in 2017, where 300 young people were asked about their experiences of authentic vs inauthentic teachers. Professor Zac Johnson who led the study said that this research indicated students do pay attention to the messages we send about ourselves in the classroom, and their perception of those messages seem to play an important role in how they connect to the content of the course.

Being your authentic self, speaking up, taking risks and owning mistakes – modelled and celebrated by teachers creates a safe space for young people to thrive. When children go home and describe their new teacher, what do you want them to say about you?

KEY TAKEAWAYS

- Authenticity is key in our profession
- When we bring our whole selves, students connect better with us
- We are role models

KEY QUESTIONS

- In what ways does your identity create connection with students?
- What barriers do you face in being authentically yourself in school?
- How can schools encourage a climate of authenticity?

COMMITMENT TO THE MANIFESTO

Create a school climate in which LGBT+ teachers can flourish without fear so that students can flourish too.

REFERENCES

Zac D. Johnson, Sara LaBelle. **An examination of teacher authenticity in the college classroom**. *Communication Education*, 2017; 1 DOI: 10.1080/03634523.2017.1324167

National Statistics **School workforce in England: November 2018**
Available at :
https://www.gov.uk/government/statistics/
school-workforce-in-england-november-2018

Local Government Act 1988. Available at: https://www.legislation.gov.uk/
ukpga/1988/9/introduction

NO OUTSIDERS – EVERYONE DIFFERENT, EVERYONE WELCOME

ANDREW MOFFAT

No Outsiders is a school ethos which has lesson plans and assembly plans to back it up. The aim is for children to leave school confident in who they are, knowing that they belong while also being respectful and accepting of others, making sure they know they belong too. Every child knows what it feels like to be left out and so if you are teaching children from the moment they enter school that no one is left out because there are No Outsiders here, it's very powerful; every child can relate to it and understands it.

My aim in this chapter is to provide practical examples of lesson plans that teachers might want to try out in classes. I always use picture books to teach equality; this is because we can focus on the characters and situations rather than our own experiences. Of course, as children get older, we can bring in personal experience if appropriate, but we can always fall back on the character and story where conversations are safe and removed.

The following lesson plans are typical of the No Outsiders plans that are in the No Outsiders resource (Moffat, 2020) but these use books that are not in the original scheme.

EYFS:

'Everybody Has a Body' (Burgerman, 2020)

The aim for the Reception child is to explore ways we are different and be comfortable with those differences. We don't need to celebrate those differences, they just are! We need books in EYFS that children can relate to and see themselves in; representation is key. *Everybody Has a Body* is a super resource to start children on a journey to acceptance. Linking to the RSE objectives about respecting others 'even when they are different', in the story we see characters of different shapes and sizes, and conclude that everyone is different and we all work together beautifully.

Text: *Everybody Has a Body* by John Burgerman
Lesson plan by Andrew Moffat

Enquiry question: How am I different?

RSE objectives: The importance of respecting others, even when they are very different from them (for example, physically, in character, personality or backgrounds), or make different choices or have different preferences or beliefs.

Starter:
- Discuss the front cover – what do you see? How are the characters the same, how are they different? Do they all look happy? How do you know?
- Ask children to describe a character without pointing to it, can we recognize which one they are describing?
- Inside the front cover there are different circles of colour; why do you think they are there?

Main: Read *Everybody Has a Body* start to finish then discuss:
- What is this book about?
- How are bodies in the book different?
- Look at the page, 'some are wide, some are tall.' How do you know there is a tall character there?
- Look at the page, 'Some are weak, some are strong.' How do you know the character is strong?
- Look at the page, 'Some are soft, some are rough.' How are the smaller characters making sure the rough character does not feel like an outsider?
- Look at the page, 'Some are bendy, some are tough' what bendy shapes can we make?
- Look at the page with the rainbow, 'Bodies come in every hue – what does that mean? Why do you think the author chose to paint a rainbow?
- Look at the last page, 'We are all different in some way, being different is okay. Being different is nothing new, it makes us special and it makes you you.' What does this mean? Can you think of examples of how we are different in our class?

Activity:
- Photocopy the inside back page and give out to children. Children choose different characters to stick in and label differences.
- Or children draw their own different characters using different colours and shapes. Children could also draw themselves and label a way they are different.

Plenary:
- The author says on the back page of the book, 'Whether your body is big, small, wide or tall, it is something to celebrate and be proud of.'
- What does this mean? Why aren't we all the same?
- What would life be like if we were all the same? Why is this story about No Outsiders?

YEAR 2

'Grumpy Frog' (Vere, 2017)

In Year Two children know how they are different and are beginning to explore empathy and resilience. This story provides a great opportunity for children to think about responses to someone who does not yet understand about diversity; how do we talk to someone who thinks differently? Frog wants everything to be green: 'You are pink!' he cries, 'I want my friends to be green!' Frog gradually learns to compromise and accept animals who are different to him. The book also cleverly links to the RSE objective referencing courtesy and manners.

Text: _Grumpy Frog_ by Ed Vere Lesson Plan by Andrew Moffat (www.no-outsiders.com)
Learning Intention: To explore the meaning of compromise Success criteria: I know what compromise means / I know how to reach a compromise/   I can accept things I may not like

RSE Objectives:
   •   the importance of respecting others, even when they are very different from them (for example, physically, in character, personality or backgrounds), or make different choices or have different preferences or beliefs
   •   the conventions of courtesy and manners

Starter:
   •   Ask if children know what compromise means.
   •   Give the children an example of a compromise: say today you really wanted tuna wrap for lunch. You had been looking forward to it all morning and when lunch time came you were so excited. But when you got to the hall, there were no tuna wraps left! Oh no! Ask the children, how do you think I felt? I was so mad! I wanted to shout and stamp my feet and demand someone to make me a tuna wrap.
   •   What do you think I did? What do you think happened? I had to compromise – what does that mean?

Main : Read _Grumpy Frog_ and talk about the story ' how is it about compromise?
   •   why do you think Frog wants everything to be green?
   •   what happens if Frog doesn't get what he wants? How does this affect the other frogs and how do they respond?
   •   why do you think no one will hop with him?
   •   'You are pink! I want my friends to be green!' How is Frog behaving?
   •   why does Frog say sorry and what is the response from the other frogs?
   •   who makes a compromise at the end of the story? What has Frog learned? How do you think this will affect his life in future?

Role play/activity:
- Ask children to role play and answer these questions to help Frog stop feeling sorry for himself, before recording their answers:
- Why isn't everything green?
- Why do I eat flies?
- Why isn't it my birthday today?
- Why won't anyone hop with me? Or:
- Children watch this clip of author Ed Vere drawing Frog and follow the directions to create their own version.

Plenary:
- Ed Vere is the author, he says this book is about 'compromise, friendship and saying sorry.' What else do you think this book is about?
- What can we learn from Frog? Why is this about No Outsiders?

YEAR 4

The Boys (Ace & Lovlie, 2021) is a companion piece to *The Girls* by the same authors and written two years previously. *The Girls* appears in the No Outsiders scheme and is a wonderful exploration of friendship. *The Boys* could not have come at a better time; at a time when toxic masculinity is at the forefront of mental health campaigns for men, we need books that show male friendship as something to be cherished and nurtured. RSE objectives about friendships are covered.

Text: *The Boys* by Lauren Ace and Jenny Lovlie
Lesson plan by Andrew Moffat (www.no-outsiders.com)

Enquiry question: Am I an island?

RSE objective:
- How important friendships are in making us feel happy and secure, and how people choose and make friends.
- The characteristics of friendships, including mutual respect, truthfulness, trustworthiness, loyalty, kindness, generosity, trust, sharing interests and experiences and support with problems and difficulties.
- That most friendships have ups and downs, and that these can often be worked through so that the friendship is repaired or even strengthened, and that resorting to violence is never right.

Starter:
- How would you define friendship? Is friendship easy?
- How do friendships change over time? Do you think friendships are different for boys and for girls? Why? (Why not?)
- Look at the enquiry question; what do you think it means? What are the characteristics of an island? How can a person be an island?

Main: Read *The Boys* start to finish and then discuss:
- The boys are very different from a young age; how are they different? (personalities / skin colour)
- 'Although they had different interests, the boys were a team. When they worked together it made all of them better.' How does this work? Can you think of any examples (boys or girls) in our class?
- How do we see the boys building their friendship?
- 'One spring the sands had shifted. The winter tides and storms had revealed hidden rocks and everything was different.' What has happened at this stage of the book? Is this paragraph just about the beach?
- Why do you think the boys started competing with each other?
- 'It felt good to be different and think about only what made them happy.' What do you think about this line? In our school we often talk about being different and we accept ways we are different, but what has happened here? What are the boys failing to do? (show interest in each other, support one another, check in.)
- 'Their successes, which had once been shared, now felt empty... the boys knew they had to be able to talk about their feelings... but it wasn't easy.' Why not? What's happened? Is success only success if it is recognized by others?
- 'They came to realise that no boy is an island and the bravest way to face problems is to talk and listen.' What does this mean? How does a person become an island?
- What do the boys do to start making their friendships strong again? (learn to be patient and kind with one another)
- 'When one of them was weighed down by sadness, the others would always be there to lift him up.' How? What sort of things might they say to each other?

Activity:
- The book compares the boys to an island. How do the boys stop being an island?
- Children draw four circles at the top of their page to represent islands and draw a boy on each. Give the boys names and write hobbies that make each one different (use the page in the book as an example where we see Tam skateboarding, Nattie rock-climbing, Rev playing music, Bobby reading).
- How do the boys on your page stop being an island?
- Below each island write questions or comments the boys could make about the other hobbies (for example, Tam could ask Nattie to show him some skateboarding tricks, Rev could ask Bobby what book he's reading. The aim is to teach children here how to show an interest in other people)
- Next consider what to do if one of your boys feels sad. Draw them on their island feeling sad but give them a speech bubble to ask for help – how do you ask for help if you feel sad? If the other boys notice him feeling sad and he doesn't say anything, what could they say? (Are you okay? You look sad, mate, everything alright?) Draw your other three boys around the sad boy on his island showing support and give them speech bubbles for supportive comments.
- Finally draw the four boys at the bottom of the page together, no longer an island.

Plenary:
- The authors of this book wrote another story that was published two years previously called *The Girls*.
- Why do you think the authors chose to do two separate books for boys and girls? What do you think their aim was in writing this second book?
- Do you think that aim has been achieved? What can we learn from this book?

YEAR 6

How do we talk about Brexit without actually talking about Brexit? *The Little Island* (Prasadam-Hallis and Starling, 2019) is a perfect resource schools can use to explore attitudes to recent news events. The aim is for our children to grow into confident adults able to put across their point of view and engage in the democratic process and this book provides a valuable stimulus to promote oracy skills. I read this book to a group of PGCE students during No Outsiders training the morning after the Brexit referendum and the response was phenomenal. These books make you want to be a teacher!

The Little Island – Smriti Prasadam-Hallis and Robert Starling
Lesson Plan by Andrew Moffat (www.no-outsiders.com)

Learning Intention: To be competent in the art of speaking and listening and participate in debate

Starter:
- What is an island?
- What countries today are islands?
- Look at the cover; what do you think the story may be about?
- There is a leaflet on the floor, 'Better together'. What's that about, do you think?

Main:
- Read *The Little Island* up to the page where the foxes attack ('Save us!') Discuss the following questions:
- The first page says, 'They worked hard and each was at liberty to live and work where they chose... it wasn't perfect and they didn't always agree, but they liked it.' What does this mean? Is this how society works today? Give examples.
- How does the unrest begin? Why do you think the geese are grumbling? Who are they blaming for the way things are? (other animals)
- Why don't the other animals stop this happening?
- When things go wrong, why do the geese keep saying, 'At least we are happy!' The foxes have come! What do you think will happen next? Predict the end of the story.

Role play:
- Once the footbridge is gone it is difficult to change the situation. If someone had presented an alternative view, do you think the geese would have changed their minds? Look at the arguments put forward in the meeting; write them up on the board:
- 'Our island was once a green and pleasant land, the apples were much redder, the grass was much greener, the sun was much warmer, the food tasted better. Now it's too busy. We should leave the rest of the farm and live on our own just as we please.'
- Ask children to consider these arguments and respond. The aim is not to agree or disagree, the aim is to consider how to effectively engage in a debate; how to listen to an argument and respond. You could set up ground rules before the debate, appoint a chair, put up hands etc. We never hear a response from the ducks; what do you think the ducks might have said?

> **Activity**: Choose one of the arguments listed above and record a transcript of two sides of the class debate demonstrating alternate views.

> **Plenary**:
> - Why is the bridge re-built at the end of the story? There is a sign placed on the island side of the bridge – what does it say, why?
> - What did the geese learn in the story?
> - Consider the meeting and the events that followed; there is no right or wrong answer to the question of the bridge but how can the animals make sure all voices are heard?
> - What can we learn from this story?
> - Why is this story about No Outsiders?

KEY TAKEAWAYS

- There are a wealth of practical resources to use in the classroom to demonstrate the concept of No Outsiders.
- A No Outsiders approach supports RSE guidelines.
- Find accessible (and enjoyable) ways to teach for citizenship in the primary classroom.

KEY QUESTIONS

- How well is our Personal Development planning embedded across the school?
- How confident are teachers in talking about the topics outlined in RSE and how can picture books help?
- How do we link this work to the Ofsted requirement to teach British values?

COMMITMENT TO THE MANIFESTO

Citizenship education should start early – and No Outsiders is a strong ethos for early years education.

REFERENCES

Ace, L. and Lovlie, J. (2021). *The Boys*, Caterpillar books.

Burgerman, J. (2020). *Everybody has a Body*, Oxford: OUP.

Moffat, A. (2020). *No Outsiders: Everyone Different, Everyone Welcome: Preparing Children for Life in Modern Britain*. Abingdon-on-Thames: Routledge

Prasadam-Hallis, S. and Starling, R. (2019). The *Little Island*. London: Andersen Press

Vere, E. (2017). *The Grumpy Frog*. London: Puffin.

WHY SCHOOLS NEED FUNDING FOR LGBT+ WORK NOW MORE THAN EVER

DANIEL TOMLINSON-GRAY

The UK's LGBT+ community is caught in a 'culture war', with huge Government cuts to funding for school-based diversity projects and different minorities pitted against each other by the British mainstream media. But there is still hope in our schools.

The Minister for Women and Equalities, Liz Truss, has suggested we should pivot from fashionable' race, sexuality and gender issues to focus on poverty (Bulman, 2020). This is part of a worrying trend, reflected in the press, where genuine issues and fears of minority groups are dismissed as part of a culture war. Perhaps through a misguided fear that more equality for us means less for them – like pie – our ruling party is scrambling to protect a straight, white status quo. The fact that genuine movements like Black Lives Matter and issues around trans rights are dismissed as 'fashionable' show just how out of touch our Government currently is.

In July 2018, the UK's Conservative government launched its LGBT Action Plan, where it claimed it was 'committed to making the UK a country that works for everyone.' The administration wanted to 'strip away the barriers that hold people back so that everyone can go as far as their hard work and talent can take them.' I was there at the launch of the Action Plan, in the garden of 10 Downing Street. For a moment, during Theresa May's speech, I heard glimpses of a policy that showed LGBT+ people matter.

Fast-forward to three years later and that 'commitment' has all but disappeared. Language directed at trans people in the press has frightening echoes of that used against gay people during the AIDS crisis. Known anti-trans groups like the LGB Alliance are uncritically offered a platform by the BBC, and are now a registered charity. Furthermore, the government's LGBT+ Advisory panel has been quietly disbanded, gay conversion therapy is still legal at the time of writing and we have a Prime Minister who once referred to gay men as 'tank-topped bum boys' (Smith, 2019).

Funding for LGBT+ bullying projects has been axed and funding for Equality and Diversity projects in schools has been cut on a significant scale. Whilst battling Covid-19, schools are now also battling culture wars in the classroom. It is a war on two fronts for exhausted teachers at the end of their tether. To counter this worrying trend, it is time to support LGBT+ teachers to be visible in schools and show there is hope for our young LGBT+ people. I co-founded LGBTed – a national network of more than 5,000 LGBT+ teachers and leaders – with business psychologist Hannah Jepson in 2018 because I believe that visible, authentic role models in schools are important.

Growing up during the time of Section 28, I was told by my school that they could not help me when I was bullied for being gay. They weren't allowed to 'promote' homosexuality in any way – which is ridiculous when you think about it. This is like suggesting we can be turned gay simply by being exposed to gay people, like being persuaded to like avocado for the first time. This is nonsense, obviously. My parents were straight, my teachers were straight, my friends were straight, and there were straight people all over my TV – but, in the words of Freddie Mercury – I was still 'gay as a daffodil, my dear.'

Later, when I was, myself, training to be a teacher, I was told never to come out to my students under any circumstances because it would 'give them more ammunition'. What kind of advice is this? This does our young people a deep disservice and they deserve better. In fact, wherever I have worked as a teacher and a school leader, the young people have been the most open-minded, accepting and welcoming of all. Only where they have been taught to hate by those they look to for guidance is this not the case. But our curriculum is still mostly teaching dead, straight, white men and very little progress has been made.

In the new LGBTed book, *Big Gay Adventures in Education*, the contributors are all 'out' teachers, or students of 'out' teachers writing about how much it benefits our LGBT+ young people when they know that some people around them are LGBT+ and are OK with it. As the saying goes, 'You can't be what you can't see.' How can you be expected, as a young LGBT+ person, to grow up to be successful, to feel valued and respected if you never see yourself represented?

At LGBTed, we relied on the Equality & Diversity funding from the Department for Education. Eight regional hub lead schools were allocated funding for school-led projects throughout their area with hubs receiving up to £250,000 to allocate over two years. We used a small share of this funding to run two successful cohorts of our Proud Leadership programme. We were determined to increase the number of LGBT+ school leaders and 75% of our participants achieved a promotion as a result of the empowerment, knowledge and skills the programme offered. This funding was quietly pulled in December 2020 with no communication and no warning. With it no longer available, we risk losing the momentum behind us and undoing the work we have done.

Since co-founding the organisation, I have been contacted by so many teachers who have felt inspired and empowered by what we do: trainee teachers have been 'out' from the outset; senior leaders have redesigned their curricula to make them more representative of the children they teach; young people have started seeing themselves represented and are beginning to feel safer. This, therefore, increased the number of visible and authentic LGBT+ leaders in schools for the benefit of the children who needed them most.

Some are arguing that, during a time of national crisis like the coronavirus pandemic, money might be better spent elsewhere – such as alleviating poverty. However, this does not take into account the fact that, for so many, discrimination *is* the main cause of poverty. Individual subjective experiences really matter when there is so little data available. So, listen to your LGBT+ colleagues, learn from them and respect them when they talk about what really matters to them.

Finally, according to Stonewall (2017), 53% of LGBT+ students said there was not an adult at their school they felt they could talk to, while 45% of young trans people had attempted to take their own life. And half of them succeeded.

These horrifying figures show that now is not the time for diversity funding to be ditched. We should not have to choose which of the most vulnerable sections of our society are worth fighting for. We cannot continue to claim that some identities are more or less valid than others. However, suggesting that fighting for equality and diversity is 'fashionable' sounds like this is exactly the way things are heading. We have to fight back in our schools and there are many ways we could do this:

- Funding modules in LGBT+ inclusion through Initial Teacher Training, ensuring that all teachers entering the profession are aware of the importance of LGBT+ inclusion and that all LGBT+ teachers feel supported from day one.
- Teaming up with other multi-academy trusts or teaching school hubs to fund work with external providers who can ensure a diverse range of voices are heard; that the work is consistently effective and that it is impactful long term.
- Actively exploring CPD opportunities for your staff that empowers them to be their authentic selves at work, funding it yourselves where it does not exist and seeing the value in this.
- Actively seeking LGBT+ staff as part of your recruitment process in order to create a genuinely diverse workforce. Don't say on your website that you value diversity if you do not.

According to the Treasury's own figures, just under 6% of the population are gay, and this includes our young people. Let us be the role models they need.

KEY TAKEAWAYS

- The government has cut all funding for Equality & Diversity projects in schools that organisations such as LGBTed relied on, so very little research is being undertaken and no official statistics exist – nor are they likely to. This means that individual subjective experiences matter more than ever. So, do your research in your setting, listen and learn about what is important to LGBT+ staff.
- We are not looking for tokenism and we are not looking to set one minority against another in any kind of culture war. We are looking for respect, support, safety and community. Create an environment in your setting where staff are comfortable to be 'out' and know they are supported by the leadership team. This should start from the top with 'out' leaders usualising representation of LGBT+ people.

- Take CPD opportunities for your LGBT+ staff seriously. Teachers value diversity in the workforce and we value being valued, whether through time commitments or financial ones.

KEY QUESTIONS

- Have you created a culture where your school, college or university empowers LGBT+ colleagues to apply for CPD related to LGBT+ inclusion? How do you know this?
- To what extent does your school, university or multi-academy trust consider CPD in the area of LGBT+ inclusion to be valuable in terms of time and money? How can you improve this?
- In what ways can your school, university or multi-academy trust help to fund work that empowers your LGBT+ staff and improves the culture for LGBT+ staff and young people in your setting?

COMMITMENT TO THE MANIFESTO

At LGBTed we commit to empowering LGBT+ teachers to be their authentic selves as visible LGBT+ role models in schools, in order to improve the school experiences of the LGBT+ young people who need us most. Let us be the role models we needed when we were at school.

REFERENCES

Bulman, M. (2020), 'Backlash as ministers vow to ditch focus on 'fashionable' fight against inequality.' *The Independent*, 17 December 2020. Available at:

https://www.independent.co.uk/news/uk/home-news/equalities-race-gender-fashionable-liz-truss-b1775517.html (accessed 21 June 2021)

Public Health England (2017), *Producing modelled estimates of the size of the lesbian, gay and bisexual (LGB) population of England*. London: Public Health England, https://assets.publishing.service.gov.uk/government/uploads/system/uploads/attachment_data/file/585349/PHE_Final_report_FINAL_DRAFT_14.12.2016NB230117v2.pdf (accessed 21 June 2021)

Smith, R. (2019), 'A comprehensive guide to Boris Johnson's infamous use of 'tank-topped bum boys' and why it's dominated this election.' *Pink News*, 13 December 2019 https://www.pinknews.co.uk/2019/12/12/boris-johnson-tank-top-bum-boys-homophobic-peter-mandleson-history/ (accessed 21 June 2021)

Stonewall (2017), *School Report: The experiences of lesbian, gay, bi and trans young people in Britain's schools in 2017*, London: Stonewall. https://www.stonewall.org.uk/system/files/the_school_report_2017.pdf (accessed 21 June 2021)

SCHOOLS SUPPORTING SOME DIVERSE CHILDREN OR ALL DIVERSE CHILDREN?

SHAUN DELLENTY

In May 1988 Margaret Thatcher implemented Section (or Clause) 28, denying vital education for LGBT+ individuals about a deadly new virus. Long repealed, the shadow of Section 28 persists, and its cost will never be known. Subsequently compassionate groups and individuals have nurtured many LGBT+ inclusive schools.

In 2016 I wrote *Celebrating Difference: A Whole-School Approach to LGBT+ Inclusion*, a book to support inclusive schools. As publication loomed, I requested an additional edit, as I sensed the political landscape was shifting against LGBT+ inclusive education.

LGBT+ stakeholders exist in our schools; this is a fact. This chapter explores how school leaders and teachers need courage to support *all* school stakeholders, *without* exception.

Surely that is our job?

PAST DAYS

When educators **choose** to enter the profession, is it to represent, educate and keep safe *all* school stakeholders? Or is it to represent, educate and keep safe merely *some* school stakeholders?

When advocating for LGBT+ inclusive schools I still meet some resistant educators, despite LGBT+ children, young people, staff, parents, and carers being represented in learning communities around the planet. Many educators (including myself) received no initial training on LGBT+ inclusion. This historical lack of relevant training, combined with the bias and prejudices of some educators and indeed governments can result in sporadic or even non-existent journeys towards LGBT+ inclusive schools.

My own LGBT+ journey spans school days struggling as a homophobically bullied child in an education system unwilling to affirm my authentic existence (due to Section 28) through school leadership to a global advocacy role nurturing inclusive learning communities and businesses. Societal progress thankfully happened in my lifetime, the equal age of consent and equal marriage. LGBT+ History Month/Pride Month are now marked in many UK schools, and in England the introduction of LGBT+ inclusive relationships and sex education, although this has not been without significant challenge. For a brief time, schools even benefited from UK government-funded anti-LGBT+ bullying campaigns, until funding was withdrawn, although still very much needed.

It was homophobic bullying in my (then) London primary school in 2009 that resulted in me formulating teacher training to prevent bullying and prejudice directed at those identifying as LGBT+, those with LGBT+ siblings and friends and those targeted for simply being 'different' which of course we **all** are. A direct response to a specific issue with *homophobic* bullying, my intersectional training intended to nurture schools safe for *everyone,* whilst exploring *everyone's* potential for prejudice, including staff. Specific problems require specific actions.

Children are beautifully unique, yet these natural differences render them *all* potential targets for bullying and discrimination. Educators have a *duty of care* to prevent bullying, exclusion and suffering to secure positive mental health, academic and life outcomes for *all*, not just *some* school stakeholders. Communicating this core duty to *all* stakeholders is vital.

When piloting my LGBT+ inclusion training in 2009, we encountered opposition from a *small* minority of parents interpreting it as an 'agenda' to 'confuse' or somehow magically 'turn' children into LGBT+, simply by opening dialogue intended to prevent bullying. Thus, time was spent clarifying with **all** stakeholders what our rationale and motives were and most importantly, what they were **not.** Black History Month had *initially* triggered similar complaints, with parental perceptions being voiced that a) we were placing a hierarchy on identity and b) raising the spotlight of awareness of societal contributions of people of colour and thus reducing awareness of white people. Some stakeholders regarded the 'protected characteristics' of the Equality Act 2010 as 'tick-box political correctness' triggering a school-wide teaching moment as to the origins of the protected characteristics stemming as they do from bias, inequality, discrimination and often hate.

In exploring communities historically stymied by oppression, schools often approach protected characteristics in silos, aspiring to raise a particular characteristic onto a more equal footing. This can trigger anxiety within *some* stakeholders that their rights, identities, beliefs and cultures are being diminished or attacked, which is **not** the intended outcome.

Effective leadership teams invest time in exploring with all stakeholders the intersections between LGBT+ identities and other protected characteristics. Rich downloadable research exists to support schools in meeting challenges to LGBT+ and racial inclusion that *might* arise: Stonewall, Just Like Us, Show Racism The Red Card, LGBTed and the Centre for LGBTQ Inclusion In Education at Leeds Beckett University all produce research exploring how exclusion and prejudice hinders mental health, academic outcomes and life-chances. Teacher unions produce relevant research and resources to be explored and deployed.

In a 'post-truth' world, as schools draw upon external research to support the case for LGBT+ inclusion and diverse schools more broadly (despite what politicians might say) this should be enriched with the lived experiences and voices of our diverse stakeholders. Communicating the benefits of inclusive school cultures, whilst positioning safety, authenticity, compassion, dignity and respect as robust core principles, is as vital as communicating the benefits that equitable inclusion has for *everyone* within a school community, *to everyone* within (and without) our school communities. Please do it with pride.

PRESENT DAYS

As Daniel has described in his chapter, England has seen recent increasing political pushbacks against LGBT+ inclusion, so called 'culture wars', protests against LGBT+ inclusive sex and relationships and toxic campaigns directed at trans people and those who support them. Divisive rhetoric abounds and genuine concerns about bias and discrimination are often dismissed by certain media outlets and some politicians as 'fashionable' and 'woke.' Schools are caught between polarised opinions on support for trans children, whilst in some global territories such as Australia, Hungary, Poland and America there has been a highly strategic reversal of progress.

With the additional impact of COVID-19, it can be *highly* challenging for schools to keep momentum around LGBT+ inclusion. Where schools return time and time again to the *individual* needs of our diverse young people, whilst spotlighting the benefits to all of compassionate, intersectional inclusion, they afford a source of motivation, inspiration, resolve and hope.

Progress is rarely linear and we can all be drawn into negative narratives. There has been very successful work on LGBT+ inclusion in many UK faith and secular schools now for over a decade at the very least and we all need to be better at shouting it and sharing the good it has done for our amazing young people. Colleagues sometimes still inform me they don't know 'where to start' or are unable to source relevant resources or best practice models, yet there are *numerous* relevant organisations, books and research publications online and many schools for whom LGBT+ inclusion is fully embedded within everyday school life. We not only have a duty to be proactive in seeking out good practice as a starting point (Google helps) it is also *vital* to share, disseminate and celebrate our own work in order to foster positive and constructive narratives and develop resilience to changing politics and societal values.

COVID-19 lockdowns resulted in many LGBT+ youths feeling isolated and vulnerable – research by ChildLine and the UK-based charity Just Like Us found that LGBT+ young people were twice as likely as their non-LGBT peers to have felt lonely and separated from those they are closest to on a daily basis during lockdown. As schools (hopefully) move beyond COVID-19, the need for affirming cultures becomes ever more pronounced, as does the need to listen with compassion to diverse youth in order to minimise the impact of future adverse events.

Despite challenges, working in LGBT+ inclusion affords the hopeful knowledge that generations of young people continue to be taught in schools that meet and value stakeholders as their *authentic* selves whilst teaching about LGBT+ identities, histories and experiences in all (not just some) aspects of school life.

These schools really *listen to* their diverse young people and value the many, not just the few.

FUTURE DAYS

How prepared are you as an individual and/or as a school to meet potential challenges, whether they arise from parents, politicians, faith groups or the media?

Policies around diversity, inclusion and behaviour (informed by stakeholder voice) must be *lived and modelled* every day in *all* aspects of school life. Government executives cannot always be relied upon for support when challenges arise, therefore schools must be clear on the moral rationale for LGBT+ inclusive learning communities and able to robustly defend them, grounding their defence in the voices, lived experience and diverse needs of those living and learning within our schools.

The UK Equality Act (2010) currently affords statutory protections for LGBT stakeholders, yet legislation can be swiftly amended or withdrawn. Were this to happen, where would you and your school stand? Would it signal a retreat to the deadly days of Section 28 or would you and your school have the courage to stand up for your inclusive ethos and *everyone* within it?

Courageous leadership requires us all to robustly steer a course towards emotionally intelligent, agile organisations that can represent and educate *all* stakeholders, meeting them *as they authentically are*, being fully present and working with complex human individuality.

Behind the 'LGBT+' and other 'diversity acronyms' and 'labels' such as 'disability' 'gender identity' 'neurodiversity' and 'person of colour' there is always a joyfully unique and complex human individual.

I fully believe this is where schools should choose to place our compassionate awareness.

Educators can choose to validate, celebrate, educate and keep safe *some* school stakeholders, or *all school* stakeholders.

What will **you** choose and how courageous could you be on their behalf?

KEY TAKEAWAYS

- Whole school approaches to LGBT+ inclusion should explore with all stakeholders the intersections between protected characteristics of the Equality Act 2010 whilst also exploring the intersections between LGBT+ and non-LGBT+ identities and experiences.
- School leadership teams must establish a moral rationale for LGBT+ inclusion in addition to educating all stakeholders as to the statutory rationale and communicate it upfront and on an ongoing basis.
- Legislation can change, schools must be courageous in riding out changes

in societal attitudes to minority groups via culture, ethos and policies. Meet everyone in the school community as they are, with compassionate listening and amplify lived experience to develop empathy across schoolwide culture. Use of up-to-date bullying and attitudinal data is vital. Knowing with precision how biases and prejudice exist within schools (and sadly they do) grounds your aims in lived experience and affords you a robust moral argument for your ongoing diversity and inclusion work.

KEY QUESTIONS

- How do you draw upon trade union training, resources and support for LGBT+ inclusion?
- Have you audited current provision in terms of LGBT+ inclusion at whole-school, resource and curriculum level? What did you find and how does this inform your strategic forward planning?
- How do you gather voices and lived experiences of the diverse range of stakeholders in your school? How are these then communicated to other stakeholders and how do they shape your provision?

COMMITMENT TO THE MANIFESTO

Learning communities without exception, must pledge to support and represent all their diverse stakeholders, including those currently falling within the 'protected characteristics' of the Equality Act 2010. They must pledge to continue to do so, should the Equality Act 2010 be in part or fully repealed. Schools must stand for their diverse stakeholders not because of political direction, but because it is the *compassionate and humane* approach, respecting human rights and the right to an education safe free from bullying and discrimination.

REFERENCES

Dellenty, S.. (2019) *Celebrating Difference: A Whole-School Approach to LGBT+ Inclusion*, Bloomsbury Publishing

Just Like Us, *LGBT+ Pupils eligible for Free Schools Meals Struggle More with Mental Health*, available at: https://www.justlikeus.org/single-post/lgbt-pupils-eligible-for-free-school-meals-three-times-more-likely-to-have-drug-or-alcohol-issues [accessed May 2021]

THE REMARKABLE POWER OF POSITIVE LGBTQ+ REPRESENTATION IN SCHOOLS

CARLY HIND

Across the last three decades, the British school system has endured the introduction and revocation of Section 28 and the fallout from this. This legislation was repealed in Scotland in 2000, and in England by 2003; in spite of this there are still huge inconsistencies within British schools and their approach to LGBTQ+ inclusion. There is still much to do to unravel the lasting impact of Section 28. In this chapter you will learn about the power of positive representation in schools and find suggested approaches to LGBTQ+ inclusion within an education setting. It is intended as a starting point to encourage reflective practice and approaches to implementing meaningful change.

* * * *

I started primary school in 1989 and left secondary school at the age of eighteen in 2003. This meant the entirety of my schooling spanned the enforcement of Section 28 in which gay relationships were referred to as 'pretended family relationships'. Clause 28, now more commonly known as Section 28, was debated in parliament in 1988 and became British law that same year (HM Government, 1988). This law meant that the 'promotion of homosexuality' by local authorities was forbidden and therefore schools felt unable to support their LGBTQ+ young people in any capacity. Looking back, I do not think I was particularly conscious that I was being personally affected by this at the time. There was absolutely no visibility of LGBTQ+ people in my schools, or in the world around me. I knew that I was drawn to women, but I could not call it what it was, because I simply did not have the language for it. It is no coincidence then that I came out at nineteen after moving to Manchester for university; suddenly I had access to a whole community of people that shared a significant part of my identity that had never been celebrated. It was not until I became a teacher and once again began to immerse myself in school life that I became acutely aware of what I had never had, the missed opportunities to see other LGBTQ+ people positively represented in a way that was not intensely surrounded by shame.

The good work taking place for LGBTQ+ in education settings is plentiful and should be celebrated, but it is most certainly inconsistent. The experiences of students will vary greatly depending on the school/ provision they attend. The fact remains that 40% of LGBTQ+ people, like me, have gone through the British education system with no teaching about matters that directly affect them (Stonewall, 2017). That means no visible positive representation in schools and little to no information about where LGBTQ+ students can access relevant information, support and guidance. In short, the message those pupils receive is that they are not worth acknowledging. This statistic makes it very clear there is still a significant way to go to ensure there is true and meaningful inclusivity within our education system.

Furthermore, it is often the case that in many schools the responsibility of establishing and running LGBTQ+ student groups, the sourcing of information and other general school-based work on relevant topics falls on the shoulders of staff who identify as LGBTQ+. Lived experience is so incredibly valuable and it is wonderful when members of staff are willing to share these experiences with students to help them safely explore their own identities. But what about schools that do not have staff members with this same confidence? What about schools that do not have supportive leadership to drive the delivery of an LGBTQ+ inclusive curriculum? Finally, and the biggest question of all, what about those students who find themselves in schools that are doing little to nothing to support those who identify as LGBTQ+? We are still missing valuable opportunities to educate and promote positivity around identity to LGBTQ+ students and the importance of allyship to non-LGBTQ+ students.

For many schools and individuals, there is vital learning that needs to take place in order to better serve LGBTQ+ people in education. If there are opportunities to visit or connect with schools that do this well then this can be particularly worthwhile. Where such connections are not possible or readily available, then you might start by considering the following:

LISTEN TO YOUR YOUNG PEOPLE

There is so much to be said for the phrase 'nothing about us without us'; students can offer a unique perspective on the experiences they have had and experiences they wish to have. It cannot be underestimated how important it is that students feel they have a voice when it comes to the ways in which LGBTQ+ people are represented within their school environment. You can approach this as something like a consultation process. Schools offer so much more than just academic studies and so different aspects of school life should be reviewed, in a transparent process, with the goal of developing a shared vision with pupils. Make clear the intentions of the process from the outset and what pupils can expect from the outcomes. A process that lacks this transparency runs the risk of not being taken seriously by pupils. Surveys can gather meaningful data but may not always be a true reflection of your full cohort. Ask your students how they would like to share their views, whether that be via tutor/ focus groups, online forums or utilising a more anonymous process such as an organised voting system.

THE IMPORTANCE OF THE WHOLE SCHOOL COMMUNITY

To truly create effective change in the school community, all stakeholders should have some awareness of what is taking place. This helps to project shared values and consistency for students. The governing body of a school has a duty to promote well-being in collaboration with the headteacher who can ensure that positive changes are filtered down through the school. For example, a school could make the decision to review its current standard of LGBTQ+ representation within the curriculum. A starting point might be to ask subject leaders to conduct a curriculum audit and disseminate findings to their respective departments with recommendations for improvements. The curriculum is such a valuable opportunity in terms of positive visibility and aspirations for your LGBTQ+ people. Allowing them to explore the work of successful LGBTQ+ people in a variety of subjects will allow pupils to see themselves in similar roles; it will empower them to feel that opportunities are available to them and not restricted as a result of their sexuality.

Following on from the shared values of the whole school community, give consideration to which of your staff members are particularly visible to students. The obvious example might be classroom teachers who inevitably have the most contact time with students, but there is also a lot to be said for involving staff in supporting roles. You could be creative with food menus and work with the dining room staff, rainbow accessories for all staff (lanyards for example) can demonstrate solidarity and acceptance, subject leaders can review curriculum inclusivity, pastoral staff can develop an inclusive tutor programme, PSHE/ RSE staff can deliver relevant information regarding sex and relationships, all staff can be involved in assemblies/ key events/ LGBTQ+ student groups. The involvement of a broad range of staff will truly help to embed a whole school ethos.

EFFECTIVE AND INTERACTIVE DISPLAYS

It can be very easy to fall into the trap of putting up some LGBTQ+ posters in order to feel like you are representing those young people and staff. The reality is that often this can be a tokenistic gesture, particularly if this is all you do. Displays can be a valuable resource if done well but they should be celebratory, informative and positively affirming. You might signpost useful, up-to-date and relevant information, spotlight current figures from the LGBTQ+ community who are doing great things, or direct students to where they can find positive LGBTQ+ representation in literature and the media.

KEY TAKEAWAYS

- It is vital that LGBTQ+ students and staff feel accurately and positively represented within their community and that their voices are regularly and meaningfully heard.
- Tokenistic gestures can create barriers, even if they are well-meaning.
- Changing the culture within a school community is most powerful and long lasting when there is a whole school approach.

KEY QUESTIONS

- How do you consider student voice in decision making and processes to ensure your LGBTQ+ students feel positively represented?
- Are the stakeholders in your school community effectively trained in LGBTQ+ inclusion and are they equipped with knowledge of inclusive language?
- Where are the opportunities within your setting to improve positive LGBTQ+ representation across the whole school?

COMMITMENT TO THE MANIFESTO

Celebrate your LGBT+ teachers and ensure they are visible, supported and involved in decision making.

REFERENCES

HM Government (1988), *Local Government Act 1988*. Available at http://www.legislation.gov.uk/ukpga/1988/9/section/28 (accessed 21 June 2021).

Stonewall (2017), *School Report: The experiences of lesbian, gay, bi and trans young people in Britain's schools in 2017*. London: Stonewall.

This study involved over 3,700 LGBTQ+ young people across Britain. Available at: https://www.stonewall.org.uk/system/files/the_school_report_2017.pdf (accessed 7 April 2021)

THE POWER OF PERSONAL STORIES

JAC BASTIAN

Stories give us an insight into other people's lives and encourage us to build empathy, which is a key driver in changing attitudes and behaviours. Through sharing LGBT+ stories in the classroom we can build empathy, challenge stereotypes and get students to consider the (often unintended) impact of homophobic, biphobic and transphobic language and bullying. Stories can also provide the much-needed intersectional representation of LGBT+ identities which has been missing from schools for so long. This can transform the culture of a school into a space where our differences are discussed, celebrated and embraced. In this chapter we will explore the power of storytelling, its role in building empathy in the classroom and how it can be utilised by educators to transform our school cultures.

STORYTELLING FOR EMPATHY AND CHANGE

Storytelling is a vital pedagogical tool that has been used to create shared values, understand differences and shape our approaches to moral and ethical issues throughout history. It has gained prominence in campaigning, communications and advertising, as well as in educational institutions as a means of changing our attitudes and spurring us to action. Studies have shown the links between storytelling and increased cooperative behaviour amongst listeners through the release of oxytocin, a chemical key to developing empathy (Zak, 2014). Campaigners have long utilised the power of storytelling to win support for their causes. In the Irish abortion referendum, 77% of surveyed voters claimed their voting intention was motivated by a personal story they had heard in the media or from someone they knew (McShane, 2018). Research has also shown good stories stick with us. We are up to twenty-two times more likely to remember a story than a plain fact (Bruner, 1986).

The sharing of stories from marginalised communities, described by Solórzano and Yosso (2002) as counter-stories, has a long and rich history in challenging dominant narratives that underpin racial hierarchies and other forms of oppression. They aim to bring personal experiences to the forefront and humanise and contextualise the impact of prejudice and discrimination on individuals and wider communities. According to Delgado (1989) stories 'emphasize our differences in ways that can ultimately bring us closer together', eliciting empathy rather than defensiveness in the listener.

Educators have long harnessed the power of storytelling to change attitudes and create more inclusive school environments. Studies in the 1960s demonstrated that the use of positive black role models in children's literature was effective at challenging racist attitudes, stereotypes and assumptions amongst white children (Litcher and Johnson, 1969). This approach has been at the heart of Diversity Role Models (DRM) educational workshops, where members of the LGBT+ community and allies share personal stories to build empathy and create environments where our differences are discussed and celebrated.

THE SILENCING OF LGBT+ STORIES

The stories we hear in school often lack representation of marginalised voices (Weale and Bakare 2020). However, one example of a story that did feature LGBT+ identities was *Jenny Lives with Eric and Martin* (Bösche, 1983). The children's book found itself at the heart of a row over LGBT+ inclusion in Thatcher's Britain which saw the introduction of Section 28 in England and Wales, effectively banning the teaching of LGBT+ identities in schools. The legacy of this pernicious law was the silencing of LGBT+ stories and education in schools that we still battle today. The Pathways to LGBT+ Inclusion Report (Diversity Role Models, 2020) found only 20% of surveyed secondary school students said they learned about LGBT+ identities and homophobic, biphobic and transphobic (HBT) bullying at school while levels of HBT bullying and language remain worryingly high. We can and must do better and storytelling can help us fill the void left by the legacy of Section 28 and help build a curriculum that embeds an inclusive ethos for all.

HOW STORIES CAN CREATE CHANGE

Sharing counter-stories provides much needed representation and visibility for those who 'may have had the same thoughts and experiences the storyteller describes, but hesitated to give them voice' (Delgado, 1989). Personal stories are naturally intersectional. As Audre Lorde (1982) said, we don't live single issue lives'. For students who exist in the intersections of multiple marginalised identities, hearing from a person who they can relate to, and who challenges stereotypes about our communities, can be a powerful and affirming experience.

Counter-stories also benefit marginalised young people through their impact on those who are complicit, either as perpetrators or bystanders, in prejudice-based bullying. Whilst delivering a workshop in an East London school I sat at the back of the class as Alex, one of DRM's role models, shared his powerful story of how homophobic language and bullying at his Glasgow school had led to feelings of fear, shame and isolation he carried with him into his adult life. After hearing the story, students discussed the homophobic, biphobic and transphobic (HBT) language they heard and what they could do differently. As I walked around the room I heard one boy turn to his friend and say, 'Maybe, when we call James a faggot, that's not okay and we should stop'. Hearing a personal story about the impact of prejudice prompted reflection and built the empathy necessary to motivate a clear change in behaviour.

This impact is not just borne out in anecdotes I've been privileged enough to witness. When a researcher visited a primary school in Ealing to conduct focus groups with pupils who had experienced a DRM storytelling workshop the previous year, they found participants could recall not only the details of the stories they had heard but also the message of the stories and the wider workshop and how it changed their peers' attitudes and behaviours. In the 2018-19 academic year, 84% of secondary students who participated in DRM storytelling workshops said they would support a friend who came out as LGBT+ while 83% of Year 5 and 6 pupils said they felt confident to challenge HBT language in their school. When asked about the impact of the sessions, it is always the stories students value the most. As one student noted: 'I will never judge anyone because I've learnt that everyone has their own story.'

EMBEDDING STORIES IN OUR SCHOOLS

The workshops DRM run are an excellent way to centre LGBT+ storytelling in the classroom to encourage empathy, reflection, openness and changes in behaviour. However, every subject, every lesson and every example can provide an opportunity to centre LGBT+ identities, relationships and people. Here are some ideas for educators to bring stories to life and foster empathy through representation:

- **Literature**: Children's literature that challenges stereotypes and provides positive representation has been shown to challenge prejudice (Litcher and Johnson, 1969). The charity Seven Stories have a wonderful Reading with Pride booklist available.
- **Videos**: Videos containing clear narratives can effectively build empathy and encourage cooperative behaviours (Zak, 2014). Our free lesson plans and Role Model Stories video series feature personal stories as a simple way of bringing narrative to discussions on LGBT+ identities.
- **Sharing:** Encouraging young people and staff to share their own stories in a safe environment can allow us to celebrate different families and LGBT+ identities in a way that is relatable and empowering. As Gary Ratcliffe, Executive Head of the Galaxy Trust told DRM (2020): 'Where possible, the discussion is always brought back to the gay people we know – in our own families, in our own school and in the wider media too.'
- **Creative approaches:** Solórzano and Yosso (2002) describe the process of composite storytelling, in which stories based on experiences or data are created to bring narrative to conversations on prejudice. Young people could

create characters through creative writing, drama or art to bring to life the diversity of families or the prejudice that people face.

- **Usualising:** Our examples, our displays, our case studies, our class names, our assemblies can all help represent different stories that have been silenced in society. A student once told me her teacher used an example of a same-sex couple in a mathematics problem and from then on, she knew she had someone she could talk to at school. Representation and stories can become a part of our daily lives in school.

KEY TAKEAWAYS

- Stories stick with us, build empathy and drive changes in attitudes and behaviours.
- There is a lack of representation and education of LGBT+ identities in schools and worryingly high levels of HBT bullying and language.
- There are many ways we can use LGBT+ stories to prevent HBT bullying and language and provide the representation and visibility that can transform the culture of our schools.

KEY QUESTIONS

- How often do you represent LGBT+ identities, relationships and families in your teaching?
- How can you bring stories which build empathy, encourage reflection and challenge stereotypes into your lessons?
- Do your resources, examples and materials reflect the diversity of families and identities and challenge stereotypes or do they reinforce dominant narratives?

COMMITMENT TO THE MANIFESTO

Use storytelling as a tool to highlight the impact of prejudice and discrimination and drive changes in attitudes and behaviours.

REFERENCES

Bösche, S. (1983), *Jenny lives with Eric and Martin*. London: Gay Men's Press.

Bruner, J. (1986), *Actual minds, possible worlds*. London: Harvard University Press.

Delgado, R. (1989),' Storytelling for oppositionists and others: A plea for narrative.' *Michigan Law Review*, 87, (8), 2411-41.

Diversity Role Models (2020), *Pathways to LGBT+ inclusion: Homophobia, biphobia and transphobia in schools today*. Available at: https://www.diversityrolemodels.org/education-services/pathways-to-lgbtplus-inclusion-report (accessed 25 May 2021).

Litcher, J.H., and Johnson, D.W. (1969), 'Changes in attitudes toward negroes of white elementary school students after use of multiethnic readers.' *Journal of Educational Psychology*, 60, (2), 148–152.

Lorde, A. (1982), *Learning from the 60s*. Available at https://www.blackpast.org/african-american-history/1982-audre-lorde-learning-60s/ (accessed 25 May 2021).

McShane, I. (2018), *Thirty-sixth Amendment to the Constitution Exit Poll*. Available at https://www.rte.ie/documents/news/2018/05/rte-exit-poll-final-11pm.pdf (accessed 25 May 2021).

Solórzano, D.G. and Yosso T.J. (2002), 'Critical race methodology: Counter-storytelling as an analytical framework for education research.' *Qualitative inquiry*, 8, (1), 23-44.

Weale, S. and Bakare, L . (2020), 'Many GCSE pupils never study a book by a black author.'. *The Guardian*, 30 September, 2020.

Zak, P.J. (2014), 'Why your brain loves good storytelling.' *Harvard Business Review*, 28 October, 2014.

EDUCATORS NEED TO BECOME EFFECTIVE LGBT+ ROLE MODELS: DISRUPTING HETERONORMATIVITY AND DEVELOPING AUTHENTIC RELATIONSHIPS

LISA JORDAN

LGBT+ role models in education can provide a beacon of hope that helps to overcome isolation through a shared aspect of identity. As an LGBT+ educator, there exists an inner conflict governing the extent of personal authenticity in the workplace. An increasingly moral pressure to come out as an LGBT+ role model is juxtaposed against the fear of discrimination and internalised homophobia as a resultant and lingering hangover from education under Section 28. An LGBT+ educator's own educational experiences and differing access to LGBT+ culture impacts upon their understanding of and ability to articulate sexuality and lead as an effective LGBT+ role model.

LGBT+ EDUCATOR ROLE MODELS

A young person who can identify with a positive representation of themselves receives the message that being who they are, and thriving is possible and their potential for self-belief is unlocked. An LGBT+ role model helps to validate the sense of self and supports a young person to find the language to express their sexuality and identity. They also provide a real and relatable example of what it means to be LGBT+ for the wider community. Role models are an example of queerness experienced in the context of intersectionality, that helps to demystify LGBT+ identities and debunk a one-dimensional stereotype of what it means to be a minority sexuality.

LGBT+ role models provide a catalyst and resource for discourse and a window into LGBT+ culture. I have frequently been surprised how many colleagues speak to me about the sexualities of their own family members. They ask me questions that they are too worried to ask them directly, during a potentially vulnerable point in their relationship. Allies can develop a deeper understanding about LGBT+ communities from role models and can access first-hand accounts of lived experiences of biphobia and homophobia. A role model can help allies to understand and access queer culture, so they too can develop open and authentic relationships in and out of the workplace.

EDUCATORS' OWN EXPERIENCES OF EDUCATION

According to the findings of the Stonewall *School Report* (2017), LGBT+ pupils in schools and colleges experienced frequent homophobic language. 45% of LGBT+ students were bullied for being LGBT+ at school. Against a backdrop of significant legislative advancements in LGBT+ rights in the UK in recent years and some shift in public acceptance and openness towards LGBT+ people, the statistics presented in this report actually represent positive progress. The percentage of pupils who were bullied for being LGBT+ decreased by 20% over the ten years prior to the report, down from 65% in 2007 and 55% in 2012 (Stonewall, 2017).

LGBT+ adults joining the education workforce now, do so under the shadow of their own educational experiences. For some, this has meant years of carefully designed behaviour modifications in an attempt to prevent and rebuff a seemingly inevitable onslaught of verbal or physical abuse. Examples of modifications include repressing and subverting mannerisms, language, speech, interests, feelings, self-expression and anything that could be a queer identifier, in the hopes of assimilating as unnoticed as possible into the heteronormative corridors. For others, it means a sense of not belonging, without the language or a frame of reference to understand and articulate their difference.

Their educational experiences are unlikely to have included positive representations, acknowledgement or the language of minority sexualities. Without being afforded the safety to be their authentic self throughout their own education, entering the workplace in an educational environment may trigger subversive micro-behavioural and subconscious stress emotive responses, placing the individual in a higher state of alert. Compounded by a continuing unclarity and inconsistency in LGBT+ visibility across schools and colleges, these responses can have a limiting impact on self-efficacy, confidence and progression into leadership.

BARRIERS TO BECOMING AN LGBT+ ROLE MODEL IN EDUCATION

The position of the role model appears to be reserved for those who are able to present a clear articulation of sexuality, including their own, with the confidence to challenge negative behaviours, not only from learners, but also from colleagues and to lead in the visible celebration of minority sexualities. The Stonewall *School Report (*2017) found that 68% of pupils report that their teachers do not consistently challenge homophobic language, therefore, a significant proportion of LGBT+ staff experience inconsistencies in colleagues' willingness to challenge homophobic language.

It takes a focused resolve to provide a consistent counter-narrative. For some staff this may be a welcome platform. However, others may not feel equipped to lead. With leadership and visibility comes additional scrutiny and the burden of minority representation, being held to account for how the entire LGBT+ community is perceived. Some potential role models may be concerned about the responses of their team, the wider staff, learners, families, communities and the potential impact on their career prospects.

An educator who is exploring and questioning their sexuality from within the profession, is unlikely to have experienced an LGBT+ inclusive education themselves and may not have accessed LGBT+ communities. I was awakened to LGBT+ history and culture as a student at university, where I had the opportunity to find and experience LGBT+ communities and see the existence of LGBT+ identities within my education for the first time. Without similar experiences, colleagues may not feel knowledgeable enough about sexuality, including their own, to feel adequately equipped or confident in supporting other people's understanding.

SUPPORTING EDUCATOR LGBT+ ROLE MODELS

Effective role models present authenticity and self-awareness. Therefore, it is imperative to create a safe environment that nurtures the way for developing role models, who may tend to respond to their learned oppression in an educational environment, with a subconscious and protective self-subversion.

In many instances, LGBT+ inclusion is driven by an LGBT+ role model who is a sole change agent, trailblazing advancements, leading on issues of visibility and awareness. Individual-led inclusion initiatives that are dependent upon the lived experience of specific personnel, are rarely sustainable beyond their tenure in post and can create inequity in learning environments. A purposeful, systemic approach, informed by lived experience, shares the responsibility and effects a robust, consistent and sustainable infrastructure for LGBT+ inclusion.

Just as Kohli (2014) suggests, there should be opportunities for teachers from diverse ethnic groups to unpack internalised racism. We should therefore seek to provide opportunities throughout ITT and CPD for educators from minority sexualities to unpack internalised homophobia and biphobia. We should seek opportunities to actively pursue and develop protective factors that can counter minority stress and raise self-belief. We should increase LGBT+ visibility and engagement in lower stakes participation that nurtures diverse LGBT+ role models.

KEY TAKEAWAYS

- LGBT+ adults entering the education workforce are impacted by their own educational experiences.
- LGBT+ educators benefit from access to opportunities to explore and unpack internalised homophobia.
- Create opportunities for LGBT+ colleagues to share their LGBT+ identities in a way that is appropriate and supportive for them.

KEY QUESTIONS

- Do you explore and support the needs of your LGBT+ educators to inspire and unlock their talents?
- Is your LGBT+ inclusion driven by an individual or supported through a systemic framework?
- What barriers to sharing LGBT+ identities exist for your colleagues?

COMMITMENT TO THE MANIFESTO

Create nurturing environments where LGBT+ educators are supported to unpack internalised homophobia, explore their authentic identity and contribute to diversifying LGBT+ visibility.

REFERENCES

Kohli, R. (2014), 'Unpacking internalized racism: teachers of colour striving for racially just classrooms.' *Race Ethnicity and Education*, 17, (3), 367-87

Stonewall (2017), *School report: the experiences of lesbian, gay, bi and trans young people in Britain's schools in 2017*, London: Stonewall. Available at: https://www.stonewall.org.uk/system/files/the_school_report_2017.pdf (accessed 4 April 2021).

SEXUALITY, BLACKNESS AND MASCULINITY

MAHLON EVANS-SINCLAIR

INTRODUCTION

If gender expression and sexual orientation existed on an 'x' 'y' axis, it could be understood that a typical manifestation of homophobia as expressed towards some men would be to read their gender expression as a proxy for their sexual orientation. The 'less masculine' (read feminine) you are in your display, the more it is taken as read that you are same-sex attracted. Acts of discrimination associated with this trope exist in interpersonal and institutional spaces, but also are cemented into the fabric of our heterosexist, often hyper-masculine, norms of society. Add to that, being a queer-identified cis-man in a Black body means that though I can understand the axes, I'm also aware that societal norms afford a very small concentration of where gender expression for Black boys and men can exist on that scale – namely at the quadrant of both hyper-masculine gender expression and very abrasive displays of heterosexuality in orientation. To exist outside of that for Black (and some other racialised) teachers who also identify as queer, can be seen as a weak spot, where role modelling can be undermined or exploited; however, it is in the incorporation of Blackness, maleness, and queerness into the art of the teacher persona where there exists a place for real transformation in attitudes and behaviours. Transformation that is needed as much in teacher training and development as it is needed in the school community at large.

INTERNAL IDEATIONS:

I reflect on not having an explicitly 'out' identity in school as a student, this being heavily informed by going to a racially and culturally diverse boys' school for the majority of my secondary school experience. Reflecting on all the boys that went to the school with me, I concluded that masculinity existed on a spectrum. We were all concerned about our individual traits and even made tenuous associations to our form classes – 'H', my own, had the all-round academics, 'P' were sporty, 'K' were expressive with the arts, 'D' had the most alternative cohort. This didn't mean that I did not get called homophobic slurs infrequently, but it meant that you could be a boy with clear hand-writing, or be concerned with being bright, or have an interest outside of football and rugby as a sport, and it was all acknowledged and respected.

One of the subjects I reflect on fondly as a student was English with Mr Bale, where I felt the most free to be my expressive self. Knowing that Mr Bale was both a white-passing man of colour and sensing that he also happened to be same-sex attracted, meant that I felt greater confidence in being supported and validated in that space. The school was very racially diverse with my cohort population being more than half made up of Black students from African and Caribbean heritage. Mr Bale encouraged academic rigour in his classroom, had no time for 'class clown' behaviours as a deflection and I always appreciated his reinforcement that to be smart as a boy was not only okay, but was in fact to be celebrated – something that included giving verbal responses in the moment without fear of judgement from others. What was so eye- opening for me was that it allowed me to confidently sit in being both a Black boy and smart and be rewarded for it, with no attachment to either my racial identity or my gender. Comments such as 'you've done well' were just a statement of fact.

INTERPERSONAL AND INSTITUTIONAL COMMUNICATION:

The inner thoughts that questioned if being Black and academically smart was somehow less masculine were something that I did not need to explore in school. It was within my ethno-cultural community of Jamaican descendents and later in my education and career journeys where notions of sexuality as expressed through gendered norms became more apparent. Whereas the tilt to macro-racism (that I had learned to navigate) came before homophobia in both queer and non-queer white-majority spaces, homophobia carried a different loading when it came from within my own Black community, adding to a sense of internalised vigilance of how to present masculinity in spaces. This gave me some anxiety about how I would carry myself when placed in my first teaching school, which was predominantly Bangladeshi/Turkish & West African, Muslim. It also gave me pause for thought when applying for my second role in a school that was predominantly Black (from both African and Caribbean descendants) and more Christian. In the first school I recall being met with comments suggesting that I was a 'sell out', for graduating, 'gay' for the inclusive ways in which I taught, and 'not Black' because of how I dressed. This was while simultaneously attempting to model that I was no less a man for these characteristics and attributes and keeping high expectations of the boys in the class, especially when it came to applying themselves to their work as much as the girls did. However, in the second school, my presentation as a different type of Black male authority figure, in addition to some of the others who presented as 'more masculine', did not have the same negative impact on my sexual orientation. The humorous, yet emotionally intelligent response of 'Thought so', that one of my form group gave me after outing myself as a non-follower of football, was the extent to which the students appraised my gender expression vis-a-vis my sexual orientation.

STRUCTURAL CONSIDERATIONS:

In maintaining professional relationships with a number of former students, a large number are from a racial background, with a few having since come out as being queer. The most striking reflection from many has been the knowledge that I was expressly queer – even if it was not the first identity marker they associated me with – and that was a reassurance for them. What it was not able to do however was make them comfortable enough to have come out earlier as they were still seeking wider structural reassurances for their own multiple identities. For some, dealing with how their race or religion was viewed by the school structure didn't leave time, or put at odds their consideration of how their sexual orientation was also forming. A zoomed-out appreciation of this is to understand that for Black (and other racialised) people, their religious or racial identities are often positioned as 'pronounced' or 'muted', in relation to their sexual orientation. This means that for those who also identify as queer in these identity groups, there exists a pervasive narrative in which there is a simultaneous hypervigilance and erasure. On one hand racism is used to perpetuate the idea that these communities enact more homophobia than the white majority population and on the other there is much minimising, to the point of erasure, the notion that in Black and other ethnic groups, queer folk exist. How this often translates in policy and its enactment is by having heavier sanctions for interpersonal instances of homophobia, such as micro-insults (slurs) in comparison to interpersonal or institutional acts of racism. This double whammy being the compounding micro-invalidation of especially queer students from racial communities. This is supported by a recent 'Just Like Us' study into the experience of LGBTQ+ students in school, with only 52% and 57% of Black and Asian LGBTQ+ pupils respectively, stating they felt safe in school on a daily basis in the past twelve months and 6% of Black LGBTQ+ pupils stating they have never felt safe. This is compared to 59% and 3% for white pupils in both categories. This also leaves Black (and other racialised) teachers who also identify as queer to often have an experience of dancing between two identities, one which is more accepted, often at the expense of having the other tolerated, both rarely being celebrated as one.

KEY TAKEAWAYS

- Masculinity, like all gender expressions, exists on a spectrum and does not have a correlation with sexual orientation. Attaching flags of gender expression to conditions of praise and reward, further narrows and codes what is valued in masculinity.
- Avoid myopic representations and portrayals of 'this' or 'that' identities when representing sexual orientation in race and gender expression. LGBTQ+

narratives need to include racial voices and narratives of race need to also be from LGBTQ+ voices.

- Challenge the notion that homophobia exists in a silo, separate from other identity markers. Pitting identities against each other makes the school environment less safe for those who intersect.

KEY QUESTIONS

- How can Professional Development be used to develop awareness of and dissuade use of giving gender-coded feedback to students about their contributions and achievements?
- How are staff encouraged to reflect on their own biases of sexual orientation as being fused with gender expression and race, especially when working in environments where they do not share the identity of the students taught?
- How is the school environment being made to be inclusive of race and religious identities as they interact with sexual orientation, so that they are not at the expense of each other?

COMMITMENT TO THE MANIFESTO

Commit to understanding the impact of multiple identities in the student population, especially at the intersection between them and LGBT+ identities.

REFERENCES

GLSEN: Research Report (2020). *Erasure and Resilience: The Experiences of LGBTQ Students of Color: Black LGBTQ Youth in U.S. Schools.* Available at: https://www.glsen.org/sites/default/files/2020-06/Erasure-and-Resilience-Black-2020.pdf (accessed 1st June 2021)

Just Like Us (2021), *Research into student perceptions of safety in school.* Summary available at: https://www.justlikeus.org/single-post/black-lgbt-pupils-least-likely-to-feel-safe-at-school (accessed 1st June 2021)

WHAT IF I DON'T WANT TO BE A CELEBRITY BLOGGER WHEN I GROW UP?

PREPARING LGBT+ STUDENTS FOR PROFESSIONAL CAREERS

MAYUR GUPTA

Growing up, I was less concerned about whether being gay was right or wrong, and more concerned about the impact that being gay would have on my future career. I grew up in an aspirational immigrant family where my parents encouraged me to earn top grades, attend a Russell Group university and achieve a prestigious business career. As a child, I never considered other options. That all changed aged thirteen when I realised I was gay and became petrified of the consequences that this may have on my career potential and life. As a teenager, I had never met any openly gay professionals and the only representation I had of gay people were musicians, celebrity bloggers and pernicious gay caricatures in media. However, I did not want a career in entertainment, and so I felt being gay would be a barrier to being a business professional and I hid my sexuality till my early twenties.

Education plays a crucial role in employment and in economic growth. According to Stonewall, 45% of young people are bullied for being LGBT+ at school and half of bullied LGBT+ pupils feel that bullying has had a negative effect on their plans for future education. Those experiences reduce the quality of education for the bullied students as they cannot concentrate as well on their classes. They will have lower incomes if they must end school early, and the poor quality of their education is likely to result in smaller gains from schooling. Without the bullying, stigma and discrimination that is common in schools, they would fare better, and the economy would benefit from their expanded skills.

It is not just LGBT+ people who benefit from LGBT+ inclusion – the business case for LGBT+ equality highlights that equal treatment is good for businesses and society as a whole. Firstly, stock market studies have shown that LGBT+ inclusive policies in businesses have a positive effect on stock performance, with Credit Suisse finding that the stock prices of 270 companies with openly LGBT+ senior management outperformed firms from similar industries. Secondly, LGBT+ people who worked in LGBT+ inclusive environments had greater commitment to their jobs, better mental or physical health, more job satisfaction and were more open about being LGBT+. More openness generates better health for LGBT+ people, and better health means that workers miss less work and are more productive. Thirdly, Richard Florida's 'creative class' theory highlights that visibility and tolerance of LGBT+ people in a country sends a signal to the world's creative and skilled people (not just those who are LGBT+) to think about emigrating to places that welcome new ideas and a diverse population.

HOW SCHOOLS CAN HELP LGBT+ YOUNG PEOPLE PREPARE FOR PROFESSIONAL CAREERS

Schools can play a big role in highlighting successful LGBT+ business role models, making career support more LGBT+ inclusive and signposting LGBT+ students to other opportunities outside school.

USUALISING LGBT+ CAREER SUCCESS:

There is an increase in good work being carried out by schools to help young LGBT+ people realise that being LGBT+ is acceptable. However, there are numerous LGBT+ young people who are still nervous about the impact that being LGBT+ will have when they start their careers, for example: is it appropriate to come out in the workplace? Will bosses and colleagues take them less seriously if they are LGBT+? Are male-dominated sectors like finance, technology and engineering more homophobic than others? Whilst there is increasing LGBT+ representation, this tends to be concentrated on celebrities and entertainers, as opposed to LGBT+ business leaders in professional services. Schools can help support LGBT+ students by highlighting and celebrating modern day LGBT+ successful business leaders.

- **LGBT+ Business Leader Biographies** One way that schools can usualise LGBT+ career success is through stocking biographies of LGBT+ business professionals in their school libraries and classrooms. For example, *It's About Damn Time* (Arlan Hamilton) for those interested in investment, *One of Them* (Michael Cashman) for those who want to go into politics, *Everybody's Business* (Jon Miller) for those who want to go into consulting and *Dutiful Boy* (Mohsin Zaidi) for those who want to be lawyers. Teachers and students can also discuss these books in classes, reading clubs, LGBT+ clubs and so on, to ensure the messages of these books become widely accessible to students.
- **LGBT+ Career Speakers**: Another way that schools can normalise LGBT+ career success is through arranging career assemblies led by openly LGBT+ speakers. LGBT+ young people aged eleven to eighteen do not tend to know LGBT+ adults in real life who they can be inspired by. When schools speak with businesses to arrange career speakers for their students, they can ask if the business could send at least one openly LGBT+ business speaker to share their story for their LGBT+ students and allies. Most businesses will

have LGBT+ networks and should easily be able to arrange having LGBT+ speakers talk at school career assemblies.

- **LGBT+ Role Model Lists**: Schools can also circulate LGBT+ Role Model Lists to their students. Famous examples of these lists include: OUTstanding Top 100 Future Leaders, OUTstanding Top 100 Role Model Executives and LGBT+ British Award Winners. This is a convenient way for LGBT+ students to learn about the most visible, influential LGBT+ business leaders in the world. The organisers who have compiled these lists have already done the hard work listing and describing the role models, so all this information is easily accessible for the LGBT+ young people viewing them.

HELPING LGBT+ STUDENTS BUILD THEIR PROFESSIONAL NETWORK:

There seems to be a gap in provision for LGBT+ career support for eleven to eighteen- year-old students. For example, for LGBT+ people who are over twenty-one years old, there are lots of great LGBT+ umbrella networks for them to get involved with. Anyone who works within or is just interested in certain sectors can join these networks to connect with other LGBT+ people who share a passion for an industry and are looking to build their LGBT+ professional network. Usually these events have keynote speakers, networking drinks, panel discussions and so on, and there is something for everyone. Some of these networks include: Intertech, Out in Tech, Interbank, Intermedia, Interinvest, Interlaw, Interengineering and Series Q. The lack of LGBT+ career support for eleven to eighteen-year-old students is problematic because it is usually during this period when LGBT+ youth struggle the most with their identities, where they seem to be receiving the least support.

Schools can support their LGBT+ students to build their LGBT+ professional network through LGBT+ and Ally clubs, signposting opportunities outside school and facilitating business mentoring for their LGBT+ students.

- **LGBT+ and Ally Clubs**: Schools can help students set up LGBT+ and Ally School Clubs for LGBT+ students to meet one another from their schools in a safe space. Many LGBT+ clubs also have a big focus on allyship. These clubs empower allies to step up to make a positive change in their school community. If your school is part of a multi-academy trust your school can see if you can work with the other schools by having an inter-school LGBT+ club to increase the numbers of LGBT+ students and allies networking and supporting one another.
- **Signposting Opportunities**: Schools can also signpost their LGBT+ students to other LGBT+ groups where students can build their LGBT+ professional network with peers the same age as them and also LGBT+ business leaders. For example, these groups can include: Mosaic, Just Like Us, Stonewall and also LGBT+ youth groups in the local vicinity to the school.
- **LGBT+ Business Mentoring Programmes**: Schools can encourage their

LGBT+ students to apply for LGBT+ focused business mentoring programmes externally, such as the PinkNews Futures Mentoring Programme and the Just Like Us Mentoring Programme, where LGBT+ students can get an LGBT+ business mentor to help them prepare for joining the working world as an LGBT+ person.

KEY TAKEAWAYS

- It is important to highlight how LGBT+ inclusion in education and employment is good for everyone (including heterosexual and cis people, businesses and society), not just LGBT+ people.
- It is important to showcase LGBT+ people succeeding in all types of sectors, including professional sectors, to provide relatable role models to all types of LGBT+ students.
- It is important to help young LGBT+ people grow their professional network of LGBT+ business leaders and strong allies.

KEY QUESTIONS

- To what extent do students understand the impact of homophobic bullying and prejudice on LGBT+ people, as well as on straight and cis people, businesses and wider society?
- How many famous, visible, successful LGBT+ business professionals do students know about?
- To what extent do your LGBT+ students have a way to build relationships with other LGBT+ students and LGBT+ business leaders?

COMMITMENT TO THE MANIFESTO

Create clear opportunities for LGBT+ students to see themselves in a wide range of careers from an early age.

REFERENCES

Bradlow, J., Bartram, F., Guasp, A. and Jadva, V. (2017) *School Report*, Stonewall and Centre for Family Research, University of Cambridge, p6.

Cashman, M. (2021). *One of Them*. Bloomsbury Publishing.

Hamilton, A. (2020). *It's about Damn Time*. Hodder & Stoughton.

Miller, J., Parker, L., Sadler, J. and Serdiville, R. (2013). *Everybody's Business*. Biteback Publishing.

Zaidi, M. (2021). *A Dutiful Boy*. Penguin Random House.

SHARED NARRATIVES: HOW STORIES AND COLLABORATION CAN EMPOWER LGBTQ+ COMMUNITIES IN EDUCATION

NICK KITCHENER-BENTLEY

LGBTQ+ staff and students alike deserve to have the very best experiences of education. This can be supported through work undertaken in a variety of contexts; clubs, classrooms and corridors. Irrespective of where and how this happens, it is mutually beneficial for all members of an educational community to coexist in a space of safety, richness and equality. This chapter will explore how I, as an openly gay teacher, sought to cooperate with colleagues and students to develop an LGBTQ+ student group and work towards creating a better environment for queer people within our school and beyond – centring on the particular advantages afforded by the collaborative nature of our work.

Looking up at the group of students speaking on our school stage in front of a cohort of around 270 of their peers on the topic of LGBT History Month, my mind shot back to my own assemblies as a teenager in secondary school. The idea that students could lead an assembly on this issue would have astonished me. And yet, here they were doing just that. How did we get here?

Firstly, I will celebrate the value of supporting LGBTQ+ members of the school community to share stories. Fisher and Stockbridge (2016) ask 'What ... are we offering students who never see themselves and/or their family structures within the educational stories?' and I believe that having LGBTQ+ staff and students enter into conversations wherein they are able to affirm the value of all individual people is of vital importance. All too often, LGBTQ+ people in schools do not feel as if they are part of a community and do not see themselves represented, so in countering this challenge, sharing stories is essential.

The previous year I had shared my own story at an assembly. I had felt *petrified* about coming out as gay – my hands were shaking, my face was flushed and my voice was trembling. Yet I was lucky to have been supported by colleagues who are wonderful friends and allies to the LGBTQ+ community; I felt emboldened by their support. So, I spoke to each year group, going through the words that I had rehearsed so many times, and the students sitting in the audience were calm, quiet and respectful. I know that every teacher is fiercely defensive about their students, but I really could not have felt more proud of the positive, supportive and kind reaction I received from the young people within our school. I propose that schools and colleges must empower their LGBTQ+ communities to have the opportunity to be open and authentic since it provides meaningful role-modelling, networks of support, and an interruption of exclusionary narratives.

I also believe representation ought to go beyond the literal sharing of stories to ensure that diversity is meaningfully embedded across the curriculum. In the summer after my first LGBT History Month Assembly, the Drama team were teaching our Year 7 students *A Midsummer Night's Dream,* including work unpacking diverse productions. Part of this involved considering queer representations in Emma Rice's 2016 Globe production, which recast Helena as a gay Helenus. Rudine Sims Bishop (1990) explores the way in which 'Literature transforms human experiences and it reflects it back to us, and in that reflection we can see our own lives and experiences as part of the larger human experience,' and it is incumbent on educators to review the extent to which the curriculum is representative of the young people we work with, and to embark on the task of ensuring we reflect the diversity of our students in the lessons we teach.

At the end of one drama lesson a group of brave and resilient Year 7 students approached me with their plan to create an LGBTQ+ student group. And it was not a coincidence, to my mind, that this idea had been posed at the end of a drama lesson. Drama offers a site where individual stories collide with cooperative experiences – and this has powerful implications for promoting diversity. Through their collaborative explorations of the play, students had engaged with the representation of LGBTQ+ identities, and I would propose that Vygotsky's (1978) argument that 'learning awakens a variety of internal developmental processes that are able to operate only when the child is interacting with people in his [sic] environment and in cooperation with his peers' (p.88), offers an important model here: the students' interactions were vital for their insightful interrogation of diverse theatre. Not only is diversifying curricula important to broaden representation, but the social learning afforded by collaborative interaction within inclusive spaces is essential to open up conversations.

This brings me to my final point about the importance of cooperative endeavours as a means to promote social justice and equality. Collaborative interaction was soon to become equally essential for our LGBTQ+ student group. In setting up the club, I worked alongside a group of wonderful colleagues who were instrumental in supporting students from across the school to join in. We have held discussions and debates, considered and thought through events pertinent to LGBTQ+ people across the world, and talked about queer people who inspire us for all sorts of reasons. Having a space to feel seen and to feel safe is of vital importance. It is important for young people to have the opportunity to talk openly about their feelings with sympathetic peers and adults. hooks (2003) celebrates community spirit wherein human diversity is championed, such that, 'finding out what connects us, revelling in our differences; this is the process that brings us closer, that gives us a world of shared values, of meaningful community' (p.197). In our school this meant that we had the fabulous spectacle of students volunteering to sell and buy LGBTQ+ 'merchandise'; walking around the school with rainbow flags, stationery, and all manner of other rainbow-themed paraphernalia!

This positivity and solidarity are vital not only for the purposes of representation but also striving for social justice. Friere (2000) has contrasted a transactional, teacher-led approach to schooling which he described as 'banking education [with] problem-posing education [which] involves a constant unveiling of reality. The former attempts to maintain the *submersion* of consciousness; the latter strives for the *emergence* of consciousness and *critical intervention* in reality.' The students' impressive collaboration, celebration and activism around LGBTQ+ equality, surely offer engaged 'critical intervention'. I propose that for meaningful community-building to occur, it is vital that students' own ideas, experiences and narratives are championed.

I would like to return to the idea of assemblies because they combine this idea of community and story. Like the drama lesson I described, assemblies serve as a form of theatre where communities gather to engage with differing stories; this is why I think they can form a key part of supporting LGBTQ+ empowerment. Our students have done a wonderfully impressive job of this at every stage; presenting assemblies on World AIDS Day, LGBT History Month and Trans Day of Visibility, and consistently speaking with power, insight and bravery. As they shared their carefully prepared presentation on the lives of LGBTQ+ people – offering their own critical intervention – I felt inspired by their support for each other. As an educator, having had the opportunity to serve the young people in our school by supporting them on their journey to realise their full potential, has been an honour. Seeing those students empower themselves and work together to strive for social change has been a privilege.

KEY TAKEAWAYS

- LGBTQ+ staff must feel supported to be able to share their stories.
- LGBTQ+ students must see diverse LGBTQ+ identities represented in their lessons so that they can make connections with their own lives and with each other.
- Students benefit from opportunities to collaborate to act for social justice, equality and diversity in their community and beyond.

KEY QUESTIONS

- How can you ensure LGBTQ+ members of your school community are supported to share their authentic lives and narratives?
- How can you ensure students see diverse identities represented in their curriculum?
- How can you ensure students have opportunities to collaborate and strive for justice?

COMMITMENT TO THE MANIFESTO

Provide safe spaces where diverse staff and students can cooperate, connect and thrive.

REFERENCES

Bishop, R.S. (1990). 'Mirrors, Windows and Sliding Glass Doors.' *Perspectives: Choosing and Using Books for the Classroom*. 6, (3), The Ohio State University.

Fisher, M.E. and Stockbridge, K. (2016), 'Spaces at the Intersection of Diversity and Controversy.' In Bloomfield, V.E. and Fisher M.E. (eds.), *LGBTQ Voices in Education: Changing the Culture of Schooling*. Oxon: Routledge. pp. 42-57

Friere, P. (2000), *Pedagogy of the Oppressed*. London: Bloomsbury Academic.

hooks, b. (2003), *Teaching Community: A Pedagogy of Hope*. Oxon: Routledge.

Vygotsky, L.S. (1978), In: Cole, M., John-Steiner, V., Scribner, S and Souberman, E. (eds.) *Mind in Society: The Development of Higher Psychological Processes*. London: Harvard University Press.

CHAPTER 10: INTERSECTIONALITY

CHAPTER EDITOR: ANGELA BROWNE

CHAPTER CONTRIBUTORS

1. Dr Susan Davis – **Re-imagining Initial Teacher Education (ITE) using an intersectional lens**
2. Lottie Cooke – **The Importance of an Intersectional Classroom**
3. Nicole Ponsford – **Smashing Stereotypes in Education: The Kerplunk Model**
4. Kiran Mahil – **How do I get a month, miss?**
5. Lee Jerome – **Intersectional Citizenship**
6. James Clarke – **Teaching at the crossroads: creating connections not walls**
7. Rich Atterton – **When Kingdoms Collide – Moving towards a deeper understanding of LGBT+ people of faith in a school context with particular reference to evangelical Christians.**
8. Emma Swift – **The Intersectional Impact of Fertility Treatment and LGBT+ Identities in Schools**
9. Audrey Pantelis – **Ceilings and Tears: How Black Female Leaders in Education are viewed and treated**
10. Abena Akuffo-Kelly – **A Toolkit for a Quiet Revolution**

BIOGRAPHIES

Angela Browne is an education leader and founder of Nourished Collective, an online space for women that provides leadership coaching, personal development programmes, community and all-round support for women. Angela is passionate about bringing nourishment to the education system and returning educators to a more balanced state of wellbeing and autonomy. Angela spent eighteen years working in a range of schools and more recently as an Interim Deputy CEO of a semi-rural multi-academy trust. She has been a headteacher in mainstream education, alternative provision and in an all-through school.

Abena Akuffo-Kelly is a computer science specialist with fourteen years' experience in a variety of school settings. She is heavily involved in activism as a school union rep and a ULR (Union Learning Rep), a local Labour councillor, a trustee of an international charity, a mother and an intersectional feminist.

Audrey Pantelis has been an educator for the past thirty years in both mainstream and SEND phases. She was the former founding Head of School of an all-age SEND school based in north west London – judged as 'Good with outstanding features'. Audrey is Director of Elevation Coaching and Consulting. She offers expertise in school and organisational improvement services – specialising in leadership coaching, SEND support and equality, diversity and inclusion strategic input.

Emma Swift is a trust-wide subject lead for a multi-academy trust, specialising in science and ITT. She started her career in the East Midlands in 2002, before moving to London, holding a variety of roles in senior leadership, then returning to Derby. Emma is the secondary subject-specific lead tutor for Physics for NSET. She speaks at a number of different events about science, curriculum and diversity, alongside supporting schools to raise outcomes and build capacity through staff development and curriculum design.

James Clarke is a secondary school teacher from North London. He is a teacher of Drama and Head of PSHE with a BA (Hons) from The Royal Central School of Speech and Drama. He is also a District Commissioner for North London Scouts and a member of the UK Scouting national Inclusion team.

Kiran Mahil is a secondary school senior leader in East London, who believes that education results in positive change. She has taught history and politics for a decade. Before teaching, Kiran worked as a political adviser, with a specialist interest in equality policy.

Lee Jerome has taught history and sociology in secondary schools and is currently Associate Professor of Education at Middlesex University. He researches and writes about citizenship education and children's rights and co-edits the teacher journal *Teaching Citizenship* for the Association for Citizenship Teaching.

Lottie Cooke is a student and activist from Southampton who works mostly on transforming the education system for it to become empowering, safe and student-led. She works with other young people in organisations like The Pupil Power, NCS and the #iwill Campaign, as well as participating in more local projects.

Nicole Ponsford FRSA is the Co-CEO and Founder of the GEC (Global Equality Collective). Previously an award-winning teacher and Harvard author (*TechnoTeaching*), she is now a Doctorate researcher, and known educational and technology thought-leader. Nicole believes that technology is the great equaliser for our time.

Rich Atterton is a school leader and a teacher of nearly twenty years' experience. He is a member of the Association of School and College Leaders council and executive. Since 2020 he has chaired the ASCL LGBT Leaders' Network and is an advisory board member of LGBTed.

Dr Susan Davis is the Pathway Leader for the Prof Doc in Education (EdD) at Cardiff Metropolitan University and a tutor on the PGCE primary programme and the MA Education. She is an active researcher, looking at quiet, shy, anxious children's experiences in primary school. She is the chair of BAMEed Network Wales.

INTERSECTIONALITY: INTRODUCTION

ANGELA BROWNE

INTRODUCTION

In this chapter, you will be introduced to the theory and everyday implications of holding intersectional identities. It is a topic dear to my heart. Indeed, this chapter marks a much longed-for account of what it is to be a human who cannot be understood on the basis of recognising that she holds one or two protected identities.

As a black girl growing up and as the black woman I became, two of the identities I hold have frequently combined to negative effect. Being a black schoolgirl often meant that I was not treated in the same way that my non-black female friends were and looking back I wonder at the presence of 'adultisation' – a force present in the lives of many black girls. As a more mature black woman I now know that where a woman may well have been considered 'fit' to take on a leadership role in a rural market town, a black woman was almost a bridge too far. Although recruiters could never confirm this, I recall all too well the feeling of not being the right fit once I had arrived at an interview and my skin colour had been duly noted.

What an understanding of intersectionality would have meant to me as a younger child, I cannot say, but for those working within an education system that still needs to do much to improve diversity, equity and inclusion, a clear recognition of how intersectionality operates is vital.

DEFINITIONS AND TERMINOLOGY

However, before you look at the following chapters, it is probably worth gaining a deeper understanding of intersectionality. You see, intersectionality is not one of the nine protected characteristics you have already explored. Indeed, it is not just any two of the protected characteristics explored in this book. Instead, intersectionality is how potentially all nine of the protected characteristics layer upon each other and present further oppressions, marginalisation and challenges for individuals.

LANDSCAPE

To understand intersectionality, you have to understand the origins of the theorist who coined the term. Intersectionality was first presented to the world stage by a feminist theorist called Kimberlé Crenshaw. Crenshaw was a graduate of Cornell University, and she had spent much of her research time focused on the development of Critical Race Theory. This is, in itself, a theory posited by her and a group of other legal scholars who understood that discrimination and racism were not things that happened in an unbiased legal system, they were not unfortunate errors that came within a neutral legal framework, but these things were instead baked into the legal system. In setting out Critical Race Theory, Crenshaw and others challenged the notion of neutrality in the law and most other systems and structures of society.

Critical Race Theory referred to a whole host of societal factors that could not exist if there were neutrality in society or the legal system. The fact that these differences and these imbalances occurred served to point towards structures of white dominance and pointed towards a legal and socio-economic framework built on inequity. Intersectionality emerged from this; it emerged out of the idea that the legal system was not neutral. Crenshaw put her theory of intersectionality to the world in 1989 in a paper she published called 'Demarginalising the Intersection of Race and Sex'.

It is important to note that intersectionality as a theory does not solely arise out of Crenshaw's specific focus on the intersections of race and gender. While this intersection frames a lot of our understandings of how intersectionality operates, as you will see from the essays in this chapter, intersectionality can and does have implications for anyone who holds multiple and intersecting identities.

In 'Demarginalizing the Intersection of Race and Sex', Crenshaw focused on a handful of legal cases in which she could evidence racial discrimination and the intersection of that with sex discrimination. She pointed to the way in which the legal system seemed in its rulings to be intent on only allowing for single identities, issues and seemingly refusing even to consider multi-identity issues. So the law ignored the fact that black women were black and female and refused to see that the intersection between those two identities could lead to multiple oppressions or a doubling down on oppression. In the essay, Crenshaw gives the example of a 1976 case in which five black women took to the courts to sue General Motors. The case is called *Degraffenreid vs General Motors*, and it provides a constructive means of understanding this complex theory.

The case refers to a General Motors HR policy that the plaintiffs argued targeted and oppressed Black women specifically, in fact almost exclusively, and this was because it was an HR policy of 'last hired, first fired.' At that time, marking a particular moment in America's civil rights movement, black women represented a group who had been hired relatively late into the General Motors workforce compared to other groups. Therefore, this HR policy negatively harshly and disproportionately impacted them, and they ended up being the primary target for mass layoffs.

However, their discrimination lawsuit was dismissed as being groundless. The court reasoned that there was no discrimination on the grounds of race because General Motors still employed black men following the layoffs. Of course, black women would not have been engaged in the same roles as black men because black men were hired to work on the factory floor.

The court also argued that sexism could not be established and was not sufficiently proved by this case because it was not the case that women had been disproportionately affected by the layoffs. This was, of course, because General Motors were still employing white women, but that was because white women held seniority. After all, white women had been in the office roles for which women were recruited for longer than the General Motors policy of recruiting black women more recently.

It was impossible in the law for these women to argue that black women were disproportionately affected by the policy. Crenshaw identified that this force of intersectional oppressions is very complex and that for some, it leads to multiple oppressions and multiple occasions of marginalisation.

VOICES IN OUR CHAPTER IN DIVERSE EDUCATORS – A MANIFESTO

We start our journey at the very beginning with **Dr Susan Davis** exploring how ITE can help teachers understand Intersectionality in 'Re-imagining Initial Teacher Education (ITE) using an intersectional lens'. **Lottie Cooke**'s 'The Importance of an Intersectional Classroom' follows to remind us of a student perspective on how teachers who understand intersectional identities can change lives. We then move to **Nicole Ponsford**, who encourages the act of 'Smashing Stereotypes in Education' through The Kerplunk Model. **Kiran Mahil**'s piece on history months is particularly important and again shows how students perceive our efforts to celebrate a range of identities by asking 'How do I get a month, miss?' We stay with subject-specific focus in **Lee Jerome**'s 'Intersectional Citizenship', a detailed look at how this subject area and its iterations can be used to bring awareness of intersectionality. **James Clarke** explores 'Teaching at the crossroads: creating connections not walls'. Then **Rich Atterton** takes us through the intersection of religion and sexuality in 'When Kingdoms Collide – Moving towards a deeper understanding of LGBT+ people of faith in a school context with particular reference to evangelical Christians'. **Emma Swift** continues with the intersection of sexuality and pregnancy/maternity in 'The Intersectional Impact of Fertility Treatment and LGBT+ Identities in Schools', a powerful piece about how multiple identities can impact on all aspects of your life. The chapter's penultimate piece is from **Audrey Pantelis** in 'Ceilings and Tears: How Black Female Leaders in Education are Viewed and Treated', where she hones in on the very intersection that Crenshaw started with and finally, with a call to arms is **Abena Akuffo-Kelly** who provides us with 'A Toolkit for a Quiet Revolution'.

CONCLUSION

Our job, therefore, with an intersectional lens is to begin to look at the interrelationships between complex identities, identities that cannot be taken apart from each other, and to start to understand the impact of that on individual lives.

This means we need to be aware of the experience in our schools for those who hold protected intersectional identities; those of being a black girl, of being a young disabled person, those of being a trans person of faith, those of being a disabled, black person. These fascinating, beautiful intersections do not necessarily seem interesting and beautiful within organisations that want to deal with identities as single issues.

As practitioners, what is required of us is to begin to dig deeper, more rigorously and more effectively, into how our curriculum reasserts ideas about single identity lives and fails to welcome and embrace the complexity of multi-identity lives, and in so doing, marginalises, silences and excludes young people who feel the challenge and the complexity of navigating their multi-identity lives.

COMMITMENT TO THE MANIFESTO

A few things that you can do as school teachers are exemplified in the takeaways at the end of each of the essays you will find in this chapter. But let us keep it simple.

Bring the lenses of intersectional identities to your school. Look through those lenses at your pastoral system, look through those lenses at your curriculum, look through those lenses at the culture you have built for staff and student and community communications, look through them at the opportunities for recruitment, retention, and promotion in your organisation. Look through those multiple lenses as though through a kaleidoscope of interesting, exciting, diverse identities, and be careful to ensure you are mindful of the challenges, the potential oppressions, the potential omissions of your work to ensure individual safety within that.

REFERENCES

Crenshaw, K. (1989) 'Demarginalizing the Intersection of Race and Sex: A Black Feminist Critique of Antidiscrimination Doctrine, Feminist Theory and Antiracist Politics.' *University of Chicago Legal Forum*: Vol. 1989 , Article 8

RE-IMAGINING INITIAL TEACHER EDUCATION (ITE) USING AN INTERSECTIONAL LENS

DR SUSAN DAVIS

INTRODUCTION

This article re-imagines the benefits that would be gained if an intersectional lens was employed within a higher education, Initial Teacher Education (ITE) paradigm. Intersectionality has emerged as an important framework for understanding and responding to educational inequities by highlighting, making explicit and observable the interconnected structures of power that produce them (Besic, 2020; Bhopal, 2020).

Employing an intersectional lens within an educational context promotes an understanding of the nature of privilege and the subsequent disadvantage that pervades educational systems and affects learners, if difference is glossed over or homogenised. We do not appreciate differences enough nor celebrate those differences. Putting learners in boxes and allocating them to those constructs is our weakness – we like to compartmentalise – but by doing so we dilute, and we repress. Intersectionality tells us that a specific learner within a school is like an onion – we need to peel away those layers to understand them and their learning needs and offer an educational experience that, as far as possible, is as unique as them.

It is fair to say that ITE programmes in the UK teach their students about inequalities that will be in place, amongst the pupils they will be teaching. However, this is usually related to the understanding of socio-economic differences. If we are looking at specific issues such as race or cultural aspects, on which a more nuanced understanding is vital, then it seems this may be less robustly and expertly explored. Arshad (2005) surveyed a large number of serving teachers in Scotland and found that teaching about race was viewed by them as only being relevant to Black and minority ethnic (BAME) pupils, learners with English as an additional language and schools with large numbers of BAME learners. She also found that the teachers were uncomfortable with the term 'race equality' and actively avoided using terms such as 'anti-racist', preferring to use more 'neutral' terms such as inclusion and diversity.

If educators are struggling to understand and teach about race, then the many complex issues surrounding intersectionality and race or intersectionality and gender would arguably be a steeper learning curve for some. Most educators undoubtedly portray a 'generalised' understanding of cultural identity and difference, but often leave those differences unaddressed, or fail to emphasise difference robustly enough, for fear of giving offence or because of lack of knowledge. This lack of interrogation and direct teaching must be explored and addressed. A commitment to ensuring educational equity and social justice is needed and ITE providers must buy into this process and be fully conscious of the role they have in educating the teachers of tomorrow. ITE programmes must equip their trainees with knowledge of the role that intersectionality plays in understanding learners within a school. Comprehension of how intersectionality defines learners and learning is key – and also that lack of knowledge will undoubtedly, disadvantage and oppress many of the learners in that system.

Working within an intersectional framework, the ITE sector can begin to account for the complex ways that race, ethnicity, class, gender, sexuality, religion, disability, physical appearance, will affect learners in an educational setting. ITE institutions have a responsibility to lead in relation to delivery of an intersectional focus in their programmes. This agenda for change needs to empower and educate ITE students about differences in the learners they will be teaching, in a deep and meaningful way, ensuring that they understand, appreciate and support these differences within their own pedagogy. The current school system where learners are categorised by one identity marker, does not provide support for that learner. Furthermore, it reinforces inequality not only within the education system but also within society as a whole. Bukko and Lui (2021, p.40) suggest that work needs to begin in ITE with a focus on developing 'critical consciousness of the systems of power and privilege in educational institutions.'

Everyday policies and practice in schools often benefit more affluent and middle-class learners, to the detriment of working-class learners. Ethnic minority learners and those with an Additional Learning Need make up a large proportion of learners from disadvantaged backgrounds. It can be argued that many trainee teachers are from advantaged backgrounds and this is especially the case with post-graduate ITE students (Wakeling, 2009) thus their understanding of disadvantage needs to be reinforced through ITE pedagogy. Young (2006, p.67) argues that we need to employ an intersectional lens when exploring any educational issues related to learner identity. She suggests that aspects of identity relating to pupils in school are often 'ignored or muffled in discourses that teachers construct about those pupils'.

The current educational system in this country has been organised along Victorian colonial ideals. This system is still based on an 'industrial' archetype of education – which is all about standardisation and conformity. We need a flexible and broad educational system, which is inclusive and equitable to all and acknowledges and celebrates differences. It is imperative to highlight equity over equality as many educators still assume that treating pupils equally is the antidote, whereas an equitable classroom and being 'equity conscious' (Jackson et.al., 2019) is fundamental here. The extent to which an educator appreciates the level of equity and inequity present in a given context such as being present in behaviour, organisational / school policy or educational outcomes is paramount. It also hinges on an awareness that if they suspect inequity is occurring, they will need to become part of the solution.

There is a growing understanding of the need for education to respond practically to the increasing diversity of British society, and to the growing citizenship agenda and wider world issues. Thankfully subjects such as sociology and philosophy are being incorporated into a wider citizenship and personal and social development agenda, and this needs to continue.

The Macpherson report on the Stephen Lawrence inquiry (Macpherson 1999) recognised the disastrous consequences of a breakdown of community and intercultural relations. It clearly set out a need for schools and organisations to combat extreme forms of cultural intolerance and racism. There is often a disconnect between teachers and their increasingly culturally and linguistically diverse student population (Durden et.al., 2016). We know this is the case in Wales where teachers are less ethnically diverse than the students they are teaching, with only 1.3% of teachers in Wales identifying as being from a diverse background (EWC, 2020). This compares with 11.8% of pupils in Wales from a diverse background.

It is imperative therefore, that ITE providers have a broad understanding of the term 'inclusion' on all its many faceted levels. This needs to include actively working to promote access for intersectionally diverse trainees. We are particularly fortunate in Wales, that the Welsh Government has recently published a landmark document written by a working group led by Professor Charlotte Williams (Welsh Government, 2021). This sets out fifty-one recommendations for the teaching profession and Welsh curriculum, including mandatory anti-racism and diversity training for all trainee and acting teachers in Wales, along with the need for BAME history to be mandatory in Wales. Thus, as a small nation, we are forging ahead with change which will only add to knowledge and appreciation of others. It is pertinent, to end with the timeless words of Audre Lorde (2012) who said – 'It is not our differences that divide us. It is our inability to recognize, accept and celebrate those differences'.

KEY TAKEAWAYS

- ITE is preparing for the teachers of tomorrow – who need to understand the connection between identity and disadvantage in all its forms.
- There are fifty-one recommendations for the teaching profession on diversity and anti-racism – these should be used as a starting point.
- Early career teachers need to recognise the way in which the national and international landscape impacts on their classrooms.

KEY QUESTIONS

- What resources and strategies are needed for trainee teachers to make them more 'intersectionally' aware?
- How do we promote an intersectional agenda in schools?
- How do we make the teaching profession more diverse and celebrate the intersectionality of teaching and school staff?

COMMITMENT TO THE MANIFESTO

Make a clear commitment to decolonising education by recognising the impact of intersectional identities and starting teacher education in this field earlier in careers.

REFERENCES

Arshad, R. (2005) *Teaching and Talking about 'Race' in ITE*. Lecture, The University of Edinburgh. Available online at: https://www.ed.ac.uk/files/atoms/files/teaching_and_talking_about_race_in_ite.pdf accessed 20.03.21

Besic, E. (2020) 'Intersectionality: A pathway towards inclusive education?' *Prospects* 49, pp.111–22.

Bhopal, K. (2020) 'Confronting White privilege: the importance of intersectionality in the sociology of education.' *British Journal of Sociology of Education*, 41:6, pp.807-16.

Bukko, D. and Liu, K. (2021). 'Developing Preservice Teachers' Equity Consciousness and Equity.' Literacy. *Frontiers in Education.* Vol 6. pp. 40 -?
Available online at: https://www.frontiersin.org/article/10.3389/feduc.2021.586708 accessed 20.03.21

Durden, T., Dooley, C. M., Truscott, D. (2016). 'Race still matters: Preparing culturally relevant teachers.' *Race Ethnicity and Education*, 19, pp.1003–24.
EWC (2020) *Ethnic minority representation within the school workforce in Wales,* Phase 2 report for the Welsh Government. Online available at: https://www.ewc.wales/

Home Office (1999) *Independent report. The Stephen Lawrence Inquiry*. Report of an inquiry by Sir William Macpherson. UK Government.
https://www.gov.uk/government/publications/the-stephen-lawrence-inquiry

Jackson, W., Kelly, P. and Nieskens, H. (2019). 'Special section: equity: more than a buzzword: it's all about ensuring that students feel loved, valued, and validated.' *Principal Leadership.* 19 (7), pp.26–33.

Lorde, A. (2012) *Sister Outsider: Essays and Speeches*. Crossing Press. Feminist Series.
Wakeling, P. (2009) 'Are ethnic minorities underrepresented in UK postgraduate study?' *Higher Education quarterly*, 63 (1), pp. 86-111

Welsh Government (2021) *Black, Asian and Minority Ethnic Communities, Contributions and Cynefin in the New Curriculum Working Group*. Final Report. Available at: https://gov.wales/sites/default/files/publications/2021-03/black-asian-minority-ethnic-communities-contributions-cynefin-new-curriculum-working-group-final-report.pdf
(Accessed 24 March 2021)

Young, K. S. (2016). 'How student teachers (don't) talk about race: An intersectional analysis.' *Race Ethnicity and Education*, 19, pp.67–95.

THE IMPORTANCE OF AN INTERSECTIONAL CLASSROOM

LOTTIE COOKE

A classroom is a difficult space to navigate for all, but particularly for students with protected characteristics. It should provide focus and creativity for students to explore their love of learning. To some extent, it was for me, but dealing with a unique bigotry from others in the room made staying on task a strenuous activity. With the indoctrination of capitalist classrooms teaching me to be submissive, quiet and obedient, I allowed these issues to eat away at my self-confidence and love of education, until I found a teacher who championed me: all of me and every identity that creates the person I am.

At fourteen, I was introduced to a teacher who brought intersectionality into every lesson, without even realising she was doing it. As a business teacher, her classroom was predominantly male and at the start of the year I was one of only two girls. I was unsure of this dynamic but I have never seen it handled so well. Instead of treating us like one synonymous group, she was acutely aware that students were all different and understanding that information empowered her to treat everyone equitably as opposed to equally. One example illustrating this was her ability to recognise that us girls who, although we were both academic, struggled to find a confident voice when explaining ideas. This allowed her to gently encourage us into classroom discussions and taught us the importance of not being spoken over, which like many young women I had already experienced countless times.

Although she could have been aware of the 'confidence gap' (Giovannoni, 2018) and the need to push girls to 'take risks in every lesson', I think we can all deduce that as a woman herself, this lived experience of a different socialisation to the dominant gender would have made it very easy to carry out this targeted teaching in an effective way. Although this evidence is anecdotal, I think education as an institution needs to understand the power of having teachers who are not just female but are an amalgamation of several identities in the classroom. Not only can they empathise and provide solutions to problems but it provides vital representation. Too many adults fail to understand that representation at a young age is vital to a healthy acceptance of our identities. If you can see it, you can certainly be it.

Egalite et al. (2015) proved this through their study on the effects of student-teacher dynamics of the same race. Overall, they found that there was a small, but positive effect on black and white students with teachers of the same race in English lessons and also found that lower ability students particularly benefited in all subject areas from having teachers of the same race. This study was completed on students from the third to tenth grade in the USA, which emphasises the fact that representation must be laced into school practices, no matter the age of your pupils. Representation is proven to have worked. I can tell you countless stories about how this has impacted me positively as a woman taught by strong women but what is more significant is the fact that where I have not felt represented in other identities, I have greatly felt the effect. It is the responsibility of our government to change the wider structure of schools to ensure representation is not a groundbreaking thing; however as teachers and students there is no reason why we cannot begin this through our schools by organising representation through staff and resources. We have an understanding of what our community needs and we can provide them with vital representation whilst we continue to lobby for structural change. This does not stop at this however; we need allyship.

My teacher approached allyship well: she is one of those special people who make up the oppressor but still works to dismantle systems that hold back her students for no good reason other than the fact that they are different. I remember a moment midway through our course when a boy made a racist insult at a girl in my class. Quite rightfully, this girl exploded with anger that she had been treated this way and instead of being stopped by our teacher, she was able to express her emotions authentically to this boy. She was given a voice to process the situation, a voice to fight against the oppressor and a voice to not limit herself to being known as just another 'angry black girl'. My teacher was then able to jump in to ensure the safety of this girl's mental health and the formal sanctioning of this boy. This happened countless times when bigotry tried to poison her classroom: it made it an unlikely safe space for many students.

Without knowing it, this teacher had taken intersectionality and made it the number one value. For issues as deep as racism or homophobia or as surface level as championing students' interests, she showed up. This is what students need: You to show up. We are experiencing an epidemic of teachers who ignore bigoted behaviour and do not value the need for equitability and instead take the approach of believing students all experience the same pathway to success. My pathway has several boulders and an electric fence at the end and yet I am expected to achieve like my classmates who have a path with a red carpet laid on top; and this is coming from a white person. Let us put extra emphasis on those students who do not have a pathway at all.

This is not self-victimisation, or a process of me making excuses: this is real life. When you recognise students' differences, you are one step closer to giving them the tools to build their own pathway through life. You will watch them learn to be proud, which is one of the most beautiful things to experience.

Be the teacher who teaches your students that it is better to be hated for who they are than loved for who they are not.

Be more Miss N.

KEY TAKEAWAYS

- Embrace the identity of every student and how it affects them: positively and negatively. Acknowledgment is the first step to empowerment.
- Every student's identity is theirs: treat it that way. Their expression belongs to them, whether this manifests painfully or unequivocally. Take that pain and turn it into pride.
- Emphasise how much you respect your students. It will only build their confidence, thus changing the world.

KEY QUESTIONS

- How can you use your vulnerability as an advantage to encourage your students' confidence?
- Are you making it a priority to continuously learn about identities that do not apply to you? If not, why?
- Are you teaching like a human or like a teacher?

COMMITMENT TO THE MANIFESTO

Teach like a human being!

REFERENCES

Egalite, A. J. et al. (2015) 'Representation in the Classroom: The Effect of Own-Race Teachers on Student Achievement.' *Economics of Education Review*, vol. 45, Apr. 2015, pp. 44–52, www.sciencedirect.com/science/article/pii/S0272775715000084, 10.1016/j.econedurev.2015.01.007.

Giovanni, C. (2018). 'Now We Must Tackle Girls' 'Confidence Gap." *Tes*, 13 June 2018, www.tes.com/news/now-we-must-tackle-girls-confidence-gap.

SMASHING STEREOTYPES IN EDUCATION: THE KERPLUNK MODEL

NICOLE PONSFORD

A collective perspective is crucial in order to ensure that schools evolve for, and around, their students, our Gen Z, global citizens of the future. DEI (Diversity, Equality and Inclusion) is a deeply personal journey, which impacts on us as individuals first– and then in groups and teams. My main takeaway after twenty years of supporting inclusion is that when it comes to deconstruction of the inequalities of intersectionality and the construction of a universal social design model, we are all constantly learning from and with one another. I call this the *Kerplunk Model,* based on the 1960s cult children's game of intersecting straws and marbles.

REBEL REBEL

We live in an unequal world with privilege and power bestowed on the minority and the majority tackling a multitude of inequalities, often linked to our identity characteristics, a lack of social mobility and access to resources. The differences in privilege (and therefore power) can be extensive and many of us do not realise how privileged we are. Power structures and systems are complex, multi-layered, and rarely will one solution fix all. But – there is always room and time to disrupt, rebel, challenge, dismantle, deconstruct and smash it up in order to change it.

MY MARBLES AND STRAWS

Intersectionality has become a personal and professional obsession for me; understanding and valuing individual differences (diversity) and how we can create environments that lead to opportunities, productivity and psychological safe spaces for all (inclusion). I call it the '*Kerplunk Model*' – all the straws and marbles that make up inequalities in our 21st century, post-COVID world.

The Equality Act of 2010 for England and Wales currently supports nine characteristics legally. I see intersectionality more as twelve characteristics – nine+ socio-economic statuses (SES), single-parent rights and menopause. Many of these are not based on appearances or stereotypes alone, as my childhood taught me. As the cis-female child of a disabled parent, with a low socio-economic status, changing parent-status and housing, the inequalities were clear – but also turned on their head as I went through education – to two grammar schools and then winning a scholarship to a private school. My identity and cultural capital changed – and also my opportunities. Although thrust into a privileged position, I never lost my experiences – the 'marbles and straws' that made and defined me.

SMASHING STEREOTYPES

It was this reason that I began teaching but I soon realised that my background was different to many of my colleagues – and therefore my viewpoint and decision-making were too when it came to understanding and empathising/ biases for students who were living with inequalities echoing those that I had experienced. This was due to the stereotyping that teachers would construct around children and their lives, that they did not truly relate to.

For me, stereotyping is just bad – however you identify, for whom you are an ally, or what your intersectional lived experience is. One person does not embody all the traits and views of a marginalised group, community, viewpoint or condition. Physiology research tells us that stereotypes often stem from our brain making mental 'shortcuts' for us. Of the eleven million 'bits' of information the brain processes a second (mainly through our eyes, then skin, then ears), fifty are processed but only seven are understood. As a result of this, we often use our bias to 'shortcut' our understanding. When this happens in education, it results in limiting opportunities for students, denying career paths and mental-health issues (at best). By challenging our own bias/ thinking on this, by increasing our own experiences and understanding of those different to ourselves, we can open up opportunities instead.

THE KERPLUNK MODEL – INTERSECTIONS WITH INTERSECTIONALITY

'Intersectionality' was first coined when I was twelve by Crenshaw (1989) in *Demarginalizing the Intersection of Race and Sex: A Black Feminist Critique of Antidiscrimination Doctrine, Feminist Theory and Antiracist Politics*. It is a term that helps us separate and then overlap the inequalities and lived experiences of people. As a result, I believe that understanding intersectionality means always getting to know an individual, so that you do not have to generalise or make assumptions based on any of their characteristics or their unique lived experience.

People are beautifully complex and that there will be parts ('marbles') that you just do not know exist, until you educate yourself in what and where they are. There is systemic thinking and orders that hold them up '('straws') but we must question them in order to understand more – and look to be able to confidently challenge barriers for the most vulnerable and marginalised young people in our society.

Now, with an aerial view on education, I see how our lived experiences influence attitudes and thinking when it comes to intersectionality in the classroom. How we might 'favour' characteristics, based on our thoughts and feelings, and how we can blindside others due to a lack of interest, understanding or education.

BREAK IT DOWN

Arming people with the words to use to hold and receive a conversation is *key* to diversity and inclusion. Talking about 'acceptable terms' to describe a group is obviously a generalisation. There are always exceptions to the rule. For example, we know that there is a huge range of diversity when it comes to neurodiversity. Naming neurodiversity conditions, a 'disorder' or not understanding what 'neurotypical' means, illustrates not only creating negative implications of a person and their abilities, but also creating the 'standard' of what a person should be, and assuming how they identify themselves. If you are unsure, just respectfully ask.

COLLECTIVE THINKING

One way of understanding the 'marbles' more is through collective thinking – this comes before the action. As Matthew Syed says in *Rebel Ideas*: 'People from different backgrounds, with different experiences, often think about problems in different ways.'

In order to understand intersectionality and its impact on lived experiences, we need to actively listen and understand what it means to others – what their perspective is and how we can celebrate their diversity to make inclusion real. Recruiting diverse teams, offering flexible working lives as we balance dependents and 'life' are all part of bringing a range of perspectives, voices and ideas to the table. It might take a different approach for you, but diversity will strengthen your leadership teams, your student voice and your communities for the better – just as they are proven to improve the workplace. (I would definitely recommend a collective approach!).

I would urge you to start looking at what Kerplunk models are in your classroom, your school and through the eyes of your students. Make yourself open to the marbles and straws that intersectionality reveals to you – and reveal the ones you have yet to learn about. Then act, get #SmashingStereotypes. And if you want any help, I am here to help you smash it all up.

KEY TAKEAWAYS

- Intersectionality is complex when you break it all down, but it's also about learning and respecting others.
- Stereotypes support assuming the lived experiences of others – get #SmashingStereotypes.
- Teacher/ adult attitudes shape student/ young people's experiences – we have to be open to change for the next generation and for one another.

KEY QUESTIONS

- How have you measured adult attitudes to Intersectionality and DEI in your setting?
- How far do you think adult attitudes to intersectionality impact young people?
- How far do you think adult attitudes to intersectionality impact on the work and life of the adult stakeholders of your setting?

COMMITMENT TO THE MANIFESTO

Consider how #SmashingStereotypes and intersectionality benefits everyone in your setting and get #SmashingStereotypes today.

REFERENCES

Physiology. Britannica. Available at: https://www.britannica.com/science/information-theory/Physiology (Accessed January 2019)

Crenshaw, K. (1989) 'Demarginalizing the Intersection of Race and Sex: A Black Feminist Critique of Antidiscrimination Doctrine, Feminist Theory and Antiracist Politics.' *The University of Chicago Forum*. Available at: https://chicagounbound.uchicago.edu/cgi/viewcontent.cgi?article=1052&context=uclf (Accessed March 2021)

The Equality Act 2010. Available at: https://www.legislation.gov.uk/ukpga/2010/15/contents

Syed, M. (2019) *'Rebel Ideas: The Power of Diverse Thinking'*, John Murray.

Reynolds, A. and Lewis, D. (2017) 'Teams Solve Problems Faster When They're More Cognitively Diverse.' *Harvard Business Review*, 30 March 2017. Available at https://hbr.org/2017/03/teams-solve-problems-faster-when-theyre-more-cognitively-diverse (Accessed March 2020).

HOW DO I GET A MONTH, MISS?

KIRAN MAHIL

Teachers utter thousands of words a day. That some are remembered means they mattered. A conversation with a student has stayed with me. It went something like this:

> *Amin**: Miss, how do I get a month?
> *Ms Mahil:* What do you mean by that? Can you explain a little further?
> *Amin:* A history month, how do I get one? There's Black History Month, LGBT+ History Month, Women's History Month. What about my history?
> *Ms Mahil:* Oh, I see. Well history months are there to reveal histories that often remain hidden. To include groups and communities that aren't usually present in our study of the past.
> *Amin:* I know Miss. I know what history months are about. I was in your assembly.
> *Ms Mahil:* Ok. Great. You understand.
> *Amin:* Not really. It's not as though we learn much about people like me who lived in the past. We don't even get taught about how my community is part of British history. Isn't that history hidden? Aren't I part of an 'oppressed group?' I want a month.

> *student name has been changed

History Months are a fixture in many schools. They are marked with events, workshops, special assemblies; all with the aim of enriching and enlightening students about those that have come before. Black History Month (BHM) is the longest-standing of them all. It has been celebrated every October since 1987. It is officially recognised by the British Government, it remembers and champions the history and achievements of the African diaspora, and educates and informs on black heritage and culture in Britain (Lochun, , 2020). A deeper reflection about that conversation with my student reveals something more powerful about their potential – to foster belonging and inclusion. For Amin, and for all humankind, there is an inherent desire to belong and be an important part of something greater than our individual selves. Can or should History Months alone be the vehicle to achieve this? How far is the history curriculum in schools designed to enable students to grapple with the complexities of the past? Who is present in the latest version of 'our nation's story'?

Using an intersectional lens for designing history curricula could make for a more inclusive account of the past. Intersectionality, coined by law professor Kimberlé Crenshaw, helps to explore where power comes from and how it collides with multiple parts of a person's social and political identity. Gender, class, race, sex, religion and sexuality are some of the multiple aspects of advantage and disadvantage. Kehinde (2021) explains that 'thinking intersectionality means recognising that there is no way to fundamentally understand society without appreciating the interlocking oppressions that shape inequality.' This sociological term has common ground with history due to the concept of power. 'History is written by the victors,' a quote often attributed to Winston Churchill, reveals the power dynamics at play in history formation. Palestinian poet Mourid Barghouti comes from a different perspective but reaches the same conclusion when he explains that if you want to dispossess a people, the simplest way is to tell their story but to start with 'secondly':

Start your story with 'Secondly' and the world will be turned upside-down. Start your story with 'Secondly,' and the arrows of the Red Indians are the original criminals and the guns of the white men are entirely the victims...Start with 'Secondly,' and Gandhi becomes responsible for the tragedies of the British.

Those who possess power tell the tale. If students are to explore the full version of the past, we must ensure the substance of what we teach is complete. Not skewed in the interest of the few hoarders of power.

An intersectional lens would also design curricula that remains true to history as a discipline. Leading curriculum thinker Christine Counsell describes disciplinary knowledge as what students 'learn about how that knowledge was established, its degree of certainty and how it continues to be revised by scholars' (Counsell, 2018). In the classroom, that means teaching students *how* to do history as well as *what* to know about the past.

History as a discipline is built on the twin pillars of interpretations (narratives about the past) and evidence (material from the past). Chimamanda Ngozi Adichie (2009) warns about the danger of a single story in her TED talk of the same name. She argues that 'the single story creates stereotypes, and the problem with stereotypes is not that they are untrue, but that they are incomplete. They make one story become the only story.'

Students are denied ever becoming historians themselves if they do not explore interpretations of the past in our classrooms. An intersectional lens to history curricula would bring to the surface different perspectives and guard against the single-story approach. Adichie explains that 'Many stories matter. Stories have been used to dispossess and to malign, but stories can also be used to empower and to humanize. Stories can break the dignity of a people, but stories can also repair that broken dignity.'

Adding marginalised voices to material used in the history classroom will make for a more inclusive and interesting history curriculum. Kimberlé Crenshaw, in her conversation with Jude Kelly during WOW Festival UK 2021, reminded us about the importance of diverse evidence. Crenshaw recalled a time when she was in class with a well-known civil rights leader. He was trying to get students to understand the incredible burden of slavery.

The example he gave: 'Imagine, you are an enslaved man and you are unable to protect your wife/daughter/sister from the sexual aggression of your owner. Just imagine how horrific that experience would be.'

I raised my hand and said, "I certainly can imagine how horrific it is not to be able to protect your loved ones. But I can't imagine it's worse than not being able to protect yourself.' This is the story of the enslaved women. It's told through the lens of their men not being able to protect them. To make that legible, we had to put a male subject in it. We couldn't just tell the story of being that woman or girl.

My survey of local history teachers suggests that while many don't feel confident using the term 'intersectionality', their curriculum intent very much aligns with the impact of an intersectional approach. They wanted to know more about how they could question and adapt their schemes of work. My advice is that it is best to do this together as a professional community and to find ways of broadening the narrative, rather than inadvertently creating a new single story.

There is growing interest in teaching more inclusive history but it is still left to a minority of educators, resulting in piecemeal change. To mainstream a history education that reveals the big story of the past, it will take history teachers working together – across school, phase, geographic and identity barriers – so scholarly connection and camaraderie can be built. As bell hooks (1994) wisely wrote, 'If we really want to create a cultural climate where biases can be challenged and changed, all border crossings must be seen as valid and legitimate.' Crucially, we must seek to refine not reduce the substance and discipline of history. As Sathnam Sanghera (2021) advises, 'Tearing down things also provokes counter-campaigns, and more would be achieved by campaigns to *create* and *build*.'

Professor David Olusoga (2020) commented that Black History Month 2020 'was infused with the spirit of that remarkable year. One in which millions of people engaged with ideas of race and racism as never before. A year in which books on race and black British history featured in the bestseller list and the idea of 'anti-racism' has caught the imagination of young people.'

This mood is emboldening some to revise what is being taught. Integrating hidden histories into the curriculum, instead of simply using History Months to carry this load is an effective way of evolving from a moment to a movement. A movement that stays true to history as a discipline but one where we are all cast as characters in our nation's story.

Amin and his generation shouldn't have to wait for as long as I did to feel fully included in the history classroom. That happened only recently. On returning from maternity leave, a colleague had devised a sequence of lessons about the partition of India. This was my story. The story of my family. My home history. A part of British history. Being validated in school history for the first time. Then I truly belonged.

KEY TAKEAWAYS

- What we know is a part of who we are. The school curriculum has a powerful role in shaping the society we live in today.
- Curriculum design is an iterative process, best done in collaboration with others.
- Teachers need to be familiar with the way the impact of intersectionality is present in the curriculum.

KEY QUESTIONS

- How far are marginalised ideas and voices part of the mainstream curriculum in your school?
- What value is placed on subject knowledge? What does that look like in relation to what teachers are encouraged to read, research and reflect upon?
- What current models of the history curriculum allow for the greatest exploration of intersectional histories?

COMMITMENT TO THE MANIFESTO

The history curriculum should be constructed to explore not just single-identity events, but instead seek to explore the multiple effects on those with intersectional identities.

REFERENCES

Adichie, C. (2009) 'The Danger of a Single Story.' *TED Talk* [Online]. Available at: https://www.ted.com/talks/chimamanda_ngozi_adichie_the_danger_of_a_single_story?language=en [Accessed March 2021]

Andrews, K. (2021) *The New Age of Empire: How Racism and Colonialism Still Rule the World.* London: Allen Lane.

Counsell, C. (2018) 'Taking Curriculum Seriously.' *Impact: Journal of the Chartered College of Teaching.* September [Online] Available at: https://impact.chartered.college/article/taking-curriculum-seriously/ [Accessed March 2021]

Crenshaw, K (2021) In Conversation: *WOW UK Festival,* 12 March 2021

hooks, b (1994) *Teaching to Trangress: Education as the Practice of Freedom.* New York: Routledge

Lochun, K. (2020) 'Black History Month: what is it, historians on its relevance.' *BBC History Extra*, 7 Oct [Online]. Available at: https://www.historyextra.com/period/20th-century/black-history-month-uk-history-when-launched-why-october/ [Accessed March 2021]

Olusoga, D. (2020) 'Black History Month is now an established part of the year. Let's celebrate its success.' *The Guardian*, 4 Oct [Online]. Available at: https://www.theguardian.com/commentisfree/2020/oct/04/black-history-month-is-now-an-established-part-of-the-year-lets-celebrate-its-success [Accessed March 2021]

Sanghera, S. (2021) *How Imperialism Has Shaped Modern Britain*. London: Penguin Random House

INTERSECTIONAL CITIZENSHIP

LEE JEROME

INTRODUCTION

For those of us who live in a democratic society it is too easy to take it for granted. We assume we should always have access to the information we want, that we should be able to voice our opinion when we want, that we should pursue a career and pastimes according to our own interests, befriend and love the people we choose, pursue the religious life (or none) we believe in, and be helped when necessary to overcome obstacles. Whilst we might recognise that these are imperfectly realised in our own society, we must also recognise that this list is a distant dream for many people around the world and that for most people in history it was probably too much to dream. Democracy holds out the promise that we can live together in a free society with millions of other people whilst we all pursue our own paths to happiness and fulfilment. Once it is lost, all those aspirations will perish too. Only within a democracy can we find ways to sustain and develop those freedoms. Educating people for democratic citizenship should therefore be seen as a fundamental purpose of schools and an intensely pragmatic project of mutual interest.

Democratic citizenship should not simply be celebrated or revered as an accomplishment (not simply seen as part of the 'best that has been thought and said' as the national curriculum describes it (DfE, 2014, section 3.1)), it must also be subjected to critique and improved through struggle. Paulo Freire (1998) noted that discrimination on the grounds of race, sex and class (and we might continue the list now with other characteristics) can be seen as a denial of one's full rights to citizenship. The fact that such discrimination can be experienced singly or in combination indicates that an intersectional approach is required to understand individuals' experiences of citizenship. This section considers the implications of an intersectional approach to citizenship education through a discussion of citizenship as status, feeling and practice (Osler and Starkey, 2005).

CITIZENSHIP AS STATUS

People who want their rights need democracy, and democracy also requires citizens – the people who form the democratic society, who contribute to the continuation of that democracy, and who reap the possible rewards of living in a democratic society. If citizens are essential to understanding how democracy works, it is therefore important that we recognise that citizenship is not achieved by chance, it has to be both learned and fought for. At a basic level it seems prudent to help young people learn about the roles, rights and duties associated with citizenship and to teach them about the processes through which citizenship is expressed. As educators we also have a role in introducing young people to the big ideas that underpin citizenship, such as the ways to balance rights in specific situations, the relationship between freedom and social order, the bonds between the individual and community and the nature of power and accountability (AGC, 1998).

But there is a danger if teachers promote the institutions, roles and processes of democracy in the form of 'textbook' knowledge as this often entails producing abstract and rather idealised descriptions without recognising that people's experiences of politics and citizenship are different. A citizenship teacher, informed by an awareness of how citizenship is differentiated in practice by people's intersectional positionality in society, should be alert to how these formal accounts fall short, how informal processes may cut across those textbook versions of government, and how citizens work to change the status quo. Citizens need to be prepared to assume their full status as citizens and help to understand how to change the institutions that define citizenship and overcome barriers to people's experience of citizenship rights.

CITIZENSHIP AS FEELING

This implies that somehow the individual citizens in a society will recognise their shared status as a common bond, some form of shared identity. James A. Banks (2017) has argued that any group (migrant or not) which has either been excluded by the state, or developed 'highly ambivalent' feelings towards it, is in danger of 'failed citizenship' (p.2). Those who fall into this category may undertake forms of resistance or opposition which threaten the survival of a democratic society, rather than seek to sustain or improve it. It is in the interests of the state then, to nurture some form of positive shared identity around citizenship. But it is equally important that this aspect of identity is not presented or experienced as being in tension with other dimensions of one's intersectional identity.

Education policy relating to the fundamental British values has been handled in some schools in a way that creates tension or reinforces feelings among minoritized students of being judged or marginalised (Busher and Jerome, 2020). Research with young people has shown that they are perfectly capable of developing nested or hybrid identities that incorporate British citizenship with intensely experienced local, global, religious and cultural identities (Hoque, 2015). A common commitment to citizenship in a plural democracy will not result from the promotion of a simplistic and unified model of 'British citizenship,' rather young people need to engage with people from diverse backgrounds who feel and experience citizenship in different ways. Teachers can create a space to reflect on what citizenship means for the young people with whom they work, and to contribute to new forms of British citizenship. But this is difficult both because of our contemporary political context, in which Brexit has breathed fresh life into a kind of 'post-imperial melancholia' (Gilroy 2004), and it is difficult for personal reasons, because teachers have to find ways to become reflexively aware of their own positionality and their own default assumptions about citizenship and identity (Peace, 2005).

CITIZENSHIP AS PROCESS

Whilst the first two dimensions inevitably encourage us to think about insiders and outsiders (we feel affinity with some but probably not all; we are citizens but others are not) a focus on process is really about our capacity to undertake political acts alone and (more importantly) with others. Democracy does not really work unless citizens act, both within the system as 'participatory' citizens (for example through voting and lobbying) and upon the system as 'transformative' citizens (through protest and demands for reform) (Banks, 2017).

In a climate where teachers may feel pressure to avoid some of these more confrontational/ oppositional forms of citizen action (McIntosh, 2020), it is also important to recognise that the Black Lives Matters movement and the School Strike for Climate movement have been largely led by young people. It is not a teacher's job to promote one form of action over another, but it is important to consider the variety of actions undertaken by citizens, the reasons forwarded by those actors, and the debates about whether they are justifiable (ethically and pragmatically). Teaching about these acts opens up debates about what it means to be a citizen, and how to relate to other citizens, for example Sam Little, one of the organisers of the Bristol BLM events in 2020 said:

> I know I have to use my privilege and my voice as a white male to stand up to the oppressors and fight for change. Being part of the LGBTQIA+ community – and considering it was transgender women of colour [Marsha P. Johnson] who fought for the rights of the community – I believe it is my duty to pay that back.
> (Devaney, 2020)

In this tiny fragment of his story, teachers can engage with his intersectional identity as a gay, white, young male citizen; as well as his historically and internationally informed commitment to coalition building and allyship; and the understanding that citizenship is a struggle. It also resonates with Freire's suggestion that many progressive social movements are actually struggling for a more complete democratic experience of citizenship.

KEY TAKEAWAYS

- Democracy requires effective citizens, but citizenship is experienced differently by people reflecting their intersectional positionalities. Citizenship education needs to reflect this real-life diversity or it will be seen as inauthentic.
- To avoid 'failed citizenship' schools should nurture young people into a diverse range of contemporary citizenship identities.
- Teachers can help young people find ways to feel and perform citizenship that make sense for them, their struggles and experiences.

KEY QUESTIONS

- Does your curriculum introduce students to the knowledge and understanding required to understand the relationships between diverse citizens, and between citizens and the state?
- How have you ensured students in your school do not experience the 'fundamental British values' as exclusionary and are supported to build diverse citizenship identities?
- Does your curriculum help students to learn about the wide array of forms of political action and to prepare for active citizenship?

COMMITMENT TO THE MANIFESTO

Education should equip young people with the understanding and agency to become effective citizens, but should not over-determine what that citizenship looks or feels like.

REFERENCES

Advisory Group on Citizenship (AGC) (1998) *Education for citizenship and the teaching of democracy in schools.* London: Qualifications and Curriculum Authority.

Banks, J. A. (2017) Failed citizenship and transformative civic education, *Educational Researcher,* 46 (7), 1-12.

Busher, J. and Jerome, L. (Eds.) (2020) *The Prevent Duty in Education.* Chans, Switzerland: Palgrave Macmillan.

Department for Education (DfE) (2014) *National Curriculum in England: framework for key stages 1-4.* London: DfE.

Devaney, S. (2020) 'These 5 young people organised Bristol's Black Lives Matters protest and they're only just getting started.' *Vogue* (11th June) https://www.vogue.co.uk/arts-and-lifestyle/article/organisers-bristol-black-lives-matter-protest

Freire, P. (1998) *Teachers as cultural workers: Letters to those who teach.* Boulder, Colorado: Westview Press.

Gilroy, P. (2004) *After Empire: Melancholia or convivial culture?* Abingdon: Routledge.

Hoque, A. (2015) *British-Islamic Identity: Third generation Bangladeshis from East London.* University of London: Institute of Education Press.

McIntosh, I. (2020) 'Black Tory MP's attack comments on critical race theory are dangerously regressive.' *The Voice* (24th October) https://www.voice-online.co.uk/opinion/2020/10/24/black-tory-mps-attack-comments-on-critical-race-theory-are-dangerously-regressive/

Osler, A. and Starkey, H. (2005) *Changing citizenship: Democracy and inclusion in education.* Maidenhead: Open University Press.

Pearce, S. (2005) *You wouldn't understand: White teachers in multiethnic classrooms.* Stoke on Trent: Trentham Books.

TEACHING AT THE CROSSROADS: CREATING CONNECTIONS NOT WALLS

JAMES CLARKE

INTRODUCTION

Over the next few pages I will challenge preconceptions that suggest our individuality, which makes us 'different' to those around us, should be seen as any form of barrier or wall to success. Declaring intersectionality should be celebrated, discussed and explored creatively through methods such as storytelling, I will guide you through my personal experiences from starting out in education, to my practice within the classroom using a recent project in collaboration with my school and the NHS. Finally, I hand over to you and set you the challenge to explore my key takeaways and questions and begin your journey of creating connections not walls within your own setting.

White, tall, glasses and a ginger beard; that is what people see when they first encounter me standing at the front of the classroom. I have become increasingly aware that our visual identity and the way we present ourselves can have profound effects on how those around us perceive and subsequently treat us. Since the beginning of my career, I have been criticised for being 'ambitious' for my approach to advancing and enriching the educational opportunities of my students. I have been repeatedly informed by those around me that this 'energy' within my teaching is because I am 'young and youthful'. No one assumes that I am doing what I do because my own experiences at school were negative or cut short due to a period of external exclusion and I want no one else to go through that. My incorrect spelling says that I am 'uneducated and not qualified to teach at A-level, as only the strongest teachers should teach at this level" as I was once told within my first year. That is until I disclose my dyslexia. Or that my 'choice' to be open about my sexuality, have a pride flag in my classroom and champion LGBTQIA+ rights, is as I was told in a whole staff briefing, me 'putting the gay agenda in their face'. My identity, my community and my values, leave me feeling like I am constantly teaching at the crossroads. It has at times made me feel detached from the education system, like an outsider who does not belong because of my identities and intersectionality, seemingly not aligning to that path of 'what a teacher should/is expected to be.'

Drawing upon my experiences of teaching Drama and PSHE, I want to explore 'what intersectionality does, rather than what it is' (Cho et al. in Hill Collins and Bilge, 2020) and suggest how we might make this transition in thinking. I propose that understanding our differences, exploring our intersectionalities within the classroom and practically performing them will help to create connections not walls. While our lived experiences are unique to us, they can in turn become a defense mechanism we use unconsciously at times, to protect oneself and block out those around us. It is, I believe, easier to find faults in people around us rather than connections. I examine the concept of border crossing in relation to the reading of the term proposed by Tim Prentki (2021) to conceptually frame my critical reflection.

In *The Applied Theatre Reader, 2nd Edition,* (2021), Tim Prentki offers insights into the concept of border crossing, a term useful to understand what I mean by teaching at the crossroads of identity constructs. Prenkti makes an interesting point which can be linked to this idea of exploring intersectionalities in the classroom. Prentki urges practitioners to 'assist participants in distinguishing between those borders which have been created by the external world so that they can be controlled or oppressed (to use Freire's term) and those which they have put around themselves out of fear, selflessness or lack of imagination.' (Prentki and Abraham, 2021: 221).

To understand the borders we put up and those that are constructed around us by others and how they can oppress our identities, we need to engage in reflective practice to locate, examine and learn from the impact of our lived experiences and bespoke narratives of self that may cause walls to form, and connections to falter.

UNDERSTANDING INTERSECTIONALITY: A PERSONAL JOURNEY

Understanding and locating intersectionality within our own identities is complex. I will not profess to offer a fully comprehensive examination of my own position (this is beyond the remit of this chapter) however I will pinpoint vignettes of experiences to offer insights into my own navigation of border crossings and how this has informed my pedagogy as a Drama teacher.

It all started when I was diagnosed with dyslexia whilst at university. Suddenly everything started to make sense to me. I could understand why I never made it to the top set blue group for English in year 6 and had to stay in the lower set red group or why I was one of the last students in my class to move beyond 'Biff and Chip' books in primary school whilst everyone else read 'adult books' like the Goosebumps series by R.L. Stine. Even at a young age, you notice your differences and the first identity borders begin to form and I know that it was these experiences that led to my own lack of confidence in English and writing as an example. When I started teaching I felt I was not as good as my peers because I could not grasp the 'academic' way of speaking or writing. My learning disability began to feel like it was a part of me that would always impinge on my chances of success. The expectation that as an educator you must write or speak in a certain way are the oppressive borders that Prentki mentions, created by both myself and society.

Reflecting on my personal experience and insecurities, upon entering teaching, I began to find that I was not alone in these feelings. 60% of students in my school are classed as having EAL (English as an additional language). Many students struggle to access the English language in a written and/or verbal way and how do these students respond? Some remain silent, others will cause disruptions as a way to communicate their frustration and others will work their hardest to try and be at the same level (or better) as those around them. Drawing upon my own challenges to accessing elements of learning, through my dyslexia, I personally felt able to empathise with their experiences and find myself meeting these students at the same 'crossroads' I'd encountered at school. This was my first experience of intersectionality in my professional teaching practice. In this case, my 'path' as someone with a learning disability and my students' 'path' as someone from a different nationality provided a meeting point at the crossroads of different identity traits through the connection of the shared experience of exclusion, frustration with learning and drive to succeed.

Our ability to show compassion, empathy and understanding is perhaps one of our greatest assets as educators, yet it is also these skills that we do not always actively seek to teach our students. Instead, our curriculum and learning are focused on an exam-based model, where an hour in a room and the ability to be able to transfer knowledge in writing to a piece of paper is the only measure of value, all that really counts. In this very approach, we create walls, which for some students are impossible to climb. Only through understanding why these walls exist within our own students and indeed ourselves can we really ensure that our students not only learn these skills but also feel empowered in their future selves to excel and overcome barriers to educational access and achieve their potential. A notable example of this theory and notion of education empowering and not disenfranchising students, can be explored further in Paulo Freire's (Brazilian educator) volume, *Pedagogy of the Oppressed* (1970).

HOSPITAL IN THE CLASSROOM (NHS CASE STUDY)

Within my own classroom and subject areas of Drama and PSHE (Personal, Social, Health, Education), I actively seek out opportunities where students can explore the intersectional connection between their own identity and that of others, who seemingly on the outside may initially look very different from their own. You first though must gain that 'buy-in', something which starts that process of taking down any initial walls that society or oneself have put up. It is through one of the oldest forms of Drama, storytelling, that many of us find a crossroads of understanding. Storytelling is universal and something all of us understand and know, an international concept which has been around for thousands of years.

A recent example can be explored through a drama project undertaken by my year 9 Drama students and patients on a medicine for the elderly ward in Imperial College Healthcare NHS Trust's Charing Cross Hospital with the specialist support of the Dementia Care Team. In collaboration with the Student Knowledge Exchange Project Team, associated staff and students from the Royal Central School of Speech and Drama and the Dementia Care Team, students engaged in a nine-week programme which saw them interact with those eighty years older than themselves. The full project title was *Innovating Knowledge Exchange: Student Involvement in Delivering Better Patient Experience in the NHS (funded by Research England and the Office for Students).*

At the heart of this project was storytelling. Every conversation that occurred always centred around the sharing and re-creating of stories. Through active listening to each other's past and current experiences, a unique and special relationship was able to be formed, one which resulted in everyone finding commonalities with each other. In other words, meeting at a crossroads. However, at the start of the project, I distinctly remembered a student coming up to me and almost being tearful at the thought of seeing an 'old person in hospital.' While we all accept that ageing is something everyone of us will experience, I found it interesting that having to physically see this made some students feel uncomfortable. At first, my initial thought was simply that it was the live link to the hospital that made students feel this way. As the project progressed however, I found out that this was not the case. In actuality, it was more linked to the idea that students felt sadness and empathy towards the patients on the screen because it reminded them of their own family.

Despite a national lockdown and learning being moved online, I became interested to see that students still continued to fully engage with this project. In actual fact, I learnt that for many, it became more about who the project was for, rather than what it was about. Exposure to others, who on the outside may have physically different attributes and belong to different communities than themselves, gave me an insight into how projects like this could be a gateway into exploring how as educators we can create connections as supposed to walls and expose students to opportunities which actively encourage them to work with opposing/different identities to their own. It occurs to me that these identities needed to meet, in order for us all to fully understand how someone who is ninety-three and is living with dementia on a hospital ward, can share similar experiences and understanding with a fourteen-year-old Iranian boy from North London.

FINAL THOUGHTS

Right from the moment we are born, we are encouraged to explore the world around us, be creative and question everything we see. As we get older, it becomes apparent that this 'luxury' is taken away from us. Instead of being able to question, be creative and explore, we are told to sit, take in information from a book and accept what we see. As educators we must champion a child to never stop questioning or exploring. We must offer and create opportunities for students' views and thoughts to be challenged. In essence, we must do this within our pedagogy to break down those barriers that stand in the way of our students building connections with those around them, by enhancing understanding and exploring our intersectionalities with those around us, which allows us to find shared experiences/understanding. We ultimately help to create a future that is filled with young people who will go out in the world, make positive changes and differences because they find what makes them similar to those around them as opposed to what makes them different.

KEY TAKEAWAYS

- We need to be exposed to opposing views and/or identities then our own to be able to fully explore our intersectionalities and not just our differences.
- Through creative methods and other dramatic techniques, we create an environment in which connections can be formed.
- Sharing stories is one of our oldest traditions in history, yet it is still one of the most powerful.

KEY QUESTIONS

- How will you offer opportunities within your classroom and/or practice, to allow students the chance to interact with others outside of their own community?
- What makes you a teacher, teaching at the crossroads?
- How can you promote border-crossing pedagogy within your practice and share this approach with your colleagues?

COMMITMENT TO THE MANIFESTO

Create opportunities outside the classroom, for all students, to learn about others, the world in which we live and share stories with those who they may not normally.

REFERENCES

Freire, P. (1970) *Pedagogy of the Oppressed*. New York: Herder and Herder.

Hill Collins, P. and Bilge, S. (2020). *Intersectionality*. 2nd ed. Cambridge: Polity Press.

Prentki, T. and Abraham, N. (2021) *The Applied Theatre Reader*. 2nd ed. Oxon: Routledge.

WHEN KINGDOMS COLLIDE – MOVING TOWARDS A DEEPER UNDERSTANDING OF LGBT+ PEOPLE OF FAITH IN A SCHOOL CONTEXT WITH PARTICULAR REFERENCE TO EVANGELICAL CHRISTIANS

RICH ATTERTON

On 2nd February 2021 Pete Buttigieg became the first openly gay US cabinet member. Mayor Pete is now the most high-profile LGBT+ person of faith in the US but for many, the idea of being LGBT+ and a person of faith can appear mutually exclusive. It is not unknown for LGBT+ people of faith to find a lack of acceptance in the LGBT+ community because of the prejudice and discrimination LGBT+ people have suffered at the hands of people of faith. It is also quite common for LGBT+ people to find a lack of acceptance among people of faith. *Vox Magazine's* Guthrie Graves-Fitzsimmons states: 'LGBTQ people of faith are often erased from our public discourse that portrays LGBTQ rights as mutually exclusive from religious belief. Buttigieg campaigning with his husband, Chasten by his side, and quoting the Bible at every turn, busted that narrative wide-open.'

Mayor Pete is a member of the Episcopal Church, a gay-affirming and inclusive denomination. To help understand the evangelical world it would be useful to listen to the continuum of feeling towards him from that world. At one end you have Bert Farias describing Pete as an abomination and his candidacy the 'death rattle of a nation' and at the other Jim Wallis welcoming him with open arms as one of a small but growing number of evangelicals who have embraced LGBT + people and are openly accepting of gay marriage. There will of course be a host of nuanced versions of both ends of the spectrum as well as the more traditional response, 'Pete is beloved of God and welcome in our churches but he has missed the mark regarding his understanding of LGBT+ issues.' David Bennett's book *War of Loves: The Unexpected Story of a Gay Activist* treats the issue with pastoral care but ultimately concludes that to honour God, you must remain celibate because same-sex relationships are sinful.

CONFLICT AND CONSENSUS

We are perhaps more used to stories of the LGBT+ culture wars from the US, be it a gay student expelled from a Christian school or student suspended for wearing rainbow jumper but there are more and more stories suggesting the culture wars are coming to UK schools and they are seemingly being driven by the perceived conflict between faith and LGBT+ rights. We now periodically see stories like 'Christian parent sues school for pride parade.' Or the more complicated dismissal case of Kristie Higgs, who claimed she was fired for her religious views on LGBT issues. Some evangelicals have recognised the need for dialogue, sometimes born out of pain and tragedy or through the courage of evangelicals like Steve Chalke, championing inclusive churches and schools through the Oasis Trust. Others however see the 'LGBT agenda' as a clear and present danger to children, subverting their right to challenge ungodly teaching.

Educate and Celebrate's report 'Becoming LGBT+ friendly in schools serving faith communities', described some useful interactions that reveal part of this conflict. One area of concern is related to faith and parents' fear that 'being gay' is a sin against the tenets of their religion. One student said in the focus group that a Christian could not be gay because they would 'go to hell'. The report also recounts the conversation with a parent at the school gate, 'It's against my religion. I believe that homosexuality is a sin. That's how I bring my son up, I don't want him being told any different.' The teacher explained 'He has to be told different, because it's part of our inclusion policy.' Another states, 'I'm not happy about my son hearing that because we don't think that that's a normal way to live.'

The report did find some common ground and concluded that everyone could 'agree that no religion condones bullying, and students of all ages became adept at talking through the issues, often independently arriving at the idea that the idea of a higher power and/or a creator could legitimately result in the existence of LGBT+ people.'

Paul Johnson and Silvia Falcetta expertly navigate the most common faith-based objections to LGBT+ inclusion in the Relationships Education guidance in primary school, helping provide a supportive and constructive way of dealing with the kinds of scenarios raised in the C and E report. In the broader context of faith and LGBT+ inclusion, the Equalities Act is your friend, Ofsted is your friend and Government guidance is your friend.

UNDERSTANDING MINDSET

For many LGBT+ people of faith there is likely to be some level of internal conflict but for evangelicals this is particularly intensified. The Bible is their moral guide or makers' manual, and unlike the fundamentalist who takes the Bible literally, evangelicals will all take it seriously. Teen evangelicals will have likely been brought up in a close-knit environment where a sense of belonging is an essential part of the evangelical experience. If you combine the potential loss of belonging with the idea you are turning their back on God, it is of no surprise that attempts to reconcile those two things can often lead to all manner of attempts at conversion therapy. Mel White in *Stranger at the Gate*, takes the reader on his journey starting with the eleven-year-old kid praying every night to not be gay anymore, through to his later years where he underwent exorcism, psychotherapy and electroshock treatment. Nothing changed. Exodus International, an evangelical umbrella organisation that supported gay conversion groups, closed its doors in 2013, with then President Alan Chambers apologising for the pain and harm caused by conversion therapy. One of its co-founders Michael Bussee was clear that in 40 years of their ministry he had never met a gay person who became straight. For many this might seem a vindication of common sense but for the evangelical desperate to not be gay it is another door for change closed to them.

They may make constant comparisons to others who have a 'normal life', have concerns about loneliness and an overwhelming fear of rejection. LGBT+ students of faith might actually find the increased level of acceptance of LGBT+ folk uncomfortable or triggering. It might not be unusual for them to react in a more hostile way when LGBT+ issues are being presented in a positive light in school, or might just be the lifeline they need.

CONVERSATIONS

So what do you do if you encounter people conflicted about their faith and sexuality or gender identity and want to talk?

1. Treat them in the same kind and compassionate way you would with anyone but remember that the conversation needs to be particularly nuanced.
2. Do not dismiss their faith because we live in more 'enlightened times.' Suggestions like 'If your faith is causing you so much bother and anguish, then get rid' are offensive and unhelpful.
3. Recognise that your advice has the potential for having life-changing consequences. Your advice might liberate a young person or it might get them sent away to stay with relatives so do not dive in.
4. You do not need to go toe-to-toe with them on the scripture. President Barlett's exegesis of Leviticus worked in *The West Wing*, but your knowledge or lack of might hinder the conversation. Asking questions is really useful here. Questions like 'Does everyone believe that about that Bible verse or belief?' is useful. Focusing on the unconditional love of God is a great starting place, whether you believe in it or not, and can be tremendously comforting.
5. You need to recognise the power and pull that religious communities might have. Advice like 'There are always other churches' although true, is initially very unhelpful.
6. Be ready to signpost; the power of your kindness will only take you so far. Stonewall has a good general page and whilst not exhaustive it does cover all the religious bases. Signposting Oasis and Steve Chalke is particularly

useful because he speaks the language of evangelicals although some no longer recognise him as one.

KEY TAKEAWAYS

- There are many conflicts between faith and sexuality, but they can be addressed.
- Use sources of support such as Stonewall to help in the journey
- Do not feel the need to 'battle' using scripture with those who disagree with your identity.

KEY QUESTIONS:

- How can I ensure I do not present LGBT+ and faith as fundamentally at odds?
- Do I understand the pastoral implications for LGBT+ people of faith?
- How can I make my classroom or lessons as inclusive as possible?

COMMITMENT TO THE MANIFESTO

Recognise the unique position of LGBT+ people working and studying in faith-based schools, particularly if they ascribe to a faith, and create conditions in which dialogue is possible.

REFERENCES

Attitude Magazine, (2020), 'Christian School Attempts To Defend Expelling Student For Being Gay'. Available at: https://www.attitude.co.uk/article/exclusive-christian-school-attempts-to-defend-expelling-student-for-being-gay/23888/ [accessed October 2020]

Baker-Jordan, S. (2020), 'Opinion: As a Gay Christian, I'm so glad to see Pete Buttigieg reclaiming religion from the far right.' *The Independent*, 15 January 2020. Available at: https://www.independent.co.uk/voices/pete-buttigieg-gay-religion-christian-democratic-debate-2020-election-a9285516.html [accessed May 2020]

Beeching, V. (2019) *Undivided: Coming Out, Becoming Whole, and Living*. William Collins.

Carlile, A. (2018) 'Becoming LGBT+ Friendly in Schools Serving Faith Communities'. Available at: https://www.educateandcelebrate.org/wp-content/uploads/2019/01/EC_Faith_Schools_Report_FINAL-.pdf, p31-3

Educate and Celebrate (2019), *Becoming LGBT+ Friendly in Schools Serving Faith Communities*. Available at: https://www.educateandcelebrate.org/wp-content/uploads/2019/01/EC_Faith_Schools_Report_FINAL-.pdf

Hodge, M. (2020), 'Girl, 15 expelled from Christian school for wearing a Gay Pride Sweater.' *The Sun*, 15 January 2020. Available at: https://www.thesun.co.uk/news/10742905/grl-15-is-expelled-from-christian-school-for-wearing-gay-pride-sweater-and-posing-with-rainbow-birthday-cake/ [accessed May 2020]

Johnson, P. and Falcetta, S., *The Inclusion of Sexual Orientation and Gender Identity in Relationships Education: Faith-Based Objections and the European Convention on Human Rights* (October 28, 2020). Available at SSRN: https://ssrn.com/abstract=3721490

Knight, L. (2019) 'Being a Gay Christian can be hurtful and gruelling but I refuse to lose faith.' *The Guardian*, 21st March 2019. Available at: https://www.theguardian.com/commentisfree/2019/mar/21/gay-christian-church-lgbt [accessed May 2020]

White, M. (1995), *Stranger at the Gate – To be Gay and Christian in America*, Penguin Books.

THE INTERSECTIONAL IMPACT OF FERTILITY TREATMENT AND LGBT+ IDENTITIES IN SCHOOLS

EMMA SWIFT

Fertility issues when you are a teacher are hard enough. The rollercoaster of building expectations, going through the painful processes, enduring the hormones, then the miscarriages. Being a lesbian and going through fertility adds layers of complexity that can be traumatic. More and more lesbians are accessing IVF either through the NHS or privately, according to the Human Fertilisation and Embryology Authority. In fact, in 2008 only 27% of treatment cycles for patients in female same-sex relationships were for IVF, increasing to 45% in 2018 (HFEA, 2020). Schools are still heteronormative spaces and going through the process for me was fraught with anxiety.

I have so many wonderful memories of 2012. Living in London during the Olympics feels like a very different time. However, 2012 was also the year that I had my first miscarriage after my first round of fertility treatment.

I was working at a secondary school in East London and even though it was widely known I was a lesbian, I did not feel safe to share my journey with my managers at the time. One line manager, whom I trusted and respected, was on maternity leave herself. I didn't feel safe talking about it with my substitute line manager, someone I did not know very well.

There were many reasons for not sharing my IVF journey. Firstly, my headteacher was Catholic and my perception of his faith was one of the reasons for my feelings. Although I had just won a national teaching award and managed a successful team, we never seemed to connect. I sensed that I did not fit into a mould of women he could engage with. He generally had either a paternal or flirty relationship with female and feminine-presenting staff, whereas I was openly gay, I spoke about my wife and I do not present in a way which is super-feminine. I felt at the time as though he did not know how to relate to me.

Alongside this was the fear that I would be seen as 'choosing' to take time off for IVF treatment. When having fertility treatment as a lesbian, there is a worry that people perceive treatment to be a choice. In fact, many workplaces in the UK still have policies that see fertility treatment as an 'elective treatment' (*The Financial Times*, 2021) and do not provide paid leave for appointments. When you work in a high-pressure environment, such as a school, being seen to choose to 'take time off' at any point is seen as selfish.

So I kept to myself that I was having fertility treatment. I did not want to field many questions about how, and why me and not my very feminine-presenting wife at the time. Straight women going through fertility treatment are not asked these questions, and while I understand why, I could not face having to explain that my outward appearance did not define my ability to want a child, to be a mother.

Another aspect of difficulty for some lesbians going through and being open about fertility treatment is the requirement to have to come out to people – your line managers, your colleagues, your HR manager. If you are not an out teacher, IVF is an endless navigation of people's responses to both your sexuality and the IVF treatment.

The hard part is not just the sense of failure and the lack of control when having fertility treatment. It is also the money. Quite simply, schools have very little understanding of the financial impact on lesbians going through IVF. The NHS assumes that the only issue for lesbians in having a child is the lack of a male partner. The fact is that while heterosexual couples have to show two years of trying and failing to conceive naturally, lesbians have to show that they have had several rounds of failed artificial insemination (AI), something that has to be privately funded, before they are eligible for NHS treatment. Private fertility treatment is expensive and there is a clear finite point when this journey is over and that is when the money runs out.

I hid my process as best I could. The scans were requested as medical appointments and most could be fit into the evenings and weekends. Even at early stages, I sensed the disappointment and disapproval of my absences. Working women face the labyrinth of HR processes all the time, with some being asked to take unpaid leave. There are so many stories out there of docked pay, and refusal of appointments (Garner, *IVF at Work and the Importance of a Safe Workplace*, 2019).

Then, at one of my scans, I was informed by the doctor that there was a problem. After a follow up scan, I was told that the embryo had died and I needed a dilation and curettage (D&C). I could not hide it when I had the miscarriage. I was signed off for the four days running up to my D&C and three days after.

This was a difficult time for me to navigate. I was coping in the classroom but not really the rest of the time, just teetering on the brink. We tried again. In these situations I just wanted to keep going but after another round and another miscarriage, I left the school. Partly because I felt that the high-pressure environment may have been contributing to my miscarriages and partly because I just did not feel that it was an environment that would understand the complexity of LGBT fertility. The experience was a catalyst for a lot of change. My marriage ended. I changed jobs. I tried to recover.

Five years later, in a new relationship,I felt ready to try again. I was working as an assistant head in a school in west London and one day a week for my trust as a subject consultant. This time I approached it differently, feeling that the school and leadership were more receptive to the idea of a lesbian having fertility treatment. I spoke with my head, HR and my line manager before it began. They were all very positive about the prospect of me being a parent.

Even though this time I felt that my status as a lesbian undergoing fertility treatment was more accepted, the amount of time that is absorbed by the harvesting and the implantation, the endless injections and medicines, in addition to the endless scans, takes its toll. The expectation to be present and to get on with things was both implicit and made explicit to me. I still carried guilt for taking time off – I had to travel to central London to go to the London Women's Clinic for treatment. This was not a choice, private treatment was my only option. I still faced questions about why it was me undergoing IVF and not my partner. I still had to come out to people I did not know or trust. I still had to justify.

Our IVF journey was not successful. Looking back now, I realise how the double whammy of being a lesbian and undergoing IVF affected my mental health, my physical health and my career at the time. The system was not, and still is not, set up to help women like me. Schools are becoming more aware of the impact of fertility treatment on heterosexual women, but there is still a significant amount of work to be done at policy level to understand how fertility treatment affects *all* women.

KEY TAKEAWAYS

- Schools can be both explicitly and implicitly unsafe spaces for LGBT staff undergoing fertility treatment.
- Heteronormative assumptions mean that LGBT staff are required to explain their fertility treatment
- Policy level support and guidance for all women going through fertility treatment is necessary to ensure parity and sensitivity.

KEY QUESTIONS:

- Does your school policy on pregnancy and maternity make specific reference to the particular circumstances that LGBT+ staff going through fertility treatment might experience?
- Is there high-quality training for HR staff and line managers on how to have conversations about fertility without being heteronormative?
- What provision is in place for women to manage the fertility process around school commitments?

COMMITMENT TO THE MANIFESTO

Schools should review pregnancy and maternity policies and make specific reference to LGBT+ circumstances in those policies to ensure that staff are safe to disclose fertility treatment regardless of their sexuality.

REFERENCES

UK IVF and DI statistics for heterosexual, female same-sex and single patients, 2020, available at: https://www.hfea.gov.uk/media/3234/family-formations-in-fertility-treatment-2018.pdf, [accessed August 2021]

NHS, *Trying for a baby when you are LGBT+* , available at: https://www.nhs.uk/pregnancy/trying-for-a-baby/having-a-baby-if-you-are-lgbt-plus/ [accessed August 2021]

Garner, M. (2019) *IVF and the importance of a safe workplace.* Available at: https://www.workingmums.co.uk/ivf-and-the-importance-of-a-safe-workplace/ [accessed August 2021]

Kyriacou, S. (2021) *Let's Break the Silence around IVF in Workplac*es', available at: https://www.ft.com/content/f4a589a0-5aa4-46af-85c0-ece7915799f9 [accessed August 2021]

CEILINGS AND TEARS: HOW BLACK FEMALE LEADERS IN EDUCATION ARE VIEWED AND TREATED

AUDREY PANTELIS

In 1965, Yvonne Connolly became Britain's first female black headteacher at a primary school in London. Potentially, the stage was set for black female educators to follow in her footsteps, but this has not been the case. Fast forward fifty or so years and the picture is not as positive as it could be. According to statistics from the Department for Education 2019, there are currently fifty-five female, black or black British headteachers currently in the education system. This from a workforce of just 3,784 female, black or black British teachers, equating to just 1.45%. This statistic is stark. The current climate regarding the attempt to dismantle institutional and systemic racism across society includes the global awareness of the Black Lives Matter movement following the death of George Floyd in May 2020 in the US. This has also provided the stimulus to examine why black female leaders in education are not represented in leadership positions, despite Yvonne Connolly's appointment. Oppression and resistance – through the concepts of white fragility, white supremacy and white sanction may be contributory factors to this and when explored further, coloniality appears to be the all-prevailing system of domination and exploitation. There needs to be an admission that this system is in operation before we can begin to unpack it and to look at the ways in which we can begin to change the status quo.

Barriers to progression are varied, complex and many for black female teachers to become leaders, their potential for leadership recognised. Ruby Hamad, in *White Tears/Brown Scars*, outlines the stereotype of black women – one that many black women in education have experienced as part of their lived experience, being seen as 'The Angry Black Woman' or 'The Sapphire/The Mammy'. The 'Sapphire' is a symbol of feminine purity, wisdom and chastity. The 'Mammy' caricature was posited as proof that black women were contented, even happy, as slaves. Her wide grin, hearty laughter, and loyal servitude were offered as evidence of the supposed humanity of the institution of slavery. Black female leaders in education are rarely seen as 'The Sapphire' and the application of unconscious bias has led to

'The Mammy' stereotype being the dominant viewpoint and any opportunity to rid themselves of this prejudicial view is thwarted in favour of the white female leader – presenting as strong and capable, but able to show emotion and vulnerability when challenged that is not seen as weakness.

Differences and distortions combine to weaken our educational landscape. The skill that black female leaders possess is the ability to maintain their professionalism, while by default they are perceived as 'unfeeling', 'aggressive', 'difficult', 'a non-team player'. The education landscape is being deprived of the black excellence, true authenticity and agility of mind that black female leaders bring to the table.

Stating that we are all 'females together' would be valued and welcomed, and at various times in history has been the norm, but unfortunately this is currently not the case. Audre Lord writes in her paper '*Age, Race, Class and Sex: Women Redefining Difference* (1984): 'As white women ignore their built-in privilege of whiteness and define woman in terms of their own experience alone, then the women of Color become "other", the outsider whose experience and tradition is too "alien" to comprehend.' TED talk speakers Jodi-Ann Burey and Luvvie Ajayi Jones discuss in their respective TED Talks of March 2021 and January 2018, of the importance of being authentic, but recognise how difficult this is. As a black female leader, the chances are that you are in education to make a difference to the lives of the children and young people in your charge. The environment can be 'hostile' and may mean that black female leaders look for the 'favour' that they require to progress, which comes at a cost, socially. This may mean looking for and accepting authority – power and privilege – from white leaders. Paul Miller (2016) talks of this in his paper *Tackling race inequality in school leadership: Positive actions in BAME teacher progression – evidence from three English schools*. Miller defines 'White sanction' as a deliberate act 'where the skills and capabilities of a BME individual are, first, acknowledged and, second, endorsed/ promoted by a white individual, who is positioned as a broker and/or mediator acting on behalf of or in the interests of the BME individual.' (p. 11).

For the majority of BME leaders, anecdotally you will hear the phrase 'I have to be TWICE as good' OR '200% better' OR 'I have to work TWICE as hard.' This is something that I heard as a young adult from my parents and something that I have instilled into my son, who is now in his late twenties. Why is it that we drive this concept forward? One possible answer is the understanding of 'black excellence' – bringing our uniqueness, our ancestry, our cultural sensitivity and social justice, not forgetting our competency – to the table, unashamedly and proudly. I have personally felt the concepts described as I have attempted to gain more senior roles in schools, in both mainstream and special educational needs settings. Having gained the post of Head of School, I experienced this first-hand when I was told by my line manager that I was a 'maverick'. You could take this statement in two ways – but as the only black leader in the Academy Trust that I worked within, you can see why I would have struggled with seeing it in a positive light. Conversely, when the school gained positive traction in and around the community, no such comments were forthcoming, but I was the same person throughout. Which person did they want?

In looking at this specific aspect of intersectionality, and from my own lived experience, I can conclude that one of the foundations of the lack of career progression is fear. There is fear in promoting strong black women at the cost of undermining white supremacy. There is fear from black female leaders being their authentic selves because of the lack of support when they do so. There is fear of recognising the differences between black female leaders and white female leaders and the linear approach to this viewpoint results in opposition, hostility, and the eventual disconnect from education by black female leaders, unable to compete with the forces that continue to oppress and undermine them. As Ruby Hamad states in *White Tears/Brown Scars* in the chapter entitled *White Tears:* 'What makes white women's tears so potent and renders black and brown women so apparently "aggressive"?' In her blog post, Ajayi explains that what makes the distress of white women so powerful is its association with femininity and helplessness. 'These tears are pouring out of the eyes of the one chosen to be the prototype of womanhood; the woman who has been painted as helpless against the whims of the world.'

So – what can we do?

KEY TAKEAWAYS

- We can recognise the leadership potential in black female leaders and capture the talent through positive action strategies to encourage leadership candidates to be identified and nurtured.
- We can make the system less adversarial by genuinely encouraging the diversity that we seek in children and young people in our black female leaders.
- We can make the system more diverse by looking at the Equality Act and ensuring that we are actively promoting strategies for positive action and living it through scrutiny of data and monitoring.

KEY QUESTIONS:

- How aware are you of the intersectional experiences of leaders in schools?
- What difficult conversations are you willing to have around how we describe intersectional leaders?
- What is the impact of intersectional leaders on your students?

COMMITMENT TO THE MANIFESTO

In order to develop and nurture future generations of resilient leaders, recognise the impact of black female leaders in education, who continue to overcome race and gender barriers.

REFERENCES

Department for Education (DfE). (2018). *School teacher workforce*. Available at: https://www.ethnicity-facts-fig ures.service.gov.uk/workforce-and-business/workforce-diversity/school-teacher-workforce/latest. [Accessed 1 Aug 2019].

Adegoke, Y. and Uviebinené, E. (2018) *Slay In Your Lane: The Black Girl Bible*, 4th Estate London

Bruce-Golding, J. (2020) *Black Female Leaders in Education, Role, Reflections, and Experiences*. University of Birmingham, Birmingham, West Midlands, UK

Hamad, R. (2020) *White Tears Brown Scars: How White Feminism Betrays Women of Colour*. Trapeze Books

Lorde, A. (1980) *Age, Race, Class and Sex: Women Redefining Difference*. Paper delivered at the Copeland Colloquium, Amerst College, April 1980

Miller, P. (2016). '*Tackling race inequality in school leadership: Positive actions in BAME teacher progression – evidence from three English schools*, p1, Sage Publishing, Vol. 48, 6

A TOOLKIT FOR A QUIET REVOLUTION

ABENA AKUFFO-KELLY

INTRODUCTION

Intersectionality has at its core the power dynamics between oppressed and dominant cultures. Yet, intersectionality can also be an instrument of power. Revolutions are not always through explosive acts of violence, disorder or mass acts of protest. Arguably many are instigated that way but the ongoing and truly transformational work is painstakingly created in the uncomfortable conversations with family members and colleagues when you push against restrictive and ingrained narratives. The work is done within you when you realise that your self-hate is an internalised manifestation of colonialism. The work is done in meetings when you stand alone as the agitator and the 'aggressive' individual who steers the narrative away from the dominant cishet patriarchal direction.

For: 'Survival is not an academic skill. It is learning how to stand alone, unpopular and sometimes reviled, and how to make common cause with those others identified as outside the structures in order to define and seek a world in which we can all flourish. It is learning how to take our differences and make them strengths – for the master's tools will never dismantle the master's house.' (Lorde, 1984). As persons who intersect various oppressed and marginalised groups we are always at the periphery, on the 'outside' of privilege. But we can push to be on the inside of the institutions that oppress us. This is a call to action. As intersectional teachers, students, parents, people we do not live in a vacuum. We are not hashtags, long-read essays, subjects of one-off inquiries, performative days and months. We are people who exist in the now.

'We do not live single issue lives.' Audre Lorde

Change will not happen if we exist in comfortable spaces, where our voices and opinions are always listened to, where we are valued and respected contributors to the conversation and when we speak we hear our words echoed. These spaces are important as they sustain us, they affirm our existence and the validity of our thought. However, that is not where change happens.

Our lack of membership in the dominant culture means that we are often at the boundaries of the most important conversations about pedagogy, curriculum structure, assessment, ECT training, behaviour management. But every single one of those conversations affect us. We teach the same students, we work under the same management structures, we all have to follow the same national curriculum. We have every right to speak on all of these matters. We may not have the level of privilege that allows us the ease of access to the higher echelons of power but there are many ways in which we as educationalists, professionals, specialists and experts in our field can have that seat at the table.

There is power in our intersecting identities. Living a life filled with contradictions, varying, and opposing levels of privilege and oppression means that we are constantly having to redefine ourselves to fit into different spaces. It means that we have a diversity of thought and experience that is not available to individuals who inhabit the dominant space. We could see that as a disadvantage but when it comes to social justice and equity our lived experiences make us specialists simply by virtue of our existence. I count myself as a specialist in being a single mother, black, a woman, an individual who identifies with the LGBTQI spectrum, and so on. When I speak about any of the above identities I do not speak as someone who has studied a degree in black history, written a thesis on gender. I do not have to, as I 'live' those identities every second of every day. That gives me an insight into what can be done to improve the lives of multiple demographics because I belong to multiple groups.

Empathy and compassion does not equal lived experience. I'm a trans-ally but I know that a trans person will speak with more passion and understanding on trans issues than I ever could because they have that lived experience that supersedes and goes far beyond any theoretical understanding of their lives. That is the power that we have; to speak with authority about our lives, and that is what is needed in so many different spaces.

There are multiple organisations that require your expertise and multi-dimensional viewpoints. For example, school governors have a level of autonomy and power that many are not aware of. They are involved in the process of recruiting headteachers, scrutinising school policies and monitoring school performance. Becoming a governor provides you with the opportunity to use your intersectional expertise to make impactful strategic change. And you are very much needed. Although 26% of pupils in English schools in 2018 came from ethnic minorities, 93% of the governance volunteers surveyed in 2019 were from white backgrounds. The typical governor is female (58.9%), white, fifty-five, or in a multi-academy trust, fifty-nine; they are also retired (32.5%) or in managerial roles. Representation is important and according to those figures more than a quarter of our pupils are not being sufficiently represented by people who share in their lived experiences, have the same reference points or cultural markers. You as an intersectional educationalist have the power to change this.

'Caring for myself is not self-indulgence, it is self-preservation, and that is an act of political warfare.' Audre Lorde

You are not alone; the struggle is real and exhausting. When, irrespective of your knowledge, your expertise and your lived experience, you are regularly ridiculed, ignored and undermined, intersectionality and activism fatigue can quickly set in. That is when you seek respite and join a community of like-minded individuals. There are many in education: BAMEed, WomenEd, DiverseEd, LGBTed, MixedEd, DisabilityEd etc. These organisations do not only offer a place to rest in the knowledge that your struggles will be understood; they also offer professional advice in regards to CPD, a personalised mentor to support you to reach your career aspirations, programs and initiatives to help broaden your horizons and reach an audience in the wider educational community. LGBTed also offers the first and only in the world educational leadership programme for teaching professionals who identify as LGBTQI+.

KEY TAKEAWAYS

- As an intersectional individual you should feel empowered. Your right to speak is not granted because of fairness, life simply isn't fair. Your voice should be heard because your lived experiences bring diversity.
- Stay informed in regards to the educational landscape and the power-brokers. Your school is not the epicentre of education, widen your scope to encompass a variety of organisations.
- Make time for self-care, inhabiting spaces where you are the minority can be emotionally and mentally draining. Take time out to seek communion with like-minded individuals.

KEY QUESTIONS:

- Have you considered how the myth of the teacher who remains professional and impartial at all times erodes your ability to be your true and authentic self when dealing with students?
- Change can happen one person at a time, what steps can you take to start on the route of decolonising the curriculum or simply being more culturally responsive?
- Which intersectional educational group will you join first?

COMMITMENT TO THE MANIFESTO

Challenge the dominant narrative by making sure you have knowledge of the power structures in education. Then use that knowledge to infiltrate those structures offering your insights as an intersectional individual.

REFERENCES

Chander, S. (2019) *Can we take back intersectionality?*, gal-dem, 12 February 2019, https://gal-dem.com/can-we-take-back-intersectionality/ [Accessed May 2021]

NGA (2019) *School Governance 2019*, NGA and TES, Sept 2019. Available at https://www.nga.org.uk/getmedia/10f021c3-7774-4e39-b2d3-84d5ae5a5115/School-Governance-Report-(WEB)-FINAL-2-9-19.pdf [Accessed May 2021]

THE EPILOGUE

It may be the case that you are now considering what to do with this book and its contents, depending on your context. Whether you have read all the chapters in this book, or whether you have dipped in and out of different sections, you may have more questions than you do answers about diversity, equity and inclusion and the protected characteristics. You may choose to do precisely nothing, which is your prerogative as a reader. If, however, you are considering next steps, there are some clear ways forward.

Here are ten ways you can use this book as a starting point for further work in diversity, equity and inclusion:

1. Start a DEI group at school – use the structure of this book as a way of structuring your meetings, by protected characteristic.
2. Embark on a student voice project using questions that you have noted, or the ones at the end of each chapter.
3. Embark on a staff voice project using the key questions at the end of each chapter – they can be grouped into themes.
4. Review your school/organisation Equality Policy and Equalities Objectives in light of the takeaways in each section.
5. Review school publicity material – website/ prospectus/ social media – in light of the recommendations in this book.
6. Evaluate your curriculum provision – academic, extra-curricular and inner – to see where the protected characteristics are presented.
7. Engage with organisations signposted in the book (and listed in our DEI directory) to support your staff and students – partnerships are vital and extra hands are always helpful.
8. Continue research on the key concepts mentioned in this book for yourself and your own development as a professional.
9. Connect with other DEI leads to facilitate local or national conversations using the #DiverseEd hashtag, through social media.
10. Synthesise chapters for your staff to hear some key ideas – and encourage them to read the book for themselves.

Throughout the book, I have been struck by the honesty of the authors contributing to our book. At times, our authors have shared parts of themselves that do not form the basis of our everyday conversations. I have seen in the writing parts of myself – feelings, thoughts and experiences that have served to demonstrate how we as education professionals have complex and interweaving experiences that ought to see the light of day more often. In reading these chapters, even if I do not share a particular person's protected characteristic, I have recognised the intensely human need to be heard.

It would be wonderful to hear your stories too.

BK

SO, WHAT CAN YOU DO NOW THAT YOU HAVE READ DIVERSE EDUCATORS: A MANIFESTO?

Bennie and I are deeply practical people – we want this book to stimulate reflections, provoke discussions and initiate actions for you in your classroom, in your school, in your trust and in your team. The book will hopefully be both the catalyst and the springboard to develop competence and confidence in this space. After wall, we do not know what we do not know until we look in the mirror, look through the window and step through the sliding door.

Our vision for the school system is clear but our provision is constantly evolving to respond to the needs of our network. Our work is underpinned by our network's shared values. Please do get in touch if you would like to collaborate with us and our growing network of Diverse Educators.

Here are twenty-five next steps for engaging with Diverse Educators – as an individual or as an organisation:

1. Follow us on Twitter @DiverseEd2020 #DiverseEd
2. Visit the website: www.diverseeducators.co.uk
3. Check out our DEI Directory
4. Get in touch if you would to be added to our DEI Directory
5. Find out more about our #DiverseEd partners
6. Register for the monthly newsletter
7. Review our collection of blogs
8. Submit a blog for us to publish
9. Use the DEI glossary (there is one for words and one for acronyms)
10. Work your way through the DEI reading list
11. Join our #DiverseEd book club
12. Follow Bennie's 365 #DiverseEd books list
13. Join us for World Book Day to celebrate Diverse Educators who have been published
14. Engage with the growing bank of DEI toolkits
15. Get in touch if you would like to create a new toolkit for our community
16. Join us at a #DiverseEd virtual event
17. Watch the previous #DiverseEd events in our archive
18. Catch up with the #DiverseGovernance webcast series
19. Catch up with the #FastForwardDiversityInclusion webcast series

20. Join us at a #DiverseEd face-to-face event
21. Let us know if you would like to host us for an event
22. Review the Statement of Intent from national DEI stakeholders
23. Read the Edurio EDI Report
24. Check out the DEI leaders programme, network and conference
25. Appoint and remunerate a DEI leader

We look forward to connecting and collaborating with you!

HW

EDUBOOKCLUB READING GUIDES

For the DEI Leaders, CPD Leaders and Teacher Trainers reading this book, we hope that *Diverse Educators: A Manifesto* will feature in your staff libraries and in-house book clubs moving forwards.

Here are twenty questions to get you started in holding a discussion with your colleagues. You could dissect it by each chapter's featured Protected Characteristic or by common themes:

1. The Editors worked really hard with the Chapter Editors to strive for balanced representation across the protected characteristics in the contributors. Which identities are missing from the book and why might this be the case?
2. Bennie references in the introduction that the volunteers were initially very female-heavy, and we had to tap a few men on the shoulder to contribute to the book. How can we get more male voices involved in DEI?
3. Hannah references in her introduction that a number of DEI leaders are not formally recognised nor remunerated, how can you use your sphere of influence in your context to address this?
4. Stories are a key part of building understanding through sharing lived experience. Which of the personal and professional stories had the greatest impact on you as a reader?
5. Role models and their visibility are a key theme throughout each chapter. For each of the protected characteristics who are the visible role models for this identity in your organisation?
6. Allyship is one of the calls to action throughout the book. How have you/ how can you advocate for others in the different spaces in which you move?
7. Representation is lacking in a lot of governing bodies, leadership teams and wider school teams in schools around the country. How might you diversify how you recruit as a school moving forwards?
8. In the Age chapter what strategies were shared that might diversify your talent management strategy?
9. From the Disability chapter what were your takeaways for countering the ableist narratives in our workplaces and in wider society?
10. In the Gender Reassignment chapter what did you learn about the importance of trans-inclusive language?

11. From the Marriage and Civil Partnership chapter, what will you do differently when you are exploring relationships in your subject specialism?
12. In the Pregnancy and Maternity chapter parental rights and parental leave were discussed, how family-friendly are your school's policies?
13. From the Race chapter what considerations will you make in your curriculum development to diversify it, to decolonise it and to ensure it is anti-racist?
14. From the Religion and Beliefs chapter what were the big questions that the contributors posed when it comes to our personal ideologies and they shape us as professionals?
15. In the Sex chapter a number of different issues facing men and women were unpacked. How have/ how will you challenge stereotypes for students in your classroom and for your colleagues?
16. From the Sexual Orientation chapter what will you do differently in supporting LGBTQIA+ staff and students in the future?
17. In the Intersectionality chapter what did you learn about the complexities of intersectional identities?
18. At the end of each of the contributions there are three Takeaways. Which resonated and which jarred the most, and why?
19. At the end of each of the contributions there are three Questions. Which stakeholders do you need to engage with topics significant to your context?
20. Each contributor has shared a Commitment to the Manifesto. What action can you commit to taking to contribute to the wider DEI agenda?

Enjoy the listening, the discussions and the learning! Come and join our World Book Day events in March each year to celebrate the published authors in our network and participate in our half-termly #DiverseEd Book Club.

HW

INDEX

S

Lightning Source UK Ltd.
Milton Keynes UK
UKHW021252110522
402819UK00005B/138